INDIAN EDUCATIONAL POLICY ITS PRINCIPLES AND PROBLEMS

INDIAN EDUCATIONAL POLICY ITS PRINCIPLES AND PROBLEMS

WILLIAM MESTON

GYAN

Published by

GYAN

Gyan Publishing House
5, Ansari Road
Daryaganj, New Delhi-110002
Phone: 011-47034999, 9811692060
E-mail: books@gyanbooks.com

Distribution Network
gyanbooks.com
India, USA, Canada, UK, Australia

ISBN: 978-93-7169-226-7 (PB)

First Published, 1936

2nd Impression 2025

Printed at: Gyan Press, Delhi.

INDIAN EDUCATIONAL POLICY ITS PRINCIPLES AND PROBLEMS
Author: WILLIAM MESTON

INDIAN EDUCATIONAL POLICY

ITS PRINCIPLES

AND

PROBLEMS

BY

THE LATE

WILLIAM MESTON, D.D., D.Litt.

Honorary Principal, Madras Christian College,
Formerly Member of the Senate, Syndicate, and
Academic Council, University of Madras,
Sometime Member of the Legislative Council, Madras

THE CHRISTIAN LITERATURE SOCIETY FOR INDIA

PARK TOWN, MADRAS

1936

NOTE

THE consideration of Indian Educational Policy to which the following pages are devoted has grown out of almost forty years' study of the subject and over thirty-five years personal contact with, and participation in, the Indian educational system. Some twenty years ago circumstances arose which called for a paper on the educational policy of the State in India. And this paper, which was afterwards published, became in somewhat changed form the first chapter of *Aspects of Indian Educational Policy*, issued in 1922. During the ten years that have elapsed since that time, educational policy has assumed new importance as the implications of the Act of 1919 have been realized, and as the way has been prepared for further constitutional advance. The nature and value of this policy are here looked at from two points of view. In Part I the principles on which the policy rests are stated; and in Part II the problems of a general character with which the policy is confronted are dealt with.

The survey of educational policy which is presented in these Parts takes us over some hundred and fifty years, from 1785 to 1930. But though so long a period is passed under review, it is naturally the latter portion of it, when an accepted policy is at work, that claims our fullest consideration. While the sources of information are numerous, as even a short Bibliography shows, there is one source which must be singled out for special mention because of its abundant supply of facts and figures—those readily accessible *Quinquennial Reviews* of Education which carry us without a break from 1892 to 1927.

It may be thought that a Third Part should have been added, one which concerned itself with the working of the Policy. But that would have called for a description of education throughout India in its different forms together with a consideration of the specific problems connected with each of them. It would also have necessitated reference to what is done in the Indian States as well as in the Provinces of British India. Only separate treatment could do justice to a subject of such dimensions and importance. This treatment, it is hoped, may be possible in a subsequent volume.

What our investigation shows is that the educational system of India rests on principles of educational policy which have only to be fully employed to secure for the country sound education and the well-being of the State. The present discussion is an endeavour so to lay stress upon these principles that India may give to them its unfaltering adherence, and may realize that it has thus been put in possession of the means whereby personal character gains in enrichment and national life in strength.

September 15, 1932.

PUBLISHERS' NOTE

THIS work is the last on which the late Dr. William Meston was engaged. It was undertaken after his retirement, and completed during a very trying illness and under great physical difficulties.

Dr. Meston hoped to see the manuscript through the Press himself, but death came to him before the work of printing was commenced, and only after some delay was the decision made that the book should still be published.

After much consideration the Publishers have felt it best to make no addition, alteration or comment. Thus, although conditions have altered considerably since the time of writing, the book is placed before the public in its original form.

CONTENTS

PART I: Its Principles

PART II: Its Problems

PART I

INDIAN EDUCATIONAL POLICY
ITS PRINCIPLES

INTRODUCTION

1. *Need for a History of Indian Education.*—The History of Education in India has been dealt with in several volumes, monographs, and articles. There are, however, indications that a more widely conceived treatment of the subject than any which has yet appeared would be valuable not only as a source of much-needed information but also as giving direction and stimulus to educational progress. The scattered facts require to be brought together, to be arranged historically, and to be interpreted critically. The efforts that are now being made to secure a new constitution for India render the present time singularly appropriate for the writing of a new and exhaustive history of Indian education.

2. *Present Consideration Limited to Indian Educational Policy.*—The following pages touch on history, but their purpose is not directly historical. They are devoted to a theme which is narrower as regards content and less extensive as regards time. They deal with Educational Policy. The attempt to formulate an educational policy is the endeavour to redeem education from what is haphazard and unrelated. It is an effort to find a foundation on which education may be based, and by means of which education may be systematically advanced. The clearer such a policy becomes and the more practical the mould in which it is run, the better is the State enabled to discharge its responsibility for the education of its people.

3. *Contents of Chapters I to III.*—How a policy grew up, how it was accepted by the State, and how it operates in the Provinces of British India, are described in the four Chapters of which this Part is composed. In Chapter I an attempt is made to disentangle the various strands which were ultimately woven into the texture

of an Educational Policy. In Chapter II the nature of that Policy, as it is stated in official pronouncements, is set forth. In Chapter III the fundamental principles of the Policy are exhibited. The period dealt with in these three Chapters covers the years 1785 to 1920. From 1785 to 1854 a Policy was in the making; in 1854 it was formulated; and from that time till 1920 it was at work as the avowed Policy of the State, that is, of the Government of India.

4. *Contents of Chapter IV.*—With the passing of the Government of India Act at the end of 1919 a new situation arises, and this is considered in Chapter IV. In educational matters the Government of India gives place to the Provincial Governments of India, and to them is granted freedom to act independently of the Central Government and to adopt the educational policy which commends itself to them. The facts of the decade 1920 to 1930 in which this freedom is exercised are examined in the course of Chapter IV, and are found to constitute a call for the voluntary adoption in the Province of those principles which had hitherto been enforced by the authority of the Imperial Government.

5. *Conclusion Reached.*—A further stage is indicated in the Conclusion. Indian Educational Policy based on the principles which have been considered, provided these principles are accepted not imposed, is seen to afford the means whereby education may achieve the most rapid advance, may fashion the strongest bond of unity, and may make the most vital contribution to national life through every Province and State of a Federated India.

CHAPTER I

Preparation for a Policy

I. Policy the Outcome of Actual Conditions

1. Educational policy in India arose out of administrative practice. Certain features of that practice stood the test of experience, and after being subjected to long and searching discussion emerged either unchanged or somewhat modified: certain found experience and discussion too much for them and were discarded. The story of this testing takes us back to the latter part of the eighteenth century. It was then that the East India Company began to be confronted with conditions which, now here, now there, called for action in regard to education. And this continued until ultimately the Company was led to a definition of its attitude to the educational administration of the country as a whole. It did this on the basis of those features of administrative practice which emerged successfully from the severe test imposed by time and criticism. What these features were we shall best learn by passing in review, however briefly, the educational developments in different parts of India, and noting the salient contributions made to educational advance by the Presidencies of Madras, Bombay, and Bengal. We shall thus see how each of these, as it dealt with actual conditions, helped towards the formation of a definite and comprehensive Indian educational policy. The period covered by this review will be some seventy years. If we attach dates to it, we may say that it stretches from 1785 to 1854. Each of the three Presidencies will be dealt with in turn; and the North-Western Provinces which, as an administrative area, became separated from Bengal in 1833, will be included in the survey.

II. Conditions in Madras

2. *Schwartz's Schools.*—We may begin our survey with that striking personality Christian Frederick Schwartz who, as he toured through South India in the half century which ran from the date of his landing at Tranquebar in 1749 to the date of his death in 1798, was not slow to recognize the important part that was played by the village school. He saw the high esteem in which Hindu and Muhammadan teachers were held, and the influence which they exerted upon their pupils. No wonder, then, that he himself decided upon the establishment of schools as one of the most effective means which he could employ to leave a deep impress on youthful minds. The schools which he set up were vernacular schools, that is to say, Tamil children were taught through the medium of Tamil, and children of English parents through the medium of English, and so with other languages. In planting his many schools he had the support of the East India Company which, while leaving the control in his hands, aided his efforts with grants of money and occasionally helped in the repair of buildings. The attitude taken by the Company towards Schwartz was continued to his successors, and the schools set up in various parts of the Presidency received generous support from Government. According to Fisher's Memoir 'the Court of Directors authorised a permanent grant of 250 pagodas each to the three schools which had been established at Tanjore, Ramnadapuram, and Shivagunga'. This was in 1787. Thus there grew up in the latter part of the eighteenth century an educational practice to meet an existing situation, and this practice, as we shall see, contained in germ one of the main constituents of an educational policy. Schools which were the fruit of private effort were seconded by grants from public funds.

3. *Sullivan's Scheme.*—Schwartz won the regard of a very large circle, Indian and European, and one of those

to whom he made a strong appeal was John Sullivan, a civilian, who was Resident at the Court of Tanjore towards the end of the eighteenth century. His admiration for Schwartz led him to foster the vernacular schools which Schwartz had founded. But it occurred to him that there was a development which might be made with distinct benefit. That consisted in introducing English into the higher classes of some of these schools which were not specifically intended for European children. It was in 1785 that Sullivan expressed this idea, and he gave his reason for the departure which he advocated. He believed, as he put it, that the teaching of English would lead to mutual understanding and confidence between Indian and European, and that it would open up to the pupils who received it a new world of knowledge. The scheme which he proposed was endorsed by the East India Company, and towards the maintenance of these English schools contributions were made from private sources, the zemindars and the rajah of the locality concerned, while an annual grant was sanctioned by the Company. It was laid down that the schools were to be inspected by one of the missionaries, and that an account of income and expenditure was to be submitted to the Government of Madras. Thus practically one hundred and fifty years ago, or seventy years before the Despatch of 1854, there was set on foot what was really an educational policy. Private effort established schools which were subject to inspection, received Government grant, and submitted their accounts to Government scrutiny. The method of extending education which arose in this way continued in force from 1785 to 1842, when it was discontinued because of the responsibilities for the advance of education through its own agency which Government had assumed. The period during which it was in abeyance was, however, short; for twelve years later it received official recognition, and was incorporated as a constituent part of the policy which the Government then enunciated. The East India Company made it quite clear why they were prepared to make grants towards education. The Directors, we read, were of opinion that the schools which Sullivan championed were calculated to enlighten the minds of the people of India. They also felt that the higher form of education would bring new and valuable ideas into the minds of the youth of India, and that it would replace the feuds of the past by goodwill in the future.

4. *Munro's Proposals.*—If now we pass over a time of wars and insecurity in the southern Presidency and come to the time of that great statesman Sir Thomas Munro, we find two important contributions which he made towards the solution of the educational problem. In a Minute which he drew up under date 10th May 1826 he calls attention to the fact that the schools in the Presidency amount to 12,498, and the population to 12,850,941, or that there is one school to every thousand of the population. When, however, it is remembered that only a small number of girls receive education, and that besides pupils attending school there are many who are taught at home, he comes to the conclusion that about one-third of the boys between the ages of five and ten are in receipt of some form of education. But the education which is given leaves much to be desired. On this we have the evidence of Mr. A. D. Campbell, Collector of Bellary, who addressed the President and Members of the Board of Revenue in a letter dated 17th August 1823. He gives an interesting account of what goes on in the schools of his district, from which it appears that while much is taught little is understood, memory being chiefly appealed to, and the books read having but the slightest connexion with the language of ordinary conversation and business. Thus the intellectual and moral effect is reduced to a minimum. Few teachers, he says, can explain the books read by the pupils; and in this sentence he places his finger on a weakness which Munro recognizes, and for which he proposes a remedy in the Minute which, as we saw, was

written almost three years later. 'No progress', he says, 'can be made without a body of better instructed teachers than we have at present; but such a body cannot be had without an income sufficient to afford a comfortable livelihood to each individual belonging to it'. He then proceeds to outline his practical proposals. First, there must be established a school for the training of teachers; and secondly, there should be planted two primary schools in each collectorate, one for Hindus and the other for Muhammadans, and as soon as possible a Hindu school in each tahsildari. It seemed to him that this scheme could be caried out in its entirety if Government would sanction an annual expenditure of Rs. 50,000. But, while he does not think that so much would be required for a considerable time owing to the difficulty of securing teachers, he has no doubt as to the benefit which the full expenditure that he mentions would yield. 'Whatever expense Government may incur in the education of the people,' he says, 'will be amply repaid by the improvement of the country'. A Committee of Public Instruction was appointed by the Government of Madras in 1826 which sanctioned a disbursement for education of Rs. 45,000. Towards the end of June of the same year the Committee announced that a central school for the training of teachers had been set up in Madras; and in the following year 'it was reported that ten candidates for the situation of collectorate teachers were being trained', and that several schools had been opened, all under Indian supervision. The proposals and activities of Sir Thomas Munro thus laid emphasis on two points in the absence of which no satisfactory form of educational policy can be initiated. In the first place, there must be facilities for the training of teachers; and in the second place, education must be generally diffused and must not be the monopoly of any particular class. Both principles were approved by the Directors of the East India Company in their Despatch of 16th April 1828. Had no adverse current set in, education in the southern

Presidency would have seen much earlier than was actually the case the fulfilment of Munro's desire for a well-trained teaching profession. And further it would have seen increasing provision for the instruction of the masses, with the result that the educational system would have been broad-based, and would have escaped the reproach that still clings to it of being top-heavy.

5. *The Company's Attitude to Elementary Education.*—The hopes which were aroused by the action of the Court of Directors in 1828 were doomed to disappointment by what the same Court did some two years later. In a Despatch dated 29th September 1830 the Directors complain that too much has been done for elementary education in Madras, and too little for education of a more advanced type. The Government of Madras is called upon to reverse its policy. 'By the measures originally contemplated by your Government', they say, 'no provision was made for the instruction of any portion of the natives in the higher branches of knowledge. A further extension of the elementary education which already existed, and an improvement of its quality by the multiplication and diffusion of useful books in the Indian languages was all that was aimed at'. They then go on to point out that the education which has the greatest influence is the education of the 'higher classes'; and that in this form of education Madras has been singularly defective. This attitude adopted at the beginning of the decade naturally becomes more marked in the course of it because of the trend of events in Bengal and Bombay. So that it is not surprising to find the Directors referring to these developments and saying to Madras: 'We are desirous that similar measures should be adopted at your Presidency'. Thus before the decade ends we see Lord Elphinstone, Governor of Madras, writing in his Minute of 12th December 1839 says: 'The principal points urged upon our attention by the Supreme Government and the General Committee are :— First, the discontinuance of the system of frittering away

the sums allowed for educational purposes upon mere elementary schools and upon eleemosynary scholars'. It almost takes our breath away to read of the expenditure which the Government of Madras was incurring in deliberately advancing the cause of mass education as being a 'frittering away' of public money. The Directors did occasionally change their minds, but surely never with such unfortunate results as when they first heartily supported the endeavours of the Madras Government to spread abroad among the people the benefits of elementary education, and then not thirty months later turned upon that Government for such an unproductive employment of general revenues. From this time on till 1854 the educational developments in Madras were marked, we are told, by the 'lack of a consistent policy'. It could hardly be otherwise.

6. *Attitude of the Company to Aided Education.*—The educational progress which had been made in Madras owed its success to two principles recognized as early as the eighteenth century. These were: There must be an education of the masses as well as of those capable of profiting by higher learning; and to secure a wide-spread system of education it is necessary for the State to give a ready encouragement to private effort. By 1830 the official frown had settled upon both principles. And the reasons for this, though two in number, were really closely intertwined. The first was the lack of funds. The argument of the Government was: 'We have at our disposal only a very limited supply of money, therefore let us spend it not extensively but intensively'. There was much to be said for this, as we shall see later. The Court of Directors in one of their letters admit that 'the minute subdivision of the Government grant amongst a multitude of establishments has the tendency of making our support altogether ineffective'. But this consideration was leading them to ignore a source of income which had done much for education in the past, and which even with small encouragement could be

counted on to do much more. And that brings us to the second reason, which is that the Government of Madras had come to think of State funds as intended for State educational effort. This was a change of attitude of which there were not a few signs. For instance, for many years, as has been already pointed out, the Government of Fort St. George made grants to the schools which were carried on by Schwartz's successors. But in 1830 the grant for 1829 was accompanied by the intimation that 'it was foreign to the designs of the Government that mission schools should be maintained at their expense or under their superintendence'. Actually the grants were not withdrawn for twelve years; but the implication of the statement is worthy of consideration. It means that the work of private effort by which the southern Presidency had been supplied with schools was to be deprived of financial support and of State inspection when the Government became itself a manager of schools. And that was what, for a time, happened. The Government of Madras decided to establish a University including a High School and a College. The High School department of the University was opened in 1841. In the following year schools under private management learned that they had drawn their last grant. The story of the proposed Madras University is full of interest, but it belongs to the history of Indian education. From the point of view of policy it is sufficient to note that the cold shoulder which was given officially to the spread of elementary education in 1830 was given officially to private educational effort in 1842. For the time being, then, a definite stop was put to a continued educational practice which had in it the germ of a beneficial educational policy. For had that practice been maintained there would have been regularly established long before 1854 a mode of administering and encouraging education which would have left neither the masses nor those capable of higher studies uncared for, and which would have spread education without undue demands on the public purse, and yet at the same time with the strictest public supervision.

7. *Attitude of the Company in* 1854.—Fortunately all that the official frown could do was to withdraw public money from the attempt to expand elementary education and from non-official educational efforts. It could not stop these efforts. To them, indeed, Madras was indebted for the maintenance and diffusion of what is fundamental in any scheme of national education. Vernacular schools were continued by those who had the welfare of the country at heart, and it was their action which made it possible for the Government, when better counsels prevailed, to embark on a definite policy with prospect of success. After the rebukes administered to the Government of Madras for their interest in elementary education, and after the subsequent absorption of that Government in its own educational efforts there is something refreshing in reading what the Despatch of 1854 has to say regarding these matters. It is at once a handsome withdrawal of the rebukes and a ready acknowledgment of the service which non-official effort had rendered in the spread of the education of the people. Paragraph 96 of the Despatch runs as follows: 'In Madras, where little has yet been done by the Government to promote the education of the mass of the people, we can only remark with satisfaction that the educational efforts of Christian missionaries have been more successful among the Tamil population than in any other part of India; and that the Presidency of Madras offers a fair field for the adoption of our scheme of education in its entirety by founding Government Anglo-vernacular institutions only where no such places of instruction at present exist, which might by grants-in-aid and other assistance adequately supply the educational wants of the people'.

8. *Contribution to Educational Policy*.—Such is a brief record of what Madras did to prepare for a definite educational policy. Conditions in that Presidency led

Government to adopt certain lines of action in regard to education, and the practice thus initiated became its contribution to accepted policy. These conditions showed that private effort is indispensable for the spread of education; and they did this in two ways. For one thing they showed what an asset to the country is the endeavour of those who, from a desire to promote education, contribute of their means to secure this object, and how rich is the harvest which the State reaps when it co-operates with this enterprise, supporting it, supervising it, encouraging it. For another thing they showed that the country itself cannot dispense with this agency, even if the Government for the time being considers that it can. Had there been nothing but official activity in the Presidency's educational field the education of the large body of the people for many a day would have gone by the board. Private effort, unsupported by Government, refused to depart from the course which it had marked out and which Government had at one time approved. It held firmly to the cause of popular education; and in time the State returned to its former position, and recognized the rightness of the action taken by private agencies. A grant-in-aid system incorporated in the educational scheme of the State and bringing with it increasing benefits not as a dream but as an actuality, was what the conditions in Madras effected. The need for the training of the teacher received due emphasis, the need for the activity of the State was fully recognized. But above all else the events of seventy years in the Presidency of Madras made it clear that if education was to flourish two things were essential—the education of the masses, and the maintenance of a system of grant-in-aid.

References

H. Sharp, *Selections from Educational Records. Part I.* Chapter iv gives Munro's Minute in full, and an extract from A. D. Campbell's letter. In Appendix A is Fisher's Memoir.

J. A. Richey, *Selections from Educational Records. Part II.* Chapter v gives many extracts from official correspondence in which may be read change of policy.

F. Penny, *The Church in Madras*, Volume i, Chapter xxii; Volume ii, Chapter xvi; Volume iii, Chapter xvii give much information concerning Schwartz, Sullivan, their successors and their schools.

J. Page, *Schwartz of Tanjore.* The times of Schwartz are presented as well as his life and work.

J. Broadshaw, *Sir Thomas Munro.* Dwells on administrative power of Munro and depicts his personality; his educational activities are summed up in a paragraph.

A. J. Arbuthnot, *Major-General Sir Thomas Munro.* In Volume ii, Munro's Minute on education is given; in Volume i, the proposals are commented on.

III. Conditions in Bombay

9. *Documents to be Considered.*—We now turn to consider the contribution towards the formation of an educational policy which came from the Presidency of Bombay. It is to be found for the most part in four official documents. The first is a comprehensive and deeply interesting Minute drawn up by the Hon. Mountstuart Elphinstone, Governor of Bombay; the second is a Report of Mr. Secretary Farish; the third and fourth are Notifications of the Government of Bombay. They all claim detailed attention.

10. *Elphinstone's Minute.*—In 1822 a 'Bombay Native School Book and School Society' had been begun, and the members of it being desirous of employing some of the funds at their disposal for the establishment of schools approached the Governor on the matter. His reply is given in a Minute which he submitted to the Directors of the East India Company when he presented them with the request of the School Book Society. The date of the Minute is March 1824. He lays it down at the very start that as regards the education of the people of India no great progress can be made without assistance from Government. The question then is: How can the assistance of Government best be supplied? There are

two ways, he says, in which Government can act. The first is that Government 'may take the education of the people entirely upon itself'; the second is that Government 'may increase the means and stimulate the exertions of the society already formed for that purpose'. To him it seems that the task requires the combination of official and private effort. Where an 'organized system' is required, and where 'regularity and permanence' are indispensable the supply may naturally be expected from Government. On the other hand 'many of the measures necessary for the diffusion of education must depend on the spontaneous zeal of individuals, and could not be effected by any resolutions of the Government'. Thus while Government should assume responsibility for increasing the number of schools, grants should be given to such a body as the School Book and School Society to enable it to improve the character of the teaching in the schools. The Society in recognition of the grants it receives should lay all its proceedings before Government and, for a reason to be stated almost immediately, should not meddle with religion or with any topic likely to excite discontent. Three important elements in any Indian educational policy are here clearly emphasized. The first is the need for State initiative and control in education; the Government must be responsible for increasing the number of schools. The second is the need for co-operation between Government and private effort if there is to be a real diffusion of knowledge. And the third is the recognition of the value of a system of grants-in-aid. While Elphinstone thus adumbrates the introduction of a grant-in-aid Code he considers it expedient to exclude one class of schools from its operation. And he gives his reason for this in very explicit terms. 'As Government has recently succeeded a Brahman government', he says, 'it is dangerous to encourage the labours of the missionaries'. He recognizes that such an attitude as this 'deprives the cause of education of the services of a body of men who have zeal and time to devote to it'. But even in the field of education, the State cannot confine itself to considerations that are purely educational.

11. *Elphinstone and Indigenous Schools.*—There can be no doubt that, while Elphinstone was keenly interested in higher education, his thought constantly turned to the education of the great masses of the people. He feared that the cessation of the wars in the Deccan might only see a continuance of that neglect of education which the unsettlement of the past years had produced. His call therefore was for a large increase in the number of schools, for he looked on this as a responsibility which the Government could not shirk. He desired to have vernacular schools established throughout the whole Presidency under good superintendence and satisfactory teachers. He saw plainly that if any stable system of education was to be built up it must have its roots in the love of the people of India for education, a love which expressed itself in the maintenance of the many schools that existed before the East India Company developed from a commercial into a ruling power. He realized as clearly as did Adam in Bengal that the general education of the people would never come within sight of accomplishment until the fullest advantage was taken of the indigenous system. It was a system which the people liked, and it was capable of development. 'At no time', he writes, 'could I wish that the purely Hindu part of the course should be totally abandoned. It would surely be a preposterous way of adding to the intellectual treasures of a nation to begin by the destruction of its indigenous literature; and I cannot but think that the future attainments of the natives will be increased in extent as well as in variety by being, as it were, grafted on their own previous knowledge, and imbued with their original and peculiar character'. These vernacular schools were to be founded, or aided, by Government. And within less than twenty years of the writing of this Minute over one hundred such schools had been established.

12. *Elphinstone and Higher Education.*—But the Minute of Elphinstone makes it clear that, while he wished for the wide extension of education, and while he considered that 'the education of the poor must be in great measure the charge of the Government', he saw little hope for the spread of education unless careful attention was given to the interests of the higher classes. 'The missionaries', he says, 'find the lowest castes the best pupils. But we must be careful how we offer our special encouragement to men of that description. They are not only the most despised, but among the least numerous of the great divisions of society; and it is to be feared if our system of education first took root among them it would never spread further, and we might find ourselves at the head of a new class superior to the rest in useful knowledge but hated and despised by the castes to whom these new attainments would always induce us to prefer them. Such a state of things would be desirable if we were contented to rest our power on our army or on the attachment of a part of the population, but it is inconsistent with every attempt to found it on a more extended basis.' And so, when in his Minute, he passes from vernacular to English schools he is not slow to express his belief that the latter provide the speediest means for the dessemination of knowledge. 'If English', he writes, 'could be at all diffused among persons who have the least time for reflexion the progress of knowledge by means of it would be accelerated in a tenfold ratio, since every man who made himself acquainted with a science through the English language would be able to communicate it in his own language to his own countrymen.' It is interesting to come upon this a decade before Macaulay took up his pen. And it is worth while remembering that these were the words of one who laboured for mass education, and who was ready to take advantage of every indigenous method that promised to advance the cause which he had so much at heart. Nor must

it be forgotten that, in the view of Elphinstone, the more higher education was fostered the more would higher administrative positions be opened to those who received it. To him education was the reparation made by Government to the people for the injury which warfare and conquest had inflicted on them. In the leaves of that tree he saw what was for the healing of the nation.

13. *Farish's Minute.*—When we pass from this remarkable Minute to our second document we find attention being directed to the slow progress which education is making among the masses. In 1825 the Collectors had been asked to send in returns as to the condition of education in the Presidency. In submitting these Farish, as secretary to Government, accompanied them with a Memorandum. Elphinstone had said in his Minute that while private agency might improve schools it was for Government to increase the number of them. But Farish points out that it would be next to impossible to establish 'numerous new schools at once'. And he gives two reasons for saying this. The first is that the Government is not able to provide the 'vigilant superintendence' that would be required. And the second is that there is not an adequate supply of teachers. 'If it be resolved', he says, 'that Government should assist in establishing schools where they are not, the first step for rendering them really useful would be to collect youths for the purpose of instructing them according to a proper system, and in proper books and branches of knowledge, and after they have attained sufficient to qualify them for the duty at a school which can be ably superintended, to appoint them to the schools for which they have been selected. . . The extension of education by this means might not be so great in the first three years as it would be by establishing schools with such masters as are now to be met with, but after that it would extend as speedily and much more efficiently'. If, then, any widespread system of education was to be undertaken

there were required not only financial resources, which the Governor thought that there were means of supplying, but also qualified teachers and efficient inspectors, which there seemed little hope of supplying at least for some time. The emphasis which this Minute placed upon professional training and an adequate inspectorate is very striking.

14. *Notification of* 1852.—There remain for consideration two Notifications of the Government of Bombay. The first of these appeared only a couple of years before the Despatch of 1854 reached India. The Bombay Board of Education intimated in 1852 that it proposed to open six new schools and that Government intended to 'defray the principal part of the expenses of the schools' in the first instance, but that this was not a permanent arrangement, for the Board had arrived at a principle which it forthwith stated. It is 'that the Government funds ought not to be laid out in maintaining schools without any co-operation from those who profit by them, but should be used to assist the inhabitants of towns and villages who are desirous to establish better schools than they have hitherto known. . . The Board therefore invite applications from the villages who desire to establish superior schools to those now in existence and who seek for assistance from Government, stating the amount per month which they are willing to guarantee to the schoolmaster. In deciding between different applications for assistance, the Board will be chiefly governed by the monthly amount offered for the schoolmaster. The Board will also make small grants not exceeding rupees five a month to the schoolmasters of indigenous schools, if the schoolmaster appointed by the village has been educated in a Government or English school, and be reported on by the Superintendent.' Thus in October 1852 is the principle of grant-in-aid stated by the Bombay Government, and the co-operation between departmental and private effort which Elphinstone saw to be the key of the situation, is made the foundation of advance.

15. *Notification of* 1854.—The Notification of 1852 was followed by one issued on the 16th May 1854. The former had related to District Schools, the latter relates to Vernacular Schools. And in connexion with their establishment the same policy is announced. Notice is given by the Board of Education that 'they are prepared to receive applications from the inhabitants of all towns and villages who are desirous of having a vernacular school established, and who at the same time are prepared to prove their anxiety for the establishment of such school by agreeing to assist in supporting it'. And the amount of support that must be given is thus stated. Half the salary of the schoolmaster must be provided by the village, the Government will meet the other half. A suitable school house must be provided and kept in repair. Contingent expenses must be defrayed, and fees must be levied. So it came about that one of the great principles of the Despatch of the 19th July 1854 was made a working principle in the Presidency of Bombay by official announcements that were issued on the 26th October 1852 and the 16th May 1854. Elphinstone saw these principles and believed in them. Perhaps if he had had in his time better teachers and the prospect of more satisfactory superintendence, perhaps too if he had been exercising his power when the foundations of government were not so 'slippery' as he felt them to be, he might have been able to put into full force, and thus a generation before the appearance of the Despatch, those principles of grant-in-aid and of co-operation between official and non-official educational activity which are so potent as instruments for securing a wide and speedy dissemination of knowledge.

16. *Contribution to Educational Policy.*—In the very effective way which the preceding paragraphs have shown did Bombay make important contributions towards the formation of an educational policy. We may say that they were four in number, and each of them vital. First, if the spread of education is to be assured,

a purely official method will not suffice. It must be achieved by the employment of the method of grant-in-aid. A great step was taken when in answer to the question: What is the best way in which Government can employ its resources on behalf of education? Elphinstone replied: By not keeping them all for itself, but by putting them out to most productive usury through aiding non-official agencies. Second, there are two functions of which the State can never divest itself in connexion with education, that of initiation and that of inspection. The prescience of Elphinstone as regards the first of these has not received the credit which is its due. After being forgotten for well-nigh half a century the principle of State initiative has come once more into prominence especially in the sphere of elementary education. It finds a place, by a happy coincidence, in the Primary Education Act of Elphinstone's own province. As regards the responsibility of the State for the provision of adequate inspection, eyes still remain shut to much that this responsibility involves. When will they be opened? Third, there requires to be a policy clearly enunciated and fully accepted regarding the training of teachers. For not a few parts of India Mr. Secretary Farish might still be writing today his Minute of a hundred years ago. There are, however, one or two provinces where his words have not gone unheeded. And fourth, local self-government must play its rightful part in the educational system of the land. While the Notifications of 1852 and 1854 anticipate the method of grant-in-aid, they anticipate also a factor which was to enter into Indian education at a much later date. It cannot escape notice that, while these Notifications call for a combination of public and private effort, and thus present an essential aspect of the grant-in-aid system, they as plainly entrust the management of the schools set up in accordance with them to public not to private bodies. The people of an area are to make a contribution for educational purposes, Government is to subsidize them in their endeavour, but the management of the schools that result from this endeavour is vested in the body that issues the Notifications, that is the Board of Education. Thus schools were to arise in the maintenance of which local and departmental finances were to combine, and of which the management was to be in the hands of a public body. When the Notifications are looked at from this point of view it will be seen that the Indian Education Commission was fully justified when it stated in the course of its Report that the system which these Notifications inaugurated 'may be regarded as the germ from which the local fund schools that now exist developed'. Thus in Bombay was sown the seed of departmental, board, and aided managements. At the same time the Notifications raise the question to which more recent events also draw attention: Would it not be in the best interests of education that the grant-in-aid system should be a comprehensive one, bringing within its sweep Local no less than Private managements?

References

G. W. Forrest, *Mountstuart Elphinstone: Official Writings.* Contains full text of Elphinstone's Minute.

H. Sharp, *Selections from Educational Records. Part I.* Chapter iv gives Farish's letter. In Appendix A reference is made to the School Book and School Society (Fisher's Memoir).

J. A. Richey, *Selections from Educational Records. Part II.* Chapter iv gives Notifications of 1852 and 1854 in full.

J. S. Cotton, *Mountstuart Elphinstone.* Elphinstone's educational proposes and reforms are dealt with in Chapter x.

IV. Conditions in the North-Western Provinces

17. *Educational Importance of the Provinces.*—Before proceeding to narrate what was done in the third Presidency, there will be an advantage in turning aside for a little to look at what was done in an area which at one time was on the point of becoming a fourth Presidency. This was the part of Bengal which in 1833 was

formed into the Lieutenant-Governorship of the North-Western Provinces. In that administration there was carried out in the decade preceding the publication of the 1854 Despatch a most successful educational experiment. It was marked by features which distinguish it from the educational development of Bengal, and demands a separate treatment which it is most convenient to accord it at this point.

18. *Thomason's Minute.*—In 1843 James Thomason who has been called 'the Father of Elementary Education in India' was appointed lieutenant-governor of the North-Western Provinces. Soon after he assumed office he issued a circular dealing with the state of education as he found it. There was very little higher education, little appreciation of it, and little need felt for it. The pressing need was the establishment of schools which would reach the great masses of the people. But how were the people in the villages to become interested in education? Thomason's reply was that the recent land settlement of the province which had mapped out every field and had given a record of each owner's possessions afforded the spur that was needed for the spread of education. Every one who had an interest in the land should be 'able to satisfy himself that the entries effecting himself were correct'. But he would be able to do this only if he could read and write and count and measure. And the means for enabling him to do this were at hand. They were the indigenous schools, the number of which could be increased and the character of their instruction improved. But this would never be done if Government sought to do everything through its own agency. 'It is important', he says to his officials, 'to carry the people with you and to aid their efforts'. In this spirit and with this aim he set to work. Let us see what he accomplished.

19. *Thomason's Schemes.*—In November 1846 Thomason issued his first scheme. According to it a school was to be set up in every village which contained not

less than two hundred houses; and the cost of maintaining the school was to be met from an endowment. This endowment was to be secured in the following fashion. The zemindars and responsible residents of the village were to endow the schoolmaster with a jageer of from five to ten acres, and when this was done Government would remit the assessment on the land thus set apart for educational purposes. This practical method of co-operation between Government and the people for the advance of education was submitted to the Court of Directors. But they shrank from an endowment in land which might become hereditary, so they rejected the plan. In its place Thomason prepared his second scheme, and this was approved by the Directors in 1849. It provided for 'the establishment of one Government school in each tahseeldaree, and a powerful agency for visiting all the indigenous schools, for furnishing the people and the teachers with advice, assistance and encouragement, and for rewarding those schoolmasters who may be found the most deserving'. It was a scheme which, it will be seen, consisted of two parts. One was the provision of a few well-staffed and well-equipped schools maintained by Government. The other was the appointment of a large number of 'visitors' who, by constant travelling throughout the province should do all in their power to encourage indigenous or privately managed schools. This service they were to render by helping people to open schools in localities where there were none, for instance, by getting good teachers for them, and by giving such advice to teachers and managers as would raise the standards of schools already in existence. All such schools were to be 'entered on the lists' of the visitors or inspectors, or as we should now say they were to be entered on the list of schools recognized by the State. The scheme was thus one which took account of every interest public and private, and which did full justice to teacher, pupil, and inspector. At first limited in its application to eight districts it spread to every part of the province, and the network of schools established and recognized bore unmistakable testimony to its value.

20. *Halkabandi Schools.*—Another aspect of what was done in the North-Western Provinces remains to be mentioned. It has an important bearing upon policy, for it may be regarded as the precursor of Local Board educational effort. The year 1851 saw the beginning in the Provinces of what were termed Halkabandi Schools. A primary school was planted in a village which was looked upon as the most central in a group of villages. It would thus be accessible to a large number of children living in the surrounding villages. But how was it to be supported? By means of a careful survey the number of children to be educated was ascertained and an accurate record of the village revenues was prepared. Ultimately an agreement was come to as regards the amount which those who owned the land could contribute for educational purposes. And we read that 'the zemindars agreed to contribute towards education at the rate of one per cent on their land revenues'. Here we have a body of people in an area imposing on themselves a local rate so as to help on the education of the locality. The result of this experiment in local self-government was that the Provinces were supplied with thousands of Halkabandi Schools.

21. *Contribution to Educational Policy.*—It would be pleasant to linger over what was done in the Oriental Colleges at Benares, Delhi, and Agra to combine oriental learning with western knowledge. The accounts of these efforts are full and the enthusiasm which pervades them it is impossible to escape. Their interest to us lies in their relation to educational policy. In certain respects they anticipated one of the distinguishing features of the 1854 Despatch; they looked on education in India as the meeting place of cultures. In so doing they made a clear contribution to the adoption by the State of a fundamental line of policy. But the outstanding contribution of these Provinces to educational policy

lay in the field of elementary education. And in that field we may notice three main strands which the educational activities of the North-Western Provinces wove into the web of educational policy. The first is the concern for the education of the great mass of the people, an education which must come to them through their own mother tongues. There can be no national system of education which does not recognize and provide adequate means for the satisfaction of this concern. The second is the responsibility which lies upon the State to take its part in what will encourage to the full the provision of vernacular education, and in so doing to work through every agency that can be depended on. And the third is the indication of one fruitful way by which elementary education may be widely disseminated. People may tax themselves for that specific purpose within a defined area, and they may be subsidized by the State for undertaking what is a national as well as a local service. Education demands for its progress the effective exercise of local self-government.

References

J. A. Richey, *Selections from Educational Records. Part II.* Chapter vi gives in full official documents connected with Thomason's schemes.

Indian Education Commission Report. See Chapter ii for references to Thomason's plans and the Halkabandi Schools.

R. Temple, *James Thomason.* What Thomason did for education is narrated in Chapter xi.

W. Muir, *James Thomason.* A full account of Thomason's work for education, including text of his notification, on pages 77-78.

V. Conditions in Bengal

22. *Appointment of Committee of Public Instruction.*—As we might expect some of the most important contributions to the formation of educational policy came from the province in which were the headquarters of

Government, the Presidency of Bengal. It is enough for our purpose if we limit the period of our survey to somewhere about a century, and take as our starting point the Government Resolution of the 17th July 1823. That is the document which states that 'the Governor-General in Council resolves that there shall be constituted a General Committee of Public Instruction for the purpose of ascertaining the state of education in this part of India, and of the public institutions designed for its promotion, and of considering and from time to time submitting to Government the suggestion of such measures as it may appear expedient to adopt with a view to the better instruction of the people, to the introduction among them of useful knowledge and to the improvement of their moral character'. The funds placed at the disposal of this Committee were £10,000 or a lakh of rupees, in addition to sums already assigned and endowments made or to be made. Even in 1823 it was perfectly clear that only a very limited amount could be done by the Committee if it had no more than an annual grant of a lakh of rupees.

23. *Aim of the Committee.*—This limitation is frankly acknowledged by Mr. Holt Mackenzie, a member of the Government, in a Note which he drew up and circulated along with the Resolution. The aim of Government is exceedingly wide in its sweep. 'Whatever can extend the knowledge of the people', he writes, 'whatever can give them a juster conception of the true relation of things, whatever can excite invention and invigorate the judgment, whatever can rouse to steady exertion and bind to honest purposes, whatever in short tends to make men wiser and better and happier here and hereafter—all are desired to be given, in due season, to the people of India'. This magnificent programme is no sooner set forth, however, than very definite limits are set to the possibility of its realization, and we speedily understand why it is that Mr. Mackenzie uses the qualifying words 'in due season'. What we should look upon

as the corner-stone of any system of national education is swiftly pushed aside. 'To provide for the education of the great body of the people', says Holt Mackenzie, 'seems to be impossible, at least in the present state of things'. Elementary education, that is to say, is beyond the powers which the State possesses. If only a lakh of rupees is available, only a part of the building can be proceeded with. And that part, it is declared, is to be at the top, not at the foundation. 'The first object of attention', the Note tells us, 'should be the limited classes who are now instructed in the learning of the country'. From the education of the small body of men who are able to combine Oriental learning with European science it may be hoped that education will in time spread to those who compose the great mass of the people. What was understood, then, by the Government when they passed their all-important Resolution in 1823 amounted to this. First, the State wishes to introduce a general scheme of education for India. But, in the second place, the State has only a limited supply of funds at its disposal for educational purposes. Therefore it intends to devote this small sum to the education of the few who can benefit by higher education, leaving the education of the masses to the indigenous agencies already in existence and to those who have a philanthropic interest in the education of India, trusting that through the education of the few education may be somehow or other passed on to the many. If these points are kept in mind they will be found to afford some help in the way of unravelling the somewhat tangled skein of educational policy in Bengal.

24. *The Realization of this Aim.*—The Committee followed in general the lines suggested by Holt Mackenzie in his Note. But before ten years had passed a serious question arose which greatly disturbed the Committee's activities. By that time the original grant of £10,000 had been increased to £100,000, and there was a clear call for expansion. But what was to be the

method of this expansion? On that the Committee was divided. Yet while there were two parties in the Committee there was one point in regard to which both parties were at one; they were of opinion that their concern was not with the education of the masses but with the diffusion of higher education. That, however, was the only point of agreement. When they went on to consider how this higher education was to be imparted there was a sharp cleavage of opinion. Was this education to be given through the medium of English, or through that of Sanskrit or Arabic? It was there tha' division most plainly appeared. The division arose ov the interpretation of certain words in the Act of 181. the Act by which the charter of the East India Company had been renewed. Section 43 of that Act laid it down that 'a sum of not less than one lakh of rupees shall be set apart and applied to the revival and improvement of literature and the encouragement of the learned natives of India, and for the introduction and promotion of a knowledge of the sciences among the inhabitants of the British territories in India'. What was the meaning of this part of the Section? What was meant by 'literature', and by the expression 'a learned native'? The question seems to us almost academic, yet it was anything but that to those who were the members of the Committee of Public Instruction during the fifteen years succeeding its inauguration. To many of them there was only one interpretation of the words; 'literature' meant Arabic and Sanskrit literature, and a 'learned native of India' meant an Indian who was highly proficient in Sanskrit or Arabic. By other members of the Committee it was held that the expression 'literature' as it appeared in the Act was subject to no such restricted meaning, and that English, far from being excluded by the Act, was entitled to take its place as a literature to which the wording of the enactment was justly applicable. The Committee was thus divided into two opposing camps. They went by the names of Anglicists and Orientalists:

and in the year 1835 each camp contained one half of the Committee. That was the state of affairs when, as the Hon'ble T. B. Macaulay tells us, the subject came 'before me as a Member of the Council of India'.

25. *Macaulay's Minute.*—Macaulay lost no time in taking up the matter. The Minute in which he deals with it is dated the 2nd February 1835. It is as clearly as it is brilliantly expressed. It is marked by his characteristic antitheses and overstatements; but it is the almost breathless contention of one who feels that he is fighting or the best education and the truest welfare of India. is easy for us, with our present knowledge, to dwell pon the false estimate that was entertained a century ago of the value of the literatures of India; subsequent investigation has shown that Macaulay's characterization of these requires to be as much qualified as does, for instance, his characterization of the Rohillas. But the point which must not be overlooked or disguised is this that Macaulay got to the very heart of the problem as it was presented to him. He did not attempt to set forth a complete educational policy for India. The State at that time contemplated no such far-reaching achievement. He dealt simply with two facts. The first was that Government saw its way to spend only a limited sum on education. The second was that the best way had to be found in which this limited sum might be expended. 'We have a fund', he says, 'to be employed as Government shall direct for the intellectual improvement of the people of this country. The simple question is, What is the most useful way of employing it? All parties seem to be agreed on one point, that the dialects commonly spoken among the natives of this part of India contain neither literary nor scientific information, and are moreover so poor and rude that, until they are enriched from some other quarter, it will not be easy to translate any valuable work into them. It seems to be admitted on all sides that the intellectual improvement of those classes of the people who have the means of

pursuing higher studies can at present be effected only by means of some language not vernacular among them. What then shall that language be? One half of the Committee maintain that it should be the English, the other half strongly recommend the Arabic and Sanskrit. The whole question seems to me to be, Which language is the best worth knowing?' It required neither the brilliance nor the rhetoric of Macaulay to point out how Sanskrit and Arabic had been employed as the basis of education from the days of Warren Hastings and with what lamentable results, or to demonstrate in regard to English that 'whoever knows that language has ready access to all the vast intellectual wealth which all the wisest nations of the earth have created and hoarded in the course of ninety generations'. There was only one answer that Macaulay could give to the problem that confronted him, and he gave it. The small sum of money which the Government had for the supply of education should be given for the spread of education through the medium of English. In this position Macaulay had the strong support of the Governor-General. The original Minute has the endorsement of a single line : 'I give my entire concurrence to the sentiments expressed in this Minute. W. C. Bentinck'.

26. *The Governor-General's Resolution.*—On the 7th March 1835 the Governor-General in Council published the Resolution that gave official sanction to the policy which Macaulay had advocated. It runs as follows. 'First.—His Lordship in Council is of opinion that the great object of the British Government ought to be the promotion of European literature and science among the natives of India; and that all the funds appropriated for the purpose of education would best be employed on English education alone. Second.—But it is not the intention of His Lordship in Council to abolish any school or college of native learning, while the native population shall appear to be inclined to avail themselves of the advantages which it affords, and His Lordship in Council

directs that all the existing professors and students at all the institutions under the superintendence of the Committee shall continue to receive their stipends. . . . Third.—It has come to the knowledge of the Governor-General in Council that a large sum has been expended by the Committee on the printing of Oriental works; His Lordship directs that no portion of the funds shall hereafter be so employed. Fourth.—His Lordship in Council directs that all the funds which these reforms will leave at the disposal of the Committee be henceforth employed in imparting to the native population a knowledge of English literature and science through the medium of English language; and His Lordship in Council requests the Committee to submit to Government, with all expedition, a plan for the accomplishment of this purpose'.

27. *An Indian Aspiration Supported.*—The conclusion thus reached officially is sometimes represented as due to Macaulay's triumphant rhetoric. Reference to the records shows the groundlessness of this assertion. More than a decade before Macaulay set foot in India, Raja Rammohun Roy had addressed the Governor-General in a letter which left no doubt as to what he and other like-minded Indians desired to see resulting from the activity of the Committee of Public Instruction. It was not the diffusion of Sanskrit literature that they hoped for, but the expenditure of the funds at the disposal of the Committee on 'employing European gentlemen of talents and education to instruct the natives of India in mathematics, natural philosophy, chemistry, anatomy, and other useful sciences which the nations of Europe have carried to a degree of perfection that has raised them above the inhabitants of other parts of the world'. Not content with writing letters or addressing Government, the Raja took part in an active propaganda for the spread of English education, and assisted by personal influence and financial help every effort that was made to impart a higher education which was western in its character

and was conveyed through the medium of English. One has only to read such a book as Pandit Sivanath Sastri's *Ramtanu Lahiri, Brahmin and Reformer*, to learn what was going on in Bengal at this time. The breath, at times the tempest, of a renaissance blows through it. Men were awakening to a new life and outlook. They were breaking through the barriers of centuries, and they found in English and its literature a thrice welcome medium of emancipation. It is surprising that any government could have stood out for so long as twelve years against the momentum of the movement. And when at last Macaulay wrote his Minute he was not finding an outlet for an English prejudice but giving practical sympathy and support to a strong Indian aspiration. In 1835 the Government of India was, by its Resolution, imposing no European sentiment but complying with a keen Indian desire that had been active for the greater part of two decades.

28. *Position of the Vernaculars.*—It has been said that the passing of this Resolution and the triumph of the Anglicist party meant a definite and deliberate obstruction to the spread of vernacular literature and education. Once more, all that we have to do is to go to the records to realize the groundlessness of this assertion. The triumph of the Anglicist party was the defeat of the Orientalist party. But the Orientalist no less than Macaulay, looked upon 'the vernacular dialects as not fit to be made the vehicle of instruction in science or literature'. The position which the Orientalist occupied was thus not one which championed the vernaculars as the media of instruction. It championed 'the expediency of letting the natives pursue their present course of instruction and of endeavouring to engraft European science thereon'. And by 'their present course of instruction' was meant the instruction of Hindus in Sanskrit and of Muhammadans in Arabic and Persian, such instruction as would qualify them to 'become moolavies or pundits', as Mr. Prinsep the great protagonist of the

Orientalists puts it. It is the instruction on which Raja Rammohun Roy pours the vials of his scorn in the letter which he addressed to the Governor-General. To seek to engraft on it western learning was to seek for what scholarship is only now able to do in a very modest way after the lapse of a century. And even if it had been possible in 1835 it would not have meant so much as the beginning of mass education through a single vernacular of India. The fact is that the Government speedily realized how impossible it was in the conditions that then prevailed, to put India in possession of a comprehensive scheme of education. This became clear as soon as a Committee of Public Instruction was set up in 1823, and the Committee saw the task before it and the funds at its command. Holt Mackenzie took the only reasonable position. The task of the Committee could be carried out only by instalments; and the first instalment was the limited field of higher education. There was some chance that funds would permit of an effective beginning being made in that field, and what had been begun could be followed up. To enter the boundless field of mass education at that stage was to court certain failure. 'In the long discussions which preceded the change in the plan of the Committee' says C. E. Trevelyan, who himself took part in them, 'there was one point on which all parties were agreed; that was, that the vernacular languages contained neither the literary nor scientific information necessary for a liberal education. It was admitted on all sides that while the instruction of the mass of the people through the medium of their own language was the ultimate object to be kept in view, yet meanwhile teachers had to be trained, a literature had to be created, and the co-operation of the upper and middle classes had to be secured'. And in taking up this position the Government fortified itself, at least in its own opinion, by claiming in its support the theory of filtration. It held that what was taught to those who were capable of receiving higher education would little by little permeate the whole. It was a comforting doctrine for a Government that had little money to spend; but it took small account of the actual conditions of Indian society or of Indian educational needs. We may agree that the Government was not without justification for the step which it took; its failure lay in not preparing without delay to take another.

29. *Auckland's Minute.*—It would be interesting to follow the swing of the educational pendulum. 'Education by means of the Oriental languages alone was clearly perceived to be vain and hopeless'. Then came doubts as to the advisability of an education of which English was 'the exclusive channel'. And November 1839 found the Governor-General, Lord Auckland, issuing an exhaustive Minute in which he reviewed the whole position of Indian education. He admits that it is the lack of funds which has led to the action hitherto taken. And he tries to keep the balance even by giving fresh stability to the Oriental colleges on the one hand, and by encouraging English education in the provincial schools on the other. As to what Adam proposed for the establishment of schools reaching the masses of the people through vernacular teaching, his opinion is that 'the period has not yet arrived when the Government can join in these attempts with reasonable hope of practical good'. To go into Auckland's Minute, however, and the reply of the Court of Directors made in 1841, while it would be valuable from the historical point of view, would lead us away from our main topic. And the mention of Adam's name recalls us to what is our immediate concern.

30. *Adam's Recommendations.*—While Anglicist and Orientalist were crossing swords in Bengal and attracting most of the attention, there was a third party which was making a very quiet but very substantial contribution to the solution of the great educational problem of the time. This was the party to which Adam belonged, those who were interested in mass education, and who

were using every endeavour to promote it through the medium of the vernaculars. Adam had been appointed by Government to report upon the indigenous schools of Bengal, and the reports which he submitted are at once a survey of what was being done in these schools and a plea for their sympathetic encouragement and reform. After careful examination of the educational conditions which he found to prevail in the districts through which he toured, he came to the conclusion that 'existing native institutions from the highest to the lowest are the fittest means to be employed for raising and improving the character of the people'. He considers that to employ these institutions for such a purpose would be 'the simplest, the safest, the most popular, the most economical, and the most effectual plan for giving that stimulus to the native mind which it needs on the subject of education, and for eliciting the exertions of the natives themselves for their own improvement, without which all other means would be unavailing'. While he admits that the schools as he found them inclined to confirm in the pupils what was 'superficial and defective', he contends that improvements can be made upon them that will draw forth the best from the pupil, and lay the 'broad and deep foundations' of a truly national education. For one thing, he proposes that the vernacular department of English schools should be formed into a normal school and that it should be regarded as an honour for a teacher to be admitted to this school. Those who were counted worthy to enter the normal school should, after undergoing the training provided, be granted the income derived from a piece of land set apart for the benefit of the school, according to conditions laid down by Village School Associations. These Associations, resembling the modern Village Panchayets, were to be the administrators of the revenue derived from the land. Then for another thing, he holds that a Government inspector should be appointed whose duty it would be to examine the schoolmasters in the schools and to distribute appropriate awards. As to funds, Adam is of opinion that voluntary contributions would be made by wealthy zemindars who, because of this, might receive remissions from Government for the land which they gave as educational endowments. Further, he points to old religious endowments which might be appropriated for educational purposes. And then he strongly advocates grants from the general revenues of the country; for, as he says, 'whence is that revenue derived but from the bones and sinews, the toil and the sweat of those whose cause I am pleading?' Even this brief reference to the reports which were written by Adam, the first of them in the same year as Macaulay's Minute, and the last three years later, is sufficient to indicate the main features of the system which he pressed upon the Government of Bengal. He emphasized as fundamental the co-operation between the Government and the people of India in the work of education. Advantage, he held, should be taken of the indigenous schools, the teachers of which (under his plan) would not continue to be untrained but would be increasingly drawn from the ranks of those who had attended Normal Schools established by Government. The management of schools would remain in the hands of the people, the control and inspection would be in the hands of Government. Funds would be allocated from public revenues so as to aid the work done, and the amount given would bear some relation to the value of the instruction imparted. It was a well thought out scheme, rich in possibilities, and making no undue demand on public funds if carried out according to a carefully graded plan of introduction. But the Council of Education in Calcutta would have nothing to do with Adam's proposals. It considered them 'almost impracticable', and was of opinion that the cost would be too heavy. So it lost the opportunity of introducing in 1840 the second instalment of the scheme which had been conceived in 1823, and in regard to the first instalment of which official action had been taken in 1835. It was reserved for the North-Western Provinces, as we have seen, to buy back the opportunity.

31. *The Vernaculars and Higher Education.*—Adam was not alone in his championship of vernacular education. During his time, as well as before it, there was a body of educators steadily at work in Bengal who were enthusiasts for an education that was given in the language of the people. These men had done everything in their power to advance this form of education by increasing the number of vernacular schools and by training a number of teachers. And yet it is interesting to notice how many of them, when the higher education of their pupils came to be considered, gave their unswerving adherence to the position which had been upheld by Macaulay and Bentinck. There was no keener advocate of vernacular education in Bengal than William Carey, yet when Alexander Duff expounded to him in 1830 his plan for imparting higher education through the medium of English, the aged missionary gave Duff his blessing. And further it has to be noted that, when Duff established his school for higher education through English, he would not admit to the English classes any one who had not previously pursued a course in the vernacular. A Bengali section was begun, and in it vernacular teaching was given not only to those who had not reached the English class but also to those who were reading in the English class itself. There was a reason for the course which Duff adopted and championed, and he was not slow to state it. Bengali, he believed, had not reached that stage of development which made it capable of fulfilling the objects he had in view. He felt that in vocabulary and ideas it was unable to perform for higher education the functions which the flexibility and comprehensiveness of the English language fitted it to discharge. He looked forward to the day which he was sure would come (and for us it has been reserved to see how justified he was in this expectation), when

Bengali enriched by wider contacts would be the natural medium of instruction for all forms of education. But he believed the time was not yet. He therefore threw his whole weight into a system of education which employed English as its medium five years before Macaulay wrote a word of his Minute. And he did this in the interests of the people of India who were seeking to open the door to progress, and were finding the Government of the twenties to all appearance shutting the door in their face.

32. *The State and Vernacular Education.*—But while the advocacy of higher education was thrown into prominence by the fierce light of controversy, steady effort on behalf of vernacular education was being carried on by unobtrusive agencies, and not least by the successors of Carey. The patronage of Government, however, was not extended to these efforts; for Government did not undertake the establishment of vernacular schools, and no regular system of aid was placed within the reach of those who, while they sympathized with what Government had achieved for the progress of education, yet considered it inadvisable that the first instalment of its programme, namely the effort on behalf of the higher classes, should precede the second instalment, the effort on behalf of the masses, by any long interval. But those who took up this position had a hard battle to fight; they could not be sure of financial assistance from the State, and Bengal public opinion, at least in the Lower Provinces, has set in another direction. As in Madras, so in Bengal, the upholders of the steady diffusion and improvement of vernacular education had to wait till the publication of the 1854 Despatch to receive the official vindication of their endeavours, and that encouragement from the State to which, in the national interests, they had long been entitled.

33. *Duff's Proposals.*—It was when the charter of the East India Company was being renewed in 1853 that the matter of education once again received serious con-

sideration. It was then that Duff appeared before the Select Committee of both Houses of Parliament and answered in characteristic fashion those who opposed and those who sympathized with the conclusions to which his experience had led him. Finally in answer to the question put to him by Lord Stanley of Alderley, 'Will you state what you would propose the Government should do towards the further improvement and extension of education in India', he gave the following statement: 'Fall back on the resolutions of Lord William Bentinck in March 1835, resolutions which, without damaging or interfering with the existing vested rights of anyone, would lead to the gradual abolition of those oriental colleges as seminaries for educational training, and thus liberate the funds so wastefully lavished upon them for the purposes of a sound and healthful education throughout the land. If the learned oriental languages are to be taught at all in the Government institutions they ought to be taught simply as languages . . . with a practical view towards the enrichment of the vernacular tongues, and the raising up of a superior class of vernacular translators and teachers.

'Then, secondly, the time has come when in places like Calcutta and Bombay the Government might very well relinquish its pecuniary control over primary and merely elementary education. . . Some of the heads of native society have now acquired sufficient experience and aptitude to enable them to carry on the management of the necessary preparatory seminaries themselves. In this way a considerable saving might be effected in the educational funds.

'Thirdly, the time has come when, more especially at the Presidency seats lectureships on high professional subjects, such as law and civil engineering, should be established, not as an integral or constituent part of the course of any existing Government College, but on such a free and unrestricted footing as to admit of the attendance of qualified students from all other institutions.

The time has also come when in Calcutta, at least, with comparatively little additional expense to Government, a university might be established somewhat after the general model of the London University, and with a sufficient number of faculties, constituted on so wide and liberal and comprehensive a basis as to embrace within the range of its stimulating and fostering influence whatever sound, invigorating, purifying, elevating studies may be carried on in any, whether of the Government or non-Government, institutions.

'Fourthly, the time has come when, in the estimation even of many who formerly thought otherwise, the Government might with the greatest propriety and advantage act on the principle recommended in the Minute of Lord Tweeddale, dated August 1846, namely, to allow the Bible to be introduced as a class-book into the English classes of Government institutions, leaving it entirely free to the students to read it or not, as their consciences might dictate or their parents desire.

'Lastly, the Government ought to extend its aid to all other institutions, by whomsoever originated and supported, where a sound general education is communicated. . . Here at home the Government does not expend its educational resources on the maintenance of a few monopolist institutions; it strives to stimulate all parties, by offering proportional aid to all who show themselves willing to help themselves. . . Without directly trenching on the peculiar religious convictions or prejudices of any parties, Hindoo, Mussulman, European, or any others, the Government educational funds would have the effect of extending and multiplying tenfold, at a comparatively small cost, really useful schools and seminaries, and of thus more rapidly and widely diffusing the benefits of an enlightened education among the masses of the people'.

34. *Bearing on Educational Policy.*—Any one who reads this reply of Duff's is bound to be struck with two or three outstanding features. For one thing Duff was

aware that he was advocating what, if adopted, would have a far-reaching influence on the progress of education in India, and just because he was aware of that he did not allow himself to forget that the East India Company had always to keep an eye upon its shareholders. Thus it is that he conjoins comprehensive plans with assurances that the Company's funds would not be subjected to any severe strain, and that indeed economies might easily be effected. There is no surer way even in our own times to block an educational project than to represent it as making heavy demands on public funds. Then, for another thing, while Duff felt strongly that the State was spending large sums on oriental colleges without any corresponding benefit to oriental scholarship, a position in which he stood by no means alone, he suggested a service which these colleges might render to vernacular learning, and by the rendering of which they might greatly help the cause of education. In doing this he voices afresh his unfailing concern for the advancement of the education of the masses through their own mother tongues. Further, he draws attention to a point which was in danger of being forgotten, namely that education had raised up from among the people of India those who were perfectly competent to undertake the management of educational institutions. And he presses upon Government its responsibility for the recognition of this fact and of what follows from it, the relinquishment by Government of its function as a manager when there are Indian non-official managers to take its place. And lastly, we cannot but note, if we compare what Duff said in his evidence before Parliament with what is laid down in the Despatch issued by the East India Company in 1854, some account of which is given in the following Chapter, how largely Duff's proposals anticipated, perhaps it might be truer to say helped to mould, the main provisions of that Despatch. In a rather remarkable way Duff contrived to bring together so much in one statement that it embraced not only the more important elements of the contribution made by Bengal to the formation of an educational policy, but also introduced ideas of his own which stimulated thought and led to action, even though it was not the action which he would himself have advocated. The general system of aid for which he pleaded became the foundation on which the educational policy of the Despatch rests. The universities which he desired to see incorporated had their place in the scheme set forth in the Despatch, and were actually established within four years of the time when he submitted his evidence. He proposed that public revenues should be released for education, and this was done in the Despatch according to a plan which did justice to vernacular instruction as well as to Oriental and English learning. The importance and value of non-official managements to which he directs attention received their due recognition in the statement of official policy which the Despatch embodies. And the principle of religious neutrality was the answer of the Company to Duff's plea for the introduction of the Bible into the classes of Government colleges. When Duff spoke, the point had been reached when practice alone no longer sufficed. Definite policy was called for. And within a year the enunciation of that policy had been definitely formulated.

References

H. Sharp, *Selections from Educational Records, Part I.* Chapter iv gives Holt Mackenzie's letter and the correspondence connected with the information of the General Committee of Public Instruction. Chapter v gives Raja Rammohun Roy's letter to the Governor-General. In Chapters vi and vii light is cast on the Anglicist and Orientalist controversy by extracts from official documents. Macaulay's Minute is given in full. Lord Auckland's Minute is given in Chapter viii.

G. Anderson and M. Subedar: *The Development of an Indian Policy.* In Chapter vi there are extracts from

Macaulay's Minute, Raja Rammohun's letter, Adam's Reports, and Trevelyan.

D. C. Boulger: *Lord William Bentinck* gives information regarding Bentinck's educational aims and policy more especially in Chapter viii.

C. E. Trevelyan: *On the Education of the People of India*. The clear statement of one who had his part in the educational controversy of 1835.

Lord Ronaldshay: *The Heart of Aryavarta*. The opening Chapters are specially valuable for a description of conditions in Bengal about 1830, and for the contrast that is drawn with present conditions.

Further consideration of the work of Bentinck, Macaulay, Carey, and Duff will be found in G. O. Trevelyan: *Life and Letters of Lord Macaulay* (where conditions in Calcutta at the time of the educational controversy are described and illustrated by extracts from Macaulay's correspondence); G. Smith: *Life of Alexander Duff* (much information regarding Duff's attitude to the vernaculars and English; also his evidence before the Select Committee); G. Smith: *Life of William Carey*, and S. P. Carey: *William Carey* (position of Serampore missionaries); H. Whitehead: *Indian Problems in Religion, Education and Politics* (reference to Macaulay's part in educational development).

W. Adam: *Reports on Vernacular Education in Bengal and Behar*, submitted to Government in 1835, 1836, and 1838 and edited by J. Long (invaluable sources of information).

Sivanath Sastri, *Ramtanu Lahiri, Brahmin and Reformer* (interesting account of conditions in Calcutta in early part of nineteenth century).

VI. Contributions Towards a Policy

35. *Provincial Activities.*—In some such way as the preceding sections have indicated did the different aspects and forms of educational practice take their rise, some in this province, some in that, according as circumstances of time and place called them forth. And having risen they took, like streams, their separate courses, till at last in 1854 they united to form the one

great flow of educational policy which then began to make its way through every part of the land. Madras showed voluntary effort at work on behalf of education, and this effort, aided by Government, steadily increasing the diffusion of knowledge. It showed attention given by private individuals and philanthropic bodies to the education of the masses in their own languages, and official and non-official agencies combining in that service of higher education which brought East and West into fruitful contact. It showed also that if there is to be real progress there must be well qualified teachers and an educational policy which is not subject to frequent change or sudden reversal. In Bombay emphasis was placed on the advantage which comes from the co-operation between public and private effort on behalf of education, on the value of trained teachers, and on the benefit of good inspectors. Emphasis was also placed upon the responsibility of Government for the initiation of educational activity, and for the most effective employment of its finances in the endeavour to advance education. And finally emphasis was laid upon the benefits which would accrue to education from local combination in town and country. The North-Western Provinces saw a general system of popular education through the vernaculars initiated and successfully maintained, with features that had much in common with both the grant-in-aid system and the local board system of later date. Bengal declared itself officially in favour of a comprehensive system of education, but resolved to confine itself to the first instalment of that scheme, namely higher education through the medium of English. Into this it threw its strength, and it was of opinion that its limited funds would be used to best advantage by such restriction of its endeavours. It was prepared to give assistance to agencies which devoted themselves to the spread of education through the medium of the vernaculars, but a policy regulating the manner of this assistance had yet to be formulated. A scheme for the development of education among the masses of the population by the employment and improvement of indigenous schools and methods was regarded as impracticable in existing conditions; but a proposal for the establishment of a university found a considerable measure of support.

36. *Principles Involved.*—As we look through the educational activities which were at work in the different provinces from 1785 to 1854 we see one or two lines of action emerging, tentatively as it were to begin with, and then receiving fuller recognition and more constant employment as time goes on, and their usefulness becomes apparent. It is worth while noting some of these, for we shall come upon them again, when the lines of action having been tested and approved take their place as principles of declared policy. One of the most important of these is the very gradual realization by the State of its responsibility for seeing to the education of the people. This has to wait till 1854 for its definite avowal; but the idea was there a generation before that and was not without effect on State activity. Then there is, though it is only faintly, a recognition of the fact that, if the State has a responsibility for education, it has a responsibility also for seeing that facilities for education are provided, that teachers are trained, and that work done is subjected to fitting scrutiny and furnished with appropriate counsel. Further, in a somewhat hesitating way, there is brought forward the thought of a large scheme of education; hesitating, for it is hardly presented before attention is concentrated officially on a small one. There is consideration of, but no definite conclusion with regard to, the task which Government itself can undertake and the work which can be carried on by others. It is not clear whether education is to be the heritage of all or the privilege of a few. There is doubt as to what place should be given to indigenous factors and what place to those which are drawn from regions beyond. But,

with all the uncertainty and hesitation, action tends in the direction of a combination of agencies as likely to be most effective, and towards a comprehensive scheme of education where the needs of none will be overlooked. The line of action, however, can hardly be described as a straight line; it is when the declaration of 1854 is reached that we see whither it has been tending. Then, again, there seems to be a growing agreement as to the most satisfactory way of employing the financial resources of the State on behalf of education; in a practical way it is acknowledged that aid given to non-official agencies constitutes a wise use of public revenues, and that it leads to a spread of education which goes beyond what the State by any agency that was purely its own could accomplish. And bound up with this is the idea that aid may be administered in more ways than one; it may help the efforts of private individuals and bodies, or it may supplement the combined efforts of those who reside in a particular locality. A generation and more has to pass before the implications of these ideas are fully realized and appreciated. And finally there is the question of the relation between education and religion, asked, considered in some of its aspects, found to lead to difference of opinion, and left unanswered. But just because it had received no answer it was waiting at the end of the period with which we are dealing for the enunciation of a principle that would reconcile the claims of religious education and the obligation of the State to maintain the position of religious neutrality. In 1854 such a principle found a place in the declaration of official policy.

37. *Preparation issues in Policy.*—Actual conditions extending over a period of seventy years had set minds thinking deeply on the subject of education and its many aspects. Issues had become clearer in the course of that time, difficulties had been faced, plans had been formed, practice had been placed on a surer footing. By the end of the period it was evident that haphazard

action was as little appropriate in the field of education as it had become in the growing field of administration. Those who devoted themselves to the cause of education saw that a certain body of principles had been disclosed, and that in the course of much testing they had proved their worth. The interests of India's youth demanded that these principles should not be lost, rather that they should become the vitalizing power of a comprehensive educational policy in the benefits of which the whole country would share. With the publication of the 1854 Despatch there came the satisfaction of this demand.

CHAPTER II

Statement of the Policy

I. Documents to be Considered

1. The period of preparation extended over some seventy years. It was a long time, but it was a time exceedingly well spent. In the course of it, educational effort and practice had wrought lasting benefit to India, and at the end of it there emerged a policy on which Indian education still rests as on a foundation well and truly laid. That policy is first stated in the Despatch which the Directors of the East India Company forwarded to the Governor-General on the 19th July 1854. When the Crown had taken the place of the Company 'the principles and policy of the Despatch of 1854 were re-affirmed by that of 1859', one of the first despatches sent out by the Secretary of State for India. A still fuller statement of policy made almost thirty years later is to be found in the Report of the Indian Education Commission published in 1883. And the list of official documents is completed by two Resolutions of the Government of India on Educational Policy, the first issued on the 11th March 1904, and the second on the 21st February 1913. Before the end of the decade in which the latter document appeared the Government of India Act had been passed, and education had become mainly a transferred subject, under the control of responsible Ministers in the various provinces. How policy has been affected by that Act we shall see when we come to Chapter IV. In the meantime the five documents which we have mentioned claim our attention, both because of their value when the responsibility for an educational policy rested with the Government of

India, and also because of what they mean to the whole of India now that this responsibility rests with each individual Province.

II. The Despatch of 1854

2. *Origin of the Despatch.*—The whole question of education came under consideration when the renewal of the Charter of the East India Company was being discussed in 1853. As a result of that discussion it became obvious that the time was ripe for a definite advance. But there was no little uncertainty as to what the nature of that advance should be. Even Sir Charles Wood, afterwards Lord Halifax, who was President of the Board of Control, was in doubt as to the proper course. He wrote to Lord Dalhousie, then Governor-General, 'asking his advice, as he confessed to being "a good deal at sea on education".' Little by little the line of advance became clearer, and the result was the Despatch on education, sometimes spoken of as the Halifax Despatch, which was issued in July 1854. The oftener one reads this document the more difficult is it to believe that it has attained the age of well nigh fourscore years. It is essentially a modern document. It provides for nothing less than a comprehensive scheme of national education in India.

3. *Object in View.*—The Despatch quickly states the reason for its promulgation. The Directors of the East India Company, through the legislation of 1853, have once again had 'the responsible trust of the Government of India placed in their hands'. And in their desire to discharge this trust the Directors recognize that it is one of their most sacred duties to supply to the people of India 'those vast material and moral blessings which flow from the general diffusion of useful knowledge'. What they have in view, they tell us, is a 'general scheme of Indian education'. For education, they believe, stimulates 'intellectual fitness, raises the moral

character of those who partake of its advantages', provides the State with those to whom may be assigned 'offices of trust', and has a most intimate connexion with 'the well-being of the people'. Education, then, as they conceive it, and as they wish it to be imparted, is closely related to life and conduct. It may be said to be marked, so far as the Despatch indicates, by three features; and in the light of what has gone before no less than of what was to follow, each of these has a significance on which we do well to dwell. To begin with, the education which the Directors have in view is one which brings the Indian mind into contact with 'the arts, science, philosophy, and literature' of the west. Secondly, the education for which the State becomes responsible is not intended for a minority, not merely for those who have a knowledge of English and seek to pursue higher studies, but for all, whatever their grade may be, who wish to benefit by the acquisition of knowledge. And third, it is an education which is to be conveyed not only through English but also through the medium of the mother tongues of the peoples of India.

4. *Three Features of that Object.*—In the three respects which have been mentioned the Despatch, as it were, rectifies certain defects of the past and sets up an aim that is still being striven after. For one thing the education which the Directors have in view is not an instrument for separating India from its past; it is intended to be a meeting place of cultures. The significance of this has come to be realized, and even so still only partially, within recent years. And Indian education has suffered through the tardiness of its recognition. For another thing, it is a complete system of education which the Directors contemplate. They acknowledge the claims of Oriental philosophy and of learning through the classical languages of India. They note with satisfaction the high attainments of some of the people of India in English literature and European

science. In both cases, however, the benefits of these studies, they remark, 'have been confined to but a small number of persons'. What the Directors wish to see is education becoming the possession of all 'the people of India in their different spheres of life'. They pledge themselves to promote elementary as well as higher education. The balance of the past is thus redressed. In the third place, while they recognize the great value of English as a means of opening the mind of India to a wide field of important knowledge they place the greatest emphasis on the part which the vernacular languages must play in a general educational scheme. 'We do not deny', say the Directors, 'the value in many respects of the mere faculty of speaking and writing English, but we fear that a tendency has been created in these districts unduly to neglect the study of the vernacular languages. It is neither our aim nor desire to substitute the English language for the vernacular dialects of the country. We have always been most sensible of the importance of the use of the languages which alone are understood by the great mass of the population. It is indispensable, therefore, that in any general system of education, the English language should be taught where there is demand for it; but such instruction should always be combined with a careful attention to the study of the vernacular language of the district, and with such general instruction as can be conveyed through that language'. In this discriminating manner is an old controversy settled and the method for the future marked out. From what shoals would the education of India have been saved, to what achievements would it by this time have attained, had these three features of the Despatch received adequate attention during the past seventy years.

5. *Control.*—But if a general system of education is to be introduced there must be administrative machinery, and the Despatch proceeds to describe what that machinery is to be. The former Boards and Councils

of Education are to be abolished and in their place there is to be created in every Province an Education Department. An officer is to be appointed 'specially charged with the business connected with education, and immediately responsible to Government for its conduct'. Thus was established the office of Director of Public Instruction in each province. Under these Directors there is to be 'a sufficient number of qualified inspectors' whose duties are to be of a twofold nature. In the first place they are to report on the state of schools and colleges inspected; and in the second place they are 'by their advice to aid the managers and schoolmasters in conducting colleges and schools of every description throughout the country'. It is specially laid down that the positions of educational officers are to be filled by those best fitted to occupy them, to whatever race they may belong.

6. *Universities.*—The Despatch then goes on to outline the educational machinery which is to be set in motion. First, Universities are to be incorporated so as to 'encourage a regular and liberal course of education', and the University of London is to be taken as their model. But not in any slavish sense. The University, administered by a Chancellor, Vice-Chancellor, and Fellows, is to consist of a number of affiliated colleges. And while the universities are 'not so much to be in themselves places of instruction as to test the value of education obtained elsewhere', the students who appear for their degrees are to be students of these affiliated colleges and will have to produce certificates of having pursued a regular course of study for a given time. Thus from the very first the Indian universities were not constituted so as to be merely examining bodies. They were to work through their colleges, and the certificates of these colleges were awarded to those whose conduct was satisfactory and who had undergone a specified course of study under competent teachers. And as if to mark the distinction between the Indian

universities and examining universities with still greater emphasis the Despatch states that 'it will be advisable to institute in connexion with the universities professorships for the purposes of the delivery of lectures in various branches of learning'. It is teaching universities that are aimed at.

7. *Colleges and Higher Education.*—Secondly, as regards the affiliated colleges any management will be acceptable provided the college satisfies the university of its ability to 'afford the requisite course of study'. And to make sure that the best standards are maintained the affiliated colleges are to be regularly visited by Government inspectors. It is further laid down that their course of study is to include 'a careful cultivation of the vernacular languages'. But colleges and institutions of higher education are not to have anything like exclusive care bestowed upon them, as has sometimes been the case. Such a policy, say the Directors, provides 'the means of acquiring a very high degree of education for a small number', and for a number who are in the main 'both able and willing to bear a considerable part at least of the cost of their education'. There must therefore be such a distribution of public funds as will prevent an undue amount being expended on higher education.

8. *Emphasis on Mass Education.*—How is this to be done? By spending far more than has yet been done on the education of the great mass of the people, those whose education has been 'too much neglected', and who by their own unaided efforts are 'utterly incapable of obtaining any education worthy of the name'. For this purpose there must be opened a large number of schools, all of them regularly and carefully inspected, and with the most satisfactory staff that can be obtained. And scholarships will be provided by the State so as to enable capable pupils to rise from the lowest to the highest stages of education. One point in the treatment of this subject deserves special atten-

tion. The Directors recognize that a very wide gap exists between vernacular and Anglo-vernacular schools; and they desire that this gap should be bridged. The medium of instruction should not be the ground, in their opinion, of the differentiation of school from school. That differentiation should be based not on the main language which they employ but on the content of the instruction which they impart. And if this is done, and if true encouragement is extended, then 'through the gradual enrichment of the vernacular languages' there will result a genuine grading of schools which will make it possible for a pupil to pass from the elementary to the higher forms of education by natural stages. There is to be nothing less than a carefully articulated system reaching from the most elementary to the most advanced form of education, a system that is to be within the reach of all.

9. *System of Grants-in-Aid.*—Is it possible for Government to provide a comprehensive system of education such as this? To this question the Directors return the only answer which they could give, and the only answer which can still be given. Nothing is more obvious than 'the impossibility of Government alone doing all that must be done in order to provide adequate means for the education of the people of India'. What then is to be done? The answer is: 'Combine with the agency of the Government the aid which may be derived from the exertions and liberality of the educated and wealthy natives of India and of other benevolent persons'. And this association of all agencies is to be effected by the adoption of the system of grants-in-aid. By this means which will draw 'support from local resources in addition to contributions from the State, a far more rapid progress of education' will be achieved 'than would follow from a mere increase of expenditure by the Government; while it possesses the additional advantage of fostering a spirit of reliance upon local exertions and combination for local purposes, which is

of itself of no mean importance to the well-being of a nation'.

10. *Conditions of Grant.*—These grants it is proposed to give to schools and colleges which satisfy Government as to the stability of their management, which impart a good secular education, which are open to Government inspection, and which 'agree to any conditions which may be laid down for the regulation of such grants'. Further, their allocation is 'based on an entire abstinence from interference with the religious instruction conveyed in the school assisted'. The amount of grant sanctioned will depend on the report of the inspectors who are to take 'no notice whatsoever of religious doctrines which may be taught in any school'. It will also depend on the 'funds at the disposal of Government', a proviso which is in theory unimpeachable, but to which in practice not a few difficulties have attached.

11. *The Educational System Looked Forward to.*—The Directors leave us in no doubt as to what seems to them the ultimate method by which the education of India is to be overtaken. 'We desire', they say, 'to see local management under Government inspection and assisted by grants-in-aid taken advantage of wherever it is possible to do so, and that no Government colleges or schools should be founded, for the future, in any district where a sufficient number of institutions exists, capable, with assistance from the State, of supplying the local demand for education. . . We look forward to the time when any general system of education entirely provided by Government may be discontinued, with the gradual advance of the system of grants-in-aid, and when many of the existing Government institutions, especially those of the higher order, may be safely closed or transferred to the management of local bodies under the control of, and aided by, the State'. This was written before 'local bodies' as we understand the term had been established; thirty years were to

elapse before legislation was to call them into being. When the Directors spoke of 'local bodies' they meant 'one or more persons, such as private persons, voluntary subscribers, or the trustees of endowments, who will undertake the general superintendence of the school and be answerable for its permanence for some given time'. In other words, what they had in mind was the only form of local management which existed in their time, that of private agencies. But now that municipal and local boards have been brought into being and possess statutory powers enabling them to maintain and manage schools, the position of the Directors takes on an added significance. The local management to which they looked forward as taking the place of what was purely governmental is no longer restricted to the private local management of which alone they had experience. It embraces now that statutory local management which has become so marked a feature of educational development. Thus the conception of the Directors has become enriched by the passage of years; their anticipation stands forth as an ideal. It is the ideal of a system of education uniting local and private managements in a common service, under the control of the State which aids them financially, guides them administratively, and counsels them by its inspecting agency. It is an ideal which is being realized, which is capable of speedy realization, and with the steady realization of which the welfare of the education of India is intimately bound up.

12. *The Encouragement of Education.*—A number of means of encouraging education are mentioned, for the Despatch thinks of the State as a power that encourages. Among these means are the award of scholarships to deserving pupils, the grant of training allowances to those with a capacity for imparting knowledge, the provision of facilities for those who have a bent for professional education, the setting up of normal schools, and (though this is expressed in very guarded

language) the prospect of positions under Government. And the improvement which the public services owe to the introduction of a system of education are dwelt on at some length. That the Directors were wide awake to those parts of the system which required special care may be gathered from the fact that they devote separate paragraphs to the importance of practical education, Muhammadan education, and the education of women. All these are to receive encouragement.

13. *Religious Neutrality.*—Passages of the Despatch quoted in the preceding paragraphs bring out very plainly what, in the opinion of the Directors, is meant by the religious neutrality of the State so far as educational institutions under non-departmental management are concerned. It implies that religious instruction may be given in these schools and colleges, but that the State takes no official cognizance of it. What it means in connexion with institutions under the management of the State is expressed no less clearly in the following sentences of the Despatch. 'Considerable misapprehension appears to exist as to our views with respect to religious instruction in the Government institutions. These institutions were founded for the benefit of the whole population of India; and in order to effect their object, it was and is indispensable that the education conveyed in them should be exclusively secular. The Bible is, we understand, placed in the libraries of the schools and colleges and the pupils are able freely to consult it. This is as it should be; and, moreover, we have no desire to prevent or discourage any explanations which the pupils may, of their own free will, ask from the masters upon the subject of the Christian religion provided that such information be given out of school hours. Such instruction being entirely voluntary on both sides, it is necessary, in order to prevent the slightest suspicion of an intention on our part to make use of the influence of Government for the purpose of proselytism, that no notice shall be taken of it by the

inspectors in their periodical visits'. It will be noted that this interpretation of 'religious neutrality' has been adopted so that the State may be free from even the imputation of proselytism. And by proselytism is clearly meant, as the context shows, using education as a means of propagating Christianity. Rather than expose themselves to the charge of being agents of the Christian faith the Directors preferred that the education given in the schools and colleges for which they were directly responsible should be 'exclusively secular'. The times did not lend themselves to a full consideration of all that is involved in the concept of neutrality. Opposing positions had found vigorous advocates, and strong feelings had been aroused. In the circumstances the wording of the Despatch was probably the most satisfactory that could be devised; and certainly it was adopted only after much consultation and deliberation. It is easy for us to say now that it might quite conceivably have been different had 'proselytism' been looked at in another light, or had the full implication of an 'exclusively secular' education been realized. It was not so easy then.

14. *Conclusion of the Despatch.*—With a summary of what has been actually accomplished in the various provinces, and a statement of what is now called for, the Despatch closes. 'The higher classes', it says, 'will now be gradually called upon to depend more upon themselves; and your attention has been more especially directed to the education of the middle and lower classes, both by the establishment of fitting schools for this purpose and by means of a careful encouragement of the native schools which exist, and have existed from time immemorial, in every village, and none of which perhaps cannot, in some degree, be made available to the end we have in view'. The Directors are under no illusions as to the likelihood of sudden or phenomenal results following the inauguration of the policy which they have enunciated. 'To imbue a vast and ignorant

population', they say, 'with a general desire for knowledge, and to take advantage of that desire when excited to improve the means for diffusing education amongst them, must be a work of many years; which by the blessing of Divine Providence may largely conduce to the moral and intellectual improvement of the mass of the people of India'. They have sown what they believe to be good seed; the harvest will come in due season.

15. *Significance of the Despatch.*—Such are the main features of this remarkable document. It has been called 'the magna charta of English education in India', but it is much more than that. It is the magna charta of Indian education. It is the proclamation by the State that it has definitely assumed a new responsibility, that of providing the people of India with every grade of education, and of encouraging that education with all the resources at its command. It supplies the means whereby what is best in indigenous education may be conserved and fostered, and whereby it may also be brought into contact with what is best in education that comes from beyond the confines of India. It puts into the hands of the country a system so well articulated that the capable child has it in his power to rise in the most natural way from the most elementary to the most advanced form of education. It enlists all managements in a united conflict with illiteracy and welcomes them as joint contributors to a common cause. It shows how a national scheme, wide in its sweep and heavy in its demands, may be brought within the financial capacity of the country. And it provides the people of India with an organization which gives unity to education without robbing it of elasticity, which establishes control but does not dethrone freedom, and which opens the way to a good secular education and at the same time makes it possible for education, when it is so desired, to be combined with moral and religious teaching.

References

J. A. Richey, *Selections from Educational Records. Part II.* In Chapter ix the full text of the Despatch of 1854 is given.

The Educational Policy of the State in India published by Satakopachari & Co. gives the full text of the Despatch.

E. Stock, *History of the Church Missionary Society.* In Volume ii, Chapter xlvi, there is an account of events connected with the preparation of the Despatch, and of discussions regarding religious neutrality.

R. B. Smith, *Life of Lord Lawrence.* Contains information as to Lawrence's attitude to the policy of religious neutrality.

W. Lee Warner, *Marquis of Dalhousie.* Touches on Dalhousie's connexion with the Despatch. Volume ii, pp. 206-209.

III. The Despatch of 1859

16. *Reasons for the Despatch.*—In 1859 a Despatch concerning education was sent to the Government of India. It emanates from the newly appointed Secretary of State for India. For the old regime is over, the despatches of the Court of Directors are ended, and the change is reflected in the language and general attitude of the communication. Though but slightly shorter than the Despatch of 1854 it differs from it in several ways. It is less a declaration, than a review, of policy. How comes it that this Despatch follows so quickly on the heels of its predecessor? For one reason because the doings of 1857 have set all men who have anything to do with India a-thinking. Have the methods of the past in government, in administration, in outlook, been such as they ought to have been? And then, as was inevitable, the question suggested itself, Has Education had anything to do with what has happened? The Secretary of State would like to be sure on that point. So far as he himself has been able to go into the matter he has received no evidence which

connects education with revolt. At the same time education always means change, and change excites suspicion. Yet all that that seems to indicate is that the methods of advancing education might have to be modified, not that the efforts to spread education should be suspended. He would be glad if the Government of India would investigate this point and let him have their opinion on it. That is one reason for the Despatch.

17. *Justification of Former Despatch.*—There is another reason. The Secretary of State has to be sure that he is right in pursuing the educational policy which was laid down by the East India Company in 1854. If there is anything defective in it, now is the time to set it right. So he has put before himself the question: Has there been that 'improvement and far wider extension of education both English and vernacular' which it was the object of the 1854 Despatch to promote? And he sees good reason, he tells us, to answer this in the affirmative. He recounts what has happened. Education departments have been created. inspecting staffs have been organized, universities have been incorporated, many affiliated colleges have been opened, secondary schools under Government management have been well attended, and the number of those under private management has been increased. As regards elementary education 'if it must be admitted that, previously to 1854, the subject of vernacular education had not received in every part of India the full amount of attention which it merited, there can be no doubt that since the wishes of the Home Authorities have been so plainly declared the officers of the Department of Education acting under the orders of the several governments have spared no pains to bring into operation, throughout the districts entrusted to their superintendence, such measures as appeared most likely to place within the reach of the general population the means of obtaining the education suited to their

circumstances in life'. Marked advance, then, has been made, and this has all taken place between July 1854 and April 1859.

18. *The Grant System and Secondary Education.*—But there is a third reason for the issue of this Despatch. Some doubts have been cast upon the advisability of advancing education by means of the grant-in-aid system. And the Secretary of State has found it necessary to go into this matter and to satisfy himself regarding the facts. He finds that so far as English and Anglo-vernacular schools are concerned the grant-in-aid system has been a distinct success, drawing forth private enterprise, increasing the number of schools, and enlisting the active efforts of communities in the spread of education. There can be no doubt as to the stimulating effect of the system on the progress of secondary education.

19. *The Grant System and Elementary Education.*—In the field of elementary education the Secretary of State is not so sure as to the suitability of the grant-in-aid system. From what he tells us in the Despatch he has not much evidence on which to go. One inspector in Bengal has come to the conclusion, evidently on *a priori* grounds, that 'it was vain to hope to base any general scheme of popular education at least in the greater part of Bengal on the grant-in-aid system under the prescribed rules'. To the same conclusion another inspector was driven on *a posteriori* grounds. And a Bombay educational officer has a sad story to tell of discouragements with which he has met and of the amount of time he has lost in the endeavour to promote aided education. The picture which certain officials have drawn of themselves and which the Secretary of State has framed in this Despatch is that of men full of desire to give effect to the provisions of 1854, beseeching people to contribute of their resources towards education, realizing that there were people then, as there are now, who see very little in education, meeting

as we unfortunately still meet those who give their promise but fail to redeem it, and finding themselves in danger of losing their position as Government servants in the undignified role of importunate beggars. It is a pathetic picture, but hardly one on which to rest a change of policy. Yet, strangely enough, that is what the Secretary of State feels not a little inclined to do.

20. *Position of the Secretary of State.*—Here is what he says. 'On the whole, Her Majesty's Government can entertain little doubt that the grant-in-aid system, as hitherto in force, is unsuited to the supply of vernacular education to the masses of the population; and it appears to them, so far as they have been able to form an opinion, that the means of elementary education should be provided by the direct instrumentality of the officers of Government according to some one of plans in operation in Bengal and the North-Western Provinces or by such modification of those schemes as may commend itself to the several local governments as best suited to the circumstances of different localities. Assuming that the task of providing the means of elementary vernacular education for those who are unable to procure it for themselves is to be undertaken by the State, they are strongly of opinion that the officers of the Department of Education should be relieved from the onerous and invidious task of soliciting contributions from the classes whose means, for the most part, are extremely limited, and whose appreciation of the advantages of education does not dispose them to make sacrifices for obtaining it'. It is an interesting paragraph. The Secretary of State is far from sure as to what he ought to do. The only thing he is certain about is that educational officials should not be sent round with the hat. And in that position he has our sympathy. On the general question, however, he seems to be drawn in two directions. On the one hand there was the natural feeling of a Government department that it

would rather work entirely through its own agency. On the other hand there was a natural hesitation as to the advisability of departing entirely from a policy which had been in existence for less than a quinquennium and which, during that short and troubled time, had done on the whole remarkable things. So the best that he could do was to state what the Government thought 'so far as they had been able to form an opinion', and to ask for fuller information. A comprehensive review was at the time impossible.

21. *Indian Official Opinion.*—This was fully recognized by those who had to do with the administration of education in India. Much interest would attach to a narrative of the considerations which led to the issue of this Despatch and of the official comments that were made on it when it was issued. This would not be difficult to compile, for there is a considerable correspondence on the subject. But we must content ourselves with three quotations that bear on the matter. When about a year before the Despatch was written the views of the President of the Board of Control and of the Court of Directors were communicated to the Government of Bengal, the Director of Public Instruction of that Province prepared a few notes and the Lieutenant-Governor wrote a Minute on the subject. The former expresses surprise at any thought of change when the system which it was thought to change had been in operation for so short a time. 'The letters and other documents', he says, 'relate to a period of about two and a half years Surely it is not to be expected that in so short a period the good hoped for from a new system of national education can be made patent to the world. This is almost as if a husbandman were to complain two or three weeks after sowing time that he had been put to a great expense for seed and had got no return for it.' The Lieutenant-Governor's Minute which bears the date of the 1st October 1858 is very incisive. This is a part of what he says as to the dis-

satisfaction expressed by the Court of Directors regarding the working of the grant-in-aid system. 'It has been found that what is denominated in the Despatch of 1854 "the great mass of the people" is not likely to be reached by the present system; the Rules apparently presuming greater general interest in the advancement of their inferiors than really exists among the wealthy classes of Natives, and larger contributions to the Schools than can be afforded by "the masses" themselves, or are likely to be given for them by their more competent countrymen'. In other words, it is the Rules under which the system is administered that are defective not the system itself. And anyone who looks, for instance, at the rules laid down by the Government of Bombay in 1858 will have little difficulty in realizing that greater encouragement required to be held out even to those who most eagerly desired to establish elementary schools. If now we turn to what took place in the presidency of Madras after the Despatch had been received, we find a very full expression of opinion on the part of the Director of Public Instruction in that province. Here is an extract from his letter of the 24th September 1859 in which he considers the terms of the Despatch. 'It is within the last four years that any extended measures have been carried out by Government for the instruction of those classes who have the requisite means and leisure for going beyond the rudiments of learning; and the period during which the grant-in-aid system has been practically in operation is still shorter. Moreover, owing to various causes, the system has had as yet but little scope to develop itself. It is only within the past year that anything like an adequate provision of funds has been sanctioned for the purpose of extending it, and this provision, owing to the necessities of the State, has been again reduced. For these reasons, I would recommend that for the present no measure should be adopted which would be incompatible with the eventual application of the grant-in-aid system to providing elementary education for the mass of the population, and that adequate funds should be furnished for extending it under the rules now in force in the presidency. At the same time, I see no reason why the experiment of a special rate should not be tried in one or more districts in which there is no immediate prospect of its interfering with the extension of the grants-in-aid system'. That is to say, it is the financial support from Government which is defective not the system itself. Thus what we find from these statements is that in some provinces it is the rules under which the grant-in-aid system has been set up that are at fault, in others it is the amount of aid given to the system by the State. It is the mode of administering the system, not the system itself, that needs to be dealt with. What these opinions make unmistakably clear is that, in the view of responsible officers, there is no desire for change, but that if there is to be a change it should be in the way of giving the grant-in-aid system the chance which it has not yet received. They also make it clear why the Secretary of State, after receiving the information asked for, made no alteration on the policy of 1854.

22. *Significance of the Despatch.*—At the same time the Despatch has a significance which is sometimes entirely missed. This significance cannot but be missed if, for example, the despatch is regarded as advocating the position that the grant-in-aid system should not be employed for the spread of education among the masses of the people. The efficacy of the system is abundantly recognized by the Despatch in the field of higher education, and when it expresses doubts as to its efficacy in the field of elementary education it hesitates not with regard to the system in general but, as the wording of the Despatch makes it perfectly plain, with regard to 'the grant-in-aid system as hitherto in force'. That is a most important qualification, and herein lies the special significance of the

Despatch. What is defective in the system 'as hitherto in force'? First, it has not been made attractive enough; second, it has not been made to apply to organized local effort. These are the two aspects in which, as the Despatch reveals, the system, so far as it has been brought into actual operation, has fallen short. It has not been attractive enough, and so educational officials have had to spend much time which could have been more fruitfully employed otherwise in beseeching individuals to take advantage of the system. What was needed was not this, but grants so generously allocated as to make their acceptance a privilege of which an ever increasing number would gladly avail themselves. The grants and their mode of allocation were such as to lead to a great expansion of secondary education, but not such as to operate in that way where the education of the masses was concerned. What was required was the putting into force of a grant-in-aid system which would meet the situation as the system which had been 'hitherto in force' had proved unable to do. If the Secretary of State had stressed this point he would have done a great service to elementary education. Elementary education needs to be fostered; and the system which the State had called into being was so worked that it failed in this essential respect. And after seventy years we have only to look at the grants assigned to one class of educational agencies to realize that what was a defect in 1859, and was hindering the advance of elementary education then, remains a defect in 1930 and hinders the advance of elementary education even now. The Secretary of State had good reason to be doubtful about the grant-in-aid system 'as hitherto in force'. It had not been made sufficiently attractive to ensure the general advance of education among the great mass of the people. But there was another reason why the Secretary of State might hesitate with regard to the system of grant-in-aid as then in force. He might justifiably doubt whether as administered it was wide enough in its sweep. Unfortunately when he sought to express this doubt, it seemed to him most natural to put it in the form of an opposition. There was, in his view, the system of the 1854 Despatch and the opposed system of Mr. Thomason. Would it not be best to regard the latter as the more satisfactory and to discard the former? Now there was another way of looking at the matter, as was suggested by one of the official replies to the enquiries instituted by the Despatch of 1859. This other way was to recognize that the two methods were complementary not opposed. Elementary education was capable of being advanced by the work of voluntary effort and by the work of local organizations. Both of them were required, and both because of their helping to supply a national need deserved encouragement at the hands of the State. Would it not then be the most natural way for the State not to discard the grant-in-aid method but only that method 'as hitherto in force'? If that were done then a far wider conception of the grant-in-aid method would take its place and supply the very thing that the country required. It would be possible to have a system of aid applicable not only to philanthropic bodies and persons who worked in the interests of education but also to groups of residents in a locality who agreed to tax themselves so as to promote education within their area. Had this way of looking at the matter been before the Secretary of State we may imagine that the last shred of hesitation that lingered in his mind as to the advisability of a grant-in-aid system for the promotion of elementary education would have entirely vanished. For he would then have seen that what was calculated to advance the diffusion of education among the body of the people was a system which linked together in the service of education private and local effort, and gave them both the benefit of generous assistance from the State. Instead of any doubts as to the advisability of the grant-in-aid system there would have been recognition of its potentialities, and recommendation of its extension. Thus seventy years ago there would have been effected the operation of a comprehensive grant-in-aid system which would have brought unity where there is still too often opposition, and concerted forward movement where there is still too much uncertain advance. But the possibilities of such a combination were not then realized and the opportunity was let slip. Elementary education has felt the effects of this ever since.

References

J. A. Richey, *Selections from Educational Records. Part II.* The Despatch of 1859 is given in full on pp. 426-450. In Chapters iv and v will be found correspondence relating to it.

J. A. Richey, *Grants-in-aid to Schools in British India* makes reference to this Despatch at p. 2.

IV. The Indian Education Commission Report of 1883

23. *Appointment of the Commission.*—No changes followed the Despatch of 1859. It 'confirmed the policy of 1854, reviewed the progress made since that date, and advocated the adoption of further steps for the promotion of primary education'. And there the matter rested for twenty-three years. The first despatch on education to be issued by the Secretary of State for India followed so quickly on the publication of the East India Company's last despatch that five years did not separate them. But almost a quarter of a century was to be allowed to elapse before another survey of educational policy in India was taken in hand. On the 3rd of February 1882 the Government of India issued a resolution appointing an Education Commission. Various considerations accounted for this step.

In 1871 the control of the Education Departments had been made over by the central government to the local governments. And the seventies were not well advanced before complaints began to be heard that there had been many departures from the avowed educational policy of the Government of India. Men and women actively interested in the education of India were becoming disheartened because the serious efforts which they were making to establish and maintain schools and colleges were not being encouraged by the State, and the cause of education was suffering. Then, the review of the situation which had been attempted in the 1859 Despatch was based on admittedly insufficient information. Further, as the resolution appointing the Commission says, 'In view of the facts that, since the measures set forth in the Despatch of 1854 came into operation, a full quarter of a century has elapsed, and that it is now ten years since the responsible direction of the educational system was entrusted to the local governments, it appears to His Excellency the Governor-General in Council that the time has come for instituting a more careful examination into the results attained, and into the working of the present arrangements, than has hitherto been attempted. The experience of the past has shown that a more critical review or analysis of the returns and reports of the different provinces fails to impart a thoroughly satisfactory knowledge of the actual state of things in the districts, and that there are many points which only an acquaintance with local circumstances can adequately estimate or explain'. The Commission consisted of twenty-one members. It began its sittings in India in 1882, and after collecting a vast amount of evidence laid its report before the Government of India in 1883. Its findings, except in regard to one or two minor matters where they thought no action was called for, were accepted by that Government in their Proceedings of the 23rd October 1884.

24. *Arrangement of the Report.*—The Report itself occupies 600 pages, the printing being a pleasure to the eyes and the paper such as to make the reader of present day reports envious. In the main volume, to which are attached several highly important volumes of evidence, the whole field is covered, with the exception of the general working of the universities, technical instruction, and European education, which by the terms of reference were definitely excluded from the investigation of the Commission. The review of what has been done as well as the presentation of the immediate situation is illuminating, the historical portions are mines of information, and the recommendations for the future are numerous without being confusing, and far-reaching without being impracticable. The Report believes in Indian education, urges its extension, and suggests means whereby that extension may be brought about effectively and beneficially. It is certainly a matter for gratitude that the history of Indian education contains two such reports as that of the Indian Education Commission and that of the Calcutta University Commission. There are twelve chapters in the Education Commission's Report. One of these, Chapter i, is introductory; a second, Chapter ii, is historical, though history is not confined to this Chapter; a third, Chapter xi, relates to legislation; and a fourth, Chapter xii, to finance; six chapters (iii-vi, ix, x) deal with the various forms of education; while the remaining two Chapters (vii and viii) are concerned with matters of administration. Some account of the recommendations made by the Commission may serve to indicate the great value of the Report, but quite as valuable as the recommendations is the statement of reasons which led to their adoption. In the following paragraphs all that can be done is to consider the main conclusions of the Commission and the grounds on which they are based.

25. *Indigenous Schools.*—With the first chapter

that records recommendations, Chapter iii, there is disclosed a very different situation from that which existed in 1859. What was, as it were, sought after then in a somewhat vague fashion has now been in part attained. Local self-government is being placed on a proper footing; and at the time when the Commission met there were being considered by the Government of India those measures which issued in the Acts of 1883 to 1885, whereby local bodies were authorized to function and were invested with statutory powers. The Commission saw in this development what promised to be of distinct value in the service of education. The Government of India had asked the Commission to consider the extent to which indigenous schools existed, and whether it was possible for them to 'be utilized as part of the educational system'. The Commission did consider these points and, as the result of its deliberations, recommended that indigenous schools should be recognized and encouraged wherever they seemed to be serving a useful purpose, that their personnel and curriculum should be interfered with as little as possible, and that the endeavour should be made to improve them steadily. As in certain provinces local self-governing institutions had begun to function, the Commission came to the conclusion that the best thing to do would be to entrust to local bodies the regulation, supervision, and encouragement of the indigenous schools. It is interesting to note that the Commission was so definitely in favour of encouraging these schools and of taking steps to secure their incorporation in the general educational system. As to the means by which this was to be achieved we may be justified in regarding the recommendation with a certain amount of hesitation. But that is because we have history to look back on. The Commission saw the beginning of local self-governing bodies and shared in the hopes which their inauguration evoked. We see these bodies in the light of what they have done and of not a few hopes still unrealized. But if we cannot credit the Commission with having hit upon the best means for fostering the growth of indigenous schools, we can credit it with having hit upon a principle which, within recent years, has proved most valuable in educational administration—the principle of decentralization.

26. *Primary Education.*—When it passes from the consideration of indigenous, to that of elementary, schools the Commission presses the claims of primary education with all the emphasis which it can command. Far too little has been done for it in the past, the Commission has to admit, and every endeavour must be made to change this remissness into steady and continued effort. And so it recommends: 'That while every branch of education can justly claim the fostering care of the State, it is desirable, in the present circumstances of the country, to declare the elementary education of the masses, its provision, extension, and improvement, to be that part of the educational system to which the strenuous efforts of the State should now be directed in still larger measure than heretofore'. But if that is to be done funds must be provided, and where are they to come from? From both public and local sources, is the reply of the Commission. For primary education is 'that part of the whole system of public instruction which possesses an almost exclusive claim on Local Funds set apart for education and a large claim on provincial revenues'. Twenty years later the same recommendations, in substance at least, have to be repeated with the admission that in the interval the attention given to primary education has not been on a level with its importance. How is it that so little resulted from the Commission's strong advocacy of primary education? Partly because secondary education was seen to open many doors, and its immediate benefits focussed thought and effort upon it rather than on the supply of a great national need. Partly because funds were insufficiently assigned. Partly because of condi-

tions that were social rather than educational. And partly because the mode of control which the Commission proposed did not answer the expectations that were cherished with regard to it.

27. *Control of Primary Education.*—It is when we come to Legislation in Chapter XI of the Report that the Commission expresses its views on the subject of control. Opinion differed as to whether the attention of Local Bodies should be confined to elementary education or should extend to secondary education as well. But there was no doubt as to the advisability of Local Bodies exercising control in regard to elementary education. What seemed to the Commission the best method by which this control might be secured was that the area of a Municipal or a District Board should be defined as a school area or district, and that the Local Body concerned should either itself or by means of a sub-committee be constituted a School Board for that locality with statutory powers and responsibilities. The Commission did not think it wise that there should be a system of dual control in respect of the elementary schools in an area, the Local Bodies having to do only with the schools which they directly managed, and the Education Department having to do only with the schools which it aided. It seemed to the Commission that there should be one controlling agency, the School Board, which would have full financial and administrative control over all the schools in the specified area. It would disburse the subsidy sanctioned by Government for educational purposes to the Local Body, and it would distribute the grants earned by aided schools. 'It should be the duty of the Boards to deal with the whole system of primary education, to watch over the wants of all classes of the community, and to provide for all such wants whether by creating schools of their own or by aiding existing schools'. Thus half a century ago there was proposed a comprehensive scheme for the control of elementary education. The most noticeable

feature of this scheme is that it is one of devolution. The control of all elementary schools in a statutory area is to be entrusted to a body which represents local interests and responsibilities. Some of the powers which have hitherto been exercised by the Education Department are, according to this plan, to be exercised by Boards in which these powers are legally vested. And not only is the scheme one of devolution, it is also one of unification. For the Boards to which control is to be entrusted are to do far more than merely disburse funds. They are to see that the educational needs of a district are supplied, that agencies work together, and that wasteful duplication is avoided. What the spread of education among the masses of the people demanded, as the Commission clearly saw, was the driving power that comes from bodies of men and women who have experience and local knowledge, who have at their disposal considerable resources, and who exercise a control that prevents waste and gives to education the strength of united action. And that driving power the Commission proposed by their recommendations to provide. It may seem strange that what it proposed is still largely unaccomplished. Yet when we look at this plan in the light of the intervening years, we have little difficulty in understanding what has placed such an interval between conception and fulfilment. For when the Commission passed from the principles of devolution and unification to means for their realization, it proposed, first, that the body controlling the all-important service of primary education should be one that had a number of other services to supply, so that primary education was only one among its many concerns; and, second, that the body exercising control should be also the body managing certain schools under its control, the sole controller being thus also joint-manager. The elements of friction were in it from the first. The scheme of devolved control, though rich in promise, was bound to lead to the disappointment of that promise because of the very nature of the Local Education Authorities proposed. As things stand even at the present day, the country still awaits the appointment throughout the country of that form of Educational Authority which will achieve what the Commission had in mind, the combination of devolved with unifying powers, the association of local with other interests, and the concentration of attention and activity on the service of education.

28. *Secondary Education.*—From primary education the Commission goes on to the consideration of Secondary Education. In the forefront of its recommendations it places the proposal that there should be a bifurcation in the secondary curriculum, thus providing on the one hand for pupils proceeding to the university, and on the other for those looking forward to 'commercial or other non-literary pursuits'. Here the Commission is half a century ahead of its time. The same ground is gone over again by the Auxiliary Committee which presented its report in 1929, and what it has to say is that 'a large number of the pupils in high schools (which prepare for the matriculation examination of the university) would benefit more by being in schools of another type', schools, for instance, which fit their pupils for 'industrial and commercial careers'. The bifurcation is thus long overdue. When is it to be undertaken in earnest? Perhaps one may hazard the opinion that it will be regarded as a practical scheme and taken seriously in hand as soon as there is clear evidence that the curriculum which is alternative to the matriculation curriculum actually leads somewhere. But to continue with the Report, the consideration of the character of secondary education brings the commission naturally to deal with the encouragement of it. For that the Commission recommends that, in addition to the teaching grants which had been in existence since 1855, there should be furniture and library grants, and that a general scheme of scholarships should be established so as to enable capable pupils to proceed to the

higher studies for which they were qualified. The Commission emphasizes the need for trained teachers and for adequate inspection. It closes its recommendations on this part of the educational field by pointing out that there is a difference between the relation of the State to primary education and its relation to secondary education. If, it says, there is need for a primary school in a district, and no agency other than a public one is available then education should be provided through that agency. But if people in an area desire a secondary school no step should ordinarily be taken by the State to provide one by its own agency; the school should be the outcome of 'local co-operation', 'preferably on the footing of the system of grants-in-aid'. The difference here stated has a bearing on educational policy that has not even yet been fully recognized.

29. *Recommendations as to Results Grants.*—There are two points in this part of the Commission's Report on which a considerable amount of comment has been passed. The first is that the Commission recommends the payment of grants in both primary and secondary schools on the basis of results. Considering the date at which the Commission met it is hardly surprising that it should have favoured the application of the Results Grant system. It was the system which had been accepted in England, and in Indian education it promised a stimulus which in certain circumstances it subsequently proved capable of exerting. But the remarkable point is not that the Commission recommended the adoption of this system but that it accompanied its recommendation with several limitations, and put it forward with a considerable amount of hesitation. Even in regard to that part of education where the results grant system has been at one time or another frequently employed, what the Commission proposes is 'that as a general rule aid to primary schools should be regulated to a large extent according to the results of examinations'. There is nothing rigid here. The aid on the

basis of results is to be made 'as a general rule', and it is to be regulated by examinations 'to a large extent'. The Commission devotes five pages of an extremely interesting nature to discussing the advantages and disadvantages of this method of payment by results. And after full consideration, the conclusion to which it comes is that 'in the lower stages of education we consider the balance to be decidedly in its favour', although it adds that it would not desire 'even at that stage to interfere with any well-considered plan for somewhat modifying it'. Then it goes on to say that 'as the higher stages of education are reached the system becomes less advantageous', and it definitely recommends that it should not be applied to colleges. So far as the results grant system is concerned, the Commission was really ahead of its time.

30. *Recommendations as to Fees.*—The other point to which attention has been drawn is the recommendation of the Commission 'that in order to encourage the establishment of aided schools the managers be not required to charge fees as high as those of a neighbouring government school of the same class'; and that 'while it is desirable to affirm the principle that fees at the highest rate consistent with the undiminished spread of education should be levied in every college aided by the State, no aided college should be required to levy fees at the same rate as those charged in a neighbouring government college'. These recommendations have been criticized on the ground that they led to the establishment of schools and colleges which were poorly equipped and to a great deal of unhealthy rivalry. When the recommendations are looked at in their setting it will be seen that such criticism requires to be revised. The Commission has been considering the way in which grants are to be allocated, and it is met with the contrast which exists between the State which, as a manager of a school or college, has behind it the fulness of the State's resources, and the private manager who has only

limited resources to draw upon but has on the basis of these established a school or college for which there exists a need that is not otherwise supplied. Now, in these circumstances, is the private manager to be penalized as regards grant or recognition because he charges a fee which is not so high as that levied at the nearest government school? The Commission answers this in the negative. And it will be generally admitted that in so doing it has given the only answer which the circumstances warranted. But it is quite obvious that a manager may employ this answer in a way which the Commission never contemplated. He may undersell and give rise to all the evils that accompany such a practice. Or he may charge low fees and to compensate for that he may admit to his college so large a number of students that good education is quite out of the question. If he acts in these ways, however, he will find himself in conflict with another recommendation of the Commission, that which aims at 'raising fees gradually, cautiously, and with due regard to necessary exemptions, up to the highest amount that will not check the spread of education'. And furthermore he will find that he has to reckon with the State which is the controller of the whole educational system, and which, in the exercise of its power of control, has to be satisfied that every educational institution aided or recognized by it charges adequate fees, maintains a satisfactorily remunerated staff, and abides by all the conditions which regulate the payment of aid and the grant of recognition. Indeed those who have blamed the Commission because perfectly reasonable recommendations have been made use of in a way that was never intended are really blaming not the Commission but the State for its failure to exercise that power of control which is vested in it and on the steady employment of which the health of education depends. The greater the extent of an aided system the greater the responsibility which rests on the State, as the Commission in another connexion makes perfectly plain, to supervise, guide and control the working of that system and to eliminate all that is at variance with the best interests of education. And those who read the Report will see that the Commission not only made these recommendations regarding fees but also consistently recommended that the State should exercise effectively its power of control, that power which safeguards education against all the misapplications to which the recommendations have been subjected. The Commission, then, it will be seen, lent no countenance by its recommendations to those unsatisfactory features of education which are fully entitled to all the criticisms which have been levelled at them. The evils arose, but the Commission was not to blame for them. In fact its Report lays stress upon the means by which they may be effectively remedied.

31. *Collegiate Education.*—By the terms of reference the Commission was precluded from enquiring into the working of the universities. Its recommendations, therefore, in regard to collegiate education are few. They relate, for instance, to the advisability of levying fees 'at the highest rate consistent with the undiminished spread of education', and of establishing scholarships which would enable graduates to undertake further studies both within India and beyond it. They base the aid to be granted not on results but on 'the strength of the staff, the expenditure on its maintenance, the efficacy of the instruction, and the wants of the locality', considerations which give education its proper setting as well as a fitting opportunity for development. And they stress the claims which buildings, libraries, and equipment have upon public funds, claims the emphasis on which does not slacken with the years, more especially since it has become recognized how dependent a true collegiate education is on the accessibility of a good library, and how important it is that scientific work should have the fullest encouragement. Besides recommendations such as these there are two of

a different character. They are the outcome of the feeling which existed among the members of the Commission that something should be done to make it quite clear that education was not a mere intellectual discipline unrelated to morality or religion. What the Commission was able to agree to, after much discussion and even then not unanimously, was the proposal 'that an attempt should be made to prepare a moral text-book, based upon the fundamental principles of natural religion, such as may be taught in all government and non-government colleges'. But the moral text-book idea soon found that it had more critics than friends; the Government of India could not see its way to support it, neither could the Secretary of State. A similar fate befell a further recommendation that 'a series of lectures on the duties of a man and citizen' should be delivered in all colleges at some time in the course of every session. The recommendations represented a gallant endeavour to supply what was recognized as a defect in a great part of the educational system of India. And though the defect was not to be rectified in the way suggested, the proposals were then as they continue to be today, calls to action in a sphere where appropriate action is still much needed.

32. *Education of Special Classes.*—Considerable space is allotted to questions concerning the education of classes requiring special treatment, and every page of this part of the Report merits careful reading. It is mainly occupied with the education of Muhammadans and the Depressed Classes. The position of Muhammadan education, the reasons for its slow growth, the measures that are calculated to advance it, and the means by which the best ends of the community may be served, are stated with a freshness, conciseness, sympathy, and insight which carry conviction and give hope for better things to be, a hope which the last fifty years have seen remarkably fulfilled. The magna charta of the Depressed Classes, so far as education goes, is

set forth in the words: 'That the principle laid down in the Court of Directors' letter of May 5th, 1854, and again in their reply to the letter of the Government of India dated May 20th, 1857, that "no boy be refused admission to a Government college or school merely on the ground of caste", and repeated by the Secretary of State in 1863, be now re-affirmed as a principle, and be applied with due caution to every institution not reserved for special races, which is wholly maintained at the cost of public funds, whether provincial, municipal, or local'. Would that the charter needed no renewing.

33. *The Education of Women.*—A chapter is devoted to the education of women in which it is urged that the conditions of aid to girls' schools should be more favourable than those in boys' schools, 'that special aid should be given, where necessary, to girls' schools that make provision for boarders', that every endeavour should be put forth to train women teachers so that men may not be required in girls' schools, that grants should be given for zenana teaching, and that 'a female inspecting agency be regarded as essential to the full development of female education and be more largely employed than hitherto'. The attitude of the Commission did much to foster the education of women. Some of its recommendations are in no need of emphasis today, so marked is the improvement which the last half century has witnessed. But in certain respects the Commission was far ahead of its time. We have only to think of what still requires to be done for the training of women teachers, and for the supply of an inspecting agency that does justice to this vital field of education.

34. *Central Point of Policy.*—Up to this point our review of the Commission's work has been confined to the various forms of education which it has considered. But there was a more fundamental matter that the Commission had to investigate. The Government

wished to know how the policy with which it was identified was being given effect to, and with what results. Administration, therefore, claimed the most careful consideration of the Commission, and to its various aspects almost one third of the Report is devoted. It was all needed, for what was disclosed called for energetic action on the part of the State. The evidence presented to the Commission showed that in the North-Western Provinces and Madras the policy of 1854 had been reversed; that in Bombay, the Punjab, Coorg, and Berar, at no time had sufficient endeavours been made to give effect to the policy; and that in Bengal, Assam, and the Central Provinces the original efforts to carry out the policy had shown no important retrogression but had also shown no further progress. The situation, therefore, was decidedly grave. A policy which had been enunciated in 1854 and re-affirmed in 1859 as the educational policy of the State had, in the course of the intervening years, been either overturned or neglected to such an extent that through the greater part of India its operation was thwarted or retarded. So serious a position could not be suffered to continue. Local governments had sought to rely more and more upon official effort, large sums had been expended from public funds to enable them to further official schemes, and through the discouragement which non-official endeavour had thus received great injury had been done to the cause of education. The Commission was convinced that there must be a radical change of attitude, a more consistent adherence to that policy which the State enunciated as its own in 1854 and which, in the view of the Commission, afforded the assured means by which the gigantic task of Indian education might be accomplished and the interests of India's youth might be fully served. Thus it is that the Commission reached what may be regarded as its central recommendation. It runs as follows: 'That whilst existing State institutions of the higher order should be maintained in complete efficiency wherever they are necessary, the improvement and extension of institutions under private management be the principal care of the Department'. The Government of India accepted this recommendation. Had the efforts of provincial governments to give effect to it been as hearty as the Government of India's acceptance, Indian education half a century later would have a very different story to tell from what it has today, in regard to influence and power no less than in regard to extent and quality.

35. *Means for Giving Effect to this Policy.*—The Commission did not stop with the enunciation of this position. It realized that the policy which it commended could be carried out only by means of the most careful provision and in an atmosphere of resolute cooperation. In both respects the recommendations of the Commission go to the very core of the matter. For instance, if private management is to receive such encouragement, does not this imply strict public control? Yes, answers the Commission, which proceeds to lay it down 'that native and other local energy should be relied upon to foster and manage all education as far as possible, but that the results must be tested by departmental agency, and that therefore the inspecting staff be increased so as to be adequate to the requirements of each Province'. A strong inspectorate is necessary, and so is a strong Education Department. The Department must take steps for the raising of fees with all due caution and respect for local conditions, it must be well informed regarding all that is going on educationally in the province, it must encourage every agency which seeks to spread education and is qualified to do so, it must act with sympathy but it must act also with authority. But how is the Department to be in possession of the fullest information available? The Commission has a definite recommendation as to the means which will secure this as well as secure effort based upon knowledge. It recommends 'that conferences (1) of officers

of the Education Department, and (2) of such officers with managers of aided and unaided schools be held from time to time for the discussion of questions affecting education, the Director of Public Instruction being in each case *ex-officio* president of the conference. Also that Deputy Inspectors occasionally hold local meetings of the school masters subordinate to them for the discussion of questions of school management.' In such a system of co-operation there lies some hope of success in the fight with illiteracy and in the endeavour to extend the bounds of knowledge. So much for control and co-operation; what as to management? It should be steady substitution of the non-official for the departmental. As regards secondary schools the further extension of them in any district should 'be left to the operation of the grant-in-aid system, as soon as that district is provided with an efficient high school, Government or other, along with its necessary feeders'. As regards schools for girls 'the further extension of female education should be preferentially promoted by affording liberal aid and encouragement to managers who show their personal interest in the work, and only when such agency is not available by the establishment of schools under the management of the Department or of Local or Municipal Boards'. As regards transference 'all Directors of Public Instruction should aim at the gradual transfer to local native management of Government schools of secondary instruction (including schools attached to first or second grade colleges) in every case in which transfer can be effected without lowering the standard, or diminishing the supply, of education, and without endangering the permanence of the institution transferred', and that Government should withdraw from the management of existing colleges in accordance with carefully prescribed conditions. The wisdom and caution with which these conditions are stated must strike every reader. They leave the impression that, if these and other recommendations of this section had been not merely enunciated but acted upon with all the energy and tact to which an accepted policy may rightfully lay claim, many of the serious defects that still characterize Indian education would be no longer there to deplore.

36. *Features of the Report.*—Thus in the form of a review of what has been done, and of recommendations as to what should be done, the Report of the Indian Education Commission presents us with a thoroughly articulated scheme of general education for India. It lays upon the Education Department of each province the responsibility for eliciting from each agency the heartiest response in its power to the crying need for the diffusion of education among the people of the land. It regards the Department as an organization which, far from working in isolation, works in intimate contact with all forms of educational activity and which seeks to enter into fullest co-operation with them. At the same time it looks upon the Department as having vested in it the powers of control, and it emphasizes the responsibility which rests on the Department to use these powers with authority. It shows us how the education of India is to be achieved only through the combination of private and public effort in a common endeavour to diffuse knowledge. It indicates the closeness of this union in the cause of elementary education where local bodies combine with voluntary agencies under one system of control to improve and multiply primary schools in town and country. It shows how in secondary and collegiate education reliance is to be placed mainly on private endeavours, and how there is to be a gradual transference of departmental institutions to non-official managers. Further it brings out how encouragement is to be bestowed by well-considered and generous grants-in-aid and the advice of a competent inspectorate. It makes clear how in this manner a system can grow up which is calculated to stimulate national self-reliance

and to make education the handmaid of ordered and assured progress. And it places within the grasp of the people a graded scheme of instruction from the lowest stage to the highest which, while subject to a wise and sympathetic control, is not subject to any rigid uniformity, but has within it the powers of self-development and self-adjustment, as well as the means of combining the fullest mental discipline with the benefits of religious teaching. A comprehensive system such as this is the one which India needs, and the Commission has shown how it may be secured. It can be realized if educational policy continues to be guided by adherence to, and systematic application of, the principles which received their first official statement in 1854.

References

Report of the Indian Education Commission.

H. R. James, *Education and Statesmanship in India.* A valuable consideration of Indian education, with certain criticisms of the recommendations of the Education Commission.

V. Chirol, *Indian Unrest.* Chapter xvii contains criticism of some of the Commission's recommendations.

W. Miller, *Unrest and Education in India.* Amongst other matters deals with these criticisms; the writer having been himself a member of the Commission.

H. Dodwell, *Sketch of the History of India*, 1858-1918. Full of suggestion, and deals with several educational considerations.

Educational Papers, a supplement to the South India Missionary Conference of 1879. Presents some of the facts which led up to the appointment of the Commission.

E. Stock, *History of the C.M.S.* Volume ii, Chapter xlvi, touches on circumstances connected with setting up of the Commission.

Calcutta University Commission Report. Volume i, Chapter iii, most informative on education in Bengal.

V. The Resolution of 1904

37. *Circumstances of its Publication.*—Twenty years elapsed between the time when the Government of

India accepted the recommendations of the Indian Education Commission and the time when the next authoritative declaration of Indian educational policy was published. During the viceroyalty of Lord Curzon every department of Indian administration was subjected to searching examination. Education felt, and still feels, the impetus which came from an enquiry that was both careful and penetrating. The results of this survey are to be seen in the Report of the Indian Universities Commission appointed in 1902, the Indian University Act of 1904, and the Government of India Resolution on Indian Educational Policy. It is with the last of these that we are now concerned.

38. *Merits and Demerits of the Educational System.* —On the 11th March, 1904, a Resolution on Educational Policy was issued by the Governor-General in Council. In the short space of fifty pages it surveys the whole field of education, giving an outline of the past, considering the efforts of the present, and developing plans for the future. Few short official documents are so rich in facts and in suggestion. A succinct sketch of Indian education, followed by references to the Despatch of 1854 and the Commission of 1882, leads on to a statement regarding the extent, the merits, and the defects of the present system of public instruction. As to extent, it is pointed out that this system supplies education to over 23,000 studying in general and professional colleges, to over half a million scholars attending secondary schools, and to three and a quarter millions of primary pupils. All this is done at a cost to public funds of little more than one million pounds. As to the merits of the system, 'it is almost universally admitted . . . that knowledge has been spread abroad to an extent formerly undreamed of; that new avenues of employment have been opened in many directions; and that there has been a marked improvement in the character of public servants now chosen from the ranks of educated Indians as compared with those of the days

before schools and universities had commenced to exercise their elevating influence'. But along with the benefits there are certain obvious defects; the system of education has not penetrated the country as it ought to have done, it has laid too much stress on examinations, too little on sound learning, it has attracted attention to rewards, and it has led to the neglect of the cultivation of the vernacular languages. There is room for substantial reform, and the object of the Resolution is to state the principles by which this reform may be effected, and to ask for the co-operation in carrying it out of 'all who are interested in raising the general level of education in India'.

39. *A Civil Service Commission.*—On one matter of policy the Resolution refuses to make any new departure. It decides against the establishment of a 'special board organized on the model of the English Civil Service Commission'. The reason given for this decision is that the examinations of such a Commission would be brought into competition with those conducted by schools and universities, and the result would be that the attraction for Government service might undo all the good that has been slowly built up by the present system, and would tend to divert the 'main stream of educational effort into a narrow and sordid channel'. Things have changed since the Resolution was issued, the importance of sound education is now more fully realized, the dangers referred to are not felt to be so threatening as was the case in 1904, and the trend of opinion is more definitely in favour of Civil Service Commissions and their appointment, as recent legislation has shown. But though that is the case there is a point on which the Resolution lays stress, and to which too great heed cannot be given, namely, that there must be no room for conflict between the general culture of educational institutions and the specialized requirements of a Civil Service Commission.

40. *Examinations.*—The Resolution adverts to the

tyranny of examinations tempting 'both teachers and pupils to concentrate their energies not so much upon genuine study as upon the questions likely to be set by examiners'. As palliatives of this state of affairs it is proposed, first, to abolish the results grant system of aid; and, second, to reduce the number of examinations preceding the university course. What some members of the Indian Education Commission feared, and what they stated quite plainly as an objection to the allocation of grants on the basis of results, namely, that from their earliest days children attending school would become familiarized with examinations and would come to regard them as the supreme test of education, has proved to be no groundless apprehension. So the results grant system is to go, and the first school examination is to be removed from the category of public tests. Events have shown that what the Resolution proposed has done something to mitigate the grosser evils of the examination system. And even for small mercies in this direction there is reason to be grateful; for there are actually those at the present day who advocate the re-introduction of a public examination for young children.

41. *Principles of Educational Policy.*—Before dealing with the different forms of education the Resolution states with great clearness the nature of the foundation on which the educational system of the country rests. 'Every agency', it says, 'that could be induced to help in the work of imparting sound instruction has always been welcomed by the State'. That is the fundamental point. What then as to the relation between these agencies and the State? 'The system of grants-in-aid is supplemented by the direct action of Government which, speaking generally, sets the standard, and undertakes work to which private effort is not equal, or for which it is not forthcoming. Thus the educational machinery now at work in India comprises not only institutions managed by Government, by District and Municipal Boards, and by Native States, but

also institutions under private management, whether aided by Government or by local authorities, or unaided. All of these which comply with certain conditions are classed as public institutions'. The policy of the withdrawal of Government from direct management and the devolution of that management on private enterprise 'has been generally acted upon', Government retaining under its own management 'a limited number of institutions both as models for private enterprise to follow and in order to uphold a high standard of education.' But if Government can withdraw from management it cannot withdraw from the responsibility for 'control over all public educational institutions', and this control it seeks to exercise 'by means of efficient inspection'. In this short paragraph three fundamental principles of Indian educational policy receive a statement that could hardly be put into fewer words. The Indian educational system, the Resolution tells us, is one provided by aided and unaided agencies supplemented by the agency of Government, not one provided by Government and supplemented by aided and unaided agencies. Second, the supplement is of a temporary character, setting a pattern and maintaining a standard, and thus ceasing to function when that pattern and that standard have served their purpose. Third, in contrast with this temporary function there is another, the discharge of which rests as a permanent obligation on Government, the obligation to control the whole system and in doing so to provide a thoroughly adequate inspectorate. The deficiencies which still mark Indian education constitute a continued call for the recognition of these principles.

42. *Primary Education.*—Turning to the different stages of education the Resolution admits that primary education is still far from receiving the attention which is its due. If 15 per cent of the population may be taken as of school-going age then 'more than eighteen million boys ought now to be at school, but of these only a little more than one-sixth are actually receiving

primary education'. What is still further disconcerting is that the spread of primary education is in 1902 slower than it was ten years previously. 'It may be said that the expansion of primary schools has received a check in recent years from the calamities of famine and plague'. But this check has not extended to secondary education. What then is to be done? Three lines of action are suggested. First, financially the advance of primary education must 'be made a leading charge upon provincial revenues'. Again, this form of education has 'a predominant claim upon the funds devoted by District and Municipal Boards to education'. The primary destination of public revenues, provincial and local, in the service of education, is the education of the masses. So far have things travelled from the days of Holt Mackenzie's Memorandum. Second, educationally, the courses require revision so as to secure that the children shall be trained by simple and appropriate methods to think and to observe, and that in rural areas the instruction may follow lines which take account of the actual conditions of the pupils. When so much is being said at the present day regarding vocational education, it is worth while recalling what the Resolution has to say as to the purposes of rural schools. 'The aim of these schools', it says, 'should be, not to impart definite agricultural teaching, but to give to the children a preliminary training which will make them more intelligent cultivators, will train them to be observers, thinkers, and experimenters in however humble a manner, and will protect them in their business transactions with the landlords to whom they pay rent and the grain dealers to whom they dispose of their crops'. Thirdly, better scales of salaries require to be provided for teachers. All these suggestions, as the story of the last quarter of a century tells us, have been acted upon, though by no means steadily or fully. Yet, in the time that has elapsed, the attendance of pupils at the primary schools of the country has more than trebled.

43. *Secondary Education.*—The enormous development of secondary education is next commented on, an increase as regards pupils of an hundred fold within twenty years. This raises the question as to whether sufficient care has been exercised in admitting schools to the privileges of recognition. If this has not been done in the past there is an obvious call for its exercise in the future. Recognition, it is laid down, must mean that a school is needed, that it is financially stable, that it provides sound education. That stress should be laid by the Resolution on recognition and its conditions is most timely. It is a part of educational policy to which even now far too little attention is devoted. Equally timely is the reference to another point, the fact that, while secondary schools have increased in number, they have shown no sign of developing 'diversified types of secondary education corresponding with the varying needs of practical life'. The Government desire to do what is possible to secure this diversity, for it has to be admitted that the attempts to bring it about that were made in accordance with the recommendations of the Indian Education Commission have not proved successful. One means which the Resolution advocates for the attainment of this greater freedom is the institution of Leaving Certificates which would in themselves 'possess definite value, and would deserve recognition not only by Government and the universities but also by the large body of private employers who are in want of well-trained assistants in their various lines of activity'. Besides relaxing in some degree the pressure of examinations, these certificates would help towards a greater variety in the school curriculum, and would lead to secondary education being regarded as much more than a stepping-stone to a college course. A great deal, however, depends on what the certificates record, how they are dealt with by the universities, and to what careers they form a passport. But into these matters the Resolution does not go.

44. *The Object of Education.*—A paragraph is devoted to the consideration of education as 'promoting the moral no less than the intellectual and physical well-being' of those who participate in it. Such an end can be achieved directly in schools where religious instruction is imparted, instruction from interference with which 'it is the settled policy of Government to abstain'. In schools where religious teaching is not given much may be done for character by 'the influence of carefully selected and trained teachers, the maintenance of a high standard of discipline and the institution of well-managed hostels, the proper selection of text-books, such as biographies, which teach by example, and above all in the association of teachers and pupils in the common interests of their daily life'. Where a school does not succeed, by one method or another, in instilling a spirit of reverence, and binding together its pupils in a healthy corporate life it is failing to realize the main object for which it was established. It is well that this position should have received official statement. We shall see something akin to it when we come to the Resolution of 1913. But it is hardly necessary to say that, from the point of view of policy, something more than statement is required. If this object is to be attained, if the formation of character is to be the main concern of education, what encouragement may schools which adopt this as their aim expect to receive at the hands of the State? Has the State a definite policy in regard to this matter? On the answer to such questions important issues hang.

45. *Medium of Instruction.*—As to the medium of instruction the Resolution lays it down that in general 'English has no place, and should have no place, in the scheme of primary education. . . A child should not be allowed to learn English as a language until he has made some progress in the primary stages of instruction and has received a thorough grounding in his mother-tongue'. With no pupil below the age of thirteen should English be used as a medium of instruction, and even

when he enters the secondary school he should maintain the study of his vernacular to the end of his school course. The object that needs to be kept steadily in view is that the vernaculars should not be allowed to sink 'to the level of mere colloquial dialects', but should become by their enrichment the means for bringing the highest knowledge 'within the reach of all classes of the people'.

46. *The Education of Women.*—The slow rate of progress which has attended the education of women indicates, as the Resolution points out, that more needs to be done for its encouragement. And so it is stated that the Government intends to set apart more funds for this form of education, in order that model primary schools for girls may be set up, more training schools for women teachers may be opened, and the staff of inspectresses may be increased. What is proposed is activity along the lines recommended by the Education Commission. In certain directions the action indicated has followed the publication of the Resolution, and not without success. The number of girls now at school is four times as many as it was in 1904.

47. *University Education.*—What is said regarding university education is simply a statement of the reforms in university administration and instruction to which effect was given by the legislation of 1904. A detailed account and consideration of these is not required at this stage; it is sufficient to mention the main features of the changes advocated. They are: smaller Senates, provision for a certain amount of election, in place of nomination, to these bodies, greater control by the universities over their affiliated colleges, and a larger exercise by them of their power to teach. Emphasis is placed on the advantages which will accrue to education, and the profound influence which will be exerted on student life, by the extension of the hostel system. Attention is drawn to the fact that the cost of the erection of hostels has been mainly the contribution of private

bodies and benefactors. And then the Resolution goes on to say: 'The necessary improvements in the universities and their affiliated colleges cannot be carried out without financial aid. This the Government of India are prepared to give; and they trust it will be possible to afford liberal recognition and assistance to genuine efforts on the part of the colleges to adapt themselves to the new conditions. They also hope that this increase of expenditure from public funds may be accompanied by an increase in the aid given to colleges and universities by private liberality, so that the policy of progressive development which was adopted in 1854 may be consistently followed, and that the influence of the improved universities may be felt throughout the educational system of the country'. The funds promised have been made available in great measure, although their amount and the mode of their allocation raise not a few questions. Private liberality has been stimulated. And if justice were to be done to the 'progressive development' of the past thirty years in the realm of university education a whole chapter would have to be devoted to it.

48. *Practical Aspect of Education.*—A considerable part of the remaining sections of the Resolution is occupied with what we may call the more practical side of education. It is mainly, though not exclusively, devoted to three forms of training. First, attention is drawn to the fact that Technical Education has hitherto chiefly confined itself to the higher branches of instruction, and that what is really needed is an education which will enable those who receive it to help in the 'development of Indian industries and especially of these in which Indian capital may be invested'. It should be not so much a special training in some technical line as a 'preliminary general education of a simple and practical kind' on which the special education may be based. Fourteen years later much the same thing had to be said by the Calcutta University Commission; and

it has yet to be taken to heart. There seems to be a strange unwillingness to do what the Resolution advocates, namely to draw 'a clear line between educational effort and commercial enterprise'. The line, however, is clearer today, and education reaps the benefit. Secondly, it is pointed out that 'India possesses no institution capable of imparting a complete agricultural education', a most anomalous position for 'a country where two-thirds of the population are dependent for their livelihood on the produce of the soil'. This glaring defect it is proposed to remedy, first, by the provision of means for research, and then by the establishment of adequately equipped agricultural schools and colleges where students will receive a thorough training, practical as well as theoretical. The recent Report of the Commission on Agriculture in India is the best commentary on the outcome of the policy which was thus set on foot. And, thirdly, the Resolution emphasizes the need for concentration on the training of teachers so that both the number of teachers may be increased and the quality of the training may be improved. Efforts will be made to establish more and better training schools and colleges, to 'maintain a connection between the training college and the school, so that the student on leaving the college and entering upon his career may not neglect to practise the methods which he has been taught', and to secure co-operation between the inspectorate and the training college. If only what is set forth here had received the attention that it deserves, how different would be the story that education has now to tell, after the lapse of a generation.

49. *Administration.*—With unerring touch the Resolution puts its finger on what were then, and what still continue to be, the two main needs of educational administration. There is a great danger that the Directors of Public Instruction may be overwhelmed by routine through the multiplication of their duties. One way to obviate that is to increase the Headquarters Staff,

and the Resolution announces the intention of the Government of India to do this. The amount of increase indicated is indeed small. But the important point is that it marked the beginning of a policy which, if it had been fully given effect to as the years went on, would have rescued Indian education from not a few of the defects that are now laid to its charge. The other need which it is proposed to remedy is that of the inspecting staff. If examinations are to be reduced in number then there must be 'an increased stringency in inspection and a substantial strengthening of the inspecting staff'. Further, if inspectors are to 'be much more than mere examiners', if they are to 'guide and advise' teachers and managers, then there must be a staff which both in number and in qualifications is fitted to render this indispensable service to the education of India. India still awaits the adequate supply of this service.

50. *Conclusion.*—In conclusion the Resolution recounts how 'in 1854 the broad outlines of a comprehensive scheme of national education were for the first time determined; how the principles then accepted have been consistently followed ever since; how they were affirmed by the Education Commission of 1882, and how they are now being further extended and developed in reference to the growing needs of the country'. The Government seeks to spread an education which will call into exercise 'all the *faculties of the mind*', which will 'form character and teach right conduct', which will be 'in fact, a preparation for the business of life'. In carrying out this aim the Government hopes that its labours 'will command the hearty support of leaders of Indian thought and of the great body of workers in the field of Indian education. On them the Governor-General in Council relies to carry on and complete a task which the Government can do no more than begin'.

51. *Features of the Resolution.*—Thus ends a Resolution which combines insight and breadth of outlook,

a high conception of education and a full recognition of what its various aspects demand, concentration on what is essential with vigorous advocacy of what is practicable. Its closing note is an index of the policy which it wishes to see in effective operation. It is a policy of co-operation, a union of official, local, and private effort, so as to build up an educational system which will be to the lasting benefit of the country. It is no new policy, only the employment of principles already authoritatively laid down, to meet new situations and to solve new problems. It is a policy which will provide a control that is sympathetic and fostering. It will put within the reach of all who are capable of profiting by it education that is advanced as well as elementary, practical as well as literary. It will spread an education that stirs the mind, strengthens the character, and promotes corporate life. It will stimulate private enterprise and initiative, it will give the strongest encouragement to non-official management, and it will supply the fullest measure of official assistance, administrative, financial, and advisory. It is a policy which ensures that education will be worth having, and that it will be, steadily and increasingly, the possession of the nation.

References

Indian Educational Policy being a Resolution issued by the Governor-General in Council on the 11th March 1904.

Lord Ronaldshay. *Life of Lord Curzon.* Volume ii. Chapter xii gives an account of the educational activities of Lord Curzon in connexion with the Resolution and University legislation.

Report of the Indian Universities Commission of 1902.

Indian Universities Act of 1904.

VI. The Resolution of 1913

52. *Circumstances of its Publication.*—Preparations for the great administrative changes which 1911 brought

to India led to a review of the policy and plans of the Government of India in various directions. Correspondence passed between the Indian Government and the Secretary of State in regard to education among other matters. And at the Royal Durbar announcement was made 'of a new recurring grant of Rs. 50 lakhs for popular education in recognition of its paramount importance'. It was felt that more than that should be done, that what was needed was a survey of the whole field of education. The result was the publication on the 21st February 1913 of the Resolution of the Government of India on Indian Educational Policy.

53. *Nature of the Resolution.*—This Resolution has two or three features which it is worth while noting before we proceed to look at its contents in detail. For one thing, although it is stated to be one regarding policy, a considerable portion of it is occupied with the presentation of facts, many of which are full of interest, but the connexion between which and policy is not obvious. Then, for another thing, so many important matters are mentioned as having been referred to local governments that the reader naturally wonders why the publication of the Resolution was not delayed till the opinions of the governments to which the matters had been referred were forthcoming. For clearly no authoritative statement can be made on subjects that are still under consideration. Enquiries into the medical inspection of pupils are commended to local governments, and so are arrangements for Vernacular Continuation Schools, and so is an examination of schemes for the training of teachers. Various points regarding European Schools, we are told, have been submitted to the local governments, schemes for girls' education have been called for from these governments, and local governments are to be consulted before definite schemes of Oriental Studies are formulated and measures adopted for the maintenance and furtherance of indigenous systems of learning. In regard to all these points, and their im-

portance cannot be doubted, the Resolution is, as was inevitable, more of the nature of an interim report than of a comprehensive and authoritative declaration of policy.

54. *Admission of Administrative Defect.*—There is a third respect in which this Resolution has a character which is all its own. It contains an admission by the Government of its failure to discharge certain of the obligations which rest upon it as the controller of the educational system. First, 'Schools', says the Resolution, 'have in certain cases gained recognition and eluded the control of inspection'. In other words, the State admits that it has failed in its power to control; it has allowed into the educational system of the land, and has kept there, schools which have no right to be there. And education has suffered, as the paragraph goes on to state in unequivocal language. Secondly, 'Above all', says the Resolution, 'the grants-in-aid have from want of funds often been inadequate'. That is to say, the State has failed to give schools the financial subvention which is of the very essence of its policy in maintaining a system of grant-in-aid. Administratively and financially the State has failed, and often failed; that is what paragraph 21 of the Resolution records without any ambiguity. And the worst of it is that, detrimental to education as the failure admittedly has been, there is no indication, in the course of the Resolution, of any steps which Government proposes definitely to adopt so as to remedy the serious administrative defects. On the financial side there is, however, what appears to be a brighter prospect. For we are told that 'the Government of India have decided to assist Local Governments, by means of large grants from Imperial revenues as funds become available, to extend a comprehensive system of education in the several provinces'. But even on this prospect a shadow rests, as all who have acquaintance with the workings of Indian educational affairs know when they read the words 'as funds become avail-

able'. The policy contained in the Resolution adumbrates no betterment in respect of control administratively, and in respect of finance the betterment is conditional.

55. *The Object of Education.*—Such are some of the features of the Resolution. Let us now look at its contents. It sets in the forefront of the Government's policy the formation of character as the main object of education. Amongst the influences which it counts on to mould character are the personality of the teacher, direct, moral and religious teaching, the corporate life of hostels, and the force of great traditions. 'The most thoughtful minds in India', it says, 'lament the tendency of existing systems of education to develop the intellectual at the expense of the moral and religious faculties'. It admits that the question of religious and moral instruction is 'the most important educational problem of the time', but with the remark that 'for the present the Government of India must be content to watch experiments and keep the matter prominently in view', it hands the problem over for solution to 'enlightened opinion and accumulated experience'.

56. *Primary Education.*—So far as Primary Education goes the Government is quite clear that it must have 'a predominant claim upon the public funds'. The State does not see its way to adopt the principles of compulsion, but it 'desires the widest possible extension of primary education on a voluntary basis', such education being given free to 'the poorer and more backward sections of the people'. To achieve this end it is proposed that 'expansion should be secured by means of board schools, except where this is financially impossible, when aided schools under recognised management should be encouraged'. The principle thus stated, it is said, is 'for guidance, with the necessary modifications due to local conditions'. And in the following paragraph the Resolution admits that 'in regard to primary education conditions vary greatly in different provinces'.

And it refers to the problems which 'present themselves where board schools and aided schools respectively are the basis of primary education'. If the statement of principle which is here made were absolute it might conceivably be regarded as constituting a departure from accepted policy. But accompanied as it is by so many qualifications it has rather the appearance of a suggestion for educational experiment. The suggested experiment has been tried in certain provinces, in others it has not. The results are interesting, and much will be said of them later. Meantime we must content ourselves with noting that the Government strongly advocates what it terms Vernacular Continuation Schools, or Middle Vernacular Schools as they are commonly called, finding in them a help towards the continuation of studies beyond the stage usually spoken of as primary, and a training ground for teachers of elementary schools.

57. *Education of Women.*—'The education of girls', says the Resolution, 'remains to be organised'. And a few suggestions are made, such as that the education of girls should be more practical and not an imitation of the education of boys. At the same time emphasis is placed on the necessity for the increased employment of women as inspectresses and teachers. But no line of policy is advanced regarding this vitally important part of the educational system of the country. Government contents itself with stating that 'the immediate problem in the education of girls is one of social development', and with calling for schemes from Local Governments. And there the matter is left.

58. *Secondary Education.*—The large increase in the number of secondary schools is commented on, and it is pointed out that, as these schools send up their pupils to the universities, every effort must be made to place them on the soundest footing. The Government intends to assist what is being done to secure this by improving 'the few schools' which it itself manages, and by increas-

ing largely the grants allocated to aided institutions. Indeed its 'policy is to rely so far as possible on private enterprise in secondary education'. What it aims at is, as the Resolution puts it, 'the encouragement of privately managed schools under suitable bodies, maintained in efficiency by Government inspection, recognition and control, and by the aid of Government funds'; and with regard to private effort the adoption of 'special measures to assist it to perform efficiently its work in the educational system'.

59. *Grants-in-aid.*—What these special measures are the Resolution states only in general terms. But there is little need for what is specific because of the principles in accordance with which the Government announces that it proposes to allocate grants. 'The Government of India', says the Resolution, 'desire that the grant-in-aid rules should be made more elastic so as to enable each school, which is recognized as necessary and conforms to the prescribed standards of management and efficiency, to obtain the special assistance which it requires in order to attain the fullest measure of utility. As larger grants become available, and as the pay and personnel of the teaching staff are improved, it will be possible for the inspecting officer to concentrate his attention more and more upon the general quality of instruction. Full encouragement can then be given to improved and original methods of teaching and courses; and gradually the earning-capacity of an institution will come to be judged on grounds of general efficiency and desert rather than by rigid rules of calculation'. Indian education still waits for these principles to be acted upon. On the benefit of their adoption it is unnecessary to enlarge. The truth is that no 'special measures' are needed to secure the advance of secondary education, only stedfast adherence by the State to those principles of control, administrative and financial, which are the very foundations of its avowed policy. There is, however, something very heartening in such a declaration

as this made by the Resolution regarding the allocation of grants. It may be remembered in days to come, and what was not accomplished by the Government of India may be realized by provincial governments.

60. *School-Leaving Certificates.*—The Resolution proceeds to commend the system of School-Leaving Certificates as a means whereby the pressure of examinations may be lightened, the real education of the pupil rather than his preparation for a particular test may be emphasized, and a school record useful for various purposes may be secured, while a combination of external and internal examinations may afford a healthy stimulus. If the certificate is to have its true value then, as the Resolution states, 'a large increase in the superior inspecting staff is required'. Nearly twenty years have gone by since this Resolution was issued and the increase in the inspecting staff still remains to be made. It is difficult to see what is gained by deploring the dominance of examinations if the State, year after year, fails to take a step which would not only help substantially to dethrone the tyranny of external tests, but would also give to the whole system that atmosphere of freedom and purpose in which true education is able to flourish and abound.

61. *University Education.*—After a brief survey of the various forms of technical and professional education, there follow five paragraphs relating to University education. That the universities have greatly benefited by the legislation of 1904 no competent observer can dispute. 'But', adds the Resolution, 'the condition of university education is still far from satisfactory in regard to residential arrangements, control, the courses of study and the system of examination'. With a view to the improvement of these defective conditions four lines of action are indicated. First, 'it is necessary to restrict the area over which affiliating universities have control'. Secondly, there must be created 'new local teaching and residential universities within each of the provinces in

harmony with the best modern opinion as to the right road to educational efficiency'. Thirdly, 'it may be possible hereafter to sanction the conversion into local teaching universities, with power to confer degrees upon their own students, of those colleges which have shown the capacity to attract students from a distance and have attained the requisite standard of efficiency'. Fourthly, it is 'desirable (in provinces where this is not already the case) to place the preliminary recognition of schools for purposes of presenting candidates for matriculation in the hands of Local Governments. . . The university has no machinery for carrying out this work and in most provinces already relies on the Departments of Public Instruction, which alone have the agency competent to inspect schools'. When one reads these proposals, proposals which go to the very heart of the matter, one cannot but regret that before much could be done to give effect to them the Government of India had passed from the position of control which it had hitherto occupied. True, some of these lines of action have been adopted by provincial governments. By them encouragement has been given to the founding of local and residential universities, the areas of affiliation have been restricted, and the transformation of a college into a university has been rendered possible. But hardly any one can deny that a policy which would have taken account of university education in India as a whole would have been more fruitful than one which left to each province a university policy of its own. Certainly it is much to be desired that every province, as it shapes its policy for higher education, would give good heed to the lines of action which the Government of India in this Resolution proposed to make its own. If affiliating universities are to be of real service to those who attend them, if their standards are to be maintained, if their ideals are to continue high, and if routine work is not to absorb the greater part of their energies, then the area of affiliation must be reduced not increased. If universities are to be a strength to the life of the nation, inspiring it with thought and infusing it with the spirit that unites, then attention must be paid to universities in which the conditions of residence are looked upon as no less vital than those of instruction. If universities are to have close contact with actual surroundings and an abiding place in the affections of the people, then few things are more calculated to ensure these results than that colleges which have ministered to a community's well-being and have spread abroad the power of worthy and living traditions, should be helped to develop, either singly or in groups, into large autonomous corporations of higher education, and to receive the rank and influence which university standing confers. And if universities are to be free to do their own work and to make clear to the country what a university really stands for in the national economy, then they must be relieved of every function which can be discharged more appropriately by specially constituted bodies or a well qualified inspectorate. Action along such lines holds out the promise of advance for the universities of India both in their internal development and in their influence on personal, civic, and national life. We have reason to be glad that they are all advocated by this Resolution.

62. *The Training of Teachers.*—The Resolution dwells on the need for a greatly increased number of trained teachers, for improvement in the rates of their salaries, and for the provision of pensions or provident funds to aid them on their retirement. But in regard to these matters, as well as in regard to the needs of the Domiciled Community, the education of Muhammadans, and the advance of Oriental studies, though all are referred to, no line of policy is indicated. It is recognized that before this can be done much consideration will have to be bestowed on these topics, a consideration in which central and provincial governments will each have to take their part. Unfortunately this

consideration, under the new constitution which followed so closely on the heels of the Resolution, has been deprived of almost all the help which the central government was so well fitted to supply.

63. *Need of Expert Advice.*—Is any comprehensive policy possible? Not unless, as the Resolution suggests, the education of the country is in possession of 'expert advice and control at every turn'. There must be departments that are fully competent to deal with the manifold problems raised by education in ever increasing number, there must be greatly strengthened inspectorates, and there must be exchange of views both inter-provincial and intra-provincial. Perhaps if the greatest war in history had not begun within eighteen months of the publication of this Resolution, perhaps too if there had not followed far-reaching constitutional changes which placed each province in the position of virtual educational autonomy, further steps might have been taken by the central government to secure that largeness of policy which it proposed to encourage. But what the central government can no longer do, the provincial governments acting in concert may carry into effect. How this is possible we shall see in the course of Chapter iv.

64. *Appeal for Co-operation.*—The Resolution concludes with an appeal to those who are interested in education to 'join in establishing under the guidance and with the help of Government those quickening systems of education on which the best minds of India are now converging', and 'to wealthy citizens throughout India to give of their abundance to the cause of education'. It is a welcome and fitting appeal at the close of what was the last resolution of the Government of India on the subject of education. It is welcome because there are passages in the Resolution which, if taken by themselves, might lead one to doubt whether the value of co-operation was fully appreciated. It is fitting because it is the final recognition by the central government of

what is fundamental in the educational policy with which it identified itself for sixty years. The first declaration of policy made in 1854 rested that policy on the partnership of official and non-official effort in the dissemination of education. The final declaration of 1913 appeals for the maintenance and strengthening of the same combination.

Reference

Educational Policy of the Government of India. Delhi, the 21st February 1913. The full text of the Resolution.

VII. Unity of the Policy

65. We have now completed our survey of the official documents in which an Indian educational policy finds expression. And this survey has made one thing clear. Though the documents are five, the policy is one. A unity pervades all the statements; not the unity of what is fixed, but the unity of what is alive. It is a policy which, when it encounters new situations, forthwith presents its means for meeting them. It is never taken by surprise; it is practical. It is a policy which through all its course has made it possible for the capable boy or girl to rise, stage by stage, from the primary school to the best that the university can give. It is stimulating. It is a policy which imposes and impresses upon the nation and the individual a responsibility which they dare not shirk for making the fight with illiteracy no losing battle. It is constraining. And it is a policy which while making its demands on the public purse combines private liberality with public finance, and by means of a carefully thought-out and fully-articulated plan makes steady, if what seems at times slow, progress towards the realization of its supreme end, namely, the placing within the reach of all of an education that stirs the mind and moulds the life. It transcends bar-

riers of circumstance and custom. It is comprehensive. How is it that this unity so marks the policy all through its story? There are various reasons. But one of them is plainly this. The policy arose out of experience; it has at every point been tested by experience; and it commends itself to experience.

CHAPTER III

Principles of the Policy

1. *Policy based on Principles.*—In the preceding chapter an account has been given of the documents in which Indian educational policy is enunciated. We have noted that these documents are five in number, and that though the last of them was issued sixty years after the publication of the first they are pervaded by an essential unity. What is at work in 1913 is fuller and more richly developed than what began to work in 1854. But the general features remain the same. This is what has marked the policy through the great changes of conditions, administration, and thought, which these six decades of Indian history have witnessed. And when we think of it, this is not surprising. For the policy set forth in these documents is based on principles. And it is to the consideration of these principles that we must now direct our attention.

I. The Responsibility of the State for Education

2. If we ask what the principle is on which the whole policy rests we find it in the opening sentences of the Despatch of 1854. The Directors of the East India Company state that by the Act of 1853 'the responsible trust of the government of India has been once more placed in our hands'. In seeking to discharge that trust they recognize that no subject 'can have a stronger claim to our attention than that of education'. And they acknowledge that to give India 'those vast moral and material blessings which flow from the general diffusion of useful knowledge' is 'one of our most sacred duties'. The recognition of this sacred duty is the corner-stone of Indian educational policy. *The State acknowledges*

that on it rests the responsibility for the education of its citizens. Its avowed educational policy is simply the enunciation of the means by which it seeks to discharge this trust.

II. The Object in View

3. *A Complete System.*—The State acknowledges its responsibility for the provision of education; what is the nature of the provision which it aims at supplying? The answer to this is twofold. In the first place, *the State aims at putting within the reach of its citizens a complete system of education.* There are States which began by recognizing their responsibility for providing only an elementary form of education, and anything which they may have done beyond this has been in response to altered conditions. But the State in India has, from the very inception of an accepted educational policy, set before itself as the object which it has in view the provision of a complete scheme ranging from the most elementary to the most advanced form of education. It has sought to place within the reach of its people secondary education as well as primary, and university education as well as secondary. And not content with that, it has so planned and arranged that in addition to general education there should be available education, professional, technical, and commercial, of great variety and of various grades. Then that nothing should stand in the way of the promising pupil it has provided systems of scholarships so as to secure 'the rise of youth of proved ability from the lowest to the highest grade of institution'. A system of education where part is linked with part, and where each grade is a rung in the ladder to the top of which all who have the ability may ascend—that is the system which the policy of 1854 accepted, and that is the system which in steadily fuller measure has been accepted and realized ever since that date.

4. *A Meeting Place of Cultures.*—But the system of education for which the State accepts responsibility is not only a complete one, it is also one in which provision is made for the mingling of cultures. *The State has in view the provision of an education which is the meeting place of what is most valuable in east and west.* In the thirties of last century, as we have seen, education was the battle ground of Anglicists and Orientalists, while a third party, the Vernacularists, urged their claims though not combatants in the official arena. By the declared policy of 1854 justice was done to each and controversy was stilled. 'We desire to see in India the diffusion of the improved arts, science, philosophy, and literature of Europe', says the Despatch. 'We do not wish to diminish the opportunities for the study of the classical languages of India', it goes on to say. 'It is indispensable that the study of the vernacular languages should be assiduously attended to', is its final position as it records the fear that there has been 'a tendency unduly to neglect the study of these languages'. What is best in the intellectual heritage of India is to be brought into contact with what is best in the intellectual heritage of the west. The Indian pupil and student will enjoy the finest that his own land can give him and he will have the fullest opportunity for enjoying the finest that other lands can bring to him. It is a great aim; so great that at times its magnitude has seemed on the point of leading to its abandonment. But the obligation still remains, is still accepted; and its magnitude has become a weighty argument for vigorous activity directed towards its full realization.

III. Means for Realization of the Object

5. *Agencies Employed.*—The State has accepted the responsibility of providing an educational system which is complete in itself and which is open to all. What means does it employ for the attainment of this end?

In the first place, in seeking to discharge this responsibility *the State works through every available and stable educational agency.* In adopting this principle Indian education starts from a position which is peculiarly its own. There are countries which recognize their obligation to educate their citizens and which discharge this obligation by themselves providing, or virtually providing, the whole of the educational facilities. But in India, while the State is the supreme controlling authority, it is only a small providing agency. It does not set up its own schools and colleges and then, when there happens to be a need, invite other managements to supply what it cannot undertake. In accordance with its declared policy it calls upon local and private bodies to provide the largest number of institutions that is within their power, it aids them financially so as to enable them to undertake this task, and it guides them by its inspecting officers so that their provision may be suitable for its purpose and worthy of the service which the needs of the country require. And the directions in which, after this, provision is still lacking are indications of the help which the State for the time being may itself render. In discharging its responsibility for the supply of a complete educational system the State goes on the principle *qui per alium per se.*

6. *Partnership of Agencies.*—But the State does more than work through every stable agency. It gives to each agency so employed a definite status. It does not subordinate one agency to another; each agency comes under the control of the State, but subject to that control each is co-ordinate with, not subordinate to, any other. It does not regard one approved agency as essential to the educational system of the country and another as incidental. Every agency as soon as it receives official approval takes its place as an integral part, a definitely constituent part, of the system. An agency may, if it chooses, take its own course, it may expend its effort and means on what the State does not consider

that there is any call for. It may elect to stand by itself, to supply what may be quite good but what the State does not at the time regard as necessary. In that case the agency remains outside the recognized educational system; it is content to take its place as unrecognized. And there it will remain until its need or its fitness has been proved, and when this occurs it will have the opportunity, should it so desire, to enter the ranks of the approved. Every agency, then, that is prepared to serve the community educationally in such ways as the community needs, and can satisfy the community of its fitness for this service, is welcomed on that footing into the great educational fellowship on which the community in its organized capacity, that is the State, sets its seal. *Every approved, every officially recognized, agency receives the status of a partner in the educational effort of the country.* So far as the State is concerned each agency has the same standing. It is an accepted partner in the great business of rendering a national service. No higher position attaches to a government school simply because it is managed by Government than attaches to a board school because it is managed by a municipality. The school which is under the management of a committee of public-spirited citizens is just as much a regular part of the educational system as the school which has behind it the resources of the State. One school may differ from another in the excellence of its teaching, the spaciousness of its playing fields, or the number of books on the shelves of its library; but while the State is quick to recognize the superiority of one school to another in respect of merit, it refuses to recognize the superiority of one school to another in respect of management. All schools, provided their managements satisfy the tests of stability and suitability laid down by the State, are recognized as fellow-members of a great fraternity, and they are given their place in that fraternity on an equal footing as long as they act worthily of it. All are partners, and there are no sleeping partners. All work for the nation, each shouldering some part of a common burden, and because of that work they have their co-ordinate place in the national system.

IV. Obligations of the System

(i) *Obligations resting on the Agencies*

7. *True to Character.*—Every educational agency which makes a contribution to which the State accords recognition comes under certain obligations in virtue of that recognition. What are these obligations? In the first place, *each educational agency comes under an obligation to be what it professes to be.* A recognized school under private management must be a school, whether aided or unaided, which has stability through the funds which its management puts into it, effectiveness through the staff which its management appoints, and adequacy through the buildings which its management utilizes or provides. It may make out a good case for receiving Government aid, or it may prefer to work without such assistance, but it must first of all show its credentials, and that in no uncertain manner, to be regarded as a true educational institution and not as a venture or money-making concern. It has no title to recognition, still less to grant, if its managers have not at their disposal funds which are satisfactory guarantee of the proper maintenance of the school. If it shirks this obligation to have a financial, not a merely speculative, stake in the education of the country it has no right to a place in the partnership; and the State has an obligation to see that, in the interests of education, it is excluded from that partnership. Similarly a board school must show that the foundation of its revenues is the money which the board or municipality puts into the school. Government may subsidize this, but what title would a school have to bear the name of, say, a municipal school if all its expenses were borne by the State

and not by the municipality? The whole point of a board school is that it is the effort of people residing in a certain locality to extend education by the funds which they raise among themselves. Every school, then, be it under board or private management, must make a definite and substantial contribution from its own funds towards the educational institutions which it manages, otherwise it is shirking its obligation and rendering itself liable to the forfeiture of its place as a recognized partner in the country's educational system.

8. *Open to Inspection.*—More is needed than the production of *bona fides.* In addition, *all recognized educational agencies come under an obligation to submit to inspection.* And this means, although it is sometimes not stated, an obligation to submit to the results of inspection. A school which is unable to bear the scrutiny of officially appointed inspectors, or which refuses to take the advice which these inspectors tender, is ill-fitted to remain within the circle of recognized agencies. If there is evasiveness, ineptitude, or persistent disregard of reasonable requirement, then there is a lowering of standard which is felt in far more than the one school concerned, and the school, weak in itself and a weakness to others, has forfeited its partnership rights. On the other hand it increases its title to these rights by the open manner in which it submits to all inspection, abides by the counsel and experience which accrue to it through inspection, and lays a steady, and in all likelihood an advancing, effectiveness before inspection. And there is a further reason for the acknowledgment by a management of this obligation. Not only must an agency give proof of its fitness both for entering and remaining on in the educational partnership to which the State admits. It must also make it plain by the work which it does and the nature of the management which it maintains to what extent it is qualified to receive the financial subvention of the State. And it is an impartial inspection which makes this plain. Whether then it be to

give proof of its fitness to continue within the educational system or to receive financial support as a member of the system, the obligation to submit to inspection is no less binding in the one case than in the other.

9. *Cooperation.*—Further, *educational agencies come under an obligation to live together in unity.* Partners divided against themselves are approaching a dissolution of partnership. There is a healthy rivalry to which education owes much and which is ever to be welcomed. And where schools in a neighbourhood show this in regard to their academic record, their sports, and their traditions, there is great gain every way. But there is a rivalry that is unhealthy, and education in India has shown not a little of it. Such rivalry is opposed to the whole spirit of the fellowship into which these schools have been admitted as well as to the purpose for the realization of which they have secured their recognized place in that fellowship. Schools are to fight resolutely against illiteracy not bitterly against one another. They are to be members of a common brotherhood not leaders of rival factions. They forfeit their place when they yield to temptations to profit one at the expense of the other, to adopt easier standards, to employ less satisfactory means of admission, to undersell by fee concessions, and to turn scholarships into virtual bribes. It would be well if schools knew that the forfeiture which they have merited was the forfeiture which must inevitably befall them. Unfortunately many a time the obligation to work in harmony is neglected because no serious result has been found to follow from failure to comply with it. But when we have reached this point we are in reality passing from the obligations which rest upon agencies to the obligations which rest upon the State. And to these we may now turn.

(ii) *Obligations resting on the State*

10. *Control.*—The paramount *obligation of the State is to control the whole educational system.* That is only

to put in other words what is stated as fundamental in the very first official declaration of Indian educational policy. For many a day the State regarded education as a field to which its obligations did not extend. And then, as the story of India's destiny unfolded itself, such an attitude was revealed as untenable. By the middle of the nineteenth century it had vanished, and in its place arose a new conception, the conception not of State aloofness but of State responsibility. To provide education for the people of the country was now seen to be a sacred trust. And when the opportunity presented itself, as it did at the time when the charter fell to be renewed, the State at once took advantage of the situation thus created. It followed up the Charter Act of 1853 by a Despatch in which it publicly proclaimed that education was a trust which it was resolved to discharge. And so in the very forefront of the Despatch of 1854, as we have already noted in paragraph 2, there it stands —the announcement by the State that it has become responsible for the spread of education and for the means whereby that diffusion may be most fittingly guided and advanced. On the day when the Despatch was signed the State acknowledged that it had come under an obligation to control education, and that obligation is one from which it has never withdrawn. The nature of the control which it contemplated exercising is evident from the very first. There was no thought of a dictatorship. A single educational system applicable in every detail to every part of India is an idea which the Despatch specifically disclaims. What was in the minds of the framers of the Despatch was, as the wording of the document makes perfectly clear, the thought of a system so directed that elasticity was of its very nature, and so guided that freedom of initiative would never be lost. By control they understood guidance, direction, counsel, encouragement.

11. *Implications of Control.*—Such a conception, it must be admitted, did not lend itself to easy realization.

From the administrative point of view unbending official control would have presented far fewer difficulties. But the idea, notwithstanding the many obstacles lying in its path, has not only persisted, it has prevailed. And in our day, when each province enjoys what is practically autonomy in regard to educational procedure, this idea has become more and more fruitful. As we shall see later, it has given rise to such living notions as Decentralization and Devolution. It has set men's minds working along new lines, such as that of control which is exercised by bodies selected or appointed for that purpose yet in such manner that the State abandons none of its responsibility. The result is a higher conception of control and a deeper realization of the need for its appropriate exercise. For not only are there fresh ideas, there are also fresh situations. While in days gone by the principal care of the State was the provision of increased facilities for education, it has now to be shared among other objects. Facilities have now to be provided where they are most required and so distributed that overlapping with its accompanying waste is prevented. Care is needed to see that the youth of the country are being educated by those who are qualified for so important a task, and that the means for obtaining such qualifications are readily accessible. Policies have to be carefully thought out and framed so as to fit the ever-changing conditions of the present day. The education of special classes has to receive due attention, satisfactory standards have to be maintained, the conditions of recognition have to be carefully scrutinized. Public funds have to be employed in such a manner that the danger of preference is as much avoided as is that of parsimony. And the State has further to see to it that it so surrounds itself with capable officers that, through them and the help which they steadily afford, the best counsel is ever at the disposal of all who labour in the field of Indian education. All these things the State has to care for. The advance of education has only served to emphasize the need for the direction of education. That need was never greater than it is today. It is the call which comes to the State to fulfil in ever-increasing measure its obligation to control.

12. *Inspection.*—A second *obligation which rests upon the State is that of providing adequate inspection for the different parts of its educational system.* The State which assumes responsibility for direction by that very fact assumes responsibility for inspection. The latter obligation is, in reality, a portion of the former, the larger, obligation. Yet because of its importance it requires to be specially mentioned and separately dealt with. How can the State know what is going on in the field of education if it has not first-hand knowledge of what institutions are doing, how standards are being maintained, and where facilities for education are insufficient? How can it know whether a school ought to be granted recognition at the hands of the State, whether it ought to receive financial support from the State, and whether it ought to remain an integral part of the educational system of the State? How is all this possible unless the State has those whose duty it is to visit schools regularly, see them at all times and test them under a variety of conditions? How can managers obtain an opinion regarding their schools which is both competent and independent if there are not those who can supply them with reports that can be relied upon for knowledge, judgment, and impartiality? How can teachers realize what education demands of them in practice, and what line of study or mode of approach will best enable them to meet these demands, if they have not the stimulus which a qualified visitor can bring them, and if they have not the advice which an experienced educational authority can place at their disposal? And how is the State to be satisfied that the funds which it provides are being utilized in the furtherance of the purposes for which they were voted and in a way that employs them to the best advantage, if it is without officers who

are in a position to find out the facts and to place them without prejudice before it? The obligation is obvious and from the first the State has accepted it, as the original Despatch amply testifies. And in the documents that follow, as education becomes increasingly complex, right up to the final declaration of the Government of India on educational policy, the responsibility for providing an adequate inspectorate is fully recognized. It is a responsibility which is pressed upon the State not only by its own declarations but also, and with ever-growing emphasis, by the insistence of facts. Consider the tens of thousands of institutions that have to be visited, the increase in that number which every year witnesses, the distances which separate school from school, the many points of staff, curriculum, expenditure, and accommodation which have to be gone into, the scores of languages and dialects which are spoken by pupils, the hundreds of teachers who require a word of counsel or stimulus; consider further the frequent changes in the inspecting agency, the temporary appointments which are inevitable, the makeshifts that have to be devised and acted upon; consider all these and the magnitude of the responsibility becomes at once as apparent as does the overwhelming need for its adequate discharge. On the manner in which the State meets this acknowledged responsibility depends the health of the whole educational system.

13. *Finance.*—There is a third obligation which the State recognizes, one which it has recognized from the moment that it became responsible for the provision of education. *The State is under an obligation to place public revenues at the service of education.* Every year sees larger and larger sums being expended on education from the resources of the provincial exchequers, until the total now amounts to twelve crores of rupees. Contrast with that the 'sum of not less than one lac of rupees' which the Governor-General was authorized to 'set apart' for education by the East India Company's Act of 1813.

But if the amount is great, it falls very far short of what the conditions of the country demand. This is not surprising when we realize what this obligation to finance education involves. It involves, in the first place, the setting apart in each province of a certain percentage of the revenues which that province is able to raise; and though that percentage now compares well with that which is set apart for educational purposes in other countries, it is still far from being sufficient to make education, what it is often called, a nation-building service. Then, in the second place, the financial obligation of the State involves such an allocation of public funds that the interests of education will be most effectively advanced while the interests of the taxpayer will be most effectively safeguarded. In the third place, the State has to consider what the agencies of local self-government are doing on behalf of education, to advise them, and to stimulate them. While its policy is one of the minimum of interference with these bodies, a policy which every consideration justifies, it is one which cannot but proceed upon some recognized relation between local and provincial revenues. And in so proceeding the State has not only to keep in view a due regard for its own funds but also the way in which it can help to develop most satisfactorily the educational service of this vitally important form of administration. And, in the fourth place, the State has so to act in its financial dealings that private effort on behalf of education may receive the fullest possible encouragement, and may not be embarrassed by the plea which lays emphasis on the inelasticity of provincial revenues. These are all exacting demands, but though the strain is heavy the State admits them all as parts of an obligation which it is pledged to discharge.

14. *Encouragement.*—A fourth *obligation which the State acknowledges is that of the encouragement of education.* No one can read the 1854 Despatch without being struck by the frequency with which the words

'encourage' and 'encouragement' as applied to education occur in it. And as the reader passes from paragraph to paragraph he realizes that, even when these words are not actually employed, the attitude which they express is never absent. From beginning to end what the document reveals is the resolute determination of the State not merely to establish education but also to encourage it in all its branches and developments. And from 1854 onwards this determination appears in one official declaration after another, and in none more plainly than in the final Resolution of 1913. But so demanding and far-reaching is the obligation that we need experience no surprise if all that is involved in it has been but slowly realized. What are some of these implications?

For one thing, encouragement is possible only on the basis of knowledge. Encouragement, therefore, involves responsibility for the maintenance of such an inspectorate and headquarters staff, for the calling of such conferences between officials and non-officials, for the setting up of such bodies by statute and executive order, that there will always be available for the State information which is full and accurate, untainted by prejudice, and having reference to every form of educational effort. That is a heavy responsibility and one which is admittedly still far from being adequately met. And there is more to follow.

For in the second place, encouragement means stimulus, and stimulus may be both administrative and financial. On the administrative side there is, for example, the stimulus which comes from official reports of the right stamp. Where these employ criticism, and in a large sphere like that of education there is bound to be not a little of this and some of it anything but pleasant, all that will result from them will be simple discouragement if their criticism is so meted out as to leave the impression that model schools are the prerogative of only one form of management, while all the badly conducted schools belong to another. Where optimism is employed it may do much, by passing hopefully over defects, to stimulate schools thus treated to reach after higher attainments. But it will soon lose all stimulating force if it is not equally suffered to play upon defects which are identical with those already mentioned save in respect of the source from which they come. The State must have sportsmanlike educational reports, and it cannot have too many of them.

Financial stimulus is a very different thing from a State educational dole. But the history of Indian education seems to show how far from easy it is to appreciate the difference. To encourage education through the channel of finance is so to assign funds from the exchequer that true educational effort is evoked on every side, varied and characteristic contributions to education are freely offered, possibilities are stirred into fulfilment, and while what is unsound receives no favour the well-conceived endeavour is not allowed to suffer simply because of a certain crudeness in its mode of expression. All this involves an attitude of discernment and of generosity. And at every point the story of Indian education calls aloud for the discharge of this obligation to stimulate education, which at times has been found slipping into the region of forgetfulness.

And in the third place, encouragement implies impartiality. Now partiality may occur in connexion with legislation as well as in connexion with finance. If education Acts, whatever may have been their intention, result in furnishing one body of educators with a guarantee which they do not furnish to another body though rendering similar service, or if they bestow on the one powers which they do not repose in the other, then the conditions created by law are unequal, and the State by continuing to administer such legislation makes itself responsible for patent discouragement.

Then again if financial resources are so distributed by the State that, for example, to a management educating 47 per cent of the children in elementary schools there is given 76 per cent of what is expended from provincial revenues on that form of education, while to the management educating 53 per cent of the pupils there is given 20 per cent of what is expended from provincial funds, then there is *prima facie* discouragement which it is for the State to remove without delay. And the matter can hardly be said to end there. For if it be found that the differentiation corresponds to a real difference of educational service, the question at once arises as to how a State which allows so much of what is, *ex hypothesi*, inefficiency to belong to the educational system is competent to control. And on the other hand if the differentiation does not correspond to a difference of service the question is raised as to whether a State which thus acts is conducting its financial allocations impartially. In the one case the State encourages those whom it ought to discourage; in the other it discourages those whom it ought to encourage.

Whether then it be in respect of information, stimulus, or impartiality, a heavy responsibility rests on the State which has included the encouragement of education among the principles of its educational policy. And that is what the State in India has done, and heavy though the responsibility be, and all the heavier as its implications become clearer, it has never sought to do other than recognize its obligation to meet it.

15. *Withdrawal from what embarrasses Control.*—Closely connected with the obligation which we have been considering is a fifth. *The State*, which is the controller of education, *recognizes its responsibility for ridding itself of all that stands in the way of or embarrasses its exercise of control.* There are several such sources of embarrassment, as we have already seen, and we need not comment on them again. But there is one large area from which embarrassment to State control needs to be driven once for all. It has waited long for this elimination; it still waits. It is the area where control and management meet. There has been no lack

of thought regarding this matter. The idea of Government withdrawing from the duties of management is by no means new. So long ago as 1854 the Directors of the East India Company stated that they had it in mind. The Education Commission, thirty years later, devoted much of its time to the consideration of the State's withdrawal from the direct management of educational institutions, and it made practical proposals as to the means by which this withdrawal might be effected. The Resolution of 1904 expresses its adherence to the principle of "the progressive devolution of primary, secondary, and collegiate education upon private enterprise and the continuous withdrawal of Government from competition therewith'. And while the Resolution of 1913 affirms 'the necessity of concentrating the direct energies of the State and the bulk of its available resources on the improvement and expansion of primary education,' it proposes that this improvement and expansion should be effected not by departmental provision but by local bodies and private agencies. There is much that could be said as to the benefits of such an educational policy as the documents reveal and contemplate; and at the appropriate place some of these benefits will be referred to. But at this point there is one aspect of the matter on which emphasis might be laid. There is a great danger that what we are now discussing might seem to be merely the pitting of one form of management against another. Nothing could be more unfortunate than such an idea. This is something far more than a matter of management. It goes beyond that and takes us straight to the vital matter of control. For the satisfactory control of the whole system the Government became responsible, as we have seen, when it accepted as a sacred trust the responsibility for the provision of education. In 1854 it was also to a certain extent and very naturally as there were then so few fitted for the task, the manager of certain institutions. But it recognized the temporary nature of this position and stated its intention of so acting as to secure eventual freedom from it. To that freedom it is pledged. In the very nature of things the State places its power of control at a disadvantage when it attempts to be not only a controller that has to deal with local and private managers, but also a controller that has to deal with itself as manager. Time has brought the managers that did not exist in 1854. The way is now open for the State to devote itself wholly to the exercise of control, and thus to provide a guidance and direction not only free from the slightest suspicion of partiality but also calculated to make itself felt through the whole system as a powerful and health-giving stimulus and support. That is what the educational system of the country so much needs, what its very defects continue to call aloud for, and what the State has now the opportunity to supply, as it alone can. When the State recognizes this and acts upon it to the full, the obligation which it shouldered nearly eighty years ago will be met. The State will have discharged its responsibility for ridding itself of what at every point embarrasses its control.

16. *Religious Neutrality.*—There is another obligation which the State regards as resting on itself, and with the mention of it the enumeration of these obligations, as disclosed in official documents relating to educational policy, will come to a close. *The State has committed itself to the policy of religious neutrality.* On this basis the whole educational structure is reared. It is a conception which has not remained stationary, and the interpretations which have been given to it will be considered in detail in a subsequent chapter. Apart from details, however, it may be said that there have been in practice, and still continue to be, two recognized features of this policy. In the first place, it is held to imply that in schools and colleges under the management of the State the education provided is 'exclusively secular'. In the second place, it means that schools and colleges under non-departmental management are

at perfect liberty to combine what will provide for the religious needs of those who study in them with what will provide for their intellectual needs, and that of this combination the State takes no official cognizance. But there is a further responsibility bound up with the principle. The State, through coming under an obligation to observe religious neutrality in education as in other spheres, and through having, in connexion with education, made itself responsible for its supply, has also come under an obligation to see that all reasonable facilities are afforded for the exercise of this neutrality in educational matters. Nothing is gained if Government simply intimates its intention of abstaining from all interference with religion while it does nothing to protect anyone from the possibility of such interference. For, the reason why Government adopts this attitude in regard to education is that no pupil may be placed in a position where the conscientious scruples of himself or of his parents may be violated. And in a system which welcomes into it all forms of educational agencies there is obviously the possibility of such violation unless the State adopts the necessary precautions to prevent the possibility becoming an actuality. And the nature of the educational system makes it easy for the State to create the necessary safeguards. For the system contains *educational institutions under public*, as well as under private, management, schools and colleges in which religious instruction is not an integral part of their curriculum as well as those in which it is. All then that the State has to do, at any juncture where cherished scruple seems to be endangered, is to encourage the establishment of institutions where religious training is not an integral part of the course. Thus will the problem receive a simple and effective solution; means will be secured for that freedom from the interference with conscientious conviction which it is the duty of the State professing the doctrine of religious neutrality to safeguard. Further consideration will be given to this matter later. Here it is enough to note that the State has never failed to acknowledge its responsibility for the maintenance of religious neutrality in the sphere of education.

V. A System Based on Principles

17. *An Organic System.*—We have now looked at the educational policy of the State in India from two points of view. In the first place we have looked at it from the point of view of its factors, of its component parts, as these are set forth in a series of official declarations; and in the second place we have looked at it from the point of view of its fundamentals, of its principles, as these are revealed in the official declarations in which the policy is expressed. This method of treatment results in two distinct gains. For one thing we see that the policy, though it has been stated at different times over a space of sixty years, forms a coherent whole. And for another thing we see what it is which has contributed to this coherence. It is largely due to the fact that the system is founded on principles which do not conflict with, but supplement and reinforce, one another; which though rising out of the past are not under the mortmain of the past but show themselves capable of application to new circumstances and changing conditions; which are not narrow in their range but bring variety, order, and vitality into the whole sweep of the internal and external relations of the educational system. And it is to these principles that education in India has been constantly recalled when there was clear evidence of departure from them. What they reveal to us is the State acknowledging its responsibility for the supply of a system of education which runs from the most elementary to the most advanced and which is the meeting place for different cultures; securing this through the operation of various agencies which it itself controls, which it encourages, and which it welcomes

to the status of partnership in a great enterprise; and finally recognition, and working for the fulfilment of, a number of obligations which rest on these agencies as well as on itself. The coherence, in other words, is due to the fact that the system is an organic, not a mechanical, system.

18. *A Needed System.*—But it may be said that the Resolution of the Government of India issued in 1913 was not only the last statement of educational policy to be issued by that Government, but that in a few years after its publication an all-India educational policy had ceased to exist. No longer was it possible for the Central Government to recall Provincial Governments to the principles of its avowed educational policy. The question may therefore be raised whether the subject which has been engaging our attention has more than a historical interest. To the consideration of that question we must now turn our attention. In the following chapter it is fully discussed. But at this point we may anticipate the result of that consideration by mentioning the interesting fact which emerges from it, a fact which shows how far from academic is the investigation which we have hitherto pursued. The fact is this. While the Government of India can no longer promulgate a policy to which it is the duty of the different provinces to give effect, the principles of the policy with which the Government of India was identified from 1854 to 1919 are the very principles the adoption of which is being pressed upon every province of India not by the fiat of a Central Government but by the facts of the educational situation with which each one of them is actually faced.

CHAPTER IV

RECALL TO A POLICY

I. POLICY UP TO 1919

1. *Growth of a Policy.*—By a long process, as we have seen, was a comprehensive Indian educational policy evolved. The strands of which it was ultimately composed began to be woven before the end of the eighteenth century. In different provinces, at different times, amid differing surroundings they disclosed themselves and claimed attention. Finally, after experience stretching over seven decades, the State (the master weaver) saw its way clearly, recognized its responsibility, knit the various strands together, and in 1854 spread before the eyes of India the texture of an educational policy fashioned so as to have its place in every part of the land. The policy thus inaugurated gave to the country a scheme of administration based upon a few clear principles. It is this foundation upon principles which has imparted vitality as well as coherence to the Indian educational system. What was laid down in 1854 was examined in 1859, in 1882, in 1904, and again in 1913; and as often as it was examined the underlying principles set forth in 1854 received confirmation. Varying circumstances brought new conditions into the sphere of Indian education; the supreme power in the land was changed, local self-government was introduced, legislative bodies received ever-increasing authority. Had the policy directing Indian education been a rigid formula, the varying circumstances would have necessitated in it frequent and, quite conceivably, fundamental alteration. But the policy was essentially a

statement of principles capable of application to changing conditions, yet not themselves requiring to be changed. Indeed their value became all the more patent as, with the passage of time and all the alterations which it brought in its train, they stood the test of experience and showed themselves adequate for ever fresh conditions. Thus it was that the policy promulgated by the East India Company in 1854 was adopted by the Government of India when Company yielded to Crown in 1858, and so constituted till the great constitutional change of 1919 introduced an entirely new situation.

2. *Nature of the Policy.*—What was the educational policy which, for a period of sixty-five years, held good in all places which the Government of India administered? And what were the changes which the legislation of 1919 introduced? The first question admits of a concise reply. The education of the country, it was laid down, was to be advanced by the State welcoming into a common partnership every stable and approved educational agency. Inspectors appointed by the Government would satisfy themselves as to the stability and suitability of the institutions maintained by the different agencies, and would tender advice to those who conducted them. At the same time the State accepted the responsibility of controlling the whole system through provincial educational departments, of taking the initiative, of providing adequate inspection, and of encouraging all approved managements by satisfactory financial support. Further, it set before itself the plan of withdrawal from the status of manager while discharging that of controller. And it pledged itself to adhere to the principle of religious neutrality through all the ranges of its educational administration. While this policy was to be carried out by the provincial governments, it was a policy laid down by the central government, and could be altered only by resolution of that government.

II. Effect of the Government of India Act of 1919

3. (1) *Education Decentralized.*—As to the second question, the answer is: the Government of India Act passed in 1919 transferred educational policy from the control of the central government and placed it in the hands of the provincial governments. The effect of this is at once clear. While the Act of 1919 'has not deprived the Government of India of all its educational functions'—for it has still educational responsibilities in regard to certain administration and universities—it has reduced these to a minimum. As matters now stand, the Government of India has no longer the power to issue a statement of educational policy the writ of which will run in every province. And not only that. While in the past the Government of India could secure the furtherance of any educational policy which it had enunciated, by means of grants to provincial governments, it lost that power by the legislation of 1919. In accordance with that legislation grants for provincial objects are not to be made by the central government to provincial governments; and so it is no longer 'possible for the government of India to influence the educational policy of local governments by means of Imperial grants.' By the Government of India Act, therefore, the Government of India was deprived of the power, which it held for over sixty years, of framing an educational policy applicable to the whole of India and of taking measures to ensure that that policy was carried out. Education, in short, ceased to be a central subject.

4. (2) *Education entrusted to Ministers.*—This was not the only change which followed from the Act of 1919. Save in regard to the small section of education which is known as 'European Education' (responsibility for the administration of which rests with a member of Council), the control of education in each province was entrusted to a responsible Minister. There is no need

for us to consider the various ways in which educational matters have been assigned to different portfolios in different provinces. That is a matter of administrative control, though it is not without a bearing on some of the more important aspects of educational advance. It is sufficient for our present purpose, however, to confine ourselves to the outstanding changes which the 1919 Act effected in regard to education—provincial control and ministerial responsibility.

5. (3) *No All-India Policy.*—So far then as a general educational policy goes, what has happened is that, by the Act of 1919, the last sentence in paragraph 2 has simply dropped out. As the Auxiliary Committee[1] of the Statutory Commission[2] puts it: 'It may be said broadly that, apart from certain matters of detail, the Government of India have, since the Reforms, regarded all responsibility for educational policy as devolved on the separate provinces, and that an educational policy for India as a whole no longer exists.' And very much to the same effect are the words of the Educational Commissioner with the Government of India who in the *Ninth Quinquennial Review* says: 'An "Indian" educational policy can scarcely be said to exist today.' But, it may be asked, if the last sentence in paragraph 2 is now dropped, do all the other sentences in that paragraph go with it? The answer is: Far from it. The carefully woven fabric was not torn into fragments by the emergence of a new constitution. In certain provinces the policy continues to operate almost precisely as it has done since 1854, while in other provinces the principles of 1854 still constitute the groundwork of the system though certain departures from them have been made. Thus, while there is no educational policy which technically can be called 'Indian', yet the principles of the policy laid down in the Despatch of 1854 are still

[1] Hartog Committee. [2] Simon Commission.

those by which the Indian provinces, for the most part; regulate their educational procedure. But, though this is the case, it has to be borne in mind, first, that changes in policy have already been initiated in some of the provinces, and secondly, that no province is under any obligation to abstain from further changes.

III. Need for an Indian, not a Purely Provincial, Policy

6. *View of the Auxiliary Committee.*—Now liberty is of the very essence of life, and departure from the old ways may mean the inflow of welcome vigour. There is no *a priori* reason for concluding that the changes in educational policy which have already been attempted are harmful or that further changes may not be beneficial. Experiment in educational practice has its place and value, and in India there is not only a place for such experiment, there is an ever-increasing need for it. Our concern, however, is not with educational practice but with the principles of educational policy. And what we have specially to enquire into is: Has the educational policy of India, after sixty-five years of central care. benefited by its ten years of provincial liberty? We receive an answer to this question in the two recent surveys of Indian education to which we have already referred, and to which further reference is made in Chapter I of Part II. And first as to the position of the Auxiliary Committee. It considers that there is a freedom unproductive of educational gains, and that if solid advance is to be achieved there must exist, alongside provincial activity and initiative, a Bureau which will perform some of the functions formerly discharged by the Government of India in regard to education by supplying 'advice, guidance, and encouragement' to the provincial governments and by helping 'to co-ordinate their efforts to deal with common problems'. It even goes further than this, for it suggests that 'consti-

tutional means should be devised to enable the Imperial Government to come to the aid of the provincial governments'. And while the Committee disclaims all idea of reinstating the Central Government in its former place of power, it draws attention to the fact, on which it has dwelt at length, 'that the money spent in some provinces on primary education has been, to a large extent, wasted'. And it expresses the opinion that 'there is no reason why the Government of India in making grants for mass education should not take measures to assure itself that such waste is not perpetuated'. A survey of the present position of education, with special reference to the field of primary education, has convinced the Committee that unhampered freedom of action in the provinces is not resulting in an educational advance at all proportionate to the expenditure of energy, thought, and money; and that there is, and will continue to be, much wasteful expenditure of effort and of public funds so long as the provinces do not accept in common certain principles by which their educational activities will be guided.

7. *View of the Educational Commissioner.*—The Educational Commissioner in the course of the *Ninth Quinquennial Review* arrives at a conclusion which, apart from the financial aspect, is virtually identical with that of the Committee. Paragraphs 36 to 40 of that Review deserve the widest publicity. They are too long to quote in full. The following are a few excerpts from them :

'It certainly seems right,' says the Commissioner, 'that under any measure of provincial autonomy provincial governments should have a voice in the manner of development of the various provincial activities in relation to the peculiar needs of the people under their governance. But it is a matter for grave doubt whether the present system, whereby the provinces have attacked their educational problems in almost complete isolation and have developed the most varying schemes for financing and controlling education in all its grades, has resulted in that forward policy or series of policies which is the most beneficial to the nation as a whole.' And again, 'although education was made a provincial transferred subject by the Government of India Act, its provincialization has not removed the need for some form of co-ordinating, advisory and informatory central agency . . . The isolation of the Government of Inida from provincial governments and of provincial governments from one another in the field of education is making its ill effects felt so that there are recently signs which indicate that opinion in favour of co-operation and mutual assistance is gaining ground.' In other words, if education is to make a really satisfactory impression on the country, there must be the removal of what constitutes a serious obstacle to the making of that impression, namely complete provincial independence in regard to educational policy. There is only one way by which that impression can be made—the acceptance by the various provinces of certain fundamental principles of educational policy.

8. *Evils of Want of Common Policy.*—The same conclusion is forced upon any one who carefully peruses the fact disclosed by the two Reviews mentioned in the preceding paragraphs. We turn over page after page, and ask : Why is our system of primary education so ineffective? and the answer pressed upon us by facts and figures is : Because there is no general policy in regard to control, financing, inspection, or training of teachers. Again as we read we ask : Why are there so many blemishes in our system of secondary education? And what the facts reply is : Because there is no commonly accepted policy in regard to control, management, expenditure, and training. Once more we are forced to ask : Why is the education of girls, of Muhammadans, and of certain other classes so backward? And the answer that springs from these pages is : Because there is no clear policy as to management, encourage-

ment of religious training, and the supply of teachers. And finally in a comprehensive way we ask: Why is it that, with all the progress that has been achieved in the last five years, there is still such appalling waste and so many millions unaffected by our educational system? And the answer does not tarry, every paragraph of these Reviews presses it home upon us: Because there is no commonly accepted policy as to the provision and the direction of education.

9. *Recall to a Common Policy.*—From the conclusions of official Commissioner, unofficial Committee, and independent investigator we have now received an answer to the question which we raised in paragraph 6 as to the effect on educational policy of a decade of provincial liberty. That answer is: After ten years' liberty there is a definite call for voluntary surrender of no small amount of that liberty if education is to have its perfect work. There is a very clear recall, not to a Government of India policy, but to what is rightly termed an Indian educational policy, a policy the main principles of which will be accepted by the free choice of each province and thus will be acted upon throughout the whole of India. There can be no mistaking it. That is what the experience of the last ten years resolves itself into—a recall to an Indian educational policy.

IV. Principles of an Indian Educational Policy

(i) *Provision of Education*

10. *The State responsible for Providing Education.*—Since that is the case, it is high time that the principles of such a comprehensive policy should be carefully disentangled and clearly set forth. All the more so because, on the one hand, further continuance of present conditions may only serve to stereotype independent provincial policies, to the lasting detriment of education; and, on the other, because the closer relationship between

provinces and Indian States to which we look forward at no distant date emphasizes the need of a large policy in the benefits of which every administration of the country may participate. Our endeavour, then, is to get at those principles on which a comprehensive system of national education may be effectively reared. Now there are two responsibilities in regard to education which the State in India has acknowledged for the past three quarters of a century: one is the responsibility for the provision of education, the other is the reponsibility for the direction of education. But the acknowledgment of a responsibility does not necessarily indicate how responsibility is to be discharged. That is what we have to look for. In other words our search now is for those principles in accordance with which the State may best meet its responsibilities for the provision and direction of education.

11. *The Provision to be Non-departmental.*—One of the things which the study of Indian education presses upon us, and which the two most recent surveys bring home to us very emphatically, is that for the State to acknowledge its responsibility for the provision of that education is not the same thing as for the State to acknowledge its responsibility for the provision of that education by its own agency. Indeed it is well and in the best interests of the country that these two are not identical. To provide education for the whole of India by its own agency is wholly beyond the power of the State. Take mass education. The tables of the *Ninth Quinquennial Review* supply us with evidence which admits of no question. The various provincial governments taken together educate in the elementary schools which they themselves manage 136,000 pupils; yet to educate this small number they require to draw upon their funds to the extent of Rs. 18 lakhs. If all who are at present receiving elementary education were pupils of State-managed schools, instead of being almost wholly pupils of non-departmental schools, the cost to the coun-

try would be somewhere about Rs. 1,200 lakhs, a sum which is in excess of the total amount of the direct and indirect expenditure of the State on every form of education through the length and breadth of British India. The thing is obviously impossible. As with elementary so with secondary education. The State educates in that field 132,000 pupils, about the same number as it does at the elementary stage. And the cost to provincial revenues is Rs. 70 lakhs. Were all the boys and girls now receiving secondary education to be enrolled in schools under State management the cost would be equivalent to about half the total sum which the State is able to spend out of its revenues on every form of education in the country. Once again, the thing is impossible. We should find much the same thing if we turned from secondary to collegiate education. But we need not labour the point. The Statistical Tables make it clear, beyond the shadow of a doubt, that the State is not able to discharge its responsibility for the provision of education by making that provision itself. But the Tables show even more than that. They emphasize what is still more significant, namely that the longer Government continues its own agency the more certainly does it stand in the way of the spread of education. For it absorbs funds which would be more profitably employed for the education of the country by other managements. This is most noticeable in connexion with the education of the masses, but it is scarcely less noticeable in connexion with secondary, women's, and non-professional collegiate education. These facts are gradually, very gradually, being recognized. The governments of the various provinces have, within the last few years, made a definite and largely successful effort to hand over the primary schools under their management to non-departmental agencies; while even among professional colleges, a change is taking place, for at the present time five out of the twelve medical colleges are under Aided or Board management, and out of the thirteen law colleges only four are managed by Government. Indeed it is possible for the Educational Commissioner to say that, with certain exceptions to which he refers, 'the expansion of education has continued to take place most largely through institutions under private management and under municipal and district boards.' There are other reasons even more cogent than those drawn from financial considerations, reasons which go to the very foundations of national upbuilding, that lend emphatic support to the position that the State best discharges its responsibility for the provision of education by seeing to it that the provision is adequately made through other agencies than its own. The very exceptions to which the Educational Commissioner refers lend emphasis to this : but we need not dwell upon them. As things now stand, Government hinders rather than helps the spread of education (at least of a non-professional character) by seeking to provide it through its own agency. We have thus arrived at one principle of educational policy, and we may state it as follows. *While it is the duty of the State to see to the provision of education, it is not the duty of the State save in exceptional circumstances, to provide that education by its own agency.*

12. *Partnership of Non-departmental Agencies.*—There are two main agencies on which the State can, and actually does, rely for the provision of educational facilities—local bodies and private managements. Of the recognized institutions in the Indian educational system 65 per cent are under private management and 33 per cent are managed by district boards and municipal councils. If the State really desires to ransom the country from the blight of illiteracy and to build up an educated nation, it has one paramount duty—the sympathetic, impartial, and unflagging encouragement of both these agencies. Each has its drawbacks, each its advantages, as a perusal of the records tells us with no lack of detail. But each has a definite part to play in the spread of education through the land; each makes

its own appeal. And what the facts garnered in recent surveys of education press upon the State is the clamant need for its discerning and untiring support, in the fullest possible manner, of these two great contributors to the cause of India's education. If, for instance, there are circumstances which have induced Government to make a present of a school building to a local body, it is inconceivable that circumstances should never arise which would make a similar present to an aided management advisable. If the methods of allocating grants differ as between the two agencies, so that preferential treatment seems to be accorded to one, then the interests of education demand an adjustment of methods so as to substitute equality for preference, and the demand is all the more keen if the inequality can be traced to the practical working of legislative enactments. What the country requires for the rapid effective advance of education is a well-balanced combination of the two agencies; 'the stability' of the one blending with 'the local flavour' of the other, as Mr. Mayhew puts it; self-governing effort and private initiative becoming mutually complementary. Now this combination it is in the power of the State to secure without difficulty. Organizations whereby this co-operation may be effected can be readily set up, and in some provinces they are already at work; but they are at present only in their initial stage, and much remains to be done to fit them for the important part they have it in their power to play. They afford the educational system of India the sole means by which local bodies and private agencies may work together in the cause of education as partners. And unless they work as partners, neither can make its characteristic contribution, and the country is the loser. Make one of these co-ordinate agencies subordinate to the other, as is happening when legislation places private agencies in the position of managers only, while it assigns to local bodies the position not only of managers but also of controllers, and we have the strange result of the State lending itself to what is practically the disparagement of an indispensable educational agency. That is the way not to advance education but to retard it. In co-ordinate managements subject to, and encouraged by, the State lies the road of progress. We have thus arrived at another principle of educational policy, namely, *it is the duty of the State to combine into a common partnership in the dissemination of education every stable agency, local and private.*

(ii) *Direction of Education*

13. *Need of Impartiality.*—So much for the provision of education. Now for its direction. And the first point which facts press upon us is that, if the State is to be, and to be accepted as, the controller of the entire educational system, *it is the duty of the State so to direct as to be above all imputation of partiality.* Unfortunately in this respect the State still labours under a handicap. As matters now stand, the State is both controller of the whole and manager of part. That anomalous position has its explanation in history, and in the light of conditions which prevailed for many years is perfectly intelligible. But the conditions have now completely altered. There are non-official bodies quite competent to manage colleges as well as secondary and primary schools. If there were not, a serious aspersion would be cast upon the education of the past three-quarters of a century. The recent developments in university administrations which have led further and further away from dependence upon Government and more and more to dependence on the work of the non-official are sufficient indication that the recommendations of the Indian Education Commission in regard to the transfer of management from departmental to non-departmental agencies are capable of a realization which strangely enough has not been given to them, although practically half a century has elapsed since they were made. In its own interests, that is in the interests of the people, the State has here a very definite step to take. Slowly, far

too slowly as it seems to many, is the State recognizing the obligation which rests upon it to take this step. It is in general withdrawing from the management of elementary schools. Out of the 200,000 schools of primary grade in British India only 2,700 are under the direct management of Government. Indeed were it not for an anomaly which it is difficult to believe can be long tolerated, the number of primary schools under State management would be less than 2,000. And so far as higher grades of education are concerned, expansion is taking place, so the Educational Commissioner informs us, mainly along non-departmental channels. He does refer to exceptions, and the more one looks at them the more one is astonished at their continuance. The current, however, it is clear has begun to flow in one direction: it has gathered no little volume. What is needed is that the State should do everything in its power to accelerate the flow till departmental management ceases to exist, and the State stands, and is acknowledged to be, the impartial director of all managements, and of the entire educational system.

14. *Need of Adequate Inspectorate.*—Let us now look at some of the ways in which the State is called on to exercise its functions as an impartial director. It may be said that, when reference was made in paragraph 12 to the encouragement of managements, stability was the only feature mentioned, and that this was not enough. That is perfectly true. If managements are to make their appropriate contribution to the educational system of India they must provide schools which are adequate for their purpose as well as stable. If they cannot do this they have no right to the status of recognized partners. But how is the State to satisfy itself as to the stability of schools and their suitability for a place in the national system? The answer is: By means of an adequate inspectorate. Now what strikes one at every turn in reading reports of what is taking place at present in the field of Education is that the State does

not possess an adequate inspectorate. It does indeed appoint inspecting officers, but it sets them an impossible task. How is it possible for less than 2,200 inspectors—and that is the total strength of the inspecting agency, men and women—to deal with over 200,000 schools, to visit them even once a year, to spend in each sufficient time to be really acquainted with what is going on, to share with teachers the benefit of their experience, and to give to managers the counsel which they so often desire? What encouragement is being given to the education of women and girls when there are provinces in which the average number of schools that an inspectress has to visit is 313, 416, and—will it be believed—1,055? What confidence can the work of the staff command when we read of provinces which have on their inspectorate quite a respectable number of untrained intermediates and matriculates? And how can the State regard itself as meeting this responsibility in anything more than in name when, as regards one province, it can be said that 'the duty of inspection (of primary schools) has been virtually handed over to local bodies,' and as regards another that the control of those inspecting primary schools has been transferred from Government to District Councils? Why multiply questions? Read what official and non-official records recently published put candidly before us, and you will find that you are faced by this sorry confession : Over the country as a whole, the State has not supplied an inspectorate at all adequate in respect of numbers, in many parts of the country it maintains an inspectorate that is not sufficiently equipped for the work which it has to discharge, and in certain provinces the State has virtually abrogated important parts of its inspecting functions. Such facts are really a call to the State to discharge adequately a responsibility of which it cannot divest itself but which at present it is meeting most inadequately. How can the State direct if it has not the agency whereby that direction may be properly exercised? At this point, then, we have come upon a fundamental article of educational policy. It is this: If the State in India is to give to its educational system the benefit of wise and salutary direction, *it is the duty of the State to possess an adequate and fully qualified inspecting agency.* To the discharge of that duty the hard facts, which are now before every student of Indian education, most urgently recall the State.

15. *Devolution.*—Let us now pass to another point on which recent records dwell at considerable length, the fact of devolution. No one can read what has been going on in connexion with the administration of education in India, especially within the last decade, and fail to be struck with the manner in which the State is transferring to others powers of direction which were formerly entirely in its own hands. This has been accomplished partly by departmental order and partly by statutory enactment, into the details of which it is unnecessary for us to enter. Suffice it to say that, throughout India, the State has deliberately handed over many of its powers of direction to universities, district boards and municipalities, and *ad hoc* bodies. Why has it done this? In regard to universities the answer is not hard to give. The transfer took place because it was both possible and advisable. It was possible because there were those who, as experience had shown, were capable of participating in the working of the universities with ability, wisdom, and devotion. It was advisable because a university is far more than a departmental organization. Thus it is that legislation came to be introduced only when there was a clear call for it, and when there were those who could carry out its provisions so as to realize most amply the aims of an autonomous university. In regard to *ad hoc* bodies the answer is that the transfer took place, for the most part, in order that all the interests concerned might have their due share in control, a consideration which, it is being recognized, can now be left out of account only to the

serious loss of education. In regard to local bodies the answer is that the control of education was regarded as a fitting field for the exercise, within prescribed limits, of a local self-governing body's functions. The result, however, of acting on this assumption has produced a peculiar situation which we must now consider.

16. *Methods of Devolution.*—In the first place, devolution of control to local bodies has affected the position of the Minister. The Auxiliary Report says, 'In consequence of the expansion of the powers of local bodies and of the devolution on many of them of a large measure of responsibility in respect of vernacular education, that branch of education has been taken to a great extent out of the control of Ministers and of the provincial legislatures.' In a number of provinces, that is to say, devolution of the function of direction by the State has become actually abrogation by the State of that function. There is no need to dwell on the evil with which this is fraught. Education is, it is true, a local service, but it is more than that. It is a national service, and the State is responsible for seeing that its national character is never lost. Yet there are whole tracts of the country in which the State is at present the abettor of this loss. Such a state of matters cannot be remedied too speedily. So much for the first point connected with devolution to local bodies. The second is one at which we have already looked in another connexion. This devolution has been secured by taking one from among the managers of schools within one area, and placing that manager in the anomalous position of retaining the status of manager while at the same time enjoying the status of controller of the whole. This arrangement might be justified if that particular form of management had shown special capacities for the position of the director, or if the State had determined to drive from the field every form of management save the one to which it entrusted the control. The first alternative is not easy to prove; the second is unbelievable.

Page after page of recent reports makes it plain that the advocate of local bodies as controllers has to deal with an array of somewhat disconcerting facts. That the State should think of dispensing with an educational agency of proved worth would mean simply that the State had resolved to fight education, not illiteracy. The whole matter of devolution to local bodies, then, calls for serious reconsideration.

17. *Need for Suitable Devolution.*—This is made all the more obvious when we remember that, not only must the bodies on which the powers of direction are to be devolved be capable of securing united action in regard to the management of schools, but they must be able to secure also a combined action in regard to the location of schools, the training of teachers to staff them, the encouragement of the education of girls and the backward classes, and the adaptation of school curricula to varying local conditions. It is when we think of what the nature of educational control is and what the nature of the bodies must be to which that control may be fittingly entrusted that we realize how far from simple is any scheme of devolution and how serious a responsibility rests upon the State when it commits itself to any such scheme. No one can read what has been recorded within the last twelve years regarding the control of Indian education and the efforts towards decentralization without feeling that many mistakes might have been avoided and much greater advance might have been secured if effort had followed certain clearly thought out lines of policy. But even failure and mistake are not without their lessons. And out of the tangle in which Indian education is at present involved with regard to its control there emerge two principles to which the recent surveys of education lend fresh emphasis. The fact is that, when a transfer of control seems advisable, *it is the duty of the State to ensure that devolution has as its result not the abrogation by the State of its educational control but the more effective and*

beneficial exercise of that power. And the other principle is this: *That form of devolution possesses especial value which leads, not to the elimination of any recognized educational agency, but to the association of them all in the fullest and most characteristic educational service which each can render to the country.*

(iii) *Financing of Education*

18. *Need for Equality of Financial Treatment.*—From this, the transition to financial considerations is natural. Here too we are in a region where, as tables and letterpress assure us, there is need for the guidance of definite lines of policy. There is no money to spare, and the requirements of education are ever growing. The most recent calculation is that the annual recurring cost of a general system of compulsory elementary education in India would be approximately 20 crores of rupees. The Auxiliary Committee which has arrived at this estimate says that the sum 'is not abnormally large'. It may not be, but the fact remains that it is only four and a half crores less than the total amount of money spent on education of all grades. And provincial funds supply practically only a half of what is needed to carry on the education that is at present provided. There are three main agencies at work, as statistics show us, and the contribution which each of these makes has its origin in three sources—the money it raises, the fees it levies, and the subscriptions and endowments it receives. If we take these sources together the result is as follows: In round figures, out of the 24½ crores of rupees spent on education in British India, 13 crores are provided by Government, 4½ by local bodies, and 7 by private agencies. Now, if we confine our attention to the contribution of the two non-departmental agencies, we see from the tables that the local bodies, which make themselves responsible for an amount of education that it costs 4 crores to maintain, receive from provincial funds 319 lakhs as subsidy, while the

private agencies, which carry on an amount of education that costs 7 crores to maintain, receive as their subsidy from provincial funds 265 lakhs. The inequality is at once apparent. And the significance of it becomes no less apparent, as we ponder the figures. It is this. There are two agencies on which rests the main burden for the provision of the education of the country—local bodies supplying 33 per cent of the educational institutions of the system, and private bodies supplying 65 per cent. Yet the one which carries the heavier burden and makes the larger contribution to the educational resources of the country is the one which, in respect of financial support, receives the smaller encouragement from the State. Now something much more important than a question of status is involved in this. The whole issue of the advance of India's education is bound up with it. Frequently it is stated that it is the lack of funds that stands in the way of educational progress. What statistical tables suggest is that it is not so much the lack of funds as the distribution of funds that is the real stumbling block. Had the encouragement of the one agency borne some relation to the encouragement of the other, even during the past decade, there would have been a much greater expansion of education than there is today. The failure of the State to maintain an equitable distribution of funds among the educational agencies of the country has had most regrettable results. It has led to the impartiality of the State being called in question, it has stood in the way of a rapid development of education, and it has kept resources which are of the greatest value to the country from being fully tapped and freely given.

19. *Present Inequalities.*—The same conclusion is forced upon us when we turn from this more general consideration to one that is of no less importance though its limits are more circumscribed. Let us look at one set of figures—those which tell us of the expenditure of the State revenues in connexion with primary education. In the province of Madras there is an endeavour, through

the statutory form of administration established there, to combine local and private support in the supply of education for the masses. That endeavour is not wholly successful, for the relative enactment requires amendment, an amendment that would present no difficulty and which would secure the fullest combination. Even as it is, however, no small amount of combination has been achieved. In the provinces of Bombay, the Punjab, and the United Provinces what we find in place of this endeavour is emphasis on the service of one agency, namely local bodies. Now it is interesting to note the results. We may take primary schools for boys, because there are more of them, and because while they are attended for the most part by boys they reckon hundreds of thousands of girls among their pupils. From the statistical tables the following facts emerge. Madras educates almost two million pupils in its boys' elementary schools, and it does this at a cost to provincial funds of 74 lakhs of rupees. Bombay educates 851,000 pupils in its boys' elementary schools (or 1,200,000 fewer than Madras) and the cost to provincial revenues is 105 lakhs. The Punjab educates 721,000 pupils in its boys' elementary schools (or 1,300,000 fewer than Madras) and the provincial cost is 48 lakhs. The United Provinces have in these schools 1,099,000 pupils (or 900,000 fewer than Madras) and the cost to their provincial revenues is 104 lakhs. The force of these figures needs no stressing. And when we take them in connexion with what has been stated in the preceding paragraph we realize that we have found a principle which the State cannot set aside, because departure from it is a disservice to education. We may express it thus: *It is the duty of the State, in its control of education, so to allocate its funds that there may be no partiality of treatment, but that each agency may receive that recognition of the work which it does together with that encouragement which will enable it to render to the cause of education the richest contribution in its power.*

(iv) *Religious Education*

20. *Encouragement of Religious Training.*—If education is to advance as rapidly in India as its well-wishers desire, and if it is to have a more welcome garb than it presents to many at present, at least one other principle of educational policy requires to be incorporated. On every side we hear the demand that there should be ample opportunities for the combination of religion with the secular education imparted. Both the Auxiliary Committee and the Educational Commissioner touch on a portion of this matter when they deal with Muhammadan education. Not a few of the remarks made in that connexion have an application that reaches far beyond the community with which the paragraphs are immediately concerned. No one can survey the progress of education in India without being conscious that no little distrust of it would be overcome if there was a closer link between learning and religion. The form of education now so largely provided is taken full advantage of, for no one can be blind to the material benefits it confers. But time and again one realizes that the education given has far too little hold on character, and that it is apt to remain a thing apart even from mental attitude. There are several reasons for this, but one of the most important is that the combination of education and religion, welcome to Hindus and Muhammadans alike, receives so little attention. If it be said that the State can do nothing because its attitude is one of strict neutrality in religious matters, the reply must at once be made that, on the one hand, the State is not only the manager of schools, it is also the controller of the whole system; and that, on the other hand, neutrality is not identical with exclusion. If the State were controller alone, it would be more easy for it to recognize the responsibility which rests upon it in this matter. It has a duty to make sure that the educational system is provided with facilities for a form of education

which appeals to every side of the pupil's nature. There are difficulties in the way of this; but the tendency has been to dwell on the obstacles, and not on the means for overcoming them, means which lie to one's hands in a system controlled by Government, but from the management of any part of which Government is steadily withdrawing. The way is open for a great step forward in this direction. Let local and private managements be combined under bodies to which Government has entrusted certain of its powers of control, and many of the difficulties which have been regarded as insuperable will disappear. By private agencies and local bodies working in union with one another, and receiving support from provincial funds on equitable terms, the State will be enabled to see at work in the educational system of the country that combination of an 'education based upon religion, the acceptance of authority, respect for persons and institutions' with 'rational teaching, liberal views, and the spirit of development' which the *Ninth Quinquennial Review* refers to as a desideratum. The duty of the State is plain: it is emphasized by facts which cannot be ignored: what is called for is the recognition of the following principle: *It is the duty of the State to encourage with complete impartiality every agency which, in the interests of the youth of the country and their all-round education, unites, in the schools that it provides, religious with secular education.*

V. An Indian Educational Policy Possible

21. (1) *Through Adoption of Common Principles.*—We began the consideration of our present subject by noting the changes which the Government of India Act effected in the administration of education. The most marked of these was that the Government of India ceased to be responsible for the educational policy of the country, and that each province became responsible for framing its own policy. We further noted that a decade

of this provincial liberty had evoked a strong desire for the enunciation of lines of policy which would be applicable to every province, that some substantial agreement should take the place of isolation. As a consequence of this desire we passed in review the educational needs of the Indian situation as revealed in provincial reports, the report of the Auxiliary Committee, and the *Ninth Quinquennial Review*. And as a result of this study certain principles emerged, few in number, fundamental in character, that held within them the promise of combined educational effort and sound educational advance. They grouped themselves round two responsibilities which the State accepts today as it has done for almost eight decades. Let us briefly set them forth. First, the State recognizes its responsibility for the provision of education. But while it is the duty of the State to see to the provision of education, facts make it plain that it is not its duty, save in exceptional circumstances, to provide that education through its own agency. Its duty is to see to it that all stable agencies, local and private, are combined into an effective partnership for the supply of the country's educational needs. By this partnership, under the State direction, full provision will be made for the education of India's youth. Second, the State recognizes its responsibility for directing the education that is provided, and for doing this in a strictly impartial fashion. That involves the possession by it of an adequate and fully qualified inspecting agency, for only thus will it be able to test, to advise, to obtain accurate information, and to satisfy itself as to the proper use of public funds assigned to educational objects. Further it is the duty of the State, when it considers a devolution of control advisable, to make sure that, in devolving its power, it does not give it away but renders its exercise more beneficial and effective; and that it does not by its mode of devolution eliminate any recognized agency but associates all agencies in the fullest and most characteristic educational service which each can render to the country. This cannot be done without considerations of finance, and in connexion with them facts emphasize the duty of the State so to allocate its funds on behalf of education that there may be no inequality in the treatment of the different agencies, but that each agency may receive that encouragement which will enable it to render to education the fullest contribution in its power. And finally, in order that education may make its appeal to the whole personality of the pupil, it is the duty of the State, while itself as the controller of the educational system maintaining complete impartiality in religious matters, to encourage every agency which, in the interests of an all-round education, unites in its schools religious with secular education.

22. (2) *Through Continuity of Essentials.*—If now we compare these principles with the principles mentioned in paragraph 2, we cannot fail to be impressed by their substantial agreement. Emphasis changes, as is only to be expected; but the fundamentals abide. The growth of local self-governing bodies, the appointment of Ministers responsible to popularly elected legislatures, and the increased demand for religious education introduce considerations which had not to be taken into account fifty years ago. They may affect the setting of a policy, but not its principles. And that is exactly what we now find. The experience of the years 1920 to 1930 has only served to show that the principles which underlay the educational policy of the Government of India from 1854 to 1919 are the principles on which must rest an educational policy which will meet most effectively the educational position of the present day. All that has happened in the field of Indian education during the past ten years constitutes, in reality, a recall, a very clear and most impressive recall, to the acceptance and employment of those principles which underlie what was the avowed educational policy of the State from the issue of the Despatch of 1854 till the passing

of the Government of India Act of 1919. In adherence to that policy lies for India sound educational advance: in departure from it delay if not retrogression.

23. (3) *Through Conference of Educational Administrators.*—But how, it may be asked, can these principles be accepted in every province of India when there is no longer the Government of India with its word of authority in regard to educational action. The principles in paragraph 21 are, it may be readily admitted, in substantial agreement with those in paragraph 2; nevertheless there is no administrative power of the present day which can re-insert the last sentence of paragraph 2 with its declaration that the provincial governments must act as the central government directs. Must the matter then remain there? I think not. For as we ponder the matter, there comes into our mind this question: Is there any central organization that can do for educational direction in present circumstances what the Government of India did for it in the circumstances of the past? And the answer to that is, as it seems to me: Yes, a permanent and enlarged Conference of Educational Administrators. Permanent, so as to secure continuity: enlarged so as to secure, in addition to provincial educational officials, non-official representatives of the various educational interests in the different provinces. In such a Conference Indian education would possess an organization which would carry weight and lead opinion. It would have once again a central authority, but no longer one which spake and it was done. It would be an authority garnering, sifting, and consolidating opinion, not imposing it; an authority of experience not of executive order; an authority winning its place not by the commands which it issued but by the co-operation which it secured. Thus would the anomalies of the present situation be discarded, the friction minimized, the waste checked. Thus, with the counsel of experienced authority freely accepted and voluntarily acted upon, the principles of educational

policy to which the conditions and needs of the present day constitute so urgent a recall will have the opportunity of recognition and adoption in every province of the land. And thus will adherence once again to an Indian educational policy become the charter of India's most striking educational advance.

References

G. B. Keith, *Speeches and Documents of Indian Policy*. Volume II, pp. 281-327 give text of Government of India Act.

Auxiliary Committee's Report. Chapter II, paragraph 21, and Chapter XV, Section 1 deal with relation between Government of India and provincial governments. Chapter IX, paragraphs 22-24 deal with religious education.

Ninth Q.R. Chapter II, paragraphs 36-40 deal with need for central control; Chapter X, paragraphs 425 and 426 deal with religious education.

A. Mayhew, *The Education of India*. Local Bodies dealt with in several places. See Chapter XV, p. 251 for reference in paragraph 12 above.

CONCLUSION

1. *Three Stages of Policy.*—We have now traced the development of Indian Educational Policy and have dwelt upon its content. And what we have found is that Indian Educational Policy has passed through three main stages, and that throughout these its essential features have remained the same. For between seventy and eighty years, say from 1785 to 1854, there are the makings of a Policy, what we might call Provincial Lines of Action. This is the First Stage. Each province finds that in one way or another attention has to be given to education, and it seeks to meet each situation as it arises by employing such administrative methods as will best advance education and extend its influence. As time goes on, it becomes plain that these modes of action are fundamentally few in number, and that there is a great resemblance between those which have been adopted in one province and those which have commended themselves to another. The Second Stage is reached when the Government, as a result of the steadily increasing claims of its steadily increasing rule, arrives at the conclusion that it must shoulder a new responsibility. It publicly acknowledges that an obligation rests upon it to give to all the people of the land the benefits of education. The first step that it takes towards the discharge of this responsibility is to set forth the procedure which it intends to adopt. And so an Indian Educational Policy takes the place of Provincial Lines of Action. This declaration of policy made in 1854 is in great measure the enunciation as principles of educational activity throughout India of what have formerly been empirical modes of administration. For three-quarters of a century this method of dealing with education continues. The fundamental principles of activity are, like the lines of

action, few in number, and are capable of adaptation to changing circumstances and new conditions. The result is the spread of education through every part of the country with increasing attention to quality, and increasing provision of all its forms from the elementary to the advanced. And then in 1920 there comes the Third Stage. It comes not as a specifically educational development, but as part of a great scheme of constitutional advance in which education shares. To the provinces is given a very large amount of administrative self-determination, and, within the sweep of this, education takes its place. The result is that what has been for so long an Indian Educational Policy becomes a Provincial Educational Policy. The change is not so marked as the change of name might seem to imply. The principles to which the Central Government adhered in its dealings with education become in the main the principles which the provinces accept and on the basis of which they continue their educational activities. But the provinces are under no obligation to adhere to these, and it is left open to them to act wholly without reference to one another, and to sanction any departure which any one of them may consider advisable. Of this Third Stage ten years have run. And the result is sufficiently remarkable. Education, it is being felt, is not limited by geography or by administrative areas. There is much that needs to be done by co-operation, much that is being lost to education by the independence that now exists, much more that will be lost to it if independence is carried any further. There are principles which have a wider range than the extent of any single province; they have their rightful place in every province, and their general adoption is what is needed so that the country as a whole may enjoy the benefits which it ought now to be reaping. They are few in number, the small body which have approved themselves in the past as fitted to meet changing conditions, to give strength to educational advance, to combine action, to stimulate interest, to deal justly with all efforts, and to eliminate waste. Conditions, therefore, make it plain that educational policy is on the point of entering on a new stage. The Fourth Stage is at hand.

2. *The Fourth Stage.*—How shall we describe that stage? The name that may be most fittingly applied to it is that of an All-India Educational Policy. Like the First Stage it will indicate lines of action; like the Second Stage it will have a wide sphere of operation; and like the Third Stage it will be the choice of the various provinces. But while these likenesses will persist, there will be two features in which it will differ from them all. First, it will operate throughout India not because the Central Government so directs, but because the Provinces so desire. Provincial acceptance will be the basis of its general application. Thus the opposition between the Second and the Third Stage will be reconciled. And secondly, it will operate throughout India because it will find the sphere for its employment not only in the Provinces of British India but in the Indian States as well. For while the States retain their autonomy as jealously as the Provinces safeguard theirs, they will recognize no less definitely the benefit of an educational system which constitutes a bond of unity through its foundation on a few general principles that are not hampering in their application. And in the acceptance of these principles within their own territories they will join with the other constituents of a united India in a common service of youth. Thus the Fourth Stage will witness combined action on the basis of a few fundamental principles which have obtained general recognition through the Provinces and States of India, and which leave room for variety both in application and in lines of development. What these principles will be our study of educational conditions, needs, and experience leaves us in no doubt. They will be those which have been indicated in the course of Chapter IV. They are few in number, fundamental in character, vital in bearing.

3. *The Constitution and Educational Policy.*—India is on the verge of a great tomorrow. She is about to enter on a new phase of national life. More than a constitution is being considered. There is present in all that is being done the moving of a spirit that stirs to growth and enrichment as yet without a parallel. In that development and enlargement there is no one factor that will count for so much as will education. And as the country stands now on the threshold of her great advance there comes to meet her that which has sprung from the impact of many minds working over a century and a half, in varying conditions, in strangely differing circumstances, yet all at one in their desire to serve the needs and aspirations of India. It is an educational policy which thus approaches to place itself in the hands of an India that is soon to become a great Federation; and it draws nigh not as an administrative rule, not as a piece of departmental dictation, not as an interesting relic of the past. It comes as the combination of living principles that commend themselves by the service which they are capable of rendering, as the channel through which enlightenment may spread with speed and with power, as the force which touches the national life to higher issues of thought and action, as the instrument of a unity which binds into one, Province and Province, State and State, and Province with State. That is what Educational Policy at this, its Fourth Stage, shows itself to be. A few principles to which education is recalled? A few principles which are fundamental to a living system of education in India? Yes, but also much more than that. A body of principles with which not merely the education, but the destiny, of India as well is intimately linked. In accepting an All-India Educational Policy which the long years have fashioned for her use, India comes into possession of that which opens to her ever fresh avenues of knowledge, ever closer bonds of national unity, and ever fuller opportunities for world-wide service.

PART II

INDIAN EDUCATIONAL POLICY ITS PROBLEMS

INTRODUCTION

1. *Will the Principles Stated Work?*—The principles which underlay the Educational Policy of the Government of India from 1854 to 1919, in accordance with which provincial educational policy has been mainly guided since that time, and to which the present conditions of Indian education constitute a challenging recall, have been set forth in the preceding Part. But are they principles which, face to face with facts, will work? Are they adequate to the situation of today? That is the matter which now demands our consideration. That is the question which we must now proceed to answer.

2. *Modes of Answering this Question*: (1) *Specific Problems.*—There are two ways in which this answer might be given. We might pass under review the working of the whole Indian educational system, and in doing this we might dwell upon the problems which emerge at each stage. We might then see what help towards the solution of these problems is afforded by the principles which we have detailed and on which we have dwelt. Thus there would claim our attention specific problems presenting themselves at different levels of education, for instance, primary, secondary, and collegiate; or problems attaching to different forms of education, for instance, general and technical; or problems arising in connexion with different classes receiving education, for instance, women, Muhammadans, and Europeans. And we should have to bring the principles which we have enumerated into relation with all these problems, and to consider how far they helped towards the attainment of the needed solution. A review of this nature is a necessity in order that Indian education may have its proper setting and perspective. To it attention will be given in subsequent

discussion. It forms part of that aspect of our subject to which we have already referred as the Working of the Policy.

3. (2) *Essential Problems.*—The second of the two ways in which the answer of which we are in search may be given is that which constitute this, the Second, Part of our discussion. It deals not with the problems arising out of specific situations in the educational system, but with problems which are raised by education as a whole. It looks at considerations which are of the very essence of an educational system, which lie at the root of its being and its well-being. It concerns itself with questions the absence of a satisfactory answer to which results in harm to education at every level, and renders it of least service to those who need it most. What some of these questions are may now be briefly indicated. Nine of them are dealt with in the following Chapters.

4. *Problems of the Administration of Education.*—To begin with, there are three questions that concern the foundations on which the educational system rests. If education were under ineffective control, or if it were in the hands of unsuitable managements, or if it were supported by a defective method of finance, it might continue to exist, but only with much depreciated value and with steadily diminishing chances of becoming a national asset. The Control, Management, and Finance of the Indian educational system, therefore, present us with problems which are of the first moment. And these problems are considered in Chapters i, ii, and iii of this Part.

5. *Problem of the Character of Education.*—Next there is pressed upon our consideration a vital problem which arises out of conditions specifically Indian. The State in India takes up a position of complete neutrality in regard to all matters connected with religion. Yet there is a desire on the part of thoughtful and anxious minds in India that education, in the best interests of the country, should not be dissociated from religion.

How can this attitude and this desire be reconciled? That is the problem which forms the subject of Chapter iv.

6. *Problems of the Power of Education.*—Then there are two facts closely related to one another, that at every turn keep meeting and forcing themselves on the attention of the student of education in India. They are the great lack of those qualified to impart education and the enormous number of those who have received no education. These facts present educational policy with two problems for which, if it is not to forfeit confidence, it must provide solutions. What can be done to give power to education? What can be done, on the one hand, to provide the country with a sufficient body of well equipped teachers? What can be done, on the other hand, to rescue it from the blight of illiteracy? With the endeavour to find answers to these questions Chapters v and vi are occupied.

7. *Problems of Changing Times in Education.*—Finally there keep crowding into the mind thoughts of what the last two decades have witnessed in India, developments to which preceding centuries can offer little by way of parallel as regards number, extent, speed, or influence. Education has felt the impact of all these, and in doing so has realized that it is face to face with problems of a wholly new type. In these changing times a new administrative system has been evolved; a new sense of nationhood has begun to emerge; a new standard of culture has made its claims felt. What can education do to meet the fresh demands of administration, nationhood, culture? In the three sections of Chapter vii an attempt is made to answer the three questions that are thus raised.

8. *Conclusion.*—The nine problems which have been mentioned and to which consideration is given in the following chapters go to the foundation of India's system of education. Examination of them makes it clear that there is no possibility of their solution apart from a larger educational outlook than has too often prevailed

in the past. That outlook, while doing full justice to what education has already achieved, must be such as to recognize with perfect frankness the immense amount that still remains to be done, and the evil plight of the country in all that affects the weal of its citizens because of widespread, unchecked, and strongly entrenched ignorance. When this standpoint has been adopted, then it becomes plain that education can succeed in its task and can free the State from a grave and ever present danger only if its administration makes steady use of a small body of essential principles. Careful and detailed investigation reveals the fact that the necessary principles are identical with those which, in a different setting and with different emphasis, began to operate in 1854, and to which the conditions introduced by the legislation of 1919 constituted an insistent recall. The question with which we began is answered. These principles, face to face with the facts of today, do work. Indeed a policy which gives to them, on the part of the State, a fuller and steadier employment than they have yet received is the only policy that will work, and it is what the present situation unequivocably demands. It assures Indian education of the means for overcoming its defects, for solving its problems, and for delivering the State from the serious menace that now confronts it. It has within it the power to place at the disposal of India a true and sound nation-building service. It is the policy which India requires. Adherence to it is what, at all costs, India must have.

CHAPTER I

The Problem of Control

I. The Problem: Is State Control Advisable?

1. The control of the educational system in India is exercised by the State. The State has occupied that position ever since it assumed responsibility for a definite educational policy in India. And the question has often been raised: Is it in the best interests of education that the control of education should be in the hands of the State? That is the problem which we have now to consider.

II. Advantages and Disadvantages of State Control

(i) *Disadvantages*

2. (1) *Officialdom.*—If State control meant that the State directly administered every part of the educational system, then it might be argued with good reason that such control was not in the best interests of education. For it would mean the supremacy of officialdom. Now officialdom rejoices in uniformity, it suspects individuality, and it delights in machinery. It loves to dictate, and where its power is installed what is novel is discounted. Education is nothing if not vital. Officialdom is the stretching forth of the dead hand. Those who read Mayhew's *Education of India* will find that he devotes a considerable amount of space to what is avowedly a criticism of the State control of education. But when this criticism is analysed it will be seen to be in reality directed not against control as properly understood (which he recognizes must be exercised), but against officialdom and State management. On both counts, his criticism, proceeding from one who was for

long a Government educational official, merits the most serious attention and consideration. Unfortunately in the history of Indian education there have been times when control has been hardly distinguishable from officialdom, and of this identification Mayhew is very clearly and also very uneasily conscious. But the identification is by no means inevitable, and it has not been a permanency. There have always been at work in India forces that, when officialdom has reared its head, have kept it in check and that have not infrequently discredited it. For one thing, India is fortunate in having had, as it still has, a number of educational officials who were first and foremost keen educationalists and who, as officials, were far-sighted and sympathetic administrators. And for another thing, India has been equally fortunate in having had, as it still has, a large number of non-officials to whom the education of India's youth has been a joy, and the spread of it their life's endeavour. Both these classes, official and non-official, have been the unsparing opponents of officialdom and the upholders of a true method of control. They have envisaged an educational system over which the State exercises a wise and vitalizing control, not one over which it domineers, and not one from which its guidance has been withdrawn.

3. (2) *Domination.*—Again, it might be argued that if State control meant nothing but direct control a system so administered might be anything but beneficial to education. There is much that might be said in support of this contention. But it would be without application to the educational system which India now enjoys. For there has been no feature of educational administration so marked as the large and increasing amount of delegated control which the past two decades have witnessed. The area of direct control that remains in the hand of the State is much less than it was even ten years ago, a fact which is often too little recognized and the significance of it too little appreciated. In paragraphs 44 to 64 of this discussion an outline is given

of the extent to which, in recent years, control has been devolved, and though the statement is necessarily brief it is sufficient to indicate with convincing clearness how far removed from State domination is the State control of education which is exercised in India: and how ample is the room that it allows for spontaneity and experiment, for differentiation of treatment and variety of development. Every year makes clearer the greatness of the distance between State control and State domination.

4. (3) *An Overburdened State.*—But the advisability of State control in regard to education would be exposed to serious doubt if it were the case that the State has far too much to do and far too little time to give to education. Mayhew sounds a much needed note of warning when he says that in undertaking the task of educational control the Government is taking upon itself 'a burden of work which, without any such increase, has often appeared unsupportable'. At the present time every provincial Educational Department is heavily burdened. But it is not difficult to see how this has come about. It arises from two main causes. The first is the large amount of work that Government lays upon its own shoulders by seeking to discharge the responsibility of management in addition to that of control. It has to attend to Educational Services with the unceasing details of appointments and transfers, it has to maintain its educational fabrics and to see to all that is connected with their upkeep, and it has to go into elaborate financial considerations on behalf of its own institutions. Thus a great deal of the thought and time which the State devotes to education is really not concentration on, but actually subtraction from, its responsibility as the controller of the educational system. And that subtraction is wholly unnecessary. And the second reason why Educational Departments are so overworked is that they are not sufficiently equipped for the discharge of their responsibilities. We shall have to consider this matter later on. At the present stage of

our discussion the important point to note is that there is nothing in the provincial Educational Departments which makes them inherently incapable of discharging to the full the function of control. All that is required is to discard tasks with which they unnecessarily burden themselves at present, and to provide themselves with adequate means for the discharge of those responsibilities which none but they can discharge. What will supply both requirements is easily within the power of the State. Let the State take the necessary action, and the point of the criticism which we are now considering will be at once turned.

5. (4) *Religious Neutrality of the State.*—Once more, State control would be wholly inadvisable if it meant that religion had to be excluded from the sphere of education. There is much in the words of Mayhew that 'the identification of a necessarily neutral Government with a system of education has robbed that system of religious warmth, colour, and significance, and that the want of this has made the education unreal and unconvincing among peoples whose life, for good or bad, is fundamentally religious'. For it is true that where Government is identified with the system in the sense of directly managing schools and colleges it quite definitely excludes religion from them. And it is also true that, as Government has frequently claimed for its institutions the title of 'model', it has created the impression among some institutions not under departmental management that they will best serve education if they follow the model which Government has set and exclude from their schools all form of religious instruction. But while these facts are true they are far from presenting the whole truth. The all-important fact to which nothing must blind us is that Government is identified with the educational system, in the sense of being a manager, only to the extent of two per cent of the schools and colleges within that system. In other words, even as things now are, there is nothing to hinder 'religious warmth, colour, and significance' being definitely

associated with ninety-eight per cent of the institutions belonging to the system. And not only is there no hindrance, there is abundant and unfettered opportunity. There are thousands of schools and colleges in which the association between education and religion is a matter of established usage. Thus while the identification of Government with education, in the sense of its managing schools and colleges, does preclude a very limited number of them from the possibility of associating religion with education, its identification with education in the sense of controlling the system, leaves it quite within the power of the overwhelming number of schools and colleges to make this combination a reality. But even granting all this, it may be said that there is a disadvantage in the controller of the system being identified with the doctrine of religious neutrality. That would certainly be true if the interpretation of the doctrine with which the State identified itself were, as has sometimes been the case, one which made neutrality the same as opposition or indifference to religion. But, as we shall see when we deal with the matter more fully in Chapter iv, there is another interpretation which is open to the State and which has indeed a far greater claim to its acceptance and support. That is the interpretation which identifies religious neutrality with religious impartiality. Adopting this interpretation the State would then be a controller that did not exclude religion from educational institutions but encouraged it while exercising strict impartiality. Thus with the State as controller there is no reason why education should be deprived of religious warmth and significance, and with a fairer interpretation of the State's relation to religion there is every reason why the State's control should lead to that encouragement of combining religion with education which is so good in itself and is so generally desired in India.

6. (5) *Unrecognized Institutions.*—There is another ground on which the disadvantage of State control might be urged. There are 35,000 educational institutions

which, as a matter of fact, remain outside that control. They are classified as Unrecognized. Now if it could be said that the reason why all these occupied an independent position was that they preferred to be free from State control, the benefit of that form of control would certainly be impugned. When, however, we analyse the figures we find that about five-sevenths of the number are schools of specifically religious, not of general, education, while another seventh is made up of schools which desire recognition but are unable to satisfy the conditions necessary to obtain it. Of the remaining seventh there are some which on political grounds do not desire to be recognized by the State. But the great majority are what we might call Oriental Schools. Their pupils are mainly engaged in oriental studies. It seems a pity that they should have no place in the regular educational system of the country. But the main reason why they have not this place is that the curricula in these schools need to be revised, or the methods of teaching to be improved, or the staffs to have the benefit of better training. Now it is such advantages that the State is eminently qualified to supply. The matter is more fully dealt with in Chapter VI; here it is sufficient to say that the existence of such schools, far from being an argument against State control of education, is really a call for an extension of that control in a sympathetic spirit. There still remain to be considered the few unrecognized institutions which do not fall under any of the classes which we have so far mentioned. These are of a high order, with an individuality of their own, and with a contribution to the country which is of distinct value. They are really pioneers; we may give them the honourable designation of Experimental Schools. They do not see how they can fit into the existing system and so they prefer to maintain independence. For the present, at least, they feel their own control to be the best; that of another might bring some benefits but it might fail to give the nurture that is required. Thus it is that the schools at Bolpur and Brindaban, and the Indian Women's University at Poona stand outside the recognized system. How long this will continue it is hard to say. But if State control is compatible with what is being done to forward that freedom in the training of teachers which is referred to in paragraph 42, it is difficult to see how it should be incompatible with that freedom in the training of pupils which these pioneer schools exemplify. The existence of these institutions is indeed not an argument against State control, but a challenge to the State so to exercise its control on the freest lines, and with the maximum of encouragement to every sound form of education, that the guidance of the State will be assured of ready acceptance at the hands of the most diverse forms of management. It would be well if there was a revision of what is now included under the heading of 'Unrecognized Institutions', and if from that class there might be transferred to the list of 'Recognized Institutions' what we have called Oriental Schools and Experimental Schools. This would mean that the State would have to provide itself with a staff capable of exercising a control calculated to evoke and foster the specific character of every such valuable type of school. But that would not be difficult, and for the cause of education it would be most salutary. Such reaction of schools upon control, whereby that control becomes possessed of a larger freedom and a more varied helpfulness, is what the conditions of Indian education demand, and what is in effect being increasingly realized.

7. *Disadvantages Potential.*—Our consideration so far has shown that, if State control meant the reign of officialdom, the universality of domination, the effort of an ineffective State, the exclusion of religion from education, or lack of sympathy with valuable development, then it would be quite possible to contend that such control was not in the best interests of education. But what we actually find is that the control which the State exercises in India does not imply any of these. Every

year sees the State taking further steps to divest itself of officialdom and unmediated direction; where the State is at present overburdened it has the remedy in its own hands; while the State, in so far as it combines management with control, is unable to give to education the benefit of religious warmth and stimulus, its control places no such obstacle in the way of institutions that are not under official management; and in the spirit of freer control that has appeared in recent years lies the assurance of growing sympathy with all forms of wise educational departures. Thus the disadvantages which have been thought to attach to the State control of education prove on examination of the actual conditions to lack cogency. What they do is to emphasize the need for true control. And what that control has it in its power to effect we must now consider.

(ii) *Advantages*

8. (1) *The State's Outlook.*—There are, in the main, three advantages which but for State control would be lost to education. In the first place, the Government is the one organization in the country which is in touch with all shades of opinion, and which refuses to none the right of access. Through its contact with those who have a definite stake in the education of the people as well as with those whose chief concern is to advocate views, and through its intimate knowledge of the many matters in a State that are not educational but have a bearing upon education, it occupies a unique position. It is able to collect information, to interpret opinion, and to unify action as no other body can. And while it can do all this, it has in the Education Department an invaluable executive. There is a tendency to ignore, or at the least to regard but slightly, the debt which education owes to the outlook of the State, and its many contacts with all aspects of national life. Yet without what the State can give to education through the medium of its control there is a very great and a very

real danger lest education should become parochial, limited in its content, and one-sided in its appeal. From this it is delivered by the experience which the State is in a unique position to gather, to disseminate, and to make effective on a large scale and in a comprehensive manner.

9. (2) *The State's Power of Direction.*—There is a second advantage which the State as a controller possesses. It has unrivalled powers of maintaining standards, giving advice, and exercising direction through the whole system by means of its administrative staff and inspecting agency. It may be said that staff and agency are not sufficient for the greatness of the task, and it must be admitted that large improvements in them are long overdue. This aspect of the matter will be dealt with fully in later paragraphs; but the result of all just criticism is to enhance the value of these agencies not to disparage them. For by them the State, even as things are, is able to put at the service of education what no other authoritative body has it in its power to give—a guidance free from the imputation of local partiality or sectional pressure, animated by sterling educational ideals, and sending into the schools and colleges of a large system the stimulus of intellectual life and vigour. And if that is the case as things now are, how much more valuable will be that service when admitted defects have received their remedy.

10. (3) *The State's Financial Power.*—A third advantage of the State control of education is that Government has behind it steady resources. It is thus able to assist education by a supply of funds showing no wide range of fluctuation. The stability of the educational system is in this way secured, and here again the State renders a service of incomparable value. It may be said that the financial support of the State might be bought too dear, or that that support might not be satisfactorily assigned. There is much to be said in favour of both contentions, and the whole matter of Finance demands full and separate treatment. But when all criticisms have

been stated and all possibilities of ill-directed finance have been admitted, there remains the fact which admits of no denial, that the educational system of the country requires a financial support which only the national exchequer can supply.

11. *Advantages Positive.*—We may conclude then on general grounds that both education and the country are benefited by the State control of education. Despite disadvantages in the exercise of this control there is nothing to indicate that these disadvantages are inherent in the connexion, or that through the application of thought and plan they are incapable of elimination or important modification. And when we look at what the State can bring to education in the supply of advice, direction, policy, unifying power, and financial support, we realize how overwhelming are the advantages of the State's control. It can do for education what no other agency in the country can do. It is bound up in every way that counts with the best interests of education.

References

A. Mayhew, *The Education of India.* Chapter vi is devoted to the consideration of the 'State Control of Education'.

A. Mayhew, *Christianity and the Government of India.* References to Religious Neutrality *passim;* see especially what is said about the Queen's Proclamation on pp. 187, 188.

III. Actual Conditions of State Control

12. *Need for Statement of Conditions.*—At first sight it might seem as if, in the words with which the preceding paragraph closed, the solution of our problem had been reached. But in reality this is far from being the case. For we have now to consider how far the control which the State exercises over education in India actually performs those services which only the State has it in its power to provide. However advisable State control may be in itself, it is anything but advisable if

the particular State with which we are dealing is unable to rise to the full measure of its responsibilities. Let us look then at the actual conditions of control in India.

(i) *Direction*

13. *The Directing Agency.*—And first as to Direction. Is the State in India able to give to education that service of Direction of which it stands so much in need? No one who reads Indian educational reports will be able to answer this question with a complete absence of hesitation. That with the money supplied a most gallant endeavour is being made year after year to provide Indian education with good Direction all who know the facts must admit without qualification. But the officials who constitute the Headquarters Staff labour under disadvantages that might well take the heart out of the most enthusiastic. Details multiply so enormously, and the staff is small. The result is that those whose power to afford the able and sympathetic guidance of comprehensive policy and specific direction would be so great an asset to the education of India, provided it received full opportunity for its exercise, have to rest content for the most part with being able to prevent the routine work of their office from falling into arrears. Thus through the organization of the department, as it is at present, the whole structure of education in India is deprived of much that would add to its strength and fitness.

14. *Total Staff too Small.*—What is the position? The Director of Public Instruction in a province is at the head of an office where there are a few members of one of the Educational Services (in no province does the number exceed five) and a large army of clerks. If we confine our attention to those whose main work is Direction, not including for the time being Personal Assistants and Registrars of Examinations, what we learn from the Tables supplied to us is that over the whole of British India the total directing staff amounts to a

score. There are seventeen men and three women. That anything effective can be done with such a small number is surprising. Much that is astonishingly good and of permanent value is being done. But with the spread of education and all that it involves this achievement is bound to deteriorate. It can be saved only by a reorganization which takes account of the actual situation. What that situation is some of the statements of the most recent Quinquennial Review and of the Auxiliary Committee's Report bring home to us most forcibly.

15. *Certain Provincial Staffs.*—Take, for example, the Bombay Presidency. There are in it about 15,000 recognised institutions, and these are attended by over a million pupils. And for the Direction of this large educational effort what provision is there? Here is what the Quinquennial Review tells us. 'Up to March 1926 the Headquarters office staff consisted of only the Director of Public Instruction and one Deputy Director. But in 1926 an Assistant Director's post was created temporarily to cope with the very large increase in the work of the department'. Two men and a temporary 'help'! All honour to them for what they have done and are doing. But what are we to think of the State which takes the view of its responsibility disclosed by these figures? Again, Bengal has well on to 60,000 recognized educational institutions attended by over two and a quarter million pupils. And its headquarters staff consists of the Director and two Assistant Directors. 'In 1926 the post of an Additional Assistant Director of Public Instruction was created on a temporary basis'. Even if it be the case that these temporary appointments are continued until they become permanent, and that this is the way in which additions to the staff are most readily sanctioned, still the impression which is left upon us as we read the reports is that the situation is being tinkered with, not really faced. And the Punjab, which is the province that has at its headquarters the largest number of officers, namely five, would doubtless be the first to admit that this was only too true.

16. *Comparison with England.*—If we look at the total number at educational headquarters for the whole of British India, and if we now include in that number Personal Assistants and Examination Registrars, the score of which we spoke in Paragraph 14 has to be increased by seven. And to show how inadequate this total is we cannot do better than make a quotation from the Auxiliary Committee's Report. 'The 27 gazetted officers', it says, 'of the Indian Educational Service and Provincial Educational Service, serving in the Headquarters offices, correspond, generally speaking, to the class of the First Division Civil Servants in England, on whom the Head of the Department is able to devolve more or less responsible administrative work. In the Board of Education these officers now number 65. In England and Wales there are some 34,000 elementary and secondary schools with six million pupils. In India there are some 200,000 primary and secondary schools with about ten million pupils'. The difference affords at least some measure of the weakness from which India suffers.

17. *Existing Needs.*—If the State in India is to control education, then, it will have to effect a radical change in the provision for one important feature of control, namely, that of Direction. Is it possible to make any real headway with the education of girls if there is no woman included in the directing staffs of the various provinces? Yet there are only three provinces that include women in their provision for Direction. How is elementary education in each province to have the attention rendered to it which is its due unless there are at headquarters, and in sufficient numbers, those who have special qualifications for dealing with it? Yet the most that can be said is that 'there is sometimes an expert officer (of this character) at headquarters'. No one who gives a moment's thought to the needs of the education of girls and of the masses would consider that the State had shown a true appreciation of its responsibilities if it contented itself with, say, one officer for

each of these fields of education. Yet even that provision does not exist. And if it did, there would still remain to be supplied the needs of training, of special classes, of the various languages, and of financial demands. The Director requires a staff that is well qualified and of sufficient size, so that he may have the benefit of their experience in connexion with all the intricate matters of educational administration. When he has got that he will really be in a position to direct, and education will be at once sensible of the benefit which will thus accrue to it.

18. *Position of the Director.*—And there will be more than the advantage of experience. The Director with such a staff will be relieved of the routine which at present threatens to paralyse him in the discharge of his duties. He will have time to devote to policy, and he will have time to explain policy. Instead of having to be content with the issue of orders, which may or may not be wholly understood, and which may or may not be attended to, he will be in a position to come into frequent personal contact with responsible educationists and educational managers. By means of conferences he will find it possible to lay before them what is intended, what new projects are afoot, what line of policy it is proposed to introduce, and so to enlist sympathy and support, or at the worst to become aware of the criticisms to which the proposed lines of action are exposed. Thus the department over which he presides will come to be, in the estimation of all who have the education of the country at heart, the recognized centre of information and the great unifying power in connexion with every educational effort. The advantage of this will be incalculable.

19. *Bearing of Administration on Control.*—At present, then, the State is making a brave endeavour to direct education, but it is doing this through the medium of a staff which is 'lamentably inadequate'. It has it in its power to remedy this inadequacy. But until it makes a real effort to secure this remedy it must not be

surprised if, on the side of Direction, its claim to control education is time and again challenged.

(ii) *Counsel*

20. *Substitution of Counsel for Authority.*—A second feature of Control is Guidance. There have been times in the past when the State has sought to supply that to school managers and teachers by the prescription of particular books and by the enforcement of codes which were largely inelastic. Time brought its own corrective. Books which the State had thought it advisable to prescribe were sometimes found to be employed for purposes that did not benefit the State; and stereotyped codes supplied the reason for much of the children's lack of individuality and the teachers' lack of interest. The day of such domination is largely over. The State has taken a more excellent way. It has substituted counsel for authority. And it has manifested this change by a change in the attitude and work of the Inspecting Officers. Thirty years ago the visit of an Inspector to a school meant the complete upsetting of the work of the school. The Inspector was in command during the days of his visit and his will was law. When he left the school he had seen the classes, or perhaps only the parts of the classes, which he desired; he had set papers and imposed tests; he had imposed a certain amount of dread, not all of it unhealthy; and he was in a position to write a report. He had not seen the school in normal conditions; he had not gauged the capacity of individual teachers; and he had not given the staff as a whole the benefit of his counsel and experience. It would be possible, without any exaggeration, to draw a much darker picture than this. But nothing would be gained by it. For the most part, what has been here indicated has passed away in the course of a generation. And what the Despatch of three-quarters of a century ago mentioned as constituting the functions of an Inspector is what is now generally recognized. He visits a school not to upset it, nor for the time being to impose his will.

but to acquaint himself with what is actually going on in it; he knows in part at least what the school aims at as well as what it achieves and wherein it comes short; and he makes the teachers partakers of his advice, ideals, and encouragement. Education is reaping ever-increasing benefits from this form of control, and the manner in which it is being exercised.

21. *Criticism of Inspectorate.*—The change to which we have referred is an indication of the endeavour which the State is making to establish its control on a sound basis. The trouble, however, is that the State continues to be better equipped to carry out the old method of control by authority than the new method of control by counsel. A smaller staff is needed to work a machine than to nurture life. And it is the small inspecting staff that the State still provides. It is not surprising, then, that criticisms of the Inspectorate are fairly numerous, and that in some cases they are not without foundation. By its present provision the State places a constant temptation in the way of its inspectorate to fall back into the inferior methods of the past. I have spoken to men who were supporting schools, some of them out of their own pockets, who yet were ready to support a hostile vote on the Budget allotment in respect of Inspection. Keen on education, even to self-sacrifice, these Indian gentlemen were in their own minds anything but convinced that expenditure on Inspection was justified. Doubtless their conviction sprang from unfortunate experiences. But no one can afford to be indifferent to the range of such criticism as this. It is not confined to members of the Legislative Council; it has not its roots in party politics; it is found even in the ranks of the teaching profession. There are headmasters who feel that they and their schools have had to submit to a real indignity through the type of Inspector who has been sent to visit them as the representative of the Education Department. And there are occasions when I have thoroughly sympathized with their indignation. There has been a vast improvement in the work of inspection in

the course of the last thirty years but there is ample room and urgent need for further advance. Improvement is necessary in respect both of the qualifications, and of the number, of Inspecting Officers.

22. *Qualifications of the Inspectorate.*—As to qualifications the position is far from re-assuring. As we go over a few of the statistics of the provinces we see that the hesitation of members of the Legislative Councils and the irritation of headmasters are not devoid of reason. The Auxiliary Committee says quite frankly: 'Inspectors who are themselves only Intermediates or men with even lower qualifications and who moreover have received no training cannot be expected to help in the work of improving the schools and the teachers; and yet we find in Bengal as many as 91 members of the subordinate inspecting staff have qualifications lower than that of a trained Intermediate; in the United Provinces 63 subordinate Inspectors are only trained Matriculates; in Bihar 84 of the Sub-Inspectors are untrained undergraduates; and in the Central Provinces 42 of the Deputy Inspectors have qualifications lower than trained Intermediates'. After this doleful array of figures there is some consolation in finding that 'in Madras and the Punjab the untrained Inspector is the exception'. The fact, however, that two provinces are attempting to do justice to the work of inspection, by appointing to that work those who have both general and special training for it, serves only to throw into relief the ominous fact that over the greater part of India the inspection of schools is carried on by a staff which is but poorly qualified to be entrusted with so important and so responsible a task. Now it is mainly through the inspecting agency that information at first-hand is collected, advice imparted, and work appraised. But if those who constitute that agency are in large part ill-equipped, they can have little experience of value to share, little advice of any moment to impart, little information that is well sifted to communicate, and little judgment that commands respect to express. Where a weak inspectorate is

tolerated year after year, and that is what is happening over a large part of India, the State while retaining the name of controller has actually lost a considerable portion of the reality.

23. *Size of the Inspectorate.*—And this conclusion receives added emphasis when we consider the size of the inspectorate. It almost looks as if some provinces enjoyed toying with the matter. In one of them we read, the last five years saw a large reduction in the number of inspecting officers; in another an increase in one class of Inspectors was set off by a decrease in another class; and in a third the end of the last five years found no more Inspectors at work than there were at the beginning of that period. It is strange how slow the State is to recognize its responsibility for what is truly an inexcusable state of affairs. In the face of what seems very like indifference the problem which we are at present considering has at times the appearance of being only of academic importance. What is to be gained, it may be asked, by discussing whether State control is in the best interests of education when official statistics confront us with the fact that where control would be most beneficially exercised there it is lamentably defective?

24. *Demands on the Inspectorate.*—In 1927 there were two and a half million more pupils attending primary and secondary schools than there were in 1922, yet in the same time the inspectorate dropped from 2197 to 2165. The schools might increase by lakhs, their teachers by thousands, their pupils by millions, but, towards the control, counsel, and guidance of this striking increase, the response of the State is a decrease in the number of its inspecting staff. That might have been understandable if the staff had been excessive five years before, or if the qualifications had been heightened. But figures make it only too plain that the inspecting agency even then was much below what the system required, and as to qualifications what we have recorded above speaks for itself. And so it comes to pass that

today the 200,000 primary and secondary schools of the system have no more than 2100 men and women to visit them, test them, advise them, and report upon them. In Bengal it is calculated that the average number of schools which have to be supervised by an Inspector in the course of a year comes to 177, and of an Inspectress 1043; while in Madras they are 177 and 106 respectively, and in the Punjab 80 and 88. No one will suggest that one visit per annum is enough for all that an inspecting officer has to do in connexion with a school; but multiply by two the most favourable of the figures now mentioned, bear in mind that for some schools one day is wholly insufficient, make allowance for the time that is swallowed up by travel, and there is hardly any need to ask the question whether schools are receiving what the State as controller is under an obligation to supply. This is especially noticeable in the realm of women's education, that form of education which ought to receive the State's most fostering care. It is wellnigh incredible, nevertheless it is a fact, that 'the average number of institutions' which an Inspectress has to visit 'is in Bombay 416, Bihar and Orissa 313, and Assam 450'.

25. *Changes in Inspectorate.*—Now these figures are based upon the total number of the members of the inspecting staff. But it has to be borne in mind that the full staff is never at work at any particular time. Changes are always taking place, vacancies occur, leaves have to be arranged for. And facts of this nature bring forcibly to our notice a feature of the Inspectorate which still further weakens its power. That is the matter of postings. As things now are, an inspecting officer may be transferred from one district to another, he may be called to relinquish inspecting on his appointment to the teaching staff of a Government institution, and he may be a teacher who has no special training for the work of the Inspectorate and who has simply to step in so as to fill a gap. In one of the most recent provincial reports it was stated that the Inspectors of

one circle had changed more rapidly than the years, and that in another there had been ten changes in the Inspectorate during the course of a quinquennium. In India, acquaintance with actual conditions is what is of especial value to an educational officer as well as to the schools which he supervises. And that can only be secured by a system which reduces transfers to a minimum and provides that transfers, when they are made, are the fitting of the right officer into the right place. The system at present in vogue fails to guarantee such results. And that means *pro tanto* a failure of the State to control.

26. *The Inspectorate and Local Bodies.*—A fresh complication has arisen within the past few years. Local Bodies have been given a large amount of control over primary education and, to enable them to exercise this control, members of the Inspectorate have been lent to these bodies. As a temporary measure there may be something to say for this; but it would require to be a very cogent reason which would withdraw from the general service of inspection any members of a body which is already all too small for the performance of its specific duties. Yet what the records tell us is that in Bombay 'the duty of inspection has been virtually handed over to Local Bodies, and to all intents and purposes Government has abrogated its powers in this matter'; while in the Central Provinces 'all Government Deputy Inspectors of schools in four districts have been placed under the control of District Councils'. The results of the experiment have not been encouraging; but our concern here is not with results. It is the principle of procedure that calls for remark. Why is an Inspector appointed by the State? For one thing, the State expends large sums on education, some on its own enterprises, some in aid of local and private endeavours. Every precaution must be taken to ensure that these large expenditures from public funds are being satisfactorily employed, and that they are fulfilling the purposes for which they have been voted. This in itself

implies that the Inspectors must bear the authority of the State when they are dealing with schools to which subsidies and grants are allocated by the State. Any departure from this would remove what is a safeguard of public expenditure, and no State, in justice to its citizens, can permit that. No Inspector who draws his authority from a Local Body provides the necessary safeguard. Whatever local or any other bodies may do, the State must have an adequate staff of Inspectors appointed by, and answerable to, itself. Public finance requires this. But there is more than public finance involved. It is imperative that Inspectors should be removed from the influence of local parties and communal conflicts. If once an Inspector comes to be regarded as a partizan in any locality, confidence in him is weakened, and his usefulness is impaired. Now the impartiality which is required in an Inspector is secured by his being the servant, not of a Local Body, but of the State. From the point of view then of public service as well as of public finance the inspectorate must be a body appointed by and responsible to the State.

27. *Inspection and the Educational System.*—The existence of a State Inspectorate does not, however, mean that no other form of Inspectorate is permissible, or that it is superfluous. The history of education in other countries shows how valuable is the work done by Inspectors who are in the employ of local Educational Authorities. It is quite within the province of a Local Body or of a private agency to appoint those who will survey the work done under its auspices. But useful as this is, it is no substitute for inspections carried on by officers specifically appointed for that purpose by the State. Local inspection may satisfy itself as to the standards maintained in an area and as to the proper expenditure of local funds. But education, as we have seen, is more than a local matter, and it involves more than the expenditure of local funds. The great system of primary and secondary education which exists in India depends for its effectiveness on the healthy life of

the hundreds of schools that combine to form it. When a school forfeits its place in this national system that is a serious loss to the school; it is also a loss to the locality; but it is more, it is a loss to the system. A school which has a place in it has fallen out, and unless it is a wholly superfluous school the system is so much the poorer. For a centre of education which was needed has to be built up anew. Whatever the cause of the closing of the school, whether the financial stringency which leads to the dissolution of a good school, or the poverty of staff which leads to the elimination of a bad one, the dislocation thus caused is a disservice to education, a disservice which extends, and is felt, considerably beyond the area in which the school affected is situated. Might not this have been obviated if the State had had at its command a really satisfactory body of Inspecting Officers? With the wide experience that such officers could have brought to bear, with the counsel which they might have furnished both to Government and to the management, they might have secured for the school more stable conditions before recognition was granted, and more favourable support from the State when it was faced with an unexpected emergency. And the result would have been a gain to the whole educational system. To secure such a result, not in exceptional cases only, but as a normal feature of the working of the educational system of the country is a need which is pressed upon the State by the educational needs of the youth of India. Local help is needed, all the local help that can be given. But something much wider is also needed. That wider contribution only the State can supply. It can render it only through a capable State Inspectorate.

28. *The Inspectorate and Recognition.*—Still another reason for the appointment by the State of an Inspecting Agency must be mentioned; and this seems the appropriate place to do so. The State has to be assured that schools are worthy of the partnership into which they were welcomed when they were officially recognized

as integral parts of the system of education existing in the country. The State assumes a very great responsibility when it places on any school the seal of its recognition. By this act it stamps the school as one to which parents are justified in sending their children, one which is entitled to present its pupils for public qualifying tests, and one which on certain conditions may receive assistance from public funds. In taking a responsibility such as this, the State must assure itself that the school is worthy of the status which State recognition confers. And that can be done only by the visits of those who are able to go thoroughly into the staff, equipment, finance, and standards of the school, and to report that they merit State approval. Recognition, in other words, is a national act. It means the admission of an educational institution to a system which is permanently bound up with India's well-being, bound up also with the honour of the State. To participate in such a system demands fitness. And the State cannot divest itself of the obligation resting upon it to see that fitness exists and is maintained. Sometimes those who speak or write on Indian education allow this obligation to slip out of view. In a recent provincial report, for instance, we find this sentence: 'The grant of aid to a school means not only that its finances are placed on a more stable basis; it implies also that the school conforms to certain standards, and is liable to periodic inspection'. That is true so far as it goes. But it requires to be supplemented by another statement, namely this, that a school which receives no grant but which has received recognition comes under an exactly similar obligation. It must have stable finances, it must conform to certain standards, and it must submit to regular inspection. Otherwise it has no right to belong to the system. And the State must see to it that these requirements are complied with. From that duty it cannot withdraw. If it fails in this it fails in a national service. Thus the recognition of a school initially, and the maintenance of that recognition subsequently, render imperative the appointment and maintenance of an adequate and thoroughly equipped State Inspectorate.

29. *Bearing of the Inspectorate on Control.*—One of the essential factors in the control of education by the State, then, is the provision of Guidance. To supply this a satisfactory inspecting agency is required. And it must be an agency appointed by the State. In this way managers will receive from experienced officers the benefit of their knowledge; teachers will be given useful hints, warnings, and encouragements; schools will be stimulated to maintain high standards by the counsel and information which Inspectors bring to them; and the whole system will reap the advantage that comes from eliminating or transforming bad schools and from building up good ones. The superiority of such a method as this over one which relies upon dictation is so obvious as to need no stressing. But no less obvious is the exactingness of this method; it demands much of the State. It means that the State requires to have at its command a large Inspectorate, possessed of unmistakable qualifications, an Inspectorate in which the authority of the State is as safe as are the country's educational interests. In all these respects the State at present shows unfortunate deficiencies. It provides an Inspectorate which is about one-half or one-third the size that it ought to be, and which has a considerable lack of the qualifications requisite for the proper discharge of the duties that belong to it. Further, the State has at points abrogated an authority which, both for its own sake and for that of the educational system of the country, can be exercised only by itself. Until the State takes steps to remedy these defects which are only too clear, it cannot regard itself as discharging in a satisfactory manner the obligations which attach to it as the controller of the educational system.

(iii) *Decentralization*

30. *The Government of India Act.*—A very marked feature of the State control of education within recent

years, and one to which we must now turn, is the substitution of provincialization for centralization. This is one of the results of the Act of 1919. For that measure made provincial governments responsible for much which, up to that time, had been done by the Central Government. It was an administrative change which was bound to come, for it was the outcome of tendencies that had been at work for years. Whether such a change should have taken place in the field of education without any preparation for it is open to question. Many who firmly believed in the advisability of the change as firmly believed in the advisability of its being effected by stages. And the educational conditions of the past decade seem to afford abundant evidence of the benefits which education has missed through the sudden and sweeping fashion in which the changes were introduced. Nothing is so noticeable as the emphasis placed upon provincial autonomy in educational matters on the one hand, and the desire for a somewhat closer degree of inter-provincial unification on the other. The operation of both tendencies merits our close attention.

31. *Central Advisory Board of Education.*—It is unfortunate that very soon after the centralization of educational control ceased, not a few of the bonds which formed an educational link between province and province also snapped. Take for example the Central Advisory Board of Education, the establishment of which in 1921 seemed a step in the right direction. It was a small body drawn from the different provinces, with a membership that was representative of non-official as well as of official educational interests. The meetings of this Board could not, in the nature of things, be very frequent, as those who composed it were widely scattered and had otherwise much to do that limited their ability to gather at a distant place. But that did not hinder them from giving of their time and thought to the matters which the Board was constituted to consider. Meetings were held from time to time, and in the

intervals items of business were circulated and had much consideration bestowed upon them. The result was that the Board 'was able to consider from an all-India point of view such important subjects as the education of Europeans and Anglo-Indians, control of degrees, standardization and equivalence of examinations, technical and vocational education, relations between universities and educational services, recruitment of university professors, national education, organization of education departments, teaching of English, mental intelligence tests, and revision of educational statistics'. The information on these subjects collected, sifted, and appraised by those who were able to bring to bear on them intimate knowledge drawn from many quarters promised to provide the Central Government with a fund of material which would be of value to it and of no less value to provincial governments. The fact that it was made available in the form of carefully accumulated experience, and not in the form of departmental orders, stamped it with a character and importance all its own. Much might have been done towards the acceptance of common lines of advance in the various provinces had the Board been allowed to function and to prove its worth. But financial considerations, it was held, required its dissolution, and what had been set up with so much promise in 1921 came to a close in 1923. And it is not too much to say that the country has had to pay far more during the past ten years for what the abolition of this Board has involved than its maintenance would have cost.

32. *The Educational Commissioner.*—As with the Board so has it been very much with the office of the Educational Commissioner with the Government of India. Not that the office has been abolished, although such a step seemed for a time not altogether beyond the bounds of possibility, but that it has been so overloaded with duties manifold and diverse that the object for which it was set up is now hardly likely to be realized. There was a large service which the Educational Com-

missioner could perform when he had an adequate staff, and when he could devote himself entirely to the educational interests of India as a whole. He was not only the officer through whom the Government of India exercised the limited amount of educational control which the legislation of 1919 left in its hands, he was also the one effective co-ordinating educational power in the country. By him and his department, information as to what was going on in every part of India, whether in actual practice or by way of experiment, was gathered and made available for all who desired to possess it. Educational questions received his attention from whatever quarter they came and they were given the consideration of those most competent to deal with them. Thus there existed for the country an Educational Headquarters which, without imposing itself on any province, was at the service of them all; and which, while respecting the administrative autonomy of each province, paved the way for inter-provincial cooperation in educational effort. But recent retrenchment has left its mark upon the Educational Commissioner's work. 'Now, in addition to his ordinary duties as educational adviser to all Departments of the Government of India, he is in charge of the Education Section of the Department of Education, Health and Lands, and has to deal with some subjects other than education. He has also to carry on, on a limited scale, the publication work of the late Bureau of Education. In addition he holds collateral charge of the duties of the Superintendent of Education, Delhi and Ajmer-Merwara'. As the Commissioner himself remarks: 'It is obvious that the arrangement under which a single officer is entrusted with so many duties of a diverse nature—specialist, advisory, secretariat, and executive—must necessarily be very unsatisfactory'. It cannot be otherwise. But what chiefly concerns us here is that a means for educational co-ordination has been stripped of a large part of its power at the very time when the provinces stand most in need of the full exercise of such a power.

33. *The Governor-General as University Visitor.*—Other methods of compensating for the absence of the help which the provinces formerly received on educational matters from the Central Government include a provision which appears in some of the more recent University Acts. According to this, the Governor-General is recognized as the Visitor of certain universities; and as Visitor he is empowered to 'cause an enquiry to be made in respect of any matter connected with the university' concerned. The power is wide and it is difficult to think of it being exercised in any far-reaching way save in exceptional circumstances. It affords, however, a means whereby a certain amount of co-ordination may possibly be secured. At the same time it does not provide the means for that review of Indian university conditions and requirements which is so much needed and would be so valuable at the present stage of development.

34. *Inter-University Board.*—The Inter-University Board does something to supply this need. It is a purely voluntary organization which arose out of a Conference of Indian Universities held in 1924. So voluntary is it that originally one or two of the universities did not join it. But with the passage of time and a fuller understanding of its aim and mode of procedure this abstention has been abandoned; and now every Indian university is represented at its meetings. Many vital topics have already been considered by the Board such as post-graduate training in technical and industrial subjects in the various universities with a view to their co-ordination, the equivalence of examinations, the relation of the intermediate stage of education to university work, and so on. It has published a useful *Handbook of Indian Universities;* and its vitality none will gainsay. The precise service which it can render to the country will become clearer as time goes on. The Board has no statutory position; its work is advisory; and for the present it has to be content with limited funds.

35. *Need for Co-ordination.*—What has been said is

sufficient to indicate that there is a strong desire, in regard to university education, that provincialization should not be equivalent to complete isolation. There is no wish that the Central Government should resume its old functions; or, if such a wish does sometimes arise its uselessness is speedily recognized. The administrative changes which the past decade has witnessed and which the future holds in prospect are decisive. But there is a wish, and more than a wish, that the educational energies of the different provinces, while having their fullest individual expression, should at the same time work together for the enrichment of the nation as a whole. And that wish can never be realized so long as present educational conditions are perpetuated. University after university can be established throughout the country all with the same family likeness; in secondary education a uniformity which all condemn is allowed to flourish; in the field of elementary education schemes are put into operation in the different provinces with an almost complete absence of reference to what is being done in neighbouring administrations. The result is at every level no inconsiderable waste of public funds, and a loss to education of that variety and adaptability of which the country stands so much in need. No one who studies what is taking place at present in connexion with Indian education can fail to be impressed with the appeal which the facts make for a co-ordination of effort. And such co-ordination is bound to remain unfulfilled desire so long as the change from centralization to provincialization is taken to mean a change from central direction to complete provincial isolation in matters relating to education.

36. *Possibility of Co-ordination.*—There is no reason however, why it should have that meaning. The Educational Commissioner and the Auxiliary Committee, as we have already seen in Chapter iv of Part I, while recognizing to the full the autonomous position of the provinces, indicate how co-ordination might be secured without any sacrifice of provincial rights. In their

opinion it might be supplied in great measure by the establishment of an agency which was advisory in character, provided, that is, the advice which it had to offer came from a well qualified source. The Auxiliary Committee, however, goes further than the Commissioner. It considers that, in regard to the advance of primary education, 'constitutional means should be devised to enable the Imperial Government to come to the aid of the provincial governments, and that the Government of India should not continue to be divested of all power to make central grants to provincial governments for mass education'. Such a view, because of its implications, calls for more than mere mention.

37. *The Auxiliary Committee's Position.*—The Committee feels that, as provinces differ in their financial ability, it would be unfortunate if a province, simply because of the limitation of its funds, was unable to make that progress in the diffusion of mass education which would be within its power if it had a provincial revenue comparable with that of some of its neighbours. In such a case, the suggestion is, the Government of India might supply the particular province with the needed revenues; and the justification of this action would be that the Central Government was simply enabling a province to fulfil a national service. This position of the Committee raises not a few questions. For one thing, the ability of the Central Government to render such a service as this depends mainly on its own power to secure additional revenue. Is it in a position to do this? Readers of the statements made by the expert who advised the Statutory Commission on financial matters will not find it easy to answer that question in the affirmative. For the conditions on which his calculations are based are normal conditions, and thus leave out of the reckoning such undesirable though perfectly possible occurrences as famine, financial crisis, or civil unsettlement. Further they refer to what may be expected to come about as the result of a steady working of a ten years' fiscal plan. So that there is a

certain element of remoteness as well as of uncertainty about this power of the Central Government. Leaving these points out of consideration, however, let us ask what would happen if the Central Government were actually in a position to make grants from its own resources to any province. Could it conceivably do this without exercising a certain amount of financial control over the province to which it made the grant? That is hardly likely. Governments are not personal donors, they are trustees. As the Committee says quite frankly: 'If the Government of India assist a province in the matter of education they should have the right to assure themselves that the money so granted is spent properly for the purpose for which it is earmarked'. Then it adds: 'This would not imply, in our judgment, detailed inspection and control, but it would imply periodical reports from officers of the Imperial Government, deputed for the purpose'. Yet it is obvious that if the Government of India is to have any assurance as to the satisfactory employment of its money no superficial investigation will suffice. And, unless the ways of Government offices are to undergo a marked change, we may be certain that sooner or later details will be called for and that statements not of a general character but of minutiae will have to be submitted. In brief, the ability of the Central Government to make the grants suggested by the Auxiliary Committee has yet to be proved, and even if that Government had funds sufficient for the purpose the bearing of this upon control would still have to be settled.

38. *A Co-ordinating Agency Possible.*—Both the Commissioner and the Committee have made it plain, and in this most educationists will agree with them, that a co-ordinating agency is one of the great needs of education in India. And search for it as we may, we shall not find the supply of that need in the Government of India or in any agency that is purely official in its composition. But, as has been already suggested, it may be found in an Advisory Board on which official

and non-official experience from the different provinces is well and authoritatively represented. Centralization in any official way is incapable of restoration, and is undesirable even if it could be restored. But co-ordination is quite capable of attainment, and the events of the last ten years within the sphere of education not only emphasize the need for it but also indicate the way by which it may be secured.

39. *Benefit of Decentralization.*—So far we have been concerned mainly with the weakness of decentralization. Let us now look at its strength. That lies in the impetus which it gives to provincial initiative and development. This advantage was for some time obscured by the financial difficulties which beset the provinces almost as soon as they had received the autonomy which the Act of 1919 conferred upon them. And it is only recently that freer conditions have prevailed. With the lessening of restrictions Ministers have now the sense of being largely in charge of their own affairs and of not having to wait till needed permission comes to them (either through legislation or financial supply), from some other source. This is a great educational asset. And it would be unfair to regard anything that has been said in the preceding paragraphs as detracting from its value. When, under the Government of India Act, transfer of educational control actually took place in January 1921, little had been done to prepare for the magnitude of the administrative change. The natural course was for each province, in the exercise of the liberty entrusted to it, to think primarily of its own concerns. Aware of its specific educational needs it sought to supply these as speedily as possible and in the way which seemed to it most appropriate. The organization which had maintained co-operation for over sixty years was swept away; for a time the Government of India and the provincial governments were spoken of as if they represented opposing interests. It was unfortunate but by no means unnatural. Had due preparation been made for the changed educational position, there would

have resulted in 1921 the full power of provincial initiative alongside of a co-ordination which would have prevented much waste of public funds and would have been to the lasting benefit of the provinces in the development of their educational programmes. Much was missed by this failure to provide in 1921 some substitute for what education lost through the sudden disappearance of all central guidance. But while that is the case, and must be admitted without hesitation, it affords no ground for throwing any doubt on the wisdom of the change, or for minimizing the gain which has come to education through the transfer of its control to provincial agency.

40. *Gain shown in Provincial Action.*—The gain has shown itself in various ways. But there are two of them that call for special notice. One is the action of local legislatures, the other the spirit of educational administration. Formerly, for example, university legislation was carried through by the Central Government. The Act of 1919 introduced a striking change. Since 1922 eight university bills have been passed through provincial legislatures, incorporating new universities or amending the constitution of the old ones, and thus fitting these bodies to render a more effective service to the community. And if the amount of legislation has been noticeable, no less noticeable has been the action of the Legislative Councils on the financial side. The individual province now sets the pace, not the Central Government. A few figures help us to realize how great a stimulus this has proved. In round figures the expenditure on education from provincial funds was six crores in 1920, in 1927 it was double that amount. It took from 1880 to 1920, or forty years, for the provinces to increase their outlay on education from one crore to six; to increase it from six to twelve required only seven years. And if we consider primary education alone, what we find is that in 1927 Madras was spending on it one crore more than it was spending ten years previously, and that in Bombay the increase

over the same period was a crore and a third; while the United Provinces had trebled, and the Punjab, Bihar and Orissa, and the Central Provinces had each doubled its outlay on this one grade of education. Then the driving force which the education of women is receiving both through the election of women to the Legislative Councils and the influence which growing public opinion is able to exert on all members of these Councils cannot be overestimated. Further, the interest which educational matters arouse is reflected in the local legislatures as a power of which the Minister finds it advantageous to become a discriminating ally, and from which he may draw a fund of strength as he embarks on his various schemes. The rise of the provinces to the great opportunities stretching out before them in the field of education demonstrates in the most convincing manner the gain which has come from decentralization.

41. *Gain shown in Administrative Spirit: One Illustration.*—With provincialization there has come something more than legislative action; there has come also the sense of greater freedom in connexion with educational administration. There is a feeling that experiments may be made, that new departures are at least not to be condemned because they are new. It is difficult to point to concrete facts, for a spirit may be felt even when its workings are hard to tabulate. Yet it is possible to give some indication of the spirit that is abroad by reference to official documents. Here for instance is a sentence taken from the Eighth Quinquennial Review. And the date of it is September 1923. The Educational Commissioner has been dealing with the effects of the Non-Cooperation movement on the schools and colleges of the country. He points out that the movement began to influence education only after the meeting of the Congress at Nagpur in December 1920. Thus it came about that the inauguration of the Government of India Act in January 1921 saw the inauguration in various parts of India of what were termed 'National Schools'. Such schools, according to the

plans of their promoters, were to have nothing to do with Government recognition and financial assistance. They were to constitute a class of educational institutions wholly independent of the State in respect of curriculum and maintenance. Now what was the attitude of the provincial Educational Departments to this experiment, which repudiated, sometimes with great vigour, the thought of any connexion however slight with the standards, supervision, and support of the State? The answer to that question is given in the words of the Commissioner, words which deserve to be kept well in mind when the question of State control in the field of education is being discussed. He writes: 'It is no exaggeration to say that, provided that the new schools did not interfere with the work and discipline of existing institutions, Directors and others interested in education would have welcomed what purported to be the inauguration of a new educational experiment'. It is unfortunate that the hopes aroused by these schools were doomed to disappointment, and that the educational system of the land was enriched by no new activity. But the important thing to note is that, had such an addition been made, the official attitude would have been summed up in the one word 'Welcome'. And that attitude was no passing phase. The writer of the Bengal Quinquennial Review of Education voices what is true far beyond his province when he says in 1928: 'The National School properly conceived and managed might make an immense contribution to the education of Bengal'. And is it being sufficiently recognized what a remarkable departure is taking place in Burma, where official recognition is being extended to 'national schools as an alternative system of education'? Official control has come to mean official welcome to well-considered experiment and well-grounded departure.

42. *A Second Illustration.*—In support of this statement let us now look at what is said by the Educational Commissioner in the Ninth Quinquennial Review when he is dealing with the Training of Teachers. He speaks

of the endeavours to increase the number and to improve the quality of those devoting themselves to this profession; and he goes on to mention what has taken place in the province of Madras. Here are his words: 'In 1923 the Union Mission Training School, Vellore, with the approval of Government adopted an experimental scheme of training for elementary school teachers somewhat on the lines of the work which is being done at the Moga Training School in the Punjab. The curriculum of the new courses includes history, geography, hygiene, civics, gardening, weaving, and cottage indutries'. This is a very condensed reference to what is really a striking instance of the flexibility of provincial control. The Training School mentioned has been allowed to have a curriculum of its own, and more than that it has been given the privilege of having its own examination conducted by a Board consisting of representatives of the Educational Department and of the management of the school. Those who pass this examination receive a trained teacher's certificate of the same grade as that obtained by those who sit for the Government examination. The school was anxious to adapt its course to those who are to teach in village schools, where conditions require attention to subjects intimately concerned with rural areas and where frequently only one teacher is available or two at the most. By the arrangement which the department has sanctioned the School can now do this in the fullest possible way, knowing that it has behind it the support of Government and that no student thus trained will suffer any handicap through his not being in possession of the certificate granted in the ordinary way by the State. The spirit which underlies this action is the spirit which underlies decentralized educational control.

43. *Decentralization: its Weakness and its Strength.*—As we close this section we take a backward glance. And what we see is that within the past ten years control of education has passed from central to provincial hands. In so doing, much co-ordinating power which was

formerly available has disappeared, and in so far as this has happened control has undoubtedly suffered. Had a well-thought-out scheme of transfer been devised the loss to education would have been less serious than it has been since 1921. Even as it is, there still remain means whereby much of the damage may be repaired, and a policy capable of wide general application may be brought into operation. But if the lack of co-ordination has to be set on the debit side of this statement of profit and loss, no less clearly must there be set down the considerations which go to swell the credit side. Decentralization has resulted in a marked increase of public funds voted and expended by the various provinces on behalf of educational activity. It has led to a noticeable development of provincial initiative in regard to the supply of educational facilities. And it has released in the realm of educational administration a spirit of freedom that robs what is stereotyped of special sanctity and gives to fresh experiment and endeavour the stimulus of welcome and support. In this freer atmosphere control becomes a power, the power of liberation.

(iv) *Devolution*

44. *Growth of Devolved Control.*—One of the most noticeable features of the control of education as exercised by the State at the present day is the degree to which that control is delegated. From being purely official it has become in great measure either non-official or official and non-official combined. This process of devolution which is to be seen at work in every grade of education gives to control a new character. If it does not redeem it from all the dangers to which education is exposed from officialdom, dangers to which reference was made in paragraphs 2 and 3, it opens the door wide for such redemption. And that is patent when we look, as we now proceed to do, at the various ways in which devolution has been, and is being, carried out.

45. *Devolution and the Universities.*—We see this devolution at work in connexion with the universities.

The Indian Universities Act of 1904 gave the universities of the country a quasi-independent position. It was an advance on the legislation which had incorporated the universities nearly half a century before, for, among other provisions, it opened the Senates to a number of elected, as distinguished from nominated, Fellows, and it empowered the universities to undertake teaching of their own. But the membership of the Senate still depended for the most part on the nomination of the Chancellor, and by the Act it was the head of the provincial government who was the Chancellor of the provincial university; while various resolutions of the Senate, in all a considerable number, had effect only when they received the sanction of the Governor-in-Council. Thus, though the benefits of the 1904 Act were fully acknowledged, a feeling remained that it still left the universities largely in official hands. Recent legislation, however, has greatly altered this aspect of university control. The universities which have been established or reconstituted within the last ten years, say since the year 1923, have a constitution which renders them to all intents and purposes autonomous. The membership of their Authorities is almost wholly elective. The Chancellor, who in general continues to be the head of the provincial government, does indeed nominate members, but their number is small, and the provision is intended to secure that interests which might be overlooked should receive representation. There are certain decisions of the Authorities which have to be approved by the Chancellor, but these are few, and the Government as such has no place in the constitution. The Senates and other bodies exercise control over constituent and affiliated colleges in regard to courses of study, qualifications of staff, financial condition, and academic fitness. Thus by these recent Acts what is, and what is felt to be, an almost complete devolution of control has been made in favour of the universities constituted in accordance with them, with the result that they have become non-official corporations.

46. *Dual Control of Universities.*—The statement that we have an example of what is almost complete devolution of control to non-official bodies in the case of those universities which have come under recent legislation is subject to one qualification. And that arises from the financial relation of Government to the universities and to the colleges which compose them. Considerable sums of money are granted by the State to the universities, and these sums are voted by the local legislatures. It is conceivable that the functioning of a university might be such as not to commend it to the members of the Legislative Council, and thus there might be a curtailment or even a cessation of the grant which the university had hitherto enjoyed from public revenues. The effect of such action might be to cripple the university, for there are few universities that are possessed of large endowments. It is obvious that this form of control, which is potential rather than actual, indirect rather than direct, must continue to exist until the universities of India have far more resources of their own than is now the case.

47. *Dual Control of Colleges.*—What is true of universities is true also of the colleges which constitute them. For the majority of these receive aid from provincial revenues. The practical result of this is not difficult to envisage. For instance, there is no process harder to carry through the various Authorities of a university than that of disaffiliating a college or removing its recognition. Almost every inspection of colleges reveals some which are so working that doubt is raised as to their right to be included among the duly recognized colleges of a university. At the same time, any one who has served on the Authorities of an Indian university knows that to act on such a doubt is far from easy. But what the constitution of the university surrounds with such difficulty Government has it in its power to effect almost at a stroke. It has only to withhold the grant which it has been in the habit of making to that particular college, and the college, dependent on

a subsidy that is now withdrawn, may have to forgo its status, perhaps even to reconcile itself to extinction. Thus with all the devolution of control in which universities participate, and that in the most healthy manner, there is still what we may call a residuary power of control vested in Government, and that of a most effective character. There is in fact a dual control, and that is a fact which requires to be faced. Are its consequences unsatisfactory? we may ask. In practice they are not, though theoretically they may be. Where universities and colleges perform their appointed functions in such a way as to forward the best interests of education no conflict of control is felt. Indeed so smooth is the working that the operation of a condominium is often wholly overlooked. But circumstances might quite conceivably arise in which, in the view of the State, a university or a college had forfeited its title to support from State funds. In taking action on that view the State would be simply discharging one of those responsibilities to its citizens of which a government can never divest itself. And this is true, whether the State acts in regard to an educational institution by withholding grant or by withdrawing recognition. Where what professes to be an educational service is so functioning that the best interests of youth are imperilled, or the larger interests of the country are being adversely affected, it is well that the State possesses a power of control which it can exercise on behalf of the well-being of its people. It is a power which may be counted on to work in harmony with every educational effort that aims at imparting sound learning and good morals. Where it has to array itself in opposition to an educational corporation or management, the reason will be found in the fact that what is professedly for the promotion of right thinking and conduct is acting in a manner at variance with its profession.

48. *Devolution of Control and High School Education.*—We may now consider control as it is applied to secondary education. And here we are face to face with

much that is confusing. In certain provinces, as for example in Madras and the Punjab, control is exercised departmentally. It is true that Secondary Education Boards have been set up in Madras, but these have no statutory position and their function is purely advisory. In certain other provinces, such as Bombay, Bengal, and the Central Provinces, there is a puzzling distribution of control between Government, the University, and specially appointed Bodies. And this dispersion of control becomes all the more difficult to follow when, as occurs in some provinces, secondary is conjoined with intermediate education. Let us look at a few of the relevant facts.

49. (1) *Departmental Control.*—Of the three main types of control found in the realm of secondary education that exercised by direct departmental agency need not detain us. The schools thus controlled are visited by Inspectors who are in the service of the State, their recognition is granted by Government, and such aid as is given comes from public funds. There is the advantage of simplicity in this, there is the absence of divided control, and there is the supervision of those who have special qualifications for the task. The health of the schools and the interests of the taxpayer are alike safeguarded. In itself this form of control, exercised as it is in Madras, Bombay, and the Punjab, does not present difficulties or raise problems. But when we consider it in its relation to the control of education above and below the secondary grade, certain questions do arise which will have to be dealt with later.

50. (2) *University Control.*—A second type of control is that which is exemplified in Bengal. Leaving out of account for the moment the Dacca University area, what we find is that 'high schools in Bengal are recognized by the Calcutta University for the purpose of the admission of pupils to the Calcutta Matriculation Examination, and are recognized by Government for the purposes of grant-in-aid'. This dual control is the outcome of an agreement between the State and the

University which was reached in 1906 and embodied in a Resolution of the Government of India published in August of that year. The working of it does not seem to have proved an unmixed blessing to education. The university has no school-inspecting staff of its own, and it has not the power to aid a school which requires considerable financial assistance so that it may remedy the defects which the university has pointed out. It can refuse to grant recognition and so may keep a school out of the educational system; but what can it do to keep a school within that system? The inspection is actually in the hands of the Educational Department, yet the university is not bound to accept the verdict of the inspecting officer. And in practice, as the Calcutta University Commission records in its Report, 'the Syndicate has been reluctant, sometimes over-reluctant, to accept those of the inspectors' recommendations which would involve considerable demands upon the pecuniary resources of the schools'. In short, as the Commission puts it, 'the plan has evidently broken down'. And that is hardly to be wondered at. For the plan fails to do justice to the sphere either of the university or of the State. The university is not a corporation which has to deal with the supervision of schools; its sphere is collegiate. It can bring pressure to bear upon school standards, but it does this by the standards which it itself demands. It has been given neither the machinery nor the powers to exercise direct control over schools, as a reference to the Acts under which universities have been established makes abundantly clear. But the State has a definite responsibility for the supervision of schools, and for this purpose public funds supply it with a service of Inspecting Officers. Strangely enough, in the situation which we are now considering, the State failed to discharge this responsibility. It even admitted its own failure in the Government Order which initiated the transfer of control. In the course of that statement it said that it had decided upon the devolution proposed because, among other reasons, there were 'a large number of private schools which receive no aid from Government and which therefore are not inspected by the officers of the Education Department'. The use of the word 'therefore' gives one pause. For whether a school is aided or unaided is, from the point of view of the State, a secondary matter. What is primary is the recognition of the school. An obligation rests upon the State to satisfy itself as to whether a school is fit for recognition, that is to say, is fit to be given, and to continue to have, a recognized place in the educational system of the country, with all the privileges which such a status confers. From that obligation the State cannot free itself without abrogating its position as controller of the educational system. Yet, as the Calcutta University Commission Report informs us, there were 300 secondary schools in Bengal which 'had never been subjected to inspection either by Government or by any other inspecting agency'. Realizing the evil of this situation the Government decided to act; and what it did was to hand over the supervision of these schools to an agency which was not provided with the means of exercising it. As might have been expected this line of action has failed of its end. It has taken the university out of its own domain, and has not pressed on the State the discharge of a responsibility which belongs to it. It is hard to see how the university, or the State, or secondary education has benefited by this step.

51. (3) *Control by Ad Hoc Bodies*.—The third type of control is that which is exercised over secondary schools by bodies set up for that specific purpose. In the Dacca University area, in the United Provinces, in Bihar and Orissa, and in the Central Provinces, that is what is now taking place. In the Dacca area and in the United Provinces, Boards of Intermediate and Secondary Education have been established; while in Bihar and Orissa there is a Board of Secondary Education, and in the Central Provinces a High School Education Board. These bodies differ in several respects but they agree in this, that they combine non-official with

official membership, that they exercise the power of recognizing schools, and that they depend for the most part on the Departmental Inspecting Agency. The advantage of these bodies is that various educational interests are represented on them, so that there is a real devolution of control. But, since the State retains the power of inspection, control is so devolved that it is not weakened. Thus the State does justice to the responsibility which rests upon it, while through official and non-official combination the basis of control is widened and strengthened.

52. *Control of Middle School Education.*—At this point we must note what seems to be somewhat of an anomaly. In the higher levels of education, as we have just seen, devolution of control not only holds good but is actually on the increase. And the paragraphs that follow show that the same thing holds true of elementary education. But between these, in what is generally spoken of as Middle School education, devolution plays next to no part. In the province of Bihar and Orissa Local Bodies have, within the past five years, been entrusted with the control of Middle Schools for boys, and there devolution stops. It seems strange that in the whole scheme of education there should remain this garden enclosed. Yet there may be an advantage in it. For there is still too much uncertainty as to what is meant by Middle School education, and how it is related to other forms. The presence of these unsettled matters may be a reminder that devolution of control can work only on the basis of clear thinking.

53. *Devolution of Control in Elementary Education*: (1) *Local Bodies.*—We may now proceed to consider how elementary education is controlled. This is done in three ways, although in actual fact one of the three preponderates. In Bengal control is exercised by the State, in Madras by *ad hoc* bodies, and in the other provinces by Local Bodies. Let us begin by considering the devolution of control to Local Bodies, reference being made to Bengal and Madras in later paragraphs. Local

Bodies act either directly or through school boards or school committees. But whatever be the method they adopt they retain in their own hands the power of the purse and the direction of the schools. Their exercise of authority will be found to work along what seem to be two divergent, if not mutually opposed, lines. Each of these calls for attention.

54. *Position in Bombay.*—In Bombay, for instance, what we find is that the Local Bodies are all-powerful and the State largely lacking in power. So much has been entrusted to these Bodies under recent legislation that, except in regard to the amount of money Government does or does not allot, the State is in the position of an excluded factor. Each District Board and Municipality appoints a chief executive officer to attend to the schools under the control of that Body. But while the appointment of that officer is subject to the approval of Government, Government has no say as to his retention should he be found to be inefficient. As to his powers there is no definite action which the Government can take under the Act, and so these have been prescribed by the Local Bodies, with the result that there is a 'disinclination to delegate powers which are clearly needed by him for a successful working of the system of control'. The legislation which is responsible for this state of matters is not seven years old, and some of its sections may be capable of a different interpretation from that which has so far been put upon them. But as things now go legislation has provided a scheme for the devolution of control which virtually amounts to the abrogation of its functions by the State. That is how the vesting of the power of control in Local Bodies seems to be working out in Bombay.

55. *Position in the Punjab.*—Very different is the position in the Punjab. There there are Education Committees, 'but the powers of control over vernacular education are vested in the local bodies and not in the committees'. And as regards the Local Bodies, nearly all the District Boards have official chairman, while the

chairman of a Municipality is appointed 'subject to the approval of the local government or the commissioner'. Then 'all schools are inspected by the departmental inspectors', and 'in practice the District Boards and Municipalities have relied very largely upon the advice and recommendations of these officers'. Thus it has come about that, through the Inspectorate, and 'the official chairmen of District Boards, Government have retained considerable control over the working of local bodies in the sphere of vernacular education'. Indeed it is quite evident that, as things now stand, what is termed a local body may not differ very much from an official body when it comes to actual working. It will be seen that the vesting of power of control in Local Bodies in the Punjab is working out very differently from what is the case in Bombay.

56. *Advisability of Devolution to Local Bodies.*—That the control of elementary education should be linked up with the system of local self-government is of great value. There is the advantage of local interest, there is the exercise of self-government, there is the machinery for the collection of taxation ready to hand, and there is an economy of organization through the employment of an existing form. But if by thus connecting itself with Local Bodies the State, in making this act of devolution, practically bows itself out, education is in danger of losing the counsel and guidance which only the wider experience of the State can supply. And if by this connexion the State retains such powers of control that a Local Body is hard to distinguish from a State Body, the question may be asked whether devolution has really taken place, and whether education is not in danger of losing that initiative and interest which are of the very essence of local effort. That the country and its youth will gain by the transfer of educational control from the State to Local Bodies, as these are now constituted, is not so axiomatic as it is sometimes taken to be. Let any one read through the records of what local self-governing bodies are doing in India, and it will not be

long before he asks himself the question: Are these bodies as we now have them the most satisfactory bodies to which the control of elementary education should be entrusted? He will see that for one thing the membership of these bodies consists almost wholly of men. Yet there is no more pressing need than the spread of the elementary education of girls. And if that need is to be supplied there must be on the bodies that provide for its realization a genuine representation of women. It certainly looks as if many a day will have to pass before the present constitution of Local Bodies will contribute to that result. Then he will see that Local Bodies are managers, and not the only managers in their areas. Is it advisable that one management should be selected as controller and no other? In regard to its own schools how can that management satisfactorily discharge the twofold duty of controller and manager? And as regards other schools is it in the best position to exercise an unembarrassed control? Is the arrangement calculated to call forth effort, from whatever source it may come, on behalf of the education of the masses? To attempt an answer to such questions is to arouse one misgiving after another. Nor is it otherwise when we turn to what the different provinces tell us regarding the actual working of these Local Bodies in their midst. A few extracts from the most recent surveys of education in four provinces makes this plain.

57. *Local Bodies in Madras.*—Madras prepared in 1928 a most careful report on the development of women's education in the Presidency. And one of the statements which it contains is this: 'In some districts where training classes for mistresses have been established for some time, a certain number of trained women are unable to obtain appointments because in many cases Local Boards appoint men in preference to women in girls' schools'. That is to say a method is adopted which does not help to advance girls' education but rather to hinder it. Then when the report deals with the question of the training of women teachers this

is what it has to say: 'It was felt that under present conditions it was not desirable for training institutions for mistresses to be managed by Local Bodies'. And the reason assigned for this position is that 'these bodies are subject to political and local factions and to change in personnel'. In this statement our attention is drawn to features of local self-government bodies which, in the opinion of the framers of the report, disqualify these bodies in regard to the exercise of management. It is hardly necessary to point out how much more they tell against the exercise of control.

58. *Local Bodies in the United Provinces.*—If we turn to the report of the Director of Public Instruction in the United Provinces for the five years 1922-1927, we find much about what he calls 'the unsatisfactory condition' of various classes in Board elementary schools. His reasons for so regarding them are given in his own words: 'The excessive or inopportune exercise by the chairman of his powers of transferring teachers is most potent in preventing the teacher from rendering the efficient service that should be expected from him. . . In some cases teachers have been transferred and retransferred three times during the year. From many divisions come reports that transfers are made to please individual members of the Board. A glaring instance is reported of a chairman who made numerous transfers of teachers in a single day for election purposes, besides making a large number of transfers on other dates on the same account. The advice of the inspecting staff in these matters is frequently unsought, and when advice is tendered it is often ignored . . The effect upon the discipline among the teachers and the tuition in the schools is deplorable'. Truly, as the Director remarks, such a record is 'depressing'. It hardly encourages one to think that a sound devolution of control has been made when it is entrusted to bodies acting in the manner described.

59. *Local Bodies in Bihar and Orissa.*—The Quinquennial Review for Bihar and Orissa has pages which

look almost like a charge-sheet. 'Unfortunately', we read, 'there have been only too many cases in which Local Bodies appear to have been actuated by motives other than the best interests of education. They may be enumerated as follows :—(here follow fourteen distinct counts among which are these) Undesirable persons have been appointed as teachers, owing to their adherence to particular political views. There have been cases of deliberate interference with those managing committees of schools which disagreed with the political views of the District Board authorities. One of the glaring instances of the abuse of power by the executive of the Local Boards is the ruthless manner in which teachers of stipendiary primary schools are being transferred'. The Director closes this part of his report by saying that 'It would perhaps be a mistake to take too pessimistic a view', and that 'matters already show distinct signs of improvement'. Even after such a 'formidable list of irregularities' (to use his own words) there is no ground for pessimism; but there is ground for holding that much more than 'distinct signs of improvement' is required to justify the vesting of educational control in such bodies as the Director has described.

60. *Local Bodies in Bombay.*—Bombay is very outspoken. 'In the case of municipal schools', runs the Quinquennial Review of that presidency, 'there is not so much lack of funds as a lack of administrative efficiency, due chiefly to the spirit of faction and intrigue that unfortunately so often prevails in municipal bodies'. And when the working of the Primary Education Act is being commented on, this is what we are told: 'In many cases the whole power of the School Board has fallen into the hands of one particular caste. . . In some cases an incompetent Administrative Officer or Supervisor has been appointed whose chief qualification for the post was his caste. . . At present there is much confusion and inefficiency, and communal jealousies might without exaggeration be described as the curse of

primary education'. Control and curse do not make good neighbours.

61. *Local Bodies and Control.*—There is no need to add to the quotations which have been already given. It hardly requires to be said that there are Municipalities and District Boards which work effectively, and have a true sense of their responsibility. But the bearing of the descriptions which have been quoted is plain. In the first place they show that the State is pursuing a policy of handing over the control of primary education to bodies about which it would be hard to say that they possess outstanding qualifications for such a trust. They are not appointed to deal with education alone; education is simply one among many services with which they have to deal. Thus the present constitution of these Bodies does not ensure that education will be accorded the thought which it so urgently needs at the present day, or that its concerns will be in the hands of those who have real acquaintance with them. In the second place, the quotations show that the State is carrying out this policy of transfer in such a way that legislation is giving to certain Local Bodies virtual autonomy. These two points confront us with serious issues. If control is to be vested in the inexperienced or the overtaxed or the independent is the State dealing fairly with Control?

62. (2) *Ad Hoc Bodies, Bengal Proposal.*—Fortunately there are indications that the policy of the State has not altogether taken the directions to which some of the facts mentioned above seem to point. We see this when we look at what is proposed in regard to the control of primary education in Bengal. The Government, we are told, intends to set up a School Board in each district. This Board will be 'essentially a non-official body with an official element'. It will devote itself wholly to education, making surveys of the educational needs existing in each district, and preparing schemes for their supply. Then it will be given power to impose and collect 'a special cess of the value of

about five pice in the rupee on the annual value of lands and net profits of mines; and the non-agricultural classes will also be assessed'. Armed with these powers the Board will be able to organize and finance primary education, and in due course to introduce and enforce compulsion. The method proposed gives promise of effective control, while it leaves the State in possession of those guiding and directing functions which are appropriate to it.

63. *Procedure in Madras.*—What is proposed in Bengal has been in operation in Madras, so far at least as regards the main points, for ten years. The control of elementary education in the province was entrusted by the legislation of 1920 to District Educational Councils. On these bodies there are representatives of all agencies engaged in the work of elementary education, official, local, and private; and to them have been committed large powers of control. They are *ad hoc* bodies, and so are free from the burden of other duties; there is only one matter to which they have to attend, and that is elementary education. They are bodies of representatives and so have in them a unifying power for education within a district. They are bodies to which additional powers can be entrusted and which may, with the additional powers, constitute an integral part of the local self-governing system of the country. They are bodies which can exercise an unequivocal control because they do not participate in management. And they are bodies which do not embody an *imperium in imperio* but are simply the executive of those powers which the State has definitely devolved upon them. The working of these bodies has not been without defects, but they are all defects remediable by legislation. Such legislation would provide, for instance, for the action of the State where the Councils fail to take the initiative, and for the appropriate relation of the State inspectorate to the Councils. It would also put the Councils in possession of funds that could be allotted to the different managements, local and private, on a definite basis.

And it would so regulate the membership of the Councils that there would be some recognized relation between work done and representation secured. By such modifications of the legislation now in force, unification would be realized, overlapping of provision would be avoided, absence of provision would be remedied, initiative would be stimulated, and economy would be safeguarded. When some such changes as these have been introduced, on the basis of experience, the educational powers of the Councils will be greatly enhanced. And more than that, the Councils so constituted will provide the means by which the State may devolve educational control without abandoning it, and may work through bodies, partly official and partly unofficial, that know their business and may be counted on to do it.

64. *Devolution: its Weakness and its Strength.*—We have now considered at some length one of the most striking features of Control, as it operates today in the educational system of India. And certainly the feature of Devolution merits all the consideration that can be given to it. For considerable as is its range at present, there is every indication that the limits of its range have been by no means reached. The great value of Devolution is increased interest in, and effort on behalf of, the education which it evoked. So long as the Control of education was to all intents and purposes an official matter, a great incentive to participate in the educational system of the country was withheld. Very different is the situation that now exists. The association of non-officials with control, indeed the almost complete reliance upon them in certain parts of the system, has introduced a form of control which brings to the service of education both strength and widespread interest. But while interest is of the highest value, and for the progress of education is indispensable, it is not synonymous with guidance and direction which is no less indispensable. If control is to pass outside the departmental sphere it can make a real contribution to education only when it is exercised by those who know

what they are administering and how they should do it. The Control which makes use of delegation without these accompaniments is a menace, not a help, to education. It hands over rule to the ill-qualified, or it retains the name of control but is without the reality. Devolution truly bestowed and well organized—and in both respects, as we have seen, this is not only realizable but is actually being realized—assures education of a Control that is at once powerful and beneficial.

(v) *Information*

65. *Information Necessary for Control.*—Control, it is hardly necessary to say, can be made effective only if it proceeds on the basis of trustworthy information gleaned from various and trustworthy sources. It is evident, as the preceding paragraphs have shown, that there has been within the last decade a large increase in the mass of information that can be drawn on. The number of those who are vitally interested in education is growing every day, and they have much to say that merits attention; while recently organized university authorities, freshly created high school boards, and local and special bodies on which responsibilities have been laid for the spread of elementary education, all mean that educational experience extends over a wider sphere than ever before. It might almost appear as if the Minister of Education, the Educational Department, and every controlling agency was likely to suffer from an *embarras de richesse* rather than from any deficiency of information.

66. *Where Information is Defective.*—But what as to the quality and adequacy of the information? In these respects much remains to be done. There are large gaps in the provision of essential information, and still larger gaps in the sifting and co-ordinating of information. And these gaps will remain so long as the State has a totally inadequate Headquarters Educational Staff, and so long as it has to be content with a wholly insufficient Inspectorate. This aspect of the present

deficiencies does not appear to have been as yet appreciated by the State. Otherwise it would hardly have permitted to continue a condition of affairs which is really a challenge to its title when it is called the controller of education. For with directing and inspecting staffs so deplorably inadequate, the trustworthiness of statements appearing in official reports may be impugned, and quite possibly not without reason. With so little time at the disposal of these officials for the collection of relevant data and still less time for the determination of their significance, policy based upon these data may fail to inspire confidence. The very foundation of State control may become liable to attack on what seem on the face of it to be legitimate grounds. That is intolerable. If the State is to control it must have the agency fitted to provide it with a fulness of well-tested experience and accurate information that can stand the assaults of the most searching criticism. At present it is not so provided; and the consequences are by no means fully realized.

(vi) *Finance*

67. *Connexion between Finance and Control.*—We have seen in a general way how State control is exercised through the medium of finance. Were the bulk of Indian universities, colleges, and schools to receive no aid from public funds, their usefulness would be seriously impaired and a large number of them would have to drop out of their place in the educational system. Thus refusal on the part of the State to sanction a grant in aid of a particular institution would be, in many cases, the surest way of leading to its discontinuance; just as the enhancement of the grant would be one of the surest ways of increasing the usefulness of the institution. Thus altogether apart from the power of recognition the State possesses through the employment of its funds an exceedingly effective means of control. Besides being effective it is also, as we have noted, capable of being salutary.

68. *Incompleteness of this Connexion.*—The trouble in connexion with this factor of control is that the ways of using it are still far too unsettled. That is what Richey's monograph on 'Grants-in-aid' published in 1923 makes very plain; and the intervening years have not helped towards anything approaching stabilization. What is needed is the enunciation of principles in accordance with which the State will act in its allocation of grants, principles on the application of which the managements can rely when they are framing their budgets. At present there is a large element of uncertainty, and where there is uncertainty there is sure to be, sooner or later, a feeling of unfairness, and where there is a feeling of unfairness there is bound to be distrust or suspicion of the agency that controls but does not make plain the terms on which it exercises this aspect of control. The State has it in its power to adopt such methods of financing education that its position as controller will not be distrusted but will be gladly accepted. What these means are will be considered in Chapter iii. At this stage it is sufficient to say that in finance as it is now administered Control has a far less effective ally than it ought to have.

References

L. A. Selby-Bigge, *The Board of Education.* Inspection in England is dealt with in Chapter vi; for the constructive aspect of the Inspectorate see p. 51.

Auxiliary Committee's Report. Administration, Chapter xvi, pp. 282-290; Inspectorate, Chapter iv, pp. 68-70, Chapter vii, pp. 159-161, Chapter xvi, pp. 291-306; Local Bodies and their Working, Chapter xvi, pp. 307-334.

Eighth Quinquennial Review. National Schools, pp. 5, 6. Administration, pp. 26-31; Inspectorate, pp. 39, 40; Local Bodies, pp. 41-45; New University Acts, pp. 52-60.

Ninth Quinquennial Review. Administration, pp. 15-23; Control, pp. 26-32; Inspection, pp. 34-38.

Quotations regarding Local Bodies are taken from provincial Quinquennial Reviews (1922-1927), United

Provinces, pp. 71-76; Bombay, pp. 58, 89-94; Bihar and Orissa, pp. 14-17.

Report on the Development of Women's Education in the Madras Presidency, pp. 31, 66.

For *ad hoc* bodies see *Bengal Quinquennial Review*, p. 59.

J. M. Sen, *Primary Education Acts in India*. For Bombay see pp. 30-38; for Madras see pp. 50-56.

Madras Elementary Education Act, No. VIII of 1920, and recent amendment. For working of the Act see *Aspects of Indian Educational Policy*, pp. 71-90.

IV. Conditions on Which State Control is Advisable

69. *State Control Advisable on Specified Conditions.* —We set out on our present discussion in order to obtain, if possible, an answer to the question whether State Control of education in India is advisable. To begin with, we examined the advantages and disadvantages of such control, and we saw that the balance easily inclines to the side of advantage. We next tested this position by surveying in considerable detail the manner in which the State actually exercises educational control. Finally from this examination and this test there emerged the answer which we set out to find. That answer we found to be: It is in the best interests of Indian education that its control should be in the hands of the State, provided that certain conditions—those, namely, which our examination revealed—are complied with. All that remains for us now is to recapitulate these conditions, and to note how far the State satisfies them as it exercises its control of education in India.

70. (1) *If Control means Direction not Domination.* —First, then, State control of education is advisable if by Control is meant guidance, direction, counsel, encouragement. That is the form of Control which, in ever-increasing measure, the State is endeavouring to exercise in the field of India's education. By the

methods of the inspections which it conducts, and the devolution which it effects, it substitutes direction for domination, advice for authority, and experience for executive order. There is still much that the State has to do before its compliance with this condition can be regarded as satisfactory. But the important point is that the condition is recognized, and that the trend of the State's administrative activity lies in the direction of its realization.

71. (2) *If Control means satisfactory Non-Official Co-operation.*—Second, State Control of education is advisable if Control provides for satisfactory non-official participation. Here again it is noticeable how steady has been the effort within recent years to secure the association of those who are independent of the State with those who are its representatives, in the work of administration and guidance. Healthy public opinion has now a channel, and an ever-widening channel, by which it may make itself felt in educational control. Indeed, what we look upon, as we take a broad survey of education, is the growth of a new conception of what constitutes State Control. It is coming to mean control by the nation, people, or community, exercised through the nation's executive. Such a departure from the former conception of control as a purely official task is most significant. It evokes a deeper interest, it helps to replace rigidity of curriculum and requirement by variety and adaptability, and it introduces the contribution of a larger experience. In all these respects State Control, as now conceived, is benefiting education. But it has also its dangers, and against these the State is not at present sufficiently proof. Control is bound to be defective if the agencies on which that Control is devolved are too numerous, uncorrelated, unrepresentative, or irresponsible. Now think of a province where elementary education is controlled by a District Board or a Municipality, secondary education by the Educational Department, intermediate education by an *ad hoc* body, and collegiate education by a university senate.

The supposition may seem far-fetched; but it is in fact a very close approach to what is actually going on. Then think of all these functioning in comparative, if not in complete, isolation. Again the supposition approximates to reality. Once more, think of some of these controlling bodies as made up almost entirely of men, although the bodies have to deal with a number of girls' schools, and of men whose concern is mainly with one type of management, though that is not the only type which the bodies control. And such a supposition is virtually a statement of fact. Finally think of some of these bodies as being so constituted by enactment that they are, however inexperienced, a law unto themselves in the administration of education. And there are circumstances, as we have seen, where this supposition is no mere fiction. Think of all these possibilities; then reflect that, as things now stand, they are more than possibilities, that to a greater or less extent one in one place, one in another, has been translated from the region of supposition into that of fact. And no effort of imagination is required to realize the harm which thus threatens education. The State which determines that its control of education is to be freed from the taint of officialdom has equally to determine that its control is to be freed from the taint of an unsuitable or unworkable devolution. At present the State in India, if it has reached these determinations, has still to go a long way till it can regard itself as having given anything like full effect to them. That is why it is necessary to say that State Control is advisable only if there is *satisfactory* non-official co-operation.

72. (3) *If Control allows for Association of Religion with Education.*—Third, State Control is advisable if it allows provision to be made for the full association of religion with education. And under State Control as it now exists, that association is not only possible, it is also in considerable measure enjoyed. For the enjoyment of this association in fullest measure what is required is no relaxation of Control. It is the growth of

public opinion, and the discontinuance of State management. And time works for both.

73. (4) *If Control is the Gift by the State of Fitting Resources.*—Fourth, State Control is advisable if the State is in a position to exercise it, that is to say, if its gift to education is an adequate inspectorate, a suitable administrative staff, and a definite policy. It is in these respects that State Control is most vulnerable. There are too few inspecting officers, there are not enough who have the qualifications required, and the system of their service is open to objection. Schools cannot be visited as they ought, standards of education suffer, and teachers are left without a stimulus and experience to which they have a legitimate claim. The headquarters staff is wholly inadequate, its power of being in touch with the various educational interests of the country is greatly limited, its ability to disseminate counsel is hampered at practically every point. As to policy, the lack of it in many directions is only too obvious. There is lack of policy in regard to consultation between province and province, so that there is an absence of strength in dealing with matters that concern the country as a whole and not merely one part of it. There is lack of policy in regard to finance so that sources which might mean much for education remain untapped, and the manner in which public funds are allocated gives rise to uneasiness. There is lack of policy with regard to control, with the result that control has become confused with management, its devolution has been envisaged without sufficient safeguards, and its scope has seemed to find far too little place for what is an integral part of it—the ready encouragement of every suitable agency for the spread of education. It is these facts which the State has to face and to remedy. There is not a single defect that has been mentioned which it is not in the power of the State so to alter that weakness will be replaced by strength and hesitating distrust by acknowledged benefit. Education is waiting for the State to exercise that power.

V. State Control a Compliance with these Conditions

74. Control on the four conditions which have been stated is the contribution which the State and it alone can give to the educational system of India. A large part of that contribution is even now being made; but an important part is not being rendered for the simple reason that the State has not yet taken to itself its inherent powers or adapted itself fully to the educational conditions of the present day. There are those who may see in this the very reason why education in India should be dissociated from the control of the State. But there is one fact which tells with compelling force against any such idea. It is this. Not only is the State as a controlling agency able to do for education what no other agency can do, but the history of its action within the past ten or fifteen years has been the record of activity along lines that lead to the elimination of those features of its control which are admittedly defective. 'The function of control', says Mayhew, no friend of officialdom, 'can never be completely surrendered by a modern State, but must be exercised in India only on the broadest lines'. And that is exactly what is happening in connexion with the control of Indian education at the present day. The State cannot, in the interests of education and of its responsibilities to parents and children alike, surrender its control; and very definitely it is endeavouring to exercise that control on the broadest lines. Definitely but, so far, not steadily. It is this steadiness of endeavour to which the State requires now to address itself. And the more it does so, the more clear will be the value and the benefit of the control thus exercised. The advisability of that control none will question.

CHAPTER II

The Problem of Management

I. The Problem: Is the Threefold System of Management Advisable?

1. The educational system of India is under one Control, that of the State. But this Control is exercised over three main forms of Management—departmental, local, and private. These three have not always existed. And as we look at the different types of management we are conscious of a problem which calls for solution. It is this: Is it advisable that the threefold form of Management which obtains in India should continue to exist? In the discussion that follows an attempt is made to reach a solution of this problem.

II. Survey of the Educational Work of Each Management

2. *Tabular Statement of this Work.*—To begin with it is necessary to be in possession of the relevant facts. These we may obtain at least in outline from the Statistical Tables of the Ninth Quinquennial Review. The position at the 31st of March 1927 was as follows:—

Institutions according to Management	Number of Institutions		Number of Pupils	
I. Under Public Management—				
i. Government...	...	4,057		334,795
ii. Board—				
District ...	63,835		3,874,694	
Municipal ..	6,093	69,928	705,295	4,579,989
II. Under Private Management—				
i. Aided ...	119,128		4,939,929	
ii. Unaided ...	17,935	137,063	674,637	5,614,566
Total ...	...	211,048	...	10,529,350

3. *Basis of Classification.*—The figures which are here given apply only to Recognized Institutions, that is to schools and colleges which have been admitted to a recognized place in the educational system of the country. They do not apply to Unrecognized Institutions, reference to which was made in paragraph 6 of Chapter I, and further reference to which will be found in paragraphs 3 to 6 of Chapter VI. It is well to note this point because of a change of classification which has been recently introduced into official tables. Formerly institutions fell into two main classes, Public and Private. The Public Institutions were those which were recognized; and they might be under public management or private management. The Private were the unrecognized. The terminology had its drawbacks. As, for example, a school that was called Public might be under private management, confusion was almost inevitable. Sometimes even in documents where one would have expected greater care a school was termed a 'private school' when what was intended was 'a public school under private management'. Confusion was avoided only by adopting cumbrousness. The classification now employed is much more satisfactory. According to it, Educational Institutions are either Recognized or Unrecognized. From the point of view of Management, Recognized Institutions fall into two classes—those under public, and those under private, management. Those under public management may in turn belong to one or other of three classes—Government, District Board, or Municipal. Those under private management may be aided by the State or they may not, and so they are tabulated as Aided or Unaided. Unrecognized Institutions stand in a category by themselves; they are almost wholly under private management, and they are almost wholly unaided.

4. *Types of Institutions*—(1) *Managed by Government*.—Confining ourselves to the Recognized Institutions of the Indian educational system, we notice that these are managed in three different ways. First, there

are schools and colleges which are managed directly by Government. They are staffed by those who are in the service of Government, and they are financed by public funds. Income from fees is placed to the credit of the State, what is required for the maintenance of these institutions is a charge upon provincial revenues, and provision is made for this year by year in the budgets which are submitted to the local legislatures.

5. (2) *Managed by Local Bodies.*—Secondly, there are schools and colleges which are managed by Local Bodies. These statutory bodies are of two main types. There is the District Board which 'exercises jurisdiction in matters of education, sanitation, roads, ferries, etc., over the area of a district', and there is the Municipality which exercises similar functions within the area of a town. The District Board may delegate some of its functions to a body which, under its general control, exercises these functions in a sub-divisional area, and is known as a Local or Taluq Board. By various enactments these bodies are authorized to raise funds for the objects entrusted to them, and among the objects on which they can spend from their revenues are the educational institutions which they maintain and manage. The increase of schools under this type of management, more especially of primary schools, is one of the most marked features of recent years. There is legal provision for the subsidy by Government of the funds which Local Bodies raise by taxation.

6. (3) *Managed by Private Bodies or Individuals.*—And lastly, there are schools and colleges which are under private management. These institutions are recognized by the State, generally through its Educational Department, and they form an integral part of the public system of education. They are managed, however, neither by State officials nor by local self-governing bodies, but by the representatives of private effort. In some cases these are individuals who find in this way an outlet for their philanthropic spirit; in others they are councils of missionary societies; in still other cases

they are committees of Indian ladies and gentlemen interested in education; and in not a few instances they are the Senates of universities duly incorporated by law. These managers are responsible for the funds by which the institutions are maintained. They put money into the schools and colleges which they have established, either from their own pockets or from donations they have secured or from endowments that have come to them as gifts as well as from the fees which they receive from the pupils. They staff their institutions in accordance with the requirements of the educational authorities, and in the great majority of cases they receive financial aid from the State. There are a few who receive no grant either because they do not wish to be beholden to the State or because their schools have not yet qualified for it. But the schools whether aided or unaided are the outcome of private effort and thus belong to the third type—those under private management.

7. *Numbers under each Management.*—We must now look at the number of institutions that come under each of these three heads, and at the number of pupils that attend them. What the figures tell us is that of the institutions which have their recognized place in the educational system of the country, 4,000 or 2 per cent are managed by Government; 70,000 or 34 per cent by Local Bodies; and 137,000 or 64 per cent by Private Bodies. Of the ten and a half million pupils who are on the rolls of recognized schools and colleges, 335,000 or 3 per cent attend institutions managed by Government; 4,580,000 or 44 per cent attend those managed by Local Bodies; and 5,600,000 or 53 per cent attend those under Private Management. Thus, the number of schools and colleges managed by private agencies is well-nigh double that of those managed by departmental and local agencies combined; while the number of pupils which they educate exceeds that of those educated in Government and Local Board institutions combined by more than half a million.

8. *Arts Colleges according to Management.*—But these figures present us only with totals, and, though they are significant a much greater significance attaches to the figures which give us information regarding the various grades of schools and colleges for which each of the managements is responsible. First, then, we turn to collegiate education of a non-professional character. There are in India over 200 colleges of general education. Some of these provide courses which lead to a degree in arts and science, in many cases to a degree with honours; others provide only for the course which lies between Matriculation and the Intermediate stage. While there is a lack of uniformity in regard to the terminology employed we may say that, in general, Degree or First Grade Colleges carry their students on to graduation in the Faculties of Arts and Science, while in Intermediate or Second Grade Colleges students receive instruction which does not go beyond the end of the second year of the usual degree course. Arranged in tabular form the statistics are as follows :—

ARTS COLLEGES ACCORDING TO MANAGEMENT

—	Under Government Management	Under Board Management	Under Private Management	Total
Number of Degree Colleges ...	34	1	104	139
Number of Intermediate Colleges...	26	1	66	93
Total ...	60	2	170	232
Number of Students attending Degree and Intermediate Colleges ...	16,101	149	55,718	71,968

That is to say, while all three forms of management participate in the provision of colleges, there are three times as many Degree colleges under private management as there are under State management, and twice as many Intermediate colleges. District Boards and Municipalities are responsible for only two colleges, and as these educate only 150 students the contribution of Local Board managements to education at this stage is most limited. In round figures we may say that of the 72,000 men and women who are in Degree and Intermediate Colleges, 16,000 are in Colleges managed by Government and 56,000 in colleges provided by private enterprise. It is to private agencies that the country is mainly indebted for the facilities which its sons and daughters enjoy in their pursuit of this form of education. If what these agencies are doing were wiped out more than three-fourths of those who are taking a collegiate course of a general nature would be without provision for their educational needs.

9. *High Schools according to Management.*—We may now consider the part played by the different managements in providing secondary education for boys and girls. The figures are as follows :—

HIGH SCHOOLS ACCORDING TO MANAGEMENT

—	Under Government Management	Under Board Management	Under Private Management	Total
Number of High Schools ...	345	218	2,124	2,687
Number of Pupils attending High Schools ...	112,920	68,776	612,505	794,201

The High Schools of the system number 2,690 and over 2,100 of these are the contribution of private agencies. Government and Local Bodies between them supply a little more than one-fifth of the High Schools of the country, about four-fifths being the supply of voluntary effort. If that effort ceased then of the 794,000 boys and girls who attend High Schools 612,000 would have to be provided for.

10. *Middle Schools according to Management.*—Secondary education includes Middle Schools as well as High Schools. And here there is a lack of uniformity in classification which requires us to come to a definite understanding if we are to have a satisfactory basis for comparison. In the educational Statistical Tables, Middle Schools are divided into two classes—English and Vernacular. In the provinces of Madras and Bombay Middle Vernacular Schools are included in the primary stage of education; in the other provinces in the secondary stage. This difference is troublesome, and especially so where, as in the Punjab, there is a definite policy which aims at 'improving the status of primary schools by the addition of two classes, so that the ordinary course will not be completed by a child at the tender age of ten or eleven and that he may be encouraged to stay at school until the age of twelve or thirteen'. This endeavour to improve the primary school leads on the statistical side to the paradoxical result that the school thus improved disappears from the list of primary schools and takes its place among those on the secondary list. For our purposes we may ally ourselves with what is done in Madras and Bombay and what is aimed at in the Punjab. We may regard what are called Middle English Schools as belonging to the secondary stage, and what are called Middle Vernacular Schools we may classify together with what are called Primary Schools under the heading of Elementary. And in doing this we are following what is in accordance with educational soundness even if it conflicts with statistical requirement. More than five-sixths of the Middle English Schools are provided by private agencies, less than one-sixth by Government and Local Bodies combined. Were private

effort to cease at this stage three lakhs of boys and girls would be without an educational home. The figures are as follows :—

MIDDLE ENGLISH SCHOOLS ACCORDING TO MANAGEMENT

—	Under Government Management	Under Board Management	Under Private Management	Total
Number of Middle English Schools ...	124	427	2,940	3,491
Number of Pupils attending Middle English Schools...	18,841	63,915	301,632	384,388

If we compare these figures with those relating to Collegiate and High School education we notice that, for the first time, the part played by Government becomes at this point distinctly smaller both relatively and absolutely. Government manages almost three times as many High Schools as it does Middle Schools, while Local Bodies manage almost twice as many Middle Schools as they do High Schools. Further, Local Bodies manage more than three times as many Middle Schools as Government does, and these schools are attended by more than three times the number of pupils who attend Government schools. And this is not something that is incidental in character. A reference to what has been going on in the course of the preceding five years shows that during that period the number of departmentally managed schools of this grade has actually diminished. At this point, then, the figures draw our attention to a stage of education where the withdrawal of the State from management is both marked and on the increase.

11. *Elementary Schools according to Management.*—It is now time to look at what is taking place at the

elementary stage, that is at the schools which in official tables are classified as Middle Vernacular and Primary. Here is what the tables inform us :—

ELEMENTARY SCHOOLS ACCORDING TO MANAGEMENT

—	Under Government Management	Under Board Management	Under Private Management	Total
Number of Elementary Schools ...	2,822	66,016	125,670	194,508
Number of Pupils attending these Schools ...	136,366	4,362,093	4,423,779	8,922,238

Several points strike us as we give these figures close scrutiny. For one thing we are impressed by the very large part which is played by Local Bodies in providing elementary education. They, at this stage, become a most important factor, and one of increasing importance. Think for instance what would happen if the contribution of private agencies were blotted out at this stage. It would mean that there would be still four and a half million children cared for in the schools that are under the management of Government and Local Bodies. How great is the difference between what we find at the elementary, and what we find at the secondary, stage. Were private agencies to desist from providing secondary education, or were they driven off the field, there would be only 265,000 out of the 1,180,000 pupils at this level who would have any school to go to. The greater part of a million would be educationally homeless. Not so at the elementary level. To all intents and purposes the number of those who attend elementary schools would be diminished simply by one half. That would fill one with dismay, but it would not spell ruin. The Local

Bodies, then, begin to pull their weight at the level of mass education. In 1927 it did not amount to the weight which private bodies were pulling, but by 1929 it had exceeded it. Yet how lamentably does the pull of both together fall short of what is urgently required.

12. *The Share of Local Bodies.*—The increased share in elementary education which is being taken by Local Bodies is a very natural development. Local self-government is becoming a factor of increasing moment in the growth of the country. And that has been shown, among other signs, by the stress laid in recent legislation upon the responsibility of Local Bodies for the service of elementary education. In 1922 the number of pupils attending the elementary schools managed by District Boards and Municipalities was 2,980,607, so that within a quinquennium these bodies have added more than a million and a third to the enrolment in their schools. They have been encouraged to do this by the assistance which they have received from local governments and by the powers which have been conferred upon them by statute. The increase in the contribution made by them to spread of mass education is one of the hopeful features of the present situation. For the interests of the country demand that education should find in local self-government an unfaltering ally.

13. *The Share of Private Managements.*—It is remarkable that the elementary schools under private management are still attended by numbers running into millions. It is also remarkable that the number of pupils has increased in the course of the last quinquennium, when so much was being done for Local Bodies, by roughly eight and a half lakhs. And to the increase in pupils must be added the fact of a fee income of over Rs. 43 lakhs, which indicates a willingness on the part of parents to send their children to these schools even though in doing so they may pass schools at which no fees are charged.

14. *The Share of Government.*—There is a point in connexion with departmentally managed elementary

schools to which the figures draw our attention. If we look back five years we find that Government then was directly responsible for a thousand fewer elementary schools than it is today. That is somewhat surprising when we remember how steady has been the trend of recent legislation in the direction of relying more and more on Local Bodies for the advance of education among the masses of the people. It almost looks as if, by a strange paradox, the Government of the country had come in the way of the legislation of the country. And the matter might seem all the more difficult to understand if search revealed to us that one province was responsible for the additional thousand, a province which, in its educational budget, had not provision for the expenditure of one pie under the heading of Government primary schools. Yet that is exactly what we find. The explanation lies in a somewhat original mode of procedure. The Madras Educational Department, by transfer or other action, ceased to manage primary schools some time ago and thus, so far as that part of education is concerned, it had no obligation to meet in the columns of its budget. The Government, however, decided to set up a number of schools for pupils belonging to the Depressed Classes and to place these schools not under the Educational Department but under a Special Officer belonging to another Department. And that is what has been done. It is difficult to imagine a proceeding more likely to weaken the control of education by the State than such a division of function; and on the side of management it marks the recession of this Government from a policy which has been adopted by virtually all the other governments in India. Had it not been for this, there would have been a still further decrease in the number of elementary schools under the management of the State.

15. *School Accommodation and Social Conditions.*—Is the best use being made of the available school accommodation? That is a question which springs to our lips when we look at what the table in paragraph 11 tells

us. We cannot but note that Local Bodies require only 66,000 schools for the education of 4,362,000 pupils, while Private Agencies which educate only 60,000 more require 60,000 more schools. When the position is stated in this way, it certainly looks as if a much better use could be made of a considerable number of school fabrics under private management. And if the numbers alone were taken into consideration there might be good reason for saying that there was unnecessary multiplication of school buildings. But unfortunately, as things are, other factors have to be brought into the reckoning. Class and community make themselves felt over large stretches of the country, and they affect both the volume of education and the manner in which that education has to be conducted. While, for example, so far as numbers go, one school alone would be justified in a locality, yet when the social conditions which prevail in that locality are considered it may quite possibly turn out that the presence of only one school would result in a number of children of school-going age in the area having to do without educational facilities. This is a regrettable situation, and it puts not a few obstacles in the way of educational advance. In certain parts of the country these obstacles have been overcome, and where the change has taken place it is education which has mainly contributed to this result. Thus while the conditions that obtain in various areas may be apparently wasteful they may prove ultimately to be the very reverse. For if they had not existed there would have been a lack of education among those most in need of it, and so there would not have been in operation within the areas that power which, the more it is taken advantage of, the more assuredly replaces waste by fruitful activity, and segregation by concentration.

16. (1) *In the Education of Girls.*—Take for example the education of girls. Changes are taking place in this field, as is shown by the fact that six and a half lakhs of girls are reading in primary schools for boys. But, after all, that is only about eight per cent of the total

enrolment; and as the Educational Commissioner remarks: 'It is noteworthy that as far back as the year 1902, 44.7 per cent of the girls under instruction were reading in boys' schools, whereas in the year 1926-27 the percentage was only 38.5'. Indeed it cannot be denied that in many parts of India parents show considerable unwillingness to send even a very young girl to a boys' primary school. And it has been found that when girls have been sent to these schools 'there is a tendency for them, in the absence of women teachers, to be neglected'. Thus while co-education is actually at work in the primary school, to force the pace would be to menace the prospects both of co-education and of girls' education itself. In other words, till the better day dawns, and as the surest means for the dawning of that day, there will be for some time to come a large number of girls' schools each of which is attended by a relatively small number of pupils. And, as it happens, the provision of these schools is for the most part the contribution of private managements. Out of 27,000 primary schools for girls 21,000 are supplied by private agencies. And as these are attended by 629,000 pupils the average number per school is not quite 30. That is a very different state of affairs from what we find, for example, in the schools for boys that exist within municipal areas, where the average number in each is 120. In a general way that explains why, with good reason, there may be four schools where in normal circumstances one would suffice. And it also one of the factors that help to explain why private effort, because of its effort to meet the abnormal circumstances, provides so many schools.

17. (2) *In the Education of Muhammadans.*—The same situation meets us when we look at education among Muhammadans. No one will contend that the existence of schools solely for Muhammadans is ideal; and many of the Muhammadans themselves are beginning to doubt whether the best interests of their community are being served by the maintenance of these schools. Nevertheless such schools have done much in the past to stimulate

education among a people that was for long looked upon as educationally backward, and it is difficult to believe that the great advance which the years 1922 to 1927 have to record would have been possible without them. Here again the part played by private agencies has been considerable. The tables that are provided by the Quinquennial Reviews for India as a whole do not supply us with detailed information on this point. But we can learn a great deal from some of the provincial reports. In those of the two large and adjacent areas of the United Provinces and Bengal we read of the popularity of privately managed schools for Muhammadans, of the manner in which they 'meet the special desires of the community', and of what is, in some respects, the remarkable growth in the number of pupils attending them. In these two provinces there are 22,000 schools of the primary grade solely for Muhammadans and these are attended by 672,000 pupils. It is a good total, and it is a question whether it could have been reached in any other way. But to get it the cost is not small; on an average a school for every 30 pupils. So long, however, as there are cases where no special school would mean no Muhammadan pupils the cost is worth the paying; and private managements have not been slow to pay it.

18. (3) *In the Education of Europeans and Depressed Classes.*—We should find very much the same result if we were to go into the figures of European education. This is largely, indeed predominantly, in the hands of private agencies. A policy of concentration, it is true, is being pursued in regard to it, and recently there have been reductions in the number of schools without a reduction in the number of pupils. That is all to the good, but there is a limit to the number of amalgamations which can be usefully secured, and the community for which these schools are provided is small and scattered. At best, the number of pupils per school cannot be high. At present in schools classified as primary it is about 60. Much less than that is the number in

schools provided for those who belong to the Depressed Classes. Things are changing even there. There is an increase in the number of children belonging to the Depressed Classes who attend the ordinary schools of the country and not those specially established for them. All the same, there are still far too many cases where a caste school and a non-caste school have to exist side by side in an area for the simple reason that were it otherwise non-caste pupils would be without the means of obtaining education. A long and not very satisfactory chapter in the story of Indian education might be written on the basis of what official records tell us regarding the pressure that has been brought to bear on Local Bodies so as to secure that their primary schools, wholly supported from public funds, should be 'held in places accessible (note the word "accessible") to all, including the Depressed Classes'. It is enough for us to notice at this stage how the considerations which have been mentioned affect school accommodation. They have placed a heavy burden on private managers, and amongst other things have made it necessary to keep open two doors when one should have been enough, but when, if there had been only one, those who were entering in would have been hindered.

19. *Bearing of the Considerations.*—When we consider what private effort is doing for the education of girls, Muhammadans, Europeans, and the Depressed Classes, to go no further, we have little difficulty in understanding how it is that, though private managements educate only 30,000 elementary pupils more than do Local Bodies, they maintain 60,000 more schools. If we took only two sets of figures—the number of girls in elementary schools specially provided for them by private managers and the number of Muhammadans in two provinces attending elementary schools specially provided for them by private managers—we should get this result: In these schools alone there are more than a million pupils receiving education, all drawn from classes for which educational progress has not been easy. And

when we remember that there are only some nine millions in the elementary schools of British India taken as a whole, we realize how important is the work that is being done by these schools, even if it is at a heavy cost in the way of school accommodation.

20. *School Accommodation and Control.*—But though social and communal conditions account for much of what seems unnecessary in the school accommodation which private bodies provide, there can be no doubt that investigation would reveal provision of school fabrics which it would be hard, if not impossible, to justify. And it is here that the factor of State Control requires to be emphasized. If the State were in a position to exercise fully its power of Control would the disparity which we have noticed have been allowed to continue? It is difficult to believe that it would. Means would have been found to place the use of school buildings and school staffs above reasonable criticism. Yet all the schools included in the table given in paragraph 11 have received the recognition of the State; in virtue of that they have taken their place in the educational system of the country. They are subject to visits from the Inspecting officers of the State; almost ninety per cent of them receive financial aid from public funds; and reports concerning them are in the hands of the Educational Departments. Thus if the number of these schools is too great for the number of pupils to be served, if school accommodation is not being used to the fullest advantage even when allowance is made for all social and communal requirements, can it be maintained that the State is exercising as it ought its function as Controller of the whole educational system? The question which we raised in paragraph 15 may be answered in part by the bodies in which management is vested; it can be answered in whole only by the body in which Control is vested; that is the State.

21. *Professional Education according to Management.*—Having considered the various forms of general education in relation to the agencies by which they are

managed, we may now look at professional education. The following figures present us with the main facts :—

PROFESSIONAL COLLEGES ACCORDING TO MANAGEMENT

—	Under Government Management		Under Board Management		Under Private Management	
	Number of Colleges	Number of Students	Number of Colleges	Number of Students	Number of Colleges	Number of Students
Law ...	4	2,103	...	...	9	5,955
Medicine ...	7	2,764	1	100	2	1,000
Education...	16	1,041	...	...	5	214
Engineering	6	1,326	...	...	1	683
Agriculture.	6	771	...	...	1	27
Commerce .	1	269	...	...	13	1,247
Forestry ...	2	129	...	...	...	...
Veterinary Science ...	3	330	...	...	...	...
Total ...	45	8,733	1	100	31	9,126

These figures are in certain respects only an indication of the share taken by the different managements in the provision of facilities for professional education. The lack of uniformity in nomenclature has the unfortunate effect of grouping under one name different ranges of educational supply. This is most clearly the case in connexion with Education or Teaching, further reference to which will meet us when we come to consider the Problem of the Teacher in Chapter V. And in regard to Medicine adjustment is necessary between the figures given in the Tables and those given in the letterpress of the Ninth Quinquennial Review. But when allowance has been made for these and all such variations, one point stands out with perfect clearness—that one of the finest contributions which the educational system of India receives is the provision which the State makes for professional training. Government is responsible for the supply of all the instruction that is given in

Forestry and Veterinary Science, and is the agency which is chiefly responsible for the education provided in the fields of Agriculture, Teaching, Engineering, and Medicine. Private agencies supply the greater part of what is required for the pursuit of Law and Commerce, and their colleges serve about a third of those who are studying Medicine and Engineering. Two things strike us as we look at the figures in the light of past records. One is that Local Bodies have now entered the region of professional training. This has happened within the last five years, and their contribution for the present is confined to one Medical College. The other is that private effort is assuming growing responsibilities in a field of education which till quite recently was looked upon as for the most part, if not exclusively, the domain of Government.

22. *Special Schools according to Management.*—All that remains to be noted, in order that our review of the work of the different managements may be completed, is their contribution of what are known as Special Schools. These are institutions not of university grade which impart training for instance in Art, Medicine, Engineering, and Industry and which give education to part-time workers, to adults and to defectives. The statistics show that these schools are provided by the various managements, and are attended, as follows :—

SPECIAL SCHOOLS ACCORDING TO MANAGEMENT

	Under Government Management	Under Board Management	Under Private Management	Total
Number of Special Schools ...	661	3,264	6,114	10,039
Number of Pupils attending these Schools ...	41,838	84,956	201,810	328,604

Were there space it would be interesting to go into the whole matter of Special Schools, but that must be reserved for consideration when the Working of the Policy is dealt with. To take them in the aggregate, as this table exhibits them, is to pass by much that is valuable, much that indicates lines along which the development of education is now moving, and much as to the responsibilities which managements are assuming for these developments. For our present purpose, however, we may regard the figures as showing that, while the country depends upon all three forms of management for the growth of its Special Schools, it relies mainly upon two of them. For Local Bodies maintain about five times as many of these Schools as does Government, and Private Agencies nine times as many. Or to put it in terms not of schools but of pupils, Local Bodies educate twice as many pupils at this stage as does Government, and Private Agencies educate more than twice as many as do Local Bodies.

23. *Bearing of Survey on Problem of Management.*—In the course of paragraphs 2 to 22 we have surveyed the educational work for which the different forms of management have made themselves responsible. And as we look at this survey four illuminating facts emerge. The first is that, whatever be the form or level of education, three types of management contribute towards its maintenance—departmental, local, and private. The second is that at any level of education the main contribution comes from two, and only two, of these types of management. The third is that at all levels private management is one of the two. And the fourth is that at some levels departmental management is the second of the two, while at other levels local management is the second. Professional, Collegiate, and High School education depend mainly on private effort and on the State. Middle, Elementary, and Special School education depend mainly on private effort and on local bodies. These facts are illuminating because of the light which they cast on the problem we are now considering. The

question before us is: Is it advisable to continue the threefold form of management that obtains in Indian education? And what we have now reached as the result of our survey makes it look as if the educational system of the country would not be the sufferer if a twofold system of management replaced the threefold one at present in existence. Whether there is anything in this we must now consider.

References

Eighth Quinquennial Review, Volume i, p. 37; and *Ninth Quinquennial Review*, Volume i, p. 45; Institutions classified according to management.

Ninth Quinquennial Review, Volume ii, Tables I and IIA: Institutions tabulated according to management and distribution of scholars.

As to the use of the terms *public* and *private*, see *Aspects of Indian Educational Policy*, p. 36.

As to classification of Middle Schools see *Punjab Quinquennial Review* (1927), p. 58.

As to Primary Schools under Government though not under departmental management see *Ninth Quinquennial Review*, p. 44.

III. Advisability of a Twofold System of Management

24. *Criticism of Privately Managed Institutions.*—In investigating whether a twofold system of management might be advantageously substituted for the threefold system now in force, we may take as our starting point the position in the educational system occupied by private management. That form, as we have seen, differs from the other two in this—that at every level of education, and not only at some of them, it is relied on for the contribution which it makes to the spread of education throughout India. There have been times when efforts have been made to disparage and displace the educational work which private managements have put at the service of the country. And there have been

times when the criticism which has been bestowed upon it has conveyed an impression of such ineffectiveness on the part of the managements as would be astonishing if it were true. In the pages of the Indian Education Commission's Report the manner in which private managements were dealt with by the State over a period of years is set down in black and white, and the record is such as to inspire the hope that it may never be repeated. And one may read reports of a much later date, and may be excused if he rises from the perusal of them with surprise that, if things are as stated, Government could have so far forgotten itself as to give these contributions of private effort a recognized place in the educational system of the country, and not only that but to have kept them there year after year. There could hardly be a more severe condemnation of the State than these criticisms if they were merited. But to be effective, criticism must be free from all trace of partiality. And to secure this in the matter with which we are now dealing two things at least are necessary. For one thing, the observed defects must be displayed against the relevant background, that is to say against the strikingly wide and varied range of educational activity for which the agencies have made themselves responsible. And for another thing, they must be brought into relation with the handicap which private managements suffer, a handicap not of their own making but due in large measure to an inadequate inspectorate, an imperfect system of grant-in-aid, and unsatisfactory facilities for the training of teachers. When account is taken of both these points, three salient considerations emerge. First, it becomes abundantly plain that the defects of private managements may be many and yet not relatively numerous, outstanding and yet not typical, obvious and yet obviously remediable. Secondly, equally plain is it that for no small share of the remedy required for these defects the responsibility lies with the State. Thirdly, no less plain is it that in so far as the remedy lies with the private managements themselves they constantly supply it, urged thereto by legitimate criticism, and correcting their defects time after time by the exercise of a vitality which seems to be inherent in them, by modes of working which commend them to pupils and parents alike, and by the manifestation of characteristics which fit them for incorporation as integral and indispensable parts of a national system of education.

25. *Permanent Value of Privately Managed Institutions.*—For private effort is a national asset. By a strange lapse of memory the Government of India permitted itself in its Resolution of 1913 to speak as if it had forgotten the rationale of private effort in education. It suggested that the labours of that form of enterprise were being utilized pretty much because they happened to be there. And it passed on without asking itself the question : Why were they there? That is a pity, for the answer to that question is bound up with what is of deepest import to India. Private effort is in India for many reasons; but the statement of two of them will suffice. Private effort on behalf of education is in India because it is the expression of a spirit which India welcomes and by which its national life is vitalized. It is the expression of an interest which does not wait to be stimulated by legal enactments but which pours itself forth in a voluntary offering to the country of managers, teachers, and funds. In it lies the assurance that officialdom will not drive the education of the people into a mould which is inexpansive and rigidly standardized; it secures a place for originality, and for personal relations between teacher and taught; and in the training of youth it makes possible the combination of good education with living religious principle. That is what private effort has meant for India during three-quarters of a century and more. That is what it still means. And the other reason is this. Private effort is in India not merely as the expression of such a spirit, but also because India cannot do without it. Notwithstanding many an official frown and short-sighted act of discouragement, it has continued its endeavour so

unflaggingly that at the present day out of the 211,000 educational institutions in the country 137,000 are its contribution, out of a total of 10,530,000 pupils 5,600,000 are its care, it trains over 6,000 teachers, and to the service of education its annual gift is not less than 240 lakhs of rupees. This plant which has thriven so wonderfully in the face of opposition that it ought to have been spared, this contribution which has been made year after year and which has met discouragement with fresh endeavour, has a place in Indian education which it has won for itself by its acknowledged merits and by the confidence which it has inspired. It has a recognized position in the declared policy of the State, though this fact is sometimes obscured. And it has an even stronger position than that. It is indispensable. Let that contribution be withdrawn and the educational system of the country would be thrown into a state of confusion. Private effort gives to India in the service of education a spirit which it cannot do without, and a contribution which is an integral part of the national life. That is why private effort appears at every level of educational activity, and that is why it must remain there.

26. *The Contribution of Local Self-Government.*—But what of local effort? What forcibly strikes one who studies Indian education during say the past half century is the increasing part played by District Boards and Municipalities. And that is what is to be expected if these Bodies are true expressions of the spirit of local self-government. Where those who reside in a locality agree to tax themselves so that they and their children may enjoy the benefits of various social services, this mode of action claims and with the best of rights, the generous recognition and support of the State. What people thus organized can do is bound to be mapped out in large degree by the funds which it is within their power to raise. This principle must not be pressed so as to exclude the special subvention by the State of localities which, though they are eager, are poor. But it does

indicate in a general way the extent of the activities in which the people of the locality should engage, and those from which it would be wise for them to abstain. The most obvious claim upon them is the education of their children. And it is to the supply of this need that District Boards and Municipalities are applying themselves with markedly increasing energy. They are now educating over four million boys and girls in the elementary schools which they manage, while in their middle schools there are 64,000 pupils, and in their high schools a still larger number. They maintain two arts colleges and one professional. They educate well on to a lakh of adults; in their technical and industrial schools they have 2,000 pupils; and they train more than a thousand teachers. Their educational activities are thus manifold, and, considering the short time during which they have enjoyed the powers now entrusted to them by statute, we may regard their work as but an earnest of what they will yet achieve.

27. *Its Title to State Support.*—Two points in connexion with Local Bodies and their educational contribution claim our attention. The first is financial. Local Bodies are performing more than a local service by the schools which they maintain, just as Private Bodies are performing more than a private service. State aid, therefore, is wholly appropriate. And provided that the aid thus given is sanctioned on certain defined principles it may be most valuable. For one thing, if the subventions of the State bear some relation to the contribution of the local body they may prove to be a real stimulus to the enhancement of local resources and thus of what can be set apart for educational purposes. And for another thing, the manner in which the State distributes its grants may be a useful guide to the Local Body as to the directions in which its educational activities might be best employed. Under control thus exercised, through the medium of finance, to which fuller reference is made in the next chapter, the work of Local Bodies will be both extended and led into fruitful channels.

28. *Permanent Value of Locally Managed Institutions.*—The second consideration that claims our attention is administrative. Much has been said in the course of Chapter i, when we were dealing with the Problem of Control, regarding the defects which mark Local Bodies as they are now constituted. We saw how serious a responsibility is taken by the State in entrusting them with large powers of educational control. But there is a difference between control and management; and there is no reason why, under good control, these Bodies should not render effective service. For whatever be the defects of Local Bodies, and however these may militate against their powers of control, the fact remains that the representatives of local effort must be managers. The body politic cannot do without them, neither can education. And, if in their present organized capacity they have their deficiencies, that is simply a call for a better constitution. And as the need for that is emphasized, the more speedily and surely will come the time of its realization. Organized local effort is as indispensable for the education of India as is organized private effort. And there can be no doubt that, on the basis of a more suitable constitution and with the encouragement which they have every right to expect from the State, these Bodies will make a contribution to the education of the country which will be characteristic, abiding, and increasing.

29. *Value of Departmentally Managed Institutions.*—Local and Private managements, then, are indispensable. What shall we say as to departmental management? If its extent is not large, amounting to some 4,000 institutions in all, it has to be borne in mind that 'from the point of view of the service rendered to education, the importance of the institutions under direct government management is out of all proportion to their number'. The equipment of government schools and colleges is well known for its excellence, the Educational Services from which their staffs have been recruited look back on a distinguished history, and the prestige of

these institutions is undisputed. Being financed from provincial revenues they have behind them the resources of the State. They have kept the standards of education high, and they have built up a tradition which has meant much for scholarship. Great administrative changes, however, have occurred within the last decade, and these have placed State educational services and State educational management in a new light, although the full force of these changes seems as yet to have failed of recognition. Still in the mind of anyone who gives them serious thought they inevitably raise the question whether it is advisable that Government should continue to be the manager of certain educational institutions while it occupies at the same time the position of controller of them all. The arguments which have been advanced in favour of Government management have followed three main lines, those of continuity, control, and pattern. To each of these we must give our consideration.

30. *Arguments for Retention.*—(1) *Continuity of Policy.*—The maintenance of State-managed schools and colleges is, it has been said, in accord with history. And the benefits arising from this form of management have been so great that withdrawal of it from the educational system would involve a breach of historic continuity that would be nothing short of positive disservice to the cause of education. There is this to be said in favour of such a position that the sudden withdrawal of the State from its position as manager would produce most harmful results. But to question the advisability of State-management is not to advocate any sudden action on the part of the State. It is to suggest the enunciation of a definite policy that would be steadily adhered to and yet carried out by stages so that there would be no dislocation of the educational machinery. The question is: Can this be done? Even at the risk of repetition we must recall some of the salient features of the past in our endeavour to give a satisfactory answer, and to place the matter in its historical setting.

31. *Policy regarding Transfer of Management.*—In the year 1854 the State announced its intention of becoming responsible for the education of the people of India. And in the official document in which it proclaimed this intention it gave details as to the way in which it would endeavour to discharge this responsibility. In the first place, it was to control the system, working through the medium of an Educational Department. In the second place, the State was to establish and maintain schools and colleges of its own. In the third place, it was to aid by grants from provincial funds schools and colleges established by private agencies provided they submitted to inspection and satisfied prescribed standards. And in the fourth place, the State did not regard its own schools and colleges as a permanency; it looked 'forward to the time when any general system of education entirely provided by government may be discontinued, with the gradual advance of the system of grants-in-aid'. For well-nigh a generation after 1854 things remained as they had begun, so far as managements were concerned. Attention, as might have been expected, was for the most part concentrated on the provision of educational facilities and thus on giving effect to the first three of the four points which we have noted above. But with the eighties it became possible to do something towards the realization of the fourth. Action in this direction received a stimulus from two sources. One of these was the publication of the Indian Education Commission's Report which, in accordance with what had been expressed in the Despatch, advocated the transfer of institutions from departmental to non-departmental management, and pointed out at length how this might be done with benefit to education and without dislocation to the system. The other was the establishment of Local Bodies, which, as was soon seen, provided a means whereby the State might transfer institutions under its own management to a form of management which was public and yet not departmental. A stimulus was thus given towards the achievement of

the full plan contemplated by the Despatch of 1854; but not a few obstacles stood in the way of its steady operation. Progress, however, has been made. Within the past forty years, and more particularly during the latter half of that period, the State has largely relinquished its management of primary and middle vernacular schools in favour of local and private agencies. And in the sphere of higher education, both general and professional, the same line of action may be seen at work. The situation is thus clear. Continuity of policy does not mean continuance in the status quo. It means continuity of action on the part of Government so as to realize the end which it stated as soon as it issued a definite educational policy—the gradual abandonment of Departmental management. Those who believe that they may find in educational history a ground for the management of schools and colleges by Government have but to call to remembrance what the facts of history are. And when they do this they will realize that relinquishment of management by the State is not the introduction of discontinuity but is in line with, and the natural outcome of, a policy enunciated by the State three-quarters of a century ago. The argument from historical continuity cannot be invoked in favour of State management.

32. (2) *Control through Management.*—But a more commonly pressed argument in favour of State management takes the following form. If the Government has no schools or colleges of its own, the contention is, it is unable to control education. This position appears in different settings. Few writers on Indian education are so accurate and informing as Mr. H. R. James, formerly principal of the Presidency College, Calcutta. Yet in his stimulating 'Education and Statesmanship in India' he refers to the recommendation of the Education Commission to the effect that 'in all ordinary cases secondary schools for instruction in English be hereafter established by the State preferably on the footing of the system of grants-in-aid' as a recommendation 'for the with-

drawal of Government from the direct control of higher education'. A statement of the same character is made by so competent and sympathetic an observer as Sir Valentine Chirol in his 'Indian Unrest'. Among the very important features of the Indian educational system which he regards as deserving of notice, he mentions first of all the fact that 'Government exercises no direct control over educational institutions other than those maintained by the State'. And in another passage which occurs in the same chapter of this book, where he refers to the Indian Education Commission, he says that 'The eloquence of the Commission was chiefly directed towards representing the important benefits that would be likely to accrue to Government and education by the relaxation of Government's control over education, the withdrawal of Government from the management of schools, and the adoption of a general go-as-you-please policy'.

33. *Confusion of Control with Management.*—It is well to know how such statements struck one who was a member of the Indian Education Commission, and whose knowledge of its inner workings as well as of its findings admits of no challenge. In his 'Unrest and Education in India', Dr. William Miller describes the assertion that the Commission advocated the relaxation of Government's control over education as a 'noteworthy misapprehension'. 'The facts', he goes on to say, 'are the other way, as will easily become plain to those who may be willing to study the Commission's Report in its entirety. That Report dwells over and over again on the necessity of such control being exercised by Government. It is constantly calling upon Government to direct and regulate and harmonise the working of all the institutions founded by that private effort which it was the principal aim of the Commission to evoke.' And further on still he says, 'It is true that under very strict limitations the Commission advocated the withdrawal to a certain extent of Government from the supply of the means of higher education; but never from its

efficient control'. These words are sufficient to indicate the real position of the Commission and to make it perfectly plain that nothing was further from its thought than a withdrawal of Government from the control of the Indian educational system. Indeed, no one can read the Report of the Commission without realizing to the full how insistent was its demand for the steady and indeed the increased, exercise by the State of educational control. The fact is that there is a great difference between Control and Management, and this difference is constantly overlooked, with the result that serious and wholly unnecessary confusion is introduced into educational discussions.

34. *Cause of the Confusion.*—It is difficult to see how such confusion arises. The State is one body, but in regard to education it exercises two functions, those of control and management. Because the State is one, these two are not one. Yet to keep them apart makes a constant demand on thought. When we are dealing with what the State is doing in the field of education we have always to be asking ourselves from what point of view we are regarding the State. Is it the State as the controller of the system? Or is it the State as manager of certain institutions within that system? It cannot be too often repeated that these two are not one. Common usage, however, tends to make us forget this. In ordinary speech to 'manage' an affair is the same thing as to 'control' it. The fact that confusion so easily enters into this discussion serves only to emphasize the need for the most careful use of terms. And this is as necessary in official pronouncements as in non-official. Let us look at an official statement in addition to the non-official ones which we have considered.

35. *Illustration of the Confusion.*—The Government of India in what is called 'The Fourth Despatch on Indian Constitutional Reforms', issued in 1919, passes in review the recommendations of the Committee on Division of Functions, one of the Committees commonly spoken of as the Southborough Committee. The recommendations

were submitted to the Secretary of State for India, and were among the material taken into consideration by Parliament when it was engaged on the legislation connected with constitutional advance. Education had its place in the report of the Committee, and the Government of India devotes a number of pages to a discussion of the position taken up by the Committee. Into that discussion it is not necessary for us to enter. There are not a few who would have rejoiced to see Educational Ministers able to give their whole time to the development of primary education, as the Government of India desired. A more effective treatment of that fundamentally important branch of education would, I feel certain, have been the result, while the lack of policy which the last ten years have seen in connexion with higher education might have been avoided. But our present concern is not with the manner in which the Government of India's advice was treated. That is to be reckoned among the things that are past, save in so far as the disregard of it extends a warning to which administrators would do well to take heed. Our concern is with a smaller matter, one which is illustrated by the following sentences taken from paragraph 107 of the Fourth Despatch. They are as follows: 'We could supplement them (the practical considerations mentioned in preceding paragraphs) by many concrete instances of the unhappy consequences of entrusting higher education too confidently to private enterprise. We have seen what has happened already in provinces where high school and collegiate education has been allowed to pass largely into non-official control. The worst developments of such a system are described in the Bengal District Administration and the Rowlatt Reports. We have recently watched the deterioration of a fine private college in Northern India under political influence.' And in the following paragraph, where the educational policy of the past is commented on, and where the Government refers to the action of its predecessors, it says: 'In particular they (our predecessors) were content to let higher education pass more and more under non-official control. For the course which they took we do not doubt that they had reasons which seemed to them good, and we have no desire now to allocate blame. We admit the errors of the past and we ask for time to repair them; and their reparation is perhaps the most urgent task before us, if constitutional changes are to bring to India the happiness for which we hope'.

36. *Results of the Confusion.*—It will be noted that in the statement of its views the Government of India, which could hardly have expressed more sympathetically its desire for the advance of education, draws attention to the evils which have resulted from what it calls the system of allowing higher education to pass largely into 'non-official control'. And to support its point it adduces instances of what prove to be unsatisfactory non-official management. It is an unfortunate confusion, for it robs the argument of its point. What the Government of India is arguing against is not really non-official control but non-official management over which the control of the State is not effectively exercised. And in that argument it will carry all who are interested in education along with it. But if there is a non-official management which is not properly controlled then the question arises, and it is a question which here the Government of India does not deal with: Who is to blame for this situation? Clearly the authority with which the responsibility for control rests. The management took its place in the educational system of the country only when the State as controller placed upon it the hall-mark of its recognition; and in taking that place it unequivocally admitted the right of the State to control. If the State has failed to exercise that control, and the whole argument of the Government of India is based upon the position that in this respect failure has occurred, then the error lies not in the passing of higher education under non-official management but in the State allowing that management to operate

without at the same time calling into effective operation those powers of control with which it, as the controller of the whole system is invested. That is certainly one of the serious errors of the past, and one too often repeated in the present. The pity is that its reparation is still delayed.

37. *No argument for State Management in Control.*—The distinction between management and control is essential to the very being and well-being of Indian education. An entirely wrong argument arises from failure to maintain it. And worse than that, a wholly unsound policy is based upon it. The Government of India desired the elimination of all bad managements in education. Before and since the Fourth Despatch the same desire, it need hardly be said, has found expression in the utterances of all who have the interests of India's education at heart. But how are bad managements to be withdrawn from the system? By that agency which put them there, the agency which has the responsibility for seeing that they are fit to be there, the agency whose duty it is to satisfy itself that they should be maintained there. That agency is the State. And if it has failed to discharge this duty of control to any considerable extent the remedy lies in a stricter attention to control. It does not lie in combining management with control. For by such a course both management and control suffer. The State is looked upon as a privileged manager, and as a controller who finds it difficult in such a position to escape the suspicion of partiality. This is disastrous. What is needed is not State management; the State has educated hundreds of capable managements. What is needed is State control, a control the beneficent influence of which is felt by every management and thus in every form of educational activity. The State requires to strip itself of a function which others are in position to discharge as well as it can, the function of management. It needs to clothe itself with the full powers of that function which it alone can discharge in its entirety, the function of control.

38. (3) *Model Management.*—But the advocates of Government's continuing to occupy the office of a manager are wont to support their position by invoking the third ground to which we have referred. It is asserted that, by acting as a manager, the State is able to supply the educational system with schools and colleges that are models. And in this way, it is claimed, the State is in a position to exercise control. The argument, if it is less spoken of than it was twenty or thirty years ago, still continues to be acted upon. So far as the actual control that can be exercised in this way is concerned, little comment is required. The control which the State can effect by means of management is obviously limited. It is limited because the number of institutions which it manages is both relatively and absolutely small; and because, quite apart from other considerations, any large increase of such institutions would make demands on the financial resources of the State that would soon sound the death-knell to further advance. Further, if it be said that a high educational standard is set by those institutions so that the influence of them is felt beyond the area in which they are located, then it must be replied that, for one thing, each case must be examined on its own merits before any such judgment can be passed with certainty, and for another thing, that it is futile for the State to set a high standard for other schools and colleges to follow unless it also sees to it that these schools and colleges are provided with means whereby that standard may be in them normally followed and regularly adopted. We might dwell on the second of these points at some length, but there is no need to anticipate what is stated so fully regarding this matter in the next chapter. And when we look at the first of these points we find that we come upon an assumption which invalidates both the procedure and the argument.

39. *The Implications of Model Management.*—The assumption which vitiates the plea for Model Schools, in all discussions of this matter, is that the State alone can

provide them. Such a position is an anachronism, and it has also the unfortunate effect of casting doubt upon the State's ability to control. It is an anachronism. For it treats the education of today as if it were identical with education as it existed say fifty years ago. And these fifty years have wrought striking changes both in the growth of educational institutions and in a clearer perception of the educational aims of the State. The perusal of Quinquennial Reviews and of Statements presented to Parliament is sufficient to make it abundantly plain that India possesses a large number of well-staffed and well-equipped schools and colleges under non-official management. These institutions exercise a wide influence, they educate numerous pupils, and they maintain high educational standards. In the increase of their number and the growth of their effectiveness there is provided the means and, as the records show, the only means, whereby there may be spread through the length and breadth of the country, and not simply in a few centres, without unnecessary delay, in a manner that will not unduly strain public resources, and in such fashion as will evoke the maximum of local and private benefaction, an education animated by true ideals, affecting all ranks, and leaving on those who receive it the stamp of character. In other words, what a study of facts as revealed in official pronouncements emphasizes in the plainest possible terms is the need, not for this particular school and for that particular college under State management being made a model, but for every institution of the system receiving such encouragement from the State that it may develop as speedily as possible into a model school or college. And when we examine closely what the precise meaning of this need is, we realize that it is a demand for State control and not for State management, a State control which the Indian educational system so greatly needs and for which it still waits. A State control is needed of such a nature that it will issue in school after school, college after college, attaining the status of a model institution. Control of that character can be the result only of continued effort, unembarrassed action, and definite policy. It is something far higher than simply undertaking the management of a particular school and supporting it from the ample resources that are at the disposal of the State. It is something far higher, and something more exacting. The pity is that the State has elected time and again, as it still elects, to take the less arduous and the less effective road. As controller it suffers the title 'model' to be applied only to a few institutions which it itself manages. And it not only refrains from conferring that distinction upon excellent institutions which are not under its management, but there is far too little sign that its chief concern is the steady increase of non-official schools and colleges that can be reckoned as effectively maintained models and credits to the system. So long as the State continues its present mode of working, the day for the coming of a model educational system to the lasting benefit of the community is being indefinitely postponed.

40. *Can State Management be Model Management?* —The assumption, then, that the State alone can establish model schools is groundless. But we must go further than that. The assumption that the State is in a position to establish schools that are models, or patterns which all ought to follow, is also groundless. To begin with, the State staffs its institutions with those who belong to an Educational Service. And those who are members of that Service must submit to its exigencies. They may be transferred from a teaching to an administrative post, and from that they may return to teaching at any time in the school year, or they may be called on to perform the work of an inspector. It would hardly be in accordance with ordinary usage to speak of a school run on such lines as a model school. Secondly, the State supplies all the resources that are required; what the school or college needs financially for its maintenance is provided out of the Government exchequer. Because of this feature State-managed institutions, far from

occupying the position of models, occupy the position of complete uniqueness. If a school under another form of management were to plead that in this respect it intended to follow a State-managed school since the Government had constantly asserted that such schools were models for its imitation, it would be speedily informed by means which there was no gainsaying, the means of finance, that in this most important respect the State-managed school was not to be taken as a pattern. And in the third place, from a State-managed school religious instruction is definitely excluded. And a school that is precluded from combining religious teaching with other parts of the education which it imparts cannot hope to be regarded as a model school in India. These three considerations, to name no others, suffice to show that a State-managed school may be a very good school, indeed an exceedingly good school, but that in more respects than one it cannot be regarded as a model school.

41. *No Argument for State Management from State Model Schools.*—Yet the use of the term 'model' still goes on. 'It is the declared policy of Government', says the Bombay Quinquennial Review, 'to maintain one full High School in each district to serve as a model'. 'With the exception of the provision made . . . in a limited number of model colleges and secondary schools', writes the Educational Commissioner in the Ninth Quinquennial Review, 'the expansion has continued to take place most largely through institutions under private management and under municipal and district boards'. How unfortunate is this use of the term will be seen in the following chapter where financial implications are discussed. And on educational grounds, as distinct from financial, the limitation of the application of the term 'model' to schools belonging to one particular form of management is as misleading as it is unfortunate. It fails to take into consideration the modern educational conditions of India, the broad needs of the whole system, and the essential duties of the State as the controller of education. It is a claim which, it is to be hoped, will

not be much longer in disappearing finally from educational reports, being recognized by the State as happily outdated.

42. *Inadequacy of Arguments in Favour of State Management.*—We have passed in review the arguments that have been urged in support of the continuance by Government of educational management. And we have seen their inadequacy. Government management has been urged on the grounds of historical continuity, control, and the work of a model. And each of these grounds proves on closer inspection to be a handicap rather than a support. To urge the State management of schools and colleges is to urge what places the State in an essentially false position. It is to advocate a departure from the historical continuity of educational policy. It is to introduce a confusion between management and control which works to the disadvantage of both. And it is to postpone indefinitely the day when either the country will be possessed of a large and increasing number of model managements, or when over the whole educational system there will be in operation a model control.

43. *Need for Concentration on Control.*—The present section has made it plain that State management of educational institutions not only fails to admit of practical justification but also involves Government in suspicions which prejudice its work as controller. And this is beyond question, even if it be admitted that the State has established and still maintains many schools and colleges which are exceedingly good in themselves, high in their standards, and valuable in their influence. That, it need hardly be said, will be admitted in the most unqualified fashion by all who have any acquaintance with Indian education, and most fully by those whose acquaintance with it is intimate and prolonged. But such things may be bought at too great a cost. And along with the admission must go the recognition of the fact that, to secure the adoption of high standards and to naturalise them in the system, there is a more excel-

lent way than that of the State establishing a few schools and colleges and making an appearance here and there as a manager supervised by itself. That excellent way is, as all the discussion in which we have been engaged has shown, the State's withdrawal from the function of management and its concentration on the function of control.

References

The Resolution of the Government of India on Educational Policy (1913), paragraph 20 gives the statement referred to in paragraph 25 above. See also *Eighth Quinquennial Review*, p. 37.

H. R. James, *Education and Statemanship in India.* For quotation see p. 136.

V. Chirol, *Indian Unrest.* The matter is dealt with in Chapter xvii.

W. Miller, *Unrest and Education in India.* The point is discussed on pp. 18-22.

Fourth Despatch on Indian Constitutional Reforms (Division of Functions), pp. 289-298 deal with education.

R. St. J. Parry, *Cambridge Essays on Adult Education.* Chapter iv deals with combination and refers to a section of the English Education Act (1918) where the combination of Local Authorities is provided for. A similar provision appeared in a draft Local Self-Government Bill considered in one of the Indian provinces.

IV. Possibility of a Twofold System of Management

44. *Transference of State-managed Institutions actually going on.*—But if withdrawal from management on the part of the State is thus plainly indicated as both advisable and necessary, the practical question remains: Are there ways by which the withdrawal may be effected? For an answer in part to this question we have only to turn to the record of what has been taking place in the course of the last few years. And when we do this we find that a process of transference of educational institutions from official to non-official management is not

merely contemplated but is actually at work. The transference is taking place at both ends of the educational ladder. Where unitary universities have been established, colleges formerly under government management have in certain instances passed out of departmental hands and have become integral parts of the universities. Then, analogous to what is taking place in connexion with higher education but on a much larger scale, is what is taking place in the field of elementary education. For there schools by the thousand have been, and are being, transferred from the management of the State to that of Local Bodies. When such a process of transference, now going on though hardly as yet pursued with steadiness, becomes extended and systematic, as part of a definite policy, we shall have received the real answer to our question.

(i) Suggested Means for Extended Transference

45. (i) *To University Managements: Satisfactory in Case of Unitary Universities.*—As to the manner of transference four suggestions have been made and these it is advisable to consider in some detail. The first suggestion is that Government should hand over its colleges to the universities in the areas of which they happen to be situated. In the case of unitary universities there is little or no difficulty. Thus 'the Muir College became the nucleus' of Allahabad University when it was reconstituted first as 'a teaching university, and then as a unitary, teaching, and residential university'. And what was formerly the Dacca College managed by Government has become the Dacca Hall, a place of residence, as the definition goes, 'provided or maintained by the university'. But the situation is not so easy where a local university is of the affiliating, not of the unitary, type. The suggestion which has been made in this case is that Government should transfer its college to the university with which it is affiliated so that it may be managed by the university. This suggestion has been

pressed, for example, by some in connexion with the Government colleges that exist in the Andhra University area. And, as the Calcutta University Commission Report shows, there were advocates of the position that Government should transfer to the University of Calcutta the Presidency College of Calcutta, to be wholly under its management. The Commissioners were unable to accept this proposal, and the reasons which they give for their decision have a general, and not merely a local, application. They call for attention.

46. *Unsuitable in Case of Affiliating Universities.*—'In the first place', say the Commissioners, 'being a university-controlled institution, the college would be placed in a wholly different position from the other arts colleges. It would not be to anything like the same extent as the other colleges a distinct corporation with a character of its own. The corporate life of the college might suffer from this, and in that case the life of the university of colleges would be impoverished. Secondly, in view of the special conditions existing in Calcutta, it would be apt to be regarded with jealousy by the other colleges, which would suspect, with or without reason, that it enjoyed preferential treatment at the hands of the university'. In considerations relating to the establishment of Indian universities the first of these reasons has hardly received the attention which is its due. It raises far too large an issue for us to enter upon here, and the natural place for reference to it is when the *Working of the Policy* comes to be dealt with. But those who promote legislation for universities do a real disservice to higher education if they fail to take account of the value which attaches to the individuality of a college. The second reason, however, is wholly apposite to our purpose. What it says in effect is this: To transfer a college from the management of Government to the management of an affiliating university is not to solve a problem but to continue it. For any authority, be it a government, a board, or a university, which controls a number of institutions and also manages one or more of them renders

the institutions which it both controls and manages liable to the suspicion of preferential treatment.

47. *Consideration of this Unsuitability.*—Let us look at this a little more closely. When the Commission speaks of the 'special conditions existing in Calcutta' it has in mind, as the context shows, not merely conditions which are peculiar to a university existing in the town of Calcutta, but those which are to be found in connexion with a university of the affiliating type. Let us suppose that a university of this type has thirty affiliated arts colleges, and that it takes over the management of say three of these, leaving the others under their existing, that is non-university, management. No prophet needs to be called in to tell what the result will be. Three colleges out of the thirty are under the immediate and intimate care of the university, twenty-seven have no such close relationship. The university which can exercise its powers to real advantage only when it exercises a strictly impartial control over every one of the colleges that compose it, is bound by the transfer which we have supposed to be effected to bestow upon one-tenth of its colleges, in virtue of its managership, a thought and attention which it is under no obligation to bestow on the remaining nine-tenths. Indeed, if it is to be a good manager, it must act in this way. That is to say, from the moment that the university assumes managership in addition to control it is committed to a course which lays it open to the imputation of bestowing on certain of its colleges a treatment which it does not accord to others. And unfortunately, as the history of Indian education in the past has shown, the imputation of preferential treatment attaching to the controller who is also joint-manager is not wholly baseless. The suggestion then that government colleges should be transferred to the universities of an affiliating constitution is one which, in the interests of the universities, must be ruled out of court. If university education is to flourish, universities must either be controllers and managers of the whole, as in the case of unitary universities, or they

must be controllers alone and not managers as in the case of universities composed of constituent or affiliated colleges.

48. (2) *Transfer to Controlling Board with Managerial Functions: Difficulties involved.*—A second suggestion is found in the Report of the Calcutta University Commission. It is to the effect that Government should hand over the management of certain of its schools and colleges to a Controlling Board. After reading the arguments which the Commission employed to dispose of the suggestion that Government should hand over the Presidency College to the management of an affiliating university, we are hardly prepared for the suggestion which it itself proceeds to make when it urges the establishment of a specially constituted Board to deal with Intermediate and Secondary Education. That Board, it proposes, should be entrusted with the duties of recognizing certain schools and colleges, of planning their courses of instruction, of conducting examinations, and of disbursing certain moneys. And in addition to this the Commission recommends that the Board should 'manage the Government institutions for intermediate training', and should have 'full responsibility for the administration of all Government high English schools, and for determining the conditions upon which grants-in-aid should be given to high schools under non-Government management'. That is to say, the Board to be called into being is to control all the intermediate colleges and high schools under its jurisdiction, and also to manage certain of them. There are arguments in favour of this suggestion and the Commission states them. But against them is to be placed the consideration which the Commission has itself stated when it refused to countenance the handing over of a Government college to the management of a non-unitary university. In the case now before us a Board, not a university, becomes controller of a number of institutions and manager only of some. One result of the arrangement would inevitably be that the impartiality of the controller would be in doubt from the very first.

The suggestion would not solve a problem; it would introduce an old problem in a new setting.

49. (3) *Transfer to Local Bodies: Conditions on which this is possible.*—A third suggestion appears in the realm of primary education. It is that the management of Government primary schools should be entrusted to Local Bodies. This suggestion is one which is being largely acted upon, and subject to two provisos is thoroughly sound. The first is that the Body must be in a position to accept and discharge the trust thus assigned to it. Should a Local Body be unable to raise the funds required, or should its educational efforts be lacking in convincingness, then there is good reason why caution should be observed before educational management is entrusted to it. Automatic transfer to Local Bodies, or to any body, is never a safe proceeding, especially where the interests of youth are at stake. Scrutiny is always necessary. The other proviso is that Local Bodies should not, in present circumstances, discharge the dual function of controller and manager. If this is not observed the spread of education among the masses of the people is prejudiced from the start. If Boards are to be managers and controllers combined then let them occupy that position in regard to the whole range of primary education, and let every other form of management at that stage cease to function. That is a procedure which it may be possible for India to adopt as it has been adopted elsewhere. But since very much has to be done before this is even feasible in India, let the circumstances of the present receive their full acknowledgment, and let the Boards be by all means managers of every primary school which Government can transfer to them and which they can satisfactorily maintain. But let this transfer in no wise interfere with other managers playing their indispensable part, or with other authorities being constituted on which the State can devolve its responsibility for control.

50. (4) *Transfer to Private Bodies: Conditions on which this is possible.*—The fourth suggestion is that

departmental institutions may be entrusted to private agencies. This also is a sound suggestion subject to the same two provisos. The ability in general to accept and discharge such a trust is evident from what has been stated in the preceding section regarding the resources which this agency can command and the confidence which its educational service evokes. But each case requires scrutiny. Can the management proposed maintain work which is abiding and not ephemeral? Is it financially stable? Is it prepared not only to submit to inspection but to carry out what, on the basis of that inspection, is demanded? These and all such matters have to be placed beyond a doubt before a management can receive a further trust. But private managements which can be depended on, and which have no hankerings after control, afford an obvious means by which the State may obtain relief from its managerial functions.

51. *The Means Available for Transfer to Non-departmental Management.*—Our examination of these four suggestions has shown us two things. First, that if Government is to hand over its schools and colleges to any other agency it must be in such a way that the anomaly which has hitherto marked the administration of Indian education may not simply re-appear in a new milieu. And secondly, that Government can prevent any such result by the transfer of institutions at present managed by itself either to suitably constituted Local Bodies or to some form of approved Private Agency. We must now look in detail at those two means whereby Government while maintaining and indeed strengthening its control may divest itself of the entanglements of management.

(ii) *Detailed Examination of Means Available for Transfer*

52. (1) *Elementary Education: Transfer admits of immediate Realization.*—We may begin with Elementary Education. It is a sphere where local self-govern-

ment has a claim to increased and trusted activity, and every year sees an enhancement of its service. A larger view than has hitherto prevailed will secure that these bodies will be dissociated both from an inappropriate constitution and from a prejudicial combination of control with management. They will then be in a position to take their fitting place in the educational system of the country and to assume steadily increasing responsibilities for elementary education. Alongside of Municipalities, District Boards, and Panchayats, there exist a large number of Private Agencies which share with Local Bodies the burden of elementary education. With generous encouragement at the hand of the State they can be counted on to carry still heavier burdens. At the stage of mass education, then, there is no reason why the State should continue to manage a school for one day longer. There are two agencies which at present impart elementary education to millions of boys and girls. They are capable of extending their service, and of so adapting it that they will be able to supply communities which have their own special needs with the forms of education that would be most welcome. Either of these agencies could undertake in the course of a few months the management of the 3,000 schools which the State still manages. And that would be all the more easy as a third of the number is to be found in a province which has no lack of suitable agencies, both local and private. Let good control be forthcoming, and there need not be in the budget of any province in British India provision for the expenditure of a single rupee under the heading of State-managed elementary schools.

53. (2) *Middle School Education: Transfer can be speedily effected.*—So far as Middle English Schools are concerned the number of them under State-management is only 124. No argument seems called for to prove that these few schools might be transferred without delay and without hurt to Local Agencies which manage more than three times that number, or to Private Agencies which manage twenty times as many. One

objection to transfer has been urged on the ground that some of these schools are connected with Training Classes for Teachers. The ground of this objection is dealt with in paragraph 56, where it will be seen that the facts show it to be devoid of force. The plain fact is, and it cannot be too quickly grasped, that so far as the transfer, indeed the speedy transfer, of these schools goes, *nihil obstat*. From all that is classified in official tables as 'Primary' and 'Middle' school education, and that means 198,000 out of the total of 211,000 institutions in the whole system, State management might disappear in the course of a few months, with this great difference that the State would be a better controller.

54. (3) *High School Education: A National or a Departmental Policy?*—As regards High Schools the State is still at work in an area where it acknowledges the appropriateness of private management. Indeed, so far as figures show, it is extending its labours at the rate of some ten schools per annum. Action such as this takes little account of present day conditions, educational, social, religious, and national. It has been upheld by various arguments, but these, as we have already seen, are not sufficient for the strain that is put upon them. Such schools are not so much models as monuments of a policy outdated whose day is done. That policy consists in following the departmental or official method. A school is established by the State, manned by State officials, financed by State funds. And what does it do? It shows what an official school can effect, what can be done by a staff which has to submit to the exigencies of a large educational service, what would be possible in the way of buildings, size of class, and salaries of teachers, if other managers possessed the same resources as the State can levy from the tax-payer, and how a school may be conducted from which religious education is excluded. It also shows how very few of these schools can be maintained because of their expense, and thus how backward would be the state of education if the citizen had to rely solely, or even principally,

upon Government for the education of his children. Now a policy which shows all this is clearly out of date. What the present day requires is not the departmental, but the democratic or national, policy. According to it the State sets itself definitely to perform two educational services. For one thing, it encourages every stable management to maintain schools and so to increase the facilities available for pupils; and for another thing, it provides a real control, so supplied with the means of imparting advice, experience, and guidance that the standard of education rises with the increase of facilities. It is in the adoption of this policy that hope for the spread of sound education lies. And the more speedily it is substituted for the departmental policy the better for the country.

55. *Transfer of High Schools possible in a short Period.*—This substitution, in the case of what we are now concerned with, High Schools, could be carried through safely and satisfactorily in a couple of years. The Government has only to hand over 250 schools to managements which it recognizes as already capable of maintaining nine times that number, managements which are constantly assuming fresh responsibilities. Within the last quinquennium Local Bodies have undertaken the management of 69 additional High Schools, and Private Managements have become responsible for 319 more. Local resources are capable of expansion, and private agencies are adding to the number of the country's High Schools at the rate of over 60 per annum with all that that involves of increasing financial provision. The capacity of the two agencies thus needs no proving; far from being exhausted it is on the increase. One of the agencies alone has in five years added more high schools to the educational system than the State itself manages. With encouragement from the State, an encouragement which they have every reason to expect, they can shoulder the responsibilities for management in this sphere that now rest on the State. Will the State give them the opportunity to do this? Then why delay? Or will

it not? Then, by such distrust of those who through the working of the educational system have become qualified for the discharge of the manager's duties, could it take any more effective means of showing how little it believes in the trustworthiness of that educational service which it has itself played so large a part in rearing? To put it in another way, either the non-official managements, local and private, are able to make a small addition to their present responsibilities, in which case delay in transfer is without excuse; or they are incapable, in which case State control finds itself on its trial. Transference of management, well conceived and steadily pursued, affords the State the surest way of proving that it is a wise master builder.

56. (4) *Training Facilities: Possibility of speedy Transfer.*—There remains to be considered a matter bound up with secondary education to which reference was made in paragraph 53. It is this. A number of Training Schools are connected with, and a number of Training Classes are attached to, Middle Schools and High Schools. Thus the transfer of secondary schools to non-official management would involve the transfer of these professional facilities as well. Is there any difficulty about this? Investigation shows that there is not. Local Bodies and Private Agencies are capable of maintaining schools and classes for the training of teachers. Out of the 1,100 of such schools and classes now actively at work, more than 600 are managed by them. A comprehensive scheme would transfer to them the 500 that are managed by the State in a way which would combine these agencies in a valuable service, which would liberate a considerable amount of provincial funds for the development of this service, and which would enrich it by the counsel of an increased, highly qualified, and sympathetic control. Such a scheme is as practicable as it is desirable. It would give a great stimulus to training and would replace present conditions, many of which are wasteful and unsatisfactory, with the steady advantages of a truly national system of training. It is

capable of attainment within a period not exceeding three years. In Chapter v an outline of such a scheme is given, the means for its achievement is described, and the benefits following from it are detailed. At this point we must be content to note its feasibility. And as soon as we have done that we realize the importance of the position at which we have arrived. For now, as the outcome of the considerations given in paragraphs 44 to 56, we see that there lies within the grasp of the State the means by which it may transfer to other agencies promptly, easily, and effectively, all the schools which it manages through the whole range of primary and secondary education.

57. (5) *Collegiate Education: Intermediate Colleges and Private Managements.*—When we turn to collegiate education the position is naturally more complicated. There have been built up by Government, colleges of university standing which are so valuable that their deterioration, not to speak of their disappearance, would be a national loss. But there is no reason why they should be lost to the country if they pass into other than official management, nor is there any reason why they should suffer deterioration if the process of transfer is attended with those safeguards which the circumstances demand. There is only one way in which the matter can be satisfactorily dealt with, and that is by facing the facts. Now the first and most obvious fact is that all the State-managed arts and science colleges, sixty in number, are not of the same grade. There are 26, or a little less than the half, of them which fall to be classified as Intermediate or Second-Grade. It might be said, subject to certain qualifications, that the Intermediate colleges have their affinity with the High School rather than with the University; and in two provinces there are colleges of this grade which do not come under university control. But be that as it may, the fact remains that Intermediate colleges are for the most part small, their courses do not extend over a wide range, and they do not present their

students for a degree. Is there any agency qualified to undertake the management of the 26 colleges of this standing which are at present managed by Government? Now seventy per cent of the total number of Intermediate Colleges in British India are in the hands of Private Managements. Some of these have been recipients of well-merited criticisms, and in their case it is really a question as to how long they ought to receive the recognition now accorded to them. But there are others of a totally different kind, managements that are well fitted by experience, tradition, ideals, and stability to perform a larger service than they now render, managements which a wise controller would definitely encourage to shoulder greater responsibilities, because of the benefit which would thereby accrue to education and the advantage that would come to the country. An addition of 26 colleges, assuming that all the 26 Government colleges were able to stand the critical tests applied to them, would not be too heavy a burden to place upon an agency that already manages 66. And financial conditions would not create any obstacle to transfer; indeed the State would be able to give the managements that became responsible for these colleges greatly enhanced grants without making any greater draft on public funds than is done at present. The expenditure might conceivably be less, for there is the contribution of the private manager to be taken into account, an item which has no place in the budgets of colleges under State management. Even, then, if there were no other agency than that which represents private effort there is available in it, as it now exists, a means by which the State might withdraw from the management of its Intermediate Colleges with certainty that the best interests of education would be conserved and that public finance would not suffer.

58. *Participation of Local Bodies.*—But Private Agency does not stand alone. Local Board management does function in this sphere even though its actual contribution is confined to a single college. The spirit

which underlies local self-government is too valuable to be lost to higher study, and the help which it is capable of giving to collegiate education demands well thought-out and steadily extended encouragement. There is one way, for instance, in which Local Bodies might make this greater contribution and in doing so might surmount the difficulties to which their present constitution subjects them. A number of municipalities and local authorities in a district might resolve to combine in establishing and maintaining a college that would serve the district; and they might, in accordance with statutory provision, constitute a committee to manage this college. That committee might have powers of co-option so that a few who had practical acquaintance with education and were resident in the district though they were not members of the Local Bodies might be invited to join it; and there might also be on it an *ex-officio* member so that the Educational Department might place at the disposal of the committee the benefit of its experience. Some such powers are not unknown in other circumstances, and the employment of them would secure a management which was the expression of the spirit of local self-government and which at the same time inspired confidence by the nature of its constitution. It would be an *ad hoc* body dealing only with the interests of the college for which it was responsible. It would have behind it a local patriotism that was not parochial but the outcome of combined activity over the area of a district. And it would have at its disposal a stable revenue, for the combining bodies would make their contributions from their local incomes raised in accordance with their statutory powers and allocated in accordance with a mutually accepted scheme. By such a method as this, and it would not be difficult either to devise it or to bring it into effect, the participation of local bodies in collegiate education might be beneficially extended. And thus with local bodies fitted for fresh responsibilities and private bodies rising to fresh opportunities, Government would be in a position to withdraw from the management of its Intermediate

Colleges and to place the whole of them in trustworthy non-official hands. And the transfer might be completed without difficulty in less than a quinquennium.

59. (6) *Collegiate Education: Possible Modes of Transfer.*—There remain for our consideration the 34 Government Colleges which prepare their students for degrees in arts and science. Some of these are known throughout India, and their staff, equipment, and buildings give to those who attend them the fullest advantage of collegiate life and learning. Obviously the transfer of these to another management can be no easy matter and one can readily see how there has been hesitation concerning it in the past, a hesitation which has sometimes amounted to an assertion of impossibility. But those who dwell on the obstacles give too scanty heed to the vitality which pervades India, to the administrative power with which experience has endowed her sons, and to the solid benefits which education has conferred on her sons and daughters alike. True, transfer can succeed only if it proceed with caution, but it can succeed. The door of success is open to it. Indeed there are at least four doors through which success may come. To begin with, private agencies manage at the present time more than a hundred degree colleges, and not a few of them have attained an academic standing that commands confidence and respect over considerable stretches of the land. To believe that agencies which have done so much are capable of doing more is not to give rein to imagination; it is only to state in words that to which figures in the various reports bear witness year after year. As it is, private agency adds to the number of colleges which it maintains on an average ten a year. It is an agency which can be relied on, which yearly adds to its responsibilities, and which is confirmed in this advance by the recognition which the State accords. To commit to it certain of the 34 colleges which Government manages would be no more than to recognize the capacity that steadily grows and strengthens its resources. Then, in the second place, as there is one degree college under

Board management, we may express the hope that the combination of Local Bodies to which we referred in the preceding paragraph may afford the means by which additional activity may be undertaken by the representatives of local effort. They may see their way to enter on fresh commitments, and in favourable circumstances there is no reason why they should not establish degree colleges that would serve a whole district. Properly organized local effort is bound sooner or later to issue in some such result as this. And well would it be for the country if the State rendered all the help in its power to hasten this development. Further, there is now in operation, as we have already noted, another method of transfer, that of the incorporation of colleges in unitary universities. And though, for the time being, there is a slackening in the establishment of that type of university, it is hard to believe that the stoppage is more than temporary. Such universities have a distinct part to play in the national life, and time, bringing as it is bound to do an increase of benefactions, will tell strongly in their favour. And thus there will be provided in increasing measure a third means whereby the State may be enabled to withdraw from the management of degree colleges. There remains to be mentioned a fourth method. It is that which is suggested by the Calcutta University Commission when it makes recommendations regarding the Presidency College in Calcutta. The Commission proposes 'that Government should cease to exercise the special and detailed control over the affairs of Presidency College which it has hitherto exercised; that the property of the college should be vested in trustees to be appointed by Government; that a fixed annual block grant should be allotted to the college, sufficient to meet the expense of maintenance and repairs, as well as the cost of salaries, pensions, etc. of such staff as may be judged necessary to maintain the educational and administrative efficiency on at least the present standard; and that a governing body, to be appointed in the main by Government, but to include one or more representatives of the University and at least two elected representatives of the teachers of the college in addition to the principal, should be established, with power to administer the revenues arising from Government grants, fees, endowments and other sources, to receive gifts, to create and award scholarships and in general to direct the policy of the college'. Such a method as is here proposed would, if adopted, give to the most highly equipped Government college in the country a management capable of directing its affairs with discretion, ability, and pride in the trust committed to it. And there is every reason why it should be adopted, for such Boards would have no difficulty in securing the services of some of the ablest and most influential men and women in the land. It is a matter for surprise that such an excellent means for rallying to the service of higher education those whose words carry weight and whose powers of administration receive widespread recognition should have been left so long untried. It is hard to think of a means which would more effectively safeguard academic interests and establish the colleges in the hearts of the people.

60. *Employment of Available Means of Transfer.*—When in paragraph 57 we began to consider the possibility of transferring to other managements the intermediate and degree Colleges which are at present managed by Government, we admitted at once that the matter was attended with serious difficulties. But as we have faced the facts we have been made to realize that these difficulties are far from insuperable. There are no less than four methods by which the transfer can be effected—private agencies, unitary universities, reconstituted local bodies, and specially created boards of trustees. Two of these are immediately available; the other two might be called into operation in the course of a few months. Before a definite policy, clearly enunciated and steadily adhered to, the greatest difficulties are found to yield. The means for transfer are as accessible as the call for their employment is pressing.

And transfer, it need hardly be said, is much more than a mere change in the name of the manager. It means that along with the transfer goes the support and care of the State, ensuring that in the discharge of its new task the sympathy and encouragement of the State are with the new management. And that support will be all the surer in the case of a State which is relieved of so much that now leads to the diffusion of its energies. With the inauguration of such a policy of transfer there will be brought into the whole realm of general education a comprehensive scheme of devolution that will leave its mark for good on every school and college in the country. For through the various means available it will operate, now in this way, now in that, in such a manner that fitting standards of educational life and work will be maintained throughout the system, that the two forms of management employed will gain in capacity for the effective discharge of the responsibilities entrusted to them, and that the State undistracted by management will place at the service of education a guidance and direction in the vigour and support of which every part will share.

61. (7) *Collegiate Education: Professional Colleges and their Transfer.*—The detailed consideration which has been given to the possibility of transferring to other managements Government colleges of general education is sufficient reason for dealing briefly with transfer as it affects Government professional colleges. The means for transfer are the same in the one case as in the other, and no more need be said regarding them here. But there are three facts which claim our attention, and on each of which much could be said if our concern at this point were not solely that of management. We can but note each and indicate its bearing on the matter with which we are dealing. First, then, though in the Statistical Tables, Colleges of Education must in strictness have their place among Professional Colleges, they are so intimately bound up with general education and are so essential to it, that transfer in the one field

implies transfer in the other. And that is what we may expect to find recognized more and more as time goes on. The second fact is what we have already noted in paragraph 21, that, while the realm of higher professional education was for long regarded as one in which Government was practically the only agency at work, recent years have witnessed a great change in this respect, a change which shows how the current is flowing. The local and private manager are now regularly represented in this field, and their work is growing. The third fact is this. There are forms of professional education which over the whole country none but Government supplies. And there are forms of it in some of the individual provinces which come entirely from the same source. Thus throughout British India the facilities for Forestry and Veterinary Science are provided solely by the State; and in, for example, the province of Madras, it is Government and it alone which is responsible for the higher training in the two branches already mentioned and also in Law, Medicine, Engineering, and Agriculture. That is to say, there are cases where Government the controller is also the sole manager. This does not affect the principle that transfer is advisable, for while Government may be the sole manager of a branch of professional education this year it may be one among other managers next year. But while it does not affect the principle of transfer it does affect the urgency of transfer in particular cases. Delay in giving effect to the principle in certain parts of the field of professional education does not necessarily carry with it the same unsatisfactory results as does delay in the field of general education. In the latter the speedy operation of the principle is the demand of definite and important educational considerations; in the former there is not at present, though we never know when there may be, a race between time and the need for the operation of the principle. Briefly then, what these facts emphasise is that the means for transferring to non-departmental managements Government professional colleges are numerous even at present, that they are steadily increasing, and that a carefully planned policy will employ them each at the fitting opportunity, and all to the fullest advantage of the educational system.

62. *Nature of 'Mission' Management.*—Before leaving this subject there is one point which deserves attention, for it indicates a change of orientation that has come about in the course of the last fifty years. The Indian Education Commission devotes a considerable portion of its Eighth Chapter to matters connected with the transfer of Government institutions to non-official agencies. And in regard to one of these it voices a conclusion in which all its members shared and to which it gives the following expression: 'We think it well to put on record our unanimous opinion that departmental institutions of the higher order should not be transferred to missionary management'. Reasons are given for this position, and one of them is so important and so apposite to our present consideration that it must be quoted. It runs thus: 'Missionary institutions hold an intermediate position between those managed by the Department and those managed by the people for themselves. On the one hand, they are the outcome of private effort, but on the other they are not strictly local; nor will encouragement to them directly foster those habits of self-reliance and combination for purposes of public utility which it is one of the objects of the grant-in-aid system to develop'. The missionary institutions here referred to are those under Christian management, and at the time when the report was written they were in very large measure maintained by grants from churches and missionary societies in Europe and America, and by the representatives of these bodies their policy was directed. At the present time there are, to give only the figures that relate to higher education, 55 colleges and 346 high schools under Christian mission management. But one important point requires to be noted. There is a steady tendency on the part of missions to devolve on the Indian Church the work for which they have hitherto

been responsible. The past half century has seen the growth of a policy which has already handed over institutions to the Church, and which seeks to effect further transfers according to the ability of the Church to receive them. As the management of institutions passes from that of the Foreign Mission to that of the Indian Church the ground on which the Education Commission based the recommendation which we have mentioned will be found to have lost its force. The institutions classed as missionary have in some degree already become, and in the course of time will more and more become, institutions 'that are strictly local', the encouragement of which will 'directly foster habits of self-reliance and combination for purposes of public utility'. Indigenous management will essentially alter the position of what have hitherto been spoken of as 'mission' schools and colleges, and the embargo justifiably placed upon them fifty years ago in respect of the transfer to them of departmental institutions will be, in the changed conditions, as justifiably removed.

63. *State-managed Institutions and a Policy of Transfer.*—This Section of our discussion has shown, as the result of detailed examination, that the appropriate means by which the State may divest itself of the management of educational institutions in favour of non-departmental managements are ready to hand and simply await utilization. Some of them have been already employed; others require time for their satisfactory functioning. Even so, the time required is in some cases a matter of only a few months, and in the most difficult cases need hardly exceed a quinquennium. The rapid developments of the past twenty years have brought appreciably nearer, the realization of what was indicated and hoped for eighty years ago. For its complete realization there is needed not the means, for they are available, but steady action in accordance with a policy that applies to all levels of education, that proceeds by stages, and that is to be carried through within a prescribed period. It is difficult to believe, after a review

of the facts which we have considered, that the launching of such a policy can be much longer delayed.

References

Calcutta University Commission Report, Volume iv. See Chapter xxxi, pp. 45-49 with reference to the proposed Intermediate Board; and Chapter xxxiv, pp. 316-319 with reference to the Presidency College.

Indian Education Commission Report, Chapter viii, Section 10, paragraphs 516-544 deal with the transfer of colleges.

V. Benefits of a Twofold System of Management

64. *How is a Twofold System of Management beneficial?*—The present discussion has been an endeavour to answer the question with which we began in Section I: Is it advisable that the threefold form of management that obtains in Indian education should be continued? The facts, to the statement of which Section II is devoted, brought us to the conclusion that there is much to be said for a twofold system of management. This conclusion we found to be strengthened as a survey of facts detailed in Section III showed that the situation would be fully met if reliance for management was placed entirely on Local Bodies and Private Agencies under the *aegis* of State control. But do the means for such a change exist? The reply of Section IV, again based on facts, is that they do, and that the only thing needed is that they should be called into use by the inauguration of a comprehensive policy. And now a final question arises: Will the education of the country benefit by the adoption of this twofold system? As we seek to answer this question, there emerge five principal gains accruing to education from reliance upon two non-official forms of management. In this closing Section we shall enumerate and examine these gains.

65. (1) *It will benefit Control.*—In the first place, Control will benefit. The suspicion which at present

attaches to the State in virtue of its cares for the education of its people, can read, without the slightest difficulty, the signs of the times. If the State does not recognize these signs it need not be surprised if its power to control is called in question. But there is no reason why this should happen. The State has the facts clearly before it, and the remedy is quite as clear. The restriction of management to the two forms of management indicated in the preceding Sections brings to education the invaluable gain of having for its direction a controlling agency that commands general confidence. And further it brings to it the gain of a controlling agency that really controls.

66. (2) *It will benefit Management.*—In the second place, Management will gain. The country will then have as the means through which its educational facilities are provided two individual but complementary forms of management. The one form of management will enable the residents of a locality to adopt that form of education which satisfies them as a whole; the other, while attending to larger concerns, makes it possible for sectional interests not to be overlooked. The one may find a difficulty not so much in giving religious education as in making it an integral part of its curriculum; the other will be hampered by no such obstacle. The one will depend for its resources on corporate taxation; the other on personal or combined generosity. The one will have behind it the benefit of local organization; the other will have the stimulus of individual initiative. The one will rely on the representatives of the people under a system of local self-government; the other on friends of the people who find their satisfaction in spreading the benefits of education. The one will provide the tradition which accompanies constitutional growth; the other will infuse into the system a growth which has its roots in soil imported as well as indigenous. Thus from this twofold and supplementary mode of management the educational system of the country will be maintained in continuity, elasticity, and comprehension. And there

will be even more than that. For the State will be free from all that is implied in attending to the demands of a teaching service, and of spending its energies on institutions which it itself has to maintain. It will thus be in a position to lay down with greater definiteness than has yet been done what is required of a management, what its responsibilities are, what recognition involves. What is needed in its anomalous position as a manager as well as the controller, and which tends to prejudice its position as the controller, will disappear with its withdrawal from management. And the State in its own interests and in the interests of education stands in need of this consummation. The situation involves finance and its allocation, but is far from being a purely financial one. The next Chapter will show some of the financial facts bearing on the position. But there are other facts which might be adduced to show how unfortunate is the participation of the State in management. For instance, in one province Selection Committees were set up to guide the principals of Government Colleges in the matter of admitting students. The object of the committees was to secure that the various communities were satisfactorily represented among the students attending colleges maintained by the State. Objection was taken to this on the ground that admissions to State colleges were being regulated by considerations which were not of an educational character. The reply to this is that the Government is manager of its own colleges, and managers may adopt any rules they please for the admission of their students provided they infringe no rule laid down by the university. But Government is more than a manager, it is the controller of the educational system of the land. Thus it may conceivably happen that the rules which Government lays down as manager may react prejudicially upon its position as controller. And there can be no doubt that, in this particular matter. the position of Government was distinctly prejudiced in the eyes of not a few whose opinion carried weight. From the possibility of such a prejudice, with the doubt which is thereby inevitably cast upon its capacity to exercise control, the State must be free. And there is only one way by which it can obtain this freedom. Then, to take another instance, the Government colleges of a province had to be closed for some time because of political agitation directed against Government. The colleges were good educational institutions, and not a word of criticism was passed on them corporately or on members of their staffs. They were doing a real service to the youth of the area, but they were looked upon as witnesses to an official position which those in the area resented, and the colleges had for the time being to withdraw from activity. This interaction indicates that restriction of management as previously indicated is a requirement of the times. Further it will be able to do what has been for too long delayed, to undertake the systematic overhaul of both forms of management, to devise means by which they may be put on a satisfactory footing, and to give them that help which will strengthen the constitution of each and raise the educational standards of both. Thus the introduction of the twofold system of management will evoke wider interest in education, will lead to greater concentration of educational effort, and will assure higher levels of educational attainment.

67. (3) *It will benefit educational Organization.*—In the third place, educational organization will benefit. Teachers will no longer be classified on these service bases which have done so much to delay the unification of the teaching profession. The profession will now become the basis, and a combined organization will be achieved. Thus teachers will gain because as a united body, they will be able to give expression to educational opinion; managements will gain because they will have a large and properly qualified body from which to make their appointments; and pupils will gain because those who teach will be no longer at the mercy of a service but will be men and women entrusted with their work simply because of their fitness for it, and because they

can give themselves wholly to it. Education will come to its own, and so will the educator.

68. (4) *It will benefit Finance.*—In the fourth place, the financing of education will benefit. The closer co-operation of public and private effort will tend to economy. Partiality in the allotment of grants and subsidies will have no chance to live, exposed as it will be to the scrutiny of people and Government alike. With that better control which will now be possible, overlapping will be discouraged and combination will be insisted on, to the great improvement of finance. Salaries, pensions, provident funds, and expenditure on buildings will come under the sweep of rules applicable to large areas; and the actual educational service performed will be regarded as a factor largely determining the manner in which public funds are to be disbursed. Money will go further, and the taxpayer will have good reason to feel that his contribution is being well spent.

69. (5) *It will benefit the Educational System.*—In the fifth place, the educational system will benefit. By the combination of two complementary forms of management it will be moulded into a coherent whole. At present, the moment an important decision has to be taken or line of action has to be followed, there comes in to upset almost every calculation the wholly non-educational division of the system into the departmental and the non-departmental. And so education is hampered, and to a much greater extent than is commonly admitted. But that distracting and weakening cleavage will disappear when the State applies itself deliberately and steadily to the welding together of the contribution made by the two forms of management, local and private, under a thoughtful, tactful, discriminating, sympathetic, and fully informed form of control. Thus will two vigorous streams of educational activity, each with its individual characteristics, pour the fulness of their power into the wide river of a unified, vital, beneficent, and national system of education for India.

70. *The Solution of the Problem.*—The problem

which we have been considering is capable of solution. And the solution which we have reached, that of a two-fold system of non-official management effectively controlled by the State, is one which promises enormous educational benefits to the country, and along with them substantial administrative and financial gains. When the State, finding in the present the means of fulfilling the anticipations of the past, sets itself definitely to incorporate that solution in its educational policy, the policy which it not merely announces but which it unflinchingly pursues, then these benefits and gains will prove to be more than promised. They will be realized.

References

Calcutta University Commission Report, Volume iv. See Chapter xxxi, pp. 45-49 with reference to the proposed Intermediate Board; and Chapter xxxiv, pp. 316-319 with reference to the Presidency College.

Indian Education Commission Report. Chapter viii, section 10, paragraphs 516-44 deal with the transfer of colleges.

CHAPTER III

The Problem of Finance

I. The Problem: How Shall the Educational System best be Financed?

1. The questions which arise regarding the financing of education are legion. The main problem which confronts the country and for which some solution must be found is: How shall the educational system best be financed so that good education may be spread as widely and as speedily and with as little waste as possible throughout the land? A thoroughly effective national system is what is required. How is the money to be got to establish it?

II. The Financing of Elementary Education

2. *How is Elementary Education to be satisfactorily Financed?*—In seeking to answer the general question regarding educational finance we shall be well advised to ask in the first place for an answer to the more specific question: How is Elementary Education to be satisfactorily financed? No one would think of denying that the most pressing need at the present time, as it has been for several decades, is the provision of adequate facilities for the dissemination of education among the great mass of the people. As the Royal Commission on Agriculture closes its chapter on Education it says: 'We are persuaded that the only hope of substantial progress lies in the mobilisation of all the available forces,

both public and private, in a determined attack upon illiteracy'. Among these forces must be reckoned money. How is it to be mobilised for this attack? Three answers have been given to this question. Let us consider them.

(i) *First Answer : Let State Expenditure on Higher Education Cease*

3. *Consideration to be Limited to State Funds.*—One answer is : There is far too much money being spent on higher education. Let Government stop all that it gives from provincial funds towards secondary and collegiate education and devote it to the spread of elementary education. Then, we are assured, there will be some chance of elementary education receiving its due. There have been those who have used the words 'public funds' for 'provincial funds' in urging this claim. But if that were taken strictly it would mean that statutory Local Bodies would have to surrender all that they expend on secondary education and to employ it wholly in the service of those who are at the primary stage. That would be to curtail the expenditure of Local Bodies in a way which is hardly consistent with the purposes for which they have been set up. And so it will be best for us to examine this answer by considering exclusively how education would be affected if all grants which the State now makes to Arts, Professional, and Intermediate Colleges, as well as to High Schools, were withdrawn and were employed for the advance of elementary education.

4. *Figures for British India.*—We may begin by taking the figures for British India as a whole. There are disadvantages in this, for these figures would afford a satisfactory means of calculation only if the different provinces could come to the financial aid of one another, and if the resources of all managements could be unreservedly pooled. But provinces are precluded from

taking such a step, and pooling is possible only within the narrowest limits. Nevertheless a general survey will be useful in the first instance, and it can be followed by greater detail so as to check the result. We need to have some facts that deal with the educational system as a whole, so that in the light of them we may examine the assertion that higher education receives so much from provincial revenues that elementary education is being starved and cut out of its rightful place. These will enable us, in a very general way, to see what amount of money might be liberated for the benefit of elementary education, and what effect this liberation would have on the education of the country as a whole.

5. *Effect on Higher Education of Withdrawal of State Revenues.*—Let us suppose, then, that provincial revenues were no longer available for colleges and high schools under any management whatsoever, departmental, board or private. What would happen? Government Arts and Intermediate Colleges for men would at once lose about three-fourths of their income; State Professional Colleges would be so impoverished that only those which prepare for the legal calling would have the needed funds at their disposal; State High Schools would be deprived of about two-thirds of the income which they now enjoy: and State institutions for women would be so hard hit that no colleges would remain and only a few high schools. Boards very possibly would be able, out of their own resources, to carry on one of the two colleges of general education for men and the one professional college which they manage; but they would have some difficulty in regard to the intermediate college; while about a quarter of their income, that derived from State subsidy, would be lost to their boys' and girls' high schools. Private effort, so far as it was aided, would find about a quarter of its income for men's and women's arts colleges gone with the disappearance of State aid; its law colleges would be slightly affected, the existence of its medical college would be rendered

uncertain, half of its income for commercial colleges would vanish; its finances for engineering and agricultural institutions would be hopelessly strained; its intermediate colleges for men would lose about a third of their income and those for women more nearly a half; while the high schools for boys would suffer to the extent of more than a fourth and those for girls by more than a third. The trouble, it is hardly necessary to say, would not stop at this point. With the inevitable diminution in the number of educational facilities the total fee income would suffer a serious diminution, and as those who studied would have to go further afield than at present, the drain on the parents' pockets would be greater. This would react immediately on the number proceeding for higher education to the institutions that survived the immediate effect of the stoppage of State grants. Thus a still heavier burden would be placed on those managements, a burden which would be almost certainly too great for some of them. And so it would go on, withdrawal of funds leading to reduction of facilities, reduction of facilities leading to diminution in the number of students, diminution in their number leading to decrease of interest in education, and decrease of that interest leading in turn to still fewer facilities. It is difficult to present this result in any satisfactory tabular form. We must content ourselves with a somewhat rough and ready method. The tables given in Volume II of the Ninth Quinquennial Review show us the number of existing institutions of the higher order and the amounts which they receive from provincial revenues. It is possible to calculate, but only in the most general way, how the number of institutions would be affected if these amounts were no longer supplied by the State, since the tables inform us what is the cost and what the income of each institution. In the following tabular statement an endeavour is made to present the result of this calculation; but, though it has been done as carefully as possible, it is at best only approximate.

I. ACTUAL NUMBER OF INSTITUTIONS OF HIGHER EDUCATION

Management	For Male or Female	Arts Colleges	Professional Colleges	Intermediate Colleges	High Schools
Government ...	M	31	43	24	315
Do.	F	3	2	2	30
Board	M	1	1	1	213
Do.	F	...	...	...	5
Private	M	97	26	59	1916
Do.	F	7	5	7	208
Total ...		139	77	93	2687

II. PROBABLE NUMBER OF THESE INSTITUTIONS AFTER WITHDRAWAL OF STATE GRANTS

Management	For Male or Female	Arts Colleges	Professional Colleges	Intermediate Colleges	High Schools
Government ...	M	8	4	5	85
Do.	F	...	...	...	4
Board	M	1	1	...	155
Do.	F	...	...	...	4
Private	M	70	18	36	1467
Do.	F	5	2	2	120
Total ...		84	25	43	1835

6. *Effect of this on Elementary Education.*—We are now in a position to frame what we may call a statement of profit and loss. The statistical tables show us that the amount spent from provincial revenues on higher

education, that is to say on high schools and institutions of the collegiate grade, is in round figures 264 lakhs of rupees. If then the proposal which we are now considering were given effect to, elementary education would benefit to the extent of that sum. Instead of receiving from the State, as it does now, a little under four crores it would receive over six and a half. That would be an enormous advantage. But on what terms would this additional grant to elementary education have been made possible? By between eight and nine hundred high schools being driven out of the educational system of the country; by the closing of all colleges for agriculture, forestry, veterinary science, engineering (with one possible exception), and the training of teachers, and by the elimination of about forty per cent of the arts colleges. As against this, small comfort would be derived from the fact that all the law colleges would continue, that one medical college would survive, and perhaps one for the training of women teachers might be saved. The plain fact which at once faces the advocate of the proposal under consideration is that, while a considerably increased number of boys and girls would receive elementary education, a very large number of opportunities that now exist to enable those who benefit by that education to climb higher would be wholly removed, the quality of education would be impaired, and the country would be impoverished by the presence in it of much talent for the development of which no means was provided. There would be a strange irony in the advance of elementary education being made the reason for the disappearance from the educational system of those very colleges which give to education what is being constantly clamoured for—a practical turn. And while the number of pupils in elementary schools would be increased, the number of teachers would be diminished because the colleges for their training would cease to exist. There would still remain training schools and classes, but they would be deprived of the men and women to direct them, while the high schools would soon realize that their day was coming to a close, as the supply of teachers to staff them was no longer to be had. This general survey, then, suffices to show us the broad outline of the picture on which we should look if all provincial resources were withdrawn from higher education and devoted to mass education. There would be a greater number of boys and girls attending schools of the primary grade but they would have fewer teachers who were competent to teach them, they would have fewer opportunities for pursuing their education beyond the elementary stage, and the chances for their becoming qualified engineers, forest officers, veterinary surgeons, and scientific agriculturists would be wiped out, while their chances of becoming fully qualified doctors and teachers would be reduced to the slenderest dimensions. To this there would have to be added the fact that the funds of the fourteen universities included in the statistical tables would be diminished by one half, so that it may well be doubted whether so many as half these universities would survive. The picture which seemed so brilliant at a first glance has lost its wealth of colour; it has become a drab monochrome. But, as we have already noted, it is a general picture. May it not be that if we paint it on a larger scale light may appear where we now see only shadow? Let us try.

7. *Detailed Examination*—(1) *Bombay.*—First, then, let us see what the west of the country reveals to us. In the province of Bombay the withdrawal of public funds from the maintenance of higher education would cut down the Government arts colleges by at least half, it would leave the law college unaffected, while the college of commerce in a town like Bombay might rally round it support which would save it from extinction; but the Government colleges for medicine, engineering, agriculture, and education would all have to cease functioning, as would also the Government high school for girls, while two-thirds of the high schools for boys would have to be discontinued. The Local Bodies would be in a position to carry on the only college they manage and

most of their high schools for boys. One, if not two, of the nine privately managed arts colleges would have to go, but the engineering college might survive and so would the two law colleges which are unaided. About a quarter of the aided high schools for boys and for girls would most likely succumb, and if funds could not be largely pooled or schools amalgamated the loss might be greater. And in return for this course of action whereby the better education of girls, the training of teachers, and the development of professional education would receive a shattering blow, the elementary education of the province would receive an addition of some 32 lakhs of rupees.

8. (2) *Bengal.*—Let us now cross the country and see what would happen on the eastern side if higher education had not the support of State funds. In Bengal more than half of the Government arts colleges for men would disappear; its colleges for medicine, engineering, education, and veterinary science would be wiped out, and so would its intermediate colleges. No Government college for women would remain, while considerably more than half the Government high schools for boys and almost certainly all those for girls would go. Local Bodies would have to part with at least one of their three high schools. About a quarter of the aided arts colleges for men would have to be abandoned, and the one for women could hardly survive. The privately managed colleges for medicine, law, and commerce would not be seriously affected, but that for the training of women teachers would not be able to stand the strain. Over half the intermediate colleges would continue to function, and three-quarters of the high schools for boys, but only about half those for girls. The result of the withdrawal of provincial funds from the higher education of Bengal would benefit elementary education to the extent of almost half a crore. It would affect higher education less seriously than in Bombay, because there are in Bengal so many schools and colleges under private management which receive no aid from public funds.

But figures take no count of quality; and a plan which robbed a province of all colleges that train teachers and engineers and reduced the facilities for the education of women would be hard put to it if it were brought to the test of India's needs.

9. (3) *The Punjab*.—Let us now turn our attention to the north and see what is to be learned from the position in the Punjab. In that province, if Government funds were no longer available for higher education, none of the arts or professional colleges managed by Government could continue to exist, and perhaps only about a third of its intermediate colleges and high schools. Boards provide no colleges, but of the high schools for which they are responsible about two-thirds of those for boys would remain and the solitary one for girls. Two-thirds of the privately managed arts colleges, including the one for women, might survive; the one law college which is unaided would be unaffected, most of the intermediate colleges would remain; more than a third of the high schools for boys would go, and about half of those for girls. Thus while by such action elementary education might be benefited by some thirty-seven lakhs, the opportunities for the further progress of those who received that education would almost wholly disappear. And were it not for the contribution made by private managements in regard to colleges, and by local and private managements in regard to high schools, the dislocation of education in the province would be well-nigh complete. What it would mean for the education of women is too patent to require comment.

10. (4) *Madras*.—From the north let us now turn to the south, and seek to visualize the conditions which would exist in Madras if State funds were no longer available for higher education. Perhaps two of the Government arts colleges might remain; but amongst them would not be that for women; while, with the exception of the law college, all the professional colleges woud have to succumb. One of the three intermediate colleges might be reasonably expected to weather the

storm; but more than half of the high schools for boys would have insufficient funds for their continuance, and almost all the high schools for girls would find their support gone. The boards might still continue to find the funds necessary for the retention of their colleges and for their girls' high schools; but wellnigh a quarter of their high schools for boys would be obliterated. Private bodies would lose about a quarter of their arts colleges and a third of their intermediate colleges for men; and they might be able, though doubtfully, to keep one of their professional colleges, that for the training of women teachers. A quarter of the boys's high schools might have to be sacrificed, and a little less than half of those for girls. At such a cost, involving among other results the substantial reduction of opportunities for the education of women and the virtual abandonment of facilities for training in medicine, engineering, veterinary science, teaching, and agriculture, about thirty-five lakhs of rupees might be handed over to the cause of elementary education in the presidency of Madras.

11. *Result of Detailed Examination in Tabular Form.*—What has been described in paragraphs 7 to 10 may be brought together in the following tabular statement. One explanation is necessary and has to be read in connexion with the table. The preceding paragraphs have referred at several points to reductions which would have to be made by private bodies if State grants were withdrawn. Thus it is said, for example, that 'more than a third of the high schools for boys would go'. It has to be borne in mind that such reductions, when they are spoken of, will take place only in cases where the institutions referred to are actually in receipt of State subsidy. Where institutions are unaided they are unaffected by the proposal which is under consideration. Thus a diminution of, say, a fourth does not mean necessarily a fourth of the total, but only of total aided, institutions. In Bengal alone, it may be stated, there are 469 unaided high schools for boys. With this

explanation we may now turn to the subjoined tabular statement.

I. ACTUAL NUMBER OF COLLEGES AND HIGH SCHOOLS IN FOUR PROVINCES

Province	Management	Male or Female	Arts Colleges	Professional Colleges	Intermediate Colleges	High Schools
BOMBAY	Government	M	5	6	...	25
		F	...	...	...	1
	Board	M	...	1	..	21
		F	...	...	...	...
	Private	M	9	3	...	141
		F	...	...	...	47
			14	10	...	235
BENGAL	Government	M	7	6	2	42
		F	1	1	1	5
	Board	M	...	...	...	3
		F	...	...	...	...
	Private	M	22	8	10	958
		F	2	2	...	37
			32	17	13	1045
PUNJAB	Government	M	1	6	8	79
		F	1	...	...	6
	Board	M	...	...	...	30
		F	..	...	...	1
	Private	M	9	1	10	192
		F	1	1	...	14
			12	8	18	322
MADRAS	Government	M	6	9	3	13
		F	1	1	...	13
	Board	M	1	...	1	139
		F	...	...	...	2
	Private	M	38	1	11	190
		F	2	1	2	41
			48	12	17	398

II. PROBABLE NUMBER OF COLLEGES AND HIGH SCHOOLS IN THESE PROVINCES IF STATE GRANTS WERE WITHDRAWN

Province	Management	Male or Female	Arts Colleges	Professional Colleges	Intermediate Colleges	High Schools
BOMBAY	Government	M	3	2	...	9
		F	...	...	...	...
	Board	M	...	1	...	17
		F	...	...	...	...
	Private	M	7	3	...	106
		F	...	...	...	30
			10	6	...	162
BENGAL	Government	M	3	...	...	20
		F	...	..	...	...
	Board	M	...	...	...	2
		F	...	...	...	...
	Private	M	17	7	7	836
		F	1	1	...	20
			21	8	7	878
PUNJAB	Government	M	...	...	3	26
		F	...	...	...	2
	Board	M	...	...	...	20
		F	...	...	...	1
	Private	M	6	1	8	137
		F	1	...	...	8
			7	1	11	194
MADRAS	Government	M	2	1	1	6
		F	...	...	...	2
	Board	M	1	...	1	105
		F	...	...	...	2
	Private	M	31	...	7	145
		F	2	1	2	22
			36	2	11	282

12. *Result of this Examination in General Terms.*—In paragraphs 5 and 6 we took a general survey of what

would probably happen throughout India if the suggestion that provincial revenues should be withdrawn from higher education were given effect to. And in paragraphs 7 to 11 we have sought to go into more detail, taking the conditions in four provinces—west, east, north, and south—and considering how such a suggestion would affect them. What these provincial figures disclose confirms, as will be readily seen, the main points arrived at as the result of the general survey mentioned in paragraph 6. We may state these points briefly. In the first place, the proposal if given effect to would benefit elementary education in four provinces financially to the extent of a crore and a half. In the second place, it would deprive the educational systems of these provinces of almost every medical, engineering, teaching, agricultural, and veterinary college. In the third place, it would affect so adversely the vigorous efforts which are being made to advance the cause of women's education that it would frustrate a large part of them. In the fourth place, it would withdraw from great numbers of boys and girls who receive and profit by an elementary education the stimulus which comes from knowing that the door to further study and achievement stands open to them. And in the fifth place, it would hamper and would very likely render impossible the working of about half the universities in the land, with results on civic and national life that do not require to be dwelt on. Confining ourselves to the most general terms, we may sum up the position as follows. Withdraw provincial funds from higher education in India, and fifty per cent of the high schools, of the arts colleges, and of the universities will vanish.

13. *Attitude to this Result.*—To such a state of affairs there would be, as we might expect, more than one reaction. There are those who would hail it, who indeed might have only one hesitation about it, namely that it did not go far enough. Critics who would like to see sixty per cent of the high schools of India disappear would be able to rejoice because what they wished

was at least on a fair way to realization. But a little reflection might be sufficient to moderate their exultation. For it would not be long in disclosing to them the fact that though the method proposed was swift to smite it was by no means so surely swift to save the educational institutions that were worth saving. The withdrawal of Government funds might leave the Indian educational system with only fifty per cent of the high schools and colleges that it now possesses, but would the fifty per cent that survived be those that ought to remain? Further while there are those who desire to see high schools reduced in number, and far fewer boys and girls going on to them, their wish in large part springs from the conviction that the present secondary curriculum is not sufficiently adapted to the needs of the country. But if fifty per cent of the existing high schools were to go the only thing that could be said with assurance was this, that there would be hundreds of high schools fewer on which to experiment with a view to securing courses that would commend themselves to educational reformers. Similarly with colleges. Grant that some of them need drastic improvement. Is abolition the best way to set about that? And while there is a pretty strong feeling that some provinces have too many universities, it must be admitted that there are others that have too few. Must then the whole idea of the withdrawal of provincial funds from higher education be regarded as nothing more than such stuff as dreams are made of? That would hardly meet the situation. For there are those who are so convinced that too much money is being spent on higher education that they would be prepared to support the proposal we have been considering until a better was forthcoming. And would that seem wholly unreasonable when, as tables in the Auxiliary Committee's Report shows us, there is a province in which, out of what it expends on education, the State assigns forty-five per cent to higher education and fifteen per cent to primary education, and another in which higher education receives thirty-nine per cent and primary education two per cent. And what answer are we to give when the Educational Commissioner tells us 'that in spite of all efforts which have been made to expand the system of primary education the increase in expenditure is still greater on higher institutions (arts colleges and secondary schools) than on primary schools?'

References

Bombay, Bengal, Punjab, and *Madras Quinquennial Reviews* (1922-1927), Tables I, IIIA and IIIB.

Auxiliary Committee's Report. See Table cxi on p. 261 for statement in paragraph 12.

Ninth Quinquennial Review, Volume i, p. 9 for quotation in paragraph 12.

(ii) *Second Answer: Let State Expenditure on Higher Education be Restricted*

14. *How is This to be Done?*—It is points such as these which lead us to consider the second answer that has been given to the question: How is the system of elementary education to be satisfactorily financed? That answer is: Restrict the expenditure of the State on higher education; do not stop it. Here we seem to be on surer ground. But are we? How is the restriction to be brought about? By a mechanical 'cut' of say twenty, thirty, or fifty per cent of what each management now receives at the hand of the State for the maintenance of higher education? By making the resources of managements the guides to restriction? By taking locality into account? Amidst so much that puzzles us, is it possible to find a principle that will lead us to a reduction of State expenditure on higher education at once equitable and beneficial? Let us look from a somewhat different standpoint at the statistics of the four provinces which we have been considering. Hitherto we have confined our attention to what would happen in these provinces if all State support were withdrawn from

the higher education which is carried on in them. What we may now consider is the actual amounts assigned by the Governments of these provinces out of their provincial revenues to the various forms of higher education that are at work within their borders. This may help us to find that principle of restriction of which we are in search.

15. *Tabular Statement of Grants to Higher Education.*—In the table on pages 312 and 313 we can see at a glance what the State expends on higher education in the four provinces of Bombay, Bengal, the Punjab, and Madras, provinces the total population of which is 140 millions.

16. *Significance of this Table.*—What this table brings home to us is (1) that these four provinces spend out of their revenues a total sum of Rs. 172 lakhs on higher education, and (2) that this amount is distributed as follows :—(*a*) on colleges of general education Rs. 32 lakhs; (*b*) on professional education Rs. 42 lakhs; (*c*) on high schools Rs. 80 lakhs; and on universities Rs. 18 lakhs. Now where is it that the money thus expended mainly goes? If we were to say that universities do not absorb much public revenue, seeing that the six universities of these provinces receive only Rs. 18 lakhs from the State, we should have to modify that statement somewhat when we came to consider the cost to the exchequer of universities in other provinces. And if we were to say that, as one quarter of the amount expended went on professional education and the remaining three-fourths went on general education, the latter made the chief demands, further consideration would be found to introduce a qualification here as well. So there is only one way to get a satisfactory answer. We must go fully into the figures which the table sets before us.

17. *Expenditure of the State on its own Institutions.*—When we do this, what at once strikes us is what the State expends on its own institutions for general education. While in these four provinces the State expends Rs. 32 lakhs on arts colleges, it spends Rs. 23 lakhs

GRANTS FOR HIGHER EDUCATION MADE TO MANAGEMENTS OF FOUR PROVINCES FROM PROVINCIAL REVENUES

Management	Male or Female	Arts Colleges	Professional Colleges	Intermediate Colleges	High Schools	Universities
		RS.	RS.	RS.	RS.	RS.
Government ...	M	3,88.289	5,85,609	...	5,64,212	...
	F	...	...	..	18.215	...
Board ...	M	...	...	...	66,356	...
	F	...	...	...	...	...
Private ..	M	1,87,000	32,000	...	8,66,426	67,772
	F	...	...	...	3,93,653	...
		5,75,289	6,17,609	...	19,08,862	67,772
Government ...	M	7,40,460	16 ,92,669	1,36,057	7,19,418	...
	F	74,118	19,566	16,122	1,81,279	...
Board ...	M	...	...	...	10,428	...
	F	...	...	...	...	...
Private ...	M	1,94,841	19,300	54,932	9,48,233	11,32,128
	F	12,600	8,274	...	2,90,166	...
		10,22,019	17,39,809	2,07,111	21,49,524	11,32,128

GRANTS FOR HIGHER EDUCATION MADE TO MANAGEMENTS OF FOUR PROVINCES FROM PROVINCIAL REVENUES—*cont.*

Management	Male or Female	Arts Colleges	Professional Colleges	Intermediate Colleges	High Schools	Universities
		RS.	RS.	RS.	RS.	RS.
Government ...	M	2,02,955	9,41,587	1,60,912	9,08,519	...
	F	40,182	...	...	1,24,483	...
Board ...	M	...	...	...	1,03,134	...
	F	...	...	...	...	...
Piivate ...	M	1,85,995	...	15,929	8,65,284	2,04,210
	F	4,800	15,226	...	1,03,916	...
		4,33,932	9,56,813	1,76,841	21,05,336	2,04,210
Government ...	M	4,25,656	8,29,590	48,440	1,65,103	...
	F	76,715	15,299	...	2,09,628	...
Board ...	M	...	...	4,000	4,65,023	...
	F	...	...	...	...	...
Private ...	M	1,92,753	17,425	35,864	7,68,593	4,15,470
	F	25,661	5,967	1,537	2,48,890	...
		7,20,785	8,68,281	89,841	18,57,237	4,15,470

of this amount on the arts colleges which it itself manages; and while it spends on high schools Rs. 80 lakhs it spends Rs. 29 lakhs of this amount on the high schools under its own management. This would be perfectly intelligible if the State by its own agency educated the greater number of the pupils and students attending high schools and arts colleges. But that is very far from being the case. It is other agencies which are bearing the main responsibilities of general education; yet it is not on these agencies that the State funds are being lavished. The facts are capable of simple statement. In the provinces of Bombay, Bengal, the Punjab, and Madras, Government Arts Colleges educate 10,667 students at a cost to State Funds of Rs. 23,09,906, and Non-Government Arts Colleges educate 41,949 students at a cost to State Funds of Rs. 9,11,912. While Government High Schools educate 59,326 pupils at a cost to State Funds of Rs. 28,90,857, and Non-Government High Schools educate 536,217 pupils at a cost to State Funds of Rs. 80,20,959. Now when the facts are thus baldly set forth we have little difficulty in seeing how it comes about that so much is being given to higher education out of provincial funds. It is because a very large amount is being given out of provincial revenues to educate a very small group of students and pupils. It is for a limited area within the field of higher education that the taxpayer is being called on to pay so much.

18. *State Expenditure on Higher Education.*—That fact becomes all the more clear when, from the four provinces which have hitherto occupied our attention, we turn to British India as a whole. The following tables show what the position is. One point has to be noted. In official tables there is given the number of students in 'Arts and Science Colleges' as a whole, Intermediate Colleges not being distinguished. That explains why separate figures for the number of students attending Intermediate Colleges are not given in Table I on page 315.

I. INSTITUTIONS OF HIGHER EDUCATION AND THEIR STUDENTS AND PUPILS

Management	Male or Female	Arts Colleges		Number of Intermediate Colleges	Professional Colleges		High Schools	
		Number of Colleges	Number of Students		Number of Colleges	Number of Students	Number of Schools	Number of Pupils
Government ...	M	31	15,702	24	43	8,682	315	105,486
	F	3	399	2	2	47	30	7,434
Board ...	M	1	149	1	1	100	213	68,031
	F	...	...	...	...	...	5	745
Private ...	M	97	54,863	59	26	8,987	1,916	570,927
	F	7	855	7	5	135	208	41,578

II. GRANTS FROM PROVINCIAL REVENUES TO THESE INSTITUTIONS

Management	Male or Female	To Arts Colleges	To Intermediate Colleges	To Professional Colleges	To High Schools
		RS.	RS.	RS.	RS.
Government ...	M	29,89,329	8,74,453	54,84,923	55,78,714
	F	1,91,015	21,157	34,865	6,19,448
Board ...	M	...	4,000	...	7,17,569
	F	...	...	...	7,416
Private ...	M	13,63,702	4,73,036	94,207	60,10,211
	F	72,529	52,091	1,46,599	16,32,264

19. *Significance of these Tables.*—These tables tell us that Government on its own Arts and Intermediate Colleges attended, as they are, by 16,101 students expends out of provincial revenues the sum of Rs. 40,75,954, while on the Arts and Intermediate Colleges that are not under Government management and are attended by more than three times that number, namely 55,867, it gives out of provincial revenues Rs. 19,61,358. I do not remark at this point on the disparity of financial support disclosed by these figures. That will be dealt with when the principles on which grants are allocated fall to be considered. At present, the bearing of the figures on the alleged excessive cost of higher education is what concerns us. And what is obvious is that if all arts and intermediate colleges were under board and private management then the total number of students attending these colleges would cost the taxpayer, *caeteris paribus*, about Rs. 30 lakhs instead of at present Rs. 60 lakhs. To complete the picture let us look at what we find in connexion with high schools. The figures for British India are these. The high schools under Government management have 112,920 pupils and the cost to provincial revenues is Rs. 61,98,162. Board high schools have 68,776 pupils and receive from provincial funds Rs. 7,24,985; while high schools under private management educate 612,505 pupils and the sum that is allocated to them from provincial funds is Rs. 76,42,475. That is to say, out of the total number of high school pupils, the 113,000 who attend Government high schools cost the taxpayer Rs. 62 lakhs and the 681,000 attending non-Government high schools cost him Rs. 84 lakhs. So that once again, *caeteris paribus*, if all the pupils who now attend high schools were in schools under non-departmental management the cost to the taxpayer would be reduced from Rs. 146 lakhs to not more than Rs. 100 lakhs. Thus in connexion with the higher education which is given in arts colleges and high schools a saving of Rs. 75 lakhs might be effected without difficulty and without hurt. Here then is a part at least of the answer

which we have been endeavouring to obtain. The main expenditure in the realm of higher general education occurs in connexion with the State's own institutions. And there, if a transfer of management were effected, the educational system would still be able to provide adequate facilities for higher education and at the same time to add three quarters of a crore to the amount available for elementary education.

20. *Consideration of the Proviso.*—But can this be done, *caeteris paribus?* Everything, it will be said, depends on this proviso. And in large part that is true. It is true at least to this extent that, if the economies proposed were effected at the cost of lowered educational standards and poorer educational provision, then they would be the very reverse of savings. But when the matter is considered from this point of view, it is seen to resolve itself almost wholly into a question of control. If the State supplies the control which encourages only those institutions that are of the right stamp, and effectually discourages those that are of a different character, and if the universities also do their duty in this respect, there is no reason whatsoever why change of management should result in any deterioration. Indeed it will be all the other way. For the change of management, by relieving the State of much that now embarrasses it, will enable the State to give to education a control which it has not yet at any time received, and the beneficial effect of that will soon be manifest in every part of the system. But there is more than that. If this truer form of control expresses itself, amongst other ways, in strong financial encouragement of institutions with power and capacity, and that is what we should expect, then we shall see, what the history of Indian education has abundantly shown, that non-departmental agencies will not be slow to respond to the stimulus which the State extends. New funds will be raised, new sources of local and private benevolence will be tapped, new levels of educational attainment will be reached. The truth is that if there is the right control there will be

the right managements. If the State does control there will be no need of the proviso, *caeteris paribus*. For other things will then be equal.

21. *State Expenditure on Professional Education.*—Now let us pass from general to professional education. Here we are on very different ground. It will not do to say that the 8,729 students who attend Government professional colleges cost provincial funds Rs. 55,19,788, while the 9,222 students who attend non-Government colleges cost only Rs. 2,40,806. Law colleges are frequently spoken of as money-making concerns, and while such a description does not tally with facts, it is true that the fees which these colleges yield, whether under State or other management, practically meet all expenses. And whatever the taxpayer may think of these colleges, at least he cannot grumble at them for taking anything to speak of out of his pocket. Then what appear in the Statistical Tables under the heading of 'colleges of commerce' are institutions which are not all on the same level, for it is only in some of the Indian universities that there is a course leading to a degree in commerce. But, as in the case of the law colleges, here again fees are so large an item that the support which commercial colleges receive from provincial revenues is almost negligible. In order to state the facts fairly we may remove from further consideration these two classes of professional colleges. And if we do that we shall find that we are left with roughly 6,000 students who are on the rolls of the forty Government colleges of engineering, education, agriculture, veterinary science, medicine, and forestry. The highly specialized nature of the courses in these colleges demands a very well qualified and therefore well remunerated staff. And while fees in medical and engineering colleges realize between six and seven lakhs, the income from that source in the colleges for education, agriculture, veterinary science, and forestry is very small. We cannot therefore look for any great reduction in the expenditure of public funds on the majority of these colleges for some time to come. But it

must be remembered that unitary universities are effecting a transfer of management in the case of certain medical colleges, and that is bound eventually to have its influence on the financial responsibility of the State. Then colleges for education, where not already incorporated in unitary universities, are capable, as we noticed in the last Chapter, of very speedy transfer to non-departmental management. So that under this head we should not be cherishing any undue optimism if we regarded a saving of, say, Rs. 15 lakhs as what a definite policy might bring about in the course of two or three years.

22. *Restriction of Expenditure on Higher Education Possible.*—We have now made some progress in our endeavour to answer the question: How may elementary education be satisfactorily financed? We have seen that to stop all the grants made from public funds to higher education and to devote the saving thus effected to elementary education would ultimately fail to achieve the object aimed at, for it would react most unfavourably on elementary education itself. But we have also seen that no such ill result would follow from a restriction of the amount expended by the State on higher education. Indeed all the facts make it very plain that there is still too much being expended on higher education compared with what is being spent on elementary education. If then there is to be a reduction in the amount which the State expends on higher education, how is this to be effected without damaging that education? The answer is: By substituting non-official for official management. There is nothing to hinder this taking place without delay in connexion with high schools, intermediate and arts colleges, and colleges for law, commerce, and education. And were this done there would be set free and made available for elementary education a sum of approximately, if not in excess of, one crore. Thus might a million more boys and girls become enrolled in the elementary schools of the country, higher education would continue to be adequately provided for, and the

lack of balance between expenditure on higher and on elementary education would be healthily redressed.

Reference

As under Section 2, i, except that figures are taken also from Tables IIA and IIB in the *Ninth Quinquennial Review*.

(iii) *Third Answer: Let Compulsory Education be Introduced*

23. *Need for Compulsory Elementary Education.*—How is a system of elementary education to be satisfactorily financed? One part of the answer to that question we have now obtained. By the adoption of the twofold system of management advocated in the last chapter, elementary education would be able to count on support from the State which would extend its sweep by lakhs of pupils. But that is not all that can be done, nor all that it is in contemplation to do. Thus we are brought to our third answer; an answer which may be expressed in the one word Compulsion. Elementary education will never be satisfactorily financed until a large measure of compulsion is introduced and every endeavour is made to reach the goal of universal compulsory elementary education.

24. *Compulsion makes Money go further.*—It may be asked: How can compulsion be of any service to finance? The reply to this is: Look at what is being done under the present system of voluntary school attendance; look at the appalling wastage of public funds which is going on every year. That is an aspect of the matter which is often overlooked. The Educational Commissioner makes a calculation as to the present cost of rendering a pupil literate. If we assume, and facts witness to the validity of the assumption, that no pupil has any chance of becoming and remaining literate unless he has had four years' effective schooling, then we find that in 1927 the number of boys who had satisfied this test, that is each of whom had in that year finished his fourth year of attendance at a primary school having passed each

year from the class in which he was to the one above, was 670,000. 'The total expenditure on primary schools for boys was about Rs. 592 lakhs of which the Government share came to Rs. 304 lakhs. This means that the cost of every scholar rendered literate was Rs. 90, of which Government bore about Rs. 46'. Now what would have been the cost under a system which compelled boys to attend school for a period of four years, and did not permit them simply to spend a year or two in school and then leave. Mayhew calculates that 'the cost per literate reckoned on teachers' salaries alone would be Rs. 60'. If that is the case, then the saving effected by compulsion would be somewhere about thirty per cent of the present expenditure on boys' schools. If the education of girls were taken into account the saving would certainly be much larger, for the wastage there is deplorable. A system of compulsory elementary education would thus mean that about thirty per cent more boys and forty per cent more girls might receive their education in primary schools without additional funds being required.

25. *Compulsion and Financial Saving.*—But if we look at the matter in another way the economy of a compulsory system seems still more marked. On the present basis, that a boy should become literate there is needed an expenditure of Rs. 90. The Educational Commissioner goes on to say: 'If the cost of literacy were to remain at Rs. 90 per scholar then taking the male and female population that should become annually literate at 3.4 and 3.1 millions respectively (and these figures represent approximately the number of children of the age of ten at which age a child may be presumed to complete four years' primary education), it would require about Rs. 30 crores and Rs. 28 crores respectively to achieve permanent literacy for all British India, that is, Rs. 58 crores in all annually'. Now let us contrast that figure with one which is given in the Report of the Auxiliary Committee. It devotes a chapter to 'The Financing of Education'; and in the course of this it

considers what would be the cost of introducing a scheme of general compulsory primary education. The calculation is based on two facts: first, that at present the average direct cost of educating a boy in a primary school is about Rs. 8, and that of educating a girl about Rs. 11; and second, that a workable scheme would affect only 80 per cent of the boys and girls of school age, for, in the words of the Committee, 'some will receive instruction elsewhere than in the ordinary schools; many others will be exempted from attendance for one reason or another; and it would obviously be both extravagant and impracticable to apply compulsion to areas in which the population is extremely scattered'. The cost of a scheme of compulsory primary education applicable to 80 per cent of the children of school-going age the committee estimates at approximately Rs. 19.5 crores in addition to the six crores that are already being spent on primary education. So that if we take the calculations of the Committee to be as accurate as is possible on generally accepted data, we may say that a scheme of what is virtually universal compulsory primary education, would cost about Rs. 25 crores. To this would have to be added the cost of administration, inspection, building, and training, all the forms of indirect expenditure on education. If we put the total cost of these at five crores, then the amount required to get practically every boy and girl to school and to keep them there between the ages of six and ten, would be roughly Rs. 30 crores. Contrast this with the figure given by the Educational Commissioner, and the economy of the compulsory system is at once apparent. Under the voluntary system Rs. 58 crores would be needed annually; under a compulsory system Rs. 30 crores. Even if these figures can claim no more than approximate accuracy, they indicate very plainly that somewhere about fifty per cent of what is now being expended every year on primary education is being to all intents and purposes thrown away. Such flagrant misuse of public funds surely cannot be much longer tolerated.

26. *How are Funds to be Secured?*—But even when we have reached this result we have answered only one part of our question. Grant that compulsion will lead to great economy, we have still to ask where the money is to come from on which the economy is to be exercised. This brings us to what is a central issue, one which we may put in this form: How much of its revenue is the State prepared to set apart for educational purposes? At present the provinces spend on education between 13 and 14 per cent of their total income. This is a figure which does not compare unfavourably with what is found in other countries. But while the expenditure of 14 per cent of their revenues enables them to do wonderful things for education, that percentage is hardly sufficient in India to keep any branch of education above starvation level. If primary education is to receive its due in India either the percentage will have to be increased, or the total revenue will have to be enhanced, or there may have to be a combination of the two. Let us look then at what is being actually done by the larger Administrations in their effort to advance education. The following figures present us with the main facts.

EXPENDITURE OF EIGHT PROVINCES ON EDUCATION

Province	Population in Millions	Total Revenue in Lakhs		Expenditure by Government on Education		Percentage of Revenue spent on Education	
		1922	1927	1922	1927	1922	1927
Madras	42·3	1175	1518	158	202	13·4	13·3
Bombay	19·2	1311	1458	170	199	12 9	13·6
Bengal	46·6	832	1050	135	148	16·3	14·0
United Provinces ..	45·3	1002	1139	156	196	15·5	17·2
Punjab	20·6	710	1086	87	151	12·2	13·9
Bihar and Orissa ...	34·0	443	574	49	72	11·0	12·5
Central Provinces ...	13·9	472	507	51	72	10·8	14·2
Burma	13·2	918	1006	46	95	5·0	9·4

27. *What these Figures Show.*—In two respects a certain amount of satisfaction may be derived from these figures. On an average these provinces spend about 14 per cent of their revenues on education and that is an advance on the percentage of five years ago. Then in 1922 there was spent on education in British India a sum considerably over eighteen crores of rupees; in 1927 it had risen to twenty-four and a half crores, an advance of over six crores. A large sum of money is being spent on education and the expenditure is progressive. Here, however, satisfaction ends. True, money is found to finance an amount of education in British India which costs over twenty-four crores. But how much of that comes from the pocket of the State? Not quite half; just under twelve crores. In other words, the legislatures of British India with a population of 250 millions vote for education the sum of £9,000,000. The estimates for the education of London alone in 1931 showed a gross expenditure of £13,000,000. There is something that calls for attention in the situation thus revealed.

28. *Possible Expansion of Public Revenues.*—If we give to it this attention we shall find that the figures at which we have been looking have a significant bearing on the financing of education. First, we notice the expansion of provincial revenues. Madras and the Punjab had each in 1927 a total income which exceeded that of 1922 by over Rs. 300 lakhs; the increase in Bengal was over Rs. 200 lakhs; and that in Bombay, the United Provinces, Bihar and Orissa, and the Central Provinces was over Rs. 100 lakhs. Most of the provinces thus seem to have sources on which they can draw for additional revenue; and the developments which are taking place through irrigation and industry hold out the promise of further enhancements. Quite apart, then, from any proposals that have been made for increase of revenue, it looks as if the provinces might count in ordinary course on having revenues that would expand in a short time to over a hundred crores; and such expansion would not be without its bearing on education. So we are

brought to our second point which we may put in the form of a question. Would it be unreasonable to expect each province, having regard to the enhancement of its revenue on the one hand and to the impoverishment which it suffers from illiteracy on the other, to set apart not 14 per cent but 20 per cent of its income for the spread of education? One province almost does that already. Some of the other services would very likely suffer for a time at least if this change took place, but the benefit would be out of all proportion to what would be after all only temporary limitations. For if sound education were to win its way into the lives of the great masses of the population, who can calculate what this would mean in improved agriculture, in expanding industry, in co-operative effort, and in changed social conditions? It is developments such as these that the country so desperately needs, and surely a few crores of rupees are not to stand in the way of their realization. And the third point is this: If the general revenues of the country can show this steady increase is there any reason why local revenues should not share in the common advance? In the course of the past ten years the amount which these Bodies have spent on education has increased at about the same rate as has the fee income of the country, and that is most certainly capable of considerable improvement. During the same period the contributions made to education by private generosity have almost doubled. Are the powers of Local Bodies being employed to the full? From the funds at their disposal are they giving to education the support which is its due? The education of the people has a special claim on Boards which are the expression of the people's organized local effort. Whether that claim is being satisfactorily met is matter for serious consideration.

29. *Allocation of these Funds.*—We might go on at this point to speak of what increased private liberality might be expected to contribute towards education. But for the present our concern is with the relation between education and public funds. And when we look at that

more closely we realise that increase of funds by itself will not suffice. There must be also systematic allotment of these funds. The State needs to lay down not only the percentage of its revenues which it intends to devote to education but also the percentage of that sum which it intends to assign to each particular form of education. In this way it would exercise a measure of control which has not yet received the consideration that the situation demands. The Auxiliary Committee, for instance, remarks on the lack of proportion between what the State spends on primary and what it spends on secondary education in some provinces, and again on a similar lack of proportion in regard to primary and collegiate education in other provinces. The Educational Commissioner has the same story to tell. Clearly education is suffering because there are no definite principles regulating the allocation of public funds. Yet such principles might easily be laid down. For example a provincial government might decide to devote not less than 5 per cent of its educational revenues to Administration and Inspection. At present five of the major provinces expend under this head less than 4 per cent of their revenues. Then if provinces earmarked for elementary education (Primary and Middle Vernacular) 40 per cent of what they have set apart for education, a step would have been taken towards recognizing the proper place of that form of education in the system. Half that percentage, or 20 per cent, might seem adequate for secondary education (High and Middle English), while half that again, or 10 per cent, might be appropriately assigned to university and collegiate education. Somewhere about 20 per cent might be required for building, scholarships, and miscellaneous charges. But that would leave only 5 per cent to assign to Special Schools and this might not be felt to do justice to them. More accurate percentages, however, would not be difficult to work out and many modifications might have to be made as fresh facts called for consideration. But the important thing is that allocation of this kind should be regarded as an essential of educational administration. While rigidity is by all means to be avoided, further delay in arriving at principles on which public funds are to be assigned among the various grades of education can lead only to financial futility. Careful allocation of funds, based on the actual data of the situation in each province, would eliminate what is at present fortuitous and would secure that what was most in the country's interests would have the substantial backing of the country's resources. And that is what is urgently required.

30. *Bearing of this on Elementary Education.*—The bearing of this more particularly on elementary education is so obvious that it requires no stressing. With enhanced provincial funds, Boards and Private Agencies would receive a financial support which, by relieving them of uncertainty, would enable them to put forth their best effort, while the training of teachers for this work would be regarded as an integral part of the arrangements for the spread of education among the great mass of the people. With definite assignments, local and private agencies would be able to frame programmes of activity extending over say a quinquennium at a time. The result would be not only a sense of stability but a stimulus to local and private liberality. There would be a fuller realization of partnership in a great national enterprise behind which was the sympathy and co-operation of administration, manager, teacher, and parent. The obstacles which now stand in the way of widespread compulsory education would be steadily weakened. And those who are working on its behalf would be able to persevere in their efforts with more heart than they have often had in the past.

31. *Benefit of Restricted Expenditure on Higher Education.*—For what is it that these answers which we have been considering yield us in the way of guidance regarding the financing of elementary education? The first answer seemed to leave us amid ruins; the second opened to us a door through which we saw a better built and better proportioned structure. By devoting its

funds for educational purposes to the fuller discharge of its function as a controller, and to the support of wholly non-official managements, the State, we realized, would be able to maintain higher education unimpaired while handing over to elementary education a sum of about a crore of rupees. Thus would the maladjustment now existing between higher and elementary education be in part rectified.

32. *Benefit of Compulsion applied to Elementary Education.*—The third answer took us further. It showed us that the introduction of a large measure of compulsion would mean the substitution of a great saving for a deplorable waste. With the expenditure of the same amount of money over 30 per cent more boys and girls would receive elementary education than is at present the case. Further it showed us expanding revenues with all the bearing of these on what the Exchequer is able to do for the advance of elementary education, on what Local Bodies will have it in their power to do, and on what private liberality may effect. In effect it showed us elementary education well financed and occupying its proper place in the educational system of the land.

33. *Benefit of the Two Answers Combined.*—But it may be said that these are only generalities. Let us get down to concrete facts. By all means. The second and third answers help us to do this very materially. As things stand at present, the State expends nearly Rs. 4 crores directly on elementary education. If to this is added the sum of Rs. 2½ crores contributed by Local Bodies, then we may say that the total amount which public funds supply for the spread of elementary education, apart from buildings, direction, and inspection, is Rs. 6½ crores. By means of this amount combined with what private liberality supplies, practically nine million boys and girls receive an elementary education. Now, to begin with, the second answer on which we dwelt, that which proposed restriction of State expenditure on higher education, indicated to us a means

whereby a sum of approximately one crore of State revenue might be, without inflicting any hardship on it, withdrawn from higher education and applied to mass education. Then it showed us that State revenues might be expected by about the beginning of the quinquennium 1932-37, if nothing untoward happened, to amount to a total of not less than Rs. 10,000 lakhs. Taking 20 per cent of that sum for education we should have Rs. 2,000 lakhs, of which 40 per cent or Rs. 8 crores would be earmarked for elementary education. Then there would be nothing surprising if Local Bodies by the same time were able to contribute towards elementary education a crore and a half more than they do today; in which case their assignment would be at least Rs. 4 crores. Thus when the 1932-37 quinquennium is still young we might reasonably expect from these three sources to have a sum of Rs. 13 crores available from public funds for elementary education. To that two other sums have to be added. First, compulsion as we have seen means a saving of between 30 and 40 per cent over a voluntary system. In terms of finance we may say that the introduction of compulsion would be equivalent to an enhanced income of 30 per cent of Rs. 6 crores, or somewhere about Rs. 2 crores. And second, there has to be taken into account the sum which is contributed by private liberality, at present three-quarters of a crore, within the 1932-37 quinquennium almost certainly one crore. Adding these two sums to the three already mentioned we see how there may be at the disposal of elementary education within the next quinquennium a sum of at least Rs. 16 crores. Now it will be recalled that the cost of a scheme of compulsory elementary education applicable to 80 per cent of the children of school-going age was calculated to be Rs. 30 crores. Thus if what our answers have disclosed is correct, the two methods which they have emphasized provide us with the means by which elementary education may be satisfactorily financed. Indeed they give us the means which, if employed without delay, would secure that during the years 1932-37 from 40 to 50 per cent of the children of school-going age would be on the rolls of the elementary schools of the country, not as casual pupils coming and going as they pleased, but as regular attenders of at least a four years' course. And when that has been done, the following quinquennium should witness what is to all intents and purposes a universal compulsory elementary school system at work throughout the whole of British India.

References

Ninth Quinquennial Review, Volume i, p. 125 for Commissioner's argument.

A. Mayhew, *The Education of India*, pp. 235-236 for consideration of cost of voluntary system.

Auxiliary Committee's Report. Chapter xiv, pp. 269-273 for estimate of cost of general compulsory education. Also Tables CIII and CV for statistics of expenditure by provinces.

III. The Financing of the Educational System as a Whole

34. *Need for Principles of Finance.*—No sooner has one question been answered than another presents itself. Our discussion up to this point has occupied itself with the financing of elementary education. That is fundamental but it is not the whole. And to the larger issue we must now address ourselves. How is the system, not merely at its elementary stage, but through all its stages, to be satisfactorily financed? Are there any principles on which it is advisable that a sound system of educational finance should be based? Twenty-four and a half crores are now being spent on education; are they being spent to the best advantage? This last is the most comprehensive question, and the importance of it claims a well considered reply. The present time stresses that importance. New constitutional conditions will soon have their effect on Indian education, and education requires to be in a position to meet adequately the

situation that will then arise. Yet if it continues to abide by some of the methods of finance which have been employed in the past, and which still find no little favour, it is bound to find its progress more and more effectually barred. The country will reap no educational benefit at all commensurate with the large and increasing outlay upon education.

35. *Is the Amount now expended Well Employed?*—In seeking for an answer to the question : Is the money that is being spent on education well employed? we may begin by asking another question. The first stage of our enquiry then is : Are Provincial Revenues being used to the best advantage in the service of education? The taxpayer has as great an interest in this as has the educationist, for it is out of his pocket that there comes the sum of nearly twelve crores which provincial governments apply to educational purposes. While there are various directions along which enquiry may proceed in order to obtain the desired answer, there are four of them which may be regarded as likely to prove most fruitful. They are the State's financial relations with itself, with Local Bodies, with Private Agencies, and with parents. Each of these will have to be considered in turn.

(i) *Is the State's Financial Relation with Itself Satisfactory?*

35. *Quotation from Auxiliary Committee's Report.*—First, then, how is it that the State, as controller of education and the disburser of public funds for education, deals with itself as manager of educational institutions? We may take as our starting point a sentence from the Report of the Auxiliary Committee. The Committee in noting the amounts spent by the various provinces on primary education takes occasion to contrast these with the amounts spent on university and collegiate education. And then occurs the following sentence : 'It is difficult to justify a recurring expenditure in Bengal of only Rs. 22.64 lakhs on 1,741,500 pupils

in primary schools as against Rs. 41.24 lakhs on 30,450 students in colleges, or even an expenditure by Government in the United Provinces of only Rs. 58.07 lakhs on 1,092,960 pupils in primary schools as against Rs. 32.81 lakhs on 12,710 students in colleges'. By reference to the educational expenditure of two provinces the Committee here takes occasion to lay stress upon what has been emphasized in the foregoing section of this discussion, and what provincial policy in general recognises, the need for a larger proportion of provincial revenues being devoted by the State to elementary education than is devoted to collegiate education. But, as we look at its statement, we feel that while it does this it also does more. It is impossible to note the figures which it quotes and the hesitation which its words express without realising that in reality these sentences of the Committee raise a question. The question is: How comes it that too much money is spent from provincial funds on university education? We must face this question, and perhaps our best way, remembering that all universities are not constituted alike, is to split it into two. In the first place we shall ask: Is too much money spent by the State on universities as such? And in the second place: Is too much money spent on the colleges that compose the universities?

36. *Does the State spend too much on Universities?* —We shall dwell in the main on the two administrations to which the Committee refers, as we seek to answer this question. Is too much money being spent by the State on the two universities of Bengal? The sum of Rs. 11.32 lakhs is undoubtedly a large gift from provincial funds. But take it in relation to the work done by the universities and it is impossible to escape the conclusion that, looked at in this light, it appears as a very good and profitable investment of provincial funds. For the statistical tables show us that by means of this grant the universities are able to carry on work connected with higher education which costs altogether Rs. 30.47 lakhs. The taxpayer has to supply a third of what is required,

and the result is two universities in full work, influencing all levels of educational activity, training teachers, and having a direct as well as an indirect effect on elementary education. And a very much similar position is to be found in other provinces. For instance, the grant which the two universities in Madras receive from the State is not quite one half of what their maintenance costs; in the Punjab the Government grant is less than one-fifth of the expenditure; and in Bombay it is not a tenth. In these provinces, then, it certainly does not look as if the State was spending too much on their universities as such. But we are driven to a different conclusion when we turn to the second of the administrations which the Committee mentions. In the United Provinces there are five universities, two of them subsidised by the Central Government, the remaining three by the Local Government. Confining our attention to these three, we note that they receive from provincial revenues the sum of Rs. 13.71 lakhs, and the work which they do involves a total expenditure of Rs. 21.81 lakhs. That is to say the taxpayer of the United Provinces has to provide almost two-thirds of what these universities cost. How is it that there is this difference between the situation in these Provinces and in those at which we have already looked? We are helped to answer this question by what we find in the Chapter on universities in the most recent quinquennial review of the United Provinces. There we are told for one thing that, apart from fees, the University of Allahabad as reconstituted 'is practically entirely dependent upon Government grant', and for another thing that 'Lucknow and Allahabad Universities are in receipt of Government block grants . . . In addition these universities receive the salaries of the government officers deputed to their service; in the event of the reversion of a government officer and his replacement by an officer appointed by the university an addition is made to the block grant in respect of the post so filled by the university'. In other words the universities of these

Provinces, though they appear in the statistical tables under the heading of 'Aided', partake more of the nature of departmental, than of aided institutions. And from this we are able to see what contributes to the difference which we have noted to exist between the financial position of the universities in the United Provinces and those in other provinces. Where the universities are truly aided institutions the taxpayer gets a good return for his contribution towards them; where they are to all intents and purposes departmental institutions the taxpayer's money is employed to distinctly less advantage. To put it in another way, too much money is being spent on universities when they are not so much aided institutions as departments of the State. That is to say, a disproportionate amount of provincial revenues is being spent on universities when, in connexion with them, the State is dealing financially, not with another, but virtually with itself. Can it be that we have here reached a principle that is of wider application than the universities as such? Let us turn to our second question.

37. *Does the State spend too much on Colleges?*—That second question is : Does the State spend too much money on the colleges which compose the universities? Again we turn to the two provinces referred to by the Auxiliary Committee. The Committee comments on the difficulty of justifying an expenditure from Bengal Government funds of Rs. 41.24 lakhs on 30,450 students when it spends only Rs. 22.64 lakhs on 1,741,500 pupils in elementary schools. But the justification is even harder than that. For, as the tables show us, the State in Bengal spends Rs. 26.79 lakhs on the colleges which it itself maintains, and they are attended by 5,226 students. On the five thousand students who are in its own colleges the State spends four lakhs of rupees more than it does on a million and three-quarters of elementary school pupils; while on the 30,000 students who are in non-government colleges it spends only a little more than one half of what it expends on its own small group,

Rs. 14.22 lakhs, on more than five times as many students as the Government itself is educating. If now we turn to the United Provinces what do we find? The Committee comments on Rs. 32.81 lakhs being spent on 12,710 students. But it is worse than that. More than a third of that sum, or Rs. 11.82 lakhs, is being spent on less than 2,000 students who are in Government colleges; and less than twice that sum is being given from provincial revenues towards the education of five times as many students in non-government colleges. Here too the facts drive us to the same conclusion. It is when the State is dealing financially with itself that too much is being expended, as on universities, so on colleges.

38. *Does the State spend too little on Elementary Education?*—We have now got our answer to the question raised by the quotation from the Auxiliary Committee's Report. And that answer is: There is not a disproportionate amount of provincial revenues spent on universities or colleges in general, but on those universities and the small group of colleges where the State is dealing with itself financially. And this helps us when we look at the other side of the Auxiliary Committee's comment. That raises the question: Is the State spending too little on elementary education? What are the figures? There are in Bengal 4,444 pupils in Government elementary schools, and on them the State spends Rs. 89,968; a million and three-quarters receive their education in non-government schools and on them the State spends Rs. 22.35 lakhs. Note the contrast: 4,500 receive almost a lakh from the State, the greater part of two millions, Rs. 22 lakhs. In the United Provinces Government primary schools are attended by 2,018 pupils and the cost to provincial revenues is Rs. 32,557; the pupils in non-government primary schools number over a million and for them provincial funds provide Rs. 57.74 lakhs. Five hundred times as many pupils at less than two hundred times the cost. We have got our answer then to the question with which we began. It is this: The State is spending too little

on elementary education when it is dealing with other managements, not when it is dealing financially with itself.

39. *Expenditure on Secondary Education.*—We have looked at this inequality of financial treatment in connexion with collegiate and elementary education. Let us now look at secondary education. Once more we may take as our starting point an extract from the Auxiliary Committee's Report. It gives a table in which there is shown, among other facts, the percentage of Government expenditure on secondary and primary education in the different provinces. And it comments on this percentage as it affects three of these provinces. We shall give the figure first and then the quotation. The figures are as follows:

PERCENTAGE OF GOVERNMENT EXPENDITURE IN THREE PROVINCES ON

Province	Secondary Schools	Primary Schools
Madras	11·71	42·55
Bombay	11·43	61·23
Punjab	34·17	16·26

Now for the quotation. 'The Punjab shows the highest figure under "secondary schools", but a large part of this is expenditure on Middle Vernacular schools and should really be shared between "primary schools" and "secondary schools". In Madras and Bombay the Higher Elementary schools which correspond to Middle Vernacular schools elsewhere are classified as primary'. This lack of uniformity in classification we have already referred to; and because it is apt to deprive comparisons of their point, the more satisfactory grouping is that which brings middle English schools under secondary and middle Vernacular schools under elementary. When we do this what are the facts regarding the three provinces with which we are dealing?

40. *Tables of Expenditure.*—The facts are as follows :

SCHOOLS ARRANGED AS TO MANAGEMENT, PUPILS AND COST TO PROVINCIAL FUNDS

Province	Grade	Management					
		Government		Board		Private	
		Number of Pupils	Cost to Provincial Revenues	Number of Pupils	Cost to Provincial Revenues	Number of Pupils	Cost to Provincial Revenues
Secondary—							
Bombay ...	High ...	8,972	5,82,427	5,145	66,356	63,606	12,60,079
Punjab ...	,, ...	27,736	10,33,002	11,444	1,03,134	79,324	9,69,200
Madras ...	,, ...	7,238	3,74,731	45,833	4,65,023	98,363	10,17,483
Bombay ...	Middle English	1,252	69,954	4,019	55,928	17,300	2,34,801
Punjab ...	,,	1,519	59,972	28,647	1,70,194	20,691	1,65,674
Madras ...	,,	816	36,292	9,670	2,31,494	22,722	2,46,280
Elementary—							
Bombay ...	Middle Vernacular	...	...	...	...	...	...
Punjab ...	,, ...	404	17,563	332,215	25,93,395	10,222	52,179
Madras ...	,, ...	...	...	...	...	...	...
Bombay ...	Primary ...	4,832	1,29,209	843,135	114,43,612	136,759	5,87,027
Punjab ...	,, ...	1,537	19,512	363,714	23,58,874	89,407	1,78,080
Madras ...	,, ...	68,475	6,47,395	903,893	40,76,165	12,43,339	38,90,020

Incidentally it will be seen that the percentages given in paragraph 39 with regard to the Punjab will have to be virtually reversed if the classification which obtains in Bombay and Madras is applied to it. In round figures the Punjab expends 15 per cent of its provincial revenues on secondary, and 35 per cent on elementary, education.

41. *Expenditure of the State on its High Schools.*—From this starting point we may look at the expenditure on high schools. We are struck at once by the large sums which the governments of the Punjab and Bombay expend on their own high schools. And the allocation of provincial funds to non-government agencies is no less striking. In the Punjab, Government educates in its high schools 27,736 pupils at a cost to provincial funds of Rs. 10.33 lakhs; non-government high schools educate 90,768 pupils and the cost to provincial revenues is almost the same, Rs. 10.72 lakhs. That is to say, when the taxpayer's money is allocated to non-departmental high schools it goes more than three times as far as when it is allocated to departmental high schools. And in the case of Bombay Rs. 5.82 lakhs from provincial revenues educate 8,972 pupils in Government high schools, while Rs. 13.26 lakhs from that source educate 68,751 pupils in non-departmental high schools. That is to say Rs. 6 lakhs of the taxpayer's money educates 9,000 pupils if they are in Government high schools, and just over twice that amount, or Rs. 13 lakhs educates 69,000 if they are in other than Government high schools. For results such as these some strong justification would seem to be necessary, and it would be well if the records could give it. In the Punjab we are told that a survey was made in regard to the distribution of secondary schools, and that 'it has borne fruit. By the provincialisation of schools (there are now 78 Government high schools as against 39 at the beginning of the quinquennium) and by timely assistance to local bodies, secondary education has been considerably advanced in backward and distant districts with the result that facilities for secondary education are now more

evenly distributed'. And in Bombay we read that 'it is the declared policy of Government to maintain one full High School in each district to serve as a model'. These statements are worth looking into. Do they help us to find any justification for the differences in allocation of provincial funds to which we have adverted?

42. *Position in the Punjab.*—In the Punjab the provincialisation of high schools on the large scale mentioned by the Director was undertaken, according to the report, because there was need of a more satisfactory distribution of high schools. Why the supply of this need should have involved a doubling of the schools under departmental management is far from obvious. Anyone who knows Indian conditions must regard it as strange that the way adopted by Government so as to exercise its power as a controller—for distribution is one of its main responsibilities as a controller—should be to become something quite different, namely a larger and larger manager. Is not such procedure tantamount to an acknowledgment by Government of its inability to carry out the specific duties of a controller? And is not that acknowledgment made all the more plain when in a later sentence the Government speaks of its 'policy' (of distribution) as 'often embarrassed by a cluster of communal schools in a single place where but one school is needed'? The situation is all too plainly serious. Had Government exercised its powers as a controller and employed non-official bodies as managers, then the provincial funds now allotted to itself could have been so used that it would have been possible for a satisfactory distribution of high schools to be effected, for high school education to have been furthered at much smaller cost, for public funds to have been made available for more needy educational objects, and for confusion between control and management with its unhappy consequences to have been avoided. By substituting management for control, as the situation which we are now considering plainly shows, Government not only deprives the country of the exercise of functions which

the State alone can discharge, but it also employs public funds in ways that are not the most advantageous. Not here do we find the justification of which we are in search.

43. *Position in Bombay.*—Shall we find it in Bombay? In that province, as we have seen, Government adheres to the policy of managing high schools to serve as 'models'. In a previous chapter we have noted that on educational grounds the term 'model' is misapplied when it is given to Government schools. And now on financial grounds we are forced to the same conclusion. If the State were prepared to serve as a model financially, if it were ready to spend on other high schools sums even approximating those which it spends on its own, there would be an immediate improvement of staffs, and managements would be afforded an all round encouragement to adopt better methods and higher standards. But that is not the way which the State takes. We have only to contrast, as has been done above, what it spends on non-departmental high schools with what it expends on its own to realize how inapposite, from this point of view, is the title 'model' as applied to these Government high schools. So long as they enjoy their present privileges, so long are they denied even the opportunity of serving as patterns.

44. *Statement from Bengal.*—We might consider high school expenditure in other provinces, but we should simply be on ground already well-trodden. In British India out of the Rs. 146 lakhs which is what the State spends on education of 794,000 high school pupils, Rs. 62 lakhs go to its own high schools which educate one-seventh of that number. Is that a satisfactory employment of public funds? Let us hear what the writer of the most recent quinquennial review of education in Bengal says. He has been considering the question of deprovincialising Government high schools and the matter of grants-in-aid. And this is the position to which he is led: 'It would appear that public money, available for secondary education, could not be more

usefully spent than in improving and extending the system of grants-in-aid'. That is a position to which consideration of what we have seen going on in other provinces and in India as a whole lends added weight. Provincial funds for secondary education throughout India, and not merely in Bengal, could not be more usefully spent than in improving and extending the system of Government subsidies and grants-in-aid. It is a statement which is applicable not only beyond Bengal but also far beyond the sphere of secondary education. The interests of the country and of education alike combine to emphasize the need for its general recognition and steady application. The present state of matters does not admit of justification. It requires thorough alteration.

45. *Expenditure on Middle and Primary Schools.*—We need hardly dwell on the rest of secondary education. It is sufficient to note that the Boards of the three provinces, Bombay, the Punjab, and Madras, educate in their middle English schools about twelve times the number educated by Government, and the cost to provincial funds is not three times what Government allocates to its own middle English schools. Nor need we dwell further upon the finances of elementary education save to remark that the Government of Madras, by the establishment of primary schools which are not under the control of the Educational Department, has expended a sum of money on the education of 68,000 pupils which, if it had been given to private agencies (which have done, and are doing, so much for the particular communities which Government desires to benefit by means of these schools), could have enabled them to educate not less than twice that number.

46. *Disadvantages of State's financial Relation to itself.*—In dealing with the general question of financing the educational system of the country we began by asking whether provincial revenues were being used to best advantage for the spread of education when the State as controller has financial relations with itself as manager.

And after looking at the matter as it affects every level of education, from the university to the primary school, we are brought to the conclusion that the relationship leads to four unfortunate results. First, the State allocates to itself a very large amount of provincial money for the education of a comparatively small number of students. Second, it allocates this money to itself so that it may be the manager of educational institutions when there are numerous other capable managers available. Third, it has only a small amount of provincial money to allocate to itself for the purposes of control, so that this function which is peculiarly its own it is unable to discharge with effectiveness. And fourth, it so allocates provincial funds that there is a marked inequality between what is assigned to itself and what is assigned to other managements. A relationship which issues in such consequences is clearly one the speedy termination of which would be to the advantage of provincial finance as employed in the service of education.

References

Auxiliary Committee's Report. Chapter xiv, p. 262 for quotation; and p. 261 for Table cxi.

The figures given are all to be found in the *Quinquennial Review* (1922-27) for Bengal, the United Provinces, the Punjab, and Bombay.

(ii) *Is the State's Financial Relation with Local Bodies satisfactory?*

47. *Revenue raised by Local Bodies.*—We have now to consider another aspect of the question whether the present expenditure of provincial revenues is satisfactory. It is that which concerns the financial relation of the State to Local Bodies. The contribution of these Bodies to education raises not a few questions, and amongst others are these : Is the revenue that they raise all that they might be reasonably expected to raise? Is the amount of that revenue which they give to education

all that they might be reasonably expected to give? A very sympathetic commentator on Indian conditions has no doubt as to the answer that must be given to the first of these questions. 'Statistics were collected shortly before the War', he writes, 'for two villages of the same population and size in Madras and Italy. The Government land revenue was much the same in each case, but Kanatalapalli in Madras paid Rs. 250 in local cess and Torre San Patrizia about Rs. 9,000. Major Jack arrived at the same conclusion from villages in Bengal and Japan. He showed that while the incidence of taxation per head was very much heavier in Japan (£1 2s. as against 3s. 4d.) the amounts levied by the local authorities were out of all proportion, being under four annas in Faridpur and more than thirty-eight times as heavy in Japan'. There are in British India some 800 municipalities and 5,000 local boards, and the total income of all these local self-government organizations amounts to Rs. 32 crores. It seems a small sum in itself for so many statutory bodies to raise. And there seems good reason for thinking that it might be considerably increased. For as one reads the records of the working of these bodies one finds reference to an increase of cesses that is 'persistently avoided', to arrears in tax collections running into many lakhs, and to 'remissions on a lavish scale'. Out of Rs. 32 crores which Local Bodies raise they expend on education Rs. 3.66 crores, or about 11 per cent of their income. Private agencies have an income of Rs. 3.40 crores from fees alone. When we think of the powers which the Boards enjoy and of the amount which they contribute to education, we cannot but feel that these powers are capable of a much more extended use than is now being made of them.

48. *Rate of its Growth.*—The same thought occurs to us as we look at the growth of the educational expenditure of these Bodies. In the decade between 1917 and 1927 the Boards increased what they spent on education from Rs. 233 lakhs to Rs. 366 lakhs, a total addition in

the course of ten years of a crore and a third. During the same period the State increased its contribution by Rs. 8 crores, the parent by Rs. 2 crores, and private liberality by a crore and a half. One might have expected the Boards to do more. They certainly quickened their pace of giving during the second quinquennium of the decade, but when the total is looked at this only serves to emphasize the comparatively small sum with which they began the decade. Further there is an additional liability which Local Bodies have now to meet, the equivalent of the fees from primary schools which they have had to forgo through the operation of compulsion within a growing number of their areas. The years that are ahead, and the tasks that belong to them, point to the need for a marked increase in the rate of their educational giving.

49. *The Support they receive from the State.*—Taking into account what the Boards contribute to education and the rate at which this contribution is made we may fairly question whether these Bodies are having a part in the spread of education which is in keeping with their aims and powers. They certainly have no reason to feel that the State denies them the stimulus of financial support. To carry on their elementary schools for boys they are subsidized by the State to the extent of Rs. 236 lakhs; another agency which educates an equal number in its elementary boys' schools receives Rs. 58 lakhs. In Bombay the Local Bodies raise Rs. 41 lakhs for their boys' elementary schools and the State helps them to the extent of over a crore; in the Punjab, Boards which raise Rs. 17 lakhs for their boys' elementary schools receive Rs. 47 lakhs in the form of State support. In the United Provinces the Government contributes towards the extra cost in which schemes of compulsory education involve Boards what is sufficient to cover two-thirds of the total prescribed outlay, which shows, as it has been said, 'that enforcement of the provisions of the District Board Primary Act will not mean a severe burden on the resources of the Board'.

When we think over such instances as these we begin to wonder what exactly is happening. Is it that the State is subsidizing local effort, or that local effort is subsidizing the State? If the attitude which the instances adduced reveal is at all general, the question may well be asked: Why trouble with Boards at all? Why work through them?

50. *Why Work through Boards?*—It is worth while dwelling on this question and seeking to obtain an answer to it. Let us consider the amount of the expenditure on Board elementary schools which is met from Board funds and the amount that is met from provincial funds. The table on page 347 lets us see the cost in seven provinces of elementary Board schools and the way in which the cost is met. (See next page.)

What that statement tells us is that the Board elementary schools in these seven provinces cost in round figures five and a tenth crores to maintain, and of this amount almost three and a third crores are furnished by the State. Thus only about 33 per cent of the sum required to carry on what are termed Board Schools is provided by the Boards themselves. If now we turn from the totals to the individual provinces we notice that in two of them for every rupee which the Boards put into their schools the State puts in at least three rupees, in two of them considerably over two rupees, in two of them over one rupee, while in the seventh the Boards contribute more than the State. These facts are significant. Take the two provinces which have the largest number of pupils in Board elementary schools, the United Provinces with their 989,000 pupils and Madras with its 904,000. Each of them needs between 80 and 90 lakhs of rupees to educate this number; but in the case of the former only Rs. 17 lakhs come from Board funds, while in the case of the latter there comes almost three times as much. This is very remarkable. For the two provinces follow different policies for the expansion of elementary education. The United Provinces rely upon Boards for the advance, Madras employs for it both

ELEMENTARY BOARD SCHOOLS IN SEVEN PROVINCES

Province	Number of Pupils	Total Cost	Contribution from State	Contribution from Boards	Total from Public Funds
		RS.	RS.	RS.	RS.
United Provinces ...	988,559	81,14,977	59,87,833	17,06,626	76,94,459
Punjab	695,929	74,93,608	49,52,269	20,63,306	70,15,575
Central Provinces ...	308,522	34,04,684	18,77,561	13,94,210	32,71,771
Bombay	843,135	173,17,537	114,43,612	53,98,507	168,42,119
Bengal	194,573	11,24,699	4,67,776	3,85,538	8,53,314
Bihar and Orissa ...	161,913	49,52,917	43,89,097	5,63,820	49,52,917
Madras	903,893	89,28,745	40,76,165	47,41,604	88,17,769
Total ...	4,096,524	513,37,167	331,94,313	162,53,611	494,47,924

Note.—The figures relating to expenditure in Bihar and Orissa are taken from the letterpress of the Report and not from the Tables, where the full figures are not entered.

Boards and private agencies. And the strange result is that, while each province has about a million pupils in its elementary Board schools, and each spends about the same amount on educating them, the province which avowedly relies on Boards receives from these Boards what is not sufficient to cover so much as one-quarter of the expenditure, and the province which avows no such reliance receives from Boards more than half of it. The Punjab relies on Board schools, yet the amount which the Boards in that province provide from their own funds would not cover one-third of what the schools that bear the name of Board require for their maintenance. From such facts we seem to be warranted in concluding that it is clearly worth while to work through Boards when they pull their weight, far from clear when they do not. Far from clear, because in the latter case there is no unmistakeable indication that a true spirit of local self-government is at work. There is unmistakeable indication in four provinces that the local self-government organizations are so completely dependent on the State for the maintenance of their educational work on behalf of the great body of the people that, if the State were seriously embarrassed financially, not only would expansion be brought to a close but what is being done at present might have to be reduced by two-thirds or three-quarters. That is a very different state of affairs from what would be found in a province where the spirit of local self-government rose to its responsibilities and expressed itself financially in accordance with that spirit.

51. *State Encouragement of Local Bodies.*—Facts such as these arouse serious misgivings as to the way in which large sums of provincial revenue are being expended on elementary education. Is it not advisable that the issue should be fairly faced? What is the object in view? So far as Local Bodies are concerned, is it that the State should run most of the revenue it can spend on elementary education through Local Boards and that the schools thus established should be called

Board Schools? Or is it that the State should encourage Boards to develop their own contribution to elementary education and in the spirit of local self-government to set up schools which have a substantial supply of Board funds as the foundation on which all else rests? There can be no doubt as to which of these alternatives provides the healthier civic outlook and ultimately secures the richer educational development. As it is, where the former alternative is the method adopted, we read of a province where there is an apathy on the part of the Local Bodies which comes very close to antipathy; we are told with regard to another where strenuous efforts have been made by the Government through Local Bodies, efforts in which the endeavour to introduce a large measure of compulsion has been conjoined with large provincial support, 'that comparatively few pupils have the persistence or the inclination to complete the full four-year course'; and of a third it is reported that the schemes of the Boards are so ambitious that provincial revenues have been unable to keep pace with them and expansion has had to be curtailed. These facts are not to be dismissed with the optimistic reflection that better days are doubtless coming for the Boards and the results of their working. If better days are to come for the Boards one thing that is essential for the appearance of these days is the adoption by the State of what would appear to be a better method of finance in regard to these Bodies.

52. *Effect of State's present Policy.*—But it may be said: What is now being done is on the basis of a policy which has been deliberately adopted. It is indeed a policy which, as Mr. Richey points out, is the reverse of that formerly employed in some provinces such as the Punjab and the United Provinces. The ground for this change, as Mr. Richey puts it, is that 'the equalisation of the facilities for primary education is of more importance than the encouragement of local effort.' And so 'instead of the Government grant being limited by its relationship to the sums which may be provided

from local funds, the financial liability of local bodies is limited and the grant from Government is determined not by the amount contributed from local sources but by the educational needs of an area'. Whether that policy is not open to the serious objection of taking an altogether too narrow view might well be considered; but on that we need not here linger. Mr. Richey was writing in 1923, and we have now the means of estimating after a lapse of years how this policy has worked and with what results. The figures at which we have been looking show us, in the provinces where the policy has been operative, a considerable number of pupils attending primary schools, a very large expenditure of provincial funds, and a contribution from local resources which is distinctly smaller. Now two questions arise out of what is thus revealed. First, Is there any necessity for such a large expenditure of provincial funds? and second, Is this the only way in which 'equalisation of facilities' may be effected? Taking to begin with the second of these questions, we may answer that there is one way, and only one way, in which the facilities for elementary education may be made available throughout any province in such a manner that no child may suffer avoidable hardship educationally. It is a way that is often overlooked. It is by Government encouraging, and at the same time controlling, every available and trustworthy agency. If the right encouragement is forthcoming we shall find means for the spread of elementary education increasing on every hand. And if the right control is forthcoming we shall find the means thus provided both suited to the task it has to perform and operating exactly in the place where it is needed. We shall see this more clearly when, later in the discussion, we deal with the State's relation to private agencies in matters of finance. But in the meantime what facts compel us to recognize is that the true method for the State to follow, if it is to combat illiteracy successfully, is to stimulate bodies, whether they be statutory or voluntary, to develop their resources so that they may render that service to elementary education which is so desperately required and which each can characteristically supply. Thus a Local Body has to be encouraged to be and to act as an instrument of local self-government. In this way it will become possessed of true self-respect and will have an incentive to perform its required and appropriate service, and thus to maintain as well as to increase its educational activity. But it will have nothing of all this if it is little more than a body stirred by State initiative, useful for the carrying out of State purposes, and dependent for its operation on extensive State bounties. Yet that is very much the role which the policy we have been noting assigns to Local Bodies. As the figures show us, if they are not the instruments of Government, they are very decidedly the dependents of Government. Nothing could be more unfortunate, because it means that the spirit of local self-government fails of opportunity for exercise and development. And so a great means for the 'equalisation of facilities' is either weakened or lost. So much for our answer to the second of our questions. And in reaching it we have made an advance towards the answer to the first. For if Local Bodies were encouraged, if the local self-governing spirit were nourished, then these Bodies would bring to the nation-building service of education their own characteristic contribution. And with the strengthening of that gift the present expenditure of provincial funds would be unnecessary. It may perhaps be replied that the endeavour of the State is to encourage Local Bodies to render this service. Good and well. Only, if that is the case statistics hardly tend to show that the endeavour as now made is succeeding. And if the reason for that policy is what has been stated that lack of success is not surprising. For equality of facilities, as we have seen, is not to be secured in this way but in one which is very different. The policy therefore fails of its end. It makes an unnecessary draught upon State funds, and it fails to encourage and guide Local Bodies to perform their specific service on behalf of the community.

53. *Allocation of Funds by the State and Local Bodies.*—But there are other facts connected with the manner in which the State allocates funds to Local Bodies that require to be recognized, faced, and altered. And one of these facts is that the State has placed the Boards of several provinces in a privileged position. It has made Boards controllers of elementary education while permitting them to retain their function as managers alongside of other managers. Thus they receive from the State revenues for distribution to others as well as for utilization by themselves. But when we examine the figures with which the table given on page 353 presents us we are left with the impression that the distribution of funds by the Boards to other managements does not follow the lines which the State adopts in its distribution of funds to the Boards. The table shows us how funds are allocated in three provinces which rely mainly upon Boards and in which controlling powers are granted to these Bodies. In addition there is given a statement of the allocation of funds in a province where no such reliance is placed upon Boards and where no such powers are granted to them.

In the three provinces which rely mainly on Boards for the expansion of elementary education these three facts are at once apparent :—First, 29 lakhs of pupils are being educated in non-departmental elementary schools, 25 lakhs or 86 per cent in those under Board management, and 4 lakhs or 14 per cent in those under private management. Second, on the education of these pupils the State spends Rs. 237 lakhs. In doing this it assigns Rs. 224 lakhs or 95 per cent to Boards, and Rs. 13 lakhs or 5 per cent to private managers. Third, for the purposes of elementary education the Boards raise Rs. 100 lakhs. When they, in their capacity as controllers, come to allocate funds they retain out of this amount Rs. 92 lakhs or 92 per cent for their own schools and they give Rs. 8 lakhs or 8 per cent to schools which

ELEMENTARY SCHOOLS UNDER BOARD AND PRIVATE MANAGEMENT IN FOUR PROVINCES

Province	Management	Number of Pupils	Total Cost in Lakhs	Contribution from Provincial Funds in Lakhs	Contribution from Local Funds in Lakhs	Total Contribution from Public Funds in Lakhs
United Provinces	Board ...	988,559	81·15	59·88	17·06	76·94
,, ..	Private ...	171,385	11·36	4·55	3·34	7·89
Punjab ...	Board ...	695,929	74·94	49·52	20·63	70·15
,, ...	Private ...	99,629	9·23	2·30	2·37	4·67
Bombay ...	Board ...	843,135	173·17	114·44	53·98	168·42
,, ...	Private ...	136,759	24·09	5·87	2·56	8·43
		2,935,396	373·94	236·56	99·94	336·50
Madras ...	Board ...	903,893	89·29	40·76	47·42	88·18
,, ...	Private ...	1,243,339	74·57	38·90	·13	39·03
	Total...	2,147,232	163 86	79·66	47·55	127·21

12

are not under their management. Such allocation, especially if compared with that in the province of Madras which follows a different policy, requires no comment. The inequality in the financial dealing of the State is obvious. No less obvious is the inequality in the financial dealings of the Boards when to them are delegated powers of control and they have to allocate grants. It is hard to find in the figures any sign that, if the Boards have freely received, they freely give.

54. *Disadvantage of Present Mode of Allocation.*—The position of privilege which is accorded to the Boards by vesting in them control is one which is disadvantageous not only from the administrative point of view, as we have already seen, but also from the financial standpoint, as now we see from the figures before us. For the privilege thus given the country has to pay dear. It has to do this in three ways. The first and clearest of these is that which has been already mentioned, namely the distrust which arises when there is inequality of treatment. Ground for that distrust the figures given provide. And distrust is expensive. The second way in which the country has to pay dear is the large amount of unnecessary expense which the present method of finance involves. Even if inequality of treatment could be remedied, there is still this fact to be taken into account, namely that there is, and can be, little or no co-operation between a privileged and an unprivileged management. The State runs its funds through Local bodies in pursuance, as is stated, of a policy of relying mainly on these Boards for the expansion of elementary education. And what is the result? Other managements are made to take the place of subordination not of co-ordination; they are not admitted to the position of real partnership in the great educational enterprise of the province. Thus in the United Provinces, where this policy is pursued without the added disadvantage of inequality in financial allocations, the number of pupils educated by private agencies is only

about one-sixth of the number educated by Boards. The policy makes against their growth. Yet, if there were six times as many pupils in these privately managed schools as there are at present, there would even then be fewer pupils in the primary schools of the United Provinces than there are in those of the province of Madras, the population of which is two millions less than that of the United Provinces. Instead, however, of taking steps to secure such co-operation, action which would involve public funds in an additional expenditure of only about half of what is now being spent on Board schools alone, it prefers to concentrate on one means by which educational facilities may be supplied. And so expenditure mounts up and the number of pupils continues to be much less than we should expect. Were we to go into the figures of the Punjab and Bombay we should have little difficulty in recognizing how heavy is the price which in their case also the country has to pay for privilege. Financially the country is a loser, its funds are not spent to best advantage; educationally it is a loser, an agency that could render it invaluable help is discouraged. And the third way in which the country has to pay for privilege is this: The controller being granted a practical monopoly has next to no incentive to economy. Were it the executive of a thorough going system of local self-government the people of the locality would see to it that their representatives practised economy. But that is not the position of a body which, the more it decides to spend, the more it can count on by far the larger share of that expenditure being met by the State. As the table given above shows us, in the three provinces which rely mainly upon Boards, and on Boards to which controlling power is given, not to speak of other powers conferred by statute, Rs. 237 lakhs of State money are required to educate less than three million pupils in elementary schools, while in the province where that reliance does not obtain the education of over two millions costs the State a third of that amount. In the former Rs. 100 lakhs of local funds are needed, in the latter not quite half that sum. What are we to say then of a policy which while avowedly one of relying mainly on Local Boards means in practice a policy of relying mainly on provincial revenues? What are we to think of a policy which fails to bring into the struggle with illiteracy the full force of a capable partner? What are we to think of a policy which leads to the uncalled for expenditure of large sums of already overstrained revenues, and gives so small a recognition, to say nothing of a welcome, to funds that are voluntarily extended and are so urgently required? What can we think of it? Is it possible, when we face facts, to think of it in any other light than as a policy which is not only narrowly conceived but which retards rather than stimulates the spread of elementary education throughout India?

55. *Relation of State to Local Bodies in financing Secondary Education.*—So far we have been considering what is being done by Local Bodies in the field of elementary education. When we turn to their activity in the field of secondary education we notice an improvement in the financial relations between them and the State. The following tables present the position.

56. *Need for a consistent Policy.*—It will be seen that at this stage the contributions of State and Board are almost equal, so far as direct expenditure on Board secondary education is concerned. But two points emerge which deserve attention. The first is that the tables do not furnish us with details as to indirect expenditure in the same way as they do in regard to direct expenditure. Thus when one reads of a school building erected by the State and handed over to a Local Body one is glad that such gifts are current, but one would also be glad to know whether such generosity of the State extends only to Local Bodies. Inspecting Officers of the State are lent to Local Bodies. Are they lent to them alone? The figures give us no means of returning an answer. And the second point is this. Is the expenditure that at present takes place in connexion with Board secondary schools well directed? In the seven provinces of which details

I. MIDDLE SCHOOLS

(1) Under State Management

Province	Number of Pupils	Total Cost	Contribution from Provincial Revenues	Contribution from Local Funds	Total from Public Funds
		RS.	RS.	RS.	RS.
United Provinces ...	91	12,950	11,245	......	11,245
Punjab	1,519	74,215	59,972	......	59,972
Central Provinces ...	8,092	4,21,256	2,74,700	......	2,74,700
Bombay	1,252	83,476	69,954	......	69,954
Bengal	1,059	62,777	54,380	......	54,380
Bihar and Orissa ...	1,013	53,431	45,225	......	45,225
Madras	846	44,230	36,292	.....	36,292
Total ...	13,872	7,52,335	5,51,768	.. ...	5,51,768
British India	18,841	11,31,785	8,17,798	8,100	8,25,898

I. MIDDLE SCHOOLS—(*contd.*)

(2) Under Board Management

Province	Number of Pupils	Total Cost	Contribution from Provincial Revenues	Contribution from Local Funds	Total from Public Funds
		RS.	RS.	RS.	RS.
United Provinces ...	455	22,364	3,600	13,842	17,442
Punjab	28,647	6,65,485	1,70,194	2,61,353	4,31,547
Central Provinces ...	7,711	2,84,497	99,695	79,161	1,78,856
Bombay	4,019	2,29,574	55,928	75,367	1,31,295
Bengal	4,988	1,00,465	3,966	51,629	55,595
Bihar and Orissa ...	3,563	55,146	......	21,210	21,210
Madras	9,670	4,82,638	2,31,494	1,07,663	3,39,157
Total ...	59,053	18,40,169	5,64,877	6,10,225	11,75,102
British India	63,915	19,99,659	6,22,369	6,77,036	12,99,396

II. HIGH SCHOOLS

(1) Under State Management

Province	Number of Pupils	Total Cost	Contribution from Provincial Revenues	Contribution from Local Funds	Total from Public Funds
		RS.	RS.	RS.	RS.
United Provinces ...	19,671	15,56,525	11,72,038	......	11,72,038
Punjab	27,736	18,38,512	10,33,002	30,685	10,63,687
Central Provinces ...	3,224	4,15,123	2,83,138	......	2,83,138
Bombay	8,972	9,66,489	5,82,427	7	5,82,434
Bengal	15,380	13,34,261	9,00,697	......	9,00,697
Bihar and Orissa ...	9,110	7,10,971	4,55,386	......	4,55,386
Madras	7,238	4,96,178	3,74,731	......	3,74,731
Total ...	91,331	73,18,059	48,01,419	30,692	48,32,111
British India	112,920	92,89,638	61,98,162	40,542	62,38,704

II. HIGH SCHOOLS—(*contd.*

(2) Under Board Management

Province	Number of Pupils	Total Cost	Contribution from Provincial Revenues	Contribution from Local Funds	Total from Public Funds
		RS.	RS.	RS.	RS.
United Provinces ...	1,541	1,01,246	34,896	32,965	67,861
Punjab	11,444	4,76,983	1,03,134	1,32,084	2,35,218
Central Provinces ...	302	38,121	12,791	14,480	27,271
Bombay	5,145	3,02,582	66,356	79,044	1,45,400
Bengal	1,562	56,041	10,428	3,317	13,745
Bihar and Orissa ..	......	......	......	......	......
Madras	45,833	21,61,666	4,65,023	5,42,557	10,07,580
Total ...	65,827	31,36,639	6,92,628	8,04,447	14,97,075
British India	68,776	32,59,828	7,24,985	8,57,213	15,82,198

are given in the above tables there are seen to be 66,000 boys and girls at Board high schools and 59,000 at Board middle schools. That seems a meagre total, yet upon it Rs. 12.5 lakhs of provincial funds are expended. That gives point to a statement made in one of the reports that Boards show a readiness to open new schools which is at times greater than their readiness to develop existing ones. And one report at least shows how the distribution of these schools is at fault. Lack of economy is the inevitable result. Obviously if provincial funds are to be satisfactorily employed, a policy of real control in regard to Board secondary schools requires to be adopted. And that is true whether we look at the individual provinces or at the figures for British India as a whole, and whether we consider the facts now before us or the facts connected with secondary schools under other managements to which attention will be given later.

57. *Unnecessary Duplication of Managements.*—What are the facts now before us? In seven provinces, as the tables show, the State maintains a number of secondary schools which educate 91,000 high school pupils and 14,000 middle school pupils, just over a lakh in all. The Boards educate a slightly larger number, in round figures a lakh and a quarter. If we take the figures for all India we see that the numbers are virtually identical. State and Board each educate in their secondary schools 130,000 pupils. Both types of schools are largely dependent on public funds for their maintenance, the Department relying mainly on provincial funds—Rs. 70 lakhs out of a total cost of Rs. 104 lakhs being met from this source; the Boards depending almost equally on provincial and local revenues—towards a total of Rs. 52 the State contributing Rs. 13 lakhs and Local Bodies Rs. 15 lakhs. When there are public bodies which maintain a large number of secondary schools, educate in them a lakh and a quarter of pupils, steadily expand their educational activities, and possess powers assigned to them by statute, the question naturally arises: Why should a State agency exist alongside of these to do the same

class of work at a distinctly greater cost? Is it because State schools are model schools? May not the Boards reply to that: 'Give us anything like the amount of public funds that you spend on your own schools and we shall soon provide you with no lack of models'. Is it because through State schools there is a better distribution of educational facilities? That cannot be, seeing that the responsibility for distribution lies with the controller not with the manager. Is it because Board schools have defects which are not to be found in State schools? Then let a little more money be spent by the State on such guidance and control as will remedy these defects. Is it because Boards have not funds for undertaking additional work? That would be a strange thing to say of an agency which within the last five years has increased its expenditure on secondary schools by three and a quarter lakhs. The fact is that there is not the slightest reason for this unnecessary duplication of management.

58. *Unnecessary Expenditure.*—Nor is there any more reason for the unnecessary expenditure which the tables reveal. The Boards put in their own funds, are subsidised by the State to the extent of Rs. 7 lakhs, and the result is that 69,000 boys and girls are being educated in their high schools. The Government educates 113,000 pupils in its high schools and to do this draws on provincial revenues to the extent of Rs. 62 lakhs. And that is not all. For those who teach in State schools belong to a State service, and the State has obligations to them not only in respect of their salaries while they are actively engaged in their work but also in respect of provision for them when they have completed their term of service under Government. Thus, at a conservative estimate, the cost to provincial funds of 113,000 pupils in Government high schools is Rs. 70 lakhs, while at a tenth of that cost to provincial funds over sixty per cent of that number is being educated in Board high schools. Why is it that in a country which has such straitened resources and such enormous

leeway to make up in the field of education, this unjustifiable expenditure goes on year after year? Realize what would be the result if the duplication of management were terminated and those departmentally managed schools were brought under Board management. In the first place, some Rs. 30 lakhs of provincial funds would be saved. And in the second place, even if only half of that sum were spent on inspection and administration, a strength, direction, and stimulus would be given to secondary schools which would add incalculably to their power in the education of the country and to their value for the well-being of the whole body politic. Such guidance would be available for all schools whether local or private, whether primary or secondary. Fresh life would run through the whole system, suitable distribution of schools would be secured, and curricula of which the country stands in need would be devised and put in operation. The time has come when the present methods of finance as applied to secondary education require to be wholly altered. And when the State takes this step so long overdue, the benefit will be seen in a far more satisfactory employment than is now the case of the educational potentialities of the Boards, a more productive use of their funds, a better system of education, and the exercise by the State of a mode of control which will be welcomed on every hand.

59. *Financial Relation of State to Boards Unsatisfactory.*—So far, then, as Local Bodies are concerned, we are in a position to give our answer to the question which we asked in paragraph 47. And the answer is that, in this connexion, public revenues are not being used to the best advantage for the spread of education. And that for three reasons. First, there is no clearly defined understanding as to the part that is to be played in the service of education by local and provincial funds respectively. The result is that funds from provincial sources are being used to do what one would think was most undoubtedly the work for which local funds ought to be responsible. Hence it is possible to find such a

statement as the following in one of the provincial reviews: '90 per cent of the increased expenditure on primary education has been met from provincial revenues'. There is something humiliating about this. The State cannot do the work of the Boards without doing a disservice to education and to still larger interests. Financially this disservice is going on today. The best interests of the country demand its termination. And the second reason why funds are being employed unsatisfactorily is that more extended powers of management are not being placed on the Boards. Any such reliance it may be said is bound up with a revision of their constitution. But why should there be delay regarding this? The sooner it is done the better. The whole tendency of the present time is to break down barriers which in the past have separated one form of education from another, so that the benefits of advanced education may be available to all who have the ability to profit by it. If this tendency is to operate more and more fully, and the Indian system of education is such that the opportunities for its full operation have been inherent in it from the first, then larger responsibilities must be laid upon Local Bodies, as is being done in other countries. There is a considerable share of secondary and collegiate education which, as we have already seen, might be transferred to them either individually or in groups. The call for this transfer was made in the last chapter on educational grounds; it is now made on grounds of finance. With a revised constitution that enabled them to assume larger responsibilities and with that wise and sustained control which the State is in a position to supply, these Bodies would come to have the place in the life of the community which it is so important that they should possess as the expression of the spirit of local self-government. And when that is done public finance will not suffer as it does at present. And the third reason why funds are being employed unsatisfactorily by the State in its relation to Local Bodies is that the State does not supply the effective control of which we have just spoken. If it did economies could be effected at once; the present wasteful threefold form of management would be abandoned; a suitable administrative staff would be appointed and the expensive overlapping and competition of the present would be brought to an end; and local funds would be drawn forth in increasing volume. We should hear less and less of funds misused, of inconclusive discussions as to the place of Local and State inspectors, of disregard by Boards of educational experience, of the intrusion of politics into the sphere of education, of delegated control ousting the State. We should have Local Bodies co-operating with a guidance on the part of the State that commanded confidence and inspired effort. And we should soon see, in these circumstances, an employment of provincial funds in connexion with the educational activities of Local Bodies that would satisfy educator, taxpayer, and administrator alike, because all would recognize that these funds were being employed to the best advantage.

References

G. T. Garratt, *An Indian Commentary*, p. 262 for the quotation in paragraph 47 and for remarks on local self-government in India.

India in 1927-28, 1928-29, 1929-30, have much recent information regarding the working of local bodies. So also have the provincial *Quinquennial Reviews*.

J. A. Richey, *Grants-in-Aid*, p. 19.

(iii) *Is the State's financial Relation with Private Managements satisfactory?*

60. *Collegiate Education and Financial Treatment.*—Let us now turn to the financial aspects of education under Private Management. Are provincial revenues being spent here to the best advantage? To begin with we may ask: How does the State deal with non-professional colleges that are maintained by private agencies? In order to answer this question the following table will

be found of use. It gives information as to what is spent by the State on the Arts and Intermediate Colleges under its own, under Board, and under Private Management.

ARTS AND INTERMEDIATE COLLEGES

Management	Number of Students	Total Cost	Contribution from Provincial Funds	Contribution from Local Funds	Total from Public Funds
		RS.	RS.	RS.	RS.
Government ...	16,101	59,13,792	40,75,954	4,015	40,79,969
Board	149	26,105	4,000	2,060	6,060
Private... ...	55,718	86,45,021	19,61,358	63,886	20,25,244
Total ...	71,968	145,84,918	60,41,312	69,961	61,11,273

What this table shows is that out of a total of Rs. 61 lakhs spent from public funds to educate the 72,000 students who attend non-professional colleges, Rs. 41 lakhs are spent on educating 16,000, Rs. 6,000 on educating 150, and Rs. 20 lakhs on educating 56,000. If we confine our attention to what is being done by the State and Private Agencies in this field we are confronted with the fact that the agency which educates 16,100 students in its arts colleges receives from public funds Rs. 40.80 lakhs, and the agency which educates 55,700 receives from the same source Rs. 20.25 lakhs. The country has Rs. 61 lakhs to spend on general collegiate education, and what the State does is this : It spends 67 per cent of that amount on 22 per cent of the students receiving that education, and 33 per cent on the remaining 78 per cent. Could the wit of man devise a more surprising allocation of public funds? So far as figures can speak what they seem to say is : 'The more you do for the education of India the less encouragement can you count on from the State'. It may be replied: 'This is not a matter of quantity only; quality is essential and must be brought into the reckoning'. The justice of such a contention will be readily admitted. But what does the contention imply? That all State colleges are better equipped and better manned than all privately managed colleges? We can hear official reports saying, 'Would that it were so'. That some State managed colleges are better than, indeed far better than, some of the colleges under private management? Yes, just as some of the privately managed colleges are better than some under State management. But let the superiority and excellence that is claimed for some of the State colleges be admitted without demur, the question at once arises: Would that superiority exist if certain privately managed colleges were to receive from the State even that amount of aid to which they regard themselves as entitled under official Codes, but which they have to forgo because of what are sometimes spoken of as the exigencies of provincial revenues? And if, with all thought of superiority swept aside, the further question were asked: What would happen if these privately managed colleges were to receive even one-half of the amount which is now being expended on State colleges? the record of what privately managed colleges have done in the face of serious discouragement and the educational position to which many have attained, would justify the reply that, by such action on the part of the State, these colleges thus supported would bring to the educational system of the country benefits to which the State's present mode of action have made it so far a stranger. Think what it would mean if the agency that now educates 56,000 students were to have 16,000 added to the number under its charge, as well as to have an additional grant of Rs. 20 lakhs. What access of life and power would come into the colleges of the land, and through the colleges into the land itself. And there would still remain some Rs. 20 lakhs to spend on pressing needs not specifically connected with colleges. Instead of that, what we now see is the State assigning to itself two-thirds of the available revenues for educating less than one-quarter of the students in non-professional colleges and giving the remaining third to agencies that are educating three-quarters of them. Thus unfortunately it gives itself the appearance of a manager who benefits because he is also controller. And further it gives the impression of a controller who stands in the way of advance because he spends so much on his own management that he has not enough to spend either on control or on the fitting encouragement of the other managements which are integral parts of the system.

61. *High School Education and Financial Treatment.*—Do we find anything of this nature in connexion with secondary education? The following tables show us how High Schools are treated financially in British India.

HIGH SCHOOLS IN BRITISH INDIA

Management	Number of Pupils	Total Cost	Contribution from Provincial Funds	Contribution from Local Funds	Total from Public Funds
		RS.	RS.	RS.	RS.
Government...	112,920	92,89,638	61,98,162	40,542	62,38,704
Board ...	68,776	32,59,828	7,24,985	8,57,213	15,82,198
Private ...	612,505	312,53,281	76,42,475	4,00,191	80,42,666
Total ...	794,201	438,02,747	145,65,622	12,97,946	158,63,568

What these figures tell us is that a sum of money from public sources of about Rs. 80 lakhs passed through departmental and board channels educates 182,000 high school pupils, and virtually the same amount passed through the channel of private effort educates 612,999 high school pupils, or more than thrice as many. There is no need to linger on this. Let everything that it is possible to say about poorly paid staff and unqualified teachers in such schools be said without reserve, and also at the same time in true perspective. Even then, if this is the way in which public money is being spent, can it be asserted that it is being employed to the best advantage? Is it surprising if a feeling is created that into educational finance there are introduced considerations the fairness of which it is hard to discern? If the State continues to employ this method of finance it can do so. But so long as it does, it will find it difficult to persuade those who are keen on the education of India that educational progress is what its method of financing is calculated to promote.

62. *Middle School Education and Financial Treatment.*—We find the same thing when we look at Middle Schools. The facts speak for themselves as they stand marshalled in the following table :—

MIDDLE SCHOOLS IN BRITISH INDIA

Management	Number of Pupils	Total Cost	Contribution from Provincial Funds	Contribution from Local Funds	Total from Public Funds
		RS.	RS.	RS.	RS.
Government ...	18,841	11,31,785	8,17,798	8,100	8,25,898
Board ...	63,915	19,99,659	6,22,360	6,77,036	12,99,396
Private ...	301,632	96,35,610	22,81,079	5,43,440	28,24,519
Total ...	384,388	127,67,054	37.21,237	12,28,576	49,49,813

From this it will be seen that Boards and Private Agencies educate almost twenty times as many pupils in their Middle Schools as does Government in its Middle

Schools, and to do this they receive from all public sources a sum which is only five times what the State assigns to itself. Or put it in another way. Send 83,000 pupils to Board and Government middle schools and the payer of rates and taxes has to provide Rs. 21 lakhs. Send 302,000, or well on to a quarter of a million more, to middle schools under private management and he has to pay Rs. 28 lakhs or only Rs. 7 lakhs more. Figures such as these indicate how difficult the State is making it to justify the manner in which public funds are being allocated at the present time. With the introduction of a policy that took a wide view of all that is being done in the educational field, we should have not only a wider expansion of middle school education, if that was thought desirable, but also surer and truer control. And until such changes come about, the increase of expenditure on education can bring little or no assurance of having any sort of connexion either with the pace of educational advance or with the quality of education which one might expect to accompany that advance.

63. *Elementary Education and Financial Treatment.*—We are now in a position to consider the financing of privately managed elementary schools. The facts are given in the following table.

ELEMENTARY SCHOOLS IN BRITISH INDIA

Management	Number of Pupils	Total Cost	Contribution from Provincial Funds	Contribution from Local Funds	Total from Public Funds
		RS.	RS.	RS.	RS.
Government..	136,366	18,27,107	17,62,302	25,364	17,87,666
Board ...	4,362,093	508,07,211	302,62,263	182,77,468	485,39,731
Private ...	4,433,779	265,11,967	73,21,537	75,05,359	148,26,896
Total ...	8,932,238	791,46,285	393,46,102	258,08,191	651,54,293

What strikes us at once as we look at these figures is that the pupils who attend elementary schools are about equally distributed between board schools and privately managed schools. Each class of school has between four and four and a half million pupils. The next thing that strikes us is that along with this equality of service there is disparity of support from public funds. Private managements educate over four million boys and girls in their elementary schools and the amount which they receive from public funds, State and local, to help them in this work is Rs. 148 lakhs. Elementary Board Schools for educating about the same number of pupils receive from State revenues alone the sum of Rs. 303 lakhs, or more than twice that amount. So striking a fact as this gives one pause, more especially in the realm of elementary education. And it is thrown into greater relief when an analysis of what takes place in the various provinces shows that privately managed elementary schools in the seven provinces of Bombay, the Punjab, the United Provinces, Bengal, Bihar and Orissa, the Central Provinces, and Madras taken together educate four million boys and girls and the amount which they receive from public funds, provincial and local, is Rs. 115.89 lakhs while elementary Board schools in the province of Bombay alone, with an enrolment of 843,000 pupils, receive from the State the sum of Rs. 114.43 lakhs, or virtually the same amount. Such inequality in the disbursement of public funds raises serious doubts as to the all-important service of elementary education being one on which the State expends its revenues in the way most advantageous either to those who stand in need of education or to those who pay out of their pockets for its supply.

64. *Financial Relation of State to Private Managements unsatisfactory.*—We have considered the figures concerned with the financing of the contribution made by private effort to the education of India. And they have only one story to tell. At whatever level of educational endeavour we look at them—collegiate, high

school, middle school, or elementary—we find the same fact confronting us. There is a differentiation of financial treatment which in the realm of higher education favours colleges and schools under State management, and in the realm of elementary education favours schools under Board management. The balance at no level tilts in favour of private effort. Such an assignment of public funds has a twofold result. It gives to the agency which is bearing the heaviest burden the smallest encouragement. And by this mode of finance it makes the State in effect, what it cannot possibly intend to be, a retarder and not an accelerator of educational advance. What has led to this situation is that various questions have been almost systematically ignored in the past, and that today, if not ignored, they have received no carefully considered answer on which to base a comprehensive policy. We must endeavour to state some of these questions and to seek for the answer which promises release from the intolerable position in which education is placed through the present manner of financial administration. But before we do this we shall complete our consideration of the financial relations of the State by looking at its dealings with the Parent.

Reference

As in last section. All the figures are taken from the *Eighth* and *Ninth Quinquennial Reviews* and from the provincial *Quinquennial Reviews*.

(iv) *Is the State's financial Relation with the Parent satisfactory?*

65. *Compulsion and Freedom from Fees.*—At this point we turn to the part which the Parent plays in the financing of education. And first as to the position created by the effort to introduce compulsory elementary education. So far as this expresses itself in legislative enactments it conjoins compulsion in education with freedom from the payment of fees. Thus in the Punjab it is laid down that 'the local authority (which introduces

compulsion) shall charge no fees in any recognized school maintained by itself'. In the United Provinces it is provided that 'compulsory primary education shall be free of charge'. The Bombay Acts have the same stipulation. In Bihar and Orissa there is this variation, that education is not to be free in areas where an education cess has not been levied, but in the areas where this has been imposed 'no fee shall be charged'. The larger the sweep of compulsion, then, the greater becomes the contraction of fee income under such legislation as this. And that is all the more certain as some of the Acts apply not merely to schools provided by public authorities but also to schools that are privately managed. The Madras Elementary Education Act of 1920 in its original form laid it down that when compulsion had been introduced into an area no fee was to be charged by a school within that area, whatever might be the form of its management. In the Punjab the local authority comes under an obligation 'if required by the managers of any school within its local area not maintained wholly out of provincial or local funds' to 'pay from its own funds the whole or part of any fees payable for primary education' in respect of any pupils attending that school. Thus unless there is a change in legislation it seems likely that before long every pupil in an elementary school, at least between the age of six and ten, will be in a position to receive his education without the payment of any fee.

66. *Local Bodies and Compensation.*—Two questions suggest themselves as we look at this situation. The first is : Is it fair that Local Bodies should be responsible for the loss of fees which privately managed elementary schools suffer through the enforcement of compulsion in an area? In the Punjab alone is this obligation definitely recognized. In Madras while compensation is not a statutory obligation under the 1920 Act it has been actually paid. There is a real difficulty involved in the position; and it would not be surprising if Local Bodies

sought relief from it. One obvious way in which this relief might come would be by Local Bodies assuming responsibilities for all the compulsory elementary education carried on within their areas. But the difficulties are no less obvious. They are administrative as well as financial. A privately managed school might desire to maintain its identity, and the interests of education within the area might lend support to the desire of the school. At the same time the Local Authorities might not see their way to undertake the fresh financial commitments that the maintenance of a number of additional schools would mean for them. And this leads us to our second question.

67. *Fee-paying Schools.*—That question is: Is it necessary that every school within an area, the elementary schools of which have been brought under compulsion, should be compelled to abstain from levying fees? Already there are those who incline to answer that question in the negative. The Madras Act has been recently amended in such a way that it will be possible for privately managed schools within an area where compulsion obtains to charge fees. And how much there is to be said for an even wider application of this liberty may be gathered from what is said by the Director of Public Instruction in Bombay in the course of his recent quinquennial review. 'It is undeniable', he writes, 'that a large percentage of the children now admitted free could well afford to pay. In view of the fact that, with their present funds, the Boards are unable to provide schools for all, it is open to doubt whether it is equitable that such children should receive education free while others who want it are unable to obtain it. . . . There is no doubt that, if the School Boards chose to levy adequate fees from all who can afford to pay, considerable sums would be forthcoming for the improvement and expansion of primary education. . . . The principle formerly followed was to secure that no child is kept away from school by inability to pay fees. So long as this condition is satisfied, there would appear to be a

strong case for the levying of fees until universal primary education of a satisfactory character has been provided'. Thus, in the interests of primary education itself, there would be an advantage in permitting schools within an area where compulsion is adopted to charge fees if they chose to do so. There are indications that well-conducted schools which levy fees do not suffer from being in the vicinity of schools where no fees are charged. They unquestionably find favour with many parents; and even if they are sparingly attended to begin with the attendance at them soon increases as they are found to satisfy a want. So long as every rupee which can be obtained for education is needed, and so long as, through lack of funds on the part of the State, a great part of that need cannot be satisfied, there is good reason for holding that the educational system would benefit by the presence of fee-paying elementary schools.

68. *Facts as to Fee Income.*—If we look at a few figures we shall see that they serve to reinforce this position. With the responsibility for elementary education which has been placed upon Local Bodies within the last few years, their resources have been increasingly drawn upon and so have those of local governments. What about the parents' contribution? Comparing the figures of 1922 with those of 1927 we get the following information as to cost and fees.

COST OF ELEMENTARY SCHOOLS

Management	In 1927	In 1922	Increase or Decrease
	RS.	RS.	RS.
Government ...	18,27,107	18,34,887	− 7,780
Board ...	5,08,07,211	3,55,17,207	+1,52,90,004
Private ...	2,65,11,967	1,94,24,786	+ 70,87,181

FEES RECEIVED IN ELEMENTARY SCHOOLS

Management	In 1927	In 1922	Increase or Decrease
	RS.	RS.	RS.
Government ...	21,367	31,926	– 10,559
Board ...	17,95,973	13,94,567	+ 4,01,406
Private ...	43,28,761	40,15,188	+ 3,13,573

It will be seen that the emphasis which is being placed upon the expansion of primary education by Board schools means an increase of expenditure throughout the quinquennium of over Rs. 30 lakhs per annum. This expenditure has to be met increasingly from public funds, provincial and local. Even though stress be laid on middle vernacular schools, as is being done in Bombay, the Punjab, and Madras, and though these may come to be recognized ultimately as the most satisfactory means for the provision of education to the great mass of the people, yet in these, unless legislation undergoes a change, the children of between six and ten are not likely to be required to pay fees. Thus a source of income, the contribution of the parents, which in Board elementary schools amounts to Rs. 18 lakhs is almost bound to undergo a shrinkage. And with Rs. 18 lakhs the Boards educate about a lakh and a half of children. The shrinkage, however, may be avoided or at any rate lessened if along with the application of compulsion there goes the increase of middle vernacular schools. Where this takes place the fee income tends to rise. So far as privately managed elementary schools go it will be seen from the above table that their fee income covers about a sixth of their cost. And the relinquishment of a sum of Rs. 43 lakhs is not to be lightly contemplated, not merely for the sake of the schools themselves, but still more because that amount means the education of about six lakhs of children, not to speak of the better class of teacher which it brings within the reach of these schools. That the parent is prepared to show his appreciation of the education given in these privately managed schools is evident by his readiness to pay for it. It would be unfortunate if the parent were denied the opportunity of expressing his confidence in, and satisfaction with, the education imparted, in the practical way which the payment of fees affords. In all provinces there are means whereby members of the backward and depressed class may obtain remission of fees, and such means are available also for parents who have financial difficulties. They are fully taken advantage of. Thus there is next to no danger that the child of any parent who is unable to pay fees will have to go without the benefit of elementary education. So that every means by which the fee income of elementary schools may be continued and expanded, provided care is taken that it works no hardship to the child—a provision of which there is no difficulty in securing the operation—is to be welcomed in the interests of those who will thus be helped to obtain educational facilities which would otherwise be denied to them.

69. *Fee Income in Secondary Schools.*—Five years ago it was possible to say, in the sphere of secondary education, that 'the parent had not been called upon to meet his share' of the increased cost. And the Quinquennial Review of 1922 could state that 'the average annual contribution made by a parent in India towards the cost of educating his son in a secondary school has only risen from Rs. 18.1 to Rs. 21.3 as contrasted with an increase in cost to Government from Rs. 6.1 to Rs. 14.7'. Such statements are no longer possible. In the years that have followed 1922 the change has been most marked. What we are now told is that 'the increase in expenditure from Government funds is Rs. 30 lakhs less than the corresponding increase in the previous quinquennium', while in fees there has been an 'increase of

Rs. 45 lakhs'. What was spent on middle English and high schools in 1927 was 32 per cent more than the amount spent in 1922; but the amount received in fees was 37 per cent greater. Indeed it may be said that the wording of the Educational Commissioner's statement in 1922 was almost truer than he realized. 'The parent had not been called upon to meet his share of the increased cost of education'. When the parent is actually called upon to do his part he may be counted upon to do it. Things have undoubtedly improved; but as we go through the various statistical tables we meet figures which cause us to ask: Is the parent yet being called upon to meet what is his share of the increased cost of secondary education? We may get an answer to that question if we consider for instance, what the fee is which on an average a high school pupil pays annually in each of the larger Administrations. It varies from province to province and from management to management, as the following table based on the figures of the Ninth Quinquennial Review shows.

AVERAGE ANNUAL FEE PAID BY HIGH SCHOOL PUPILS IN SEVEN PROVINCES

Management	Province						
	Punjab	United Provinces	Bombay	Bengal	Central Provinces	Madras	Bihar and Orissa
	RS.	RS.	RS.	RS.	RS.	RS.	RS
Government ...	28	19	43	28	41	16	28
Board ...	20	22	29	27	36	24	...
Private ...	20	29	39	26	50	27	24

Much might be said by way of commentary on these figures. Two remarks must suffice. First, even the highest amount which the parent pays in those provinces for the education of his child in a high school is a comparatively small recognition of a great benefit. Second, does it not look as if, in connexion with high school education, provincial and local funds were being employed to meet a considerable amount of the cost that ought to be defrayed by the parent?

70. *Fees in Arts Colleges.*—The same question occurs to us when we consider the fees that are being paid in Arts Colleges. The following table gives us some of the relevant information.

AVERAGE ANNUAL FEE PAID BY ARTS COLLEGE STUDENTS IN SEVEN PROVINCES

Management	Province						
	Punjab	United Provinces	Bombay	Bengal	Central Provinces	Madras	Bihar and Orissa
	RS.	RS.	RS.	RS.	RS.	RS.	RS.
Government ...	99	94	122	130	77	89	87
Board ...	...	...	...	...	...	54	...
Private ...	90	72 or 131	132	73	91	97	70

As the majority of the universities in the United Provinces are not of the affiliating type, an element of uncertainty is introduced into calculations dealing with the arts colleges of the province and the fees paid in them. But if we look at the other six provinces we cannot help being struck with the fact that in three of them it is possible for a non-departmental college to obtain from its students a higher fee than does a departmental college. Does not this place the State, as a manager among other managers, in an unfortunate position? And does it not look as if public funds were being called on to some extent to do what it is the plain duty of the parent to do? And is not that a duty which the parent is prepared to perform, and which he does perform when the opportunity is given to him, as the figures show? Why then withhold the opportunity?

71. *Action on the Part of Government.*—Some governments seem to feel that the drain on public funds is too great. In one province, it is stated, fees have been raised in certain departmental institutions since the Ninth Quinquennial Review was published; in another an effort was made to do this, but without success. The Government of Bombay itself tells the story. 'In order to give the lead to the aided institutions', it says, 'Government proposed recently to raise the fees in their colleges and high schools, but owing to an adverse vote in the course of the discussion of last year's budget which was repeated in the discussion on the budget for the current year, the proposal was turned down. Meantime certain aided colleges realizing the remedy have increased their fees without waiting for Government to adopt their measures'. This is rather a pitiable tale. The State sets out to give a lead to private managements; in the result, the aided managements give a lead to the State. The frank official statement brings many a question to one's lips. What is the connexion between the adverse vote and the refusal to adopt a course which sound educational considerations demanded? Had the members of the Legislative Council any notion of the position of the fee income in Government colleges? Is it not possible for Government as a manager to do what other managers do, namely to bring its scale of fees into line with the facilities which it affords and for which it pays? It would be difficult to find anything which proved so conclusively as these two sentences taken from the Government's own account how unfortunate is the conjunction of State control with State

management. It tells adversely even in the matter of fees.

72. *Financial Relation of State with Parent Unsatisfactory.*—In closing our consideration of the financial relation between the State and the parent we may note that there is another reason besides that of the general financing of education why the contribution of the parent should receive an attention which is not at present given to it. Every educational report lays emphasis on the large number who proceed to higher education without having any special qualification for its pursuit and with little power to benefit by what it imparts. While those with suitable capacity deserve every encouragement, those who are not so gifted would have a real service rendered to them if they were discouraged from entrance upon a course both long and expensive, and unlikely in the end to bring them advantages for which they had hoped. Much of the evil that is now all too patent, many a sore disappointment and much heartfelt discontent, might thus be avoided. Many factors would contribute to this result, as for example alternative courses, new openings, higher standards of study; but amongst them would have to be included what we are now considering, the levying of appropriate scales of fees. That, combined with the system of scholarships which the State has established, and the concessions made in respect of the able children of needy parents, would mean that no barrier was placed in the way of the capable pupil, while at the same time it would have a deterring effect on the not inconsiderable number whose parents would benefit, as would they themselves, by the choice of a line of study different from that which is usually spoken of as 'higher education'. Whether, then, we take into account such a consideration as this, or whether we think of what has been already dwelt on, the present level of fees now levied, the readiness of the parent to pay for the education of his children, and the manner in which public funds are being employed, we are led to the conclusion that the State's

financial relation to the Parent cannot be regarded as satisfactory, and that it calls for definite modification.

References

All the figures are taken from the *Quinquennial Reviews*, central and provincial. The quotation from the statement of the Bombay Government is taken from the Resolution of the Government in the Educational Department No. P. 36 of 7th June, 1929.

IV. Issues to be Faced

73. *Statement of the Issues.*—We have now completed our survey of the financial relations of the State with itself, Local Bodies, Private Managements, and the Parent. This survey has been sufficient to convince us that the present system of financing is unsatisfactory, and has besides the unfortunate effect of rendering the position of the State equivocal. Is there any means by which the State may be relieved from this position, and by which the financing of education may be placed on a satisfactory basis? We shall be helped in our search for such a means if we can find answers to three questions pressed upon us by our consideration of the methods of finance that are now employed. The first of these is: Is it the policy of the State to spread elementary education solely through the medium of Board schools? The second is: Has the State a definite policy in regard to grants-in-aid? And the third is: Has the State a definite policy in regard to educational administration? It may be argued and not without reason that the second question really includes the first. But clearness demands that they should be treated separately. And it may be said, also not without reason, that the third has been already dealt with under the Problem of Control. But considerations of finance require that because of its bearing on provincial expenditure it should be dealt with also under the Problem of Finance. These are the three issues, and we must now face them one by one.

(i) *Is it the Policy of the State to extend Elementary Education solely by Board Schools?*

74. *Present Position.*—What answer are we to return to the question: Is it the policy of the State to have only one medium for the advance of mass education, the medium of the Board school? If we betake ourselves to facts, the answer which they supply is that there is no agreement on any such policy. The wording of one part of the Government of India Resolution of 1913 indicated that, subject to certain provisos and exceptions, the expansion of elementary education was to proceed by means of Board schools. But no generally adopted line of action followed from this declaration of the central Government. Nor was it otherwise when six years later each province became responsible for its own educational policy. What did appear was not agreement but difference. It was as if the provinces fell into two groups so far as their attitude to the mode of spreading elementary education was concerned. And that continues to be the case at the present day. As the Educational Commissioner puts it: 'In Madras, Bengal, Burma, and Bihar primary schools are mainly provided by private agencies, while in the other provinces (Bombay, United Provinces, Punjab, and Central Provinces) they are mainly provided by local bodies'. The South and the East rely chiefly on private managements; the North and the West mainly on board managements. There is no agreement throughout British India on a policy which makes Local Bodies the sole means whereby the expansion of elementary education is to be secured.

75. *Lines of Action open to Provinces.*—Can we go further than that? Yes, if we consider what has been done, and what is being done, by provinces in which the policy adopted is to advance the education of the great mass of the people through the medium of Board schools. Two lines of action were open to the Government that decided to adopt such a policy. On the one

hand, it could have decided to send all its funds for the promotion of elementary education through the channel of Local Bodies, and to assume complete responsibility for the supply of this form of education within the province exclusively by their agency. In that case every school contributed by a non-local body would have been of an entirely private character and, in the eyes of the State, a work of supererogation. Thus quite logically it would have received from the State no regular financial aid. On the other hand, the Government of the province might have decided that the main emphasis was to be placed upon the work of Local Boards, but that, because of existing lack of facilities, it was advisable to depend to a certain extent on private managements as well, the contribution of managements thus depended on to receive from the State full encouragement both financial and administrative. In that case these private agencies which were recognized as co-operating with the Government in the work of elementary education would have been given to all intents and purposes the same status as, though a more limited extent of activity than, the Boards. Now what the facts reveal to us is that it is neither of these lines of action which has been adopted. Where it has been decided to advance elementary education by placing emphasis upon Local Bodies, private managements have not been eliminated; yet where they have been allowed to remain they cannot be said to have been encouraged. A little detail will make this clear.

76. *Lines of Action actually Taken.*—We may begin by looking at what takes place in the four provinces which rely mainly upon Boards for the expansion of elementary education, namely the United Provinces, the Punjab, the Central Provinces, and Bombay. To help us in this consideration, as well as to facilitate comparison with some of the provinces such as Bengal and Madras which do not rely on Boards, it will be advantageous to have the following tables before us.

I. ELEMENTARY SCHOOLS UNDER BOARD MANAGEMENT IN SIX PROVINCES

Province	Population in Millions	Number of Pupils	Total cost	Cost to Provincial Revenues	Cost to Local Funds	Total cost to Public Funds
			RS.	RS.	RS.	RS.
United Provinces ...	45·3	988,559	81,14,977	59,87,833	17,06,626	76,94,459
Punjab	20·6	695,929	74,93,608	49,52,269	20,63,306	70,15,575
Central Provinces ...	13·9	308,522	34,04,684	18,77,561	13,94,210	32,71,771
Bombay	19·2	843,135	173,17,537	114,43,612	53,98,507	168,47,119
Total ...	99·0	2,836,145	363,30,806	242,61,275	105,62,649	348,28,924
Bengal	46·6	194,573	11,24,699	4,67,776	3,85,538	8,53,314
Madras	42·3	903,893	89,28,745	40,76,165	47,41,604	88,17,769
Total ...	88·9	1,098,466	100,53,444	45,43,941	51,27,142	96,71,083

II. ELEMENTARY SCHOOLS UNDER PRIVATE MANAGEMENT IN SIX PROVINCES

Province	Population in Millions	Number of Pupils	Total cost	Cost to Provincial Revenues	Cost to Local Funds	Total cost to Public Funds
			RS.	RS.	RS.	RS.
United Provinces ...	45·3	171,385	11,36,566	4,54,644	3,34,072	7,88,716
Punjab	20·6	99,629	9,22,796	2,30,259	2,36,839	4,67,098
Central Provinces ...	13·9	28,570	4,53,535	93,688	26,608	1,20,296
Bombay	19·2	136,759	24,09,091	5,87,027	2,56,016	8,43,043
Total ...	99·0	436,343	49,21,988	13,65,618	8,53,535	22,19,153
Bengal	46·6	1,549,305	56,74,834	17,37,864	9,05,912	26,43,776
Madras	42·3	1,243,339	132,49,800	38,90,020	12,790	39,02,810
	88·9	2,792,644	189,24,634	56,27,884	9,18,702	65,46,586

What is it that we learn from the figures? In the first place, the totals make it clear that while, in the first four provinces emphasis is placed on Board schools, these are not the means exclusively employed to develop elementary education. Of the pupils in the elementary schools of these provinces, 28.4 lakhs are in Board schools and 4.4 lakhs are in schools under private management. That is to say, for more than an eighth of those who are receiving elementary education provision is made by non-Board managements. In the second place, the privately managed schools cannot be said to receive financial encouragement at the hands of the State. While they educate between a sixth and a seventh of the number educated by the Boards they receive from public funds, provincial and local, one eleventh of what the Boards receive from provincial funds alone. Such an allocation of funds cannot be regarded as giving private managers much hint to continue contributing towards the supply of what is admitted to be one of the most pressing needs of the country. In the third place, glancing from the totals to the individual provinces we find that there is only one of these provinces that accords to private managers equality of financial treatment with that accorded to Board managements. And if we turn from the tables given in the Quinquennial Review of that province to the letterpress we find that what is there stated could hardly be read as encouragement even by the most optimistic of private school managers. One of the official opinions quoted, it may be remarked, envisages a time when such schools will have no place in the system. In the four provinces, then, which rely mainly on Board schools for the advance of elementary education private agencies are not eliminated. They take their place alongside the Board schools and educate something approaching half a million pupils. Yet though they do this they are not encouraged, discouragement being either financial or administrative. The policy that is pursued neither makes exclusive use of the Boards nor gives encouragement to other agencies to supplement the work of the Boards. It falls between two stools.

77. *Such Policy ignores what is fundamental.*—Would it not be well to recognize that this is the inevitable result of such a policy? The result cannot possibly be different because the policy takes account of only one factor. It dwells upon one means for the supply of a need, although there is more than one means available; and it fails to dwell upon the immensity of the need. But the fundamental point is this immensity. So long as that is not grasped the question as to whether one means is to be mainly relied on, when there are two available, is almost wholly academic. In theory there is no fault to be found with the official who looks forward to a time when the whole responsibility for the elementary education of his province will be borne by Board schools. But when, as the figures show, not three per cent of the children of school-going age in that province are actually at school, such looking forward can hardly be said to belong to the realm of reality. And when we are dealing with elementary education and policies for its spread we have to come face to face with facts, however much we may dislike them. In the four provinces mentioned above there is a population of 99 millions. Consequently there should be 13 million boys and girls at school. Actually there are 3 millions. That is to say, not only are there millions who do not attend school but there are ten millions for whom, if they wished to attend school, there are neither school buildings nor teachers available. It is facts like these that must dictate policy. It is the crying need and the utter inadequacy of its supply that must tower above all other considerations. And in the presence of facts so wounding to a nation's self-esteem to propose to rely for the remedy on one agency, the resources of which are wholly inadequate to a task of such magnitude, and to discourage another agency which with proper care is capable of taking no small share in the task and of contributing out of its own resources towards its accom-

plishment—to do this is to ignore essential facts, to propound a short-sighted policy, and, worst of all, to deprive large sections of the community of opportunities for the desperately needed education of their children.

78. *Effect of a comprehensive Policy.*—How different is the situation presented in those provinces where another policy is adopted. In the four provinces to which we have referred as mainly relying on Boards for the spread of elementary education a little over two and three-quarter million pupils are educated in Board schools at a cost to the State of Rs. 242.6 lakhs. In the two provinces of Bengal and Madras where no such reliance obtains, the same number of pupils is being educated in privately managed schools and the cost to the State is less than a quarter of that amount, or Rs. 56 lakhs. Where the State seeks to lay the main emphasis on one form of management it fails to advance the spirit of local self-government, it introduces inequality of treatment, it discourages contributions that would otherwise be forthcoming; in effect, it offers an obstacle to educational progress. Where the State seeks to follow no such policy but to rely on every approved agency, and to draw them all together under its control into a common service, each agency develops and presents its characteristic contribution, provincial funds are spent to good advantage, and the State, by the line of action which it has adopted, gives to the advance of education a stimulus which is shown in quickened progress and in the larger opportunity which the State enjoys for the exercise of beneficial control.

79. *Financial Consequences of Boards as Controllers.*—There is, then, no consistent policy in favour of relying solely on Local Bodies for the spread of elementary education. Further, there is no consistent policy of relying mainly on them. And it is well that this is the case. For we have seen how far removed is such a policy from the best interests of educational progress. How far removed, receives fresh emphasis from what has become of late a feature of policy in certain provinces, that of

making Boards controllers while allowing them to continue in the exercise of powers of management along with others. If a definite line of policy had been adopted which dispensed with every management save that of Local Bodies there would have been no difficulty in that management exercising a delegate control, combining in itself and in itself alone both functions. But that is not the line which has been followed. And the result is what every one must see to be inevitable. To put it bluntly the Board as controller is felt to be favourable to itself as manager and unfavourable to other managers. Can any one who looks at the financing of education say that this is a groundless prejudice? In the United Provinces, the Punjab, and Bombay where Boards are in control, they secure for their own schools which educate 25 lakhs of pupils Rs. 224 lakhs from the State, while the privately managed schools in these provinces with 4 lakhs of pupils have to be content with Rs. 13 lakhs. And while on the schools under private management Boards expend Rs. 8 lakhs, on their own schools they spend Rs. 92 lakhs. Could any method be more calculated to make managements other than Local Bodies feel that they are under a control which says to them as plainly as financial dealings and figures can say it, that there is one, and only one, management which is to be cherished whatever be the cost, and even if it brings into its schools only three millions out of a possible thirteen millions? Could there be any line of action more likely to generate suspicion regarding the impartiality of the controlling power? Could there be any policy better devised to place unnecessary obstacles in the way of educational advance? Does not this mode of working render imperative a reconsideration of the whole position if primary education is to have that place in national life which it must have, if national life is not to be a chimaera?

80. *Attitude of the State.*—Any one who looks at educational figures and surveys is bound to realize that the time for such a reconsideration has most assuredly come

He will find, as he reads official reviews, page after page in which criticism follows criticism of the provision made by private managements, until he will find it hard to understand how it is that, if their sins are so scarlet, the confidence reposed in them is so widespread. And if he turns from letterpress to statistical tables he will note, what he could not have known otherwise, how small is the support which these managements receive from provincial funds. And then his eye will be caught by what these surveys have to say about the provision made by Local Board managements. He will read of 'abuses', 'perversity', 'defects', and worse. And he will have his curiosity stirred as to how the State treats these managements whose iniquities are thus confessed. The reading of a few pages will satisfy that curiosity. He will learn that to these managements State revenues are generously supplied. What is he to think of such a situation? He is forced to one or other of two conclusions. Either, serious defects attach to only one form of management, in which case the recognition and support of another indicates the misuse of powers of control and a culpable waste of State funds. Or, serious defects are not confined to one particular form of management, in which case an allocation of State funds which is determined by reference to the form of management and not by reference to the educational service rendered is wholly out of place. If the first supposition is correct, the State which supports a second form of management is shown thereby to be no competent controller. If the second supposition is correct, the State which assigns funds on the basis of management is thereby shown to be no impartial controller. The policy of depending on one form of management exclusively or mainly for the provision of elementary education not only fails to employ public funds to the best advantage; it exposes the State, in its capacity as controller, to the charge either of incompetence or of partiality. Such a policy, in the interests of the State and of education, calls for speedy reconsideration and fundamental modification.

81. *No generally accepted Policy of Reliance on Boards.*—Clearly then what is needed, as the facts we have been considering press upon us now from one point of view, now from another, is a thorough examination of the lines along which the financial policy of the State in regard to elementary education has been moving of late and still continues to move. We began by asking whether it was the policy of the State to adopt one medium for the advance of elementary education. We found that, while there was no general avowed policy in favour of relying on one form of management, there was a tendency for several provinces to rely in the main on one management, that of Local Bodies. And we also found that where such a line of policy has been developed, the system of provincial subsidy adopted by the State has been such as to result in preferential treatment to these Bodies, while the administrative system employed by the State has been such as to give them preferential treatment in respect of control. Thus a singular situation has arisen. By placing emphasis on one means of advancing mass education, the State has poured out its funds in aid of that one means until in one province it has actually had to curtail expenditure on schemes of expansion. Yet though the State has spent so freely on Local Bodies, there is little sign that it has thereby succeeded in evoking and rallying to its support that spirit of local self-government the development of which is one of the greatest assets that the education of any country can possess. And at the same time, by the line of action which it has adopted, it has not only drawn into Board Schools a comparatively small number of boys and girls of school-going age, it has also in large measure deprived itself of the vigorous support of another form of management which, even while not encouraged, has made no inconsiderable contribution to the education of these provinces, and which by its encouragement in other provinces has done yeoman service in the cause of elementary education. The policy of reliance on one form of management for the expansion of elementary

education is partial not comprehensive; it spends provincial funds generously but not to best advantage. It is not a policy for general adoption. The interests of the country call for another and totally different line of action. What that is will be evident when, as we now proceed to do, we seek to give an answer to our second question.

(ii) *Has the State a Policy regarding Grants-in-Aid?*

82. *Lack of Agreement as to Principles.*—That second question is: Has the State a definite policy in regard to aid? So far as official statements go, one would rather gather that it has. But when one looks into such a monograph as Richey's 'Grants-in-aid', and still more when one looks at financial tables in official reviews, one begins to have doubts on the matter. It is not only that the action of the government of one province differs from that of another—that would be both intelligible and natural—but that there seems to be a lack of principles regulating the disbursement of grants and subsidies which find general acceptance among provincial governments. One would have thought, for instance, that the State would have employed grants-in-aid for the advance of education in every instance where it was possible to secure a suitable management to aid. And one would also have thought that, in general, the State would see to it that the grants bore some kind of relation to the amount of work done. On two such principles, neither of them rigid and both of them fair, a system of financial dealing might well be built up which would evoke the maximum of educational effort, which would lead to valuable co-operation, and which would utilise provincial funds to the best advantage. Yet we search in vain for signs of the widespread employment of either principle.

83. *Illustration from the State and Elementary Education.*—Let us take another glance at elementary

education. This is a field from which the State is withdrawing, a field in which good and stable managements abound, a field within which there seems every reason why the first of our principles should operate to the full. Yet if the State is withdrawing it is very slow to take the final plunge as the following table shows.

ELEMENTARY SCHOOLS UNDER STATE MANAGEMENT IN 1922 AND 1927

Year	Number of Pupils	Total Cost	Contribution from Provincial Revenues
		RS.	RS.
1927	136,366	18,27,107	17,62,302
1922	108,364	18,34,887	17,83,402
	Increase : 28,002	Decrease : 7,780	Decrease : 21,100

The State still increases the number of pupils whom it educates at this stage, and it spends seventeen and a half lakhs from its own resources on them. The sum is large; as things now go too large. The best that can be said for it is that it is some Rs. 21,000 less than it was five years before. All the same it is surely high time that the State should dissociate itself entirely from the management of elementary schools and should give effect through the length and breadth of the country to the principle that where there is a capable management to aid there aid shall be employed.

84. *Illustration from Boards and Elementary Education.*—What about the second of our principles in the field of elementary education? Let us look at what the non-departmental agencies are doing in that field and what advance they have made in the course of five years. The following table gives us the facts.

ELEMENTARY SCHOOLS UNDER BOARD AND PRIVATE MANAGEMENT IN 1922 AND 1927

Year	Under Board Management		Year	Under Private Management	
	Number of Pupils	Cost to Provincial Revenues		Number of Pupils	Cost to Provincial Revenues
		RS.			RS.
1927	4,362,093	3,02,62,263	1927	4,433,779	73,21,537
1922	2,980,607	2,21,97,201	1922	3,574,871	51,40,063
	1,381,486	80,65,062		858,908	21,81,474

From these figures it is plain that, within the quinquennium, Local Bodies have virtually blotted out the difference which existed between them and Private Bodies in regard to the number of pupils attending the elementary schools under their management. Local Bodies have added to the pupils enrolled in their schools at the rate of 2.8 lakhs per annum, while in schools under private management the increase has been only 1.7 lakh. In great part what this means is that Local Bodies had a considerable leeway to make up and they have done it. So that now, so far as the burden shouldered by the two forms of management goes, there is equality. But, as we have already noted, equality of support does not correspond to equality of burden. If we look not at the total figures but at the subsidy, we see that it, as the table shows, has been going up at the rate of Rs. 16 lakhs per annum to Local Bodies and at the rate of just over Rs. 4 lakhs to Private Agencies. It would have been interesting to see what would have happened had there been some equality of subsidy from the State, if even the rate to Private Agencies had been Rs. 8 lakhs instead of Rs. 4 lakhs, or if the total amount placed at the disposal of these Agencies had been a crore and a half (half that given to Local Bodies) instead of Rs. 73 lakhs. The growth of Board schools is not difficult to understand when we look at these few figures.

Far more difficult is it to understand how there is such vitality and advance in schools under private management, considering the meagreness of the support which they receive from the State and the absence of relation between subsidy given and work done. There can be only one explanation, a desire for the spread of education that refuses to be baulked. Whatever official statements may say there can be no doubt as to what statistical tables say. Their figures spell discouragement to a capable, vigorous, and undismayed agency. It can hardly be that this is what the State intends. But it is the result to which it is being driven by the absence of adherence to a clearly defined policy. Were the State to lay it down that its subsidies from provincial revenues were to be made impartially to every approved educational agency, and that these subsidies were to be related to the service rendered, the present anomaly would cease and elementary education would have a steady and valued driving force behind it. Boards would be encouraged to exercise to the full their statutory financial powers, and Private Agencies would be stimulated to enhance their contribution to the education of the people, a contribution which even under present discouragement is so marked. Between 1922 and 1927 two million pupils were added to the elementary schools of the country. There is no reason why, in the course of a quinquennium, a policy of grant-in-aid based on sound principles should not result in the addition of two millions to the enrolment of privately managed schools alone.

85. *Present Attitude a Hindrance to Education.*—The responsibility resting on the State for the formulation and maintenance of an equitable system of aid requires to be pressed with unsparing energy. Either memories are short as regards the past, or eyes are deliberately closed as to what is the present position of elementary education in India. Government and Boards have been at work for several decades, they have had allocated to them large sums from provincial revenues,

they have had the backing of most favourable statutory enactments, and what they are able to show as the result of all these factors operating so generously on their behalf is a total of four and a half million boys and girls attending their elementary schools. It is a lamentable result when we remember that the number of children of school-going age is over thirty millions more. There is, however, one bright spot in this dark situation. The number of boys and girls actually attending elementary schools is not four and a half millions but nine millions. How does it come about that the number is doubled, and that the resulting total has some appearance of being presentable? It is because an agency that is an integral part of the educational system of the land but which has no statutory powers, whose only financial right is to dip into its own pocket, and whose effort has met and still meets with strange discouragement at many points, believes in education so heartily and works for it so unflinchingly that it brings millions into the elementary schools of the country. For this service it receives from provincial funds Rs. 73 lakhs while for a similar service the State and Boards receive Rs. 320 lakhs. Is it not time that such an allocation of public funds should be acknowledged as inequitable and in need of radical alteration? Is it not time that the failure of the State to advance elementary education should be traced to its indubitable source, to its reliance in large areas of the land on a line of action that extends preferential treatment to an educational agency the response of which is limited, and to its lack of encouragement of an agency which with no statute to support it brings to the service of elementary education crores of rupees, lakhs of teachers, millions of pupils, and all the force of private initiative? Is it not time to recognize that when the State has about four crores to spend on mass education it acts in a way prejudicial to the public interest if it gives over three crores to one agency which educates four and a half millions and three-quarters of a crore to another agency which educates a similar number? And if that is what is happening at present is it not time to realize that education is being jeopardized by such a procedure, by such failure to abide by definite and salutary principles? Yet what is happening now is nothing new. We have only to read through the pages of Indian educational history to find its parallels in the past. How long is it to be allowed to continue? How long is it to receive the countenance of the State? How long is the State to allow those who examine its workings to say of it that it has pledged itself officially to the spread of elementary education, but that financially it has committed itself to a mode of action which discourages its spread? There can be but one answer to that : The State will allow this wholly indefensible situation to continue until it sets itself resolutely to carry into effect a financial policy which brings aid into effective relation with the extent and character of educational service rendered.

86. *Lack of Policy in High School Education.*—Let us now turn from the field of elementary, to that of secondary, education. If we consider what has been happening in regard to high schools during the quinquennium 1922-27 this is what the figures tell us.

HIGH SCHOOLS IN 1922 AND 1927

Year	State Management		Board Management		Private Management	
	Number of Pupils	Grant from Provincial Revenues	Number of Pupils	Grant from Provincial Revenues	Number of Pupils	Grant from Provincial Revenues
		RS.		RS.		RS.
927 ...	112,920	61,98,162	68,776	7,24,985	612,505	76,42,475
922 ...	86,447	49,65,906	45,498	3,53,901	462,965	56,29,327
ncrease ...	26,473	12,32,256	23,278	3,71,084	149,540	20,13,148

We have already seen how into this field, which by common consent stretching over several decades is one where reliance on non-departmental effort is specially appropriate, the State enters as a manager. Unsatisfactory as is this from the point of view of management, it is no less unsatisfactory from the point of view of finance. To add 26,000 pupils to its own high schools during the five years mentioned, the State has allocated to itself from its own resources Rs. 12 lakhs. To the Boards which have added almost as many, it has assigned not Rs. 12 lakhs but less than a third of that amount; while to the agency which has added 150,000 it has assigned Rs. 20 lakhs. Such differentiation of treatment is simply discouragement of effort. Yet it looks as if it were almost impossible for the State to see the situation in this light. It is useless for it to say that in so allocating its funds it is spending largely on 'model' schools, when there is no more in this 'model' theory than there was in the old 'filtration' theory which the State once espoused with detriment to educational advance. Equally useless is it for the State to say that 'The steady fall in the proportion of expenditure from "other sources" indicates that the grant-in-aid rules, in spite of recent economies in the assessment of grants-in-aid, are still generous', when its generosity amounts to this that, as the relevant figures show, it allocates in this particular case the same sum to secondary schools under private management which educate 100,000 pupils as it does to those under its own management which are attended by 29,000 pupils. The wonder really is that private effort should manage to achieve so much in all directions as it does year after year while it receives such financial treatment at the hands of the State. And the wonder also is that the State which is the controller of education can allow this to go on year after year. A policy of grant-in-aid that applies equally to all acknowledged and recognized educational agencies, whatever the management may be, is what is required both to advance education and to deal fairly with the taxpayer's money.

87. *Lack of Policy in Middle School Education.*—The financing of Middle English Schools for the past quinquennium is presented in the following table.

MIDDLE SCHOOLS IN 1922 AND 1927

Year	State Management		Board Management		Private Management	
	Number of Pupils	Grant from Provincial Revenues	Number of Pupils	Grant from Provincial Revenues	Number of Pupils	Grant from Provincial Revenues
		RS.		RS.		RS.
1927 ...	18,841	8,17,798	63,915	6,22,360	301,632	22,81,079
1922 ...	14,934	8,10,143	43,806	4,46,987	232,432	22,03,556
Increase ...	3,907	7,655	20,109	1,75,373	69,200	77,523

There is one satisfactory feature disclosed by these figures, the fact namely that the State is adding little to its responsibilities in this field. In five years it has enrolled not quite 4,000 additional pupils, while its financial commitments have increased by not much more than Rs. 120 per mensem. But why should it be educating even 19,000 pupils, more especially when to do this the State assigns to itself from its own revenues over eight lakhs of rupees? And why should it do this when there are Boards which educate three times as many and receive from the State two lakhs less, and Private Managements which educate sixteen times as many and receive from the State less than three times what it allocates to itself? And as if this mode of assigning grants was not sufficiently puzzling, the figures add to our bewilderment by showing that, while during the quinquennium private managements have added to their schools more than three times as many pupils as have Boards, the additional grant given during that time to the Boards by the State is more than double that given to Private Managers. Once again we are brought face to face with the fact which is being steadily ignored, namely that the State has no clear policy of grant-in-aid and that because of this, education fails to make the advance which is within its power, as well as to achieve results commensurate with the sums of public funds expended on it.

88. *Lack of Policy in Collegiate Education.*—The need for a definite policy which has been revealed to us by consideration of the financial aspects of elementary and secondary education, makes itself felt as strongly when we look at the facts concerning Arts Colleges. The facts are presented in the following table.

ARTS AND INTERMEDIATE COLLEGES IN 1922 AND 1927

Year	State Management		Board Management		Private Management	
	Number of Students	Grant from Provincial Revenues	Number of Students	Grant from Provincial Revenues	Number of Students	Grant from Provincial Revenues
		RS.		RS.		RS.
1927 ...	16,101	40,75,954	149	4,000	55,718	19,61,358
1922 ...	11,123	33,78,579	296	20,143	34,514	15,27,944
Difference.	4,978	6,97,375	147	16,143	21,204	4,33,414
	Increase		Decrease		Increase	

This table indicates that District Boards and Municipalities are finding the demands upon them for the advance of elementary education so exacting that they are unable to finance collegiate education as they have done in the past. This is much to be regretted. For one thing, without adequate participation in collegiate education the spirit of local self-government fails of its natural exercise. And for another, until the Boards regain their strength in this region, which is admittedly one for the contribution of non-departmental agencies, that contribution will have to come almost entirely from private managements. And so it does, as the figures show. But how it does, the system of financing that now prevails makes it difficult for us to understand. For in this sphere the State has been pressing its own advance, adding to its students at the rate of almost a thousand per annum, and for its service drawing on provincial funds at the rate of an additional lakh and a third every year. Thus while what the State expends on arts colleges under its own management is steadily rising, it is also rising out of proportion to the work done. To add a thousand students per annum to its arts colleges the State assigns itself out of its revenues Rs. 1,40,000; but if four times that number are added to colleges under private management though under public control, as has occurred in the course of the quinquennium, the subsidy which the State gives to these colleges is Rs. 87,000. The discrepancy, even when fullest allowance is made for difference in status and equipment of colleges, is so startling that if a policy is asserted to exist then the only description of it that is at all applicable is: A policy that encourages an agency on the shoulders of which the smaller amount of educational responsibility is carried, that places at a disadvantage the agency which tackles the larger task, and so in effect a policy that discourages the spread of higher education. Now there is no likelihood that the State would desire to associate itself with any such policy. All the more reason therefore that by its financial allocations it should separate itself once and for all from even the semblance of such an identification. And thus all the more reason still, that it should be the clear and unflinching exponent of a policy which links the education of the country with a system of grant-in-aid that does justice to the needs of the situation and the work actually accomplished.

89. *Ill Results of Lack of Policy.*—We might complete our survey of education by looking at the financial aspects of the State's policy in regard to professional, technical, commercial, and special forms of education. But, by comparison, the amount that is expended on these branches is small, and the consideration of them confronts us with no fresh principles. We may therefore content ourselves with the result of what we have passed under examination in this section, the all-important realm of general education. Here is the mainstay of the educational structure. And what have we found in regard to it? That through the length and breadth of it no comprehensive policy of grant-in-aid exists. That the operation of the grant system as at present administered is a virtual discouragement of much educational initiative and vigorous effort. That provincial revenues are not being employed to the best advantage, and that education is made to suffer, seriously and wholly unnecessarily.

90. *Need for Policy based on Principles.*—The worst of it is that this situation is not a matter of today or the day before. It has been pointed out again and again through the story of education in India. And while official documents have criticized the action of provincial governments, budgets have been slow to express that criticism in terms of rupees. The policy of grant-in-aid set forth in the Despatch of 1854 was treated for years with such neglect that, almost a generation later, several governments came under the strong criticism of the Indian Education Commission for their manner of administering it. The evidence before the Commission showed that in many cases the amount of grants to well managed aided schools and colleges had been restricted and reduced, while on Government schools and colleges in the same area public funds were being liberally expended. The recommendations of the Commission which

the Government of India accepted were intended to secure that there would be no repetition of any such procedure on the part of local governments. And to a certain extent they were successful. But only to a certain extent. In their Resolution of the 4th November 1899, that is to say some fifteen years after the publication of the Commission's Report, we find the Government of India commenting on departures which the State has made from the position of impartiality. And it adduces a very striking instance. The Governor of one of the provinces, it tells us, was addressing his Legislative Council, and in the course of his remarks regarding education he made the following statement: 'It has been said with some truth no doubt that, whenever it is a question of providing money for a Government institution, money is forthcoming; but whenever it is necessary for other institutions the reply is always unfortunately *non possumus* . . . If twenty-one people are knocking at the door of Government for relief, who is the person that is likely to receive attention from Government first, Government institutions or what I may call strangers? Of the twenty-one it is only natural that Government should be a little more tender-hearted to its own particular child. But when its child has been fed, I think we may be able to extend our attention to the other twenty'. On this the Government of India comments: 'This is surely not to make the improvement and extension of institutions under private managers "the principal care of the Department". The Governor's language would be appropriate in the head of a rival concern, but in the Home Department Resolution, dated 18th June 1888, it was distinctly laid down that "in this as in all other matters it is the policy of the Government of India to avoid entering into competition with private enterprise".' This quotation is significant. Here is the head of a province with a whole Education Department to advise him who not only supports the policy of illiberality towards aided education which that Department has been pursuing, but justifies it on the ground that departmental educational effort and private educational effort do not belong to the same family. One of them is a child of the family, the other is an alien. The Government of India puts its finger on the fundamental misconception which runs right through the Governor's speech. The official spokesman of this province, it says, places the State in the position of an educational rival. There is no comprehensive policy here. The eye of the State is not concentrated on education as a whole and the steps to be taken to advance the education of the whole country. The eye of the State is fixed on a department of the State. And now another generation has passed. No speech from an authoritative source has again given utterance to so complete a misrepresentation of the position and duty of the State with regard to education. But if there has been no such speech there have been, and there still are, figures that unfortunately set forth virtually the same position. What the Education Commission saw and what the Government of India saw is very much what we are looking upon once again today. A policy of grant-in-aid which is intended to be applicable to all grades of education and to work on principles that deal equitably with every approved management under the control of the State so as to bind all together in a great educational forward movement is being treated with financial discouragement. And the Government of India has now no status in the latter. The responsibility for a change of attitude therefore rests on each provincial government. Yet, can any one say that that responsibility is being fairly faced? Criticism of managements and contrasts between managements have their undoubted place in educational discussions, and within that place are to be welcomed. But prior to these there must be, as the facts make only too plain, another form of criticism, and the need for it cannot be too strongly pressed. There is need for the State, that is each provincial government, to turn the light of criticism upon itself, to institute a severe and searching examination of the method which it adopts in disbursing provincial revenues, and of the policy with which it definitely associates itself in eliciting and subsidizing educational effort. When the State brings itself to do this, and looks the facts squarely in the face, it will speedily recognize that its attitude must be radically altered; that either it must establish education as a whole upon principles of aid which are equitable, impartial, comprehensive, and stimulating to every approved educational agency, or it must give up all thought of being regarded as the controller of Indian education.

(iii) *Has the State a Policy of Educational Administration?*

91. *Connexion with Former Issues.*—We have arrived naturally at the last of the three issues which we saw had to be faced and to be satisfactorily dealt with if the present system of educational finance was to be put on a proper basis. The consideration of the first issue has shown us that the method now employed for the financing of elementary education will have to be thoroughly changed if the country is to bear no longer the stigma of a great reproach. The consideration of the second issue took us into a wider field, the financing not merely of elementary education but of education as a whole. And there we were led to realize that there would never be a system of educational finance that would do justice to the interests of education and the position of the State until there was established and administered impartially by the State a comprehensive policy of grant-in-aid. But if that is to be the case, and the need for the enunciation of such a policy has long been known, why is it that there has been such delay in taking a step on which there depend consequences so momentous? This question, to which our line of consideration has brought us, is simply another way of stating our third issue: Has the State a definite policy in regard to educational administration? What we have now to do is to seek for an answer to that question.

92. *The Essentials in this Matter.*—There are many matters which it would be tempting to consider in a discussion of this issue. One of the appendices of the Calcutta University Commission's Report provides a number of most interesting points which might be regarded by some as germane to our theme. And it might even be contended that our question required us to investigate the bearing on administration of vested interests, the sense of prestige, and the working of officialdom. But while all these are not without their attraction to any one who is dealing with the subject now before us they are not of fundamental importance. Administration is based upon what are known as Direction and Inspection. And it is on these, in their financial aspects, that we must concentrate attention. We shall thus get to the heart of the matter, to what is essential.

93. *Financing of Direction Inadequate.*—And first as to Direction. It will hardly be believed that the immense educational system of British India is carried on under a Direction which costs only fifteen and a half lakhs of rupees. That simple fact explains much. If the State makes up its mind to do what is unnecessary—to give a few thousand boys and girls an elementary education through its own agency—it has no difficulty in finding for this object seventeen lakhs of rupees out of the taxpayer's pocket. If it decides to enter the field of collegiate education as a manager, even in certain cases as we have seen to be placed in the position of a rival manager—once again doing what is unnecessary—it has at its command well on to half a crore. But if it seeks to occupy the position of a Director, and none can do that but the State itself or those to whom the State grants so much as may fittingly be delegated control, all the funds which it has at its disposal for this vital and most necessary task do not amount to one-fifth of what it expends on the heterogeneous items that are grouped together as 'Miscellaneous'. Not only that, but in the course of five

years the expenditure on Direction has grown by no more than a lakh and a half. A sum of Rs. 30,000 has been added annually to the expenditure on Direction, while the pupils in primary schools alone are increasing at the rate of 400,000 per annum. And as if that were not startling and saddening enough, there is one other fact which has to be taken into the reckoning, namely that when retrenchment operations are set agoing Direction comes in for a large share of their attentions. From such attentions it most certainly requires to be delivered. While the State can find large sums with which to perform unessential services, in the sphere of education, all it can obtain for an essential service, one which it is its duty to render, is a mere starvation allowance. Education needs to be wisely directed, it needs the men and women who can take counsel together regarding its interests, it needs those whose sole task is to look before and after, to appreciate the significance of relevant facts, to frame comprehensive schemes, to be in touch with all who are contributing to educational progress and activity, and to consolidate opinion that carries weight and leads to action. But while education needs all this, and needs it urgently, the State will not pay for it. It is not simply that it does not pay for it. And it is not that it is without funds to pay for it. It has funds; but it expends far too great an amount of them on objects which, so far as it is concerned, are unnecessary. Thus is education poorly served; it is deprived of that Direction of which it stands in such sore need; and it is mocked by a method of finance which, while appearing to give, in reality withholds.

94. *Financing of Inspectorate Inadequate.*—And what is true of Direction is equally true of Inspection. At present Rs. 83 lakhs are all that are expended on this vital service. And that figure is only six and a half lakhs more than it was five years before. Facts such as these make it look as if it were almost a matter for regret rather than for thanksgiving that the past quinquennium

has been marked by striking educational development. For during that time the State has taken no thoroughly appropriate means to test the quality of that advance, to afford guidance to those who are engaged in it, and to supply information on which future developments may be fruitfully based. It spends Rs. 88 on the primary and secondary schools which it itself manages, when there is no call for it to do anything of the sort, and then it says as plainly as figures can say it that it has not enough money to provide the country with that all-important service of Inspection which there is a call for it to provide that is steady, pressing, and louder every year. The fact is that Inspection is being starved when there are actually funds which, if they were being properly utilized, would give to it the nourishment, health, and strength which are so much required and which would mean life to education. Thus the real state of education remains in considerable part unknown, the Department is deprived of the full information which it ought to possess, and the schools have to go without an essential stimulus. Thus also though much appears to be given to education from provincial revenues year after year, and decade after decade, yet when we look closely at it we see that the present method of financing the inspecting agency takes away from education in great part even that which it seemeth to have.

95. *No Policy of Educational Administration.*—In the light of the facts which we have been considering we are in a position to return an answer to our question: Has the State a definite policy in regard to educational administration? And the answer is: So far as finance goes, and it is a guide which can usually be depended upon, the only policy which the State has is one of starvation. If this policy goes on unchecked, Direction will soon become merely nominal, and Inspection wholly superficial. The significance of this lack of policy can hardly escape any one who has the interests of education at heart. Because there is no consistent policy regarding the way in which elementary education is to be

financed, the means for the supply of that great national need is entirely unsatisfactory. Because there is no comprehensive scheme for the financing of education in general, resources are being applied in a manner which produces results wholly incommensurate with the funds expended, where it does not actually block educational advance. And why is all this? Because the State will not spend money on that which is fundamental—the provision of Guidance. On essential services it stays its hand. If the financing of education is to be set right there must be a thorough change at the fountain-head itself. The system of Indian education, it has been often said, is topheavy. The system of the financing of Indian education is in a still worse plight. It is a pyramid seeking to stand on its apex.

Reference

Figures and references are to be found in the *Eighth* and *Ninth Quinquennial Reviews;* in the provincial *Quinquennial Reviews;* in the *Indian Education Commission Report*, Chapter viii; in Richey, *Grants-in-Aid;* in the *Calcutta University Commission Report,* notes at end of Volume v; and in the *Resolution of the Government of India on Quinquennial Review*, 1892-97 (4th November, 1899).

V. The Remedy for Unsatisfactory Educational Finance

96. *Present Mode of Financing Education Unsatisfactory.*—We have now considered the financing of the educational system of India in its more important aspects. We have dealt with the allocation of public funds over all, and within the different grades, and we have been brought face to face with serious weaknesses in this allocation, weaknesses revealed by the statistical tables with their unadorned presentation of facts. These facts make it plain to us that the answer to the questions with which we began: Are provincial

revenues now devoted to education being expended to best advantage? cannot be in the affirmative. But fortunately the facts have done more than lead us to a negative conclusion. They show us how provincial revenues may be so spent as to do justice at once to education and to the taxpayer. Let us consider how this may be.

97. *How it may be Remedied*: (1) *By the State Spending on Control.*—In the first place, the facts press upon us with irresistible force the need that exists for real educational control by the State. Until the State concentrates on this its funds will continue to be subject to waste and the progress of education to delay. Control is guidance, and that is what the State affords in ways which are at present far too limited and ineffective. How can it be otherwise? How can guidance be given except on the basis of strong staffs of experienced educational administrators? And such staffs have never existed. The amount of money that is at present spent on them is perhaps enough to provide a good machine; but what education needs at its head is brains and proper supply of them. Brains, however, have to be paid for, and that is a payment to which the State seems to find it hard to reconcile itself. Again, how can guidance be given except on the basis of information carefully garnered and judiciously sifted? But the means by which such information can be gathered and its results disseminated are not to be had without dipping deep into the public purse. And here once more the budget provision fails. Such economy at the source issues in lack of knowledge, lack of information, lack of guidance, lack of policy. In fact nothing could be more uneconomical. The present parsimony is sheer wastefulness; it needs to be stopped speedily and finally. Guidance is the place where the State must spend upon itself if education is to be a national power. And if even the crore which is all that it now devotes to Direction and Inspection were doubled that would be still a small enough provision, but it would be at least one step along

the right path. The State would at any rate have begun to give to the educational system the essential service of control.

98. (2) *By the State ceasing to spend on itself as Manager.*—The second point which the analysis of educational financing presses upon us is that the State must devote itself without distraction to control. The entrance of the State into the realm of management simply creates large financial outlays without corresponding educational benefits. And it has the further effect of prejudicing the action of the State as controller. As we have gone through the figures at each educational level we have seen how unfortunate is the endeavour of the State to allocate funds to various managers when it itself continues to be one of them. It spends money upon itself for the discharge of functions which other managements are quite capable of discharging, and in such a way that the claims of elementary education are not safeguarded; while the money which it expends on other agencies bears no clear relation to the amount or nature of the work done. Thus by its financial dealings the State not only fails far too much to give to managements the guidance which it is the duty of a controller to supply, but it also fails far too frequently to give them that aid which is calculated to inspire educational effort and initiative and to secure educational continuity. Further there is created the impression that far too much is being spent on higher education when the figures make it plain that what is really in great part happening is a large expenditure by the State of public funds on its own institutions. Were the State to abandon management then without the addition of another rupee to the budget there would be available what would enhance most definitely the effective and beneficial power of the State as controller of the educational system, and also what would enable other managements to shoulder larger responsibilities and to do this in a most capable and telling way. If the country is to have a healthy educational budget, and thus a healthy educational

system, the State must note what figures have pressed upon it decade after decade; it must relinquish management and give itself wholly to control.

99. (3) *By the State Ceasing to Finance Delegated Control Combined with Management.*—In the third place, the State requires to see that when there is a delegation of control this must be so arranged that the control is not delegated to a management which is one among a number of managements. Delegation which neglects this safeguard leads to financial unhealthiness and educational retardation. The State, as we have seen, itself endeavours to effect this combination, but, as circumstances increasingly show, to the disadvantage of educational finance. The same result is bound to follow if, through devolution, a corresponding combination arises in connexion with a body other than the State. And if the State not only permits the establishment of a control which is also conjoined with part managership but also lends most generous financial aid to this combination, an aid which, it may be, is more generous than that which is given to other managements, it throws its weight on the side of what works to the detriment of education. It helps to set up an *imperium in imperio*, with all its hampering effect on the State's endeavour to control; it extends to one management a preferential treatment which prejudicially affects the activities of other managements; and it fails to draw into the service of education all the resources of finance, activity, and personnel which are ready to place themselves at its disposal if only they receive that encouragement to which they have a just title. Without the expenditure of an additional rupee another million of children might have been receiving the benefits of elementary education at the present time had the State faced the financial facts to which several quinquennia, and more particularly the one that is just past, have been drawing its attention in the most pointed manner, and had it decided that throughout the country, as has been done in certain parts of it, control should not be

conjoined with management if that management was only one among others.

100. (4) *By the State Basing Its Finance on a System which Evokes and Coordinates Effort.*—The fourth point which considerations of finance make abundantly clear is what might be expected from the financial bearing of the preceding three paragraphs. The State must not only become in reality the controller of the whole educational system; it must not only see to it that control, whether direct or delegated, is not prejudiced by being associated with management; but it must also set itself resolutely to frame and to give effect to a comprehensive scheme of subsidy or grant-in-aid in accordance with which it will make its educational allocation from provincial revenues. Its fundamental principle will be so to assign public funds that every capable agency recognized by the State will occupy the position of a true partner in the educational enterprise of the country. Thus finance will be employed as a great bond of unity. It will link together all forces prepared to do battle for education against ignorance and will form them into a united national contingent. No force will be disparaged, each will make its individual contribution, and all will be encouraged to give the most characteristic and the best service that is in their power. Further, finance will be the medium of healthy rivalry, stirring every unit to emulation in the contribution it can make to the one great end. Thus Local Bodies will have ground for satisfaction not in the fact that they are Local Bodies, but that, as representatives of local self-government, they are able to render under statutory enactments and out of their resources an ever-growing service to the education of the country. And Private Bodies will find ground for satisfaction not in the fact that they testify to individual generosity or corporate liberality but that they are able to bring, in steadily increasing measure, the voluntarily offered resources of those who believe in education to the upbuilding of a comprehensive national system. Again, finance

will be the instrument not of preferential treatment based on name or official position, but of a preference based on work systematically done and educational service adequately rendered. And if there is any differentiation there will be only one ground for that, namely the difference in effort made and energy sustained. Thus there will be inaugurated a definite and carefully articulated policy which will take the place of the present combination of what is in part legislatively unilateral and in part strangely haphazard. There will be a policy which will unite effort of every kind, local and private, drawing forth the fullest contribution which each can make to education, discouraging none, stimulating all. And there will be a policy by the working of which finance will be so administered that there will be no possibility of the State retarding rather than accelerating the spread of education. And all this unity will have its centre in the State as controller, a controller that represents the nation, that admits to the service of education only fitting agencies for a task so high, and that to such agencies, when they are admitted, gives the steadiness and stimulus of its full and impartial support, whatever be the form of management to which they belong.

101. (5) *By the State Securing the Co-operation of the Parent.*—Finally, the facts which we have surveyed emphasize the need which exists for the State to secure the fullest financial co-operation of the parent. This is all the more necessary because of what the State has done for decades, that for which it has received far too little recognition. For the State has given of its funds year after year so that scholarships are available for pupils of talent and of slender means, and it has also made provision, regulative and financial, whereby substantial concessions may be enjoyed by any one who experiences a handicap because of the community of his origin. When such opportunities exist and when to these is added the contribution of private benefaction, it is for the State to ensure, to the fullest extent of its

powers, that the responsibility which belongs to the parent is not shifted on to other shoulders; in such a way too that the parent who decides to send his child on to higher education may be under no misunderstanding regarding the expenditure which he will be called on to meet. The strict and equitable levying of fees assures the taxpayer that his money is not being misapplied, satisfies the self-denying parent that he is not being asked for a sacrifice which others find it easy to escape, helps to warn off from certain forms of study those who would have their abilities better employed otherwise, and makes to the educational system a contribution of which it stands in need, and by means of which it is able to extend its benefits to all, be they rich or poor, who can profit by them. The State by its manner of financing and the terms on which its grants-in-aid are supplied is in a position to safeguard for the country this valuable educational asset.

102. *Resumé of Changes required for Satisfactory Financing of Education.*—We have now reached an answer to the question which we asked ourselves in the first paragraph of this Chapter. That question was: How shall the educational system of the country best be financed so that good education may be spread as widely and as speedily as possible throughout the land? The answer is: By a very fundamental change in the mode of financing which now prevails and has prevailed for too many years. That mode fails to give to education results commensurate with the amount expended, and more especially fails to lay what is the foundation of a truly national system, the education of the great mass of the people. The reason for this is that it does not provide for a genuine controlling agency, and that, because through associating management with control, it exercises preferential treatment at every level of the educational structure, thus leading to the uneconomical distribution of large State funds and to the discouragement of bodies which are prepared to make substantial contributions to education from private sources. It is

therefore a method which calls for radical alteration. And the alteration can be so brought about that no dislocation will be created by it. By a policy which places the State in the position of accepted and unchallenged educational controller, and which separates control from management, the change can be swiftly and smoothly effected. There are managements in sufficient number and with sufficient experience to meet the demands of the new situation. The process of transference to these is capable of realization within a period which it would be easy to specify, and which, as the preceding Chapter has shown, need not be long. The result would be a striking change in the employment of public funds, a change which would lead to the employment of these funds effectively, economically, and equitably. Provincial funds would no longer be spent lavishly on the few and meagrely on the many; private agencies would no longer be made to feel that the more they worked for education the less would they be encouraged; district boards and municipalities would become the genuine expression of local self-government in the sphere of education. A sense of partnership would be created. Under impartial control fully established and adequately financed there would be assured guidance and direction such that the causes of unwholesome rivalry would be removed, undue emphasis on one form of education to the disadvantage of another would be abandoned, and true proportion would be secured. Thus in the course of less than ten years elementary education would extend its borders till it embraced some sixty per cent of the boys and girls of school-going age, the facilities for higher education would be increased and enhanced, and the alternative courses that are so desirable would become an integral part of the system. Thus would the State, Local Bodies, Private Agencies, and the Parent so enter into financial combination that in the service of education public revenues would be utilized to the country's greatest advantage.

103. *Demands of Sound Education and of Sound*

Finance Identical.—It will be noticed that, in this discussion, the main lines of policy which have been shown to be necessary in the interests of sound finance are the same as those which, in the discussions of the preceding chapters have been shown to be necessary in the interests of sound education. What educational advance demands is what the satisfactory utilization of the taxpayer's money requires. Thus do the interests of the State, the citizen, the educator, the parent, and the child converge. And when the policy which these combined facts press upon the country becomes the policy with which the State identifies itself and for the realization of which it marshals all its resources, then India will at length see in its midst no mere working of educational machinery but the steady growth of a living educational system. For it will see a system towards the vitality and development of which there will contribute the united forces of sound education, good administration, national sentiment, local patriotism, private generosity, and unwasteful finance.

CHAPTER IV

The Problem of Religious Neutrality

I. The Problem: How are Education and Religion to be Combined?

1. One of the problems constantly confronting the Indian administrator, demanding the attention of the Indian educator, and exercising the mind of the serious Indian parent, is: How are education and religion to be combined in the educational system of India?

II. The Desire for Combination

2. (1) *On the Part of the Parent.*—To the thoughtful parent the question is far removed from the realm of purely academic interest or political capital. From the lips of Hindus, Muhammadans and Christians there comes an earnest cry for a closer association of religion with education. And the ground for their earnestness may be said to be two-fold. In the first place, the Indian mind finds it hard to think of an education worthy of the name which is dissociated from religion. The schools of the past owed their distinctive features to what was taught in the precincts of Hindu temple and Muhammadan mosque, and to the sages who there gathered around them bands of learners and found the beginning of wisdom in the fear of the Lord. And where Christianity has come the church and the school have gone together. The close association of education and religion has thus a historical support which long connexion has hallowed, and which the thoughtful parent desires to see maintained. It is woven into the texture of the national life. And the other ground is really the same position urged from a different standpoint. Parents complain that old loyalties are being set aside, and that reverence is passing. And they say tha

this is very noticeable in the case of those who have had the benefit of education, and who repay the sacrifices made by parents for the provision of that education, by a very general, if not a complete, disregard of those things which give to life its worth. They ascribe this attitude in large part to the secular character of the education which is now being imparted, and they urge, often with pathetic earnestness, that there may be a return to that form of education which finds its support in religion.

3. (2) *On the Part of the Teacher.*—What the parent feels, the teacher, so often himself a parent, also feels. For the faithful teacher is ofttimes sorely grieved at the result of all the effort he expends upon the training of youth. He is dissatisfied with an education which quickens intellectual development but which leaves an all too slight impress upon life and character. He looks with distress at the gulfs which separate communities and which education in its corporate aspect seems so powerless to bridge. And he longs for that manifestation of a civic conscience, of lofty political aim, of the love of truth, of responsibility for the diffusion of education, which, he feels, ought to follow in the train of all true teaching.

4. (3) *On the Part of the Administrator.*—And the administrator shares with the parent and the teacher in a similar longing. If education is without its telling influence on the springs of conduct the progress of the country is retarded. And the administrator wishes to see it advanced. Thus it is that the Government of India in its Resolution of 1913 speaks of the provision of religious and moral instruction as 'unquestionably the most important educational problem of the time.' And it is highly significant that the Viceroy in a deeply impressive speech made on the 17th July 1926 appealed 'in the name of religion' to those 'who direct the education of the young' for the creation of an atmosphere in which the plant of national life may attain its fairest growth.

III. The Difficulty of Religious Neutrality

5. *The State's Position.*—So much for the longing. Alongside of this must be set another fact, the fact that in educational matters the attitude of the Government, central and local, in India is one of strict religious neutrality. As soon as the State arrived at and promulgated an educational policy, it stated this fact most clearly. It said for example, that all schools managed by Government were founded for the benefit of the whole population of India, and that in order to effect this object it was indispensable that the education conveyed in them should be exclusively secular. It laid down that inspectors were to take no cognisance of the religious instruction imparted in any school. And all this is felt to be in accord with the spirit of the Proclamation made by Queen Victoria in November 1858 in which she stated that no one was to be 'molested or disquieted, no one to be in any wise favoured, by reason of their religious faith.' The attitude of the Government of India before the inauguration of the reforms of 1919, is the attitude of the provincial governments of the present day when education is in the hands of a Minister responsible to the legislature of his province. Place, then, side by side these two facts: the desire for religious education and the neutrality of the Government in all educational matters. And it will be at once conceded that we are confronted with a serious and difficult problem, for which a solution is urgently required.

6. *This Position in Education.*—In seeking for a solution we must first examine the nature of the neutrality which the State professes and the ground on which it is maintained. The *Imperial Gazetteer of India*, in Volume IV, Chapter xiii, puts the position very clearly so far as it applies to education. It says:

'The existence in India of creeds differing widely from one another and from the faith of the ruling power has made it essential for the State to assume a position of strict religious neutrality in its relations with public instruction. This principle was emphatically asserted in the Despatch of 1854 and has ever since been rigidly enforced. No religious instruction is given in government schools; and provided only it imparts sound secular instruction a private institution is equally entitled to government aid whether it teaches the religion of the Bible, the Shastras, or the Koran.'

In even more succinct form the policy of Government has been stated to be 'abstention from religious teaching in publicly managed schools, abstention from interference with religious teaching in privately managed schools'. And the reason for this attitude was given quite frankly so long ago as 1854. It has been adopted, as the Despatch of that date tells us, so as 'to prevent the slightest suspicion of an intention on our part to make use of the influence of government for the purpose of proselytism'. Here then we have the whole matter in a nutshell. It amounts to this : there are so many faiths in India that Government feels that it cannot support them all, and any recognition of religion which falls short of this would expose Government to the suspicion of sectarianism or proselytism. So in matters of education, so far as Government is concerned, there is to be no recognition of religion at all. One could not help feeling that there was a note of finality in the declaration which the Government of India made in 1904, that 'in the Government institutions the instruction is, and must continue to be, exclusively secular'.

7. *Neutrality and Secularity.*—There is one point in connexion with these statements which cannot but arrest the attention of those who are engaged in a search for the solution of the problem now before us. It will be noted that, in certain circumstances, a neutral policy is regarded as identical with a secular education. Such an identification is peculiarly unfortunate. True, the limits within which this identification was at first regarded as operating were definitely circumscribed; it held only in the case of educational institutions managed

by Government. True also, these limits were thought of as certain to become more and more circumscribed until their contents would ultimately vanish; for one has only to read the Despatch of 1854 to realize that what was contemplated was a steady transfer of departmental institutions to non-departmental agencies. But when all that is granted it has still to be admitted that there are three directions in which the consequences of this identification have stretched far beyond the limits originally thought of and have worked to the detriment of Indian education. In the first place, what was thought of as a temporary expedient has been suffered to become a permanent feature of the educational system of the country. Not only did the sweep of official management increase, its tenacity also increased. The Indian Education Commission Report, to mention only one official document, affords striking confirmation of this statement. And with the increase of departmentally managed institutions there came of necessity an increase in the number of schools and colleges where neutrality in regard to religion became identified with pure secularity in the type of education imparted. This is unfortunate, but there is a second consideration still more unfortunate. What was contemplated in the Despatch of 1854 by schools under public management was institutions under the educational department of the State. About thirty years afterwards there arose schools under Local Board and Municipal Board management. These were also looked upon as schools under public management; and under that classification they still remain. Thus it came about that the same interpretation was applied to them, and they became further exemplifications of the position that, being under neutral management so far as religion went, they could impart only what was secular so far as education went. And as if this was not enough, a third factor had to be reckoned with. The State which manages certain institutions also controls all institutions. There was, and not unnaturally, a tendency to regard Government the controller as assuming towards neutrality the same attitude as Government the manager. Thus many came to think of Government as not merely neutral but as the upholder of a purely secular system of education throughout the country. Those who read Mayhew's *Education in India* are left in no doubt as to the harm which has accrued to education in India from this reading of the attitude of the State. It may be a misunderstanding, but, if it is, it is one into which an observer might readily fall, and from which, if it desired, Government might as readily extricate itself. This at least is certain that, owing to the attitude of Government, neutrality has no other meaning than that of secularity over a considerable range of the educational system of the country. It would be difficult to calculate the evil which has followed from this identification. Clearly if such identification exhausts the concept of neutrality then there may well be serious hesitation in looking upon neutrality as a safe guiding principle.

8. *Neutrality and Indifference.*—Fortunately there has never been a time in the development of an educational policy in India that neutrality has meant secular teaching only. We have already noted that the principle of neutrality has been defined as 'abstention from religious teaching in publicly managed schools, abstention of interference with religious teaching in privately managed schools'. Thus in all schools which are under private management there is complete freedom to impart religious education. Only with such teaching Government does not concern itself. Thus if, in the case of publicly managed institutions, religious neutrality means opposition to religious teaching, in the case of privately managed institutions it means indifference to it. This second meaning of neutrality, it must be confessed, escapes the unattractiveness of the first only by a hair's breadth. But, the champion of the Government will reply: No other meaning comes within the region of practical politics. Take neutrality in either of these senses and you get something that works; take it in any

other and you are either up in the air or down in chaos. And he will quote the position taken by the Indian Education Commission in regard to institutions managed by the State as given in Chapter viii, paragraph 526 of its Report:

The declared neutrality of the State forbids its connecting the institutions directly managed by it with any one form of faith; and the alternative of giving equal facilities in such institutions for the inculcation of all forms of faith involves practical difficulties which we believe to be insuperable.

And very likely to this there would be added the statement that as soon as a Government begins to meddle in things religious its days are numbered.

9. *Neutrality and Exceptional Arrangements.*—So now we have got at what the State means by its doctrine of religious neutrality in regard to education. It shuts it out of publicly-managed institutions; it shuts its eyes to it in privately managed ones. And it adds that this is the only practical position. The only practical position? Is that really the case? Then why this admission as to 'exceptional arrangements' which are made in certain Muhammadan schools under public management? These exceptional arrangements include such a facility as the provision of a mosque for worship. Nor any one who has seen the sacrifices which Muhammadans make in order that their children may be instructed in their faith has nothing but admiration for the stand they take and the means they employ to secure their end. The matter, however, which is now before us is not what Muhammadans themselves do but what a Government professing 'complete neutrality in matters of religion' does for them. Looked at from this point of view the 'exceptional arrangements' made for these schools under public management, the schools of one community, suggest partisanship rather than neutrality. A policy of strict neutrality admits of no exceptional arrangements. It looks as if we have no sooner arrived at some kind of understanding regarding the Government's position

of religious neutrality than we are confronted with facts which make us ask whether the actual attitude is identical with the professed attitude.

10. *Lack of Clearness as to what the Situation Requires.*—The same question forces itself upon us when we look at the efforts made by the State to safeguard the religious scruples of pupils and their parents. There are many ways of doing this. No Government in India has gone so far as would one of the Universities had it accepted a resolution moved in its Senate. The proposal, if it had been carried, would have had the effect of denying the privilege of affiliation to any college which made some form of religious education an integral part of its curriculum. The motion, though rejected by an overwhelming majority, had its supporters. To some, therefore, the best means of safeguarding conscience is to cut these colleges entirely out of the educational system of the country. To others the best means seems to be to deny to such schools and colleges any aid from public funds. To others, again, the most satisfactory means seems to be to deny such institutions aid unless they are prepared to make exceptional arrangements. And so on it goes, for the simple reason that there are two questions which are not clearly faced and clearly answered. These questions are: first, Do we wish schools and colleges where religious education is an essential part of the course which they provide? And, second, How are we to have these in such a way that they will fit into the Indian educational system without encroaching on religious scruple? Instead of answers to these questions, what we find is for the most part a number of discussions as to how a method of safeguarding conscience in the educational system of one country is to be introduced into the educational system of India where the conditions are vitally different. Indian education, in regions far removed from that of conscience, has had to pay the penalty again and again for efforts at transplantation, however well meant. When the specifically Indian conditions are fairly faced, and not

until then, we shall be in a position to solve the problem that is now before us. There is no need for elaborate statistics. Let the main point be kept steadily in view. The State is not able, as in England, to overtake by statutory agency even the elementary education of the country. It therefore calls into partnership with it—partnership be it noted, not subordination—a network of private agencies. These have their definite status in the educational system, and from that status they can be dislodged only by failure to occupy the position of partner or by the denial of all the principles on which the educational system of the country rests. Not only have they a position which the State guarantees them, they have also the position which comes from bearing the responsibility for the education of one half of the pupils who are studying in the elementary schools of the land. A very similar situation meets us when we turn to secondary education, for there are practically twice as many pupils in secondary schools under private management as in those under public management. Let one other fact be recalled. A full system of compulsory education obtains in England; in India compulsion is the exception. Into such a system as this it has been proposed, on more than one occasion, that there should be introduced the means for safeguarding conscience which have been found to answer in circumstances totally different. It is advisable that we should look at one of those attempts.

11. *Exemplified in Legal Enactment.*—In one of the provinces of India a clause has been introduced into the educational code which provides that, if a school which gives religious instruction accepts grants, it must give exemption from that religious teaching to any pupil whose parent or guardian objects to it, and intimates his objection in writing, this objection to be intimated ordinarily at the beginning of a term. It further lays down that the religious teaching is to be given at the beginning or at the end of the secular instruction imparted. If these conditions are complied with, aid from

public funds is available; if not it is withheld. At first sight it looks as if we had reached a solution of the problem with which we started. But when we look more closely we find not only that the old tangle remains but that the emergence of a new element is rendered possible—that of insincerity. For such legislation makes it permissible and legal for a manager of a school in which religious instruction is imparted to exempt from attendance at such instruction all who desire to be exempted, and yet in every part of the school course to bring to bear the particular attitude and influence of his religion. It would be within the power of every managing body, Hindu, Muhammadan, Sikh, and Christian, to make the definite form of religious instruction optional but so to concentrate their religious forces on every other aspect of the work and life of the school that submission to these was compulsory on the part of the pupil. The manager that acted in this fashion would be acting in a strictly legal manner; and he would be entitled to receive grants from public funds. The conscience of others would be respected up to the limits laid down by statute, but the object of the statute would be wholly defeated. No manager who stated unequivocally that he gave an education in which religion was an integral part of the curriculum would be in a position to claim or expect to receive any aid from public funds towards the maintenance of his school. But a manager who refrained from what is technically called 'religious instruction', but made religious instruction in a non-technical sense intensive in its power and pervasive of the curriculum of every pupil would suffer no disadvantage, but would be entitled to enjoy the fullest participation in the allocation of public funds. This form of legislation, then, is futile. It is introduced in order to safeguard conscience, and that is precisely what it fails to do. The solution of our problem receives no help from this expedient.

12. *Failure of State to Supply Alternative Facilities.* —We cannot, however, leave the matter there; we must probe it still more closely. Under the type of enactment

which we have been considering, grant from provincial revenues cannot be given to a school which makes some form of religious instruction an integral part of its curriculum. And the reason for this, we are told, is that a management which makes religious instruction an integral part of a school course either will, or may, compel pupils to take a form of education which they do not wish. But such an answer does not settle the question. It only forces us to ask another one. And that is: Who is to blame for this situation? The answer generally given, either implicitly or explicitly, is: The management. Is that answer correct? Is it true that a management which has planted a school in an area, and thus supplies needed educational facilities, (for we are not dealing with unneeded schools; their day is soon done) is to blame because there are people in that area who desire another type of education than that which the school supplies? Most certainly not. The blame attaches not to the management which, of its private resources, makes this educational contribution, but to the authority which fails to provide a sufficient number of schools, and thus fails to make alternative facilities available. It is the State not the management that is to blame; the responsibility rests on the State. If anyone is to be penalised it is the State not the management. For the State has fallen short in two respects: from the point of view of education it has failed, because it has not encouraged a management which has supplied an educational need; from the point of view of policy it has failed, because it has not foreseen and provided for an important educational contingency and situation. We shall revert to this later. Meantime we cannot but remark that there is something ironical in a management which seeks to provide the kind of education that is so much asked for being told that it is to be penalised because it is the only one in a certain area. As if the management could split itself in twain and so provide for the requirements of those who wish something different; or as if it could continue one and yet deny itself by making religious teaching alternative when it looks upon education as defective unless religious teaching is integral. It is, of course, always open to the State or its representatives to turn round and say to such a management: 'If you take that position we have no difficulty in dealing with you. We shall give you no grants from public funds; you can exist on your own, and sink or swim.' And to this the management will be well entitled to reply: 'If I have to support this my contribution to the education of India entirely from my own funds there is a considerable chance that I shall sink rather than swim. But do not hesitate. And when I have sunk you will have blotted out a school which made religious teaching a vital part of the education which it imparted. And you will have obliterated a management which refused public funds on conditions which would have made that acceptance insincere. Derive such comfort as you can from the reflection that you have lost such a school and such a management to the educational system of India.'

13. *Resulting Confusion.*—We began by stating a problem, and the more we have investigated that problem the more complicated we have found it. We have seen how the difficulties in the way of a solution have arisen and increased in number. In the first place Government proclaimed itself to be neutral in regard to the form of education imparted. Then as a manager it laid down that the maintenance of neutrality in the schools which it managed meant the maintenance of secular education only. By this attitude it could not but imperil its position as controller, although it made it clear that neutrality as a controller meant, in respect of schools not under public management, nothing more than indifference or toleration. Then it included schools under Local Board and Municipal management among those which were subject to the same interpretation of neutrality as applied in its own schools. Next it did not adhere with consistency to its own declared policy of neutrality. And finally it sought for a solution of difficulties which

had arisen through its lack of forethought and provision in forms of legislation which placed at a disadvantage schools that made religious instruction an integral part of their education. Everyone who has followed the course of events in connexion with this matter is bound to admit that a more unsatisfactory tangle it would be difficult to imagine. And so long as matters are approached along the lines which have hitherto been adopted so long will the tangle remain. The only hope for a solution is to begin as we have suggested above, by obtaining a definite answer to the question: Is the government of the country definitely prepared to encourage schools which combine religious with secular education?

IV. Religious Neutrality Impartial Encouragement

14. *Need for Encouragement of Religious Education.*—We start, then, to re-think the position by asking Government for a clear pronouncement on the subject of its attitude to schools imparting religious education. What is that attitude to be?—opposition, indifference, or encouragement. A wise and far-seeing government will be forced to admit by the logic of facts that an attitude of encouragement is the only one which holds out the hope of a system of education at once acceptable to the people and beneficial in its influence. As it is, education in India has to many the appearance of a good, but of an exotic, plant. And the influence of education has told more on the side of intellect than of life. What education requires to redeem it from both defects is its connexion with religion. An attitude of aloofness, apathy, least of all opposition, will not suffice. A government which adopts the policy of encouragement has behind it the support of thinking parents, teachers, administrators, and lovers of their country in all walks of life. In other words the form of neutrality which it behoves the Government to adopt is one which has been strangely enough left too much in the background. Yet it is the adoption of a

form which will be of incalculable benefit to the whole educational system of India. That form is Benevolent Neutrality.

15. *Encouragement Consistent with Neutrality.*—Almost as soon as this position has been stated we shall hear the old objection: When Government adopts this attitude it will be regarded as a partisan and all confidence in it will be gone. Yet when we look at what is going on in various parts of India we shall see that, even now, some approximation is being made to the identification of the doctrine of religious neutrality with the position of benevolent neutrality. For instance, twenty years ago it could be said regarding the province of Madras that 'under existing rules and orders no classes for religious instruction can be held within the walls of any school under public management'. Within ten years that was no longer true. By a Government Order of the 15th July, 1922, it was laid down that while one religion was not to be fostered at the expense of another and that while public funds were not to be utilized for imparting religious instruction, it was within the power of a Local Body to permit this instruction, to be given in the school premises. Further, it was stated that if the regular teachers of the school were prepared voluntarily to undertake this form of instruction, that was the most satisfactory way of imparting it. So, if religious teaching is desired, pupils have no longer to go to some other place than the Municipal or District Board School to which they belong. They may have it in their own school and from their own teacher. And while in Bombay the pupil of a Municipal or Local Board School who desires religious instruction has to be content with 'well-constituted outside bodies', and cannot have the help 'of a teacher in the service of Government or a Local Body', he may nevertheless have provision for that instruction within his own school premises. A development in some such directions as these is what is called for; and we are only at the beginning of it. The coming years will see great changes; and in the meantime it is

possible to indicate four lines along which Government may advance towards the encouragement of religious education without departing by one jot or tittle from its position of strict impartiality. (1) In the first place, encouragement may appropriately and in a strictly constitutional manner come along the line of the Teaching Grant. If a school wishes to combine religious with secular instruction it will require a larger staff than if it had not that combination. Such an enhancement of staff would afford a legitimate claim for an enhancement of grant. The scale of grant permissible, the size of staff to be recognized, the qualifications of the teachers and the hours during which they taught, would all be brought under the operation of the grant-in-aid code. But subject to these rules no management would suffer because it had a staff which enabled it to do justice to the moral and religious as well as to the intellectual education which the school imparted. (2) In the second place, encouragement may proceed along the line of the Building Grant. For a school which lays emphasis on the religious aspect of education will conceivably require appropriate accommodation. The State cannot be asked to bear the expense of erecting chapels, mosques and temples; but it can make a grant towards the erection of a classroom or assembly room which will help materially towards that corporate feeling or that sense of reverence which religious education fosters and which is so valuable as an aid to learning and as a preparation for life. (3) In the third place, encouragement may advance along the line of the Library Grant. For a school which embraces religious teaching within its curriculum must have books in its library, and enough of them, to give reality to its teaching. Grants, therefore, for religious books while they would conform to accepted rules would not be taboo. And if this were the case schools would be the first to rejoice in the encouragement.

16. *Encouragement through Finance.*—These are three effective ways in which encouragement may be

given to schools that impart religious education without encroaching in any way on the impartiality of government. And they have this advantage. A grant is sanctioned only when a management incurs a definite expenditure, and it bears some recognized relation to that expenditure. Under such a system encouragement advances *pari passu* with the contribution made by the management. In this way two great gains are secured. On the one hand encouragement is given without wasteful expenditure of public funds; only as managers give do provincial revenues give. On the other hand only schools which are really in earnest are encouraged; for the Government helps those who help themselves.

17. *Encouragement through Provision of Facilities.*—(4) The three methods which have been mentioned are all concerned with finance. But there is a fourth method for the encouragement of religious education which is not of a financial character. It is the method of providing facilities. For many a day after 1854 the chief energies of the State were directed to the establishment of schools so that the spread of education might be advanced as rapidly as possible. In the enormous territory that had to be covered it is no wonder that the multiplication of schools took precedence of all other considerations. Questions of the distribution of schools and of the safeguarding of conscientious scruple within schools were not so much as thought of. They arose when the circumstances of the country made further postponement impossible. Yet such questions had been, in part at least, foreseen and an answer had been adumbrated in the 1854 pronouncement. Inherent in the policy which is there laid down is the duty of the State to see that adequate facilities are provided for the children that attend school, facilities adequate in character as well as in number. This is clear when we remember that no State can lay it down that it is determined to maintain neutrality as regards religion in education unless it is prepared to take practical steps to render this neutrality effective. Unless it is ready to do

this the profession of neutrality is either meaningless or untrue. If, as in India, the State aids schools without regard to the religious teaching given in them and so leads to situations in which conscientious scruple may be violated, its profession of neutrality is without meaning, for neutrality means no action, whereas in actual fact Government is taking a definite line of action. And if the State refuses to aid schools which supply a definite form of education which is healthy and beneficial to character because some people do not wish it, the profession of neutrality is untrue, for the State is now taking sides. If the State wishes to escape from the dilemma of making a profession of neutrality, which profession is belied by its acts, only one way is open to it. It must recognize the obligation which rests upon it to see that such facilities are provided for those who attend school and college as will make it possible for them to obtain a sound education and yet one which does not impinge on the sanctity of conscience. How, in practice, these facilities are to be provided will be considered in paragraph 22. Meantime enough has been said to show that it is perfectly possible for Government to encourage religious education without in any degree departing from its position of neutrality. Indeed it is only in this way that it can maintain a strictly neutral position.

V. The Working of Impartial Encouragement

18. (1) *Relinquishment of State Educational Management.*—We have seen that an encouragement of religious education in the schools of the country, carried out in a thoroughly impartial manner, is the surest way in which the Government cannot merely profess but actually exhibit its policy of religious neutrality. We must now give attention to the steps by which this benevolent neutrality may be incorporated in the educational system of India. Four steps may be mentioned. (1) The first is the relinquishment by

Government of its position as manager of educational institutions. This is a line of action already urged on many grounds which there is no need to re-state here. It is enough to say that so long as Government takes the position that only secular instruction can be given in the schools and colleges which it manages it need never profess to be neutral in regard to religion. For the attitude towards religion demanded by these institutions, though bearing the name of neutrality, is actually one of exclusion. And in the circumstances, exclusion is opposition. In order to be really neutral Government must abandon its position of manager while adhering to its position as controller of the whole educational system. And the sooner the process is initiated the better, for no Government can risk for long the imputation of being partial.

19. (2) *Equality of Treatment for Local and Private Managements.*—The next step is to place schools under board management and schools under private management on equal terms as regards their eligibility for grant or subsidy from the State. The school under Local Board and Municipal Board management derives its income from three main sources: fees, funds derived from taxation, and Government subsidy. The school under private management also derives its income from three main sources: fees, private contributions, and Government grant. In principle, therefore, there is only one point which distinguishes the two forms of management. In certain local areas people agree to tax themselves, in a statutory fashion, so as to maintain a number of services, one of these being schools; and the schools so maintained are schools under local management. In certain places certain people agree to give out of their own pockets, in a voluntary way, what will maintain schools; and the schools thus maintained are schools under private management. Both these classes of schools may levy fees, and both are eligible for financial help from public funds. Let the conditions on which this help is granted be the same for each type of school,

bearing some definite relation to what each management puts into its schools, that is to say bearing a relation to what the Board supplies from funds raised in accordance with statute, and to what the individual or committee or association supplies out of its own pocket, and then the irksome differentiation which at present exists in the allocation of grants to the two forms of schools will be done away.

20. *Bearing of these Two Conditions.*—But it will be said: What bearing has all this on the matter we are now considering? It seems to be no more than a purely financial arrangement. A little consideration will show that this is far from being the case. The arrangement is indeed a financial one, but it is much more than that. For the moment this arrangement is come to, then the present classification of schools, which has very obvious disadvantages, will give way to a classification from which these disadvantages are eliminated. At present schools are classified as Schools under Public Management and Schools under Private Management. And those under Public Management are divided into those under Government and those under Board Management. If Government divests itself of the functions of management, as has been urged in paragraph 18, then Board Schools will be the only representatives of what is termed Public Management. But if these receive grants from public funds on the same terms as schools maintained by private agencies, then both types of schools fall under the general heading of Aided Schools, and the need for reference to public management disappears. So far as management is concerned there are simply two classes—those under Board and those under Private (or preferably Committee) management. And what is the bearing of this on our present problem? It means that, when Board schools are looked at in this manner, there is no reason why religious instruction should not be given in them. Such instruction would be given in accordance with regulations laid down by the management, that is by the Board, the representatives of those who within

a specified area tax themselves to render public services of which education is one. But religious education, however regulated by the management, could be given in these Board schools without a question, as is indeed being done in certain Board schools already. Thus it would result that all schools of the national system, those under Board as well as those under Committee management, would be able to combine religious with secular instruction.

21. (3) *Delegation of Control to Ad Hoc Bodies.*—When these two steps have been taken, the next one is the delegation of control. The State is fittingly recognized as the Controller of the educational system of the country. It alone is in a position to advise, to direct, and to aid, the cause of education both in its own sphere and in its relation to other parts of the administration. But it may exercise that control either through its own agency or through a delegated agency. And it is becoming every year more clear that when Government vests its powers of control, or at least a substantial part of them, in bodies on which there are a considerable number of non-officials who have an intimate knowledge of local conditions and a certain stake in the education of the area concerned, there is a great advantage in this delegation of function. It is true that such bodies cannot to begin with, or even for some time, discharge their duties with the ease that marks a long established department. But they bring to bear on their task a large amount of educational experience, administrative capacity, and local knowledge. And these are of the utmost value for the stimulation of educational activity within an area, and for the maintenance of such activity economically and without friction. Such bodies have already been called into existence. We need instance only the District Educational Councils in Madras which deal with elementary education, and the High School Education Board in the Central Provinces which deals with secondary education. Amongst other matters, such *ad hoc* bodies would survey the field

under their control, would distribute grants from provincial funds, would see that overlapping was prevented, and would encourage the appropriate agency to provide the kind of school that is needed for a particular locality. They might have powers to levy a cess as is proposed in Bengal, but the multiplication of bodies with powers to impose taxation is to be avoided, as far as possible; and the same end would be gained if the proceeds of a certain tax were placed at the disposal of these bodies for educational purposes. The bodies would be authorised to recognize schools, to refuse recognition to a school in an area already well provided, and to take steps for the establishment of a school in an area either not supplied with a school or though supplied with a school yet not possessing a school of a type for which need exists. In this way control would be exercised with a due appreciation of local requirements, with a full knowledge of financial resources, and with a keen desire to advance appropriate educational development. It would be a control delegated not to bodies, such as Local and Municipal Boards, which have many other services to render, but to bodies able to give their exclusive attention to matters connected with the training of the young. And it would be a control delegated not to bodies that constituted simply one group among several exercising managerial functions but to bodies able to give themselves wholly to that guidance and direction which matters connected with the training of the young demand. Thus while Government would remain the ultimate controller, to which appeal could be made in specified circumstances, it would reap the fruit of delegated authority in quickened interest, educational cooperation, and effective administration.

22. (4) *Provision of Different Types of Schools.*— We are now ready for the fourth step. Government management being relinquished, local bodies being in receipt of grants-in-aid on the same terms as privately managed schools, and *ad hoc* bodies being appointed to exercise control over education, we have next to give

attention to one important function of these bodies to which as yet only indirect reference has been made. That is the function of providing such facilities for pupils that both education may be available and conscience may be respected. Now, at first sight, the provision of such facilities seems to be too intricate for any body to arrange adequately. But closer investigation shows that this is not the case. In actual practice what we find is that there are those who desire for their children an education of which religion is an integral part, or to which it is an addition, or from which it is excluded. And when we realize this we see that only two types of institutions require to be provided: one in which religious instruction permeates the whole, and one in which religious instruction is confined to one period distinct from those assigned to the ordinary secular instruction. The first type will satisfy those who wish for religious education as an essential part of the whole education imparted; the second will satisfy both those, who being allowed to absent themselves from the religious period, will obtain what they desire—a purely secular education, and those who desire in addition to their secular education a separate course of religious instruction. As matters now stand in India, arrangement for the provision of both types is comparatively easy. In the first place it will be necessary to decide upon the area within which such alternative facilities are to be provided. The area suitable for primary schools will be very different from that suitable for secondary schools; but when the area has been defined the nature of the facilities to be provided within the area will not be difficult to settle. In actual fact the number of cases where alternative facilities are desired and do not exist is far from large. But let us take a definite case. Here is a school, the only one in an area, and it makes religious instruction an integral part of its course. There are parents who object to the instruction given. What is the Controlling Authority to do? It may follow one or other of two courses. It may ask the management of the school, we shall call it a Committee School, whether it is prepared to grant any exemptions in respect of the religious instruction imparted in it; or it may arrange for the establishment of a second school which is more in harmony with the wishes of parents than is the existing school. Let us look at these alternatives. There may be circumstances in which the management of the Committee School is prepared to grant exemptions from the religious instruction given in certain periods stated in the time-table, though in the nature of the case it is unable to grant exemptions from the religious education which is not confined to any one hour but pervades the whole. The management might act in this way rather than face a pupil with the alternative of choosing between an education of a type abhorrent to its parent and no education at all. Even so, such exemptions would be only for such time and in such circumstances as seemed to the management to justify it. But the manager might be of opinion that the objection to the form of teaching was based on other grounds than those of conscientious scruple, or that while there was only one school in the area there was room and need for more. In this case he would intimate to the Authority that he intended to maintain his type of school without even temporary departure from its avowed character. It would now rest with the Authority to decide what action it would take. If it was convinced that the opposition to the Committee School was fictitious it would leave matters as they were. But if it was convinced that the opposition sprang from conscientious motives it would arrange for the establishment of another school, in this case a Board School. And the establishment of this school would settle the matter one way or another. For in a short time the emptying Committee School would show that its presence was not desired in that area. Or the well attended Committee School and the filling Board School would show that both were needed. Thus facilities would be available, and conscientious scruple would be respected.

23. *Objections Considered.*—Three objections may be taken to this mode of procedure. (i) It may be said that by the provision of alternative facilities there might in certain circumstances be two schools each of them with a somewhat small attendance instead of one school that was full. That is possible, though not, as things now are, probable. But when all is said that is said in official reports regarding the size of schools there is no reason for lamenting the possibility of two schools in each of which a large amount of individual attention can be given to the pupils. There is rather ground for rejoicing that such a possibility may be realized. The lack of it is what is stultifying much of the education of the present day. And it must not be forgotten that each of the schools thus at work in an area is, in the conditions described, either an actual or a potential centre of religious education. (ii) It may be said: How is any Authority to induce a Local Board to become responsible for an additional school? And if there is a difficulty with regard to a Board which possesses funds under statute will there not be a much greater difficulty in connexion with a Committee which has to take funds out of its own pocket? The difficulty seems great when stated, but it exists only on paper. This is obvious when we consider what is sometimes said, that Government can bring pressure to bear on a Local Board, but can bring no such pressure to bear on a private body. When this is fairly faced it will be found that the pressure in both cases is the same. When a new school has to be added to the existing list, there is only one form of pressure that achieves its end, and that is financial subsidy from public funds. Let Government through the educational Authority concerned help a Board or a Committee generously and the school will be provided. (iii) It may be said: It is easy to lay it down that in certain circumstances an additional school is to be provided, but not so easy a thing to do the actual providing.

And even when every known consideration has been taken into account by an Authority, circumstances beyond calculation may so operate as to make the additional school, when established, unnecessary. That may be the case; but just because of such a possibility, Authorities will act with caution and with a due sense of the responsibility resting upon them for the expenditure of funds under their control. And it must not be forgotten that, as matters now stand, one of the most familiar, as it is one of the most depressing features of official annual reports, is the record of schools which are opened, last for a little time, and then close. And next to that, and far more difficult to deal with, is the record of schools which should never have been established but which are just able to live, in reality cumberers of the educational ground. It is situations like these that Authorities with statutory powers will be able to deal with effectively, because they have the intimate local knowledge that is required. And they may be trusted to weed out the schools that are unnecessary as well as to establish no school which is unnecessary.

24. *Agreement the Solution of Hard Cases.*—By means of the steps that have been described it will be possible to advance education, to safeguard conscientious scruple, and to maintain State impartiality. But it is conceivable that after all hard cases may still arise. The remedy for hard cases, however, is not legislation; it is agreement. And that is a service which the proposed Authorities will be able to render in ever increasing degree, as they extend their experience and grow in administrative power. Their capacity for reconciliation of interests will also increase; and with the increase of that capacity will come the decrease, and finally the elimination, of hard cases. And what these Authorities will do in the sphere of primary and secondary education, the Government and the Universities will do in the sphere of collegiate education. Thus it will be found that the principles of control which we have advocated are capable of application to every form of education and of

affording also the best means for dealing with hard cases.

25. *The Demands of Religious Education.*—The bearing of the preceding considerations on schools which make religious education an integral part of their curriculum is very obvious. If they are of the right stamp they will win the confidence of parents. This is true, as has been abundantly shown in the past, even where the religious education imparted has been different from that based upon the faith of many of the parents. Where the religious factor is recognized as educative not as propagandist, the welcome given is widespread and sincere. But to produce this result there must be a staff which by academic qualification, personal influence and numerical strength is able to make the religious education in the school telling in every part of its work. Where the personnel of the staff and the influence they exert is able neither to win the confidence of pupils and parents nor to send forth those who are fitted to fight a good fight in the battle of life, the school may as well discard its claim to impart religious education. That is the very thing which it is not doing, and it may go. But where schools not only make the claim but also substantiate it by the power which they exert and with which they inspire their pupils, the place of a school which thus makes religious education essential to its being is secure in the hearts of pupils and parents alike.

VI. The Solution of the Problem

26. *Principles which render Solution Possible.*—There are two facts which everyone who knows India and is interested in its education, realizes sooner or later. The first is that a real desire exists for the combination of religion with education. The second is that Government has adopted the attitude of religious neutrality in all branches of its administration, including education. The existence of these two facts confronts us with a

problem which urgently demands solution. That problem is: How is religious education possible in the Indian educational system when that system is controlled by a Government which has identified itself with the policy of religious neutrality? The problem, not easy in itself, has been complicated by a number of causes. Among them may be mentioned the fact that 'religious neutrality' has had more than one significance attached to it, that Government has been prejudiced by its dual position as a controller of education and an educational manager, that Local Bodies have often been reckoned as subject to the same limitations as are schools managed by Government, and that a form of legislation has been proposed or enacted which fails to take account of the foundations on which Indian education is reared. Further, it cannot be denied that little determined effort has been made by Government to render operative the important implications of the policy of neutrality which it professes. Full consideration of these various points has made it clear that a solution of the problem is possible only if two definite principles are accepted by Government. The first of these is that neutrality means a readiness on the part of Government to encourage the combination of religion with education while in so doing it remains strictly impartial. The second is a recognition by Government of its responsibility for providing adequate educational facilities so that with the advance of education there may be no violation of religious scruple. When we examine the Indian educational system we find that both principles are of a practical character, and can be given expression to in that system in a way which, far from prejudicing education, enhances its value, commends it to an ever widening circle, and gives it a place in national life which it has not yet secured. In this way, by the recognition and employment of these principles, the solution of our problem has been reached.

27. *Benefits of the Solution.*—Much might be said regarding the benefits which accrue to education from

this solution. But we must content ourselves with mentioning only four of them. And with a brief indication of the nature of each of these advantages we may appropriately conclude our consideration of this vitally important problem.

(i) Religious Neutrality will no longer be regarded as necessarily involving at any point a purely secular education. Thus the charge of a 'godless' system of education will not be possible, or if it is made it will be untrue. A serious stigma under which Indian education has laboured will thus be removed.

(ii) While there will be perfect freedom there will be an encouragement of religious education without the impartiality of the State being impugned. The abandonment by the State of its office as manager, and the recognition of Local Board management as coming under the category of Aided management will make it possible for the State to advance the cause not only of schools which confine themselves to intellectual training but also of schools where religious sanction affords a driving power to mental and moral life.

(iii) All form or appearance of coercion will be removed. Through the provision of facilities, no pupil of a school will be coerced into the abandonment of what is most sacred. And no manager of a school will be coerced into the abandonment of a cherished educational ideal.

(iv) Religious education, the need for which recent analyses of the religious situation in India have only served to emphasize, will receive its rightful place in the educational system of the land. It will not be regarded as the instrument of partisanship and propaganda. It will be conceived of as the great means whereby the search for truth is quickened, individual character is strengthened, corporate life is built up, and national life is enriched by those who have learned to do justly. to love mercy, and to walk humbly with their God.

References

Various aspects of the combination of religion with religion and of the State's attitude are presented, dealt with, or referred to in the following:—

A. Mayhew, *Christianity and the Government of India,* Chapter xiii, and throughout the book.

R. B. Smith, *Life of Lord Lawrence.* In the Chapter which deals with 'Lawrence as Pacificator' (latter part).

Imperial Gazetteer of India, Volume iv, Chapter xiii.

Indian Education Commission Report, Chapter viii, section 9, paragraph 512, and section 10.

E. Stock, *History of the Church Missionary Society,* Volume ii, Chapter xlvi.

G. O. Madras, No. 836 Law (Education) Department of 15th July 1922.

Press Notice, Bombay, No. 3601, Educational Department of 5th July 1921.

In the *Quinquennial Review of the United Provinces,* 1927, at p. 135, the statement occurs that 'religious instruction was made compulsory in all primary schools of the Moradabad municipality for boys of school-going age'.

V. Chirol, *Indian Unrest.* Chapter xx deals with 'the Question of Religious Education', and suggests a plan.

Report of the Commission on Christian Higher Education in India. Chapter on 'Change in India'.

S. K. Datta, *Asiatic Asia.*

CHAPTER V

The Problem of the Teacher

I. The Problem: How is India to have an Adequate Supply of Properly Qualified Teachers?

1. Every country has its heaven-born teachers. To pass these through the routine of the Normal Schools savours of sacrilege. But the number of teachers who are made, far outruns the number of those who are born. And an educational system has to concern itself, in large part, with what is usual rather than with what is exceptional. Indeed, its stability and power as a system is bound to depend, to a great extent, on a body of well-trained teachers. For the earth-born are lifted no inconsiderable distance above the soil by the experience wherewith a professional training enriches them. And even the heaven-born do not lose their wings entirely by being brought into contact with some of the standards of the earth whereon they have to serve. The education of India is far too important to be left in the hands of amateurs. But, unfortunately, that is pretty much what is happening at present, as a study of the facts presses home upon us with an insistence which we cannot escape.

II. The Present Situation

2. *Facts as to Numbers.—What are the facts?*—Here are some of them. First, as to *numbers*. In round figures, eleven millions of the youth of India are receiving education in its recognized schools and colleges. And they are receiving this at the hands of 400,000 teachers. When we consider the number of subjects that have to be taught, the number of institutions for general and professional education that have to be staffed, the number of langu-

ages in which instruction has to be imparted, and the number of special arrangements which are still necessary so that fitting opportunities for education may be within the reach of all classes and communities, we cannot but conclude that India has far too few teachers. Statistics might easily be marshalled in support of this conclusion. But let one set of figures suffice. In the presidency of Madras there are over 28,000 primary schools each of which is taught by a single teacher, and 20,000 of these schools have four or more classes. In some of the classes there are seventy to a hundred pupils. In Bengal there are over 39,000 single-teacher schools with three classes in each school. Bombay, which has done much for its teachers, has more than 5,000 Local Board single-teacher schools; and in the United Provinces there are more than 10,000 such schools. The single-teacher school has still a place, and in not a few conditions a most useful place, in the elementary education of the country. But we cannot help noting that the number of these schools now runs into over a hundred thousand; nor can we help reflecting that if that number were diminished, education would benefit. Now that number can diminish only when there is a larger number of teachers available.

3. *Facts as to Qualifications.*—So much for numbers. Let us now turn to *qualifications*. Of the 400,000 teachers at work in India, 183,000 are classified as trained, and 217,000 as untrained. These figures mean that by far the greater part of the youth of the country is being educated by those whose main qualification for teaching is the light of nature. Of those who are engaged in what is both the most difficult and the most responsible task that exists in India to-day, fifty-four per cent are unskilled workers. And if we look at what is fundamental in the system—the primary school—we find that 'only forty-four per cent of the total number of teachers in primary schools for boys, are trained'. While of those who are trained, only about twenty-eight per cent have completed the Middle School course. In other

words 'a very large proportion of the teachers possess general qualifications which are scarcely superior to those of the pupils in the highest class of the primary stage'. And when we pass to other grades of schools, what are we to say of one province in which only twelve per cent of those who teach in Middle Schools are trained, while in the High Schools of another province a similar percentage holds? It may be said that within the last five or ten years there has been a distinct increase in the number of teachers who have undergone training. Statistics support that statement. In 1922 there were 40,000 more trained teachers than there were in 1917, and in 1927 there were 55,000 more than in 1922. Thus in ten years there has been a gain to the system of 95,000 who have passed through some form of professional training. But any little grain of comfort which we might derive from this, is rudely snatched from us when we look into the most recent tables and note two facts. The first is that there are 24,000 more untrained teachers in the schools of India now than there were ten years ago. And the second is that, while the trained teachers have increased by six per cent in the course of the last five years, the number of pupils receiving instruction has increased by twenty-five per cent. Clearly the supply of qualified teachers is not keeping pace with the steadily increasing demand.

4. *Facts as to Salaries.*—And if we look at *salaries* we find a state of affairs which is most disheartening to read, and obviously most detrimental to the best interests of education. More will have to be said regarding this matter, and in the meantime it must suffice to mention a few facts drawn from recent statistics. The average monthly pay of teachers in boys' and girls' primary schools is Rs. 15 As. 4 in Madras, Rs. 8 As. 6 in Bengal, and Rs. 11 As. 5 in Bihar and Orissa. Thus over a large tract of country reaching from the extreme south of India to the borders of Tibet, a teacher in a primary school may think himself well off if he receives on an average a salary of Rs. 12 a month. On the

western side of India Bombay provides a welcome bright spot. The scales of pay there run from Rs. 20 to Rs. 60, the average being Rs. 47.

5. *Resulting Problem.*—Even the few facts which have been mentioned make it perfectly plain that the number of teachers is insufficient, their qualifications are not high enough, and their salaries are inadequate. The facts, therefore, confront us with a problem which we must now consider. The problem which calls for attention and solution may be stated in this form: How is India to secure an adequate number of teachers, and of teachers properly qualified?

III. Need for Attractiveness of Teaching Profession

6. *Advantages and Disadvantages of Teaching Profession.*—The first and most obvious answer to the question is: India will not have a satisfactory supply of teachers till the teaching profession is made really attractive. There are, indeed, features of attraction in it as it now exists. A teacher who impresses himself on his pupils has a reward to which there are few parallels in any walk of life. He wins a loyalty and affection which are an abiding strength and stimulus. He has the privilege, accorded to few, of seeing his work prospering in his hand. He has the incalculable benefit of always being with the young, and his concern is with living beings rather than with lifeless things. For the refreshment of his mind he can count on one vacation, at least, every year. Yet for these advantages, it must be conceded, he pays a heavy price. Thousands of teachers in India are unable to live on the salaries which they receive. Even in a well conducted school, the management which thinks that it has been doing well by its teachers is awakened one day to the galling fact that a considerable number of the staff are enmeshed in a web of debt. And it very likely finds that the energy which should be reserved for the school is being expended on attention to proceedings in a court of justice. Many

are without books, save the class-books supplied by the school. Lack of provision for old age makes retirement a spectre, and delay in retirement may be working against the progress of the school. Many live in villages where intellectual stimulus is practically non-existent, where the help that might be derived from sympathetic supervision is infrequent, and where the opportunities for entering on some form of attractive speculation are disastrously inviting. Not a few find themselves at the mercy of village feuds, or embroiled in political factions. Many more find it hard to decide who is the master whom they have to serve. Caste feeling has many ways of dealing with a teacher who affects to neglect it. To a considerable number, even among the higher ranks of the profession, the parent of wealth presents more than one disturbing problem. In fact, one who contemplates entering on the work of a teacher has to reckon on preparing a balance-sheet of advantages and disadvantages which it is far from easy to adjust. And so long as that is the case, India will have thousands of teachers who are not gripped by their vocation, and, as a consequence, thousands of pupils with whom school leaves no stimulating memories. Can anything be done to help the teachers and, through them, the youth that attends the schools of India?

7. *Insufficient Salaries.*—One thing clearly must be done. The teacher must be able to live by his teaching. It is true that teachers are able to augment their incomes by undertaking duties which only those who are literate can perform. Their help in the Postal and Co-operative Credit Departments is most valuable, and their assistance as family tutors helps to stimulate the desire for learning. No one would grudge them the small additions to their purse which such activities would bring to them. But the existence of these opportunities affords no reason why any management should be content to offer an unsatisfactory salary to one whose primary duty is that of teaching. In the course of a discussion which took place in a provincial legislature some years ago

regarding the low salaries that were being paid to teachers, the lowness of the salaries was not denied, but it was pointed out that certain village teachers were able to combine with their scholastic work other duties and thus to draw a total salary which was not unsatisfactory. No wonder that the Head of the Department was promptly asked whether he considered this a good arrangement. Most certainly, no management can escape from the responsibility of giving the teacher whom it employs a living wage. And yet cases have been mentioned of teachers under training who received a stipend larger than the initial salary paid to them when they ceased to be students and took their place in the schools to which, after their training, they were appointed. Such anomalies, however, must be rare and, in the nature of things, they can be of short duration. But the fact remains that in 1927 there were a thousand fewer men attending Training Schools and Colleges in India than there were five years before. I once listened to a discussion which took place during a meeting of an Educational Authority as to whether additional normal schools should not be provided in order to make good the shortage of teachers. After it had gone on for some time a member drew attention to the purely academic character of the debate. There were, he said, in that part of the country, normal schools already in existence sufficient to afford training for all the teachers whom that small district required. The real trouble was that a sufficient number of teachers would not go to them. And the reason was well known. Teachers did not consider that, after completing their training, they received a living wage. Official figures tell the same story. Some of them have been quoted already. Here are others drawn from a recent Report. 'In the Punjab the average salary (of a primary school teacher) is comparatively high (namely, Rs. 25); but twenty-five per cent of the teachers in local body schools receive less than Rs. 20. In Bihar and Orissa the pay of primary teachers is so low that even in municipal schools the average pay is only Rs. 18.

In the Central Provinces the average salary in aided schools is as high as Rs. 20, but in some of the aided schools it is as low as Rs. 8.' And here is a quotation from the latest Bengal Quinquennial Review: 'The salary of the schoolmaster in Bengal is a miserable pittance, often lower than that of a menial servant or that of a casual labourer. Here figures are available which need no comment. In the Chittagong division, the average salary of a High School teacher is Rs. 51.7, of a Middle School teacher Rs. 18.2. In Rajshahi 70 per cent of the High School teachers receive between Rs. 20 and Rs. 70, and the actual average is Rs. 44.5'. Truly the figures need no comment, but they raise many questions.

8. *Need for fixing Minimum Salaries.*—The figures, however, tell us something more than that salaries, in a large number of cases, are sadly insufficient. They tell us that salaries are being settled in what might be termed a sectional manner. Government fixes a set of salary scales for its teachers, municipalities and district boards do the same for theirs, and private managers make their own arrangements with those whom they employ. Government draws upon public funds to enhance the salary which sorely needs enhancement, local bodies have the rates to draw on, and private bodies their own pockets. But there is no general agreement, no dealing with the matter in what might be called a national way. It certainly looks as if the prime desideratum for even an approach to effectively grappling with this situation was a concensus in regard to what would be considered fair scales of salaries for different grades of teachers in different provinces, and, if need be, in different areas of these provinces. There is little likelihood of making these scales obligatory for a long time to come, even after general agreement has been reached. But one thing is possible. The State can lay down that it will neither recognize nor aid any school which gives its teachers salaries which go below the minimum of each scale agreed upon as reasonable. By adopting such a course there would be a twofold advantage. In the first place, a living

wage would be secured for every teacher of every grade; and, in the second place, a maximum of agreement and a minimum of compulsion would be employed.

9. *Trained Teacher to be Considered.*—In speaking of a minimum salary I am thinking only of a minimum salary for a qualified teacher. If the profession is to have its proper status it must be a body of those who enter it by the recognized avenues. Self-election to the profession is surely out of date; most certainly all recognition of such self-election is. It will not be long before only those who have satisfied the required tests obtain a footing among those who are accounted to be really qualified teachers. And if it be said that efforts to secure this will only place additional temptations in the way of managers to fill up their staff with untrained teachers for whom no minimum salary is prescribed, the reply is easy. Government, as the controller of the whole system, has only to lay it down that recognition will not be accorded to schools which regularly employ untrained teachers, and the practice will cease. We shall have an opportunity of referring to the untrained teacher later, but meantime our concern is with the teacher who has qualified for admission to the ranks of an honourable profession. And it is for such a one that the laying down of a minimum salary is indispensable, if the country is to have good teachers and a sufficient number of them.

10. *Adjustments Necessary.*—I do not forget that no regulation can be made which may not require adjustment in some particular. For instance, there are Teaching Orders that receive only a subsistence allowance, and there are those who are prepared to render honorary service. But subject to arrangements in such cases which in no way contravene the general principle—and there is no serious difficulty in the way of making such arrangements—the prescription of a minimum salary for each grade of qualified teachers will be found as easy of enforcement as it will be beneficial in result.

11. *Rate of Increment.*—When a minimum salary for each grade of teacher has been authoritatively fixed a

step will have been taken, even if it be only a first step, towards giving to the teaching profession the attraction which, in common with every human activity for the sake of others, it ought to possess. But in advocating this step I realize that many questions are raised as soon as agreement has been reached in regard to initial remuneration. They present matter for serious thought, and many minds are actually at work upon them. The most striking statement in this connexion which I have seen within recent years is one which occurs in the recent Quinquennial Review of Education in the United Provinces. It runs as follows: 'Inspectors report that the work of teachers in Government schools is not of the standard that may reasonably be expected. . . . For the first two or three years after appointment the teacher generally works well; his initial zest has not worn itself out and, further, he has not yet been confirmed in his appointment. But after confirmation . . . secure in the tenure of his post and in the enjoyment of an annual increment accruing to his salary without effort on his part, he too often becomes slothful and maintains his work just a little above the standard of positive inefficiency. The difference in quality between the work of a teacher of ten or more years' service in a Government school and that of his brother of similar standard and service in an aided institution is not as a rule sufficient to justify the wide difference existing between the pay drawn by the two teachers'. Clearly we have to see that the initial salary attracts, but that is not enough; as clearly the system of increments must be so devised that it stimulates.

12. *Provident Funds.*—We must content ourselves with noting this point; further consideration of it is impossible, for another aspect of the matter now demands our attention. It is this. A teacher must have some assurance not merely as to what he is to receive at the beginning of his career and throughout his working days, but also as to what is to befall him when his career terminates. Such an assurance means the institution of

Provident Funds for teachers. Much has been done in this direction within the past few years. In the United Provinces and in the Punjab provident schemes for teachers of primary and secondary schools are already in existence. In Madras the scheme which was introduced in 1923 applies to colleges as well as to schools. In Bihar and Orissa such a fund has been provided for secondary schools; while in Bengal, provident funds are encouraged by means of special grants-in-aid to schools which maintain them. In the direction of these schemes there is diversity of method, but a general similarity of plan. A contribution from the teacher, usually a fixed percentage of his salary, is supplemented by contributions from the management and the government. In this way, every teacher to whom this scheme applies, knows that at the end of his service there awaits him a sum of money which by careful investment will provide him with a good retiring allowance and at his death will be available for those dependent on him. In this latter respect the Provident Fund has an advantage over the Pension which dies with its holder. Since so much has been done within a few years to inaugurate Provident Funds we may look forward with confidence to their being established at no distant date in every province, and to a teacher's appointment being made conditional on his contributing to that one which is in operation in his province. We may even see schemes become quickly inter-provincial as well as intra-provincial.

13. *Government Initiative.*—By means of the two provisions now mentioned two great steps will have been taken in the direction of placing the teaching profession on a basis which affords, at least, the attraction of a living wage and of security for the future. The initiative in regard to both steps will obviously have to be taken by Government,—whatever be the agency through which it decides to work—for both make demands on public funds and both are connected with provincial areas. Several governments have already taken action,

as we have seen, in the matter of establishing provident funds. Similar action in the matter of a minimum salary has elements of intricacy and difficulty, but governments will find that they have a large body of opinion on their side when they resolve to deal with this question, so that notwithstanding all its difficulties the matter will be carried through in an atmosphere of sympathy.

14. *Organization of Teachers.*—There is a third step which follows naturally from those which have been mentioned. There is pressing need for the organization of teachers on a professional basis. At present teachers tend to be organized according to managements. Some are Board teachers, some are Government teachers, others again are Mission teachers, and so on. These divisions cut across one another, and they divert attention from the service of teaching in which all are enlisted to the service of the manager by whom each happens to be employed. As a result, jealousies arise and rivalries exist, in which jealousy for education and the friendly rivalry which advances it play at most a small part. What is needed is the maintenance in each province of a Register of Teachers, on which only those who have the requisite qualifications will be permitted to have their names entered, and in which the classification will be according to general grade or special subject. To have one's name on such a Register would be a guarantee of qualification and standing. Its benefit to the teacher would be equalled only by its advantage to managements. To them it would afford a much-desired guidance, and it would give them at a glance the information for which they so often ask in vain. Naturally, if the information was to be accurate, the Register would require periodic revision. But this would not be difficult to carry out. A specified fee would be paid by every teacher on enrolment, and copies of the Register would be readily purchased. Thus there would be funds for publication and revision. And if, at the office of the Registrar, there was maintained an Employment Bureau

for Teachers, the benefit accruing to the profession would be great.

15. *Existing Services.*—But, it may be said, what is to become of those who are at present members of one of the Government Educational Services? Much will depend upon the effort which Government makes to relieve itself of the function of a manager of schools and colleges. When it inaugurates a definite policy with this end in view, and every year affords increasing testimony to the advisability of such a line of action, it will at the same time inaugurate a policy in support of the organization of teachers on the basis of their profession and not on the basis of their management. And it is hard to believe that Government will much longer stand in the way of the accomplishment of so valuable an object. But, in the meantime, what is to be done? Simply this, that so long as Government occupies the position of a manager it will fall into line with other managements in regard to the scales of salaries which have been introduced by general consent into the areas within the jurisdiction of that Government. The minimum salary agreed on will be the minimum salary which Government will grant, and as regards increments and maximum salary it will act as other managers do. Like them, too, it will give the teachers employed by it the benefit of a Provident Fund in place of a Pension. It may be asked whether Government will maintain scales of salaries exactly corresponding to those maintained by other managements. The only answer that can be returned to this question is that, provided it complies with the requirement as to the minimum salary, it will be at liberty to allow varieties of scales, in the same way as other managements, until stabilization is reached. And that is not likely to take a very long time. The uselessness of one management trying to outbid another will speedily be learned. Uniformity may be neither possible nor desirable, but soon such a measure of uniformity will be attained that strong reasons will be required to justify departure from it on the part of any management.

16. *Increased Educational Expenditure Necessary.*—It must be frankly acknowledged that before the steps which have been advocated in the preceding paragraphs can come within the realm of realization, the expenditure on education throughout the country will require to be augmented. And this augmentation will have to come from every source—from the State through its taxes, from the Municipality and the District Board through their rates, from the Private Agency through its contribution, and from the Parent through fees or their equivalent. The country that wishes good teachers has to pay for them; and the Government has no treasury that is miraculously supplied.

17. *Need for Educational Associations.*—There is one other way which will serve to enhance the teacher's status. That is the formation of strong Educational Associations or Guilds. The methods which have been mentioned up to this point, depend to a large extent on the initiative of Government. This method depends wholly on the action of the teachers themselves. It is in their power to form and maintain Elementary Teachers' Associations, Secondary Teachers' Guilds, and such like, which will be a real force not only in the educational world but also in the country. Much has been done already in this direction: but much more is possible. The Associations could do a great deal for the teacher by making known in the proper quarter hardships or handicaps under which the profession labours. Facts are always welcome, and in the long run the statement of them leads to their being properly dealt with. But Associations which give the public the impression that they exist only to improve the financial prospects of their members, or to support measures calculated to lower educational standards, or to be persistent knockers at the door of the Treasury, alienate sympathy and fail to win support. The main reason for the existence of such Associations is to band together men and women in a common effort to make education a great and beneficent power in the shaping of young lives. With that as the

supreme end in view, other functions which the Associations may discharge with advantage will take their proper place and will meet with due recognition. And this will be all the more certain when the organization of teachers is professional, not sectional. A homogeneity will be possessed by the profession which does not exist at present. The object of teachers will no longer be, on the part of some, to concern themselves with their position in a Government service, on the part of others to think mainly of their prospects under a municipality or a private committee. It will be to help on in a united manner the cause of education as a whole. And in this way they will render the greatest service to the pupils for whose benefit they have been appointed, to the parents who have entrusted so much to their care, and to the profession which is of such incalculable value to the country.

IV. Need for Effectiveness of Teaching Profession

18. *Training Required.*—In the preceding section we have considered means whereby the teaching profession may be rendered attractive, and so may draw to it those who find in it a satisfying life's work. Another question now claims our attention. It is : How is the teaching profession to be rendered *effective*? To that question one reply may be at once expected, and it will be given in some such terms as these : If the teacher is to discharge his work effectively he must be trained for it. If he is to be a fit teacher he must be fitted for his task. 'Teaching is a skilled craft.' We have already noted that 54 per cent of those who are engaged in teaching the youth of India have received no special training for that work. Some of them are devoid of all but the most meagre general education, and of not a few it can be said that they are not far in advance of the pupils under their charge. Statistics show that there are, in round figures, 190,000 elementary schools, attended by eight and a quarter million boys and girls, and

that there are, again in round figures, 312,000 teachers in these schools. That is to say, the average staff of an elementary school is roughly a teacher and a half. What we do find is that of the 190,000 elementary schools there are not quite 80,000 which have more than one teacher. India then has a system of elementary education in which there are a lakh of schools that have only one teacher, and in which, at best, only every alternate teacher has any sort of training for his work. When we keep this in mind, our uppermost thought must be one of marvel that education has advanced as it has done. There must be some exceedingly good material in the profession, otherwise progress such as has been made, even within the last five years, would have been utterly impossible.

19. *Training not always Appreciated.*—But when all is said, the figures quoted above mean nothing if they do not indicate a serious educational handicap. The number of those engaged in laying the foundation of the educational system of the country is far too small, and the number of those who have any adequate notion of how to set about laying it is lamentably smaller. Yet there are those who read in the figures no tale of woe. We read for instance that a committee appointed in one province to consider retrenchments included in its report a recommendation that training colleges should be abolished. The opinion of the members of the committee which submitted this recommendation was 'that a teacher's own capacity and education were his chief qualification, and that training made little or no difference'. We are not told whether this conclusion was arrived at on *a priori* or on *a posteriori* grounds; and we have all to admit that it may be with teachers as it is sometimes, say, with doctors: the product of a course of training may not command our confidence. But for the doctor in this unfortunate position we find ourselves prescribing more training not less, and more attention to that training on his part. We shall have to say more on this point in regard to the

teacher later on. At this point it is sufficient to note that the provincial government concerned refused to accept the retrenchment proposed. It is good to know that there are governments who regard economies in education as tending only to poverty.

20. *What is meant by 'Trained'.*—There is one other point which calls for notice in this connexion. While 45 per cent of those engaged in teaching are classified as 'trained', the significance of that designation is not constant. There are training schools, for example, which devote a considerable part of the time of those who attend them to a general, not to a professional, education, in order that those who take that course may be at least somewhat in advance of the pupils whom, after training, they will teach. Formerly there were even those who were regarded as trained, not because they had undergone a course of training in the work of a teacher, but because they had passed a prescribed written examination. While that avenue to the ranks of the nominally 'trained' is largely closed, some gates unfortunately still remain open, as we shall see later; and as what is past cannot be wiped out at once we may take it that there are yet among these who are included among the trained, some who can lay claim only to being certificated. All this complicates matters, and calls for definite action. Not only is the bulk of the teaching profession in India made up of those who are practically amateurs, and not only are there those who, though designated trained, have never been trained, but of those who have been trained there are hundreds whose general qualifications are of a somewhat tenuous character. If action seems clearly to be called for, along what lines should that action proceed?

21. *Provision for Training.*—Let us look at the existing centres of training. They bear different names in the different provinces, and even one with some experience in dealing with statistical tables finds it hard to be quite sure of the facts. According to the tables given in the Ninth Quinquennial Review there were in 1927.

15 training colleges for men with 1,142 students attending them, and 6 for women attended by 166 students, while there were 529 training schools for men with 21,610 students and 115 for women with 4,664 students. Thus the training colleges train about 1,300 men and women, and the training schools over 26,000. These figures seem to invite questions. For example, if, as they seem to show, training colleges have an average attendance of 60 students, and each training school an average attendance of about 40, what is the reason of this disparity? Are the means for training being satisfactorily employed? And how is it that, when we compare what was being done in 1927 with what was being done five years before, the quinquennium sees a decrease in the number of those under training? Then, what is the distinction between a training school and a training college? If we take this last question first, we realize how far from easy is an answer to it. We might have thought that a college trained graduates and a school undergraduates; but in that we should be mistaken. There are institutions bearing the name of College which in addition to training graduates have a department for undergraduates; and there are training Colleges which do not present candidates for university degrees in education. Then again certain of the training centres which are included among the Training Schools are in reality Training Classes attached to schools of general education. The classification at present adopted is certainly confusing. Some uniform system might be adopted by Government in their tables with advantage. Even if this led to an institution which served both graduates and undergraduates appearing statistically as two, the information thus conveyed would be decidedly more accurate than that with which we are supplied at present. There would be a distinct advantage in the nomenclature applied to institutions for training being in some sort of harmony with the nature of the training imparted. In what follows we shall seek to deal with

institutions for the training of teachers, so far as possible, in accordance with the functions which they discharge.

22. *Contribution of the Universities.*—If, to begin with, we look at the top of the educational ladder we find that real progress is being made. The greater number of the universities now confer degrees in Education, and these degrees are conferred, mainly though not exclusively, upon those who have gone through a prescribed post-graduate course in education. As a result of the provision made by the Indian universities there are over 700 men and women appearing annually for the degrees granted by them in this subject. The greater number of these have attended a recognized course, theoretical and practical, of at least one year's duration, and those who participate in this course prescribed by the university have the advantage of that general education which a graduate in Arts or Science possesses. Further, not only have the facilities for this higher form of training been increased, but the curricula offered have been brought more and more definitely into touch with Indian conditions and fresh educational methods. The problems of compulsory education, the development of backward areas, the requirements of village community work, and the various forms of school organization and administration are among the subjects that are now included in the courses qualifying for a university degree in teaching. Then there have been enlarged facilities for specialization, as for example, in phonetics, manual training, nature study, and domestic science; while opportunities exist for more specific study of methods in the teaching of history, geography, languages, mathematics, and science. Nor would even this all too brief indication of progress in higher training be complete without mention of the fact that recent years have seen the addition to the system of special Training Colleges for women. By the institution of these women receive a most welcome attraction to the profession.

23. *The Untrained Graduate.*—But while progress is being achieved in regard to both the quantity and the quality of the provision for the most advanced form of teachers' training, alongside the record of advance must be set two considerations which require to be kept in mind lest what has been already stated should issue in unwarranted complacency. The first is this, that notwithstanding all that is being done, there are less than six thousand graduate teachers with professional qualifications on the staffs of the high schools of India. The great majority of the 237,000 pupils in the high school departments proper, that is in the stage beyond the middle school, are thus being taught by those who have received no special qualification for the task on which they are engaged. Yet surely the high school stage is one that makes a rightful demand for those who are equipped for teaching in a way that admits of no question. The demand is justified whether we consider secondary education as terminating a school career or as affording a fitting approach to what the universities impart. It is most unfortunate that at this very point a grievous weakness reveals itself. Not only is the number of trained graduates inadequate, but it would take five years, at the present rate of output from training Colleges, for managers of high schools to be in a position to secure enough trained graduates to replace the untrained graduates at present on their staff. And before the five years were up a few hundred more high schools would have been added to the total that had to be supplied. The unsatisfactory situation is thus not only being perpetuated, it is being rendered more unsatisfactory with the progress of time. And there is no reason why it should not be ended. All that is needed is the co-operation of high school managements and college principals, together with departmental control. Trained graduates are essential for high school classes. It lies with managers to provide them, or, in default to incur the penalty of the withdrawal of recognition. And it lies with college principals to see

that they refuse to admit as students pupils from schools inadequately staffed. If action of this kind were taken and persevered in for five years there would result an almost revolutionary change in educational conditions. The benefit would be at least threefold. In the first place, if colleges would have nothing to do with schools which made it a habit to employ unqualified teachers, the level of undergraduate education would be at once raised. Thus one long-standing university problem would be helped towards a satisfactory solution. In the second place, the high schools would become staffed only with those who were qualified for their responsible task; the most advanced form of school education would be rescued from the hands of the amateur. Thus an important problem of secondary education would be brought nearer a solution. And in the third place, there would be an increase in the number of trained graduates sought for and employed. Thus some help would be given towards the solution of the pressing problem of unemployment.

24. *The Private Candidate.*—The second consideration to which attention must be called is this. Out of 700 graduates who appear for a university degree in Teaching there are over 100 who are classified as 'private'. The 600 who come under the heading of 'public' are stated to be those 'appearing from a recognized institution'. We may, therefore, conclude that the 100 who do not fall under the heading of 'public' are chiefly, if not wholly, those who appear from an institution which is not recognized, in other words from an institution which is not satisfactorily equipped for the requirements of educational training, or from no institution at all. Here is another pivotal weakness, and one, responsibility for which lies at the doors of the universities. Scorn would be heaped upon them if they granted a degree in medicine to anyone who had attended only lectures or who had done only reading in private. Is there any reason why they should escape scorn if they confer a degree in Teaching on anyone who has had no

practical training or who has had training in an institution on which the university is not prepared to set its seal of recognition? The time has clearly come when, in the interest of such a national service as education, the universities require to make it plain that they will have nothing to do with so-called 'private' candidates for degrees in education. Let the universities lay it down that they will admit to their colleges of general education only those who come from properly staffed schools, and that they will confer degrees in Teaching or Education only on those who have combined, in a way satisfactory to the university, practical training with a theoretical course, and the whole educational system will receive an immediate benefit in which the youth of the country will most fully share.

25. *Training for Undergraduates.*—We may now pass from those institutions, or those departments of institutions, which train graduates for the teaching profession, and consider those whose students are undergraduates. Statistics show that, in round figures, there are 26,000 men and women who are attending courses that will fit them to become teachers in middle and primary schools. Five years ago there were 27,000; and whatever may be said as to the better quality of the teacher now available, or as to the benefits of concentration in training centres, we should not be facing facts if we did not admit that the loss of a thousand teachers in the course of a quinquennium, which has seen unprecedented efforts on behalf of mass education, discloses another serious weakness in our educational administration, and forms an additional plea for attention to the attractiveness of the service of teaching. Yet this is not all. Even to make the admittedly inadequate provision which at present exists for the staffing of middle and primary schools, 290,000 teachers are required in elementary, and 42,000 in middle, schools. But what does this provision imply? It means that on an average there can be only two teachers in fifty per cent of the primary schools, and four teachers in each middle school. Now

these staffs are subject to constant change, as the heads of schools know only too well. Every year numbers leave the teaching profession through the operation of an age limit, because their health is not sufficiently robust, owing to the lure of another career, and, in the case of women, on account of marriage. We may take it that the number of those who retire from the teaching profession annually is not less than five per cent of the whole, and almost certainly it exceeds this. But if we keep it at the smaller figure we may say that every year sees nearly 17,000 lost to the ranks of the country's educators in primary and middle schools. Now, as we have seen, there are 26,000 teachers in training for these grades, and their period of training generally extends over two years. The result is that we cannot count on more than, say, 13,000 teachers with appropriate qualifications annually leaving the training schools so as to be available for employment in these schools. That is to say, what statistics tell us is that the training schools are every year supplying the primary and middle schools of the country with 4,000 fewer teachers than these schools are annually losing. The conclusion to which we are forced is that, if the schools of these grades, as they now exist, are to have staffs that do not fall wholly below the present unsatisfactory minimum, they must draw more and more on the untrained teacher. That means a steady deterioration of primary and middle school education, a deterioration bad enough as things now are, and still worse with every increase of pupils. Realizing this, we cannot escape the question: How is the country to be benefited by the spread of education in circumstances such as these? If every year is to see increasing reliance placed upon the untrained teacher, the country is being made to pay large sums of money for which it receives no real return, and the boys and girls of the country are being given less and less of an education that will be of real service to them in the battle of life. And if compulsion is to be introduced on any wide scale while present conditions continue, it will only mean that children are being legally compelled to receive an education which will not be for the country's betterment. It is difficult to believe that, were the country awake to what is in store for it, not to speak of what is now being done in it, it would suffer existing conditions to continue, or its money to be voted in the present unfruitful manner.

26. *Ill Effects of Lack of Training.*—We have noted in paragraph 23 how the lack of trained teachers in high schools affects adversely the work of these schools and thus in turn hampers the work of the universities. In the last paragraph we have seen how it is that high schools are in their turn affected by the admission to them of pupils who, through the shortage of trained teachers, have been insufficiently instructed to enter upon a high school course. And we further have had impressed upon us by the medium of figures that compulsory elementary education, if applied to India as a whole, in present circumstances, would be equivalent to compelling the country to accept that poor education which cannot be dissociated from a system that is mainly in the hands of the amateur. Thus at whatever stage we touch the education of India, be it at the university or in the primary, middle, or high school stage, we find one persistent, disastrous, and paralysing weakness—the absence of the teacher who is trained for his responsible duty. If education is to be rescued from the blight which threatens its whole advance and power, then every effort must be exerted to supply that which will effectively remove the blight. And if the effort is to be effective, it must take place along carefully considered lines. To the consideration of these lines we must now apply ourselves.

V. Outline of Policy for Securing Trained Teachers

27. *Lack of Policy.*—What we are in need of for the supply of the trained teacher is a definite *policy*, and so far as it is possible to discover from reports and reviews

of education, India seems to suffer in the most marked degree from a singular absence of any such policy. At whatever aspect of the matter we look we are impressed by the lack of concerted action. In a domain where we might reasonably expect the operation of a general and steady response to a national responsibility we are confronted with what partakes too much of the nature of the casual and ill devised.

28. *Provincial Training: Effort and Lack of Effort.*—Take for instance provincial action in this matter. The latest statistics show that, throughout India, there are 27,500 men and women attending the various schools and colleges that train teachers. And of that number 10,800 are in the training schools and colleges of Madras. If to this large number which Madras provides we add the 3,600 who are under training in the Punjab, we realize that two provinces supply more than half the trained teachers who are being prepared for this all important service to the community. Out of the eight major provinces, then, two are doing more to give the country a supply of those who are vital to its well-being than the other six provinces taken together. Let us put it in another way. Two provinces with an aggregate population of seventy millions are training 14,400 teachers per annum, while six provinces with an aggregate population of one hundred and eighty-eight millions, or wellnigh three times as great, are training only 12,400. These facts indicate a strange lack of distribution, a very unequal sense of responsibility. And when, as has been already pointed out, we have to set alongside this inequality of distribution an actual diminution of supply during the last five years in some provinces, we realize the seriousness of this provincial weakness in educational matters. Very obviously the lack of properly qualified teachers cannot be explained by lack of funds. Something much more fundamental is wanting, and that is a national policy. The attainment of a large measure of provincial autonomy in regard to education does not seem to mean the attainment of a

large measure of accepted responsibility. Provinces have their Ministers of Education and their Educational Departments; why do they not have their comprehensive educational policies? The nation must have its teachers; but it cannot have them till each province takes its due share in this national service.

29. *Training supplied by Local and Private Agencies.*—Within provinces we find the same absence of plan. Two somewhat astonishing facts confront us. For one thing, while provincial governments are more and more devolving upon local bodies the control of large sections of the education of the country, there is not a single training school maintained by a Municipality or a District Board in Bengal, Bihar and Orissa, and the Central Provinces, while the solitary training institution under local management in the province of Bombay is stated, in the tables, to have four students. Little more than one hundred women are being trained to become teachers by the local bodies of the country; and the total number of their students under training, men and women, does not reach the figure of 1,200. What are we face to face with here—policy or *laissez-faire?* The second fact is one which will come as a surprise to many. It is this: five times as many teachers are being trained by private agencies as by local bodies, while the number of women teachers trained by private agencies is greater than the number trained in Government and Board institutions combined. What statistics tell us is that Government trains 20,100 teachers, Local Bodies 1,200, and Private Agencies 6,200. The two facts mentioned in this paragraph lend emphasis to the need for a definite and widely accepted policy in connexion with the training of teachers throughout India.

30. *Need for the Co-operation of these Agencies in Training.*—Now the figures to which we have called attention, if they are in many respects disquieting, are in other respects stimulating. They provide us with data from which valuable guidance may be derived, more especially if we take them in connexion with the general

trend of education throughout the country. What that tendency is the most recent figures make fairly plain. First, elementary and secondary education are almost wholly in the hands of Board and Private managements. Second, while the number of pupils at the elementary stage is about equally divided between them, the balance has inclined since 1930 in favour of the Board schools. Third, the number of secondary pupils in privately managed schools continues to be largely in excess of those attending board schools. From these facts two conclusions seem to follow naturally. The first is that the educational strength of the country lies in the partnership of these two agencies. And the second is that what appears in the realm of general education might be reflected with advantage in the realm of the training which is given to those who impart this general education. In other words, let the main burden of training teachers for elementary schools fall upon local effort, and the main burden of training teachers for secondary schools fall upon private effort, the work of both being subject to government control, support, guidance, and inspection. If this were generally accepted we should have clear lines along which the professional training of teachers might advance with effectiveness, economy, and a minimum of friction. And certainly we should have a definite policy.

31. *Responsibility of Local Bodies for Elementary Training.*—If local effort is to be responsible largely for the advance of elementary education, it must be responsible for all that that involves. For the time being we shall not deal with the constitution of local bodies; and, when local effort is referred to, it must not be taken for granted that Municipalities and District Boards as at present constituted are the bodies to which reference is made. The term is used to signify statutory local bodies in which the control or management of educational institutions may be vested. It is obviously the case, there is a growing tendency to commit to local bodies by legal enactment a large measure of responsibility for

the advance of elementary education. If, then, the principle which we have enunciated were acted upon, this would involve the transference to these bodies of a large measure of the responsibility for the training of the teachers who are to staff these schools. Statistics, however, show no sign of such transference; indeed the most recent figures show less sign than there was five years ago. The tabular statements of the year 1922 indicate that there were four times as many teachers being trained by Boards as there were in 1927. But such retrogression, if disappointing, only serves to emphasize the need for the matter being dealt with in a regular and comprehensive, rather than in a shifting and haphazard, manner. And this is possible without dislocation or financial embarrassment. Local bodies manage at the present time 3,600 Vernacular Middle Schools, and their number is being steadily added to. If the location of these schools receives the attention which is their due and which, one would gather from reports, has hardly been accorded to them, they will be more and more planted at strategic points, points where they will exert most influence in combating the illiteracy of a locality, points where they will serve to link up the work done in several surrounding elementary schools. Now, if to these Vernacular Middle Schools, thus strategically situated, there were added, according to need, training classes, then there would have been set afoot the beginnings of a truly effective system of teachers' training.

32. *Advantages of Recognizing this Responsibility.*—This method of dealing with the matter would have at least four advantages. In the first place, there would be no unnecessary expenditure. The staff at each selected centre could be so appointed that adequate provision would be made both for the ordinary teaching of the school and the training carried on at it without there being overlapping, and the school would serve as the practising department. In the second place, the classes for training would naturally develop into fully equipped

centres for training as soon as it was clear that at this place, or at that, the appropriate location for the training of teachers had been found. Indeed by beginning with normal classes attached to middle schools it would be possible to experiment as to the most fitting place for a training centre, and when the experimental stage was ended a decision could be come to without hesitation as to whether the class should be discontinued or transformed into a permanent centre. If the latter course were decided on, the centre would be established and organized in places where the ordinary conditions of the pupils were to be found. There would thus be none of that artificiality which is sometimes inseparable from the training school being situated in a place removed from the environment of the pupil. In the third place, the association of the student under training with the pupils attending the school would help to keep the thought of teaching before the pupils, and would lead them in many cases to consider the advisability of fitting themselves for such a career. And in the fourth place, by this method there would be a concentration of training centres without overcrowding, with the result that each one who was being trained would receive the fullest individual attention.

33. *Need for Local Educational Authorities.*—Doubtless there are those who would admit all these advantages, but who would set against them the disadvantage of transferring the training schools from departmental to local board management. It will be said, for example, that local bodies have a more or less political complexion, and that this does not make for satisfactory educational conditions. Or it will be said that some of these local bodies have such an intimate relation to departmental plans that they are rather instruments of official than of local policy; and if so, why change? Much might be said in regard to both points; and further, it might be conceded that local bodies have not fulfilled many hopes that clustered round their inauguration. But, when all is said and done, the fact remains

that local self-government is the basis of all good government; and that, though a particular method or expression of it may have been less successful than was anticipated, yet that affords no reason why a more appropriate expression of it is not to be sought for and given effect to. Without going further into this matter at this point we may content ourselves with saying that there is need for statutory local bodies which are concerned wholly with education. This is recognized in the Madras Elementary Education Act of 1920 which has set up *ad hoc* District Educational Councils; while Bengal proposes to set up a School Board in each district. To relate these Bodies or School Boards to local administration would involve no difficulty. All that is needed is that by statutory enactment these *ad hoc* bodies should have due representation of local bodies, as at present constituted, or under any revised constitution, as well as of other educational agencies in the area; that they have satisfactory financial provision; that they give their whole attention to the one service of education; and that they have an effective administrative organization. In these ways the interests of education would be advanced, and local interest in education would be conserved and indeed stimulated.

34. *Combination of Local and Private Effort in Training.*—A further advantage would accrue from this method of dealing with the training of teachers. As we have already seen, private effort trains five times as many teachers as does organized local effort. Now there are practically 1,200 Vernacular Middle Schools under private management. To certain of these, chosen because of their location, training classes might with much benefit to a locality be attached or in connexion with them a training department might be established, as is being done in a number of cases at present. The increase of facilities which would result from this would be in line with the needs of the country. No agency can be neglected if real progress is to be made, and co-operation between local and private effort in the pro-

vision of training classes and centres according to a carefully thought out plan is essential to the national well-being. But if to Local Bodies as at present constituted there was delegated the control of the whole of elementary education and the training connected with it, we should have a denial of the principle of co-operation. Local Bodies would be made the controllers of all the training classes or schools connected with elementary education, while they would themselves be the managers of a certain number of them. This anomalous position would react to the detriment of the controller, and thus to the detriment of education as a whole. But if, instead of perpetuating this anomaly, elementary education with its attendant training is entrusted to *ad hoc* bodies, in the way suggested in the previous paragraphs, then, however close may be their connexion with District Boards and Municipalities, they will by their concentration on education eliminate friction between control and management, while they will evoke such concerted action on the part of local and private effort as will assure elementary schools of adequate staffs of well qualified teachers.

35. *Women and Educational Authorities.*—Another benefit that will come from the plan now advocated is that statutory school boards or councils would number women as well as men among their members. At the present time one of the greatest difficulties in the way of the advance of women's education, so far as that is carried on by Local Bodies, is that for a woman to be elected to one of these bodies is still very much of an event. The incorporation of education committees or *ad hoc* boards which have a statutory position and a connexion with local sentiment and effort, will put an end to this difficulty. The constitution of these bodies has only to provide for the due representation on them of women, and a step of distinct importance will have been taken. It may be said that Local Bodies even at present have powers to appoint Education Committees, and these may contain a certain number of persons who

are not members of the Local Bodies. That is true, but these committees are advisory, and their advice the Local Bodies are under no obligation to accept. There is little encouragement for anyone to serve on a committee when he knows that the recommendation made by it on the grounds of educational experience may be thrown out by a body with whom other considerations have greater weight. But in statutory bodies on which the representation of women with the needed knowledge is normal and effective this difficulty will not arise. And by the establishment of such bodies the elementary education of girls will soon become aware of what it has gained.

36. *Transfer of Departmental Training Schools.*—It may be thought that in this discussion there has been a failure to take into consideration the position of Government. Figures, however, show that in this connexion the work of Government has not been overlooked. The withdrawal of Government from direct management of primary schools is the explanation of this fact. There are in round figures 190,000 primary schools in the educational system and of these less than 3,000 are under departmental management. If the policy at present in operation is maintained this number will before long disappear from statistical tables. Then, Government manages only 130 middle vernacular schools out of a total of a little over 5,000. Government is slowly transferring to other agencies its management of primary and middle vernacular schools. How many training schools for teachers of the primary grade Government maintains we are unable to learn from the published tables. What we do know is that there are altogether 417 training schools managed by Government, and perhaps we may take it that the schools for teachers of the primary grade does not exceed 250. The transference by Government of its vernacular middle schools to non-departmental management would help to solve, by a very quick process, the matter of maintenance of roughly one half of the Government training schools for primary teachers, and

there would be little difficulty in finding suitable managements to undertake the responsibility for the maintenance of some hundred training schools throughout India. Transference, it is hardly necessary to add, carries with it, quite as much as does recognition, responsibility for fitting financial support.

37. *An Effective Training Policy.*—As the result of the investigation which we have conducted in the preceding paragraphs, we reach the conclusion that there is no reason whatsoever why the present haphazard arrangements in regard to the provision of properly qualified teachers should continue. What is needed is that Government should vest the control of elementary education, under appropriate safeguards, in statutory boards and that the control of elementary education should include that of the training of teachers for service in elementary schools. These boards would encourage all agencies to participate in the endeavour to multiply the number of schools for the great mass of the population, to place them in the positions where they are really required, and to staff them with teachers who, knowing their work, are able to make education attractive to the children. Backed by such encouragement, local and private effort would combine to do for elementary education what is so urgently needed but what, through lack of policy, is being left undone or done with disheartening lack of advance. The education of girls would receive the attention which is its due, and, through the appointment of women with educational knowledge to the boards, would not be relegated to a place of subordination. Further, the boards having only education to deal with would be able to act with a minimum of delay; while the transference of normal schools and classes at present under the management of government to local and private management would facilitate financial arrangements, and make for us a scheme of mass education that would be recognized as extensive, effective, and economical.

38. *Better Financial Arrangements.*—Certain matters still call for consideration. What was referred to in the last sentence, for instance, requires expansion. In the absence of tables giving details as to the expenditure incurred by different managements on the training of the different grades of teachers, we have to be content with the information supplied in regard to undergraduate training as a whole. From the tables we find, for instance, that the number of women teachers being trained in training schools (not colleges) under private management is 2,600, while the number being trained in training schools under departmental management is 1,950. From provincial funds the privately managed schools receive Rs. 4,46,400, while the Government institutions receive Rs. 6,93,900. That is to say, private agencies train 650 women teachers more than do departmental agencies, and they receive in grants from provincial funds two and a half lakhs less. In other words, if the funds which Government expends on its own normal schools were at the disposal of approved private managers then, without additional cost, about 1,400 additional teachers might be trained. And if we look at what is being expended on the preparation of men teachers, we find that the institutions managed by Boards and Municipalities are far from being economical, for this reason, that the number of students in each of their normal schools is so small—an average of less than a dozen per school; yet, even so, if these schools had at their disposal the amount which Government spends on its normal schools out of provincial revenues, then about 10,000 additional teachers could be trained without increase of cost to provincial funds. These calculations are only an indication of what may be done with the funds which are at present being given from the different provinces year by year towards training schools, if the management of these schools were transferred from departmental to non-departmental bodies. I have said that it is an indication, for exactness of statement would require detailed acquaintance with the needs of the

different provinces and with the financial position of Local Boards and private managers. Enough, however, has been said to show that under non-departmental management a large advance in training would be possible without further expenditure from provincial revenues. And when to this is added the fact that, under the scheme proposed, there will be less diffusion of training schools, and second, that there will be more co-operation between training schools and schools of general education, it will be seen that definite economy will be secured all along the line. Thus the policy advocated gives promise of utilising private and public funds with most advantageous results for those who furnish it, and for the country.

39. *More Variety in Training.*—Another consideration in favour of this policy requires to be emphasized. Not only will a satisfactory distribution of training schools be secured, but variety in training will become more general. As things are at present, rigidity of training is accountable in no small degree for that lack of spontaneity which is so often deplored. Where normal schools are attended by numbers of students that render individual attention practically impossible, the standardization of instruction becomes almost inevitable. Those who receive that form of training can hardly escape the feeling that they are pretty much cogs in a wheel. And very much the same thing happens when one training school is the facsimile of another. Then localities as well as instruction become standardized. The differences between urban and rural conditions tend to be glossed over when large centralized training schools, and those for the most part in towns, are the rule. The results are, they cannot but be, disappointing. One reads in reports of men and women who apply to primary schools the methods which are suited only to secondary schools. One hears of teachers fresh from the training school, where a full equipment for each class has been looked on as a matter of course, completely nonplussed when called on to teach in a village school where all the classes are taken often by one master and, in most cases

by not more than two. In these circumstances what was beneficial in the training school curriculum is apt to be forgotten or to lie unemployed. It would be different if training schools brought their students face to face with actual conditions. But how can this be done if one curriculum is laid down for every school in a province however much localities may differ and however great may be the differences among schools in these different localities? Let a good training class be established as part of a school which is being carried on in a definite locality, a school which answers the needs of those who live in it, and the students under training there will be in contact with actual educational conditions and they will be prepared to meet these in the most effective manner. The courses in the training schools and classes will be laid down with reference to the conditions that prevail in the areas within the jurisdiction of the several statutory bodies. Thus, while there will be much in common between one course and another in a province, there will also be a considerable amount of what is special. And when this variety is regarded as natural and not exceptional, when more experiments are carried on as they are now being conducted in certain provinces of India, it will be found that many of the difficulties which stand in the way of the progress of elementary education have wholly disappeared.

40. *Stricter Conditions of Admission to Training.*—Another general consideration claims attention. The lowering of the conditions of admission to training schools and classes, wherever it is found, is a tendency to which strenuous resistance must be offered. In several places one hears of disquieting efforts to secure for training schools quantity rather than quality. In present circumstances that is not hard to understand: but the phase can be no more than temporary. Some day, and a day not very far distant, the rate-payer will awake to the fact that he has a say in this matter quite as much as the head of a training institution or the

head of an administration. He will realize, what he is only beginning to grasp, that a lowering of the standard of admission to training schools means simply a raising of the amount of money which has to come out of his pocket. For poor instruction on the part of the teacher means lack of progress on the part of the pupil, and lack of progress on the part of the pupil means money spent to no purpose. That is what all recent reports press home with irresistible incisiveness. And when at last the taxpayer sees this point, and takes the action which is within his power, there will have arrived one of the red-letter days in the story of education in India.

41. *Duration of Training Course.*—And this consideration suggests another which needs to be fully gone into. In many of the training schools the course is one of two years. And when we examine this what we find is that, as is frankly admitted, the first of these years is occupied with the endeavour to supply deficiencies in the general education of the students under training. Such an admission is the strongest possible plea that could be urged for putting an end to a situation so unsatisfactory. If a great part of what is being done in the training schools is what should be done in the schools for general education, then let it be done there, and let normal schools be what they are intended to be. It is most uneconomical to have two parallel courses of general education going on under different names. And if the standard of admission to the training school were kept at what it ought to be, then this method which adds unnecessarily to the burden of the taxpayer without adding to the efficiency of the teaching imparted to the taxpayer's child, would simply be dropped. And if that result followed, training would be cut down by one year, or rather would be restricted to the one year that is now devoted to it. Thus several lakhs would be at the service of educational authorities for the provision of additional training facilities. And training schools would be training schools.

42. *Responsibility of Private Managements for Secondary Training.*—Turning now to training of the secondary grade, we may take it for granted that, under any scheme of reorganization, training will continue to be given in the larger centres of population, as at present, but will not be restricted to these. Classes which provide training for secondary teachers will be attached to suitable high schools in rural areas, and the opportunities for doing this are manifold. This is the field in which private agencies provide the great bulk of the education of the country. There are altogether 2,687 high schools and of these 2,124 are under private management. In round figures eighty per cent of the high schools are managed by private bodies, and twenty per cent by Government and Local Bodies. If then we follow the line suggested in connexion with elementary education, the responsibility for the training of secondary teachers will rest mainly, though not exclusively, with private managements. If the schools under departmental management are transferred to managements, local or private, which are stable and adequate—a transfer which, on other and more general grounds is to be welcomed—then Local Bodies and Private Managers will combine to train all the secondary teachers required for the service of Middle Schools. Here again statutory Boards or Committees, as is already the case in certain provinces, will have a large amount of control vested in them, and will form the means by which training will be organized in appropriate centres, with curricula suited to different localities. Under a satisfactory scheme which might possibly secure in certain cases combined action on the part of Board and Aided Schools, training schools connected with some of these High Schools and training classes attached to others would meet the situation, provide teachers for boys' and girls' secondary schools, avoid waste of money, increase the number of qualified masters and mistresses, and associate training with actual conditions. It is becoming every year more obvious that considerable changes in the High School course cannot

be much longer delayed. As soon as something is done to give effect to such recommendations as are made, for instance, by the Agricultural Commission and the Auxiliary Committee, we may expect to find alternative High School courses which will be readily taken advantage of. Thus a stereotyped course leading to the university which is practically all that lies before a high school pupil at present will give place to courses which provide alternatives adapted to varied capacities and outlets. In addition to that which prepares for the university we may hope to see a course that forms an introduction to agricultural study and practice, another which is of service for an industrial career, and so on. In this way teachers who receive their training at centres connected with High Schools will be in contact with variety, and this contact will react on the curriculum which they pursue, and the teaching in the Middle Schools to which they are appointed. Thus will the secondary education of the country become more and more suited to the needs of the people.

43. *Spread of Training in Vernacular Languages.*—There is, however, an objection which may be at once raised to this part of what is suggested. It may be said that High School education is largely given in English, and that association with such schools will not be for the benefit of those whose main work as teachers will be carried on in the mother-tongue. Prophesying is easy, but not necessarily convincing. Nevertheless, it is impossible to read reports of what is going on throughout India without recognizing the tendency to extend to High School education that emphasis on the vernacular which is usual at the Middle School stage. Quite patently, as we might expect from what is stated in Chapter vii, there will be far more vernacular teaching in the High Schools of India during the next ten years than there has been during the last twenty. We need not fear, therefore, possible evil results from the association of those under training with pupils who are receiving a High School course. They will find themselves in

an atmosphere that is congenial not antagonistic, whether we consider the studies on which they are engaged or the progress of the country to which they are giving their lives. And this will prove all the more certainly to be the case as the training schools and classes for secondary teachers become associated with High Schools in well selected rural areas.

44. *Work of Universities for Graduate Teachers.*—As regards the training of graduates there is little to say in addition to what has been already said in paragraph 22. Attention has there been drawn to what the universities are doing, and in increasing measure, to provide training facilities for graduates. Not only are good courses now available, but the variety of courses is being steadily added to, while the specialized lines of study included in the educational curricula of the universities are on the increase. The larger the burden of this kind which the universities are able to shoulder the larger will be the service which they will render to India's schools, and indirectly, but none the less potently, to the well-being and advance of the country.

VI. What This Policy Involves

45. *Two Implications.*—We have now outlined a policy by the adoption of which in the different provinces the training of teachers may be helped forward. Responsibility for the separate parts of this progress has been assigned, and the means for concerted, effective, and economical action has been suggested. The policy promises to give us an increase in the number of well trained teachers, and of teachers who are in contact with the actual conditions of their pupils. It thus supplies the answer of which we were in need when we took up the matter in paragraph 27. We must now note, at somewhat greater length than has been hitherto possible, two *implications* of the policy that has been outlined. It involves for one thing, as we have seen, the setting up of *ad hoc* educational authorities; and, for another thing, the withdrawal of Government from the

management of schools. To these points we may now turn.

46. *Multiplication of Educational Authorities.*—A policy which involves the setting up of new educational authorities may be deprecated on the ground that the multiplication of such bodies does not make for the satisfactory administration of education. There is much to be said for this view. Controlling authorities may be so increased in number, and their functions left so devoid of correlation, that real control may be rendered practically impossible by the very machinery that was set up for its existence. But bad as such a situation may be there is one that is worse, and that is the one at present in existence. A few examples will make this clear. In the presidency of Madras, District Educational Councils control primary education; the Educational Department controls secondary education, while District Secondary Education Boards give advice with regard to it; and the University, in large part, the Educational Department, in an important part, exercise control over collegiate education. In the United Provinces, Local Boards administer primary education; the Board of High School and Intermediate Education controls certain aspects of secondary education and a certain amount of what in other provinces is regarded as university education, and the Educational Department controls other aspects; while the University has to do with degree courses. In Bengal, the Education Department controls primary education; 'there is a complicated and triple control over secondary schools'; and one university controls collegiate education while a second controls degree education. More need not be said. It is perfectly obvious that the matter of control demands the fullest reconsideration. The present form of its delegation carries with it no assurance of real control. And what has been suggested above, even though it does involve the appointment of special bodies, has many advantages compared with the methods now in force. For one thing, the *ad hoc* bodies which it is proposed to constitute will have some form of

connexion with Local Bodies, even if it be no more than the statutory representation of these Bodies upon the new authorities; and still closer modes of relation might be devised which would bring out the connexion between the *ad hoc* authorities and organized local effort. In the second place, one authority might be large enough to work through two committees, one dealing with primary, the other with secondary, education. In this way there would be no multiplication of bodies, and there would be opportunity for a more intimate bond between the two forms of education. In the third place, these authorities would help materially to correlate local and private educational effort. In the fourth place, they would deal with the training of teachers as well as with the general education given in the schools where the teachers would be employed. And in the fifth place, their constitution would be such that the Educational Department would be in the position of the State which had delegated certain powers to these Authorities, but in doing so had not abrogated its own functions. Thus the policy proposed reduces the number of controlling authorities to a minimum, does not deprive the State of its function as a controlling agency in respect of education, but rather enhances it, and while bringing elementary and secondary education into relation with one another, brings training into relation with both. Thus a well articulated system of control and administration is secured.

47. *Transfer to Non-Departmental Management.*—This is emphasized when we consider the second point mentioned in paragraph 45, namely, the withdrawal of Government from the management of schools. It may be objected that, if Government transfers the schools at present under its management to the management of non-departmental agencies, it loses its powers of control. Certainly if this transference took place we should have no more Government Model Schools. But, provided the system was properly administered, we should have Model Schools under various managements and that would

mean the achievement of a much more valuable result. Certainly, too, the departmental services of teachers would cease; but again there would be a more valuable result, namely the organization of teachers on a professional, not on a service, basis. And the valuable results would not cease there. They would be seen also, and very strikingly, in connexion with the administration of education and the inspectorate.

48. *Effect on Administration and the Inspectorate.*— The benefits to administration we need not recapitulate; they have been stated in sufficient detail as first Control and then Management occupied our attention in Chapter i and Chapter ii of this Part. But these benefits though immeasurably great would be still further enhanced by the benefit which would be derived from the position occupied by the Inspectorate under the new conditions. On the educational authorities which have been advocated, inspecting officers will sit, in accordance with the constitution of these bodies, and in such manner as to secure that their experience will carry the weight to which it is entitled. Thus the State which expends so much from provincial revenues on education will be able to make its position clear and its expert advice felt. The taxpayer will feel that his money is being rightly spent and the parent that his child is being well educated. But more than that will result. There will be an increased inspectorate which will not only be responsible for the duties usually assigned to it in connexion with general education but which will be able also to do much in the way of encouraging and directing the teacher. It will be possible for the members of the inspecting cadre to devote more time to the training centres and to guide teachers with that combination of friendliness and experience which will have a distinct influence on the whole of their subsequent teaching. Freed from a large amount of the office work which now ties them down in mind as well as in body they will be the bearers of new ideas and fresh methods and tried experiments to teachers. And what this will mean to

men and women who, in certain cases, see from year's end to year's end few with any vital interest in their work, it is impossible to rate too highly. Inspectors will also be able to attend vacation courses for teachers and to impart a stimulus as valuable as it will be welcome. More might be said, but what has now been mentioned makes it abundantly clear that the State's withdrawal from management will mean an incalculable increase in the power and worth of the control which the State will exercise over education.

VII. What it does for the Training Centre

49. *Vacation Courses.*—Up to this point we have said little regarding the Training Centre; but that is simply because the subject is so vast, and several of its aspects, and these important ones, fall to be considered under organization rather than under policy. It need hardly be pointed out, however, that, if the lines of action here advocated are given effect to, few parts of the educational system will be so conscious of the resulting benefits as will the Training Centre. This will be speedily seen both in the work which it does and in the influence which it will exert. Let us content ourselves with noting two of these benefits, one in connexion with Vacation Courses, the other in connexion with Special Courses. There is great need for Vacation Courses. Universities have done something in the past to organize such courses, and they have been serviceable to teachers in High Schools. That the number of these courses might be increased and that they might become a regular contribution of the universities to the larger life around them is much to be desired. And doubtless this is one of the great services which the universities will render in increasing measure as they enter more and more fully into the deepest life of the nation. But great as is the help which the universities have it in their power to provide, it is likely to be most efficacious in connexion with teachers of the higher grades. The teachers of other grades must not be forgotten; and for

them what are spoken of as Refresher Courses require to become more of a recognized institution. There is no reason why, with a certain amount of planning, every teacher within, say, a revenue district should not have the advantage of such a course at least once in five years. If these courses were conducted at different places in different years, as could quite easily be done, travelling to attend them would be a comparatively simple matter. And, if they were held at times when the hostels attached to schools were not occupied by their usual residents, terms of attendance would be still further simplified. The presence of inspectors at such courses, as has been suggested in the preceding paragraph, and as actually occurs in certain countries, would increase the attractiveness of the study which these courses would supply. The award of a certificate would be both useful and stimulating. While those who took advantage of these 'refreshers' would find not only the gain of added knowledge but also the great gain of contact with fellow-teachers in different spheres and with differing experience.

50. *Special Courses.*—There remains to be noticed one other service which a training school can render. It is the appropriate centre at which courses in special subjects can be provided. Vacation courses have their vitalizing function to perform, as have also refresher courses, but their duration is, at best, limited. Now there are subjects which a teacher is unable to take while he is undergoing training but with which, as time goes on, he sees the benefit of being acquainted. A year's leave, or even half a year's, might afford him the opportunity which he desired, provided there was a place where he might have the instruction of which he was in want. It might indeed be possible for him to arrange an exchange with a teacher whose school was near a training centre at which the particular subject was taught, and that he might be able by means of an adjustment of hours to take out the course without encroaching on his teaching work. There are certain subjects such as some of the aspects of agriculture, drawing, methods

of learning a language, arithmetical processes, physical instruction, domestic science, wireless, welfare work, moral and religious training, which a teacher would like to have some grasp of, either because he had never studied them before or because they were newer methods with which he desired acquaintance. By making provision for teachers who are ready, even at some cost, to avail themselves of such courses, training centres will be in a position to send forth fresh streams along channels which time or lack of stimulus may have rendered stale and it may be very nearly stagnant.

51. *Limits of Present Discussion.*—Did this consideration of the teacher and the teaching profession extend to matters concerned with suitable curricula, this would be the appropriate place in our discussion to dwell upon them. But the area of our consideration is more limited than that. It confines itself to policy and administration. By this limitation we restrict ourselves to considering the foundation on which suitable courses may be laid, the framework into which they may be most effectively fitted. We have set before us the consideration of a definite problem, and in the sections which have preceded we have outlined a solution. There will be no little advantage if we now recall what that problem is and the nature of the solution to which we have been led. To this we shall devote our closing section.

VIII. Advantages of Solution Proposed

52. *Summary of Solution proposed.*—The facts which were stated in Section II placed very forcibly before us the problem : How is India to secure an adequate number of teachers and of teachers properly qualified? In Section III we saw how, by means of suitable salaries, provident funds, and appropriate organization, men and women might be attracted in sufficient numbers to the teaching profession. But the schools of the country need not only a great increase in the number of those on their staffs but also a great increase in the number of those who are properly equipped to take their place on

these staffs. The deficiencies in respect of qualification were impressed upon us by the facts considered in Section IV. So, in Section V, we set ourselves to consider how the deficiencies might be remedied most satisfactorily. We found the means of remedy in the adoption of a definite line of educational policy. That lay in the direction of linking up local and private effort not only in the common service of providing the elementary and secondary schools that are required but also in concerted action for the provision of trained teachers to staff these schools. That responsibility we saw could be rested mainly though not exclusively on local bodies for elementary education and its needs, and on private bodies mainly though not exclusively for secondary education and its needs. To bring about this co-operation *ad hoc* controlling bodies would be established, and, while the State would make this devolution, it would so effect it that it never divested itself of its responsibility for controlling the whole educational system. The exercise of this control we saw in Section VI would be rendered all the more salutary and effective by the withdrawal of the State from the management of schools; while its power through an increased inspectorate would be not only increased but also, from an educational standpoint, more telling. Section VII indicated certain ways in which still further guidance and stimulus would be associated with the line of policy here advocated. Thus we have been led to a solution of the problem with which the facts of India's schools confront us when we realize how deficient these schools are in the number and qualifications of those who teach the rising generation. And the solution as it has been unfolded has disclosed its soundness both by providing means for meeting a situation which calls for speedy and concerted action, and by pointing the way to a solution of other outstanding educational problems, such as those of control, management, and the suitability of education imparted to those who receive it. We may bring our consideration of this matter to a close by enumerating the benefits that will accrue from the adoption of the solution which has been now set forth.

53. *Advantages of this Solution.*—In the first place the line of policy which has been proposed is practicable. It can be put into effect without delay and without dislocation of any existing educational machinery. The sooner it is adopted the more speedily will it give to the schools that supply of well qualified teachers the absence of which is at the present moment proving so harmful to the spread of education in the land. All that is needed is that Government should resolve to extend and complete a process which it has already begun. It has quite definitely set itself to withdraw from the management of elementary schools; the time is ripe for it to take similar action in regard to secondary schools. Acting on this as its avowed policy in each province, it will secure that, in the course of a short time, and by a perfectly natural development, the two great educational agencies of the country, local and private, will be united in rendering a common and much required service to India. They will not only manage schools of general education, they will also unite to supply these schools with teachers by means of a system of training schools and classes which the State will aid, encourage, and guide. Each agency will have its appropriate place in this great system, and in place of unwholesome rivalry and unsuitable location there will be healthy combination and strategic setting. Then, too, the State will come to its own as a controlling agency. Government in each province will escape the suspicion of being a rival or favoured manager. It will be able to devote itself to educational administration with a freedom from those aspects which are inseparable from its function as a manager, that will emphasize and lead to its ready acceptance as a true and trusted controller of the whole system. And when Government does really guide, when it has a staff of inspectors that bring to the schools under its supervision the benefit of wise direction and varied experience, when its knowledge is at the service of every

institution, then Government control far from being a fetter to education, will be a stimulus of ever-increasing value. Further, the State will be able to exercise its control through the medium of bodies whose only concern is with education. Undistracted by other interests they will discharge a task for which existing means are inadequate. And not only that. The devolution to special bodies will be such that Government will abrogate none of its functions, and the sphere of the Minister of Education will be unimpaired. Control will be delegated, it will not be dispensed with. Training and general education will be brought into helpful contact, and training into contact with actual needs. Local interest will be stimulated; power will be mobilized; teachers will be not only qualified, they will be qualified for their specific spheres; the education of girls will receive the attention of which it stands in need. And finally, with teachers on a professional rather than a service basis, and the different agencies acting in combination, funds will be economically but at the same time fruitfully employed. There will be a large increase of training centres well staffed and well controlled, with the result that the country will reap the benefit in a steadily growing diffusion of education, and in a steady advance of its standard and quality.

54. *Teaching a Vocation.*—We have, through this consideration, found the solution of the problem in regard to the teacher with which the Indian educational system confronts us. There is no reason why India should not have in her schools an adequate supply of teachers and of teachers adequately qualified. The policy set forth in the preceding sections shows how this may be done. But there is just one thing to be said in closing. All the training of teachers, however greatly it may be increased and however greatly it may be improved, will fall short of the greatest service which it can render to the country if it is only a means whereby those who receive it find in teaching simply a profession. The true result comes when it enables the

men and women who receive it to find in teaching a vocation.

References

L. A. Selby-Bigge, *The Board of Education* contains much that has an important bearing on the training of teachers and the connexion of the inspectorate with this. Its applicability to India may be judged by reference, e.g., to p. 152 and pp. 248 ff.

Quinquennial Reviews give information and statistics as to teachers and their training in the Chapter dealing with 'Professional Education' (Volume i) and in the Tables (Volume ii).

Eighth Quinquennial Review, Chapter vii, pp. 141-152; Table IX; Tables 51-62.

Ninth Quinquennial Review, Chapter viii, pp. 172-187; Tables VI-A and VI-B; Tables 55-66.

Auxiliary Committee's Report, Chapter iv, Section vi, paragraphs 54-60, and Section viii, paragraphs 74-81 (primary); Chapter v, Section viii, paragraphs 42-47 (secondary); Chapter vii, Section viii, paragraphs 58-68 (women).

CHAPTER VI

The Problem of Illiteracy

I. The Problem: How is Illiteracy to be Overcome?

1. *The Menace of Illiteracy.*—Up to this point it is those who are educated or who are receiving education that have claimed our attention. Not that we have forgotten the numbers who cannot be brought under one or other of these classes. But even when we have referred to them it has been for the most part incidentally, or in so far as we were considering means whereby the sweep of education might be extended. We have, in fact, looked at one picture, one of brightness and of hope, but one into which there enter only a few millions of the peoples of India. We must now look at another picture, one dark and disquieting, one into which hundreds of millions are crowded. It is the picture of India's illiteracy, of India's ever present handicap. How menacing is this handicap three recent pronouncements bring home to us most vividly. A short time ago it came as a painful surprise to many who had heard of the constitutional development of India, and who had thought of the country as making great strides on the road to democratic government, that the voters for provincial Councils amounted to less than three per cent of the population. How is it that the number of what we might call parliamentary voters is so limited, more especially when the framers of the constitutional changes a dozen years ago laid it down that the franchise should be as broad as possible? The answer is to be found in two sentences of the Report of the Indian Statutory Commission. They run as follows: 'The present franchise is too limited in its scope to provide the material

from which to build any adequate scheme of representative government. Its only justification is that it was a beginning, and that, in spite of the mandate that a "broad" franchise should be aimed at, illiteracy and the restricted supply of competent persons to conduct the elections compelled the adoption of limits producing this result'. Turn now from politics to another fact of Indian life. Over seventy per cent of the people of India are engaged in, or connected with, agriculture. Yet great masses of those who are thus dependent on the land live in a condition of anxiety that often borders on despair. Not far in the offing hangs the cloud of starvation; while after centuries of toil how much still requires to be done that the eyes of India may look on telling agricultural advance. How is this? Let the Royal Commission on Agriculture in India give the answer. 'We desire to emphasize our considered opinion', say the Commissioners, 'that illiteracy presents the most formidable single obstacle to rural development in the widest sense'. Now let us look at another facet. Industrialism, we are often told, is making for itself a place of growing importance in the life of India. Some twelve per cent of the people are concerned with the various forms of industrial development; a much enhanced reliance upon it is needed if provision is to be made for India's rapidly increasing millions; yet the rate of advance is singularly slow. Why is this? One answer to the question will be found in the Report of the Royal Commission on Labour in India. Here is what the Commissioners have to say. 'In India nearly the whole mass of industrial labour is illiterate, a state of affairs which is unknown in any other country of industrial importance. It is almost impossible to over-estimate the consequences of this disability, which are obvious in wages, in health, in productivity, in organization, and in several other directions'. Political development, agricultural development, industrial development, all of them are vital for India; yet all of them, according to competent and sympathetic witness, lag. Is there anything that can be done to remove a handicap so menacing to the truest welfare of the people? Observers from three fields who have the interests of India at heart unite in one answer which they return to this question. And that answer is: Banish illiteracy.

2. *The Census and Illiteracy.*—The Census of 1931, shows that out of a total of 270 millions in British India there are in round figures 23 millions who may be classified as 'literate'. That is to say, there are 23 millions who can write a letter to a friend and read his reply; for such is the test adopted for the purposes of the Census. In addition to the numbers thus recorded there must be mentioned those who, though unable to write, are able to 'decipher the pages of a printed book with more or less difficulty'. And further it must be said, as the Auxiliary Committee states, 'that there are large numbers of persons in the country who, though not classified in the Census as literate, not only manage their own affairs and those of their families competently, but are fully capable of taking an intelligent part in public life'. But when we make all allowances it certainly looks as if we had to admit that in 1931 out of every 1,000 inhabitants of British India there were 900 who could lay claim to not even the most elementary form of literacy. In the Census of 1911 the number of illiterates stood at 940, and in that of 1921 at 920 out of every 1,000. In a picture so dark it may be questioned whether much satisfaction can be derived from contemplating what is merely a slight difference of shade. Yet it is but fair to recall that the first Census was taken in India only sixty years ago and disclosed the fact that the literates amounted to no more than nine millions of the population. Also it is worth while remembering that, despite tremendous obstacles, almost three and a half millions have been added to the rolls of recognized schools during the past decade. So that it is impossible to escape the conviction that, if the citadel of illiteracy has still its flags flying, the sappers and miners are unceasingly if unostentatiously at work. Yet

if their work is to have any prospect of success it must proceed on the basis of facts, not of wishes or of hopes. What are the facts?

3. *The Extent of Illiteracy.*—A few of these facts are easy to state. There are over eleven millions receiving some form of education at the present time. This includes pupils in every kind of educational institution, public and private; and it means that 4.1 per cent of the population of British India are at school. According to the calculation made in the *Ninth Quinquennial Review* where the material has been worked over afresh, the percentage of children of school-going age to the total population is 14. From which it follows that if literacy is to have a real chance the number of those that are now receiving education needs to be more than trebled. Side by side with this must be set a few other significant facts. In the course of the past decade the number of pupils has been growing at the rate of about 330,000 per annum. But during that time the population has been growing at the rate of some 2,300,000 per annum. The increase in population is about seven times the increase in the number of pupils. It can hardly be said that education and population are running a neck and neck race. True, owing to vigorous efforts, the rate of increase in the number of pupils during the second quinquennium of the decade was almost double that during the first; but whether our comfort from this fact will be long-lived depends very largely on whether the acceleration proves to be not only sustained but considerably enhanced. There are still other facts that have to be brought into the reckoning. Of the eleven millions now at school more than one half are studying in the first or most elementary class. And out of that class, lakhs upon lakhs do not proceed, except in so far as they proceed to leave school. It is recorded that 'of the 34.5 lakhs of scholars who completed their first year primary course in 1922-23 only 12.2 lakhs spent another year at school in a higher class'. And conjoined with this appalling waste is the fact that the average attendance in boys'

primary schools is 77.8 per cent of the total number of scholars enrolled, a percentage which was the same in 1927 as it was in 1917. Between dropping off in apparently wholesale manner, and not attending even when they do not drop off, pupils can scarcely be said to give the educational system of their country much of an opportunity to show its worth. So we are not surprised when this further fact confronts us: 'The number of literates in the age group 10-15 in the Census of 1921 was approximately only half the number of pupils in the age group 5-10 at school five years previously'. And saddest of all is the touch of unadorned reality succinctly presented to us in the following sentences. 'In 1921 less than one woman in fifty in British India could read and write. . . . In no province does one girl out of five attend school; in some provinces not one out of twenty or twenty-five'. From these few facts, and their number might be easily increased, we have no difficulty in realizing the main features of the situation. The number of those actually under instruction is not one-third of the children of school-going age. Even with the most strenuous efforts on its behalf education lags far behind the growth of population; the disparity between the education of men and women seems to be increasingly emphasized; among those who receive education too few remain at school long enough to become effectively literate; and there is a 'rapid relapse into illiteracy'. The situation plainly presents a problem of serious import for the country. That problem is: How is Illiteracy to be overcome?

References

For quotations see *Statutory Commission Report*, Volume ii, p. 89; *Agricultural Commission Report*, Chapter xv, paragraph 483; *Labour Commission Report*, Chapter iii.

India in 1927-28, 1928-29, and 1929-30, give much information, and important tables as to illiteracy.

Ninth Quinquennial Review. For population of school-going age, see Volume i, pp. 146-8.

Auxiliary Commission Report. See especially Table LXIX on p. 145.

II. Contributions to the Solution of the Problem

(i) *The Contribution of Indigenous Education*

4. *Conditions a Century Ago.*—In seeking to find a solution of our problem we must first consider whether we may expect any help from a consideration of the educational conditions which prevailed in India before the inauguration of a definite educational policy. The year 1823 which, as Sir Henry Sharp reminds us, may be regarded as a turning point in the history of Indian education, saw the Government making a grant to a society in Calcutta that had been founded for the 'diffusion of useful elementary knowledge'. And Howell speaks of that grant as 'the first recognition on the part of the Home Government of the claim of education for the masses'. In 1823 the Committee of Public Instruction was set up, as we have already seen, and various enquiries were instituted. Between 1822 and 1826 it was reported that in Madras one out of every 67 of the population was at school; in Nagpur one out of 80; and in Bombay one out of 133; or from 1.5 to .8 per cent of the population. Adam who travelled over a number of districts in Bengal from 1835 to 1838 in order to lay the facts regarding the position of education before the Government, calculated that the percentage of children of school-going age who were actually attending school ranged from 2½ to 16 and did not exceed the higher figure. Accounts of what passed for education indicate the poverty of the instruction received. Whether the schoolmaster was a regular official of the ancient village organization is still an unsettled matter and calls for fuller investigation on the part of the historian of Indian education. But whatever view of this particular point may be taken, it is perfectly clear that, at the date of which we are speaking, there were a number of schools of a purely indigenous character at work in the country.

One has only to read Elphinstone's correspondence, Adam's reports, and Munro's minutes to realize this. But while such schools existed in various parts of India at the time when the East India Company awoke to its administrative responsibilities, we have not sufficient data to give us any certainty as to their exact number or distribution. Incidental remarks lead us to believe, what the conditions of the country readily suggest, that schools started in one place were often shifted to another to meet the exigencies of the times. The breakdown of the Moghul Empire, with all the unsettlement that came in its train, turned India into a country of camps from one end of it to the other. 'Our literature, art, and even true religion perished', writes one Indian historian regarding this time. The latter years of the eighteenth century and the first decades of the nineteenth saw the people of India in large measure pupils in a hard school, for it was the school of war and its attendant miseries.

5. *Position of the Indigenous Educational System.*— The maintenance of the indigenous system, under conditions which would bring out the best that there is in it and that would make its teaching a real influence in the life of the people, was vigorously advocated by Munro in Madras during the eighteen twenties and by Adam in Bengal during the eighteen thirties. It is interesting to note that both laid emphasis on the improvement of the teacher as the first essential in any scheme of advance. But while such men strove to enlist the support of Government in schemes for the diffusion of education among the masses by the utilization and improvement of the indigenous system, they had but little success in their efforts. The attitude of Government is easy to understand. With a limited amount of money at its command for educational purposes it decided to concentrate on the first stage of an ambitious programme. It gave itself deliberately to the promotion of education among the higher classes. The result was that other stages of the programme were left untouched for the greater part of a generation.

Thus it came to pass that the education of the masses was left officially to the tender mercies of 'filtration', to the good offices of private agencies, and to the individual efforts of keenly interested and enthusiastic officials. Filtration proved to be a theory that did not work; officials were subject to transfer and had for the most part too much to do without the additional burden of educational administration; private agencies fortunately continued to espouse the cause of the masses, and they have made provision for that form of education from that day to this.

6. *Potentialities of the System.*—But the story of conditions a hundred years ago holds out no hope that by simple re-instatement our present problem is to receive a solution. Even if the best features of the indigenous schools could be restored, we have to realize that the education of today has to prepare those who attend school for circumstances very different from those which prevailed a century ago. *Pial* schools still exist in the Madras Presidency; other provinces have their *maktabs* and *tols;* and there are many who bear witness to the usefulness of these within a definitely limited sphere. But a system which tended to place memory on a kingly throne, and which availed for the days when villages were for the most part self-contained and knew an isolation to which there is at present scarcely a parallel, has at its best a restricted service to perform. To exert a real influence on the great body of the people in our day it stands in need of a supplement. And if this supplement is made then we shall see that, while the whole system cannot be retained, there are potentialities in it of which our present day system will do well to take advantage.

7. (1) *Identification of the Teacher with the Village.*—Is there any feature of the past which, even in changed conditions, we might well recall with advantage? One feature certainly: The position of the Teacher. In the village life of the past the teacher was somebody. He generally belonged to the village; more than likely he

owned a piece of land in or near the village; and with all the concerns of the village he identified himself. He wrote letters for the villagers, was able to help them in calculations as to their lands and its requirements, and could give them information which they were happy to have regarding the world beyond their own immediate neighbourhood. Ignorant fathers had to thank him for what he had done in furthering the interests of sons whose lots had been altered by his teaching. His attainments might compare unfavourably with those of a very young elementary teacher of the present day, but he had a place which his experience and judgment gave him in the formation of opinion. His character was one of the village assets. He was no mere visitor, hoping against hope for transfer to another place, and finding in his school a more or less satisfactory lever for his own advancement. Out of this book of the past we may well take several leaves when we seek to formulate our present-day schemes for the removal of illiteracy. To introduce into our Indian villages teachers belonging to a service the exigencies of which are to be regarded as paramount and the prospects of promotion in which, involving constant changes, are ever being kept in view, is to make the teacher in himself a centre of unsettlement and, as regards the village, more or less, an outsider. Not in this way is the illiteracy of the country, entrenched as it is in the villages of the country, to be even seriously encountered, much less triumphantly overthrown. The man who identifies himself with his village, with its needs, with its aims, with the means for the removal of its limitations, and with the endeavours for its well-being, he it is whom the present situation most definitely demands. Is the country to get him and, having got him, to retain him? That is a question which is hardly being faced as things now go. Indeed it is difficult to see how it can be so long as Educational Services receive the amount of official attention that is now bestowed on them, and so long as indigenous schools, or the 'relics' of them that are still with us, are relegated quinquennium after quinquennium to the Chapter in official Reviews of education which bears the heading 'Miscellaneous'. When we read provincial educational reviews we are frequently left with the impression that among those who administer education there are those who would not be sorry to see the end of such schools. It is as if they said: 'Attrition is at work on them; may its work prosper'. Now these schools are relics, but there is no reason whatsoever why they should be fossils. It is perfectly natural that they should be classified as 'Unrecognized', but that name settles nothing, indeed it only raises another question. Sooner or later educationists must come to grips with that question: What is to be done with these schools? Are they simply to be pressed or pushed or cold-shouldered out of existence? That is what seems to be contemplated as the proper mode of dealing with them in cases where satisfaction is expressed that the number of unrecognized schools is diminishing. If that is the right attitude, why make any reference to such schools in reports relating to a system of which they do form an integral part? Why not treat them as non-existent and leave them to their fate? Yet these schools continue; even official information speaks of them as being attended by several lakhs of pupils. And the number who attend them and who do not come within official ken is probably as large as, if not larger than, that of those who do. If what we have to deal with here amounts, at a conservative estimate, to half a million boys and girls attrition seems a poor instrument, the cold shoulder an unfortunate attitude. What is to be done? Retain what is best in these schools, drop what is unsatisfactory, modify what is capable of improvement? There is some hope in such a method. For then we shall be able to rejoice not in a shrinking body of schools but in an enlarged system enriched by schools which have hitherto had no part in it, but which are now fitted for that place. One of the distinct advantages of such a policy would be that the village school would have, as in days gone by, teachers who identified themselves with the interests of the village and who made the village school a force because, far from being an exotic, it had become an organic part of village life. That is one leaf which, in our conflict with illiteracy, we shall be well advised to take out of the book of the past.

8. (2) *Provision for Religious Education.*—And the second leaf is suggested by what is said in official tables in explanation of some of the terms employed. Unrecognized schools, we are told, 'are for the most part indigenous institutions for education of a religious character'. They are schools which the people feel that they have an interest in because religion, which enters so intimately into all their doings, has its place in the school curriculum. There can be no doubt that one source of the vitality of these schools is to be found in the association of what they teach with the spirit and facts of religion. If we are to have village schools which make their appeal to the regard and support of the parents, and so form powerful means of substituting literacy for illiteracy, then we must see to it that from these schools religion is not excluded. To what extent religion was combined with the ordinary instruction which these indigenous schools imparted in days gone by is a matter which will repay fuller investigation than it has yet received. But without making any attempt to pursue this line of research we may content ourselves with noting one or two relevant facts. The schools were constantly carried on within the precincts of temple or mosque, or in close connexion with a place of worship. The day's work was begun with prayer or other religious observance; and lessons were enforced by appeal to the stories and sanctions of religion. The relation between the ordinary features of a school curriculum and the requirements of religion had thus an emphasis which was none the less real because it was so natural and unstudied. Nothing would have been further from the thoughts of the people amongst whom these schools were established than that any regulation should exist which definitely shut out from the schools religious practice or teaching.

We have got to come back to this position once again, for not until then will the people feel at home with their schools. They will think of them as something that is in the village but hardly of the village. To change this presents not a few difficulties but most of these difficulties will be found to vanish as soon as it is known that, within the school, religion is not to be treated as something apart, and that provision for instruction in it will be either provided or welcomed. In this way it will be possible to do much that will make the village school an integral part of the life of the community, and thus a mighty force in the overthrow of illiteracy.

9. (3) *Residential Quarters.*—There is a third leaf which it would be well to take out of the book of the past—the association of teachers and pupils in a common place of abode. That would hardly be necessary if all the pupils belonged to one village. But where, as is so frequently the case, villages are too small to warrant the establishment of a separate school and where central schools have to be resorted to, the opportunity for a considerable measure of life in common will arise, and to take advantage of it will be both fitting and beneficial. What is done today cannot be a mere replica of the past; conditions have changed too much for that. But where simplicity is maintained, where all extravagance in building is avoided, where the standard of living is in accordance with that which prevails in rural as distinct from urban areas, then something of the old relation of guru and chela may be usefully reproduced in a new setting. If, for example, through appropriate adaptation of the hostel system such community of residence were made possible in a village with a thousand inhabitants, and there are thousands of such villages through India, not only would the education of that village be advanced, but the education of the many small surrounding villages with no schools of their own would be put on a new footing. A residential institution of this kind would be in truth a centre of education. The village atmosphere

would be preserved, study and residence would be combined in buildings that would cost a minimum to erect, and that it would be within the power of the village to maintain, while the economies that would be possible would enable the school more frequently than is now the case to have at least a second teacher. Thus suitable education would be available, a low rate of expenditure would be preserved, and the attraction and service of the village would be potent and ever present motives. Ideas that make an appeal to the heart of India would lie at the heart of the education of the country, and that education would have an attraction which up to the present it can hardly be said to have exercised.

10. *Advantages of this Method.*—The adoption of such a method, one which is in line with India's thought, would help to remove some of the difficulties that now stand in the way of those who seek to combat illiteracy. It would benefit the teacher. As things go, a teacher is often placed in a village where he has few if any whom he can consult on educational matters. The maintenance of a hostel would more than likely provide him with companionship and stimulus in common work. Thus teachers would be more inclined to take up work in the villages. It would benefit the pupil. When a village became an educational centre there would be far more opportunity for pupils to engage in games which called forth the team-spirit and stirred esprit de corps; and at the same time they would be brought into contact with wider interests and thus be enabled to rise superior to what was purely local or communal. It would benefit the smaller villages. It would hold out some hope of really tackling illiteracy in villages with few residents; it would put education within the reach of many for which separate schools could not possibly be supplied by any agency of the present time. With benefits such as these an old Indian institution could be adapted to meet the needs of the present. School buildings and hostels are often regarded as unsatisfactory today unless considerable sums are expended on their outward appearance

and their inward convenience. The result is that rural resources are soon overpassed, the village is deprived of what it ought to receive. A little planning will obviate this danger; and it will do this principally by securing that school and hostel are a real village institution, a true educational centre, a veritable community home. This combination of school and residence, both thoroughly village in character, will confront illiteracy with a force that is as destructive to entrenched ignorance as it is attractive to the mind and tradition of India.

11. *The Maintenance of the Teacher.*—As to the maintenance of the teacher we can hardly expect that there will be a return to the days when the school master received no small portion of his salary in kind. Nor can we expect him to become the power which the villages nowadays require if he has to keep himself in life by what farming or extra village appointments may bring to him. The teacher will find that in modern conditions his influence is weakened if his salary is dependent on charity or on the good will of another. But when, as has been suggested in Chapter v, recognized scales of salary and suitable provident funds have been provided the teacher will have the advantage of remuneration on which he can live and of the independence which results from earning it. At the same time he will have in the village a home and not a caravanserai.

(ii) *The Contribution of Women's Education*

12. *Increase in the Number of Women Teachers.*—The past has shed light on ways along which the problem of illiteracy may be approached with some hope of at least partial solution. Is there any feature of the present day which may open up further avenues of hope? Undoubtedly there is a very clear one: The education of women. Far too little has been accomplished in this realm, as we have sorrowfully to admit. But when we realize that every inch of the way gained has meant an alteration in social outlook quite as much as an educational advance, we find less reason to be discouraged.

And from the point of view of the problem with which we are dealing there are not a few signs of brighter days ahead. For instance we all deplore the enormous number of girls in primary schools who go no further than the lowest class. But while we do this we must not lose sight of the fact that the past quinquennium has seen more than 50,000 girls added to the Middle and High School classes of the country. This has a most important bearing upon teaching; for an addition of 10,000 girls per annum to the ranks of those who go beyond the primary stage means that there is a great widening of the field from which well equipped women teachers may be drawn. And reference to statistical tables shows that this is not a matter about which 'may' is all that can be said. There are at present 500 more women under training than there were five years ago, and 2,000 more than there were ten years ago. Here then we may believe that the morning star is really shining. It would shine better, however, if forces followed the cosmic example and showed signs of arrangement. There are more women teachers in Madras than there are in Bombay and Bengal together, or than in the United Provinces, the Punjab, Bihar and Orissa, and the Central Provinces taken together. That is not the result of accident. Where definite plans have been made and carried out the facilities for the training of women teachers have been increased in certain cases and within a short period as much as twofold, and they have been fully taken advantage of.

13. *Need for Policy in regard to Training.*—The very marked increase in the number of girls entering the middle and high schools of the Indian system is not only most valuable in itself; it is also about as distinct a call as there could be for the inauguration and systematic support of a clearly conceived policy in regard to training. In Section VI of the preceding Chapter the outlines of such a policy have been indicated. Training classes attached to Middle and High Schools for girls in accordance with a plan will have two telling results.

For one thing girls will receive an incentive to proceed from their general studies to those of a professional character. The influence of this will be felt in many a quarter of the land, more especially if the training classes are added to schools of general education at really strategic points. And for another thing, the establishment of these classes will lead in time to the formation of fully equipped training schools and colleges in increasing number and suitable locations. Already some of these are being so conducted that the association of undergraduates with graduates under training is rendered possible. The benefit of this companionship, with all its bearing on illiteracy, it would be hard to overestimate. Definite plans, then, are what is needed to take advantage of the present situation, to encourage every stable agency prepared to impart a thorough training, and to give to the country the supply which it so desperately needs of women teachers.

14. *Bearing on Illiteracy.*—But it may be asked: What is the bearing of all this on the problem of Illiteracy? The answer is twofold. First, the more women teachers there are the more girl pupils will there be. At present it can be said that 'the percentage of girls under instruction of the total female population is 1.5'. Five years before it was 1.1. One of the reasons for this lamentable state of matters is that in the present conditions of society girls who have to go to schools which are mainly staffed by men are not likely to continue long at school. But increase the number of women teachers, and you increase the number of girls who attend school and the length of time they remain there. Thus the stranglehold of illiteracy is decreased; for it must never be forgotten, as the Auxiliary Committee points out that 'the school-education of each additional girl counts more towards the future than the school-education of an additional boy'. And second, elementary education, be it for boys or for girls, will never flourish and spread as it ought to do until women, who are recognized in all countries as having a special capacity for teaching the

young, are given that place of influence in the educational system of India. And everything must be done to achieve this result. There are few things which will so contribute to it as the training, the systematic training, of women teachers. By this means an ever increasing number of girls will be attracted to school, and not only that, they will increasingly remain there till they have become permanently literate.

15. *Training of Widows as Teachers.*—And now another fact claims our attention. Indian women are taking more and more to the teacher's calling, as we have seen, but this only serves to emphasize a question which at some places is even now acute. Women are ready to be employed as teachers in towns or in the villages to which they belong. In these they have the companionship of relatives or friends. But what are they to do when they are offered appointments in places where neither friends nor relatives reside? The unmarried woman teacher often finds that the social difficulties in the way are such that she has no option; to accept the appointment is impossible. Thus schools which might become the abodes of life and interest in the hands of well qualified women teachers become too frequently places of dullness and stagnation under those who have no special aptitude or qualification. Is there any way in which this difficulty may be surmounted? The training of widows is one of the methods which has been suggested, and which to a certain extent has proved successful. The country owes much to what is being done for the furtherance of this object by the Government in the city of Madras, by the Seva Sadan Society at Poona, and in the Industrial Widows' Home at Lahore. What has been done is but the initial stage of an advancing effort that is bound to leave its mark on social as well as on educational conditions. There is no need to stress its importance in the conflict with illiteracy. Time will do that and in no uncertain fashion.

16. *Sisterhoods and Settlements of Women Teachers.* —Yet even if these teachers were available in much greater numbers than is the case at present, and if they were prepared to take up many of the appointments which unmarried women teachers find it impossible to accept, there would still be a very large place, as there is a deep need, for teaching sisterhoods. A number of women teachers having their headquarters at a central village would not only be able to do wonders for that village but would also be able to give their services in the villages round about with comparative ease and with incalculable benefit. In these days of cars and motor buses, going to a school several miles away in the morning and returning to headquarters in the afternoon or evening is now feasible to an extent that would have been regarded as incredible even a few years ago. By means of sisterhoods and present day transport, hamlets which could not maintain a teacher of their own, or which were such that lack of satisfactory conditions took from them the hope of having a woman teacher in their midst, would be able to enjoy the services of one whose residence was so situated as to render daily visits from her perfectly practicable. The place at which this body of teachers resided would be more than a centre for the visitation of schools; it would become a centre of village development. In turn it would be visited for information and ideas by those who belonged to adjacent villages. Its benefit to the women of these villages would be bit by bit recognized. And with the interest of the mothers aroused, the desire for education would be stimulated in quarters where hitherto the power of conservatism has held almost undisputed sway. Some of these sisterhoods would be established on a religious basis—an idea to which the East is no stranger—and the combination of religious with secular education thus supplied would be an added commendation of their work. But, apart from religious orders, we may expect to have in the villages before very long settlements of women to whom the great possibilities of rural India make an irresistible

appeal. Indian women have become acquainted with hostel life through the residential colleges which they have attended and through the hostels attached to training schools in which they have lived. It seems a natural step for those who enjoyed hostel life while they were under training to continue that life after training in places where enthusiasm will be able to devote itself to a great cause, and where companionship will afford the atmosphere of home. When conditions are thus secured which render residence in comparatively isolated positions free from the difficulties that they have hitherto presented to the woman teacher, the result will be seen in the growing number, attraction, and power of elementary rural schools.

17. *Hostels and the Spread of Education.*—The residential system for teachers, both men and women, requires to be emphasized as a method in keeping with Indian tradition and as an effective means of diffusing education especially in scattered places. It may seem incongruous to bring into combination with this method, which has its roots in the past, that of employing the modern motor bus and car. But we have to take things as we find them in modern India. And from one point of view at least, the motor bus may be said to be effecting a silent revolution, intellectual and economic. In this revolution there is an ally which education cannot afford to miss. And if emphasis is placed, as it ought to be, on the help which new means of transport supply, no less emphasis must be placed on what hostels for teachers can effect. Yet strangely enough, when schemes for the expansion of elementary education are being considered the provision of residential quarters for women teachers tends to be wholly overlooked. Thus it is often taken for granted that numerous villages can obtain the services of no woman teacher, and what is taken for granted is asserted as a fact, with the result that education suffers and illiteracy receives a further lease of life. The assumption is many a time purely gratuitous; the erection of a few hostels for women

teachers would speedily expose its groundlessness. Such hostels promise at least a partial solution of a situation which is sometimes spoken of as insoluble. And if money has to be spent on them, is the fight with illiteracy to be the only campaign in the world that is to cost nothing?

References

Eighth Quinquennial Review, Volume i, p. 116 (dearth of teachers); and Chapter vi, Volume ii, Tables IX and LI.

Ninth Quinquennial Review, Volume i, Chapters vii and viii, pp. 182-86; Tables VI-B and LV.

Auxiliary Committee's Report, Chapter vii, more especially Section viii.

Report on the Development of Women's Education in the Madras Presidency.

(iii) *The Contribution of Teachers' Training*

18. *The Lack of Training.*—We have now looked at the contribution which the past, and at the contribution which the education of women, enables us to make towards the banishment of illiteracy. A third contribution now calls for attention, that which comes from the training school and normal class. From what was said in Chapter v, it has become only too plain that illiteracy is actually being disseminated under the guise of education. Few things could be more ironical. Owing to the small number of pupils in elementary schools who proceed beyond the lowest class, there is a paucity of those from among whom teachers may be selected for training. Among these only a limited number can be provided for in the existing training schools. But the number of boys and girls attending primary schools is greatly on the increase year after year. Thus as the number of teachers sent out by the training schools has not been sufficient to staff the primary schools in the past, and as the training schools are not keeping pace with the increase of pupils over a considerable portion of the country in the present, the lower classes tend to fall more and more

into the hands of those whose only instructor in the art of teaching has been the light of nature. The lowest class thus makes miserable progress. Only 40 per cent of it reaches Class II, 75 per cent of that reaches Class III, 75 per cent of that Class IV, and finally 60 per cent of that Class V. This in turn affects not only the number of those who become literate but also the number of those from among whom teachers may be selected. And so the vicious circle remains unbroken. There is one place at which to break it effectively, and that is at the training school. That must be preached in season and out of season, and being preached it must be acted upon. Otherwise within the next ten years illiteracy will be not a problem to solve, but a disease for which a life and death operation is required.

19. *Improved Methods in Teaching.*—On the subject of training we need not traverse the ground already covered in the preceding Chapter. But there are three points that call for specific mention because of their bearing on the spread of education in rural areas, the places where illiteracy has its stronghold. And the first is the improvement in the methods of teaching. Why is it that so many lakhs of boys and girls never get beyond the lowest class? They enter it, they remain in it for a couple of years or more, and then they leave school. The reason partly is that their parents have no objection to their being at school so long as they cannot add to the family income; but when they are old enough and strong enough to do that then their school days are over. Economic conditions, then, afford part of the reason for what is commonly spoken of as stagnation, a part the decisive character of which is too frequently overlooked in educational discussions. But another part, and no small one, is to be found in the fact that often at school the mind of the child has received little if any stimulus. Nor can it well be otherwise if traditional methods still rule the teaching given in the village school, methods which may have been suitable for conditions gone by but which are valueless for the conditions into which the

children of today are born. Yet there are methods well known and in all good training schools regularly employed, which enable the elements of reading to be quickly mastered and the essentials of arithmetic to be speedily grasped. When are these methods to spread from the academic to the practical sphere? Only when there are far more well-equipped training schools and thus far more thoroughly well-trained teachers. And when that day comes, and there is no reason why it should not come soon, two results at least will follow. The three R's will be so taught as to stir the interest of the child from the beginning. He will soon realize that he is having more than a drill which simply marks time. He will not be slow to discover that keys are being put into his hand that open doors of ever fresh discovery. And with the strong curiosity of the child he will press on. School will become a place of conquest; and he will not suffer himself to be withdrawn from it till he has tasted more and more of the fruits of victory. And the other result will be that, with the employment of better methods, the curriculum will be shortened. In most provinces five years seem to be regarded as necessary for the completion of a primary course. But good teaching should make it possible to cover an even better course in four years. Indeed what is being done in the Punjab might become the rule throughout India. With the stirring of the waters which would come from the introduction of a less lengthy and a better imparted course, much of the present stagnation would go. There would be the *Open Sesame* to advance. and the whole system would be aware of a new vitality. But the vitality will not drop from the clouds. Its place of origin is the training school.

20. *Training Essential for Compulsion.*—The second point which needs emphasis is this. If compulsion is to become at all general, then it will be a curse and not a blessing unless along with it there goes a great increase in the number of thoroughly well-staffed and well-equipped schools for the training of teachers. Is

it sufficiently realized that to compel a boy or a girl to attend school for four years in conditions that are now far too common is to force incompetence upon the youth of the country, to compel the warping of growing minds, and to inflict injury for which even decades can scarce provide a remedy? Compulsion will be simply child-condemnation if training is allowed to remain as it is at present, the ally not of literacy but of illiteracy. If, however, training centres are multiplied and if large numbers of them are established in close contact with rural conditions, compulsion will have an entirely different complexion. The teacher will have something to give to the child which will fit into his natural surroundings and which will at the same time quicken his power of apprehension. Progress will be natural, stagnation abnormal. The child will advance, and what is of almost equal importance, the parent will see that he has reason to be proud of this advance. And with the co-operation of the parent thus secured the battle with illiteracy will be half won.

21. *Training links Education with Life.*—The final point is this. When, as the result of changes advocated in the preceding chapter, training centres are able to provide a variety of courses, to cast aside the all too prevalent rigidity, and to supply what the actual conditions of the pupils demand, education will be seen in a new light by the great mass of the people. It will appear as something intimately connected with their own circumstances and at the same time bringing them into relation with a larger life. For where the training schools and classes become true training centres a link between education and life will become ever more manifest. While the professional aspects of the teacher's work will receive their due emphasis, no less will be the emphasis placed, for example, upon the importance of welfare work, or the advantage of a knowledge of printing, or the possibilities of wireless, or the immense value of music. It will be seen that education pays, that it pays for the child, the parent, the village, and

that its payment is rendered in the currency of life. When that is seen another step will have been taken in the conquest of illiteracy. But for this to be seen, the right training centres have first to be seen, and in sufficient number. When is the country to be cheered by this sight?

References

Ninth Quinquennial Review, Vol. I, Chapter viii (i): The Training of Teachers.

Auxiliary Committee's Report, Chapter iv, paragraphs 74 to 83.

(iv) *The Contribution of Mobilized Resources*

22. *What the State is doing.*—We may now look at another contribution towards the solution of the problem of illiteracy. It is the contribution which comes from the marshalling by the State of all the resources that advance the spread of Primary Education. So desperate is the need here that there can be but one cry: All hands to work. And what the hands supply it is for the State to encourage, to guide, and to combine. What is the State doing in these directions? In the Chapters dealing with Management and Finance many details have been given, and it is unnecessary to go over that ground again. But our immediate concern is with 'Primary Education' at this point, that is with education as given in the four or five years of what is generally known as the primary stage of education. It is in connexion with these that the struggle with illiteracy is being fought most acutely; in connexion with them it will be fought to a finish. To these few years then and to what is being done in them we confine our attention throughout this Section. What is the State doing in the way of marshalling all available resources to cope with these all important years? Four main points claim our attention. First, the State is slowly relinquishing any direct contribution of schools managed by

itself within this field. Second, the State recognizes two agencies as providing what is needed for the supply of primary education, but its attitude to them is largely one of discrimination rather than of combination. Third, the State has adopted a policy for the mobilization of financial resources which it is difficult to reconcile with the number and magnitude of the interests involved. Fourth, the State brings to primary education the resource of control, but it shows a lack of policy in regard to the employment of this resource. The first of these points has been already fully dealt with in the Chapters on Finance and Management. But the other three require separate treatment, and to that we now turn.

23. *Administrative Discrimination Hinders Combination.*—The second of our four points draws attention to the fact that the State, through gradually withdrawing from the maintenance of primary schools, has entrusted the provision of these schools to two main agencies. It has given to each of these its official recognition, that is to say, it has satisfied itself that the schools which these managements establish conform to its requirements, it accepts these schools as integral parts of the educational system of the country, and it gives to the pupils who attend them credit for the amount of study which they have done in them. But, while it has given this recognition impartially to both agencies and this status to their schools, it has carried its equality of treatment no further. It has, for instance, in certain large areas entrusted a delegated control to one of these agencies, not in any part of the country to the other. In some localities the legislation which is in force gives precedence to one of these agencies, the same one, over the other in regard to the receipt of State aid. In other localities the effect of legislation has been to render one of these agencies, again the same one, practically autonomous and thus in great measure independent of State control. It may be possible to explain how all this has come about; nevertheless that this discrimination should

tell wholly on one side is distinctly unfortunate. Two agencies are given the status of recognized components of the public educational system, and then what is presumably regarded as an advantage is extended to one and not to the other. Such discrimination would be intelligible if one was less capable than the other or had in it essential defects; but in that case the State would be seriously at fault in having granted recognition. Or it would be intelligible if, without having in it essential defects, the agency discriminated against was possessed of little stability and could not be relied upon; but in that case how could the State have reconciled itself, either in conscience or in policy, to placing upon so broken a reed the *imprimatur* of its official recognition year after year? Here certainly is one weakness, and a very serious one, in the campaign which is being waged with illiteracy. Two divisions of one army are ready for the conflict and they have both been given the regulation uniform. But as soon as they come into action one is backed steadily from headquarters, the other is largely left to make its own way. No wonder that defeat often seems nearer than success. The strategy is wrong. The combing out must take place before the uniform is served out. Then each unit will know that it can count without fail on the resources of headquarters. The present disparity of treatment is a sign of poor generalship. And the State cannot afford to have its generalship in doubt, least of all in the conflict with illiteracy. In that fight there must be combination not discrimination.

24. *Financial Discrimination a Source of Weakness.*—Let us now look at the third of our points. The State has a policy of financing, but the working of that policy is such that the most is not made of the financial resources at the command of the State in the battle with illiteracy. The following table shows what the two agencies relied on and recognized by the State for the spread of primary education are actually doing and how they are being dealt with financially.

PUPILS AND COST OF PRIMARY SCHOOLS ACCORDING TO MANAGEMENT

Agency or Management	Number of Pupils Educated	Contribution from Provincial Revenues	Contribution from Local Funds	Total Contribution from Public Funds	Income received from Fees
		RS.	RS.	RS.	RS.
I	3,851,054	262,29,495	159,07,505	421,37,000	10,66,152
II	4,286,089	70,92,866	61,93,194	132,86,060	42,37,823

From this brief table it appears that the agency or management (I) which educates in its primary schools the smaller number of pupils received from the State well on to two crores of rupees more than the other (II). Even if what that other agency (II) receives from Local Funds as well as from the State is set along side of what Agency I receives from the State alone, the total amount thus received by Agency II, it will be seen, is just one half of what is assigned to Agency I. Obviously this is not a method of finance calculated to do the most for the forces which are arrayed against illiteracy. The discrimination which we noted in the preceding paragraph as marking the attitude assumed by the State administratively to the two agencies is found to be marking it also financially. The force which shoulders the larger responsibilities receives the smaller share of the State's financial support. Such procedure is remarkable, and is all the more so when we turn to the column which gives the fee income and realize the significance of its figures. Agency I has frequently in the past given education in its primary schools at reduced rates or without charge, and at the present time it is not permitted to levy fees in areas where compulsion is introduced. Thus it provides an ever increasing means whereby children may obtain an elementary education without any payment. This fact throws into relief what is happening in connexion with Agency II. It provides primary schools which are under no obligation to impart free education; yet though the number of schools which are under this obligation is every year increasing, this Agency, Agency II, has millions of pupils in its schools and a fee income of over Rs. 42 lakhs. There can thus be no doubt as to what parents think of these schools. But the parents' recognition of their value, a recognition for which they are willing to pay, only serves to emphasize the unsatisfactoriness of the financial attitude which the State assumes to the Agency that provides these schools.

25. *Further Illustration of this Weakness.*—How little the present mode of financing primary education is calculated to marshal the resources which are available for the rout of illiteracy, may be realized from two other considerations. Each of the two agencies makes a definite financial contribution to the spread of education. The one does this by means of the funds which it raises in accordance with statute and of such fees as it collects; the other by the amounts which it gives out of its own pocket and by the fees which it levies. And the State gives to each a grant from its funds in token of the national service which each is rendering. Let us then put side by side the contributions of the two agencies and the amount of subsidy which they receive. The following table gives the information.

MANAGEMENT CONTRIBUTION AND STATE AID

Management or Agency	Contribution of Agency	Subsidy from the State	Subsidy from Local Funds
	RS.	RS.	RS.
I	174,07,549	262,29,495	.. ..
II	111,40,939	70,92,866	61,93,194

Agency I to educate 3,851,000 children puts in Rs. 174 lakhs and the State for that service gives it a subsidy of Rs. 262 lakhs. Agency II to educate 4,286,000 children puts in Rs. 111 lakhs and is subsidized by the State and other statutory funds to the amount of Rs. 133 lakhs. The discrepancy of support thus revealed needs no comment; could a better means be devised for delaying the combination of resources with which to combat illiteracy effectively? The other consideration connects itself with what is pivotal in every discussion concerning illiteracy, the education of girls. The facts are capable of presentation in brief tabular form.

STATE SUPPORT OF GIRLS' EDUCATION

Management or Agency	Pupils in Primary Schools for Girls	Contribution from the State	Contribution from Local Funds	Total Contribution from Public Funds
		RS.	RS.	RS.
I	347,890	25,93,588	29,44,591	55,38,179
II	596,538	13,00,676	10,53,676	23,54,352

Could any mode of employing public money be hit upon which would be more likely to result in the retardation of girls' education? And if the State not merely adopts this mode of finance, but persists in it year after year, is it not in fact withholding strength from those who seek to extend the bounds of education and to defeat the forces opposed to it? As the figures which we have been considering plainly show, the State fails to mobilize effectively available financial resources, and so it prolongs the day of illiteracy's power.

26. *Weakness of Control.*—Our fourth point is that the resources of State control are imperfectly mobilized As we have already noted, the State has delegated control, which is in itself a most wise procedure. But it

has done this in such a way that in some cases it has very little power over a misuse or ineffective employment of the control so delegated, which is a most unwise procedure. Again, it has carried out this devolution in such a way that control is prejudiced through combination with management. And finally, while it occupies the place of controller, the State, according to the testimony of its officials, seems to keep within the educational system a number of schools which ought never to have secured recognition from it, or which, though at one time fit to obtain that recognition, have now no title to retain it. The continued recognition, accompanied in some cases by continued subsidy, of schools which do nothing to remove illiteracy is working untold evil, and for the presence of that evil the responsibility must lie at the door of the State, so long as the present conditions are allowed to exist. It cannot then be said that the State is mobilizing the resources of control.

27. *Mobilization of Resources still Awaited.*—The overthrow of illiteracy depends on large measure on the contribution which comes from Mobilized Resources. And that contribution waits for the State to make it. In one respect the State has done what is helpful, for it is withdrawing from the management of elementary schools and is entrusting the provision and maintenance of them to two non-departmental agencies. But there its helpfulness receives a check. It has adopted towards these two agencies an attitude of preferential treatment, administrative and financial, and such an attitude spells discouragement and uncombined resources. The generalship of the State has been such as to bring into the field two great forces wherewith to crush the power of illiteracy. But it has not been such as to combine these forces When its word of command should have rung out with authority there has been a note of weakness which has spread lack of confidence through the ranks. The attack loses zest; for can the attackers be sure of headquarters support? The battle goes on with all too

doubtful advantage; for what can be expected of eager combatants who are given the cold shoulder? The sallies are fitful; how can they be other when over the far-flung line a liaison officer is so seldom to be seen? As we look round on waste, stagnation, inconclusive action, and the immense amount of land that still remains to be possessed, we are constrained to say : The State has splendid forces wherewith to change all this. When does it intend to mobilize them?

References

Auxiliary Committee's Report. Chapter xvi, pp. 314-6, for consideration of Bombay Primary Education Act, 1923; see also *Bombay Quinquennial Review* (1927), pp. 7 and 94 on same subject.

Madras Elementary Education Act, 1920. See especially financial clauses in Chapter iii of the Act.

Ninth Quinquennial Review gives the figures referred to in Volume II, Tables II-A, II-B, III-A, and III-B.

(v) *The Contribution of Legislation*

28. *Limits of a System without Compulsion.*—Closely associated with the contribution that comes from combination of resources is that which comes from Legislation. The object of both is that there may be no waste of effort in the life and death struggle with illiteracy. Legislation has been invoked principally to secure the introduction of compulsion in the sphere of elementary education and to establish the appropriate machinery for its inauguration and extension. The voluntary system, it is felt, succeeds up to a point, and up to that point succeeds quite as well as, and in certain cases better than, some forms of compulsion. But it has its limitations. Did it not occur in an official statement made by a Superintendent in one of the provinces during the Census of 1921 we should be inclined to smile at the assertion that 'the cost of each of the additional literates in the province in the last decade was Rs. 4,000'. We seek to brush the words aside. But a little

consideration convinces us that the Census Superintendent has told us nothing but the bare truth. The lack of correspondence between expenditure and result is due to the fact that the children who enter school are under no obligation to remain at school for at least four years, the minimum period within which literacy may be attained. Thus lakhs upon lakhs of rupees are being expended annually on teachers and buildings, for lakhs upon lakhs of pupils who leave school before they have a grip of the three R's, and who at the next Census will undoubtedly be counted among the illiterates. Between thirty and forty per cent of the children who have received some form of education are said to relapse into illiteracy within a few years of leaving school. A system which allows this to go on year after year stands condemned as doubly wasteful. It fritters away the financial resources of the country, and it does not secure for the country what are among its most valuable resources—children who are able to read and write.

29. *Permissive Nature of Present Legislation.*—To remedy this state of affairs, so detrimental to the best interests of the land, educational legislation has been introduced in all provinces save one. It has taken the form of Acts which aim at a complete system of compulsory primary education within the provinces to which they apply. But while that is the object in view, the Acts which are in operation are all permissive in character. Educational Authorities are set up and are given statutory powers to introduce compulsion, but in general it is for these Authorities to say when and to what extent this compulsion is to take effect. Thus compulsion may be adopted in one area and not in another, and within the area where it is adopted it may be made applicable to boys and not to girls, to Hindus and not to Muhammadans, and so on. That there should be variety of treatment is only what might be expected, for not only is there the marked distinction between urban and rural districts, but there is also a difference between area and area in respect of

financial capacity, educational facilities, employment of these facilities, and occupation of parents. But variety of treatment may be so emphasized as in effect to make compulsion nominal. Enabling Acts seem to be steps in the right direction, but what are we to think if they come to be looked upon as enabling delay? When the slow progress of elementary education is made the subject of remark or criticism there is a tendency to draw attention to the Acts now in force, and to say that advance cannot be quicker than the rate at which these Acts are taken advantage of. The machinery is there. But what if it is not set in motion, or being set in motion it is worked indifferently or intermittently? Is the country, it may be asked, any the better of the machinery which the Acts have provided?

30. *What it has Accomplished.*—The answer to that question is a decided affirmative. First, because of the amount that has been already accomplished; and second, because of the guidance afforded for further legislative action. First, then, as to what has been already accomplished. It must not be forgotten that the first Primary Education Act came upon India's statute book only in February 1918. Yet though time has been so short, the difficulties so great, and the road so unfamiliar, we cannot but be struck by the fact that by 1927 there were 114 municipalities which had adopted some form of compulsion in the areas for which they were responsible, and two years later the number had increased to 138. The Acts therefore have proved of distinct service within urban areas, of which, as we have already seen, there are some 800 in British India. It is not only that municipality after municipality adopts compulsion, but that it is encouraged to persevere in the policy by the results of what it has done. 'In one year after the introduction of compulsion, the number of pupils in Bombay city increased by over 6,000'. 'In Bihar and Orissa compulsion has been introduced into only one municipality, but the figures for the year 1926-27 show that out of a total of 2,200 boys of school-going age as many as

2,139 are at school.' 'Schemes for compulsion introduced in the Punjab have appreciably contributed to the remarkable rise in the percentage of boys under instruction from 4.77 in 1922 to 9.32 in 1927.' Extracts such as these from official reports indicate that a few years' working of the existing Acts is leading to beneficial educational changes in urban areas.

31. *Weaknesses of Present Legislation.*—But the same cannot yet be said of rural areas. Up to 1927 compulsion had been introduced into any of these in only four of the larger provinces. 'Very little progress has been made', we read, 'in the enforcement of compulsion in rural areas, except in the Punjab and the Central Provinces. In the former province compulsion has been followed by increased enrolment and the reduction of wastage. In the latter province pronounced success has attended a number of schemes in rural areas, though in a few areas attendance has not appreciably improved.' Now as it is in rural areas that illiteracy is so largely entrenched, it is worth while looking through the records to see whether we can discover any reasons for this disappointing state of affairs. We shall find that they are mainly two. First, 'the reluctance of local bodies to make use of the law to compel pupils to attend school'. Second, the unwillingness of local bodies 'to initiate schemes by which compulsion may be financed'. Initiative and finance, these are the points at which, by common consent, legislation requires strengthening.

32. *Initiative and the State.*—First as to initiative. When the State has delegated certain of its functions regarding elementary education to local authorities, is it precluded from taking action if it is convinced that, though the local authority is reluctant to take the necessary steps, the time is ripe for the introduction of compulsion into the area? That question is really answered as soon as it is put. If the bodies exercise a control which has been delegated to them by the State, then the source of that control resides in the State, and

the State is not relieved of its responsibility for the exercise of this control by the fact of delegation. If the authority which has received delegated control acts in a manner which does not approve itself to the State delegating the control then the State will have to resume control. The situation may be delicate; but that is not the point. What is relevant is that a body was appointed to help the State in the more effective discharge of its duties, and that this appointment, as it turns out, is not providing the State with the help anticipated. In that case, obviously, another arrangement will have to be made. For the interests of the State, that is the interests of its people, are supreme. Local self-government was not devised so as to occupy a place of virtual autonomy, but to co-operate with, and advance the well-being of, the State, that is of its citizens. This relation between the central and the local government, in the field of primary education, finds expression in the Bombay Primary Education Act. For there it is specifically laid down that if the local authorities are unwilling to bring in a scheme of compulsory education, of the need for which the government is convinced, the State can call upon the authorities to take the necessary action. When local authorities do not discharge duties which the education of the people call for, their inaction is a call for State action. It is well that this point should be clearly stated in legislative form. But, whether it be expressed or not, the fact remains that the State by exercising the power of delegation does not deprive itself of the power to initiate action or of the responsibility for exercising that power wherever it may be necessary.

33. *Initiative and Co-operation.*—The State has the right to initiate. But when it becomes its duty to initiate, how is that duty to be carried out? One of the reasons, as we have seen, which have been given for the unwillingness on the part of a local authority to initiate compulsory educational schemes is the difficulty of obtaining the necessary funds. What is to happen

in these circumstances if the State calls for the local body to take action? If it pleads poverty is there to be a deadlock? That might be the case if the State were a controller whose sole duty was to issue orders. We have seen reason to hold that the State takes a very different view of its controlling power from that. State control, as Chapter i has shown, is State help. And State initiative, which is part of this control, is a form of State help. It means the recognition by the State of the obligation which rests upon it to take action by co-operating in action. It is the expression by the State of its readiness at every point, and most of all where it sees the need to be greatest, so to enter into combination with suitable agencies that, for instance, in the field of education these agencies will be able, by the State's co-operation, to give to the country educational facilities the supply of which has become a necessity. This co-operation will be rendered in two ways: administratively, by guidance; financially, by grants from its own funds to aid local resources. It is with the latter aspect that we are now concerned, and that we have now to consider. And as we do this we are led into a much wider field than that which treats of the relation existing between the State and a local authority. For we are at once confronted with the question: What is meant by 'local resources'?

34. *Local Resources and Local Board Resources.*—There has been a tendency at times to treat this question as one which answers itself. Local resources, we are told, are the resources of Local Bodies, that is of Municipalities, District Boards, and Taluk Boards. And on the basis of this answer a considerable amount of educational practice and legislation has been built up. In certain provinces the Government enters into agreement with the Local Bodies as to the amount which they will raise for primary education, and the amount of the subsidy which the State will supply; in others, rules framed under the Elementary Education Acts prescribe the proportions in which the cost of providing primary

education shall be divided between the local authorities and government'; in others again, legislation lays upon government the obligation of contributing a sum not less than that which local bodies raise by means of an education tax. The principles on which the distribution takes place are not what concern us at this point. What is here important to note is that in all these cases there is only one form of local support that is brought into the calculation, that which comes from Local Bodies. But this use of terms, while it may have a technical justification, is one which hardly does justice to the actual conditions. Local funds, if we employ the term in no restrictive sense but simply to mark off what is raised locally from what is contributed centrally, are of two kinds—those which are raised by Local Bodies in accordance with statutory powers, and those which are supplied by Local Committees and Individuals as voluntary contributions to the service of education. It would seem as if this second form of local resources were, for all purposes of financial consideration, regarded as non-existent. When we think of the present position of elementary education we cannot but feel some surprise that so great an omission should be allowed to pass without comment.

35. *Advisory Board's Recommendation.*—It is not that the fact of these resources has been wholly overlooked. The Central Advisory Board of Education, in the course of its short existence, dealt with the relation between provincial and local funds when it was considering the ways in which the spread of elementary education was to be advanced. And it made a number of recommendations for submission to the governments of the different provinces. The first of these was that the provincial government should decide what the minimum amount of money was that should be spent in each area, and having done this should further decide how much of this minimum should be met from provincial, and how much from local, funds. And in a note appended, there is a sentence which shows that the Board was

not insensible to the existence of local resources other than the resources of Local Boards, although it was not prepared to recommend the official recognition of a third source of income. The Note runs as follows: 'It was recognized that in some areas, particularly in Madras, a substantial portion of this minimum expenditure not met by Government would actually be met from private funds, but local bodies should be held responsible by Government for seeing that the portion not met by Government was actually forthcoming from whatever source.' That is to say: That, first, the contribution towards the required minimum will come from three sources, Government, Local Bodies, and Private Bodies; second, that the Government will be responsible for the portion of the contribution which stands in its name; and, third, that Local Bodies will be held responsible for their own contribution and also that which comes from private sources. In other words the amount from private sources is so substantial that it forms an indispensable part of the minimum provided from local sources, but those who contribute it have no responsibility in the matter. The suggestion presents us with a wholly novel situation. It distinguishes between local resources and Local Board resources, but it places the responsibility for the provision of the two not upon the two agencies that supply them but entirely upon one of them. Had an attempt ever been made to give effect to this recommendation of the Advisory Board we can readily anticipate what would have been the result. The Local Bodies would have most naturally protested against a proposal to lay at their doors a responsibility which in no way attached to them. Their responsibility, they would have said, ceased with the raising of the funds which they were authorized by statute to collect. To go beyond that was not in the bond. If they were to be held responsible for the non-Government portion of the minimum required then that must be a minimum which they were in a position, out of their own resources, to supply; they could not possibly be responsible for a minimum which had to be provided not only by themselves but also by another contributing agency. Thus Local Bodies would have denied with justification responsibility for what was not theirs, while those who were really responsible would have felt that somehow Government had so acted as to grant them relief from the discharge of their responsibility. The plan would have been found unworkable. The method proposed admits that there is a distinction between local board funds and local funds, but having done this virtually obliterates the distinction. There is but one way to get over the difficulty. It is to recognize that the responsibilities are as distinct as are the sources. In the preceding Section it was urged that the pressing need for a wide expansion of elementary education called for the mobilization by the State of all recognized agencies, board and private. The corollary of that is what we have now reached. That is to say, the situation calls upon the State to mobilize the financial resources of these agencies in a regularized fashion, and so to subsidize them that local board funds and local funds may contribute in combination to the fullest spread of elementary education within the areas where the agencies that raise them are at work.

36. *Organization of Private Agencies.*—But it may be said: 'How is the State to deal with Private Agencies? The name is one which applies to no homogeneous body. There are individuals and committees, there are teacher-managers and generous donors, there are Hindu societies and Muhammadan associations and Christian missions. Is it possible for Government to deal with bodies so numerous and constituted so diversely?' Yes, there is no difficulty when the situation is frankly faced. In any one area it is, for the most part, only a small number of these agencies that are actively engaged in educational work. And for another thing, nothing has been more noticeable within, say, the last two decades than the efforts put forth by these agencies to secure grouping and organization so

that they might act with greater unity and speak with greater common authority. The time has indeed come when the Government of a province might appropriately announce that it was not prepared to give official recognition to any management unless it had a statutory constitution or was registered under some of the Acts on the Indian statute book relating to companies and associations. Were this done much that is now complicated in educational administration would be greatly simplified. And so far as the matter now under consideration is concerned, the result of such action on the part of Government would be most beneficial. In any district the State would be able to come into direct contact with the representatives of local resources as easily as with the representatives of local board resources. Approved organization would work as smoothly and as effectively in the one case as in the other.

37. *Benefit of Mobilized Financial Resources.*—The means is thus available whereby in each of the districts or areas which compose a province the Government may obtain full information as to the resources, local board and local, that can be relied on to come to the assistance of elementary education and its expansion. And by taking advantage of this means and acting upon it the State will achieve several valuable results. It will facilitate the exercise of its inherent power of initiative. It will relieve Local Bodies of burdens which are either not theirs or should not be laid upon them; it will give Private Agencies a sense of closer and more responsible partnership in the education of the country; it will strengthen the combination of effort on behalf of a truly national system of primary education; it will pave the way for the introduction of a steadily increasing range of compulsory school attendance; and it will press back the frontiers of illiteracy.

38. *The State Subsidy.*—The amount of local support that may be depended on having been settled in the manner suggested, the Government is now in a position to state the amount of subsidy which it is prepared to

supply from its own funds. That subsidy will doubtless vary from district to district, the amount of it being larger in areas that are undeveloped, sparsely populated, or lacking in prosperity, than in areas where the conditions are favourable. And it will be such a subsidy as will make it certain that within the areas into which compulsion is introduced there will be not only readily co-operating managements but also well-equipped and well-attended schools. It is far more important to have even a limited number of these schools than a greater number with imperfect equipment and a staff of inferior qualifications. For the State will not allow itself to forget, what has sometimes been forgotten, that its objective is the removal of illiteracy not merely the increase in the number of pupils attending schools. In the province of Bengal it was found recently that, though the pupils enrolled in the primary schools had increased by nearly 370,000, the number of those who reached the fourth year of attendance had actually declined. Good schools well-attended have a remarkable effect. They lead to the desire for more of their kind, as developments in the Punjab have clearly shown. And so compulsion comes to have less the look of compulsion than of compliance with an expressed wish. By the generous subsidy of the State from its own resources, then, there is ensured a corresponding and growing readiness on the part of those in the locality to give of their resources, whether these come through statutory bodies or through recognized and registered private organizations.

39. *Need of a Comprehensive Plan.*—We have now seen how two great obstacles to the spread of compulsory primary education may be overcome. By the exercise of its inherent power of initiative the State may remedy local lack of action. And by the mobilization of resources, local as well as local board, the State will find itself able to solve many of the difficulties which are the result of the present defective financial policy. But when these obstacles have been overcome the

success of compulsion is not automatically assured. For anything like success there is required in addition a comprehensive plan, one which takes full cognizance of all the conditions and facts. It must not, for instance, resemble the plan which after having been provisionally introduced into one State was revised because it was found in practice to work out almost exclusively in the interests of one class of the community. Nor must it be like a plan at work in another State which, according to the Census Commissioner of 1921, tended to intensify the division between those who lived in urban, and those who lived in rural, areas, although, it need hardly be said, no thought of this had attended its inauguration. To avoid such anomalies, and to spread elementary education widely and among all classes of the people, there is required a plan which applies to all within the areas affected and which advances by regular stages. This is perfectly feasible whatever be made the unit of advance, the individual town or municipality, groups of villages, or special areas. For instance if a beginning were made with the municipalities of British India, compulsion introduced into these would secure that 10 per cent of the children of school-going age would be actually at school. If then compulsion took within its sweep villages which have between 5,000 and 2,000 residents about 16 per cent more would be affected. Extend the compulsion to villages with from one to two thousand inhabitants and an additional 12 per cent would be brought into the schools. To act in this way and by some such stages would not be difficult, and it would mean that very speedily the half of the population would have the benefit of a system which assured to their children no less than four successive years of study in a primary school. Combined with this method might be that of grouping villages. Elementary education might be made compulsory in groups of two or more villages which had a combined population of, say, 1,000, and which were not more than a mile distant from one another or from a village which was regarded as the central one of the group. In this way another 20 per cent of the population might be reached. And still more might benefit if areas in which, for example, certain forms of industry are carried on were scheduled for compulsion. This would affect both urban and rural districts. Compulsion introduced into the wards of municipalities where factory workers live would make itself felt not only among the children brought up in these wards but also among the children of their relatives outside the city with whom the closeness of contact maintained is one of the features of Indian labour. Then much would result if the Labour Commission's recommendation that compulsory education should be introduced in the coalfields were given effect to, or if what the Commission has to say regarding children in plantations received due attention at the hands of the educational administrator. There is no plan that may be expected to escape every difficulty. Parents of one community may object to their children going to schools attended by children of another community. Opinion differs as to the best way of dealing with pupils of the Depressed Classes. Co-education has its own problems. But while a plan which is a perfect paper plan is almost as sure to fail as a perfectly rigid plan, one which took account of actual facts, which was introduced step by step as circumstances revealed its suitability and its practicability, which admitted of flexibility in its application, but which after its introduction was adhered to with inflexible steadiness, such a plan in the course of a decade would bring within its operation not less than 70 per cent of the boys and girls of school-going age, and would have behind it the momentum of public sentiment, the backing of provincial legislatures, and the growing appreciation of parents.

40. *Forms of Local Educational Authorities.*—How can this flexibility of plan be secured? Legislation has a part to play in answering that question. There must be Local Educational Authorities, for they alone have intimate acquaintance with the actual conditions. There are those who say that no separate bodies for this

purpose are required, that Local Bodies, as now constituted, are quite competent to do all that is necessary. Such a position is unfortunate. For one thing it takes all too little account of the need that exists for definite and undistracted concentration on education. And for another, it hands over the administration of education to bodies which in present conditions are only partially representative of the locality, and which may contain next to no representation of educational interests. Legislation is needed to set up Authorities which represent the different classes within the locality and which are able to devote themselves to the one concern of education within the locality. Such authorities may vary in constitution from place to place. Some may resemble the present Local Bodies, others may be more of the nature of Village Panchayats, others may have a specific *ad hoc* constitution. Legislation, or rules framed under the Acts, will give to the country that variety of Educational Authority which differing conditions demand, and without which the advance of elementary education will be deprived of much of its driving power. But when legislation has provided the country with Authorities that really meet the situation, there will then be secured such flexibility and adaptation to local circumstances, based upon experience and knowledge, as will guarantee that compulsion, when it is introduced, will work. It is for this end, and for this alone, that flexibility has here been urged. That feature attaches to the plan not to the policy. The policy is the introduction of compulsion; it may be achieved in various ways. But when, in an area and after full consideration by those best qualified to give it, the policy has been adopted and compulsion has been introduced, the duty which then rests on the Educational Authority is to give effect to that policy, not to devise means of exemption from its operation.

41. *Limitations of Legislation.*—The reason why the advance of compulsion by stages has been emphasised is that the surest way to deprive elementary education of the beneficial contribution which legislation may make

to it, is to invoke legislation in areas where, even if passed, it cannot become operative. Law inoperative is law weakened. And that is what would result if an attempt were made at the present time to render compulsion generally applicable to areas where, say, the total population did not exceed five or six hundred, where revenue was well nigh negligible, or where there was a difficulty about the supply of teachers of the right stamp. But if there are regions where, as things now are, reliance cannot be placed on legislation, that constitutes no reason why within them illiteracy should go unchallenged. It is well to recognize what law can do and what its limitations are. Where law can make to education the contribution of a backing power then it is by all means to be taken full advantage of. But where conditions are such that it cannot exercise that power then it is for educational effort and device to show its worth. Areas into which compulsion cannot enter are areas into which the capable teacher can enter, or into which suitable means of transport may enter, or into which a link with another village may enter. And there they should enter. For with their entrance the power of illiteracy will be lessened, and the road which law cannot traverse now will be made less difficult for its advance in the days to come.

42. *What Legislation can Effect.*—Our consideration, then, of this contribution towards the solution of our present problem has brought home to us the precise part which legislation can play in putting down illiteracy from its seat. It has made it clear that in this matter the State has an obligation of which it cannot divest itself. If statutory bodies fail to take appropriate action, the State must not fail. Then, there is another principle which legislation can embody, and that is the adoption of such methods of finance as shall secure the participation of all recognized agencies in schemes which introduce and maintain compulsory elementary education in area after area. A third is the appointment of Educational Authorities which do full justice to the interests concerned. And a fourth is the recognition of a plan

as essential to the working out of every scheme which involves compulsion. Legislation can secure all these, and in such a way that the State will be placed in no false position. It will not come under any obligation to compel the youth of the country to attend schools that are poorly equipped, inadequately staffed, or insufficiently inspected. But it will come under an obligation to see that there is a steadily growing number of areas in which, through the backing of public opinion and local sentiment, the children will be kept at school for not less than four years, and the schools which they attend will provide a sound elementary education imparted by competent teachers. With the contribution of Legislation thus rendered, illiteracy will not be slow to read the writing on the wall that portends its steadily approaching doom.

References

Mayhew, *The Education of India*, p. 299 for reference to remark of Census Superintendent mentioned in paragraph 28.

Full information regarding the nature of the Primary Education Acts is given in *Seventh Quinquennial Review*, *Eighth Quinquennial Review*, pp. 106-8, and *Ninth Quinquennial Review*, pp. 129-32.

The recommendation of the Advisory Board referred to is given in *Eighth Quinquennial Review*, pp. 44, 45; and in Richey, *Grants-in-Aid to Schools*, p. 20.

(vi) *The Contribution of Adult Education*

43. *Extent of Adult Education*.—So much for the young. What as to those who are older? This leads us to consider the contribution of Adult Education. At present it is a small contribution. And such as it is it gives the impression of having behind it too little of a clear, directing policy. There are, for instance, a number of Night Schools in each province, but the pupils who attend these are not wholly adults. There are amongst

them children of school-going age who, being unable for some reason to go to a day school, seek to supply that lack by attendance at a night school. If we look at statistics we find that there are over three lakhs of pupils belonging to what may be called the adult schools of the country. But as we are told that these schools are really for adults in only four provinces, we shall not go far wrong if we reckon the number of adults who are receiving education in some form year after year as being nearer two lakhs than three. About half of these are to be found in villages. If the teaching of a lakh of adults were marked by concentration of resources its influence would be considerable. Diffused as it is at present through the length and breadth of India its power to stay illiteracy cannot but be distinctly limited. Of the other lakh no small part comes, as reports make clear, from among workers in industrial centres. These help to swell the ranks of the literates in the towns, and as we have already noted they have an indirect effect on the illiteracy of the villages. But there is much wastage both of effort and of money, and a great call for study of conditions and the enunciation of guiding principles. The position of adult education in other countries has much to give India in the way of information, warning, and encouragement. To take advantage of it would seem to be a counsel of common sense. Whatever will redeem Adult Education from the present uncertainty of treatment is calculated to increase its extent.

44. *Progress of Adult Education.*—If the number of adults attending school seems small, the rate at which that number has increased is rather striking. The movement for adult education in India may be said to be about ten years old. Yet within the second quinquennium of that period the total number of grown-up people who are enrolled in schools has increased by roughly 30,000. An increase of 6,000 per annum brings with it no small reason for hope. And what is interesting is that many come to school with such a desire to learn that they make surprising progress. The progress, it

is recorded, is much in advance of what is common in the ordinary day school. And connected with this is another noteworthy fact. It is what one would expect, but it is always good in connexion with education to know that there are expectations which are actually realized. Where adult education gains any hold in a village it is found to react on the village school and to an increase of interest on the part of parents in the education of their children. Both in urban and rural areas there is encouraging indication that adult education repays the trouble that is bestowed upon it, and that it brings to the spread of education among the young a potent incentive.

45. *The Help of the Universities.*—Is there any way by which Adult Education may be steadily advanced? There is no doubt that the Universities have a part to play in this effort which will be more and more recognized as time goes on. At present the Departments of Economics in the Universities are only beginning to receive the attention which that subject deserves; while Departments of Social Study and Service have still to be instituted. But there are courses of lectures and demonstrations which might well be given under the auspices of the universities, calculated to turn the thoughts of men and women, while still undergraduates, to a service which their country imperatively requires and which they have it in their power to render. The Royal Commission on Agriculture in India appeals to 'both past and present members of Indian universities to apply themselves to the social and economic problems of the countryside, and so to fit themselves to take the lead in the movement for the uplift of the rural classes'. The Royal Commission on Labour in India is of opinion that the universities might do much to carry on investigations into the conditions, for example, of industrial groups, 'their income and expenditure, their families, their indebtedness and its causes, their migrations, their absenteeism and its causes, their sickness, their housing and the interrelations of such fac-

tors'. And one of the results of such investigations would undoubtedly be a clearer understanding of the precise service which adult education was likely to afford to those engaged in industry, and of the best way in which that service might be rendered. But even now, while larger plans have to wait for their realization, there is much that might be done by undergraduates returning for their college vacations to their native villages. Were guidance given during the college terms, the villagers might reap the benefit of such direction in a two months' course given by keen and interested youth. It might at the least prevent not a few from relapsing into illiteracy, and to not a few it would bring the impetus of a new hope. The pity is that there is little or no provision for any such guidance in the colleges of the country; and the rural areas are deprived of a sterling advantage, while the youths themselves miss what would be a valuable stimulus to them and what would constitute a much needed link between the intelligentsia and the life of the villages.

46. *The Help of Co-operative Societies.*—One great means of advancing Adult Education lies in the employment of the Co-operative Movement for that purpose. This line is one which is being taken advantage of with marked success in the Punjab. And what is now being tried in the United Provinces is an indication of the help which this method can give to those who are engaged in fighting illiteracy. At selected places, where there is a suitable teacher and where a co-operative society already exists, Co-operative Adult Societies are being organized. The members of these societies contribute twice a year at harvest times, 'each according to his means, but not less than eight annas a head'. The money thus raised helps to furnish a school library and to put books within the reach of those who attend it. The school meets twice a week, and the teacher gives instruction in the three R.'s and imparts information on subjects of general interest. Government grants subsidize the scheme, and thus in a steady and economical

way the benefits of education are brought within the reach of older folk who have had no such advantages in their youth. And Co-operative Societies are only at the beginning of their usefulness.

47. *Need of a Plan.*—The field of Adult Education is full of promise, but to realize that promise far more thought and labour will have to be bestowed upon the field than it has yet received. Suggestions are to be found in provincial reports and in the recommendations of commissions. But concentrated action, and action in accordance with some plan, is what is supremely needed. And that means central direction. It may be granted, as many hold and suggest, that the efforts to advance Adult Education in rural areas should be in the hands of 'co-operative societies and associations of public-spirited individuals who are anxious to promote the development of the countryside' rather than in those of the Department. But are such efforts, whether they be in the country or in the town, to be left to undirected and uncorrelating initiative? That would be simply to carry into adult education errors of administration which have had bad enough results already in the sphere of primary education. To avoid such errors there must be guidance, and that is where the Education Department can perform a singularly valuable service. Its officials know the field, they can point out what it is that the different parts of the country require, what form of educational activity might supply most effectively the needs thus disclosed, what agency was best suited to provide it, and what combination of forces it was most important to secure. They are in a position, both through their own experience and through information gained from others, to prepare schemes, to indicate where encouragement will be forthcoming, to help on co-operation, and to press upon Government how public funds may be most usefully employed for the objects proposed. It is this kind of guidance and co-operation which Adult Education most requires. The provision of it means the establishment at educational headquarters

of a section devoted to Adult Education and its advance. The setting up of such a section in every provincial Education Department would mark the beginning of a great concerted advance before which illiteracy would not be slow to withdraw from positions of which it has held age-long possession.

References

Eighth Quinquennial Review, Vol. I, Chapter v, pp. 124, 125.

Ninth Quinquennial Review, Vol. I, Chapter vi, where under (*c*) a special section is devoted to Adult Education.

R. St. J. Parry (Ed.), *Cambridge Essays on Adult Education*. See especially Chapter iv on Organisation by Mansbridge, and Chapter v on Democracy and Adult Education by Mastermann.

Agricultural Commission Report has a section on Adult Education in the course of Chapter xv, pp. 529-31.

Labour Commission Report refers to the education of half-timers and workers in Chapter iii.

(vii) *The Contribution of Literature*

48. *Lack of Suitable Literature.*—The endeavour to overcome illiteracy ought to receive a large, vital, and steadily growing contribution from Literature. The pity is that it does not. An official speaking of the contents of some of the libraries in India which he had sampled said that they 'would hardly tempt him to literacy even on a desert island'. The same idea is expressed in more orthodox official language when it is said that, while lack of funds accounts in some measure for meagrely stocked libraries, 'the dearth of suitable literature in the vernacular is probably mainly responsible for the poor equipment'. And according to the Madras Library Association, 'the present state of our country demands imperatively that books of an informational nature should be circulated in large quantities by our libraries. But there are few such books in Tamil'. The supply of books which will make their appeal to those whose

appetite has been whetted, whether in a primary school or in a night school, or which will serve to whet that appetite, is exceedingly limited; their range is small, their suitability still largely an ideal.

49. *Increase of Production.*—There is much that is disappointing in this, but nothing unparalleled. Those who can look back to the literature in, say, Britain about the time when elementary education became compulsory will have no reason to feel at all hopeless regarding what is now going on in India. The past generation has seen a remarkable literary development that has not been confined to any one part of the country. In India far more books can now be obtained in the various vernacular languages than was possible twenty years ago. And very noticeable is the effort to spread, through the medium of the vernaculars, information both general and scientific in a way that will meet the needs of those who have had few educational opportunities. That these efforts should still fail many a time to supply what is most required will occasion no surprise, while the lack of encouragement with which they meet readily explains that dearth of suitable literature which all deplore.

50. *The Encouragement of Literature.*—A full discussion of the relation of Literature to education would require a volume to itself. Our present consideration confines itself to educational policy as concerned with illiteracy, and for that a paragraph must suffice. We wish to know whether there are any means which may be employed with some prospect of success so to encourage literature as to make it an effective instrument for the overthrow of illiteracy. Three means suggest themselves, and within our limits we can do little more than mention them. They are the employment of rewards, the inauguration of library schemes, and the expansion of Text Book Committees. And first, the payment of those who are prepared to produce books by which the illiterate may be stimulated to seek for education, and by which the literate may be encouraged to retain and increase the benefits of such education as they

have received. In Bombay and in the Punjab about four or five thousand rupees are being allocated annually by the provincial governments as rewards to the authors of suitable vernacular literature. An extension of this method throughout India, and on a scale which will bring to men and women with some literary ability the assurance that time and care devoted to the exercise of this capacity will not go unrecognized is what is greatly needed. The far-reaching benefit of such action on the part of provincial governments would very soon be seen in the increase of authors and in the larger production of the type of literature that is required. The second means to which we shall refer is the working out of rural library schemes. The more these schemes are promoted in a regular and progressive manner the more will they give to the country suitable librarians and suitable literature. The principal requisite of every district library scheme is a 'well-trained, resourceful, and enthusiastic librarian'. He will soon make himself acquainted with the tastes and needs of his district. And when these become known, and when it also becomes known that the library is anxious to secure for its shelves what will minister to these tastes and supply these needs, no long time will be allowed to elapse before the libraries have what the people need. Even as it is, no small amount is being expended from provincial and private sources on the maintenance of libraries at the present time, but there is always the danger that where there is no plan money will be uneconomically spent. And in the matter with which we are dealing every rupee is needed. If illiteracy is to be really tackled, the time seems opportune for the drawing up of library schemes which are looked at from the point of view of the province as a whole, which are related in some degree at least one to another, and which will be realized in accordance with a definite policy and the growth of resources. The third means is a fuller use of the existing Text Book Committees. Each province has one of these Committees, and they do a very large amount of work in scrutinizing books sent in by different publishers and authors, and in deciding as to their suitability for use in class or in library. There is a great deal of talent on these Committees, and if the scope of them was enlarged so as to cover the field of Adult Education and Village Libraries, that talent would have a still wider opportunity than it has at present of rendering an important service to the country in general, and to the campaign against illiteracy in particular. Such an enlargement of the functions of the Committees would involve the appointment of a small number of salaried men and women keenly interested in village welfare work; but there would always be those who would gladly lend their services in an honorary capacity. The Committees thus enlarged would be able to build up at, say, the office of the Director of Public Instruction in each province a central library which would be the means of keeping schools, welfare centres, co-operative societies, and community organizations informed of every suitable book that was issued, its contents, cost, publishers, and distinctive features. In this way what is still so defective in respect of publishing in India would be, in part at least, remedied. There would be an increased chance of the right kind of book being sold, and thus of men and women having some inducement to give themselves to writing. Such a department as this, worked with no more red tape than a private enterprise, but with as great a sense of responsibility as if it were a State undertaking, would put the kind of literature that is needed into the hands of thousands who have left behind them every form of schooling, as well into the hands of those who will thus be able to make the best of the education which they are still receiving.

51. *Combination of Effort.*—The three means of encouragement indicated in the preceding paragraph, it will be readily seen, are far from being unrelated. The more that is done for libraries the greater will be the stimulus given to authors; and the more authors of the right stamp are encouraged the more deeply appreciated

will libraries become and the more will they increase in number. While the stronger the efforts put forth at headquarters the more effectively will what is done by library and author be placed at the service of the community, and the more fully will the people of the country be put in possession of a power that steadily lifts from their shoulders the handicap of illiteracy. Further, they are methods which have a peculiar appropriateness in a situation which demands mobilization of all forces, because their effective exercise requires the combination of what is official with what is non-official. They call for the organization and financial encouragement of the State, and at the same time they present to private endeavour and liberality a matchless opportunity. And this also is certain. The more these methods are employed the more surely will others no less fruitful disclose themselves for consideration and support. The fact is, and what has been indicated in this short Section simply goes to emphasise it, that we are only at the beginning of Literature's contribution to the conquest of illiteracy.

References

Ninth Quinquennial Review. See under Libraries in Chapter xii, and Text-Book Committees in Chapter xiii, section v.

S. R. Ranganathan, *The Five Laws of Library Science.* See especially Chapter ii.

(viii) *The Contribution of Community Work*

52.—*The School a Community Centre.*—The last contribution to which we shall refer as helping towards success in the conflict with illiteracy is the contribution of Community Work. Like that of Literature it is still in its infancy, but its strength is great beyond its years. The Commission on Village Education in India which reported in 1920 gave it as its opinion that 'one of the greatest opportunities open to missions in India at this time is the working out in practice of the conception of the school as a community centre'. It is that opportunity which is now being taken advantage of, and in increasing measure, by Governments as well as by Missions. The idea of it is that the village school is far more than a place where children are taught the three R's. It is a place where those who have not had the benefit of education in their youth may reap the benefit of a night school. It is a place where those who are no longer able to profit by the study of books may gain fresh and useful ideas through ear and eye. It is a place where information is given and received through reading-room, library, informal conversation, lectures, discussion, agricultural demonstration, lantern slide, and cinema. It is a place that is the headquarters of all effort that makes for thrift, sanitation, health, and higher standards of life. It is a place where, in favourable circumstances, teachers are trained so that, with the spirit of service to the village, they may go forth to pass on their enthusiasm to other villages. Those who teach in the school and those who have benefited by its teaching build up around it the credit societies which foster self-respect and mutual confidence, the co-operative organizations the members of which pledge themselves to keep their children at school, or to fight against malaria, or to stamp out the hookworm, and the groups that become acquainted with First Aid or improved methods of farm work or village crafts. Thus the thoughts of the people are drawn to the potentialities of the village, the desire to remain in it is stimulated, and the effort to realize its possibilities becomes more steady. In such an atmosphere illiteracy feels itself ill at ease.

53. *Forms of Community Work*.—From different sides this contribution is being made. It is the thought which underlies the training now being given at the mission station of Moga in the Punjab and in the village uplift work carried on at Gurgaon in the same province. 'The experimental work in the Punjab', says the Auxiliary Committee, 'has led to the establishment of similar

centres at Vellore in Madras, Manmad and Ankleswar in Bombay, Bhimpore in Bengal, and at Umedpur in the United Provinces'. As time goes on, it will be possible to give an account of much that has passed beyond the experimental stage and to estimate its precise influence. But the present mention of this work would be not only all too brief but also wholly defective if it found no space for reference to the Rural Community Board which has been established by the Punjab Government. This body, mainly official in its personnel, is connected with Rural Community Councils throughout the province, the membership of which is mainly non-official. Through funds supplied by the Central Board, the Councils maintain propaganda work in connexion with education, agriculture, veterinary science, and co-operative societies. The cinema is being pressed into their service, nor is dramatic talent overlooked. Extension of such effort is bound to involve a fair amount of expenditure. But even the little that has already been done makes it plain that it is worth every rupee that has been spent upon it. It also makes it plain how beneficial it would be if similar organizations could be established in all the provinces of India.

54. *Requisites of Community Work.*—If, however, the endeavours to extend community work are to prove successful, experience seems to indicate that there are three points that require to be kept in mind wherever they are inaugurated. In the first place, they must be connected with organizations, and not only with individuals however enthusiastic and capable. Changes in India, for one reason or another, are so frequent that to depend wholly on one person's interest and initiative is almost equivalent to upholding the temporary not the permanent. In the second place, the very largest association of non-official activity with these endeavours is what will lead to their steadily widening development. Interest tends to wane if they come to be looked upon as only what has been brought into view by the latest turn of State machine. And in the third place, though it is

unwise to depend wholly on individuals, it is utterly hopeless to depend wholly on organization. Personality tells here, and without it there would soon be nothing to tell.

55. *The School as Community Centre a Principle of Unification.*—The contributions which have been considered in this and in the two preceding Sections may be approached from so many points of view, and they run into so many engrossing ramifications, that there is no small danger of their being regarded as likely to confuse rather than to unite, and as being at best interesting and useful rather than important or essential. Adult education is represented as valuable on political grounds, the library movement is advocated as a means of checking the drift from the villages to the towns, community work at times draws support from a regard for national health. Among those who desire the welfare and prosperity of the villages of India, one lays stress on the printed book, another on the dispensary, one concentrates on the children, another pleads the cause of the adult. Is there any way in which the danger of confusion may be avoided and a true perspective may be gained? There is one method, and that is by never losing sight of the desperate handicap from which India suffers through the presence within her borders of hundreds of millions who are unable to read or write. That fact never forgotten, its significance unflinchingly recognized, the suggestion that any of the contributions which we have been dealing with in these Sections is ornamental or superfluous is seen at once to be a complete mistake. They are all needed, not one of them can be dispensed with, if the battle with illiteracy is regarded not as the field of the freelance or of the casual sniper but as a campaign in which the national honour no less than the national life is involved. All essential, yet all essential in co-operation. And how is that to be secured? By holding fast to that idea which is as fundamental as it is illuminating—the position of the school as a community centre. In the light of that

conception, the education of child and of adult, the employment of library and literature, the banding together of co-operative effort and individual initiative, reveal their specific appropriateness. They no longer seem to stand in each other's way, or to tend to confusion in thought or act. They fall into their proper places, places assigned to them in virtue of their relative importance, as essential parts of one great plan which aims at nothing less than leading the whole community, through the instrumentality of schools rightly conceived, out of the bondage of illiteracy into the liberty wherewith knowledge is able to make them free.

References

Village Education in India, Chapter viii, 'The School as a Community Centre'. See especially pp. 80-2.

Agricultural Commission Report, Chapter xiv, 'The Village'. See especially paragraphs 428, 429; and for the part of the universities, paragraph 426.

Auxiliary Committee's Report, Chapter iv, section viii, paragraphs 91-6 for Community Work.

F. L. Brayne, *Village Uplift in India*, pp. 115-42.

J. E. Woolacott, *India on Trial*, pp. 38-9, for work of Co-operative Societies.

Ninth Quinquennial Review, Chapter vi devotes paragraphs 238-42 to Rural Education.

III. How These Contributions are to be made Effective

56. *Resources Available but Not Employed.*—The survey which we have now completed brings home to us two indisputable facts and leads on to a third. The first is that the country either possesses, or has it in its power to be in possession of, resources sufficient to meet and vanquish illiteracy. The second is that, except at a few points, these resources are being employed far too feebly and with but small appreciation of the urgency of the conflict with illiteracy or of the weighty national

issues that hang upon it. The forces are there or can, without difficulty, be mobilized. But when they are brought into action there is no clear plan of campaign, available reinforcements are not called to the colours, and the sinews of war are poorly supplied. Why is this permitted to continue? Why is it that there is in effect treason in the camp? Why is it that the records of the paymaster's office show year after year so many strange entries? Why is it that when unity is of the very essence of success, independence, not to speak of rivalry, rears its head? It seems to be taken for granted that the universities may be counted on for something that will better conditions, that well-to-do people will help with the institution of libraries in the villages, that there will always be those who, urged by their enthusiasm for education, will establish schools even though they receive next to no encouragement, and that through the loose organization now in existence a real contribution may be expected from local bodies and provincial legislatures. And while all this continues to be taken for granted year after year, the trade and agriculture of the country suffers, a literate electorate is not built up, and the youth of the country fails to rank as an outstanding national asset. The situation is far too serious to be left any longer to the mercies of haphazard treatment or inadequately organized effort. And so we reach the third fact which our survey keeps pressing and pressing upon us—that which is at the foundation of any true educational policy—the need for capable and comprehensive organization and direction.

57. *The Education Department as a National Server.*—It is well that we have reached this third fact; for with it we come to the kernel of the whole matter. The survey of our resources, actual and potential, as it has been made in this Chapter, might leave us enlightened, hopeful, but yet somewhat embarrassed. Are all the contributions which we have mentioned, to be employed simultaneously? If not, what is to be the order of their exploitation? Is each of them of the same

value? If not, who is to decide their relative importance? Are they sufficiently developed? If not, who is to draw them forth? These and a score of similar questions which cannot be kept back, leave us with no certainty as to the reply that will be given, and, what is worse, with no certainty as to the action that should be taken. For that certainty will come only when the State deals with illiteracy nationally. And how is that to be done? By the State giving to the education of the land the fulness of its initiative, its guidance, its co-ordination. By making the Education Department of each province the great rallying point not of official action but of national service. That is a conception of the Education Department which, as we now clearly see, should have been operative and effective long before the present day, and most of all in connexion with the struggle to remove from the country the handicap and blight of illiteracy. It means a headquarters staff that, by its size and qualifications, can give itself fully to the consideration and devising of means for the solution of this grave and menacing problem. It means an inspectorate that can really visit, guide, encourage, and report. It means enlisting the services of men and women, officials and non-officials, administrators and educationists, welfare workers and those acquainted with finance, who will carry out the duties assigned to them either individually or in groups, being either directly responsible to the State or in the exercise of a power which the State has delegated. It means that there will be an organization that will link education to village conditions, to effective central and local administration, to the training of teachers, to the fitting distribution of funds, to community centres, to the requirements of the grown-up as well as of the young, and to those traditions of learning which have their roots in the very soil of India. Thus having a centre round which it revolves, educational control will be a service which initiates action and which co-ordinates every resource and contribution. To control so exercised and to encouragement so supplied agencies will respond loyally, and responding will work in accord. The forces will be mobilized, the sinews of war will be made available impartially and effectively, there will be something which deserves the name of a united front. Illiteracy will know itself at last to be on the losing side.

58. *The Department so Organized renders Resources Effective.*—But it will be objected: 'This is a beautiful dream. It is, however, only a dream. No province could possibly realize it'. In truth it is the one who thus objects who is the dreamer. It is he who does not face facts. No one who weighs what facts have pressed upon us in the preceding pages can come to any other conclusion. For he will call to mind that every province year after year is throwing away lakh upon lakh of rupees on a mode of elementary education which is without a shred of result on illiteracy. He will recognize that Government continues to spend lakhs of provincial funds on parts of education from which it should have long ago withdrawn. He will acknowledge that on certain parts of education there is an economy of provincial expenditure that impoverishes the system as a whole. And remembering all this he will admit that it is no dreamer who asserts that there are funds which have only to be employed and not, as at present, wasted, to result in the inauguration of a control which is a national service, which transforms casual endeavour into ordered advance, wasteful expenditure into adequate supply, and unrelated efforts into co-ordinated effectiveness. The State has but to discharge its fundamental obligation to education, the Province has but to employ aright the resources which are actually at its command, the Education Department has but to act as the server of the nation, and not only will the forces that are needed to spread enlightenment be brought into the field but they will also be so marshalled as to be co-operant to that end. The plain fact is that the means by which illiteracy may be driven from its seat of power are gathering in might every day. The contributions which

will ensure its defeat are even now borne in the hands of a growing multitude of willing offerers. The resources of head and purse, of reflection and initiative, which have it in them to remove a handicap that blights and paralyses, continue to be laid before the nation in almost embarrassing profusion. What then is lacking? Only one thing. The State must control.

CHAPTER VII

Problems of Changing Times

INTRODUCTORY

At this stage in our discussion a new situation confronts us. The changed and changing conditions of the present day supply their own educational problems and present to educational policy their own tests. Constitutional reforms, the growth of a sense of nationhood, and the development of fresh standards of culture, all serve to place the principles of educational policy in India on their trial. We have to see how they will stand this searching ordeal. And the better to do this we shall deal separately with the three problems that thus arise and call for solution.

(i) *The Problem raised by Constitutional Reforms*

I. THE PROBLEM: HOW IS EDUCATION TO BE MOST ADVANTAGEOUSLY ADMINISTERED AMID CHANGING CONSTITUTIONAL CONDITIONS?

1. And, first, let us consider the bearing of recent constitutional reforms on Indian education. The changes connected with them present the educational system with a new problem. It is this: How is the education of India to be administered most advantageously in the conditions created by recent constitutional changes?

II. THE SITUATION AND ITS DIFFICULTIES

2. *Education under a Responsible Minister.*—That is a question which did not arise before 1919. Prior to the passing of the Government of India Act of that year, an officer generally with educational, and certainly with administrative, experience was placed at the head of the

Educational Department of each province. This officer, known as the Director of Public Instruction, was responsible to the Executive Government of his province, and more specifically to the member of that government who, as one of his many duties, held the portfolio of education. But the provincial government did not possess autonomy in regard to education. Matters of policy in general, and more detailed matters as well, were dealt with by the Government of India, and the decisions of that government were binding on the provincial government, while each province might, and did, receive financial aid from Imperial funds. This, however, was not all. From the decision of the Government of India appeal might be made to the Secretary of State for India. So that, in the last resort, the India Office and the British Parliament had to be regarded, on the administrative side, as integral parts of the Indian educational system. A complete change was effected when, with the passing of the 1919 Act, education (with a few exceptions) became a 'transferred' subject. The ladder of educational administration no longer stretched from the earth of a provincial department to the Olympus of Whitehall or Westminster. Its stature became very much shortened. The Director of Public Instruction was now made responsible to a Minister, and the Minister was in turn responsible to a popularly elected provincial legislature. In all but two or three exceptional matters, the decision of the Minister, or more accurately of the provincial government in the Ministry of Education, became final. No appeal from it lay to the Government of India or the Secretary of State. And, once more, this was not all. When Legislative Councils were established in the various provinces the interest which education evoked was seen in resolutions introduced and interpellations submitted, and these had their undoubted influence on the action of Government. But the Executive was not bound to give effect to all that a Council resolved on. A very different state of affairs was created by the Act. The Minister could obtain the funds necessary for the carrying on the work of his department only if they were voted by the Council. And if he was pursuing a policy which did not commend itself to the Council he might fail to obtain their assent to the expenditures which he proposed. Thus while formerly there were matters in connexion with which the opinion of the Council might be accepted, there now came to be matters in connexion with which its opinions had to be accepted. Thus an entirely new situation has arisen. The Minister for Education is head of the educational system of each province, he is responsible to the local legislature, and in educational matters each province is a law unto itself.

3. *Administrative Difficulties.*—The situation, it will be seen, is not an easy one. The Minister has in all likelihood been elected a member of the Council, not because of his record in the realm of education, but because of his public spirit and activity. As a member of the Council he was almost certainly appointed to the Ministry on the score of administrative gifts. But to a special acquaintance with education or the details of educational administration he may quite probably advance no claim. And not only is there his own inexperience : there is always the fact that he has to carry the Legislative Council with him. How is education to be administered in these conditions? Within him, the sense of freedom in shaping educational policy cannot be separated from the sense of responsibility as a member of a government charged with the maintenance of national stability. Around him are thoughtful councillors and irresponsible critics. And ever by him are the other members of government who, while they encourage him in many ways, have a knack of curtailing ambitious schemes and of reminding him that there is a limit to what is in the power of provincial revenues. How is it possible for an educational system to be administered by one who is a politician rather than an educationist, whose activities are limited by considerations of government as a whole, and whose power may be terminated

by the adverse vote of his constituency? Clearly the Minister can make a success of his department only if he has those on whom he can rely for counsel and the fruit of experience. Where shall he find these? The answer is: In the Education Department, in Statutory Bodies, and in men and women who, having the education of the country at heart, place their knowledge at the disposal of the Minister, either individually or jointly.

III. Means of Meeting These Difficulties

(i) *Information*

4. (1) *Unofficial Opinion.*—Let us look at each of these available sources of information. And first of all let us consider what may be called unofficial opinion. In every country there are those who have no doubt as to the value of their advice on matters educational, and they are not deterred from expressing it even though it be in conflict with what experience suggests or conditions render feasible. But there are also those whose interest is genuine and who speak that they do know. And there are others who have a stake in the education of the country, who see what it is doing or failing to do for their children, who help towards the maintenance of a school, who devote time to the management of some institution or group of institutions. The danger that has to be avoided is the growth of an impression that such opinions never get the length of the Minister's ears. There is only one thing as unfortunate as the belief that the Minister is surrounded solely by official views, and that is the belief that he is at the mercy of any crank. But even the risk of the crank has to be run so that the unofficial view may always be sure of a hearing.

5. (2) *The Press.*—On the power wielded by the press it is hardly necessary to dwell. There is a constant need in India for thoughtful writers on educational subjects

both in the daily papers and in weekly and monthly journals. In not a few cases this need has been realized and to a great extent supplied. But much still remains to be done. And there are few more valuable services that responsible newspapers can render to the cause of good education than the association with them of a number of educationists whose views, even when they may not command assent, certainly inspire respect. The influence which a well-informed press is capable of exercising on the formation of public opinion in regard to educational policy and advance has not yet been recognized to anything like the degree that is both possible and desirable.

6. (3) *Educational Organizations.*—In order that particular views may receive the attention that is due to them, combination of forces is what is most needed. There are now in existence Teachers' Guilds, Associations of Teacher-Managers, Councils of Missionary Education, Councils of National Education, Associations of Muhammadan Education, and other organizations with similar aims. There is a very great advantage in the banding together in this manner of those who, while possessed of and working for ideals, base their opinions upon hard facts. And this advantage is enhanced, it is hardly necessary to add, when the opinion given represents the views not merely of an individual but of a number who have brought to the consideration of the matters concerned experience, balance, and community of interest. It would be well if the Minister made it clear that the views of such associations would always be welcomed, and that, before any important educational plan or decision was made, he desired to be supplied with all the information that these bodies were prepared to place before him. Such an intimation from the Minister would make it plain that unofficial opinion was expected to make its contribution, and that every well thought-out plan would be well weighed. It would help towards the formation and maintenance of educational associations and guilds. And it would place at a discount the views

of the irresponsible and the inexperienced. But if this is to be done in any regular and serious fashion, it is obvious that headquarters staffs require to be greatly strengthened. The need for this is emphasised not only by this consideration but, as we have already seen, by many others: so that it suffices merely to mention it.

7. (4) *Educational Conferences.*—Educational Conferences convened for special purposes are so clearly useful that the lack of them over considerable periods is rather astonishing. The advantage of conferences of educational officials, more especially of an inter-provincial character, cannot be over-estimated. For nothing could be more useless and wasteful than that, in matters concerning the advance of knowledge, provinces should act as if they formed a series of watertight compartments. But valuable as such conferences are, there is always a danger that they may present only one point of view. And a similar danger attaches to a conference composed wholly of non-officials. Where education gains is when a conference becomes the meeting place of responsible officials and non-officials, so that in the interchange of opinion and experience from various standpoints, conclusions are reached which register wide agreement and carry the authority of educational worker, thinker, and administrator. And if such conferences were needful in the past they are still more needful now when the head of the system of education is one who, with all his recognized public gifts, would be the first to confess that in order to discharge his functions aright he must have the considered views of those who have made education the special subject of their study and concern.

8. (5) *The Universities.*—Let us now pass from the unofficial sources of information which are at the disposal of the Minister to those which have their origin in legal enactment. Among these the most outstanding are the Universities and the Local Bodies. The universities have been incorporated by special Acts of the legislature. And the majority of them have received a constitution that

renders them, to all intents and purposes, autonomous. On their Senates and other Authorities there is to be found a body of opinion so varied, extensive, representative, and experienced that the Minister who did not accept its conclusions would require weighty reasons to justify his refusal. It is difficult to think of bodies that are better constituted than these to give really trustworthy advice on matters connected with the different branches of higher education in the country. Yet it is always possible that an educational matter may have to be ultimately decided on grounds that are not purely educational. Thus while the views of the university may tend in one direction, and while it is vital that the Minister should be in possession of these views, it may nevertheless be that, in the conditions of the time, the action of Government will have to tend in another direction. This may happen, for instance, when a Government is pressed financially; and it might quite conceivably occur when local feeling runs high, communal sentiments are strained, or political tension is marked. These circumstances, however, are exceptional. And in general nothing is clearer than the benefit of the advice which the Minister has it in his power to obtain from the universities. And this benefit has been enhanced by the establishment, under recent legislation, of Academic Councils. The Senates as constituted under the Act of 1904 did an amazing amount of work: but it was beyond them to marshal the carefully collected and well tested information which the Academic Councils, with their full representation of those actually engaged in collegiate education are able to supply. The institution of these Councils appears to me the greatest forward step which university legislation has taken in the last quarter of a century. And for the Ministry of Education the help of the Councils is invaluable.

9. (6) *Statutory Bodies.*—Passing from the universities we may now look at other bodies set up by statute. The growth of these during the past twelve or fifteen years has been very noticeable. Boards of High School

and Intermediate Education, of Secondary Education, and for the award of School-Leaving Certificates have been set up, and these are able to provide the Minister with a large amount of reliable information in regard to education above what is elementary and below what qualifies for university degrees. Then in the case of elementary education there are Local Bodies in all the provinces, with functions laid down in various legislative enactments, and in one province there is a statutory body which is concerned solely with elementary education. The need of such bodies, from the point of view which we are now considering, hardly requires to be stressed. If the Minister is of opinion that conditions require a new educational development, he must be assured that the step which he contemplates is practicable, that it will benefit the system as a whole, and that it will have general support. Where is his assurance to come from? Partly from non-official sources, which we have already considered; partly from his own department, to which our attention will be given later; and partly from such bodies as those with which we are now dealing. But if these bodies are to give him real assistance they require to have both the confidence of the people and a membership which has a very considerable acquaintance with education. Now most of the Boards which have been constituted for secondary and intermediate education are *ad hoc* in character. Dealing solely with education, they have a membership with qualifications that few are likely to dispute. And as the members represent many interests, thus making sure that matters will be considered from all relevant points of view, their work inspires general confidence. In secondary and collegiate education, then, the Minister has no difficulty in obtaining views that will carry weight and will be sure guide as to what is good educationally and feasible administratively.

10. (7) *Ad Hoc Bodies.*—When we come to the all-important matter of elementary education, we are conscious of a difference. The tendency of recent legislation

has been to entrust the control of this vital service to bodies on which there rests the responsibility for a vast amount of work. The result is that, as education is only one of the many functions which these bodies have to discharge, it can receive only a portion of their attention. Further, those who are elected to these Local Bodies owe their appointment rather to their position in the community or to their acquaintance with local politics than to their knowledge of educational requirements. Thus while the popular factor may be secured there is less assurance regarding the experienced factor. Even when the attempt is made to overcome this defect by appointing educational committees of the Boards, on which there may sit those with experience in education who are not members of the Boards, the position is not wholly satisfactory. The Boards, it is true, have, through these committees, the benefit of advice from those who know what they are dealing with, but the Boards are under no obligation to take that advice. And there is something that is anomalous in the position thus assigned to the most disinterested advocate and champion of education. Matters might be bettered if the Educational Committees of Local Bodies were given definite statutory powers, but some ingenuity might be required to reconcile the possession by the Committee of certain powers inherent in it with its status not as an independent Committee but as a Committee of a Board. This difficulty tells in favour of setting up bodies which are concerned solely with education. Whatever may be the best course fifty years hence, there can be little doubt that, as things now are, there is a very urgent need for the appointment of bodies that are able to give to the advance of mass education their undivided attention. Such bodies may be kept in close touch with local areas and local interests; but the all-important thing is not their connexion but their responsibility for the discharge of one task, that of spreading elementary education. *Ad hoc* bodies which have now their recognized place in secondary education are needed still more in the field of primary education. The advantage of their existence will become more plain as time goes on and their work is steadily accomplished. And their establishment will be welcomed by the politician as much as by the educationist: but to none will they be of such value as to the Minister of Education.

11. *Relation of these Bodies to the Minister.*—One thing, however, is clear. If such bodies are to be set up care must be taken that the constitution which they receive does not confer on them a position of virtual autonomy. The present situation, as recorded in recent reviews of the working of Local Bodies in the sphere of education, makes disappointing reading. What is it that has led to this? Very largely, I should say, the tendency that exists to regard education as simply a local service and therefore on a level with the construction of roads or the provision of dispensaries. It is a tendency which wherever it appears, and it is by no means confined to India, makes it look as if the most important matter for education was not the development of individuality but the maintenance of orderly administration. And as soon as that idea gains any power the next step invariably follows, the endeavour to fit the administration of education as easily as possible into the other forms of administration connected with Local Self-Government. The idea is specious: it seems to take thought for education, in reality it saps its vitality. In India this has to be guarded against at all costs. For there, let any subject have but the appearance of being amenable to mechanical rule, and soon mechanism rules the day. The smooth working of the machine is hailed with delight, and the absence of the disturbing element of life is invoked to justify the procedure. And it is from the possibility of such a plight that the education of India has to be rescued. For much recent legislation has led it perilously near this danger. What has the country gained if, after striving steadily for representative and responsible government, it receives, on the one hand, a

responsible Minister of Education, and, on the other, legislation which to all intents and purposes excludes the Minister from no inconsiderable portion of the educational field? The Minister is there to let into the whole system the breath of life: what if he is surrounded by machinery which frustrates that purpose? There is need for very definite action to enable the Minister to exercise his functions unhampered, and to secure for elementary education, bodies that know their subject and can assist the Minister. Until this is done, the education of the great mass of the people will suffer, as it is suffering today. If the Minister is to be in full possession of all relevant facts, and to have the means of giving effect to decisions based on them, there will require to be not a little careful revision of the legislation regarding the constitution of local educational authorities.

(ii) *The Education Department*

12. *Value of the Department.*—We have now surveyed all the sources of information of a non-departmental character which are available to the Minister—individuals, associations, conferences, universities, and statutory bodies. And so we are brought to consider what must ever be the most responsible source of all—the Educational Department. If it is properly equipped it has unparalleled means of securing accurate information regarding every form of education, the work of every institution, the utilization of funds public and private expended on education, the working of managements, the standards aimed at and attained, the composition of staffs, and the precise nature of local problems. Where the Minister cannot obtain all this information fully and speedily, it becomes him to enquire into the constitution of his Department. Were the Education Ministers of the various provinces to make it their first care that they were at the head of Departments thoroughly satisfactory in respect of numbers, personnel, and stability, they would render to education a service

for which it has already waited too long. The need for a re-organization is patent to all.

13. *Reorganization Required.*—Along what main lines shall this re-organization proceed? First of all, the Minister will require to safeguard the Department from the criticism against which no Department is at present proof—the fact that it is overweighted. Its duties are so multifarious that routine and details rather than larger matters of policy engross attention. It needs relief from the functions of management and all the difficulties and thought which these involve and for which outside the Department there is ample provision. It requires to give itself to administration and to that work of direction which is so much clamoured for, but all too little given. It must have a staff which can supply the information that is necessary and which can pass that information through the sieve of judgment and experience. Further, the Minister will have to see to it that where delegation of function is advisable it will most certainly operate, yet not in such a manner that the Department will abrogate those functions for the exercise of which it must always be held responsible. And finally the Minister will need to take care that, while various bodies are appointed and to them different duties are assigned, the Department is so organized that it will never cease to perform the all-important task of unification, to link in ever closer bonds the different stages of education, and to mould an aggregation of units into an articulated system. By acting in such ways as these the Minister will ensure that his Department is so constituted as to meet the changed conditions of the day. A reorganization which strengthens his Department by additions to its personnel, by elimination of functions that can be overtaken by others, by devolution where that is advisable, and by constant aiming at the exercise of wise unification,—that is what no Minister can afford to delay. He will need considerable funds for it, but what he devotes to this will be well spent money. For it will put the Minister, and that

means the country, in a position to take any educational advance on the basis of a maximum of sound information collected in a minimum of time.

14. *The Department and Continuity of Policy.*—And now we are ready to listen to the question which all along has been waiting for an answer and which will no longer be restrained, the question : What is the relation between the Ministry of Education and the Department of Education? We have said that the Minister is a politician. Is there anything calculated to secure that educational policy will not be dictated by, or made subservient to, political exigencies? Complete freedom from the operation of party politics it may be impossible to secure. The past history of education in various countries, and the story of it in some countries at the present day, makes it unlikely that Indian education will be able to escape the flow of every political current. But there is much reason to believe, and the history of education is our warrant, that education can be so administered as to avoid the dangers of party politics and to participate in the benefits which political changes so often reflect. Were it not so there would be no such position as that of Education Minister. Citizens jealous for the true nurture of the country's youth would resent the whims of an individual or the linking of education with the passions of the moment, and they would refuse their sanction to an office which afforded an opportunity for the exercise of either. This accounts, for example, for what we find in England. There the official designation of the Minister is President of the Board of Education. The Board, of which he is President, with its large and well equipped staff, stands between the country and the caprice of a Minister. From it he knows what he can and what he cannot do in the field of education, whether a line of policy which he favours will founder on the rock of finance, or come into immediate collision with local interests, or prove so complex that competent administration will break down under it, or fail to give to the youth of the country the

return which he had anticipated, or commend itself to ratepayer and educationist alike. And as the Board in all important matters goes over the ground through the enquiries of capable Consultative Committees, the reports of which are published and widely read, and as it has always at its service a highly qualified inspecting staff, no Education Minister could hold his position in England for a day if he set himself to disregard the Board or to depreciate its counsel. The question, then, naturally arises: Is there in India anything corresponding to the Board of Education in England?

15. *Duties of the Director of Public Instruction.*—It may be said that there is the Education Department. And, on paper, that is perfectly true. But we must see whether we can go further than this. For while a recognition even on paper of so important a relation is useful, it will not by itself suffice. And it is when we look at the organization of the Education Department that we come to real grips with the matter now before us. The permanent administrative officer of each department is the Director of Public Instruction. And what are his duties? 'He is the expert adviser to the Minister in matters of policy, and in many provinces he takes his place beside him in the Legislative Council. He is responsible for the administration of education in a province of which the population may be anything from seven to forty-six millions of people. He has to deal with a large number of districts, with a number of colleges, and with thousands of schools, some under public and others under private management; he must keep in touch with the different parts of the province by frequent touring. He has delicate negotiations with a large number of local bodies entrusted with duties in regard to primary education. He has often to advise Government departments other than his own in regard to the appointment of suitable applicants for the posts under their control and in regard to educational questions which affect them.' What, then, is the relation between the officer by whom tasks so manifold are discharged and the

Minister of Education? Executive action has sought to give some answer to this question, and so doubtless has use and wont, though what part custom has played in the course of the past ten years is matter more of conjecture than of certainty. Let us see what answer it is that executive action has returned.

16. *Relation of the Director to the Minister.*—It is an answer that has varied. The Calcutta University Commission was of opinion that 'in view of the increased responsibilities which would devolve in the future upon him, the Director of Public Instruction should be a Secretary to Government.' And in Bengal, when the Reforms were introduced in 1921, the Director was made an *ex-officio* Deputy Secretary to Government. But a year of this arrangement led to the conclusion that the combination of offices was too heavy, and the experiment was abandoned. In the United Provinces, however, these two offices are still combined. In the Punjab the Director is Under Secretary and there is no Secretary to Government concerned with education, so that he deals directly with the Minister. And so does the Director in the Central Provinces, who holds the position of a Secretary to Government. As things stand, then, there are only three provinces in which the Director has a recognized position in the Government Secretariat. And it is in these alone, so far as the matter is determined by executive action, that all educational matters dealt with by the Ministry of Education pass through the hands of the Director in the ordinary course of business. In the remaining provinces, so far as one can see from the outside, there is an absence of any such connecting link between the two officials. It may have been established by convention, but we are not told. And if the nexus is loose or non-existent then we may have provincial ministries and departments functioning without consultation, acting as if they were independent entities, and even being played off one against the other. Anything more deplorable than this it would be hard to imagine. How

seriously would the education of a province be prejudiced if a measure could be dealt with by the Minister without any reference to the Director, or if the Director could be represented as the official who refused suggestions or applications which the Minister himself did not desire to accept but which, on various grounds, he preferred not to oppose officially. If there is even the possibility of such things happening, it is high time that this possibility was ended by a clearly understood and unambiguously worded statement of the relationship of the Minister and the Director.

17. *Contribution of Department and of the Ministry.*—The fact is that when an educational problem has to be solved, or an educational measure has to be introduced, the Ministry and the Department has each a definite contribution to make. There are considerations of a general character which the Minister, in touch with a far-spread constituency, is able to supply, and there are considerations of a more specific character which the Director, in touch with educational conditions, has it in his power to furnish. Neither contribution is by itself sufficient: co-operation is essential. The Minister is in office today and he may be out of office tomorrow; indeed he is all the more likely to be out of it if, in dealing with an educational matter, he has not based his action on the counsel which the Educational Department is alone in a position to place at his service. The Department, on the other hand, is a permanent body. It contains those who are conversant with education and its administration. It is the one competent bureau of educational information which exists in the province. The officer who directs it has at his command not only his own experience but that also of a number of educational officers, and this he can collect on practically any aspect of education in the shortest possible time. Yet with all his knowledge of specifically educational matters, the Director will be the first to admit that the Ministry is in the best position to weigh considerations of popular feeling, reaction to taxation, and

'the swing of the pendulum'. Clearly, then, either through rules of procedure or by constitutional enactment or by the instrument of an unwritten but scrupulously observed convention, the relation between Minister and Director admits of unequivocal definition.

18. *Department and Ministry Interdependent.*—And if the relationship admits of this definition it demands it. For there is something much more involved in this than the interest of a Ministry or of a Department. It concerns all who have a stake in the education of the country, as well as all those who are receiving that education. It will not do to say that the Director cannot be a Secretary because the Director must tour, while the Secretary is not a touring officer. Nor will it do to say that a double function of this nature is a load which no single individual can carry. True, the Director must tour; if he did not he would be deprived of much that now makes his office so valuable to the cause of the country's education. True, even as it is, the Director is overburdened; but that is in large measure because the Department continues functions which it should abandon and is supplied with a headquarters staff that is wholly insufficient. But let all that and much more be granted, and the fact still remains that not until this matter receives a thoroughly satisfactory treatment will the interests of the country's youth be fittingly safeguarded. There is no reason why there should be delay. Various ways are open, and different methods may be adopted in different provinces; but though the means may vary there is only one end. The Ministry and the Department of Education must be interdependent, not independent.

IV. The Solution of the Problem depends on Information and Co-operation

19. We began by seeking an answer to the question with which recent constitutional reforms have faced educational policy. That question is: How is education to

be administered most satisfactorily in the conditions which these reforms have introduced? And as we looked at these conditions we found that the question was not really a single one. It resolved itself into, at least, two: How is a Minister of Education who is elected on political grounds to shape an educational policy that is not dominated by party politics? and, How is a Minister whose tenure of office is dependent on popular support to shape an educational policy that will be independent of the vicissitudes of a particular Minister? And though the Despatch of 1854 knew nothing of Ministers and popular legislatures, it has in the principles on which it is grounded that which gives us an answer to both questions. For woven into its very texture is this assertion: A true educational system can be built up only on the basis of information and co-operation. And if we translate that into language applicable to the changed conditions, brought about by the introduction of constitutional reforms, in the realm of education, this is the answer that our questions receive: Education will be administered in a way which is adequate to present day conditions if the Minister works upon information supplied to him by individuals and bodies that have the authority of knowledge and experience, and if he and the Department work in close co-operation. Thus will there be secured the soundness of the educational system and the continuity of educational policy.

References

L. A. Selby-Bigge, *The Board of Education* describes the functions of the Board of Education in England, as well as those of the President of the Board, its permanent officials, and the Local Educational Authorities.

Calcutta University Commission Report, Vol. IV at p. 35 is given the recommendation as to the position of the Director of Public Instruction.

Ninth Quinquennial Review, Chapter ii, paragraph 32 gives an account of the duties of the Director of Public Instruction.

Auxiliary Committee's Report, Chapter xvi, section i, goes fully into the functions of the Minister for Education, the Secretary to Government, and the Director of Public Instruction, and their relations to each other.

(ii) *The Problem raised by a growing sense of Nationhood*

I. The Problem: Can the Indian Educational System become a National System?

1. For many a day men will continue to discuss how it is that, among a number of people or peoples living in contact with one another, barriers which used to separate them are found somehow to have broken down, and in place of division there has come a unifying sense of nationhood. Analysis of the phenomenon is still admittedly incomplete; but the phenomenon itself is indisputable. And that it is making its appearance in India today no careful observer will care to deny. With many a setback, the idea gains ground. That it should be slow in permeating a country so wide in area, so diverse in population, so unequal in development, need cause no astonishment. The wonder indeed is that, notwithstanding the tremendous obstacles which menace its advance, its achievement is already so striking. If it is not possible at the present time to speak of India as a nation, it is possible to say, and with ever-growing truth, that the sense of nationhood is becoming a steadily determining factor in the lives of the millions who inhabit that sub-continent which stretches from the Himalayas to Cape Comorin. And this significant fact of the changing times in which we live brings, among the many problems that it raises, one for education. It is this: Can the educational system of India become a truly national system?

II. Answers to this Question

2. (1) *Impossible.*—It is common knowledge that there are those who would reply to this question by the

categoric assertion that the thing cannot be done. They hold that the present system is bad, that it is essentially bad, and that a truly national system can be built up not by altering the rooms of the present building and adding new ones, but only by razing it to the ground and building the whole fabric afresh. India is not alone in having had advocates of such a view. There have been in the past, and it looks as if there still were, those whose aim it was to overthrow an existing system of education and to substitute for it one that subserves political ideals or makes a severely local appeal. Such limiting ideas as these, however, have found little lodgment in Indian minds. The thought of comprehension in education is what appears in the resolution of the Indian Congress held in 1906 when it expressed its conviction that 'the time has come for people all over the country to take up the question of National Education for both boys and girls, and organize a system of education suited to the requirements of the country, on national lines and under national control'. Even more striking is the embodiment of comprehensiveness in the bold experiments of Dr. Rabindranath Tagore as he seeks to make his Santiniketan and Viswabharati the centres of that peace which broods over world-wide intellectual and cultural co-operation. Change not iconoclasm, breadth not limitation, these are among the ideas that keep stirring thoughtful minds who side by side with India's education place the sense of India's nationhood. They are found to be at work among the thousands whom the present system of education in India has moulded, among the educated men and women who sit on University Senates, Local Bodies, and Educational Committees all over the land, as well as among those who support the Ferguson College and the activities of the Seva Sadan at Poona. For them, '*Impossible*' is no answer to our question.

3. (2) *Possible on certain Conditions.*—The answer which they would return is rather 'It is quite possible that out of the existing system of education, there may

be evolved one which will suit the changing conditions of Indian life. To do this, however, it must satisfy certain conditions. It must possess certain features'. What are these? we ask. And this is the reply which a wide consensus unites in giving. If education is to be national it must be available for all who are of school-going age and give opportunity to all; it must be under Indian control; it must have the means for expressing itself through the channel of personal relationship between master and pupil; it must be animated by a religious spirit; it must be conveyed through the medium of a mother tongue and be the medium of Indian culture; and it must be marked by applicability to life. Does the Indian educational system possess these features? That is what we must now consider.

III. Consideration of Features of a National System

(i) *Available for All*

4. *Efforts to secure this.*—There is no need to linger over this first point, that the Indian system of education, if it is to be national, must be available for every child of the nation who is of school-going age. The efforts which have been made to realize this condition have frequently been overshadowed by the immense amount that still remains to be done. Yet let it not be forgotten that between 1922 and 1927 two and three-quarter millions were added to the number of those attending school, and the result of forty years' effort prior to that added only six and a half millions to the total. Neither let it be forgotten that not only does every year add to the number of areas within which compulsory elementary education is at work, but every year sees the Indian system of education becoming more self-contained. Stage by stage the learner can advance from the primary to the secondary school and to practical training till he can take his well-equipped place in the world

of business and practical affairs, or from secondary school to collegiate course till he has it in his power to take advantage of a steadily increasing provision for higher study, literary and professional, for scientific investigation, and for many-sided research. Year by year Indian education proves more available for all, and provides ever fresh opportunity for all.

(ii) *Under Indian Control*

5. *The Minister of Education.*—The second feature of a national system, that it must be under Indian control, requires but little in the way of comment. Not a twelve-month passes without Indian control becoming more and more an integral component of the Indian educational system. The control now lies in the hands of a Minister who is responsible to a popularly elected legislature. When the provinces become not merely as now largely autonomous, but as is certain at no distant date, fully autonomous, the position of the Education Minister will carry with it an increase both of responsibility and of power. He will have to share with his colleagues joint cabinet responsibility, he will have to take his part with them in securing revenue either by the imposition of new taxation or by a more satisfactory incidence of the taxation already in force, and he will have to stand or fall by the policy with which he identifies himself. But if he is to do all this he will require to be *the* Minister of Education, and not, as at present, *part* Minister. The arrangements which have been made in some of the provinces for the discharge of this office seem almost to put a premium on lack of control. In one province primary education is an item in the portfolio of one Minister, higher education in that of another. Or one Minister deals with general education, another with, say, medical education. One form of education is not in the hands of a Minister at all. And as if these were not enough to advertise the absence of unifying control, what are we to say of education being made only one of the matters for which the Minister is

responsible? Such anomalies were perhaps inevitable in the early stages of a new constitution. That they should survive these early stages is unthinkable. The Indian control of education requires that the Minister in charge should deal with education, the whole of education, and nothing but education.

6. *Educational Authorities.*—When we take stock of what is going on outside the Ministry of Education we realize to how large an extent powers of control are entrusted to Local Bodies and Educational Authorities with Indian chairmen and a membership either wholly or predominantly Indian. The Senates of Universities have now only a sprinkling of members who are not Indians. Recruitment of the educational services from abroad has been discontinued for years. To any one who looks at what is taking place at the present time, and compares it with the conditions that existed twenty years ago, no fact is more patent in connexion with Indian educational administration than that Indian sentiment is now not only vocal but decisive. In this respect, conditions could hardly be more favourable for a development of education which is in fullest harmony with Indian aims and Indian ideals.

7. *Indian Legislatures.*—Nor must we fail to lay stress upon the increasing powers of Indian legislatures. Dip into any official report and notice how one statement follows another witnessing to the influence exerted on education by the Legislative Councils, the Legislative Assembly, and the Council of State. 'Every Government, both provincial and central,' we read, 'has by bills, resolutions, budget discussions and questions in its legislature paid constant attention to educational policies in India, and there can be little doubt but that the manner in which educational policy has been kept in the public limelight has resulted in a greater measure of attention being focussed upon such problems as mass education, women's education, physical education, and the educational needs of special communities. The transfer of education to popular control and the criticism

of an opposition has, except in cases where the policy of obstruction has been adopted, tended to accelerate progressive developments.' Or again, 'The greater publicity which has of late years been given to the details of educational policy and administration and the non-official opinions expressed through the activities of the local legislatures, have had considerable effect on the shaping of educational policy'. Official and non-official opinion and experience combine to make that power felt in the sphere of educational development. And when the federal system of Government which promises to be the next stage in Indian constitutional advance is definitely introduced, the range of Indian control will be felt in every state and province of the federation and with increasing unifying power through the whole administrative fabric. Already Indian education is under Indian control, and every year strengthens that control.

(iii) *Marked by Personal Relation*

8. *Demand for the Personal.*—A third essential of a truly national Indian system of education is the demand that education should not be an impersonal matter. If education is to be a possession which the nation treasures then at the heart of it must be the personal relation between teacher and pupil. The Indian mind ever turns to the time when, in the story of the country, learning was pursued for its own sake, and long years of training in places far from the busy haunts of men inspired that love of knowledge which built up the great philosophic systems, gave power to a comprehensive religion, and reared a unique social system. The glories of Taxilla still warm men's hearts, the influence of Islamic schools still haunts them. No wonder that when effort after effort is made to establish a national system of education, features of these great days should have their place in the picture which imagination paints for the future. And it is not wholly the past which has its weight. The *pial* school of South India has attached to it today the support of present confidence

and traditional regard. In the Presidency of Madras there are known to be about two thousand of these schools, and the number of their pupils cannot be far short of a lakh and most likely exceeds it. In the north of India there are growing demands for the provision of *pathasalas;* and recently in one district alone the number of pupils attending these took a leap of a thousand within a single year. And as with Hindus so with Muhammadans. 'The system which begins with the Mulla school or Maktab and finishes with the Madrasa had its roots firmly imbedded in the country long before the present system was introduced, and it remains in most respects almost unchanged from what it was a century ago.' Some 10,000 boys and girls attend these schools in Sind alone, and doubtless there are thousands more that have no place in any return. The *pathasalas* and *maktabs* may lack in educational power, but they retain their place in the affections of the people for several reasons, and chief among these is the feeling that the teacher is one of themselves, that into the school there is carried something of the atmosphere of the family. A supporter of national education puts the matter quite plainly. 'The relations of teachers with each other and with students should be those of members of a joint family (*gurukula*).'

9. *Aversion to the Mechanical.*—In India people are ready, none more so, to yield deference to a *guru* : but they are also ready, none more so, to withhold that deference from one who is a *guru* only in name. And while none rejoice more in personal contact between the teacher and his disciple, none are less likely to fall into the mistake of confusing physical proximity with mental fellowship. Thus they are not slow to discern in much that goes by the name of the tutorial system in Indian colleges at the present time the presence of what is often mechanical, a piece of routine. Against that the heart of India revolts. Why is it that the indigenous schools have such a hold upon the people? There is in them,

it cannot be denied, a great deal of poor teaching and lax discipline. And to plead for the grant of public funds on their behalf seems to be very much the same thing as to advocate the cause of ill-equipped and poorly conducted schools. And yet it is not wholly so. For the people of India desire their education to be fulfilled with life. They see in it something more than an intellectual discipline, though that they esteem highly. They see in it one of the chief means whereby life comes into contact with life, so that the whole horizon is enlarged, social habits are built up, loyalties of mind and spirit are fostered, and the individual is early led to value common service. Such aims as these are not to be lightly esteemed, nor the way of reaching them to be disparaged. That way may be at times crude, but it makes for a right goal. It is far better than education made to order, regulated by machine-like precision, and with as much of the vital spark in it as the equipment of a factory. Education of that kind lends itself to standardisation : it is capable of yielding results that can be tabulated and it affords data which are of immense help for the composition of a superficial report. Is it surprising that there should be a deeply seated desire on the part of the people of India to get away from an education which is often very efficient and often deadeningly impersonal? People sometimes ask : why is it that, when really good teaching is available, parents prefer schools where the teaching seems decidedly inferior? There are some answers to this question which, if they were put into words, would not be very creditable to the parents. But there is one which is all to their credit, although it is frequently felt rather than stated. We may express it thus : Because they consider that education is something larger than teaching, even though that teaching be exceedingly good. And when parents express their preference for a school not nearly so well organized as the Board school that is next door to them, that is no reason why the educator should be misled, or why, the administrator should take his seat with the scorner. The distrust felt by so many in India for an education which, with all its merits, has its affinities with mechanism rather than with personality must command respect. And if the present educational system of India cannot do away with this distrust it cannot hope to become truly national.

10. *Teaching as a Vocation.*—But there are at least two methods which the present system has it in its power to employ for the removal of this distrust. And both of them are actually being used with acknowledged benefit and ready appreciation. The first method lies in winning to the staffs of India's schools those who look upon teaching primarily as a vocation. Much has to be done to improve the status of the teacher: but that much is not entirely a matter of high salaries. It is frankly admitted in a recent report that higher salaries do not necessarily mean better teachers. The teacher has as great a right as any one to live with freedom from anxiety, for he has so much to give—time, thought, knowledge, experience, his own soul also. But what is the motive behind this giving? Remuneration or service? All through India's chequered story there have been those who found in teaching an opportunity without parallel for being of service to their community and especially to its youth. And today the same ideal has its scores of devotees. For that we cannot be too thankful. But we must not stop at thanks. We must take measures which will secure for education the maintenance of this ideal, and the fulness of its operation. And that can only be done at the fountain head: the key of the situation is the training school and college. Over its portal must be written as its watchword 'Service'. And within its walls men and women must find a vocation.

11. *Colleges, Centres of Life.*—The second method by which distrust in the present system may be removed is by the recognition of schools and colleges as centres of life. One of the great benefits of the Indian University Act of 1904 has been that the connexion between

collegiate instruction and collegiate life has received steady and growing emphasis. A glance at the laws of universities which have been established or reconstituted within the past twenty years is enough to show how strong is the desire and how real the effort to combine study with residence. In universities of the unitary type, corporate academic life is an accepted feature. By the system of Halls with which undergraduates are associated, whether they live within the university or not, a personal bond is established and maintained between the members of the staff and the students under their care. And while unitary universities possess unique means for the fostering of this relationship, there are colleges of affiliating universities which are not far, if at all, behind them. Every year sees increasing pressure being brought to bear on the constituent colleges of these universities to provide adequate hostel accommodation for their students, and residences for 'the head of the college and some members of the teaching staff in or near the college or the place provided for the residence of students'. And the pressure is bearing fruit, as not merely regulations testify. It will come as a surprise to many who hear of nothing but the unsatisfactory aspects of Indian collegiate life that a third of the students attending the Arts Colleges of India reside in recognized hostels. So much is said in criticism of the present system, of the miserable conditions in which many students live, and of the great divorce between academic work and personal contact, that the other side of the picture is all too frequently ignored. If we have to admit, as has the writer of a recent provincial report, that there are parts of the country, and these not isolated, where 'intercourse between the teacher and his pupil is of a purely official kind "the closing bell rings and each goes his own way" ', it is also true that there opens to the view of all who are interested in Indian education, centre after centre of healthy academic life and happy personal relationship between the teacher and the taught. There are 72,000 students attending

Arts Colleges and of these 24,000 live in College hostels. Even in professional colleges the same spirit is at work, for of the 18,000 who are studying in the various professional colleges of the country 7,000 are members of recognized hostels; and that is all the more remarkable as nearly half of the students in higher professional colleges have taken their Arts degrees and, in one sense, are no longer *in statu pupillari*. While then much still remains to be done let it be laid to the credit of Indian education that over 30,000 of its college students enjoy the stimulus and strength of residence within the college circle. And the remarkable thing is that, while there has been an addition of over 50 per cent to the number of Arts College students within the past five years, the hostel accommodation provided has kept pace with this and has even gone a little ahead. Thus it is quite clear that, as the result of definite planning and considerable expenditure, there is being witnessed in our time a striking realization of the ideal which cannot envisage true education apart from the happy intimacy of *guru* and *chela*.

12. *Schools as Centres of Life.*—What is occurring in colleges does not stop there. There are a lakh and a half of boys and girls attending secondary schools who live in hostels or boarding homes connected with the schools. That is not a large number when we remember that there are one million two hundred thousand pupils belonging to the secondary grade. Yet keeping in mind how largely such schools are attended by those who live in their immediate neighbourhood, and how many of the pupils are thus able to reside in their own homes, we cannot but be impressed by the fact that one in every twelve of those who are pupils of secondary schools is accommodated in a hostel. Even at the primary stage there is such provision, and 20,000 take advantage of it. The cold medium of figures tells us that the grand total of pupils and students on the rolls of schools and colleges is just over eleven million, and the grand total of residents in approved hostels is

227,000. That is not a great number. Still, those who are examining the educational system of the country cannot ignore it. It means that even as things are and taking into account all forms of educational institutions, general and professional, collegiate, secondary and primary, technical, commercial and special, those in town and those in country, those which are next door to the pupil's homes as well as those which are miles distant, the school for the infant as well as the college for the post-graduate, there is in connexion with them a place of residence for one out of every fifty of those who constitute their enrolment. And every year sees a yet more vigorous effort to increase that provision, and to make the centres of learning centres of personal contacts and influence.

13. *Residence and the Personal Relation.*—It is quite possible that, at this point, some one may say: Even if the present number of residential quarters were doubled or trebled, there might still be an absence of that personal contact between teacher and taught which is so essential to the Indian conception of what constitutes true education. True. Hostels are sometimes built after what has been called the 'barracks pattern', and the last idea they suggest is that of normal homelike conditions. Those who live in them may be a well disciplined contingent: they may fail, however, to give us the impression of that combination of freedom and co-operation which is of the very essence of the family. While there is truth in the criticism, there is no less truth in the fact that the lesson of experience is being steadily taken to heart. In the endeavour to supply a great want, mistakes have undoubtedly been made. But look at some more recent hostels and see how the mistakes are receiving both atonement and remedy. Even in the construction of the fabric the idea of what these buildings mean for the personality and common life of the residents is clearly the dominating thought. Yet to what buildings can effect, however well adapted to their purpose they may be, there is

a limit. To convert limitations into opportunities is the task of those who are concerned with the management and the inmates of hostels. And how well that task is being performed, how great a national service is being thereby rendered, is evident to all who study educational conditions and their influence on life. It is manifest in at least three ways. For one thing, in many cases, and their number is growing, members of the staff live in the hostels, and the personal contact between the student and his teacher which has behind it centuries of happy Indian tradition receives daily exemplification. For another thing, there is an increasing feeling against the purely communal hostel. The result is that the hostel becomes a microcosm of the nation, various sections of the community combined in intimacy and in the pursuit of a common end, the experience and judgment of the senior mingling with the freshness and enthusiasm of youth. And for a third thing, a hostel has generally a playing field, and there team work exercises its beneficial power. A new sense of commonalty, which transcends what is communal, comes to vigorous and triumphant life.

14. *The Personal and other Loyalties.*—There is a criticism of another kind which may be here voiced. It may be said that to foster the personal feeling is to endanger other loyalties: the pupil, for instance, may become more attached to his teacher than to his school or college. Such a danger is always present, and an unwise teacher may encourage it without realizing the evil that is being wrought: but the wise teacher will see that he steers clear of it. In this, as in so much else, all or nearly all depends on the teacher and what manner of man he is. Where a school or college is well organized, where stress is laid on common work, where its aims, traditions, and demands are emphasised, personal devotion to members of the staff will not conflict with whole-hearted devotion to the *alma mater*. The more intense loyalty will generate the larger. Many looking at schools and colleges have seen such a growth.

and they have rejoiced, for there they looked on the source of a nation's strength. Where they saw no such growth they were looking not on a false relationship but on a defective administration.

15. *Full Opportunity for the Personal Relation.*—What has been said is sufficient to indicate that, while India has a system of education which can be conducted in a largely, if not wholly, impersonal fashion, and which can be the instrument of what is purely official, such use of the system is far from belonging to its essence. It is indeed a misuse. It is a failure to realize or to utilize the great opportunities which are inherent in the system. Every day is making these opportunities more patent, and every day is seeing them more fully taken advantage of. The asset of personality is coming to be recognized at its true value: and the time of youth's training is being thought of not only as the years in which information is imparted and the mind is quickened, but also as those in which, and with far-reaching results, personal contacts are formed, between those who teach and those who learn, which mould character, fashion links with ancient and valuable ideals, and lay the sure foundation of a nation's welfare.

(iv) *Imbued with a Religious Spirit*

16. *The Educational System and Religion.*—A fourth essential of a truly national system of education in India is that it should be animated by a religious spirit. There can be no doubt that the dissociation of large portions of the educational system of the country from any contact with religion keeps that system from obtaining its true place in the regard and esteem of the people. To a greater degree than is desirable it fails to make a genuine appeal to many of those who should be its keenest supporters. They feel that there is in it a tendency to a cleavage between education and what is deepest in life. This tendency will receive fuller treatment when the changing Ideals of Culture are dealt with. In the meantime it is sufficient to stress the fact that

if the system of education which exists in India is to have its real power and true place in national life it must have an intimate connexion with what is an integral part of the Indian character—the attitude of looking at all experience *sub specie aeternitatis*. Is there anything to hinder the association of Indian education in a really effective way with this outlook and discipline?

17. *Means available for Association of Religion and Education.*—In seeking to answer this question we do well to remember that the policy of religious neutrality professed by the Government and the lack of consistency which it has shown in the meaning of that policy, combined with the dual function of control and management which it continues to discharge, have all tended to withdraw attention from a most important aspect of the Indian system of education. And it is because of this that there has been a readiness to think of that system as being in its very nature godless. When facts are faced, such a view is found to be wholly untenable. Let attention be shifted from what is done by the direct action of Government in its capacity as a manager to what is done by non-Governmental agencies. Out of 232 Arts Colleges in British India 170 are under private management; out of 6,000 secondary schools 5,000 are privately managed, and out of 195,000 primary schools 126,000 are under similar management. What do these figures mean? They mean that in three-fourths of the Arts Colleges, five-sixths of the secondary schools, and seven-elevenths of the primary schools of the country, religious instruction either is, or may at once be, an integral part of the training they give. Much has already been done to render effective this portion of the system and to maintain schools and colleges in which secular and religious instruction go hand in hand. The latest Quinquennial Review tells us of over 14,000 schools and colleges under Hindu, Muslim, Christian, and other Missions, attended by more than eight lakhs. And not only is the number of these on the increase, but pressure is now coming from the side of Local

Bodies. Arrangements are being made in various parts of the country whereby pupils attending Board schools may combine with their other work religious instruction. So that a large section of institutions under public management are finding appropriate means for making some such provision in this respect as has always been open to schools and colleges under private management.

18. *What is still required.*—All that is now needed is, as has been urged in Chapter iv, that through the abandonment of management Government should concentrate wholly on control, and, in the exercise of a strict impartiality, should so lend encouragement to the association of religion with education that through every part of the system there would be the fullest opportunity for the spread of an education that would make its appeal to what lies deepest in the national life of India. We may hope that the day will soon come when this change will be effected, with its far-reaching results. But in the meantime till the day comes when Government renounces its function as an educational manager, there is much that can be done in preparation for it. The institutions for which Government is responsible constitute only two per cent of the whole. Through the remaining ninety-eight per cent without a day's delay there may be breathed the fulness of the religious spirit. Thus to speak of the educational system as godless is simply to confess that the fault lies not in the system but in those who have failed to use it aright. Let the means that are now available for the association of religion with education be employed with steady application and thoughtful endeavour, and there will soon be a national system of education which will take account not only of the intellect, but also of the springs of character, and of those relationships human and divine which give meaning to life and value to knowledge.

(v) *Capable of preparing for Life*

19. *Lack of Clearness in the Idea.*—A fifth feature which is regarded as essential in an educational system

that claims to be national is that it should be capable of application to life. Much has been said and written about this feature to the accompaniment of confused thought and the advocacy of useless expenditure. One has only to read the report of discussions on Vocational Education at an Imperial Educational Conference to realize how fluid is the notion, how tentative the best conclusions that can in the meantime be reached. A report on Indian education published in 1923 made reference in one paragraph to the success which had attended the preparation of more practical schemes of school work, and in another to pupils who beat their teacher because he sent them to work in the school garden. At times one would almost think, from the trend of speeches and suggestions, that schools in India were expected to turn out competent farmers, excellent book-keepers, and skilled mechanics. Critics have used language which seemed to imply that time devoted to the three R's was time misspent, and that boys and girls who left school without the knowledge of a trade were victims of a system that was fundamentally unsound. What is it that lies behind all this? In large part a feeling that a great deal of the education given to the youth of the country bears too little relation to life.

20. *Education and Life.*—This feeling is more easy to state than to substantiate, and it is sometimes so stated as to ignore the important part in practical life for which the present system of education has richly equipped hundreds of thousands. Thousands of graduates have gone out from the universities of India to take their place, an increasingly responsible place, in the public services, in the administration of the country, in the various professions, and in private enterprise. Thousands have gone out from the high schools of the country to serve in schools, in places of business, in forests, in railways, in hospitals and dispensaries, in management of property, in engineering projects, and in the development of commerce. And those who have taken their share in these varied forms of activity have

not been living in the clouds, but have been in closest contact with what is real and practical. Indian education evidently does fit thousands for life. Why is the assertion so often made that it does not?

21. *Limited Range of Activity.*—In seeking to answer this question there are a few facts of fundamental importance which must never be allowed to slip from memory. To begin with, we must remember how the people of India are employed. 'About 72 per cent of them depend upon agriculture for their livelihood, 11 per cent on industries of one kind or another, 7 per cent on trade, while the remaining 10 per cent depend upon the various professions, liberal arts, administration, and domestic service'. Now consider what these figures mean. They mean that there is a very large range of what is in other countries developing life from which the great mass of the people of India are shut off. Trade and industry are indeed growing, but how slowly. And into these avenues of enterprise and investigation what stimulus is there for youth to enter? Were agriculture conducted on scientific lines what a field would be opened for effort, experiment, and welfare. But custom, which at times invokes the aid of religious sanction, lends its weight to a fragmentation of holdings that is wholly uneconomical, to methods of animal husbandry that cause poverty to stalk the countryside as a spectre hard to exorcise, and to forms and methods of trade which hold out too little prospect of return and too little room for experiment. Thus it comes to pass that the area within which youthful energy may find that stimulating exercise in which it rejoices, and which brings to it the very vigour of life, is almost mercilessly curtailed. Too true is it that, as conditions now are, a very large portion of the youth of the country instead of seeing attractive lines of expansion look forth on *culs de sac.*

22. *Its Expansion needs Capital.*—In the light of these facts the dissatisfaction so often expressed with Indian education is seen to be a composite feeling. It

is a combination of two wishes. The first is, 'We wish to see our country develop its great resources and so to enter upon the great heritage which we believe to be its birthright'. The second is, 'We wish to see our children receiving such instruction as will enable them to play a worthy part in this national advance.' Now it is obvious that the first of these wishes goes far beyond the realm of education, and indeed is related to it only in an indirect way. The development of industry, for instance, depends upon capital which schools cannot supply, on technical knowledge which a general education does not impart but for which special institutions are being made available in accordance with demand, and on combination, patience, credit, power to deal with men, tact and sympathy which co-operative societies can do much to build up and which schools that have true ideals of education can greatly foster. But, if there is no capital, industry languishes, and technical knowledge finds no outlet. A road along which education might run with profit is barred. Agriculture, again, if it is to give to the country the true value of its contribution, requires a steady supply of capital which schools cannot provide, skilled knowledge which special institutions will impart so soon as their establishment is justified, and a willingness to run counter to hampering custom which schools of general education can do much to stimulate. But without capital agriculture goes steadily downhill and special schools to promote it receive next to no support. To the school of general education another path of usefulness is closed.

23. *What Education Cannot Do.*—To the criticism then that India's education has too little connexion with the actual conditions of life the reply which the preceding considerations suggest is: Increase the avenues of practical life, and then examine the charge. The country has launched out into many lines of practical effort. It has achieved, and is still achieving, great feats of engineering and irrigation, it has a network of well provided hospitals and dispensaries, its schools run into

hundreds of thousands, its railways cover thousands upon thousands of miles, its telegraphs link one end of the country with the other, it has its tramways, its telephones, its mills, its factories, its mines, its forests, its plantations, its banks, its shipping companies, its experimental farms. And for the staffing and carrying on of these, Indian schools and colleges have supplied the men and women required, and with a competency which every year sees enhanced. What is it, then, that is at fault? Education? No. Where the opportunity occurs, education supplies it. Opportunity? Yes. Let but the agriculture and trade and commerce of the land be developed, as India has it in its power to develop them, and we shall soon hear little of the assertion that Indian education is wedded to books, divorced from life. When that development does take place, and the boundaries of enterprise and national service are enlarged, it will be found that those who enter in to exploit most fully, successfully and beneficially the increased territory will be precisely those whom the schools and colleges of India have fitted for the momentous task.

24. *What Education Can Do.*—Education cannot supply the capital that will make this development possible. Indeed it is having far too little capital expended upon itself. The tax-payer gives twelve crores, the rate-payer three and a half—the princely total of less than sixteen crores. And yet people wonder that education does not do more. Should not their wonder rather be that, with so little expended on it from public funds, it does so much? And while among the things which it cannot do is to provide capital for a much-needed national development, there is much that it can do, that it is doing, to bring nearer the day when that capital will be raised. Education is opening the minds of those who receive it to a realization of the vast undeveloped resources of the country, it fills them with a desire to advance the economic welfare of their land, and it indicates to them the means whereby that advance may best be made. It is forming and directing public

opinion. It is pointing to developments which but a few years ago would have been unthought of. It is appealing to those whom it influences for service in directions which, if they involve a break with custom, bring promise of a better day for the country. That is what education is doing to assist the mobilization of that capital through which great avenues of national progress and achievement are to be opened and kept open. But education is not content with this indirect service, great though it be. It has a direct contribution that it makes, and this it renders in a twofold way. For one thing, it provides the schools and colleges where professional training and technical skill can be obtained and where agriculture and the various forms of science that enter into commerce can be studied. And this contribution which is practical as well as theoretical is being made with an increase in range, effectiveness, and appeal to which every year bears witness. And for another thing, the present system provides the schools and colleges of general education which are performing a twofold task, the significance of which is often missed. On the one hand there is at work in the secondary schools of the country a spirit which manifests itself in unceasing efforts, some of them most successful, to combine training of hand and eye with that of the mind. In one province there are 12,000 pupils belonging to secondary schools who along with the ordinary curriculum work at carpentry, printing, spinning, bookbinding and such-like. In another an agricultural bias has been given to the ordinary education imparted that has been welcomed in scores of schools. What was begun in the middle school has found its way into the high school. Slowly, but none the less steadily, secondary education is coming to be recognized not as the exclusive domain of a merely literary training but as the sphere in which the practical combines with the literary 'to develop accurate observation, to create aesthetic taste, and to arouse an interest in manual work' which will make education the guide to well-directed activities when school days are past. And on the other hand, notwithstanding all the handicap of too rigid curricula and the too pressing influence of public examinations, those who attend the secondary schools and the arts colleges of the country are being given, as the result of the greater attention that is now paid to ideals in study and in corporate life, increasing opportunities for laying the foundations of sound knowledge, for building up character, for thinking for themselves, and thus for becoming equipped to take their full share with discrimination and understanding in the great developments that lie ahead. Such is the contribution which education is rendering to the country by means of its schools and colleges, general and professional. And if it is a contribution which every lover of his country would wish to see much enhanced, it is one which shows with growing clearness that inherent in the existing system of Indian education is the means whereby the land may have the benefit not only of those who think but also of those who work all the better because they have been taught to think. Let the system be rightly used, let it escape from much of its present bondage to public tests, and of its capacity to enter with advantage into the practical affairs of life none will be left in doubt.

(vi) *Imparted through the Mother Tongue*

25. *Special Consideration Required.*—One essential of a national system still remains to be dealt with, that of its being imparted through the medium of the mother tongue and being the instrument of the country's culture. But it cannot be dealt with here. Its place is not at the end of a discussion, for it raises the whole question of Changing Standards of Culture. And to the consideration of a question so important an independent section must be assigned. It is the subject of our closing Problem. Our consideration there will show how in increasing measure, Indian Education is coming

to the minds of Indians through the languages of India, with all their appeal to the spirit of India.

IV. The Indian Educational System inherently National

26. *Potentialities of existing Educational System.*—We began by asking whether it was possible for the educational system of India to become a truly national system. And our discussion has given us the answer. The present system has in it the features which a country such as India, animated by national consciousness, demands. It is under Indian control, it has a steadily enlarging place for that personal relationship between teacher and taught which is sanctioned by age-long tradition, it provides the means for its permeation by a religious spirit, and it supplies the training ground for character, for thinking, and for practical activity. And, as the following section will show, it is steadily gaining in strength as the medium of India's culture. Thus as its sense of nationhood gains in strength and summons to ever greater responsibilities, India has no need to go afield in search of a system of education which will fit it to give to that summons an adequate response. It has but to take the system which is ready to its hand, to call into exercise all its important features, to realize all its great potentialities. And as it does this, with fresh emphasis here, new application there, at one time with an altered setting, at another with an implication fully developed, it will find itself the unchallenged possessor of what supplies the nation's deepest needs and ministers to the nation's truest life.

References

Ninth Quinquennial Review. For allocation of duties to Ministers see Vol. i, Chap. ii, paragraphs 28, 31. For influence of Legislative Councils on Education see Chap. ii, paragraph 41. For students living in hostels see Vol. ii, Tables 16-A and 16-B. For statistics of Mission Institutions see Vol. ii, Part ii, Tables 1, 2 and 3.

Eighth Quinquennial Review, Vol. i, paragraphs 225, 226 for reference in paragraph 19.

Auxiliary Committee's Report. For branches of education not under the control of the Education Department see Chap. xvi, paragraph 18.

A. Mayhew, *The Education of India*. For the influence of personal loyalty see opinion expressed on p. 116. The passage was written in or before 1926.

Report of Imperial Education Conference, 1923. For consideration of Vocational Education see pp. 38-46.

Quinquennial Review of United Provinces. Pathasalas and their growth, see pp. 100, 101. Salaries and teachers considered in their relation on p. 41.

Quinquennial Review of Madras. Reference to number of secondary pupils engaged in carpentry etc., p. 67.

Quinquennial Review of Punjab. Schools with agricultural bias. See pp. 83-5.

Quinquennial Review of Bengal. Reference to relation of teachers to pupils referred to in paragraph to be found at p. 115.

(iii) *The Problem raised by changing Standards of Culture*

I. The Problem: Is the Indian Educational System the Medium of Culture?

1. *Obvious changes due to Education.*—A hundred years have seen astounding changes in what men were wont to speak of as the 'unchanging East'. Of few parts of the East can this be said as truly as it can of India. And there some of the most outstanding changes must be placed to the credit of education. Illiteracy is the ally of a poverty-stricken country and a dominated people. With the growth of education material prosperity expands, and political consciousness arises. So has it been in India. She is steadily advancing in education, and her people growingly participate in advances which increase her wealth, her comfort, and her development. They eat in ever-increasing measure of the tree of knowledge, and they rise to new conceptions of a citizen's duty and their country's destiny. But even if such changes as

these which the past century has brought were unalloyed gains, the educational system of the land would have somewhat limited, though genuine, ground for self-gratulation. Education must do more for a country than help it towards changes in standards of living and mode of government if the changes which it introduces are to touch the heart of the people.

2. *Education and Culture.*—Has education in India benefited the country in other ways than those of which we have spoken? Has it caught the imagination? Has it stirred aspiration? Has it added to the store of ideals? Has it enriched life? In these questions Indian education faces the most testing problem which present-day conditions present for solution. Is the educational system of the land making for the culture of the land? On the answer to that depends the justification or the condemnation of the education with which the State has been identified more or less definitely for a century, and in a fully defined fashion for the past seventy-five years.

II. Two Admissions as to the Working of the System

3. (1) *Divorce from Religion.*—Now it must be admitted that there are two respects in which the carrying out of India's educational policy has kept the people of the land from feeling altogether at home in the education provided for them. The first is the absence of religion, the second is the separation from the culture of India. And the remarkable thing is that in neither respect is it the educational policy of the country that is at fault, but simply the manner in which the State has given effect to it. So far as the first of these admissions goes, the policy provided for a supply of schools and colleges in which religious instruction could be given without the slightest hindrance: it made it possible for that instruction to form an integral part of the education which those who attended these institutions would receive.

And while it contemplated alongside of these a number of schools and colleges managed by Government, in which the government attitude of religious neutrality would be maintained, it looked forward to the gradual but steady transfer of such institutions to managements which adopted no such attitude. Thus it not only established an educational system in which there was ample opportunity for an alliance between education and religion but it anticipated the adoption of action which would lead most definitely to the extension of that opportunity. What is it that has limited this opportunity and foiled in great measure this anticipation? It is official action. The State, as we have seen in Chapter iv, interpreted religious neutrality in regard to the educational institutions which it managed as meaning the exclusion of religion : then it increased the number of these institutions, it did not diminish them : then it spent on them large sums of public money so that their prestige was enhanced out of proportion to their number : and then it spoke of these schools and colleges as 'models'. Thus it came to pass that, through the action of the State, there was created an impression that a model school or college was one which definitely divorced religion from education. Is it surprising if, in these circumstances, it has had not a few followers? At the door of the State, then, lies a twofold responsibility. Its procedure has made a separation between religion and education which is alien to the Indian view of education. And it has stood in the way of giving effect to the policy which would have entirely removed the feeling that the Indian educational system was departing from Indian educational ideals.

4. *Recall to Principles.*—Times are changing. At one point after another, the mind of India has made itself felt. What is needed is not this divorce, it says. There must be an alliance : education and religion must go hand in hand. So shall we feel that our education is more truly a possession of our own. And the stronger that demand becomes, the more fully does the adminis-

trator realize that he must sweep aside the overgrowth of official action, that he must get back to the principles which were enunciated three-quarters of a century ago, and that he must not be satisfied till he has given them free course. Then will a great step have been taken towards making Indian education India's education.

5. (2) *Divorce from Culture.*—But now another admission has to be made. It is this: that in the past there has been too great a divorce between the system of education prevailing in India and the culture and tradition of India. If we seek for the reasons of this they are not difficult to find. The main reason is that the system had its beginning precisely in such a divorce. This was no accident, it was the outcome of a deliberate purpose. And that purpose owed nothing to the intervention of the State: it was conceived and executed by India's own sons. A century ago, in the city of Calcutta, there appeared a ferment of intellectual life which was almost volcanic in its force. The vigorous Indian minds among whom it manifested itself cried aloud for freedom, and only in one direction did it seem to them that they could find the larger liberty of which they were in search. Not in the literature of Bengali, their mother tongue, for 'anything said or written in' it at that time was 'despised in consequence of the medium through which it was conveyed'. Not in the Sanskrit system of education, for that, they considered, far from enlightening their countrymen only served to keep them in darkness. Not in Hinduism, for against it they rose in revolt, and to defy what it enjoined they set themselves with an energy that was well-nigh frenzied. Not in any of these did they feel that liberty was to be found, or the cravings of their minds satisfied. That liberty, that satisfaction was to come, so they asserted by their act as well as by their speech, only through Western knowledge, only through the medium of the English language. This was the position in Calcutta a century ago. This was the stan-

dard of culture which was then acknowledged not only by the young and eager but also by such thoughtful and experienced men as Raja Ram Mohan Roy and Babu Ramtanu Lahiri. This fact we have to keep steadfastly in mind. From it consequences flowed some of which could hardly have been foreseen.

6. *Macaulay's Minute and his Expectation.*—One of these consequences was Macaulay's Minute. When he wrote it in 1835 he was not initiating a new policy, he was but speeding an Indian movement which had been in existence for nearly twenty years and which had steadily gained in strength. He used in that Minute, with his characteristic exuberance, expressions to which no one with the knowledge we now possess would ever think of subscribing. But while these words are not forgotten and are frequently quoted, there are others which, strangely enough, seem to have few that remember and fewer still that quote. Yet no one who wishes to understand the forces that were then at work, whether among Hindu youth or government administrators, should forget what Macaulay had in mind when he gave his support to those Indians who advocated 'English' education. Such men he looked upon as 'interpreters' on whom devolved a very definite responsibility. What was that responsibility? It was, in his own words, 'to refine the vernacular dialects of the country, to enrich those dialects with terms of science borrowed from the Western nomenclature, and to render them by degrees fit vehicles for conveying knowledge to the great mass of the population'. A hundred years ago Macaulay saw that the standards of culture which prevailed in the Calcutta of his day would change, and that the great medium of this change would be refined and enriched vernaculars. What he supported was a preparation for this change.

7. *Lines of Official Action.*—But while Macaulay saw this and so acted, the action which government took was calculated to emphasize only one part of the programme which Macaulay and his brother-in-law

Trevelyan had in mind, and which Holt Mackenzie had outlined a dozen years before. It acted as if the conditions in Calcutta were similar to those existing in the rest of Bengal, in Bombay and in Madras. And soon it seemed to take it for granted that the money expended by the State on the diffusion of Western learning was to be utilized in the establishment of schools maintained by the State itself. Now, in both these respects, what was done was unfortunate. There was no movement in any province corresponding to that which the second and third decade of the nineteenth century saw in Calcutta; so that what was educationally beneficial in that city was not necessarily most advantageous for other parts of the country. And while the State had only a limited amount of money to expend on education, and so could undertake only one part of its comprehensive programme if it spent all that money on itself, it might have done a great deal towards the realization of the full programme if, instead of becoming directly responsible for schools in which that truncated policy was exemplified, it had aided schools which could combine with their already existing vernacular departments the inculcation of Western teaching. But while it is easy from the vantage ground of history to make such comments now, a glance at the political history of India during the first half of the nineteenth century makes it very plain that the period did not readily lend itself to consistent policies or comprehensive views.

8. *Theory of Filtration.*—There was another direction in which the official action which radiated from Calcutta failed to meet the situation. Much criticism, and not a little sarcasm, has been levelled at the State because of its reliance on the doctrine of Filtration. It has indeed been suggested that this doctrine was all the more readily made use of because it fitted in with financial considerations. But there is no government which does not believe, and which has not good reason for believing, that the learning which is at one time the privilege of the few will be shared in course of time by the many.

If the State in India a hundred years ago failed to realize fully the implications of caste or community it has not been alone in this, as even our own times remind us. The error lay not in the doctrine of Filtration but in the application of it. Filtration comes through the teacher. That is what the State in 1835 did not recognize : it is what several provinces in India have still failed to recognize. Had the proposals of Sir Thomas Munro made in 1822 received the attention which was their due, and had normal schools been set up, as he advised, at strategic points, how wide by this time would have been the sweep of elementary education and how deep the impress on education of the finest Indian spirit. The opportunity was in large measure lost, and Indian education is still paying for that loss today.

9. *Change of Official Attitude.*—But if the action of Government tended to emphasize that divorce between education and Indian tradition in which the Calcutta movement had its origin, it is remarkable how speedily the Supreme Government made atonement. The Despatch of 1854 is often thought of as being very much an announcement that, among the imports of India, there had now to be reckoned that of educational machinery. In reality what the Despatch gives us is a programme of national education and the principles whereby it may be realized. That this programme, with which the State officially identified itself, remains after the lapse of three-quarters of a century so largely unaccomplished is one of the tragedies of Indian education. And the reason for this failure is simply that, time and again, the State in India has refused to act upon the principles which the Despatch sets forth. On that failure it is not for us to comment at this point. What we have to note is that the idea of a divorce between Indian tradition and education in India finds no support in the Despatch. Instead of that we have presented to us a very different conception. Education is to be the meeting-place of East and West. While, says

the Despatch, 'English should be taught where there is a demand for it, such instruction should always be combined with a careful attention to the study of the vernacular language of the district and with such general instruction as can be conveyed through that language.' The mother tongue and English are looked upon as 'the media for the diffusion' of a liberal education. At the same time, say the Directors, 'we do not wish to diminish the opportunities which are now afforded in special institutions for the study of Sanskrit, Arabic and Persian literature, or for the cultivation of those languages which may be called the classical languages of India.' Though its influence in this direction passed far too long unnoticed, largely through the concentration of attention on organization rather than on principles, the Despatch in reality marks the turn of the tide from the divorce between Indian education and Indian culture to the combination of them. Slow, much too slow, has been the realization of this function of the Despatch: but within recent years the swelling of the tide has brought it into clearer prominence. It is worth while looking at some of the signs of the flowing current.

III. Efforts to ensure Combination of Education and Culture

10. *Growing Use of the Vernacular.*—And first, let us consider the statement which is so often made that Indian education is imparted by means of a foreign tongue. What are the facts? The *Ninth Quinquennial Review* gives a diagram of the stage at which, in each province, the mother tongue ceases to be the medium of instruction and English takes its place. And it also gives us a table of the numbers of those who are in attendance at each stage. If we compare the diagram with the figures what we find is that, out of the ten million odd pupils and students tabulated, nine and a half million at least are being educated through the medium of a vernacular and six hundred thousand, or just over half a million, through the medium of English

Education is thus being given to the overwhelming number of those who receive it not through an alien language but by means of a mother tongue. And one of the most striking indications of how the employment of the vernacular is on the increase is afforded by a comparison of the figures in the 1927 Review with those of the 1922 Review. Five years ago, out of a total of seven and a half millions under instruction, sixty-eight lakhs were being educated through the medium of a mother tongue, and seven and a half lakhs through that of English. That is to say the number of pupils or students attending schools and colleges of general education in 1922 who were being taught in English was 10 per cent of the whole, in 1927 it was 6 per cent. Thus although there has been an addition of almost three millions to the total under instruction the percentage of those who receive their education through the medium of English has decreased almost by one half. The significance of this can hardly be exaggerated.

11. *Place of Vernacular in the Educational System.* —But we cannot stop at this. It may be said, for instance, that the figures which have been adduced apply only to institutions for general education and not to all the institutions of the system. Then let us take account of the 350,000 who study in professional, technical, and special schools and colleges. Of that number somewhere about 260,000 receive their education by means of a vernacular, while there are over 50,000 who belong to European schools where English is the recognized mother tongue. Thus, so far as statistics can help us, the conclusion which we reach by means of them is that of eleven millions who are under instruction in recognized and unrecognized schools and colleges about 700,000, or very little more than 6 per cent, are being educated in a language which is not the vernacular of the pupil. But even here we cannot stop. For now we have to consider not merely tabular statements but the record of what is actually taking place so as tc

secure a fuller use of a mother tongue in the service of education.

12. *Universities and the Vernacular.*—What is it that the record tells us? Two significant facts in connexion with the universities, and several in connexion with the high schools. We notice, for example, that the Act which incorporates the Andhra University provides 'for the ultimate use of the vernaculars as the media of instruction and examination'. When this provision will become operative perhaps no one knows, but a considerable step has been taken when a goal such as this has its place in a legal enactment. Then, the Osmania University has gone beyond what is purely legislative. It has constituted a Bureau of Translation which employs a large, well-qualified staff, engaged in preparing books in Urdu that 'embrace the whole range of university studies'. At present about a score of high schools in Hyderabad State are educating their pupils with a view to entering upon their studies at this University where Urdu is the medium of instruction and English is taught as a second language. We shall have more to say regarding universities later. But this reference to what the Andhra University proposes and the Osmania University is actually doing makes it perfectly clear that we are at the beginning of a new chapter in the story of Indian universities and their relation to the mother tongue.

13. *High Schools and the Vernacular.*—As regards high schools, there is action on every side. While not many pupils have as yet taken advantage of what is permitted in Madras,—study by means of a vernacular in all non-language subjects of the high school course, and answering in vernacular the papers of the School-Leaving Certificate Examination—a beginning has been made. And there is more than a beginning in Bombay where pupils may, if they choose, answer the history paper of the School-Leaving Certificate Examination in the vernacular, and thirty per cent of those appearing in that subject have actually done so. In Bihar and

Orissa the vernacular is being used in the high school classes of certain schools. In the Central Provinces the vernacular is compulsory in the high school classes of schools under government management: and, though aided schools are under no compulsion, several of them have voluntarily adopted the vernacular as the means of instruction in these classes. These are but a few of the relevant facts, and every year is adding to them. In the light of them we see clearly how things stand. Ninety-four per cent of those who receive their education in India are now receiving it by means of one of the languages of the country: the percentage is on the increase: and what is taking place mainly in the high schools of the country is stimulating that increase.

14. *Educational Advance through the Mother Tongue.*—Thus a hundred years have wrought a remarkable change. A century ago a form of education appeared in Calcutta which, under the influence of Indian students and reformers, began in a definite divorce between that education and Indian culture. When the State made itself responsible for the introduction and maintenance of a comprehensive educational system a quarter of a century later it sought to undo the one-sidedness of the past by emphasizing the place of vernacular languages within that comprehensive scheme. Far too little attention was given to what this official declaration involved, and for well-nigh half a century the endeavour to give it practical effect showed small sign of having behind it official driving power. But time, backed by what education has itself accomplished and by the constitutional changes which have their origin in the influence exerted by education, has added its weight to the value of a policy which was in danger of being overlooked. And today we stand at what looks like the beginning of a new era. If the constitution of the Andhra University and the working of the Osmania University mean anything, if what is going on among the high schools of the various provinces means anything, this certainly

admits of no denial, that throughout India there is being steadily built up a system of education which, from the elementary to the advanced stage, has set itself to employ the languages of India as the means by which its diffusion is to be effected.

15. *Connexion between Language and Culture.*—But almost certainly some one will say at this point: 'True, there is evidence of the growing use of the vernaculars in the education of India. But is it not the case that "the high school and undergraduate courses are essentially Western courses, unrelated to Indian life as it was lived before the advent of the British"? There are signs that the education given is becoming increasingly connected with Indian languages: but what signs are there of its being connected with Indian culture?' To begin with, the employment of Indian languages is a sign. This is often overlooked because the significance of it is not fully appreciated. To use a language is to do more than simply utter words and sentences. It is to create, even though it be unconsciously, a definite atmosphere. The teacher who in his intercourse with his pupils employs a certain medium of expression is doing more than that, he is employing a medium by which his pupils are brought into the environment which belongs to that medium, into the atmosphere which, wherever it goes, it breathes. New facts may be presented by means of a mother tongue, but it is in familiar surroundings that they are introduced. Another culture may be drawn on but it makes its appearance in the midst of a culture which is the pupil's birthright. Thus were the present movement to go no further than the stage which it has now reached, that is to say, the increasing use of the languages of India in the higher education of the country, it would mean, that in ever-increasing degree the culture which is connected with these languages is becoming an integral part of that education. For some time there might be little realization of what was happening, but before long, and especially through the re-organization of training

schools and colleges, it would be manifest that what was taking place was a steady filling up of the gap between the education and the culture of India. The efforts which are now at work, and which the past ten years have seen so vigorously increased, make it certain that another ten years will not have passed without there being in large numbers of the schools of the country, perhaps in the majority of them, such use of vernacular languages that the knowledge imparted from the primary to the high school level will be effectively related to the 'real thoughts and aspirations' of the pupils.

16. *Influence of a growing Vernacular Literature.*—That then is one sign, the full implication of which is only slowly being appreciated. And in the growth of literature there is another, no less significant. The hope which Macaulay cherished regarding the vernaculars has been amply fulfilled in the province with which he was more immediately connected. The education which he supported has made its influence tell on the Bengali language till its power of expression has won the widest acknowledgment. How different is it today from what it was a century ago when none were more contemptuous of the use of Bengali as a vehicle of culture than an important section of those whose mother tongue it was. A great literature has sprung up of which every Bengali is justly proud, and the excellence of which is so great that those who cannot read it in the original are glad to enjoy it in translations. And what is happening in the north-east of India is happening also in the south. Most noticeable is the enlarged output of Dravidian literature. It is as if a renaissance were taking place before our eyes on the eastern portion of the country, north and south. And when we read of what the Bombay, Punjab, and United Provinces Governments are doing to stimulate the development of vernacular literature, we realize how eager and how steady is the effort which is being made in every part of the land not only to extend the power of

the vernacular languages, not only to set forth through them the larger outlook and the wider knowledge which changed conditions and experiences have brought in their train, but also to link all this with India's heritage of mind and soul. The growth of Indian literature is a second, and most impressive, sign of the closer link that is being forged between the education and the culture of India. In a few years every class room will show it.

17. *The Universities and the Study of Indian Languages.*—A third sign is the action of the universities. There was a time when the vernacular languages received but scant attention at the hands of the universities, and when the classical languages were dealt with as if scholarship had been stationary for about half a century. At the present day far more time, far more care, and far more thought are being devoted to these great portions of India's possessions. There is still an immense amount that the universities have it in their power to do so as to be the exponents of an enriched culture through the media of the spoken tongues and the treasures which the classics of India reveal to patient study. But we have only to look at what has been done in recent years to realize how striking is the change which is actually taking place. Madras University has not only made the study of a mother tongue compulsory on all who read for an Arts degree, but it has established an Institute of Research in Oriental Languages and Literature. The large provision made by Calcutta University for post-graduate work in Pali, Persian, Sanskrit, and Arabic, as well as in Indian history and culture is well known. The Universities of the Punjab and Dacca have departments of classical study, while Rangoon has special courses in Buddhist philosophy and law. The Benares Hindu University has its faculty of Oriental Learning and the Aligarh Moslem University its department of Islamic Studies. Every sentence of this statement might be expanded with advantage, and even then, we should have gained anything but a complete idea of what the

universities are doing to remedy a serious defect. The fact is that the universities are applying themselves most resolutely to the provision of means whereby what has very largely stood in the way of an alliance between study and the thought which influences life may be removed with all possible speed. Now at one point, now at another they are quietly filling up the gap which was caused by the original cleavage. And what they have done, far from being a final effort, is simply the earnest of still more strenuous and successful achievement.

18. *The Next Step.*—We have seen how significant are the changes that are occurring in the high schools, how in all parts of the country the pupils of these schools have increased and increasing facilities for taking their whole course of study in their mother tongue. And not only that. They now have it in their power to answer in the mother tongue papers set at the examination that enables the successful candidates to matriculate at two, at least, of the existing universities. It is not difficult to foresee what the next step will be. Are those who have pursued their studies in a vernacular language from the time that they entered an elementary school up to the time when they completed their high school course, and even up to the time when they were declared eligible to enter on a collegiate course, to be told at that stage that they must now submit to a change which amounts to a serious dislocation between their new studies and those that have gone before? Are they to be told that the language which has carried them so far can carry them no farther? There are circumstances so well known that there is no need to detail them here which make it necessary to give as the answer to that question: Yes, for the present, it must be even so. But matters quite clearly cannot rest there. There will be a demand for universities in which instruction is given not through English but through the medium of a mother tongue. And that demand it will be impossible to resist.

19. *Contributory Factors to this Result.*—Even at the present time there are, quite apart from the high schools, several facts which point to the same conclusion. Let us look at three of them. First, there is the fact of the Indian Women's University at Poona. Into the constitution and standards of that university, which is a purely private institution and is not related to any of the universities incorporated by law, this is not the place to enter. It is mentioned here simply for one purpose. It has shown that, where the mother tongue is regularly employed, there is an increase in the number of women who take advantage of the facilities thus offered for higher studies. This fact requires to be carefully pondered, and its significance for Indian universities realized. Alongside of this has to be taken the fact that, in some parts of the country, the Intermediate Classes, that is the first two years of what has generally been looked on as the Arts and Science degree course, have been separated from the colleges that teach up to the degree. This has been done in two ways which need not be described here: the result is the all-important matter. And the result is that classes which over the greater part of the country are still regarded as parts of the university course are, in areas where the separation spoken of has been given effect to, brought into close relation with the high school classes. At present, it certainly does not look as if this line of action was likely to be widely adopted. But the fact remains that it is actually at work in certain parts of the land. And where that is the case the conditions which prevail in the high school will have their influence on those that prevail in the Intermediate Classes. And the manner in which the mother tongue is employed is one of these conditions.

20. *Local Universities.*—The third fact is that within the last fifteen years there has been a noticeable development of what may be called Local Universities. For about half a century the older universities had affiliated to them colleges which were often at distances of hun-

dreds of miles, and in areas where the spoken languages were very different from those that prevailed in the locality where the headquarters of the university were situated. That state of affairs has not yet ended, but very marked modifications have been introduced within recent years. Let three instances suffice. One is the establishment of a unitary university at Dacca in the province of Bengal. The second is that up to 1916 the United Provinces and the Central Provinces were served by one university; now the Central Provinces has its own university, and in the United Provinces there are five, four of them being unitary. And the third is that until 1916 the University of Madras was the only university in an area which now has five universities. One of the results of such a development as these facts indicate is that, among the students who attend the modern universities and the colleges of which they are composed, there is a greater homogeneity as regards the languages they speak than was the case two decades ago. And that is bound to have its effect. A university established in an area where one vernacular language prevails is in conditions favourable for its adoption of that language as the means by which it conveys instruction to its students. If that language is employed by the great number of the surrounding high schools, and if it is also the language which has admitted to matriculation, its extension into the college courses becomes every year more likely and more natural. The matter is far from being a simple one, and there are many considerations which have to be taken into account besides those which have been mentioned. But no one who is alive to the trend of public opinion and educational development can fail to see the significance of what is now taking place in connexion with the larger employment of the mother tongue in the higher reaches of the educational system. A time is certainly coming when an Indian boy or girl will be able to take the whole of his or her education from the 3 R's to the Arts degree by means of one of the vernacular languages of the country.

21. *What has been Achieved.*—Much has been already done to bring the educational system of India into relation with the culture that has its roots in Indian soil, and much has been done to prepare for still further advances in this direction. But perhaps the greatest achievement of all is simply the realization of the fact that great as has been the value of Indian education there is a weakness in it precisely at that point where it should be strong. It should grip the people's mind, it should stir their ideals, it should integrate their lives. That educators should admit that to a great extent it has failed in these directions is most significant. It means that those whose heart is in the education of India are determined to remedy this failure. They have begun already. The next decade will see the gap between education and culture much narrower than it is today.

IV. Part Played by English in this Combination

22. *Facts not to be Overlooked.*—Up to this point we have dwelt upon the increasing use of a mother tongue in the education imparted by the high schools. And we have seen reason to believe that what has been done in the high schools will not stop there but will become operative at the university level as well. Does that mean the adoption by all the Indian universities of vernacular languages as the media of instruction to the exclusion of English? Facts do not indicate that this is likely to be the case. It is likely that in several parts of the country the university will be able before long to carry on the education of its students by means of the vernacular language which has taken them through the high school course: in several parts of the country, but not in all. Two facts have to be kept in mind,—the service which the English language renders, and the presence in the educational system of what are classified as European schools. Both these facts claim our attention.

23. *Service rendered by the English Language.*—There are certain parts of the country in which the alternative before a pupil who wishes to have a high school course is either such a course through the medium of English or none at all. No administration or management could possibly face all that would be involved in providing schools and staffs adequate for the instruction, in these localities, of every pupil through his own mother tongue. These multilingual areas are the despair of the educator. A recent writer who knows Indian conditions well and who yields to none in his desire for the largest possible employment of the languages of India in the education of her youth speaks of the problem presented by these areas as being 'perhaps insoluble'. It is doubtless one of those problems which will be solved by action, but at present we have to face and to acknowledge the fact. Where an attempt has been made, as it has been made in at least one province, to employ one of the most generally spoken vernaculars as the medium of instruction in the high school, 'the result has been that in many areas the language of the minority has been sacrificed, and owing to this difficulty English has necessarily had to be retained in certain places as the medium of instruction'. When the question of minorities crops up the educator, no less than the statesman, has to walk with caution. At the high school stage, then, in a number of localities throughout India the only feasible method of imparting the education required is by the employment of the English language. This fact, it is hardly necessary to say, has an obvious bearing on university education in these localities. Then, there is the case of the Indian parent who is subject to frequent transfers. His duties take him now to one linguistic area, now to another. The consequence is that he is not long enough in any one place to give his children an education based on some one mother tongue. He naturally falls back upon English as the one language which does not change amidst all the other changes incidental to his location, and English becomes the first

language of his sons and daughters as they proceed with their higher education, first at the high school, then at the university. Further, there is the fact which is very significant that the number of Indian pupils who desire admission to 'European schools' is steadily on the increase; indeed the number of those admitted has almost doubled in the course of five years, and has necessitated modifications in the 'European Code'. The service of English in all these cases, and the list of them might be extended, is so clear that there is no need to emphasize it. Finally, there is the fact of the European schools themselves. And to that fact we now turn.

24. *European Schools in the Educational System.*—What are termed 'European Schools' are few in number, some 400 all told, and they are attended by only a little more than half a lakh of pupils. Yet it is generally acknowledged that they play a larger part in the life of the nation than these numbers taken by themselves might suggest. And those who maintain these schools are not only convinced advocates of them but also generous supporters of them. What is the significance of these schools? I cannot but feel that the real significance of them is frequently missed both by their supporters and their critics. One respects the vigorous efforts which are made on their behalf by individuals and organizations that contribute so liberally to their maintenance: and one has every sympathy with the ideals of education which are cherished by those who plead so earnestly on their behalf. But are the interests of those for whom these schools are intended best served by the present mode of administration which, as it were, segregates these schools, gives them a special code, and removes them from the control of the Ministry of Education? Are the schools likely to receive that place in the education of India which they ought to occupy if they are looked upon as an *enclave*? Then the critics no less than the supporters so often seem to miss the real point. One of them says very bluntly 'The government contributes Rs. 13.2 for every Indian student, while it contri-

butes Rs. 100.6 for every European student'. To him there is preferential treatment here and he resents it. He fails to notice that these 'European Schools' are attended by 10,000 Indian pupils, so that expenditure is far from being wholly on behalf of Europeans, and he also fails to note that while in the case of European schools 65 per cent of the cost is met from private sources and fees, in the case of Indian schools the percentage is only 35. But such lines of argument are unfruitful, just as some lines of support are unconvincing. Is there any way in which the matter may be dealt with more satisfactorily?

25. *The English Language a Mother Tongue.*—The whole situation is removed from all that is communal or divisive when it is recognized that English is the vernacular of some 250,000 of the people living in India. It is therefore one of the mother tongues of the land. In virtue of that fact, schools in which English is so employed have a claim to a place in the national system just as schools in which another mother tongue is similarly used. That they have a right to a place will not be denied: to what extent they should have a place is a matter which cannot be settled in the abstract. It must be decided on the broad principle of the national service which they render. In some localities they may be able to render no definite service, and so they will receive little or no support from provincial funds; in other localities their service may be considerable, not only making provision for the pupils whose vernacular is English but helping to solve the problem of education in multilingual areas, or satisfying a desire which may be felt by not a few Indian parents. What are now termed 'European Schools' supply a vernacular need and render a national service. It is these considerations which assure them of their place in the national system.

26. *Significance of these Schools.*—In the past the tendency has been to find the significance of these schools in what may be called their nationality basis. That is as unfortunate as it is unnecessary. Unfortu-

nate, because if India is to have a truly national system of education there must be everything to suggest comprehension within that system, nothing to suggest what is foreign to that system. And unnecessary, because as soon as the ground of distinction is recognized as being one not of nationality but of language, then these schools at once take the place which belongs to them as component members of the national system. In these circumstances it would seem fitting that these schools should drop the name which is now given to them. The dropping of that name would not be the dropping either of their character or of their position. It would emphasize the fact that they were integral parts of a system to which they brought their characteristic contribution. It would make it plain that they were English schools within an Indian system, not European schools which were somehow on a different basis from Indian schools. With the dropping of the present name would naturally go the disappearance of these schools from a place on the Reserved List; they would be in charge not of a member of the Executive Council but of the Minister for Education. Then, the number of those who, though their mother tongue was not English, would be admitted to these schools would not be subject, as at present, to a prescribed percentage laid down in a special Code. It would be settled entirely by the capacity of the applicants to profit by the education imparted and by the capacity of the school to carry out the objects for which it was established. Further, it would be the duty of the Ministry to see that the financial support given to these schools was such as to enable them to discharge their specific function. This would certainly involve a considerable outlay from provincial revenues, for recruitment of appropriate staff might not be easy in India, and the number of pupils might quite possibly continue to be comparatively small. But each province would doubtless decide what percentage of its educational expenditure was to be devoted to this, as to every other, form of education, and the number of schools that could be maintained would be settled in large measure, by that decision. Yet not wholly, for, with the schools having an assured place in the national system, the very large contributions that are now made towards their maintenance by private donors would be almost certainly enhanced.

27. *Bearing of these Considerations on the Universities.*—Our discussion up to this point has carried us along two seemingly parallel lines. On the one hand, we saw that, as the result of the growth of local universities and of what is happening in the high schools, there is the prospect of the establishment at no very distant date of universities in which the instruction given will be imparted through the medium of some of the Indian mother tongues. On the other hand, it is clear that as the result of English being one of the mother tongues employed in India and because of the national service which it renders, there will continue to be high schools in which English is the medium of instruction. And this will lead naturally on to universities where English is similarly employed. Thus there seems to be every likelihood that if the languages generally spoken in India receive the attention that is their due, and continue to be cultivated with that increasing care which is now being paid to them, there will be a very remarkable development of education along linguistic lines. It is a development that will tell in three directions. To begin with, the pupil of a high school within an area where, say, Bengali is the language mainly spoken will find that he can not only obtain his secondary education through the medium of that language but that he can also proceed to a university where Bengali is the language employed. That is one course which will lie open to him. A second will be this. Having taken English as his second language in his Bengali High School, he may then prefer to go into a university in which English is the chief medium of instruction. There will very likely be few of these universities, and he may have to go

some distance to secure admission, but the choice will be available and it will be in his power to take advantage of it. And third, he will find that there is before him more than a choice of universities based on the language in which their study is conducted. He will realize that the choice gives him the opportunity of entering universities each of which possesses a definite character, has about it the atmosphere inseparable from the language in which instruction is given and through which thought is conveyed, and brings those who enter it in contact with a tradition, an outlook, an impetus that stirs ideals and leaves its impress on his inmost being. The present position of each university being but a pale replica of its neighbour will be gone. Each will have a definite function of its own to perform, and in the consciousness of the part which it can play, the spontaneous contribution which it can make to the nation's well-being, there will flow through the universities a fulness of life and vigour which will make them the objects of the people's pride and cause them to be cherished as one of the nation's greatest assets.

28. *A Great Opportunity.*—Our consideration of what is taking place in the field of Indian education helps us to realize how striking is the opportunity that is now before it as a power for enriching mind and integrating life. The lines along which Indian education is moving point to fresh developments of the highest moment for the well-being of the people. For long it has been recognized that in the schools and colleges of India the streams of varied cultures meet. But there has been too long a tendency to emphasize one of these,—that which comes from outside the country—with the inevitable result that education has taken on an alien look, and being removed from its appropriate setting has come to be prized because of its utilitarian value. This has occurred through failure to give due effect to a line of policy enunciated more than two generations ago which made provision for the association of

education with religion and with the languages of the country that were in common use. Today there is a clear realization of the ill effects of this failure. And efforts are being made to secure more fully both associations. Greater facilities than was formerly the case are now provided for the association of religion with education. And within the last few years how steady have been the endeavours to bring education into intimate relation with the vernacular languages of the country, not only in the more elementary but also in the higher ranges of learning. Much has still to be done, but no one can be blind to the direction which advance is taking. The emphasis which is being placed on the mother tongues of India is making it more and more possible for education to become an integral part of the life of the people, the medium for thoughts which do not lack in appeal and for ideals which have a constraining power. Thus if what is now taking place is not weakened by obstacles, but finds in them rather the reason for an increase of activity, the prospect is one which is remarkably stimulating. The development that is in process has only to be continued and strengthened, and the result will be a threefold benefit. In the first place, Indian education will still be the meeting place of various cultures, but in such manner that, while each makes its distinctive contribution, that which appeals to Indian thought and enriches its ideals will have the most telling influence. In the second place, through greater attention to, and employment of, the languages in which so much of the wisdom of India lies stored, education will be robbed of its alien appearance and will advance along lines which do justice to the various aspects of the nation's heritage. And, in the third place, though each aspect will receive opportunity for its fullest development there will run through the whole system the unifying ideal of national service. Eighty years ago it was seen that India might have a system of education which would effect all this.

After many days the vision is in process of being realized.

V. Obstacles to this Combination

29. *Inequality of Opportunity.*—The vision is in process of realization. But it is confronted with at least three obstacles. First there is the fact that the education of women lags far behind that of men. So long as this inequality is tolerated, so long will education fail to exercise effectively its power of culture. It is not only that the woman misses what ought to be hers, but that being without appreciation of that which has been denied to her she stands in the way of the full intellectual development of the man. Thus on two counts is education the sufferer. And what should be the ally of ideals that enrich the life of family and the State tends to be valued only for what it will fetch.

30. *Standardization.*—A second obstacle is to be found in that lack of elasticity which has too often characterized the Indian educational system. Where there is rigidity education is slow to show itself in any aspect that stirs the imagination and ministers to moral growth. Much is said about the influence which examinations exert, but the real trouble is that one test serves too many purposes. Paradoxical as it may seem there are too few examinations. That which is the best means of indicating what a boy or girl has done at the secondary stage is not necessarily the best means of indicating whether he should be admitted to a university. But it is frequently taken to be. And the result is that both high school and university suffer. There is required a greater diversity of test, a diversity that corresponds to a greater variety in the courses provided and a fuller recognition of the different ends to which education leads. There is little chance of this being accomplished until there is much more decentralization of educational control. Things are making in that direction. Before long we may expect to have throughout the coun-

try thoroughly competent Local Educational Authorities. With their establishment a better day will dawn for both primary and secondary education, both in their character and in their influence on thought and life. And the establishment of Civil Service Commissions in the various provinces, a great administrative advance of which a beginning has been made, will enable the universities to give themselves to their proper work, that of spreading knowledge which probes and moulds, and will relieve them of any responsibility for the provision of tests for those who seek to enter the public service. There is clear evidence not only of restlessness under, and distrust of, standardization in the field of education, but also of a readiness to think out, and give effect to, plans whereby it may lose much of its present power. And with well-thought-out plans in more general operation there will be a growing recognition of the power which resides in education to enrich life and an increasing endeavour to give to that power the fullest opportunity for its expression.

31. *Sectionalism.*—A third, and a most grievous, obstacle is to be found in the spirit which emphasises what divides. Education which can see with difficulty beyond the limits of community or nation is education which has been stripped in large measure of its great and beneficent unifying force. Now it is quite possible that, just because of this, some may hesitate, as to the advisability of Indian education developing along the lines which our present discussion and consideration have emphasised. May it not be, those who hesitate will ask, that the effort to lay stress on culture will lead only to the identification of education with what is acceptable to this community or to that? and may not that be all the more likely when the education of the country not only follows much more than hitherto linguistic lines and comes into closer association with religion? No one who is acquainted with the conditions of any country would ever think of minimizing the possibility of such dangers. They are to be found in every land; it is not in India

only that they are to be feared. But in India the possibility of danger may be translated into the reality with remarkable speed and bitterness, when persistence in lowered standards has been allowed to rob education of its ideals, or when currents of strong feeling sweep across the country. There is but one means by which Indian education may be rescued from this danger; and that is by recalling it to one of its fundamental principles. Nearly four score years ago the charter of Indian education laid it down that the system to be introduced was to be marked by this essential feature: It was to be the meeting place of cultures. The enunciation of this position showed Indian education the means by which it might be delivered from a danger to which it was then exposed, the danger of becoming education in India without becoming Indian education. Too slowly has the power of this principle been recognized: too slack has been its application in the intervening years. But where it has been employed, there has education flourished, and there have its ideals flourished with it. Today few features of Indian education are more marked than the effort that is being made to give this principle free course. And the education in India, under its power, is becoming in increasing volume the education of India. But its sweep does not stop there. The more the principle is employed the clearer becomes the synthesis which it effects. It takes the sharpness from what have been too often bitter antagonisms, and reveals them not as enemies and dividers but as, in combination, making available a completeness of knowledge which either in isolation was powerless to provide. It brings them together, in their variety of outlook and tradition, as mutually indispensable contributors to the realization of a richer mental and spiritual heritage. It withdraws from Sectionalism the power to separate, replacing the stifling air of exclusiveness by the freer and more life-giving air of comprehension. Education in India, as it lays stress on the manifold ideals bound up with the land, and claims kinship with the stimulus of diverse religions, has but to remind itself of the rock whence it was hewn. Threatened by the dangers of narrowness and disruption it has but to recall itself to that principle which is inherent in it, and by the operation of which it rises above all that tends to sunder. Indian education is the meeting place of cultures. To that it must hold. By that it will flourish. And so will the life of the nation as well.

VI. Growing Connexion between Indian Education and Culture

32. The student of Indian educational policy cannot help being struck with the fact that the developments which are now taking place in the field of Indian education serve to give effect to a purpose which was conceived many years ago. Great obstacles stood in the way of the attainment of that purpose, and the actual steps which should be taken so as to achieve it remained for long far from clear. The road is clearer today. India feels that she cannot have an educational system which gives her the impression of having about it something alien; and she is taking the right way to remove the sense of aloofness. She is making provision for her education to be brought into close relation with the languages of the land and with their large store of thought and inspiration. Her universities are playing their part and are enlarging the sphere of that provision and so are her high schools. A recognition of the true significance of what are at present called European schools and of the place which English has among the languages employed in India contributes to the same result. There is thus being steadily built up a truly national system of education from its most elementary to its most advanced stages. It is pervaded by no mechanical uniformity, but by a variety which takes account of thought expressed in various tongues and animated by various beliefs. Yet that variety it brings into a unity of service of mind and spirit, the service of a people's well-being.

In high school and university heads and hands are at work to rear the fabric. The men and women who place their time and experience at the disposal of educational authorities are the pledge that public opinion is behind this great endeavour. In the training school and college there lies the certainty that it will not fail. And thus efforts initiated nearly eighty years ago to put an end to the cleavage, even then of considerable duration, between Indian education and Indian culture, after encountering many a difficulty and overcoming strange neglect, are now receiving a reinforcement which is the earnest of their approaching success. For they can have but one result, that to which they are at present tending—an education which has its roots in the soil of India, yet claims kinship with truth wherever it may be found; and which, while it fails not in action or in public utility, gives the most striking proof of its worth for the sons and daughters of India in the intellectual resources which it builds up, the ideal satisfactions to which it invites, and the discipline and enrichment of the spirit to which it admits.

References

Lord Ronaldshay, *The Heart of Aryavarta*. See the opening chapters for conditions in Bengal a century ago and now.

A. Mayhew, *The Education of India*. See especially Chap. xiii: 'Education and Culture'. Developments are referred to which have advanced since the book was written.

V. V. Oak, *England's Educational Policy in India*, p. 107. Criticism of cost of European schools referred to.

H. Sharp, *Select Educational Records, Part I*. On p. 116 towards the close of Macaulay's minute.

Eighth Quinquennial Review, Vol. i, Chap. iii, paragraph 103 for reference to Indian Women's University.

Ninth Quinquennial Review, Vol. i. Diagram showing when English becomes medium of instruction faces p. 89. Intermediate Colleges are dealt with in Chap. iv, pp. 85-8. High Schools and the Vernacular, Chap. v, paragraphs 100-2. The Osmania University, Chap. xiii, paragraph 556.

The Universities and Oriental Study, Chap. xiii, pp. 273-6. The Andhra University, Chap. iii, paragraph 98. In Vol. ii see Table ix for students at different levels. (In the *Eighth Quinquennial Review* it is Table x.) Vol. i, Chap. x, paragraph 411, deals with European Schools and the attendance of Indians.

Central Provinces Quinquennial Review. See p. 31 for reference in paragraph 23.

CONCLUSION

I. Need for Changed Educational Outlook

1. *Criticism of the Indian Educational System.*—'No country', it has been said, 'is satisfied with its educational system'. And a very good thing it is. Where there is no criticism, education is in danger of mistaking stagnation for stability, and of regarding smoothness of working as more to be desired than the strenuousness of advance. To these dangers the education of India has, in common with that of other countries, been constantly exposed, and from them it has been in great part delivered by a dissatisfaction which has become more vocal as the years have sped. Within the present century, to go no further back, there has been a steadily growing interest in education which has been accompanied by the most outspoken and vigorous criticism of educational methods and results. Weakness at every stage has been laid to the charge of the system of public instruction, its form of administration has been impugned, its effects have been deplored. It has been represented as doing too little for the great mass of the people, for developing a type of secondary education largely out of touch with the actual conditions of those who receive it, and for establishing universities which, whatever else they may have done, can hardly be said to have raised the level of scholarship in the land. It has been found fault with for having but slight connexion with what is practical, for leaving a weak impress on character, and for running along grooves where there is too little contact with Indian tradition and culture. It has been challenged for the hundreds of inferior schools which it contains, for the thousands of ill-qualified teachers whom it allows to experiment on the youth of the land, and for the miserable supervision with which it rests content. It has been accused of wasting lakh after lakh of public revenues, and of blocking whole

pathways of advance by the plentiful employment of red-tape. It has been decried for the small extent to which it has entered with benefit into the lives of women and girls, for the rapid decline into illiteracy of thousands whom it has drawn within its sweep, and for the unemployment to which those who are its products are being increasingly subjected. The system has been denounced as godless, expensive, ineffective. And while there is never any lack of those who urge its improvement, now at this point now at that, there are also those who seem to think that improvement is past praying for.

2. *Criticism and Perspective.*—Nothing but good can result from a ready acknowledgment of all the truth but may be contained in these criticisms, and from a vigorous endeavour to make that truth effective. Now if that endeavour is to succeed there are two facts which must receive serious consideration. The first is the fact of achievement. That during the short period of less than three generations the Indian educational system should have touched so many million men and women, should have brought to them facilities ranging from the most elementary to the very advanced, should have made it possible for hundreds of thousands to prepare themselves for positions of responsibility in the various professions and in the public services, in commerce and in industry, in administration and in learning, and should have enabled numbers of them to occupy these positions with an ability and distinction that is admitted not only in their own land but also in the councils of the world, is an achievement which, if it is sometimes obscured, is nevertheless so striking as to be fraught with international significance. That is the fact which it falls to the lot of the historian of Indian education to record with the fulness of detail which is its due. And the second fact is one which it is for the investigator of Indian educational policy to exhibit in all its bearings. The fact is this. At the very heart of education in India there lie principles of educational

policy which have only to be employed to redeem education from admitted weakness and to display the strength which is inherent in it. That is the fact on which we must now concentrate our attention.

3. *Neglect of Principles of Educational Policy.*—It is a fact which is constantly forgotten or neglected, as the story of India's education abundantly testifies. For its neglect there is one explanation which has been frequently adduced. It is to the effect that these principles have passed into neglect because they are not fitted to do what is claimed for them, or in other words they are unable to afford solutions for the serious problems which Indian education lays before them. This form of objection, it will be seen, is simply the return of a negative answer to the question with which we began this part of our discussion, the question which, in the first paragraph of the Introduction we put in the form: Are the principles of policy on which Indian education is built adequate to the situation of today? Now in order to answer that question we adopted the method of detailed examination. We have devoted seven chapters to a full consideration of difficulties, each of them of capital importance, which arise in connexion with the control, management, finance, religious character, provision for teaching, extent, and changed setting of Indian education. At each point we brought recognized principles of educational policy into immediate touch with these difficulties and the problems thus presented. The result has proved sufficiently striking. It is that at every crucial point these principles meet the situations, be they of old or recent origin, and afford means whereby the problems raised may receive satisfactory solutions. Also at every point where there is departure from or neglect of these principles, the difficulties experienced still remain in the way of the educator, and the defects of the educational system remain unrelieved. Thus candid and detailed examination leads but to one conclusion. And that conclusion is: If the educational problems of India are ever to be

solved, it can only be through the application of those principles of policy which, though they have been too little employed to their full extent and have been far too frequently neglected, have been utilized to a greater or less extent for three-quarters of a century and are of the very essence of Indian education. To explain the neglect of these principles, then, by the assertion that they are not able to bear the weight that is put upon them is to give a reason which proves to be devoid of cogency the moment that it is brought to the test of fact. The true reason must be sought for in another direction.

4. *Defective Outlook the Reason of this Neglect.*—In what direction, then, shall we seek for this reason? In the direction of what State responsibility for education really involves. In 1854 the State came to the conclusion that a new responsibility rested upon it in India. Up to that time it had admitted and had discharged many responsibilities. But with the Charter Act of 1853 it deliberately added to these, and proclaimed in the following year that it had become responsible for the education of the peoples within the Indian territories committed to its care. What that obligation involved was only slowly realized as years advanced, and even today the full force of that conception has not yet been grasped. In order to discharge the obligation which it accepted in 1854 the State installed and set to work an educational machinery which has done much for the attainment of the end contemplated. It is possible, as we have seen, to derive no small satisfaction from what this power-station, established in the middle of the nineteenth century, has effected. There is good reason to be thankful for the eleven millions who are enrolled in the educational institutions of the land; there is no less reason to be thankful that, notwithstanding the financial stringency which India has experienced and the slow development of her educational equipment, there are in India over twenty millions who are able to stand in the ranks of the literate. But there is another side to

this. Thankfulness which expends itself on what is behind, and does not summon to what is before, has outlived its usefulness. And there is a danger lest that may be the stage which Indian educational administration has now reached and at which it may incline to rest. In other words there is a danger that the colossal task which still confronts Indian education may be forgotten in a pre-occupation with present methods, present machinery, even present advance. And that the danger is far from imaginary is brought home to us by the perusal of scores of Indian educational reports. Were we to rely upon what these reports place before us, we might be pardoned if we came to the conclusion that education had so far prospered that the supply of agencies was abundant, and the most important matter for consideration was which of these agencies might be most speedily and most fittingly dispensed with; and as if funds for educational purposes were so abundant that nothing was more pressing than to make it clear beyond the shadow of a doubt that further large contributions from agencies which have already given lavishly might continue to be offered, but would no longer be welcomed. Alongside of such an impression as this, created by what meets us in so many official records, set the meagrest outline of what is the actual state of affairs. Thirty million boys and girls who are of school-going age never darken a school door, and what is more they have no school door to darken. There are a hundred million of women on whom education has never so much as cast a single ray of light. There are in the whole of India some three hundred million people who, if they receive a most elementary letter in their own tongue, are unable to read it far less to answer it. The nine million children in the primary schools of British India are in the hands of a totally inadequate number of teachers, sixty per cent of whom have no special qualifications for their task. Over thirty per cent of those who are enrolled as pupils of schools in any one year are found some ten years later enrolled among the illiterates. The total amount spent on education in British India is in round figures no more than Rs. 27 crores or £20 million, of which the whole sum that comes from provincial sources is Rs. 13 or ten million pounds. Add to startling facts such as these the present plight and weakness of what ought to be the strength of India—its agriculture and its industry; add too the appalling story told year after year by the tables of Vital Statistics, a story only too closely connected with the absence of education. And then look the situation fair in the face. There is no disguising it. It is a situation so grave that it menaces the very foundations of national life. How is it to be met? By casting aside the conception of State responsibility for education which has hitherto sufficed, and by substituting for it the one which does justice to threatening facts which can be no longer ignored. Eighty years ago the State understood by its responsibility the obligation to provide for what was in the highest degree beneficial. It was a conception of the State's duty which was ahead of its time and which wrought wonders. But it is a conception which the events of the past three decades have been steadily rendering inadequate. Yet this inadequacy there has been in many quarters a failure to realize. That is the reason why principles of educational policy which bring with them the strength of which the educational system stands in need have been ignored and neglected. They have been passed over because there has not ruled and stirred education a growingly adequate conception of what is involved in State responsibility for that necessary provision. Facts have not been faced. Principles therefore have received neither the recognition nor the exercise which is their due. To receive that nothing less than a changed outlook will suffice. The State must provide for a national necessity.

II. Principles bound up with this Outlook

5. *What a Changed Outlook Requires.*—What is it that the changed outlook demands, that outlook which

recognizes, without flinching, the fact that, if the State does not provide for such education as will meet the conditions that now obtain, the very life of the State itself is threatened? At least three things. In the first place it demands that the State must provide a central Controlling Authority. In the second place it demands that the State must draw forth a sufficiency of Co-operating Agencies. And in the third place it demands that the object aimed at shall be nothing less than a comprehensive National System of education. What the fuller conception of State responsibility in regard to education which is forced upon us by the simple facing of facts requires is Control, Co-operation, and Comprehension. We must look at each of these in turn.

6. *The Notion of Control.*—To begin with, there is no hope of any satisfactory dealing with the present situation which leaves millions untouched by education and thus exposes the State to dangers too great to admit of exaggeration, until the State recognizes its obligation to control education in deed as well as in word. It cannot allow what is a necessity for its own existence to fall into hands which, however well-intentioned, may be irresponsible. A national need demands a national effort. The State must itself control. Is that because it has the power to dominate education? No. But because, as no other body has, it possesses the means to serve education. A fuller conception of State responsibility brings with it a clearer conception of State control. It is the State service of education. For the State to control education, then, signifies that to education it will extend the steady and generous service of initiative, guidance, direction, encouragement, and finance, and yet in doing so will exercise the most anxious care that State interference is reduced to a minimum. That is the conception of control which the situation of the present day makes so real. Such control it is no easy thing to realize. But it is the control which Indian education must have.

7. *The Notion of Co-operation.*—So much for the con-

ception of State control which the conditions of our day reveal, and to the exercise of which they issue an insistent summons. But this control does not operate in empty space. It is, as we have seen, a service. Whom does it serve? The answer to that question brings us most naturally to the second of the essentials of responsibility which we have noted, that of Co-operation. The State is in education the controlling authority, and that control it exercises over co-operating agencies. Now when we look at the agencies as they are at present marshalled in the educational field we cannot help being struck with several features of the scene that bring hesitation rather than reassurance. For one thing and only too clearly, there are too few of them. Then again, while some of them are of the highest value and have stood the test of many a conflict, there are others which promise weakness rather than strength. Further, when we look at them as a whole they march but little in step with one another, and a concerted attack is about the last thing of which we could think them capable. And all the time what is required is a sufficient number of schools and colleges, and a sufficient number of them working in co-operation with one another. And that can never come about until the changed outlook of which we have spoken is universally adopted. So long as the thought of control concerns itself mainly with the working of an official department there will be not only the absence of true control, there will be also the absence of co-operating agencies. There will be agencies, but in patently insufficient numbers; and there will be agencies, but little working among them for a common purpose. The controlling authority will consider that it has discharged its functions when it can show that it has expended on education in the course of one year a larger sum than it expended on it the year before, even if that expenditure has run for the most part along only one channel; when it has seen that its own officials, their services, and their institutions have received due attention; and when it passes judgment on the contributions made to education by non-official agencies. But that is an outlook which must go for ever. It is responsible for encouragement being meted out to a part not to the whole, so that the supply of a sufficient number of agencies becomes forthwith a complete impossibility. It is responsible for establishing at the very centre of educational administration a method of preferential treatment such that, while the operation of a certain number of agencies is assured there is also assured the presence of those conditions which effectually block the way to co-operation. And as if that were not enough, co-operation receives something approaching a *coup de grâce* when the controlling authority proceeds to follow it up with discriminatory judgments. As soon, however, as facts are really faced and State responsibility becomes lifted out of these narrow and constricting grooves, as soon as it moves not in the small space where purely official machinery is at work but in the large field where the eye sees not a vestige of educational power but only the black cloud of menacing ignorance which hangs lowering over the existence of the State, a complete change of outlook is effected. It is realized that the existing agencies are but a fraction of what is required. Agencies greatly enhanced in number and adequacy are needed, the country must have them, the well-being of the people is at stake, the being of the State is challenged. The controller must definitely adopt such a line of action that these agencies are supplied, and that they no longer operate in isolation, opposition, or discrimination. They must operate in sufficient numbers and they must co-operate. That is what Indian education must have.

8. *The Notion of Comprehension.*—Thus we are led to our third essential, that of Comprehension. Nothing less than a comprehensive scheme will suffice for the removal of a comprehensive menace. If the nation's foe is to be routed it must be by an educational system which affects the whole nation. The State has under-

taken the responsibility for the education of its people. It must therefore see that as speedily as possible there is not a child of school-going age that is left without the elements of education. But can it stop there? There are some who consider that it can and ought. But a little reflection shows how utterly impossible it is to entertain any such idea. The State must see that the elementary schools of the country are staffed by those who are qualified for the duties assigned to them. Otherwise the State would only be setting up machinery whereby one of its most valuable assets was being daily brought under influences from which it ought to have been most sedulously shielded. To obviate harm so far-reaching as this, that is to say in order to have teachers able to do justice to the millions of pupils entrusted to them, the State must see to it that there is provided an education which goes beyond the elementary stage of the pupils. In other words, if only to secure an elementary education which will avert a national menace, secondary education is a necessity. Nor can the matter rest there. There must be those who can instruct teachers, and there must be those who can review and guide the work of teachers. And for them there must be available the type of education which will fit them to perform their necessary and responsible tasks. Other considerations quickly enter in and assert their right to attention. The agricultural and industrial interests of the country cannot be allowed to hang in the air or to be the concern of those who are devoid of education. The vital statistics of the land are not tabulated only that a department may pass on them its comments: until they are linked with education they might as well be thought of as fatal. The capacity, which by cultivation becomes life to the State, cannot, unless the State denies itself, receive in the form of a stunted educational system its death-warrant at the hands of the State. Thus from such considerations there follows a conclusion which there is no escaping. If the State is to be delivered from the grave situation which now confronts it, it must accept responsibility not merely for the provision of education in general; it must be responsible for seeing that there is within the reach of its citizens a supply of education which takes account of the actual needs of the country, a supply which is provided not in isolated courses but in correlated groupings, a supply which is adequate in the higher no less than in the more elementary stages. If illiteracy is to be effectually countered, if the State is to rest on foundations from which the present elements of decay are eliminated, then it must be in possession of a comprehensive national system of education. That is what the Indian educational system must be.

9. *The Larger Outlook and Appropriate Action.*—We have sought to gain some conception of the larger outlook to which the conditions of the present day summon us in the realm of education. And what we find as the outcome of our consideration is this. The State must so control or serve education that there is raised up a large body of co-operating agencies which place themselves at the service of the country, and put it in possession of a comprehensive scheme of national education. That is what is involved in the State's responsibility for the provision of education in India. And it is to the realization of this conception that the State must resolutely bend its energies. The State, on pain of denying itself, can do nothing less than this. How then is it to do it? The directions which its activity must take are not hard to trace. All the greater reason therefore why they should be set forth with a plainness which does not become blurred through unnecessary detail or featureless generality. And that is what we shall now endeavour to do.

(i) *The Establishment of a National System*

10. *Comprehension in Extent.*—If the State places before itself not the limited considerations of depart-

mental working but the disaster that impends over the nation because of the enormous extent of the educational field that lies fallow, not to speak of the poor results produced by not a little of what is actually under cultivation, then the picture on which it must drill itself to look is that of a national scheme of education, a scheme which aims at nothing smaller than the education of all its citizens. It is large maps that must hang in the Educational Offices of the various Provinces, and by reference to them that the work of the Departments must be done, their judgments passed, their reports compiled, their achievements rated. Not until this first step has been taken is there any chance of the conflict with illiteracy and all its woes, being joined on terms that carry with them the slightest hope of victory. Only when such a plan dominates the educational administration of the State will success be seen in its true perspective, failure in its undisguised injury, and hindrances in the light of calls not to acquiescence in their continuance, but to renewed effort for their removal. In the past we have heard enough and to spare of the difficulties which lie in the way of universal elementary education, of the chronic lack of funds, of the poverty of agencies. Let all these difficulties be admitted; for all are true. But set over against them the shame to which the country is exposed, the frustration of hope and advance to which it is condemned because the obstacles are neither truly faced nor looked at in their real significance. Then it is that action stands revealed as a necessity, and delay as not merely lamentable but a lasting reproach. And to escape that reproach, to avoid the method of isolation, independence, or haphazard that has marked and marred the development of education in the past and has left behind it a baneful heritage, the State will not rest content till it has set before itself a large plan, and has determined that to the realization of that plan all its resources will be devoted. The plan which the State will recognize itself as being under the necessity of adopting, if it is to discharge the responsibility which it has undertaken, will include at least two provisions. In the first place, there must be provision for a system of elementary education which will reach every boy and girl of school-going age and will keep them at school from, say, their fifth to their tenth year. It is a provision that will have to take effect in stages; but whatever be the method of its realization, that is the aim and nothing less, and its approach to the achievement of that aim is the measure of the Department's success or failure. In the second place, there must be provision for the placing of secondary and collegiate education within the reach of all who are capable of taking advantage of it, and of so doing this that every barrier that is now in the way of those who have the necessary ability will be wholly removed. A plan such as this, with its twofold provision, is the minimum plan which any State that seeks honestly to be responsible for the education of its people can contemplate. If the State is prepared to be content with something less than this aim, or, having adopted the aim, to dawdle over its realization, it might as well candidly confess that what it said eighty years ago, and has said many a time since, is a mere verbal profession. If the State is satisfied with concentration on what is official or even quasi-official, then let it say so, and we shall have no difficulty in understanding why tarry the wheels of education's chariot. But if the State has learned from past experience the futility of identifying itself with any such attitude to education, if it recognizes without qualification the straits in which it has itself been landed by such narrowness of outlook, if it makes no disguise of the crumbling foundations on which as a consequence it is now engaged in rearing itself, then there is one thing which it will do, and to the carrying out of which it will give itself with all the power that it can command. It will put before itself a national plan, embracing elementary and higher education, and it will strain every nerve to realize it. Also it will frankly admit that by its manner of achieving this plan the working of the Educational Department must be judged, and the well-being of the State itself decided.

11. *Comprehension in Appeal and in Administration.*—So much for what is the first stage in the effort of the State to discharge its responsibility for the education of the people, an effort pressed upon it as it looks not at the working of departmental machinery but at the actual conditions of leanness and menace which, because of its present educational practice, now confront the State. Yet this instalment of the State's duty, which, though it is essential, cannot be regarded as anything more than initial, is not likely to go far on the way to realization if the plan is marked by comprehensiveness only of extent. Two other features of comprehension claim our attention. In the first place, the education which the plan contemplates must be such that, while welcoming into it the best that can be drawn from every source, it maintains a clear and steady connexion with what is true to Indian thought, culture, and tradition. The plan will be no less comprehensive in its appeal than in its scope. The education given in India will be Indian education. In the second place, the success of the plan demands that there should be set up such machinery that the plan will be more than intra-provincial. It must be inter-provincial. The country must not be the arena of conflicting plans of educational advance. There will be no endeavour to perpetuate the reign of the stereotyped, but every endeavour to establish the reign of harmony. The well-being of the country will be no less important than the well-being of the individual province. A comprehensive national plan, then, comprehensive in its extent and content, national in its provision and service, that is what, as the result of the larger and truer outlook, the State will place before itself as the only plan which will satisfy it, and the plan for the realization of which it will work,

cost what it may, even to the casting aside of much that up to the present moment has been looked upon as characteristic of the State's mode of educational activity.

(ii) *The Provision of Agencies*

12. *The Function of the State.*—But if a truly national system is to be called into being, there must be the agencies that are capable of transferring such a plan from the region of purpose into that of fulfilment. What that involves for India as a whole has never yet been fully faced. We search through many pages of reports for a clear recognition of what a national system actually requires, and our search is but partially rewarded. The reason is not far to seek. To face this matter squarely is to be brought face to face with the seemingly impossible. And States naturally do not care to contemplate what has even the appearance of being beyond them. Yet it is only when the State in India, under the compulsion of undeniable facts, is brought to fix its attention on what has for it in the realm of education the look of an impossibility, that there at length emerges some glimpse of hope. There is some chance then that the shallow optimism no less than the outworn methods of the past may be swept aside. There is a chance that when the State realizes the apparently hopeless task for which it is responsible, that of building up a comprehensive national system of education, a task of which it has as yet touched but the merest fringe, it will no longer shut its eyes to what, with regard to agencies, constitutes its real function. The clouds of menacing darkness which keep sweeping over it, as the result of its failure to deal fully with the situation in days gone by, serve but to press that function upon it, to throw it into clearer relief. It is of a twofold character. First, the function of the State is not the provision of agencies but the encouragement that will secure their provision. Second, this encouragement must be so expressed as to

secure the provision of suitable co-operating agencies. The function of the State is to encourage the operation and the co-operation of agencies.

13. *The Encouragement of Agencies.*—The State, confronted with what is needed to counter the hurtful presence of illiteracy and to restore well-being to the body politic, in other words with the establishment of a national system of education, is at once brought to realize that the provision of this system goes wholly beyond the power which it commands. That is plain in connexion with even the very limited educational effort which is at work in the country at the present day. The State has not resources sufficient for the provision through its own agency of a tithe of the educational facilities now at the service of the people. But when this is said, and it is not only said but has been recognized as the simple truth with a definiteness which the years have only confirmed, the whole has not been said. What then is that whole? It is this: The State has not the funds to provide through its own agency for the establishment of a national educational system, but it has the funds whereby it can so encourage agencies that this provision will be made. It is on this encouragement, then, that the State must concentrate, for it is that encouragement which opens the door of hope on what seems otherwise a hopeless situation. Devoting itself to encourage by the channel of its revenues every agency that has proved its fitness, or that has within it the seeds of fitness for the work that has to be done, it will see what is required accomplished. Agency after agency will rise up, will equip itself for the task, will place its resources at the service of the State. The look of impossibility will vanish. The time past has sufficed to show that all doctrinaire notions as to the means that are to be employed, all analogies with other countries which however attractive are devoid of strict applicability to India, all identification of official support with one source of supply when there are others equally to be

depended upon, that all this has had but one result. It has cramped education, it has wrought the havoc of the present. All such acts and attitudes must now go by the board. Faced with a need which remains unsatisfied, with a disaster which draws ever closer, the State is hedged up to one line of policy. It must send forth its encouragement on every side, with all its fullness and steadiness, without trace of narrowness or suspicion of partiality, to every agency, whatever its name, source, or constitution, that can be brought into the service of the country's need. And while it recognizes only one region from which this encouragement is excluded, the region of incompetence, it will also count it as one of its duties so to act that wherever there is an agency which can be turned from incompetence to capacity, it will be no fault of the State if this transformation is not effected.

14. *The Co-operation of Agencies.*—Every competent agency is to be encouraged. But the reason for this encouragement must never be lost sight of. It is that all the agencies thus drawn forth and encouraged may work together for the inauguration of a national system of education. The State must encourage agencies not only to operate but also to co-operate. To be partial or preferential in its mode of encouragement is simply to undo all the benefits which encouragement is calculated to yield, and for the diffusion of which encouragement is pressed upon the State by the relentless logic of facts. If the State places its financial resources at the service of one agency in a manner which works out more favourably to it than does its service to another, and if this difference of treatment cannot be traced back to a difference in educational work done, then the State is extending encouragement indeed, but in such a way that there can be no co-operation of agencies. It is a form of encouragement that makes for conflict not combination; for the discouragement not of incompetence but of competence, actual and potential. It is employing its own

resources to the ultimate defeat of its own purposes, and these purposes the very objects for which the State, if it is to live, must strive. There are two ways in which this mode of encouragement may work to the detriment of the ends which the State has in view. Alongside of other agencies the State may set up an agency which has a specially intimate relationship with itself, and which has therefore in respect of encouragement priority of claim over all other agencies. Or it may decide to send its encouragement through one particular channel when there are others quite as suitable which it might also employ. In either case the encouragement of the State becomes partial from the very first; and what is done under the name of encouragement turns out in actual working to be the bearer of official discouragement, and that on no small scale. And that cannot be what the State wishes; it is certainly not what its interests require. Clearly then if the State wishes so to exercise its encouragement that it will secure the co-operation as well as the operation of agencies, there are two principles in accordance with which it must act. For one thing, it must work through purely non-official agencies. And for another, it must extend to all non-official agencies equality of treatment. Where a number of agencies are employed then these must be solely non-official; for official and non-official agencies occupying by their very constitution different relations to the State, relations which assure official agencies of a support and attention not assured to those that are non-official, are precluded from co-operating save on discriminatory terms; and that is no co-operation at all. And a non-official agency which, either through legislative enactment or administrative practice becomes the recipient of a treatment more favourable than that which is meted out to another, is precluded by that very fact from entering into whole-hearted co-operation with that other. Thus what we have already noted in the preceding paragraph receives added confirmation. We saw that to supply by its own means the agencies needed for a national system is wholly beyond the resources of the State. We now see from another point of view that if the State is ever to secure this national system it must abandon, and without delay, all thought of employing its own agency. For if it persists in such a course it seeks to build on a foundation the components of which cannot cohere. That is to court disaster. If the foundation is to be well and truly laid, if the structure is to be secure, and present conditions show how desperately both are needed, there is but one way to take. The national system must rest upon, be built up by, non-official agencies, on each of which the State relies, all of which it welcomes on a common footing, none of which it admits to the status of privileged relation. Thus, and not otherwise, will all be able to work together on equal terms, and by the encouragement of the State to build up in real co-operation that comprehensive educational system in the absence of which the vital interests of the State have become so seriously jeopardized.

15. *Organization of Agencies.*—There are two points in connexion with the co-operation of agencies to which our consideration draws attention and on which, more particularly in the light of past educational history, emphasis requires to be placed. The idea of co-operation has always been inherent in the educational system of the country since the day that it was inaugurated. But it is only when the facts of illiteracy are faced without disguise that co-operation appears not only as what is desirable but also as that which is imperative. To set up agencies and then allow them to dissipate their strength in rivalry is more than unfortunate. It is a reflection upon the State's power of control. In the majority of cases it indicates a radical weakness in the State's employment of its revenues on education. We may therefore rejoice that a clear realization of what illiteracy really means brings with it a true conception

of co-operation and its necessity. But, if to be assured of combined, instead of diffused or even antipathetic, action, the State has to deal with a number of diversely constituted agencies in area after area, each of which requires to be separately approached, then its procedure is bound to be cumbrous, its operations to be subject to delay. This, however, would be avoided if agencies, in order to be recognized, were required to be definitely organized. A large number of non-official agencies now at work belong to the type of organization which we associate with local self-government. Whether, as now constituted, that type affords the best means of co-operating with the State, the means whereby its relation with the State once established may be most fruitful for the cause of education, admits of serious doubt. But be that as it may, here is a form of organization with which the State can readily establish relations and which, with or without modification, may be encouraged in such a way as to bring to education the contribution of a large and unified service throughout considerable tracts of the country. But no such organization exists in connexion with the other form of non-official agency which we generally speak of as Private Management. Yet there is no reason why in any locality that agency should not be as definitely organized as is Local Board Management. Private bodies might be required, for example, in a way that is as reasonable as it is advisable, to be grouped, within a district or smaller defined area, in recognized and legally constituted units. Thus, by approved organisation easily secured and easy to maintain, it would be possible to provide as sure a legal status for Private Bodies as for Local Bodies. And this would enable the State, by means simple and speedy, to draw forth from a number of separate agencies the great strength of real co-operation.

16. *Legislation and Agencies.*—One of the great obstacles in the way of co-operation stands out clearly as soon as we investigate the legal standing of the

different educational agencies. The fact is that, so far as legislation goes, it exists in all essential points in regard to only one of the forms of co-operating agencies. This is not confined to finance, but it comes out most plainly in connexion with it, where priority of allocation from provincial revenues to Local Bodies, with all that this inevitably means for other bodies, proves to have the support of legal enactments. Such a one-sided arrangement is unfortunate in itself, anything but a strength to the State, and a constant hindrance to the spread of education. That, notwithstanding this, there should be the measure of combination that at present exists among bodies which differ so much in the status enjoyed by them in the eyes of the law, is a striking testimony to the desire of agencies to operate and co-operate in the spread of education even under adverse conditions. It is also an indication of what would happen, and of how education would benefit, if the conditions were altered and the two forms of agency were alike in legal status. Co-operation in educational effort which has been so often weakened by prevailing modes of legislation would then be seen to establish itself in the most natural fashion, and with a stimulating power which would be felt through the whole system. If the State is to face the devastating effects of illiteracy with a strong and vital combination of agencies, then without delay it must make a courageous effort to revise every legislative enactment of the present time which has the practical effect of discouraging that combination. It must see to it that law becomes a bulwark, not a barrier, to education; a friend, not a foe, to the co-operation of agencies.

(iii) *The State as controlling Authority*

17. *Need for Control.*—What a realization of the facts which stare the State in the face makes abundantly clear is, as we have now seen, that the State must set itself to aim at nothing less than a comprehensive national scheme of education, and to encourage in the

most whole-hearted manner the incorporation within that system of a full supply of co-operating agencies. But when the State has begun to act in both these directions its efforts, however vigorous, may yield no results at all commensurate with the energy expended, if no action is taken by the State along a third direction, that of guidance. A national system demands national control. A comprehensive system of co-operating agencies requires a co-ordinating authority. This is a service which the State and the State alone can render, and this is the service which, when it is rendered, puts the State in possession of a system of education that will bring back to it the well-being which at the present time is undeniably slipping from it.

18. *Conception of Control.*—Just as the facing of facts, however unpleasant, brings with it an enlarged conception of the educational system which India must possess, and a fresh conception of the manner in which agencies are to contribute towards the establishment of this system, so it also brings with it a clearer conception of what is involved in the control of education by the State. State control in the conditions of the present day stands revealed as a service of co-ordination. The situation with which illiteracy faces the country is one that fills with misgiving all who have the interests of India at heart. Not only is the power of illiteracy widespread and devastating but the effort to thwart it is far from being as potent as the circumstances demand. At times there is created the impression that it lags behind the strength which illiteracy itself exerts. In the records of over a century illiteracy reveals itself as one of the greatest and most unbending barriers to the progress of India; in the period which stretches from 1920 to the present day it has served to constrict the path of constitutional advance on which India then entered; and it meets the fresh opportunity of the present day with a dark cloud that is little suggestive of a silver lining. It constitutes a call which leaves the State no

option. The State must enter the field of education to co-ordinate all the available forces so that with unbroken ranks they may attack and overcome the legions which still shamelessly fly the colours of illiteracy. The situation demands such an exercise of power on the part of State that its resources of experience, guidance, direction, and finance will be placed at the service of education in the spirit of no rival or partial administrator or grudging paymaster, but in that of a generous giver, an impartial director, a wise adviser, and a supreme combiner. Such is the role which the State can play, which it alone can play, and which, as facts make clear beyond a doubt, it must play.

19. *Administration and Inspection.*—In order to realize what this conception of Control involves, we must now go with a certain amount of detail into some of its outstanding features. And, in the first place it is obvious that the State can neither lay claim to the control of education, nor justify that claim if it is made on its behalf, unless it places at the service of education administrative and inspecting staffs which are equal to the responsibilities that rest upon them. There must be those in the Office of each provincial Educational Department who have the experience that commands confidence, the contact with actual conditions which drives away all suspicion of pure officialdom, and the first-hand acquaintance with education which renders their judgment a valued factor in every educational plan and movement. And these officers there must be in such numbers that they are readily accessible, that they are prepared to consider proposals no less than to give advice, that they are felt to be the supporters of all who seek to make schools and colleges what they should be for the country, and that they proceed in their directing work by no hand to mouth expedients but by framing well thought out policies which they have time to explain, willingness to modify, and tact in executing, so that they carry with them all opinion that counts and

all managements that render a genuine contribution to education. And what is true of administration is as true of inspection. There must be those who as the result of their knowledge and qualifications and numbers are able to impart to schools and those who teach in them the stimulus of information and suggestion, who gain the confidence of those who are connected with education by their personal interest and wise counsel, and who wherever they go bring standards that are seen to be worth striving after and ideas that are worth the effort to incorporate. For such a service as this the substitution of a circumlocation Office or of an Official Bureau is very easy and has been on occasion offered. It is however to gain nothing; it comes perilously near to losing everything. And if the State can look at what the present condition of education means for it and for its people, and yet make no effort to supply education with the service of an administrative and inspecting staff that is qualified and adequate, then it is failing in what is fundamental and, whatever be its intention, is actually helping on its own undoing.

20. *Standards.*—State control of education, then, is seen to be the service of Guidance. That comes out very clearly in connexion with the maintenance of educational standards. A number of the agencies now at work are found, when that work is examined, to have no real title to a place in the educational system of the land. What is the reason of this? In large part because the State does not guide. It has not a strong enough inspecting staff to supply it with accurate information as to the actual condition of schools; nor a strong enough administrative staff to enable it to carry out the changes that are necessary. The result is that throughout India there are no clearly recognized standards of staffing, stability, and attainment; and even if there were, there do not exist the means which would ensure that they would be given effect to. The present method of

control supplies at too many points an opportunity for departure with impunity from sound and wholesome educational standards. In effect what it comes to is that the State is lending its support, either by financial aid or by official recognition, to places of learning which fail to comply with reasonable standards and have forfeited any right to a place in the educational system of the land. That is to say, in the light of present day conditions, the State is becoming contributory to its own disintegration. How is it to escape from this intolerable position? By so exercising its control that every agency which maintains true standards will be certain of steady and stimulating encouragement, and every agency which continues to depart from these standards will be certain of forfeiting aid and recognition. This implication of control follows naturally from what has been said as to the necessity for the provision of satisfactory administrative and inspecting staffs. But it requires specific mention for two reasons. First, because failure to maintain right educational standards is sometimes so represented as to leave entirely out of account the part which the State is under an obligation to perform. And secondly, because until this matter receives the attention which facts demand, the efforts which the State is making to spread education may result in nothing so surely as the weakening of the State itself.

21. *Devolution.*—But the control that will work must be a control that can bend. If it is to face frankly and deal suitably with the facts of the present situation, if it is really to grip, it must be adaptable, and it must have behind it the authority of competent public opinion. Illiteracy has shown slight readiness to disappear before a control which is mainly official or which trusts to centralized domination for its power. The facts which have been facing the country for the past two or three decades, and which, to its cost, it has been so slow to recognize, have made it abundantly clear that the day of such methods is over. They let us see that

control is not, and cannot be official ordering. Control is and must be national service. And what is national has a place in the guidance of education for everyone, be he official or non-official, who has a title by knowledge and experience to participate in the advance of education. Thus simply under pressure of facts, control is bound to become more and more devolved. There are circumstances when it will be most satisfactory for the State to act directly through its own qualified officers. There are others, and they are daily on the increase, when what is needed is control exercised through bodies specially fitted for the task. These are needed because of their capacity to evoke educational interest, their power to marshal local educational sentiment, their suitability for the application of specific educational experience, their ability to bring about a combination of educational forces. They are needed because flexibility is required, because concentration is required. Thus it is that a clear realization of the position of education in the country today, and of the country's needs leads to a larger conception of the Local Educational Authorities which the country must possess. There has been a tendency in the past and it still strongly persists, to think that if devolution is to be carried out at all it must be through the medium of the Local Body as we know it. But education to be effective requires for its administration various forms of local controlling bodies. That this fact has been too long overlooked, to the detriment of education, is now being pressed home upon us with a new emphasis as we have awakened to the immense power and devastating range of illiteracy. The stereotyped has had a long day. With minor modifications it has had a run of fifty years. But that it is unable to deal with the present situation can no longer be concealed. Yet when other directions have been suggested, and attempts at variation have been made here and there, so strong has been conservative feeling that these have been received with an encouragement, that has been wavering and with criticism that has been unnerving. And so it will be till facts in their undisguised significance are faced. Then it will be seen that, criticism or no criticism, diverse types of controlling authorities the country must have. It must have them so as to secure the teachers that are needed for the varying localities and their varying requirements. It must have them to spread elementary education with that adaptability to different conditions which is an essential of its growth. It must have them so that the dull level of secondary education may be succeeded by a variety that sends vitality through the whole system. It must have them that education may be brought into relation with life, and into association with religion, so that in a more congenial atmosphere it may truly thrive. And it must have them that there may be that representation of interests and that concentration on education which have far too long been kept out of the reckoning. Clearly if the disaster which threatens the State is to be avoided, there must be a new conception of educational authorities, their constitution and their functions, and the State must set itself, at all costs, to act without delay in accordance with that enlarged and truer conception of control.

22. *Initiative.*—But devolution will not settle the matter. The sole reason for its employment is to aid the State in the discharge of its obligation. It is not that there should be set up a power parallel to or co-ordinate with the State. Neither is it that by devolution the State should wash its hands of a responsibility which is far from easy to meet but which never ceases to rest upon it. The bodies to which control has been delegated may fail. They may shirk decisions, they may be blind to opportunity, they may act mechanically, they may quail before unpopularity, they may claim virtual autonomy. They may fail by slackness, incompetence, or self-assertiveness. But such failure is not the end of control. It is simply a reminder of the fact,

too often forgotten, that devolution is devolution. The State devolved control in order to make that control more effective and beneficial in its working for its citizens. Where that result is not obtained, for one reason or another, devolution for the time being has ceased to operate. But the State has not. Its responsibility does not cease. And to discharge it the State calls into exercise its power of initiative, and the difficulty is tided over, the impasse is ended, the work is done. There is nothing arbitrary in this, no assumption of autocracy. The State may do the work through its own officials for the moment, or it may help on the hesitating body to do it, or it may devolve the work on another body. Whatever the method which it employs, the State by its exercise of initiative simply gives expression to the truth that behind all modes of working lies the solicitude of the State. One instrument of this solicitude may fail, but the State will not fail. It will find the way by which what its citizens need will not be left undone. The initiative of the State in connexion with education is but the State's service of Guidance.

23. *Finance.*—So also in another form is the financing of education by the State. It is a service of supply. There are at least three ways in which this will show itself. In the first place, as the result of the maintenance of a satisfactory staff for administration and inspection, public subsidies will be withdrawn from institutions that fail to conform to prescribed and accepted standards. And the lakhs of rupees which are thus saved will be ready for the encouragement of schools that can be depended on to advance the education of the country. Education in India has been kept too long waiting for that guidance. In the second place, when the State makes no distinctions between contributing agencies save those of capacity, but places them all on the common footing of co-operating agencies, and when it works through bodies which are not sectional but which exercise a thoroughly representative and effective

devolved control, then funds will be distributed on the grounds of accepted principles. Thus they will avoid the expensiveness of preferential treatment. Public revenues will be allocated on the basis of true service rendered to the cause of education; they will go further and do more for the citizens and the country. And in the third place, the encouragement which will mark the exercise of the control thus instituted and the generous support which will accompany its working, will lead to the tapping of resources hitherto untouched. Local Boards will see how great a gain will accrue to them from a considerably increased educational expenditure of their funds. And Private Bodies will not be slow to recognize how well repaid is the enhancement of their liberality. By this service of supply, the expression of a wise and watchful control, the education by which the State is weakened will steadily lose its place, that whereby it is built up will be resolutely advanced. The State will rest on firmer foundations.

24. *Concentration on Control.*—The enlarged conception of Control on which we have been dwelling has revealed features too often neglected but none the less, perhaps even all the more, demanding emphasis because of the educational situation of the present day. The country is heading for disaster unless there is a very marked change in that situation. Such a change there can be if the State sets itself to control, if it determines to place at the disposal of education a truly national service of guidance. Such a service, we have seen, affords the means by which the country will be in possession of a sufficient number of qualified and co-operating agencies to provide it with a comprehensive system of national education. There is no other way in which this can be done. That fact constitutes a summons, which it dare not neglect, to the controlling authority to concentrate on control. It is a summons which has been far too much disregarded in the past. The result is writ large on every page of India's educational history.

Control has been mingled with some other function and the twofold harm that has issued therefrom may be read in the menace of today which hangs over the well-being of the State. Control has become devoid of power, and the needed agencies are not to be had. The State has attempted to control but has not thrown its unhampered energy into it. It has delegated control but time and again has saddled that delegation with the very conditions that have proved its own inveterate handicap. Not thus is the country to be served. If the facts of the present day are really faced, the State will look on all that pertains to education in a way very different from that which it has too often adopted in the past. And the clearest sign of its changed outlook will be this. The State will discard for ever its present unsatisfactory attitude to control, and it will replace it by one which makes the State the accepted controller because it gives to education a lead, a guidance, a service, into which it throws itself with unencumbered concentration.

III. These Principles found in the Indian Educational System

25. *Changed outlook and Principles of Educational Policy.*—What our consideration has shown us is that the State is being threatened with a process of undermining which, if not effectually stopped, is bound to result in disaster. It has also made it very clear to us that if this menace is to be removed it must be through the instrumentality of an education the administration of which is based on certain principles. These principles are capable of succinct statement. First and foremost, the State must aim at nothing less than a comprehensive system of national education. The system must be comprehensive, the whole being so carefully articulated that not only is there provision for a full scheme of compulsory elementary education but also opportunity for every one who can profit by it to advance from the elementary school to institutions of secondary and

collegiate grade. The system must be national in that while it affords a meeting place for what is best in the cultures of other lands it presents education in the setting which does the fullest justice to Indian thought and tradition. Secondly, the State must so act as to draw forth all the agencies that are required for the firm establishment of this national system. It must see to it that these agencies are enlisted from every source that can furnish what is required, that no agency thus recognized and employed is placed at a disadvantage in respect of financial support or administrative dealing as compared with another, and that all are welcomed to their place in the educational system as partners and contributors to a common end. And it must so make use of its revenues that no agency which can possibly contribute to educational development will be left unnoticed or unencouraged, and that when such agencies become parts of the educational system of the land they receive State support impartially and in accordance with the service which they render. And thirdly, the State must control. It must so control that as speedily as possible it will divest itself of every function which hinders it from giving to control undivided attention and care. It must be in a position, by the staffs which it gathers round it, to direct, guide, stimulate, and unify the national system. It must so exercise control that management is not confused with control, that religious neutrality is not identified with religious exclusion, and that devolution does not mean abrogation of responsibility. It must so control that while it encourages the contribution of every stable agency it admits to the enjoyment of a place in the national system only those that comply with recognized conditions and maintain approved standards. And it must so control that while it unifies it does not stereotype, while it directs it does not destroy individuality, and while it finances it incurs no suspicion of favouring.

26. *These Principles Inherent in the Indian Educa-*

tional System.—Such are the principles of educational administration which, when we look at the grave situation that confronts the State, force themselves upon us as those which the State must adopt and on which it must act with steadiness and without delay if it is to escape the menace which threatens its very foundations. And as we examine them in detail we cannot but be struck with the fact that we are looking at no new principles. They prove to be the principles to which, as we found in the closing chapter of Part I, educational policy is being recalled if it is to deal at all satisfactorily with the situation which has resulted from the operation in the field of education of the Government of India Act of 1919. And the matter does not stop there. What we realized to be necessary to meet adequately the position that has obtained ever since 1920 was found in turn to be nothing new. Analysis showed that the principles required for this purpose are the very principles that are embodied in the Educational Despatch of 1854, the first declaration by the State of its educational policy in India. It is true that certain of these principles have taken on a fuller significance with the flight of time; their content has become plainer with each new set of conditions in which they have found themselves; and the emphasis on individual principles has varied with passing years. Such changes in significance and emphasis are only what is always to be found where we are dealing with living ideas. In expression they alter, in essence they remain unchanged. Through different forms of statement the principles abide; they are there today in the educational system of India as they were there well-nigh fourscore years ago when the State for the first time admitted its responsibility for providing education to the people of India. The principles are there, an integral part of the educational system, sometimes brought into clear relief by the conditions which they were called on to meet, sometimes pushed into the background by some form of officialdom that did not care for their operation; sometimes given effect to, at other times treated with neglect. But through many vicissitudes they keep their place, never authoritatively discarded, never officially disavowed, constantly employed. Age has not withered them; the passage of years has served but to emphasize their vitality. And the reason of this is not far to seek. They remain, they live, because they are necessary. When the education of India is faced with a situation that is critical, analysis of the situation reveals the fact that it constitutes in essence an appeal to the country for the fresh recognition and full application of these very principles. Give them that unfettered opportunity which, in accordance with the verdict of their history, is nothing but their due, and their vitality becomes at once apparent and communicates itself to every detail and the whole range of educational activity. Keep them unused or suffer them to have a strictly limited application, as has happened time and again in the educational story of India, and the result is ever the same—education suffers and the State suffers with it. What the country has to settle is whether the shortsightedness which in the past has so often resulted in this injury to education and to the organized community is to receive further support or whether it is to be set aside as definitely unworthy and destructive. There is at the heart of the Indian educational system what is organic not mechanical, a body of living and life-giving principles which there abides and ever calls to be employed. The critic has only to go to it to find his criticisms forestalled and answered; the reformer has only to go to it to find there the means for securing the benefits that he advocates; the administrator has only to go to it to realize that here his problems far from being insoluble are being placed on the road to a fitting solution. And critic, reformer, and administrator alike, when they ponder this body of principles, grasp its significance, and appreciate its power, cannot but stand amazed at their own blindness in having failed so often and for so long to take into their reckoning and to employ with resolute wholeheartedness what has all the time been lying to their hand for their country's weal. Ready to their hand is the means by which education may flourish and the State may be in health. Yet there has been a strange unwillingness to get at essentials, a strange preoccupation with a distorted perspective. Are critic, reformer, and administrator to go on contenting themselves with a circumscribed view of education which concentrates attention on the working of a government department and concerns itself with matters of machinery? Or are they to rise above all this, to look fairly in the face the situation, the gravity of which can not be overstated, which now confronts the State because of the conquests of ignorance and the blight of its working? And are they then as frankly to look on this body of living principles which lies to their hand, which calls aloud today as in the past for recognition and utilization, and looking on it to use it to the full? Few questions that present themselves to the India of our time are so momentous. For the answer that is returned to it means national health or national sickness.

IV. The Times demand their full Employment

27. *Urgent Need for Employment of These Principles.*—The present is a time when in the clearest possible fashion the critic, the reformer, and the administrator are brought to the parting of the ways. The country remains in the grip of an appalling ignorance which thwarts at every point its fruitful development, a position so serious that the patriot's eye can be no longer closed to it. Yet at such a time as this a great constitutional advance is to be made, involving the exercise not only of far-reaching provincial powers but also the growth of federal control which is to affect the States as well as the Provinces. How can the country meet these tremendous responsibilities, how can it impart

strength to a union so great as to be devoid of parallel? How can it do this when illiteracy threatens to undermine the foundations on which the federal units rest, or it may even be to provide them with a foundation which has not the consistency of sand? Certainly not by thinking of education any longer as a purely departmental effort or by dwelling on the working of official machinery. There is only one way in which it can be done. The State must be definitely regarded as a central authority which gives to education so adequate, so steady, so impartial, so ungrudging, so adaptable, and so untramelled a service of direction, encouragement, information, finance, and initiative that it calls forth and receives in response the abundant service of approved and stable agencies, drawn from local and private sources, co-operating on a common basis for a common end, and placing at the disposal of the State the fulness of their resources and the energy of a wisely guided and consistently encouraged effort. That is to say, the way in which healthy education may be widespread through a healthy federation is by the adoption of, and by adherence to, those principles which are inherent in the Indian educational system, which have been there for over seven decades, and which only await their unfaltering employment to disclose their power. The ready acknowledgment of what education has achieved no less than the courageous admission of the much that it has left undone is found to call for an enlarged outlook and a new beginning. And that new beginning can be no other than the giving to the principles of educational policy which this discussion has set forth, as it has found them at the very heart of the educational system of India, an opportunity for their unqualified and complete and steadfast operation. And when the Indian educational administration becomes a genuine attempt to work from that new beginning, the results of that attempt will not be long in doubt. For it will be nothing less than the calling into exercise of the means whereby not only will education be made sound and general, its deficiencies be diminished, its problems be placed on the road to solution, but also whereby the land will see the menace that confronts the State removed, the larger responsibilities awaiting it more confidently shouldered, and the unity of federation the highway of a nation's strength.

BIBLIOGRAPHY

The following sources of information have been consulted.

I. Statements of Educational Policy

1. *Despatch from the Court of Directors of the East India Company to the Governor-General of India in Council*, dated the 19th July, 1854.
   See Nos. 8 and 11.
2. *Educational Despatch from the Secretary of State for India*, dated the 7th April, 1859.
   See No. 8.
3. *Report of the Indian Education Commission*, 1883.
4. *Proceedings of the Government of India in the Home Department (Education)* under date the 23rd October, 1884.
   The Government Order on No. 3. *See* No. 11.
5. *Indian Educational Policy*, being a Resolution issued by the Governor-General in Council on the 11th March, 1904.
6. *Educational Policy of the Government of India.* Resolution of the Government of India (Department of Education), dated the 21st February, 1913.

II. Despatches, Memoranda, and Correspondence connected with Educational Policy

7. H. Sharp (Ed.), *Selections from Educational Records*, Part I. 1781-1839. (Bureau of Education, India), 1920.
   Contains, *inter alia*, text of Holt Mackenzie's Note, 1823; Munro's Minute, 1826; Macaulay's Minute, 1835; documents relating to Anglicist and Orientalist controversy; Auckland's Minute, 1839.
8. J. A. Richey (Ed.), *Selections from Educational Records*, Part II, 1840-1859. (Bureau of Education, India) 1922.

Contains Despatch of 1854; Despatch of 1859; University Acts, 1857; and a large number of minutes, letters, and resolutions.

9. G. Anderson and M. Subadar, *The Development of an Indian Policy*, 1818-1858, 1921.

Contains extracts from minute of Mountstuart Elphinstone, from reports of W. Adam, and from Despatch of 1854; letter of Raja Ram Mohan Roy to Lord Amherst; and text of Macaulay's Minute.

10. G. W. Forrest (Ed.), *Official Writings of Mountstuart Elphinstone*, 1890.

Contains Elphinstone's Minute in full.

11 *The Educational Policy of the State in India*, Madras, 1904.

Contains Despatch of 1854; extracts from the Report of the Indian Education Commission; and various Government Orders.

12. A. J. Arbuthnot, *Major-General Sir Thomas Munro*, 1881.

Munro's Minute on education is given in Vol. ii, and a comment on it is made in Vol. i.

13. G. Smith, *Life of Alexander Duff*, 1879.

Contains in addition to information regarding Duff's activities an extract from his evidence before the Joint-Committee of 1833.

III. Reports Dealing Specifically with Education

14. W. Adam, *Reports on Vernacular Education in Bengal and Behar*, submitted to Government in 1835, 1836, and 1838. Calcutta, 1868.

Full text of Adam's reports on indigenous education.

15. *Progress of Education in India.* First to Ninth Quinquennial Reviews.

The Third (1892-1897); Fourth (1897-1902); Fifth (1902-1907); Sixth (1907-1912); Seventh (1912-1917); Eighth (1917-1922); and Ninth (1922-1927) have been consulted.

16. *Report of the Indian Universities Commission*, 1902.

17. *Report of the Calcutta University Commission*, 1917-1919.

Vols. i to v have been mainly consulted, the other volumes mostly for specific references.

18. *Interim Report of the Indian Statutory Commission* (Review of Growth of Education in British India by the Auxiliary Committee appointed by the Commission), 1929.

19. M. P. West, *Report on the Survey of Primary Education, Bengal*, 1918.

20. E. E. Biss, *Report on the Expansion and Improvement of Primary Education in Bengal*, 1921.

21. E. E. Biss, *Second Report on the Expansion and Improvement of Primary Education in Bengal*, 1922.

22. *Report on the Elementary Education Survey of the Madras Presidency* 1924-25, 1925.

23. *Report on the Development of Women's Education in the Madras Presidency*, 1928.

24. *Education in India*. Various dates from 1914 to 1929.

A series of Annual Narratives, published by the Bureau of Education, India. Most of the thirteen issued have been consulted.

25. Reports on the Progress of Education in Bengal, Bombay, Madras, the Punjab, the United Provinces, Bihar and Orissa, and the Central Provinces. Various dates.

The provincial reports on public instruction. Many of these have been consulted in their annual form, and all of them for the quinquennia 1917-1922 and 1922-1927.

26. J. A. Richey (Ed.), *Grants-in-Aid to Schools in British India*. Bureau of Education, India, 1923.

An Occasional Report in which grants systems in the different provinces are given in detail, with an introduction.

27. *Village Education in India*. The Report of a Commission of Enquiry, 1920.

The report of a commission appointed by the missionary societies in Great Britain and North America.

28. *Report of the Commission on Christian Higher Education in India: an Inquiry into the place of the Christian College in Modern India*, 1931.

The Commission was constituted by the International Missionary Council.

IV. Reports into which Education Enters

29. *Reports of the Franchise Committee and the Committee on Division of Functions.* Fourth Despatch on Indian Constitutional Reforms (Division of Functions). 1919.

In the Despatch from the Government of India to the Secretary of State the recommendations of the Committee on Division of Functions in connexion with education receive consideration.

30. *Report of the Royal Commission on Agriculture in India*, 1928.

Besides devoting one chapter to Education, the Commission deals not only with education in general but also with such forms of professional education as agriculture, forestry and veterinary science, and with such topics as illiteracy and adult education, while it presents the rural conditions which are the background of much of the education in India.

31. *Report of the Indian Statutory Commission*, 1930.

The comprehensive character of this Report finds place for much that has a bearing on Education. There is a chapter on the Growth of Education in Vol. i, and in Vol. ii there are references to the Financing of Education. The Commission is careful to say that it has concerned itself 'primarily with education and its organisation in relation to political and constitutional conditions and potentialities of progress'.

See No. 18.

32. *Report of the Royal Commission on Labour in India*, 1931.
The Commission presents the conditions of those engaged in factories, plantations, mills, etc., both adults and young people. It makes recommendations as to the application of compulsion in certain cases, the education of half-timers, etc., and it shows how illiteracy affects industry.

V. Legislation and Administration

33. *Imperial Gazetteer of India*, 1908.
In Vol. ii Education is dealt with.
34. C. Ilbert, *The Government of India*, 1922.
'A brief historical survey of parliamentary legislation relating to India.' While not dealing with Education, it shows at various points the administrative framework in which education has its place.
35. G. B. Keith (Ed.), *Speeches and Documents on Indian Policy*, 1922.
Amongst other documents in this collection there are in Vol. ii extracts from the Montagu-Chelmsford Report and the text of the Government of India Act of 1919, with the Select Committee's Report and various related speeches.
36. *Report on Indian Constitutional Reforms*, 1919.
There are a few references to Education; and the position of Education as a Transferred Subject is among its proposals.
37. *Reports on the Administration of the various Provinces*. Various dates.
In these in addition to what is reported from year to year there is a good deal of standing information as to the administration of public instruction.
38. *India in* 1920-21, 1921-22, and so on annually.
Statements prepared for presentation to Parliament, and *inter alia* full of information as to educational administration, local self-government, and legislative enactments. These have been consulted up to 1929-30.

39. J. Matthai, *Village Government in British India*, 1915.

Describes the various manifestations of village self-government in British India, a chapter being devoted to Education.

40. Lord Ronaldshay, *India. A Bird's Eye View*, 1924.

Local self-government is dealt with, and more attention to indigenous methods is advocated; there is a description of a panchayat at work.

41. J. M. Sen, *Primary Education Acts in India.* A Study. 1925.

Gives with comments the provisions of the various primary education acts passed up to 1925.

42. K. T. Shah and G. J. Bahadurji, *Constitution, Functions, and Finance of Indian Municipalities*, 1925.

A general consideration of the working of municipalities, sections being devoted to their powers in regard to Education, and their financing of Education.

43. L. A. Selby-Bigge, *The Board of Education*, 1927.

Much information in small space regarding the working of the Board of Education in England. The consideration given to a number of administrative problems calls for attention because of analogous problems in India.

44. A. Mayhew, *Christianity and the Government of India*, 1928.

Amongst much else, the Government of India's doctrine of Religious Neutrality is considered in its statements and implications, and the whole position is made the subject of comments, searching and illuminating.

45. G. T. Garratt, *An Indian Commentary*, 1930.

A survey of Indian conditions in the course of which consideration is given to important points connected with local self-government administration.

46. W. Meston, *Aspects of Indian Educational Policy*, 1922.

Deals among other subjects with the State and Private Effort, the Madras Elementary Education Act, and Nos. 17 and 27.

VI. History

47. H. Dodwell (Ed.), *Cambridge History of India*, Vol. iv, 1930.

The first, and as yet the only published, volume of the two in which India is considered in connexion with the history of the Empire. The historical conditions of the latter part of the eighteenth and the earlier decades of the nineteenth century are fully described, so that the background of educational development is clear.

48. V. A. Smith, *Oxford History of India*, 1919.

Books VII to IX present the conditions from 1760 onwards amid which education effort was carried on and educational policy was formed.

49. H. Dodwell, *A Sketch of the History of India from 1858-1918*, 1925.

Tendencies and influences at work in India from the end of the East India Company's power to the coming of constitutional reform are set forth with much clearness, and a section is devoted to Education.

50. E. Stock, *History of the Church Missionary Society*, 1899, 1916.

These four volumes are a perfect storehouse of facts, historical and biographical, that cast much light on the progress of education in India.

51. J. Richter, *History of Missions in India*, 1908.

Much historical information regarding education for which Christian missions have been responsible in India during the eighteenth and nineteenth centuries; educational problems also receive treatment.

52. F. Penny, *The Church in Madras*, 1904, 1910.

These three volumes throw much light on what was done by the East India Company as well as by the Crown in the Southern Presidency. Educational development is treated in considerable detail and with much suggestion.

53. Jadunath Sarkar, *India Through the Ages*, 1928.
Gives a fresh presentation of various lines of development in the history of India, with several references to Education in its appropriate setting.

VII. Biography

54. J. Page, *Schwartz of Tanjore*, 1921.
Gives a narrative of the times in which Schwartz lived and the conditions amid which he carried on his schools.

55. Sivanath Sastri, *Ramtanu Lahiri, Brahman and Reformer*.
An account from first-hand sources of the circumstances attending the beginning of Western education in Calcutta, and of those who took part in it during the early years of the nineteenth century.

56. J. Bradshaw, *Sir Thomas Munro*, 1894.
But a short reference to Munro's educational efforts in a book mainly occupied with the civil and military aspects of his career.

57. J. S. Cotton, *Mountstuart Elphinstone*, 1892.
Contains a full account of Elphinstone's educational activities, and of what he did as founder in Bombay of the 'system of instruction both in the vernacular languages and in English'.

58. G. O. Trevelyan, *Life and Letters of Lord Macaulay*, 1878.
In this standard biography detailed information is given towards the end of Vol. i of Macaulay's life and work in Calcutta, his educational aims and proposals.

59. D. C. Boulger, *Lord William Bentinck*, 1892.
Contains several references to his educational policy, and specially its connexion with other parts of his administration.

60. S. P. Carey, *William Carey*, 1923.
Many references to Carey's educational work; the aims of Serampore College are clearly set forth.

61. W. Paton, *Life of Alexander Duff*, 1923.
Reference is made to Duff's educational objects and methods.

62. W. Lee Warner, *Life of the Marquis of Dalhousie*, 1904.
References to Dalhousie's interest in and work for education occur in Vol. i; while in Vol. ii special reference is made to his connexion with the Despatch of 1854.

63. W. W. Hunter, *The Marquess of Dalhousie*, 1890.
Dalhousie's work for education is brought out as an integral part of his administration.

64. W. Muir, *James Thomason*, 1897.
Reprint of an article contributed to the *Calcutta Review* in 1853 by one who worked with Thomason; full account of what Thomason did for education in the N. W. P.

65. R. Temple, *James Thomason*, 1893.
Contains an account by another who was intimate with him of Thomason's educational achievements.

66. B. Mallet, *Thomas George, Earl of Northbrook*, 1908.
Northbrook was private secretary to Sir Charles Wood, and had his part in drafting the Despatch of 1854; reference is made to this.

67. R. B. Smith, *Life of Lord Lawrence*, 1883.
The minute written by Lawrence which shows his attitude to religious education is given in Vol. i. Reference to this will be found in No. 50.

68. W. W. Hunter, *The Earl of Mayo*, 1891.
Gives his views on education and what he did for it.

69. Lord Ronaldshay, *Life of Lord Curzon*, 1928.
Much information is given regarding Curzon's educational work, including reference to his conferences, his university policy, and his drawing up of the Resolution of 1904. *See* Vol. ii.

See further No. 12 (for Munro); No. 13 (for Duff); No. 52 (for Schwartz, Bentinck, etc.).

VIII. Comment

70. C. E. Trevelyan, *On the Education of the People of India*, 1838.
Valuable as a narrative of what took place in Calcutta about the year 1835 by one who had a considerable part in it.

71. F. W. Thomas, *The History and Prospects of British Education in India*, 1891.

A large number of facts regarding education in India is given, and conclusions are reached as to the means for the spread of education, in regard to its nature and management.

72. *Educational Papers*. A Supplement to the South India Missionary Conference Report, 1880.

Comments on the educational policy of the Government of Madras prior to the appointment of the Indian Education Commission.

73. V. Chirol, *Indian Unrest*, 1910.

Five chapters deal with education, its growth, character, connexion with religion, provision for the masses and for women; certain findings of the Indian Education Commission are considered; and certain suggestions are made.

74. V. Chirol, *India*, 1926.

Two chapters are devoted to education which is dealt with in its various relations.

75. W. Miller, *Education and Indian Unrest*, 1911.

As one who was a member of the Indian Education Commission the writer brings out the position of the Commission regarding the control of education; shows also what the nature of Indian educational policy is; and deals with many points raised in No. 73.

76. M. G. Cowan, *The Education of Women of India*, 1912.

A detailed review of women's education more especially in Burma, and northern and western India, with a consideration of its character, methods, and relation to religion.

77. H. R. James, *Education and Statesmanship in India*, 1797-1910, 1917.

An independent and stimulating consideration of educational conditions in India; questions of control and management are dealt with, as well as certain positions of the Indian Education Commission; nor are the achievements of education left unrecognized.

78. F. E. Keay, *Ancient Indian Education.* An Enquiry into its Origin, Development, and Ideals. 1918.

A historical survey of various forms of Hindu and Muhammadan education, their growth and character, together with a consideration of the development of indigenous elementary education.

79. Lajpat Rai, *The Problem of National Education in India*, 1920.

The problem is felt to arise from the difficulty on the one hand of building on old foundations, and on the other of remaining in isolation.

80. Har Dayal, *Our Educational Problem*, 1922.

The 'unnatural and artificial' character of the Indian educational system is dealt with.

81. H. Whitehead, *Indian Problems in Religion, Education, and Politics*, 1923.

A large range of educational problems is included in this volume; and while the benefits of the educational system are acknowledged, the writer points out the defects which are due to the giving of higher education to a limited class and the neglect of the villages.

82. Lord Ronaldshay, *The Heart of Aryavarta*, 1924.

In the earlier part of this volume the relation between Indian education and culture is discussed; and the great change in outlook is revealed in its significance.

83. V. V. Oak, *England's Educational Policy in India.* 1925.

'An attempt to scrutinize educational policy in India by means of an analytical study of educational finance'.

84. A. Mayhew, *The Education of India.* A Study of British Educational Policy in India, 1835-1920 and of its bearing on National Life and Problems in India To-day, 1926.

Gets at the really vital matters of education in India: the place of the mother tongue, the connexion between education and culture, the evils of officialdom, the animating power of religion, the education of the masses; and surveys the whole with a freshness that characterizes every part of the volume. There is also much valuable historical information.

85. M. Olcott, *Village Schools in India*, 1926.
Considers the conditions of village education, ways of extending and improving that education, and the training of teachers for it.

86. S. R. Ranganathan, *The Five Laws of Library Science*, 1931.
Full of enthusiasm and practical suggestion for libraries and for their extended service; with an indication of the bearing of libraries on adult education.

87. Cumming (Ed.), *India*, 1931.
The chairman of the Auxiliary Committee contributes an article on Education to this volume; and other writers deal with such subjects as Agriculture, Finance, Commerce, and Labour.

88. J. A. R. Marriot, *The English in India.* A Problem of Politics, 1932.
The writer regards the problem with which he deals as being intimately connected with Macaulay's Minute; education both in a chapter devoted to it and at various points throughout the book is subjected to criticism.

IX. Articles

Many articles in the usual works of reference, as well as in periodicals, monthly and quarterly, have been consulted; also many pamphlets, addresses, memoranda, and representations to Government on educational subjects.

LIST OF STATISTICAL TABLES

INDEX

F

G

O

P

Q

R

S

PRINTED AT THE DIOCESAN PRESS, 1936—C10142